Also by Scott Eyman

John Ford: The Searcher 1894–1973

Print the Legend:
The Life and Times of John Ford

The Speed of Sound:
Hollywood and the Coming of Talkies

Ernst Lubitsch:
Laughter in Paradise

Mary Pickford:
America's Sweetheart

Five American Cinematographers

Flashback:
A Short History of the Movies
(with Louis Giannetti)

The Lion in his domain: Mayer's office at MGM, 1948.

(Bison Archives)

The Life and Legend

LION OF HOLLYWOOD

of Louis B. Mayer

SCOTT EYMAN

Simon & Schuster
New York   London   Toronto   Sydney

SIMON & SCHUSTER
Rockefeller Center
1230 Avenue of the Americas
New York, NY 10020

For information about special discounts for bulk purchases,
please contact Simon & Schuster Special Sales at
1-800-456-6798 or business@simonandschuster.com

Designed by Elliott Beard

Manufactured in the United States of America

10   9   8   7   6   5   4

Library of Congress Cataloging-in-Publication Data
Eyman, Scott, date.
   Lion of Hollywood : the life and legend of Louis B. Mayer /
Scott Eyman.
      p.   cm.
   Includes bibliographical references and index.
   1. Mayer, Louis B. (Louis Burt), 1885–1957.   2. Motion picture
producers and directors—United States—Biography.   I. Title.
PN1998.3.M397E94   2005
791.4302'32'092—dc22
[B]   2005042472
ISBN 0-7432-0481-6

For Chuck Adams

"It was something of a miracle and something of a joke. They had come from the Ukraine and Poland and Austria-Hungary . . . but it was they, more than anyone else, who reached the fantasies of America, indeed of the entire world—a universalism of taste which shaped the century and which they could shrewdly exploit because they innocently shared it."

—*World of Our Fathers*, IRVING HOWE

"When people think about the studio system they should realize it was not a prison; it was not full of buttonhole makers, people who didn't know anything, who were crass, who crushed artists into the ground. That was not the case. . . . Louis B. Mayer knew that the coin he dealt in was talent. He would husband it and be very patient with it and put up with an awful lot of nonsense if he really believed in it. Of course, he was tough, and he could be ruthless and very disagreeable but . . . he and Thalberg built up this extraordinary concentration of talent which was MGM, and when Mayer left the whole studio began going to pot. I think people don't understand how a place like MGM had to be fed, sustained and organized every day."

—GEORGE CUKOR

PROLOGUE

IN THE SUMMER of 1944, when he looked out his window on the third floor of the Thalberg Building, Louis B. Mayer saw a studio—his studio—that covered 167 acres. Lot 1 encompassed seventy-two acres, housed all the thirty sound-stages, office buildings, and dressing rooms, the seven warehouses crammed with furniture, props, and draperies. Lot 2 consisted of thirty-seven acres of permanent exterior sets, including the town of Carvel, home of the Hardy family, and the great Victorian street from *Meet Me in St. Louis*. Here was the house where David Copperfield lived, there the street where Marie Antoinette rolled to the guillotine.

Lots 3, 4, and 5 were used for outdoor settings—the jungle and rivers that provided the backdrop for Tarzan, much of *Trader Horn*, the zoo that provided the animals, including the lion that heralded each and every Metro-Goldwyn-Mayer film. Connecting everything was thirteen miles of paved road.

In periods of peak production, which was most of the time, the studio had six thousand employees and three entrances to accommodate them—the gate between Corinthian columns on Washington Boulevard; another one farther down Ince Way; and a crew gate on Culver Boulevard, where the workers punched time clocks.

MGM owned forty cameras and sixty sound machines. Thirty-three actors were officially designated stars, seventy-two actors were considered featured players, and twenty-six directors were under contract. "Anywhere from sixteen to eighteen pictures were being shot at one time," remembered actress Ann Rutherford. "They were either shooting or preparing to shoot on every soundstage. . . . You could stick your nose into any rehearsal hall or soundstage, and it was just teeming with life."

The studio had its own dentist, its own chiropractor, its own foundry. It made its own paint, its own rubber molds. There were shops where old cars could be fabricated and assembled; electric, glass, and plastic shops. If a prop could not be found in the vast warehouse, it could be made overnight, or purchased; the studio spent $1 million a year buying props.

About 2,700 people ate in the commissary every day, while the research department answered about five hundred questions daily. The studio's laboratory printed 150 million feet of release prints every year. Power was supplied by an in-house electrical plant, which was of sufficient size to light a town of 25,000.

MGM maintained a police force of fifty officers, with four captains, two plainclothesmen, an inspector, and a chief—a force larger than that of Culver City itself. Each member of the MGM police was trained to recognize all contract players and to salute each star.

The MGM police had a slightly different mandate than most police forces. Part of their job was protecting the studio's assets from the public, but they also had to protect those assets from themselves. No matter what an MGM actor did, police chief Whitey Hendry had to beat the local police to the scene, where publicity chief Howard Strickling would make arrangements to keep the story out of the papers. To do this, the studio had paid informants in every local police department.

Twenty years earlier, when Mayer had moved onto what was then the Goldwyn lot, the studio had consisted of forty acres, five stages, six cameras, six stars, a half-dozen directors, and six hundred employees. In the intervening years, Louis B. Mayer and his lieutenants built a company that was regarded by the public and his peers alike as the pinnacle of the industry.

"It was *the* studio in this town," said screenwriter Bernard Gordon. "When I came out here in 1939, I drove by MGM and I thought to myself, 'By God, *that's* Hollywood.' No other studio compared, and Mayer was the boss. Metro-Goldwyn-Mayer. *Mayer!*"

Each studio had its own specific ambience, and MGM's was a luxury that was a synonym for quality. The songwriter Harry Warren used to have a stock story about the difference between Metro and the competition: "At Warner Brothers, you come in the gate at seven in the morning. The guards on the walls keep their guns aimed at you. At 7:05, Hal Wallis calls out, 'Have you written that song yet?'

"At Metro, the birds sing. The grass is green. Everybody smokes a pipe and has the Book-of-the-Month under his arm. Nobody works at Metro. You watch the flowers grow."

For the audience, MGM was predominantly a means of escape. In the 1930s, MGM came to symbolize an alternate reality from the drabness and squalor of the worldwide Depression, an escape into a dreamworld of Park Avenue swells. During World War II, MGM movies were serving simultaneously as escape and rallying cry—*Mrs. Miniver* rallied support for England and, by implication, the internationalist cause, while the home front was bolstered by *The Human Comedy* and Andy Hardy.

For audiences at home and abroad, MGM was Hollywood at its most Hollywood in the best sense of the word, proved by the fact that MGM grosses were reliably leagues ahead of its competitors' and had been since the company was formed in 1924.

The year before, in 1943, MGM had released thirty-five pictures, among them *The Human Comedy, DuBarry Was a Lady, Girl Crazy, A Guy Named Joe, Bataan, Lassie Come Home,* and a full roster of programmers. In 1944, Mayer was riding herd on a group of pictures that included *Meet Me in St. Louis, Gaslight, National Velvet, Thirty Seconds Over Tokyo,* and *The White Cliffs of Dover.* Although there was a war on—actually, *because* there was a war on—profits for the MGM division of Loew's, Inc. for 1944–45 (the financial year ran June to July) would be an astonishing $22.4 million on a gross of $98.1 million, compared to $14.5 million in profits for Paramount, $10.9 million for Fox, $3.4 million for Universal.

Within the industry, when Paramount or RKO made a particularly good picture, it would be said that "it was of MGM quality"; at a sneak preview, when the MGM logo of a roaring lion appeared, there would be a spontaneous burst of applause from the audience.

Singer Tony Martin asserted that "Being . . . at MGM was the movie equivalent of being a pitcher on the New York Yankees—you were first-class, everybody knew you were first-class and there was no reason not to be grateful for having the privilege."

"Warner Brothers had its stock company, sure," said Ann Rutherford, "but who wanted to rub elbows with Guy Kibbee and Hugh Herbert, bless their hearts? . . . Most of the contract people at MGM stayed and stayed and stayed. Why? Because the studio looked after them. Warner Brothers wouldn't—they were always spanking somebody or selling them down the river. From the time you were signed at MGM you just felt you were in God's hands."

"It was almost feudal in the way it was so self-contained," remembered actress Janet Leigh. "Everything was grown inside. It was a complete city. There were doctors and dentists, there were people to teach you acting and singing and dancing. There were people to help you with your finances. You could live there. And the people were like family, because everybody was under contract, not just the actors and producers, but the electricians. If I finished one picture, I might find a different crew on the next one, but the one after that would probably have the same crew from the first picture. You had a sense of being surrounded by friendly, familiar faces; you had great continuity."

"MGM functioned like General Motors," remembered actor Ricardo Montalban. "It was run with such efficiency that it was a marvel. It was done by teamwork; they could project the product, and the product was not any individual movie, it was the actor. They created a persona that they thought the public would like; they tailor-made the publicity to create a persona throughout the world. It was amazing."

The key to the smooth running of this machine was detail, a sense of the overall that kept employees functioning whether they were working on a picture or not. An actor who wasn't assigned to a picture was still expected to be exercising, attending acting, dance, music, or speech classes, working in screen tests with prospective talent, promoting the studio's releases, or slipping into a tux to fill an empty chair at a studio dinner.

And none of this vast, smooth-running organization mattered as much as it ordinarily would have that summer of 1944. Louis B. Mayer, sitting in his office with white leather walls, a custom-designed wraparound desk, and an adjoining soundproof telephone room where he could consult with New York a half-dozen times a day, had a serious problem: He believed that his most popular young leading man was homosexual.

This issue had arisen before, when MGM had to finesse the fact that two of its top stars, William Haines and Ramon Novarro, were gay, but that had been more than fifteen years ago. The movie business had expanded exponentially since then—weekly movie attendance had increased by a third, from 65 million in 1928 to 85 million in 1944. Now, there was more at stake.

Van Johnson had been handed the job of replacing Lew Ayres in the Dr. Kildare movies, then landed a supporting part in *The Human Comedy*. The fan mail had perked up, and the fan magazines were avid for interviews and photographs.

Johnson was an engaging personality, a competent actor. And he was an ex–chorus boy who was, claimed one MGM employee, "notorious on Broadway." Mayer knew it was only a question of time until MGM's money would have to be used to buy somebody's silence. The studio had done that before, with William Haines, an experience Mayer had vowed he would never repeat.

For Louis B. Mayer, homosexuality was not necessarily an insurmountable obstacle. As with many people of his time, Mayer believed that homosexuality was a psychological aberration that could be successfully treated—especially by a good woman. As Mayer's suspicions about Johnson grew, he ordered every available, beautiful woman on the lot thrown at the young actor in an effort to establish his heterosexual bona fides.

Nothing.

But now there was a chance . . .

On April 1, 1943, during the production of A Guy Named Joe, Johnson had been badly hurt in an auto accident on Venice Boulevard and had spent a month or so recuperating at the home of his best friend, MGM character actor Keenan Wynn, the son of the legendary comedian Ed Wynn. While recuperating, Johnson had sparked to Evie, Keenan Wynn's vivacious, entertaining wife. He had told anybody who would listen about how sweet she had been to him after his accident, how he envied Keenan's taste in women. Word got back to Louis B. Mayer. Word always did. Ida Koverman, the dreaded Mount Ida, Mayer's executive secretary and protectress, sent a limousine for Evie Wynn.

Mayer's office was designed to intimidate and it succeeded splendidly. The anteroom, where the secretaries sat, was grand enough, but behind the mammoth walnut doors the sanctum sanctorum was even grander. Evie Wynn entered and saw that the office was huge and white—completely white. The carpet—all sixty long feet of it—the walls, the ceilings, desk, chairs, sofas, and lights were all snowy and pristine, with silver accents that combined to suggest a moderne temple.

At the end, behind a white-leather-sided crescent-shaped desk, sat the five and a half feet and 175 pounds of Louis (always pronounced Louie) Burt Mayer, who made the decisions that helped shape the parameters of the American Dream for twenty-five years of the twentieth century.

He looked rather like a very small, very charming white penguin, and he had soft, silken hands that disguised the fact that he had done manual labor for years.

"I have thrown June Allyson and Gloria De Haven and Sonja Henie at Van," Mayer began. "He will only marry you. I'm here to see if we can't work something out. What would make you happy?"

The tone was unthreatening—a sophisticated, fatherly man of the world talking to his female equal, offering up his concern, his vulnerability, asking her help so they could protect each other's interests.

Evie Wynn was surprised but not flabbergasted. "I had thought about Van a lot at that point," she would remember nearly sixty years later. "Keenan was always busy; his work was his life. 'Go with Van,' he'd say. So Van and I would go to parties and premieres, and Keenan went into the background. I think Keenan thought Van was safe. Maybe he knew about his proclivities, but he never said anything. Van was thirty years old, and my head was turned."

Mayer went on to explain sorrowfully that MGM was in a difficult position. Character actors were a dime a dozen, and the studio had to economize wherever it could. Keenan, for all his great talent, was expendable.

But perhaps there was a solution. If Evie divorced Keenan and married Van, perhaps the studio could make some . . . accommodation. If Evie did this thing that would benefit her, Van, and, coincidentally, the studio, Keenan would be signed to a new contract that would pay him far more money than any character actor on the lot. That was only fair; he and Evie had children, after all.

Moreover, he would guarantee Keenan good parts in good movies—no B films, no throwaways. And, as a final sop, there would be no unsalaried layoffs, the three-month hiatus that was a nominal part of all but the most gold-plated stars' lives. MGM would pay Keenan fifty-two weeks a year for seven years.

He wanted Evie to think about this situation, think about it very carefully. Everybody would win; nobody would lose.

"He was very fatherly," said Evie Wynn. "And I was scared to death. I did stick up for Keenan. In retrospect, I can see he was arranging my marriage to Van just as Universal did later for Rock Hudson. That was a farce. Ours was a real marriage. I was in love with Van, but I wouldn't have married him if I'd known he was homosexual."

Evie promised to think about it. Suitable arrangements were made. About a year after the meeting in Mayer's office, Evie and Keenan Wynn were divorced, and in January 1947, she and Van Johnson were married.

Mission accomplished.

For Louis B. Mayer, arranging marriages was a normal part of his job. Coping with occupational hazards like alcoholism, suicide, and outré sexuality was as much a part of his job as negotiating contracts with stars and directors, as devising and promoting the accepted myths that first bewitched, then defined, several generations of Americans.

For Louis B. Mayer, it was just another day at the office.

There was no middle ground about Louis B. Mayer, not then, not now.

"You are talking about the devil incarnate," the normally mild-mannered Helen Hayes would say. "Not just evil, but the most evil man I have ever dealt with in my life. He was an untalented, mean, vicious, vindictive person. He deliberately undermined people, went after individuals who were good box office for Loew's, Inc.: Buster Keaton, Billy Haines. He turned everyone against everyone else, establishing himself as a kingpin, without having anything to offer himself. And he would lie to your face."

"Louis B. Mayer was a Jewish Hitler, a fascist," said Ralph Bellamy. "He had no feeling for any minority, including his own. No feeling for people, period. When he found that Lew Ayres was a conscientious objector he was furious. He informed everybody that 'Lew Ayres has some kind of phobia about killing people.' And he killed his career."

Others had a different view. Adela Rogers St. Johns described him as having "absolutely infallible judgment. And that's the only thing that is required of a producer. . . . He headed the greatest studio that ever existed, and he was the only immovable figure in it."

"Everything that has been said about him has been the case for the prosecution," asserted the director Clarence Brown. "Louis B. Mayer . . . made more stars than all the rest of the producers in Hollywood put together. . . . He knew how to handle talent; he knew that to be successful, he had to have the most successful people in the business working for him. He was like Hearst in the newspaper business. . . . He made an empire out of the thing."

Sam Marx, an MGM story editor, said that "Mayer is [an overly] maligned man. His reputation is far worse than it should be. He once said to Hearst, 'We have two strikes against us—we can write a check for a million dollars and it's good.' He was a true capitalist and a devout Republican, but he wasn't as violent as people thought he was. He had to be strong to do his job, and he couldn't do that without making enemies."

Even Helen Hayes had a disconnect between the man she hated, and the organization he had created and ran. "It was *the* great film studio of the world," she said. "Not just of America, or of Hollywood, but of the world."

Perhaps in trying to understand the man who created this great studio we should look for middle ground, areas where some general agreement can be found. Mayer was, first of all, a superb manager. "Mayer was a great executive and could have run General Motors as successfully as MGM," said screenwriter-director-producer Joseph L. Mankiewicz.

"Mayer was a man born for success," said the producer Armand Deutsch. "He was a fierce man, beneath a variety of exteriors. Sometimes his eyes would just *blaze*. The thing that distinguished him and that made MGM the greatest was the insistence on being the best. He was a showman. And the engine that drove this factory, that sent forty or fifty films a year into the marketplace, was Louis B. Mayer."

He was a businessman, but a businessman with a specific vision. He was unusual for a movie mogul in that he took an overt moral position in his movies— a provincial nineteenth-century Victorian propriety. An ardent purveyor of what would today be termed family values—indeed, as the main mover behind the Andy Hardy movies, Mayer was one of the defining agents of those values— he was not above being attracted to some of the beautiful women that crowded the MGM lot. But such was his personality that he tended to fall in love with them rather than maintain an essentially mercantile relationship. As with every one of the Jewish movie moguls, no matter how *haimish* he seemed to be, the first wife was eventually discarded and a *shiksa* enlisted for the job.

What Mayer wanted in his movies—and usually got—was an idealized vision of men, women, and the world they lived in. Mayer fervently believed that movies were not a reflection of life, but an escape from life. He believed in beauty, glamour, the star system, and materialism.

Marriage was sacrosanct and mothers were objects of veneration, hence completely desexualized. When MGM made *The Human Comedy*, Mayer's favorite of the eight hundred movies produced under his aegis, Fay Bainter was cast as the mother of a five-year-old. At the time, Bainter was a matronly woman in her mid-fifties.

But Mayer was a businessman before he was a moralist, so MGM was the proud home of the tomcat sexuality of Clark Gable, the easy availability of Jean Harlow, the wry, common-man persona of Spencer Tracy, the wounded vulnerability of Judy Garland, the shopgirl heat of Joan Crawford, and the ethereal Greta Garbo—a personal discovery of Mayer's, as were Hedy Lamarr and Greer Garson.

To get the vision he wanted, Mayer would implore, he would beg, he would placate, he would scream, he would threaten. And once in a while, if imploring, begging, placating, screaming, and threatening didn't work, he would allow the actor or director or producer to go ahead anyway. If they failed, he would be sure to say, "I told you so." And if they succeeded, he would just as invariably admit he had been wrong.

Even while he was alive, his values and the kinds of movies he loved were being supplanted. Since his death in 1957, he has been ruthlessly caricatured as a vulgar, roaring tyrant, a metaphor for the banality that New York intellectuals found in Hollywood, even as they scrambled to earn the salaries paid by those vulgarians. Respected film critics have thrown around the word "evil"—a word that should probably be reserved for the people who herded Jews into boxcars—about Mayer, as if he were Edward Arnold in a Frank Capra movie.

All this overlooks the fact that Mayer, more than any film producer of his generation, had a deep and instinctive understanding of the mass audience's taste and needs, and built the most successful operation ever devised to meet those tastes and needs.

Sophisticates in New York or Los Angeles might scoff at Andy Hardy or the let's-put-on-a-show MGM musicals, but Mayer knew that formula works. Then, as now, people—especially Americans—like stars, spectacle, and optimism, if possible with a little sentiment attached. They do not want to be challenged or instructed, but comforted and entertained, and the aesthetic quality of a film is less important to its commercial success than its fitting securely within an existing category—and certain categories are more easily manufactured than others.

Variety's estimation of Mayer's achievement is irrefutably accurate: "Placed in his proper perspective, he was probably the greatest single force in the development of the motion picture industry to the heights of prosperity and influence it finally attained."

He was many things—tycoon is insufficient. Elia Kazan, who knew something about feral ambition, compared Mayer and the rest of the men who created the Hollywood studio system to those who thronged to Alaska during the gold rush, "desperate men in a bare-knuckle scramble over rugged terrain, roughnecks thinly disguised, men out of a book by Frank Norris or Theodore Dreiser, alike in reach and taste . . . but, when they felt they had to, ready to go for each other's throats." In Mayer's case, literally.

He was a man with a manic intensity and creative vanity. Competition was everything, and the movies were the vehicle by which he would justify his beliefs. He competed with the other moguls to see who'd make the best or biggest grossing picture of the year, who would sign up the hottest star or writer or director. Usually, it was L.B.

He liked his drama melodramatic, his comedy laced with a strong dose of sentimentality. He loved swaggering, charismatic hams like Lionel Barrymore and Marie Dressler. He loved the respectability the studio gave him, and he delighted in the reflected glory earned by hosting meet-and-greet luncheons for visiting dignitaries. When Charles Lindbergh or George Bernard Shaw came to Los Angeles, they visited MGM. He had the essential narcissism of a child; there was no higher form of praise than for him to say of someone, "I like him; he can talk to me."

And he loved music and the movies that featured music. In his most far-sighted creative act, he made a songwriter named Arthur Freed the associate producer of *The Wizard of Oz*. When that film lost $1.1 million in its initial release, Mayer promptly gave Freed his own unit, for no good reason other than he had a hunch.

Freed responded by rolling out a series of films still venerated as the high-water mark of the form: *For Me and My Gal, Girl Crazy, Meet Me in St. Louis, The Harvey Girls, The Pirate, Easter Parade, The Barkleys of Broadway, On the Town, An American in Paris, Singin' in the Rain, The Band Wagon,* and *Gigi* — cumulatively, Mayer's greatest contribution to posterity.

For all of his idealism about the movies, inside the business, with the possible exception of Columbia's boss Harry Cohn, there was no one in Hollywood who was more feared. He was a great hater, and once you got on his list, it was very hard to get off. And if he hated you, he would try his best, not merely to get you out of MGM, but to get you out of the movie business.

Mayer came out of Russia and into the movies laboring beneath a miserable education. His grandson Daniel Selznick remembers Mayer's notes accompanying Christmas and birthday presents as being ungrammatical — misspelled, and with no capitals at the beginning of his sentences.

To survive he had had to be aggressive; to flourish he had to be ruthless. Empire builders by definition have to fight for money, fight for power. They may be kind to animals and small children while doing all this, but make no mistake: if, in the line of business, somebody has to get hurt, it won't be them. Business, as Charlie Chaplin observed in *Monsieur Verdoux*, is a ruthless business. There should have been no surprise in any of this — show business is a jungle, and Metro-Goldwyn-Mayer's symbol was a lion.

"No one got to know Mayer but Mayer," said Fredericka Sagor Maas, a writer at the studio in the mid-'20s. "He was a chameleon — strong and brutal. His people respected him highly, but he could destroy you with his pinkie and he damn well knew it. He brooked no contradiction or anything else that would diminish his power. And he was obsessed by his fear of [Loew's, Inc. chairman] Nicholas Schenck, who was more powerful than he was."

What he wanted was the same thing as what he needed, and to get it he would do anything he deemed necessary. As one MGM employee remembered, "Typically, he tried every angle. If Mayer couldn't get in the front door, he tried the back. If he couldn't get in the back, he'd try the chimney. If he couldn't get in the chimney, he'd try to blow the house down."

"He was always acting," said MGM star Esther Williams. "He was the best actor on the lot, but since I wasn't marrying him I didn't care if he was sincere or not. But you believed him at your peril."

Jack Warner was always Jack Warner, Sam Goldwyn was always Sam Goldwyn, Darryl Zanuck was always Darryl Zanuck. But Mayer was different things to different people. If you needed a father, Mayer would be your Daddy. If you needed a demanding coach, Mayer would set the bar six inches higher and tell you he knew you could vault over it. He would sob and wail, he would listen and offer advice. He could be whatever he needed to be. He always saw the endgame, and always saw that endgame in terms of what he wanted, what the company needed. He was Hollywood's greatest closer.

The value Mayer cherished was a clannish loyalty. The employees of MGM, from Clark Gable to the night watchman, were family, part of his personal empire. He never wrote a movie, never directed a movie, and couldn't have even if he wanted to. He never pretended to tell writers what to write or art directors what to design. But he grew up in a time when a businessman recognized good workmanship when he saw it, and that was what L.B. respected. He had a horror of hoodwinking the customer; he believed in giving good weight. He never stopped feeling and smelling the goods. He would never pretend to understand cinema—he usually disliked it when he saw it—but he understood movies and the people who buy them and live in them as few others have.

The problems of an uncreative man in a creative industry would seem to be insoluble, but unlike many businessmen, Mayer had a knack for abstract thinking, and he was a master at manipulating people, many of whom were inherently unstable, into giving him what his studio needed. His supreme gift was his understanding of the nature of stardom and the needs of the audience, bred by his years of being an exhibitor.

MGM movies didn't have the best scripts or the best directors. Most of them weren't even the best movies, but they assuredly had the largest concentration of the greatest stars, the illuminated personalities who meant the most to what Norma Desmond in *Sunset Boulevard* would call "those wonderful people out there in the dark." For the audience, MGM represented what the movies should be.

For years, Mayer was regarded as merely a businessman, the one who coordinated, who set budgets and gave approvals for Irving Thalberg, the boy wonder who ran MGM production. And when Thalberg died in 1936, people in Hollywood waited for Mayer to stumble and fall.

It didn't happen. The studio went from strength to strength, making even more money, making even better pictures. For ten more years, MGM thrived, until changing times and tastes conspired to destroy, first Mayer, then, incrementally, his studio.

It is easy to smile ruefully at, or be horrified by, a man like Mayer. He has been demonized in memoirs and relentlessly caricatured in popular art— Michael Lerner's definitively hilarious turn in *Barton Fink*—as the archetypal emotional tyrant. And enough of it is true to give the stories the resonance of fact.

"He could be grating," said Evie Johnson. "He was a bulldog; you had to believe what he believed. His opinion was the right one, and no debate was possible. Socially, as a dinner partner, he was a lot of fun—ingratiating and kind. But you had to remember he was also a despot who used the carrot-and-stick approach."

Producer David Lewis, a protégé of Irving Thalberg, called him "brilliant, seductive, unprincipled. A rattlesnake was tame compared to Mayer. But all in all a man of genius, one of only three such men with whom I crossed paths in the motion picture business."

Yet, to walk the streets of MGM during the Mayer era was to visit Olympus. There was Garbo with a retinue holding up the train of her dress; there the three Barrymores, or Clark Gable, who seemed to carry some sort of masculine spotlight that illuminated him from within. And there were the problem children—the alcoholic, impetuous John Gilbert, the crude, crass Wallace Beery, who physically abused Mickey Rooney until director Sam Wood challenged him to a fistfight.

In what we seem doomed to regard as the movies' Golden Age, MGM defined Hollywood in ways that transcend any individual movie. Some of those things are intangible—glamour, gloss, the specific sound of the MGM orchestra—but some are not. Louis B. Mayer defined MGM, just as MGM defined Hollywood, and Hollywood defined America.

His is an extraordinary story, symbolized by the immense difference between the place where he began and the place where he finished. Dealt a miserable hand at birth, he made it to America and climbed the ladder of the most exciting business in the world.

———————————

I began this book knowing little of Mayer besides the oft-repeated stories, but the man that more than 150 interviewees told me about was far more complex than the one-dimensional ogre of legend.

The bell can't be unrung, of course; it's not that all the famously negative stories of Mayer are false, but, rather, that there was another Mayer—one willfully undocumented because he was less like an absurd comic heavy in a movie, more like a human being. This aims to be a portrait in three dimensions.

Mayer's creation was MGM—the stars, the stories, and the way they were presented that led audiences the world over to applaud the moment they saw the MGM lion. More than Thalberg, more than any of the actors, Mayer was the constant, the man who set the tone.

Even today, with the studio divested of everything except its name, the words Metro-Goldwyn-Mayer still resonate with the glory of Old Hollywood—a town that wouldn't have achieved half the renown it did without Louis B. Mayer.

PART ONE

"Business is not an exact science."

—LOUIS B. MAYER

A formal portrait of the rising young Haverhill, Mass., exhibitor.
Mayer had an oil painting made from this photograph
and hung it in the lobby of the Colonial Theater.

(Harold B. Lee Library, Brigham Young University)

Chapter
ONE

HE WAS HUNGRY, always hungry.

That was the sum total of what Louis B. Mayer remembered about his early childhood. Since he was never a man to dwell on the past, and he had the kind of mind that could ignore or blot out what he didn't wish to remember, he would always tell family and friends that his memories were few and dim—just that he was hungry, and thirsty for milk.

No human being leaves his childhood completely behind, but unlike many self-made men, Mayer never enjoyed talking about his childhood, for it was a time of deprivation and talking about things always made them seem real. Long before Hollywood, the story of Louis B. Mayer is indissolubly linked to Russian anti-Semitism. Without that, his family, not to mention millions of others, would never have left their homeland.

Among these despised Jews was one who would come to be known as Jacob Mayer, designated officially by anti-Semitic regulations as a "nonsettled petit bourgeois." Jacob was born around 1847 and grew up to be an extremely short man—barely five feet—with a bad case of short man's disease. In those days, the family name could have been Baer . . . or Meir. "Only God knows," said one of Louis B. Mayer's daughters, "where the Mayer came from."

In 1881, Tsar Alexander II was assassinated by a group of conspirators that included at least one Jew, prompting an outbreak of even more virulent anti-Semitism, culminating in pogroms in 150 settlements in six western provinces. By now, Jews were forbidden to settle in villages, to buy real estate out of the town where they lived, forbidden to open stores or shops on Sundays or Christian holidays. They were, however, still eligible for conscription, obligated to serve in the army for twenty-five years. In 1882, Alexander III declared the May Laws, which prohibited Jews from purchasing or even renting land. All this meant that any Jew with a modicum of intelligence or drive knew it was imperative to get out of Russia.

Between 1881 and 1890, 240,000 Jews left. Eighty percent of these Eastern European Jews who migrated came to America; between 10 and 13 percent went to Canada. The usual route for Jews from the Ukraine and southern Russia was to cross into Austria-Hungary illegally, then take a train to Warsaw or Berlin, then on to Hamburg, where they could purchase a steerage steamship ticket to the New World for $34. The passage took between eight and fourteen days, depending on the weather.

Among those making this trip was a young boy named Lazar. The standard MGM biography of Louis B. Mayer would give July 4, 1885, as his birth date, and Minsk as his birthplace, for reasons that remain mysterious, as he wasn't born on that date or in that town.

Mostly, Mayer was vague about his birthplace. But on his petition for American naturalization in 1912, he broke down and specified the town of Dumier, also known as Dymer. (Dumier is the Ukrainian name, Dymer is the Russian name, and Dimer is the name in Yiddish.) Under any name, Dumier is in the northern Ukraine, about twenty-five miles north of Kiev and about that far south of Chernobyl, not far from today's border of Belarus. Today, Dumier has about ten thousand people, only ten of whom are Jewish. (In 1926, the Jewish population was 238, many of whom would die at Babi Yar.)

In the 1901 Canadian census, while Mayer was still living with his parents in Saint John, New Brunswick, his father gave July 12, 1884, as his son's birth date. If Jacob knew when his son was born, then Mayer knew when he was born, which is why Louis's chosen date of July 4, 1885, was so close to the truth. The small smoke screen of one year and eight days could be attributed to any one of several possibilities:

1. Jacob gave different dates for Lazar's birth at different times, so the boy was genuinely uncomfortable specifying a date. (Birth certificates for this area from the late 1800s to World War I were lost during World War II.)

2. It was part of Mayer's sense of showmanship. As many people noted over the years, he was a superb actor, a closet performer who came roaring

out of the closet at the slightest pretext, and being born on the fourth of July has a certain ring to it.

3. He needed to believe in a myth of self-creation, which, in his case, was not that far off the mark.

It's improbable that Mayer didn't know the specifics of his birth—there wasn't an ounce of vagueness in his makeup, ever. Perhaps the reason is contained in a remark he made many years later: "In the beginning, I had to be older. Later, I wanted to be younger."

It's possible that Mayer specified Minsk because, while Dumier was the technically correct response, the family had moved to the Minsk region soon after his birth, possibly in order to facilitate their emigration from Russia. It was easier to leave Russia from a region other than your own, because then you didn't have to account for military service, whether or not your taxes were paid, and so on. It's probable that the family moved around in the general area of Vilnius/Minsk/Kiev (think Jacksonville/Atlanta/Nashville) when Lazar was young, so stories about where he was "from" could easily vary. It's also possible that they were reluctant to be specific because of some generalized insecurity as Jews.

In 1874, Jacob had used a broker to marry Sarah Meltzer, an Austro-Hungarian girl born in 1851. The family had three children in Russia: Yetta, born in 1878, Ida, born in 1883, and Lazar. Sarah Mayer lost several children in infancy, and Lazar would always be her most cherished child. Jacob, Sarah, and Lazar are all religious names, so the family were definitely practicing, devout Jews, as were many others in their vicinity. There are some Meirs and Mayers in tax and property records that survive in the area. There's a Gershevich Mayer in a 1784 property tax record, possibly a distant ancestor. The surname was not unknown, but it's not common in surviving records either.

The family reached landfall in England in 1886, followed by stopovers in New York and Boston. Jacob stated on his immigration papers in 1921 that he was a resident of Long Island from 1887 to 1892, which would explain why his last two children were born there: Rubin/Rudolph in April of 1889, and Gershon/Jerry in Brooklyn in April 1891.

It's almost certain that Jacob was working as a peddler during this time, selling scrap off a cart, like many of his landsmen. Peddling was difficult and dangerous work. Merchandise on a peddler's back—notions, dry goods, spices, old clothes—could weigh a hundred pounds and it was common for a peddler to walk ten to fifteen miles a day. Late in 1891 or early 1892, the family moved to

Canada. Family legend has it that Jacob got into some kind of trouble—both violence and a convenient fire were mentioned—and had to light out for the territory. By the time they arrived in Canada, the family name was Mayer, and Lazar's name was Louis.

Saint John, New Brunswick, is on the Bay of Fundy, one of the world's great natural wonders. One hundred billion tons of water flow into and out of the bay twice a day, forming rip currents and whirlpools that power a vital natural ecosystem. The Bay of Fundy has shaped the environment and culture of the entire region.

The feeding grounds around Campobello, Deer and Grand Manan Islands make the Bay particularly rich for marine mammals. Up to fifteen species of whales arrive every summer to eat and mate, while the tides create large blooms of plankton.

Saint John is one of the only ice-free seaports on the east coast of Canada, so it has always had an important shipping business. It was a quaint old town, with streets paved with rectangular blocks of quarried granite—an old-fashioned city, a place where people knew their neighbors.

Jacob's move from New York to Saint John was something Mayer could never rationally explain, probably because he never asked his father what he had been thinking.

The Mayers were naturalized as Canadian citizens in 1892, but the first documentary evidence of the family's existence in Saint John comes in the 1895–96 city directory, where Jacob Mayer is listed as a "pedler" (sic). The Mayer family was living in the crowded tenements of the town's North End, the equivalent of New York's Lower East Side. Most of the directory references show Jacob as a dry goods merchant or a junk dealer, with a work address of 74 Smythe Street (about a mile from his residence), later on Paradise Row (about a five-minute walk from home), and finally on Main Street—right next door to his house. Jacob began picking up other people's castoffs, anything he could carry or drag, then resold it door-to-door. Locks, metal, nails—anything.

The most lucrative salvage objects were the shipwrecks that drifted into the Bay of Fundy. As soon as Louis and Jerry were able, they were taught to dive for ripped pieces of metal, then drag them to shore. This went on all summer throughout Louis's adolescence, while Jacob stockpiled the steel so he could spend the winter selling it. In later years, Mayer would tell friends that he had developed his barrel chest by diving for salvage without benefit of scuba gear.

Louis would imply that he was as hungry in Saint John as he had been in Russia. He would tell friends that he used to press his nose against the windows of shops that sold noodles, unable to afford any himself, dreaming of the day when he would have all the noodles he wanted.

Louis would never deny that he had been in the scrap business, but he objected to stories that he was also a rag picker. "I never picked rags. Never! All we did was pick up scrap metal." Because of the catch-as-catch-can nature of his childhood, he would develop a somewhat extravagant sense of the importance of breeding and manners—people could get contracts at MGM, not because of any demonstrable talent or even force of personality, but because they had the sheen of gentility that Louis referred to as "class."

Jacob Mayer was like his son in some ways, unlike him in others. Like Louis, he was short and chunky, but Jacob was also hunched over, almost as if he had a spinal defect, and he had a solemn, phlegmatic personality. He talked in a labored, almost asthmatic manner.

His wife, Sarah, was also small and round, but where her husband was placid, Sarah was industrious. She supplemented the family's meager income by buying chickens from farmers and selling them to the poor families in the North End. Amongst the Jewish community of Saint John, it was considered a rather degrading way of earning money, but Sarah didn't care. She had children to feed, and besides, she could always keep the occasional chicken for some of the soup that her son loved so much. Louis would come to resemble her emotionally as well as physically.

The Mayers regularly attended temple, and Louis occasionally reminisced about the various cantors he had known, and how they had achieved their effects. His feelings about his religion were hard to pin down—although putatively a good Jew, one who often alluded to Jewish liturgies and would quote Hebrew prayers and sprinkle his conversation with the occasional Yiddish phrase, he rarely went to temple as an adult. Yet, he once proudly showed off a beautiful, hand-illuminated copy of the Haggadah he had just bought.

As late as 1880, there were only eight Jewish families in Saint John, but the Mayers were part of a considerable Eastern European influx in the last decade of the nineteenth century. Many of the Jews that came to Saint John arrived, not because they necessarily wanted to live there, but because it was a major port of entry for immigrants, and had many economic and family ties with Boston, which was virtually a sister city for many in the Jewish community. Saint John was also slightly cheaper than traveling all the way to New York.

By 1896, there was a sufficient Jewish population to form their own congregation. When a synagogue was built in 1898, among the elders of the Jewish community placing the Torah in the Ark was Jacob Mayer, who was, an early history of the community revealed, regarded as a pillar of the Jewish community in spite of the fact that he "carried on a small junk business at the foot of Main Street. He struggled hard to earn a living."

There was a fair amount of Jew-baiting among the population of Saint John, and there were times when Louis and his brothers, Rudy and Jerry, would have to fight their way home through nests of hostile Irish and German kids. Louis learned that you have to fight—not just for what you want, but to keep what you already have.

In later years, Louis would tell of a tussle with another boy at school. The fight ended in a draw, but Louis headed home with thoughts of revenge, just biding his time until he could get another shot at the child. When Sarah found out what had happened, she took him "to the end of the beautiful valley [!] we lived in and asked me to repeat the words I had been mumbling to myself the afternoon before."

"Damn you," screamed Louis into the valley, with the echo coming back. Sarah told him to shout the words "Bless you" with the same force. Those words seemed to come back with a stronger echo.

"Which do you prefer, my son?" asked Sarah. "It is entirely up to you. That is the way life is. It always returns to you what we say to it. If you shout at your fellow man, 'Damn you!' life and your fellow man will shout it right back at you. If you say to life, to humanity, 'Bless you,' then your life will be the echo of these words. 'Bless you.'

"As the years went by, that law was confirmed in my experience. If I put in hatred, meanness, revenge, I would get it back. If I tried to speak of love, kindness, forgiveness, they would be returned to me."

The story had obviously been polished to a fine, metaphorical sheen over the years, but the alternating strains of aggression and benevolence that would make the adult Mayer so hard for many to take certainly ring true. He would always be torn between taking revenge on the world that had made his childhood so brutal, and playing the benevolent *padrone* surrounded by the earned riches of success.

Louis became a familiar figure around the streets of Saint John: a small, energetic boy carrying a large, coarse bag over his shoulder. He kept his eyes on the ground, scanning the area in front of him for anything metal—nails, discarded pipe, a horseshoe. When he saw something, he would dart forward, grab it and toss it into the bag. It was his now, but he had to have more, so he would keep moving quickly, so nobody else could get to the precious metal before he could. The habit of a rapid pace, almost a trot, would stay with him all his life.

John Wilson owned a tin business on Sidney Street and one day in the mid-1890s he found one of his employees hanging on to a ragged, crying child. He had a battered cart, and on the side of the cart was a sign that said "Junk Dealer."

"I caught him in the yard stealing scrap metal," the employee said. "I'm getting the police."

The boy was terrified, sobbing and begging them not to call the police. "I didn't mean to steal anything. I thought you'd thrown the metal away."

"He wasn't stealing," said Wilson. "I gave him permission to take that metal. We're partners, aren't we, son?"

This *beau geste* resulted, first, in young Louis having access to Wilson's foundry for all the tin and copper trimmings he had no use for. Second, they became lifelong friends.

The older man gave the boy a piece of advice he would hold dear: "When you come to the end of your rope, tie a knot and hang on." In other words, never, never, never, never, never, *never* give up. It was a maxim Louis would follow until the last weeks of his life, and it is probable that Wilson was a far more sympathetic father figure than Jacob Mayer. "Mr. Wilson was my best friend," Mayer would say, "my first partner." Whenever Mayer came to Saint John in later years, he placed flowers on Wilson's grave, just as he did on his mother's.

It's obvious that Louis was an industrious child, taking control because his father couldn't or wouldn't. John Wilson remembered that he was impressed with the boy's good manners and bright personality. Louis's own stories of his childhood revolved around his work ethic and respect for the dollar.

He remembered that he saved up pennies until he could buy a little red wagon. When his mother saw it she asked him what he intended to do with it. "Put it to work," he replied.

"When?"

"Tomorrow."

And so the red wagon delivered bits of iron and brass to the small salvage business Jacob Mayer had started. Louis became enamored of baseball, and saved a penny and a nickel at a time until he had enough to buy a glove, and he made all his friends wait outside so they couldn't see how much he was paying. He wore the glove on his belt, and he became the kind of ballplayer managers love—scrappy, intense, making up in desire what he lacked in ability.

Mayer remembered a hotel dining room he passed regularly on his scrap rounds. He would stop and look at the luxurious environment—silver candlesticks, pink lamp shades. He vowed that one day he would go into that dining room and order an expensive meal. Years later, when he had more money than he had ever dreamed of, he was back in Saint John. When he went by the hotel to fulfill his childhood fantasy, he found that it had been torn down. "That," he would remember, "is the definition of the tragedy of success."

One writer has claimed that Mayer had a good education and graduated from high school in 1902. But a review of the graduation lists of Saint John High from 1899 to 1902, as well as the accompanying class photos, not to mention a roster of all graduates prior to 1914, shows no sign of Louis Mayer. The school records list Louis as a student in the fifth grade in 1895, but there is no evidence to suggest that Mayer's education extended past 1897, when he was just short of thirteen. There are three references to Louis in the school records—once he was listed as a "Good" student, the other two times as "Fair."

Louis attended the Winter Street school, where he was taught by Ada Cowan. "I knew you'd be a successful man some day," Cowan remembered when Mayer came back to Saint John in the 1930s for one of his very occasional visits. "Do you remember the time I asked my pupils what they'd do if they had $20?"

Mayer thought for a while, then laughed. "I remember that day," he said. "One lad said if he had $20 he'd buy a bicycle, and another said he would buy a pony, and I said that if I had $20 I'd go into business."

Mayer had to leave school—there was a family to support. He always said his only regret was not having left at the age of ten, so he could have gotten a two-year head start on all the other kids who quit school at twelve.

After he left school, Louis subsidized the scrap business by working part-time as a mobile merchant, a sort of early Fuller Brush Man. He carried a basket full of stock—combs, cards, stationery, which he peddled from house to house.

By the time Louis was fifteen, Jacob decided to let him make all the deals for the family business, probably because he spoke better English than his father. This meant that Louis had to travel to Halifax and the other Canadian ports in search of salable scrap. He also had to make semiannual trips to Boston to sell the machinery and metals he had salvaged. Louis boasted that there came a time when he had two hundred men working for him, helping him raise such sunken ships as the *Alpha* and the *City of St. John.*

The family lived in five different places in Saint John. The first three years were in apartments for one year each, then they lived at 28 Acadia Street from 1898 until 1902. Finally, in 1903, they moved to 724 Main Street, which became known as the Mayer Building, where they lived until 1914. All these houses and buildings were within a couple of blocks of each other, so young Louis's childhood was circumscribed to the point of claustrophobia. (This area was leveled for urban renewal in the 1950s and 1960s; nothing remains of the buildings L. B. Mayer grew up in.)

"In most people, you can perceive the child," said Mayer's grandson Dan Selznick. "You can look at them and say they were such-and-such kind of a child in relation to their parents, who were the following. With this particular person, even though I've seen pictures of my grandfather as a child, it's very hard to get a sense of what the fabric of that family was."

"It was a crappy childhood," said Mayer's nephew Gerald. "They were poor. My grandfather barely spoke English, and he hadn't been trained to do anything at all." It was young Louis's ambition and drive that was supporting the family. In April 1899 "Louis Myer" was arrested for running a junk business without a license. It was a classic catch-22, because as a minor he couldn't apply for a business license. So Louis was hauled before a judge, and when the judge heard about the young boy supporting his family, he had Jacob set up a business so the boy could say he was working for him.

Jacob Mayer was very hard on Louis, much easier on Jerry and Rubin. What Jacob and Sarah produced was an aggressive Momma's boy capable of a deep and lasting affection for women but who was a trifle uneasy with men. From men he expected deference, loyalty, obedience. He wanted retinues more than he needed friends.

Aside from being physically grueling, this was a spiritually desolate way for a child to grow up; there was no room for intellect or even dreams, just muscle, brute strength, and enough aggression to ensure that Louis got to the metal before anybody else did. The only way to make something positive out of it was to think of it as a kind of atavistic game — these were the steps necessary to get out of Saint John, to get to someplace more hospitable, someplace warmer: the United States, where everybody was rich, or could become rich.

The contempt many had for a lowly immigrant junk dealer made the young boy belligerent, and junk dealing itself made him endlessly resourceful and opportunistic. Out of this crucible was Louis B. Mayer formed.

"Jacob beat my father," Irene Mayer Selznick would say. "He was always down on him for being so hardworking. It left my father suppressed." The physical and emotional abuse left Mayer eager for revenge against the world, but he would be the kind of man who had to go through life justified. The only way to show his father and everybody else who had underestimated or abused him how wrong they had been was to succeed. He would have a lifelong crusade for power; if he could not dominate a situation, he tried to avoid it, but he also spent his life in flight from acknowledging his own pursuit of power.

Education could not be the vehicle by which he would lift himself up. His tastes in reading would never be more than basic, and he always had trouble with grammar—the fact that Yiddish was spoken at home and English everywhere else might have made the situation worse. The combination of his own lack of affinity for school, and the fact that his hapless father was a Hebrew scholar of sorts gave him a deep-seated distrust of abstract knowledge. He would come to believe in the wisdom of experience, the common sense of the streets.

For the half-million Jews arriving from Eastern Europe at the turn of the twentieth century, work in America's big cities tended to be limited to the clothing trade, which was in the hands of the Ashkenazim—German Jews who had emigrated fifty years earlier, prosperous, cultured people who found it relatively easy to reestablish themselves in America.

But the Eastern Europeans were largely illiterate, fervently religious, and politically radical. They made Gentiles and Ashkenazim equally nervous. Back home in the *shtetl* they had raised haggling to an art form, which begged the question of what they would haggle about in America. It wouldn't be theater, because the theater was in the hands of Frohman, Ziegfeld, and Belasco—Sephardic aristocrats by birth or pretension who specialized in seducing the carriage trade into their theaters.

The movies . . . *that* could be haggled over.

Louis was a dreamer and the movies are the greatest medium of dreams ever invented, as he would have known, for the movies came to Saint John in 1897. They took your mind off your troubles yet they satisfied the dramatic and emotional demands of just about everybody. Watching those beautiful shadows move across the screen, accompanied by the ardent music that supported and accented the movements of the actors, was a safe embrace, a shelter from the outside world—like being led into a tranquil, flowing dreamworld. There was something here, something that could be made . . . and certainly something that could be sold.

Louis began hanging around the York Theatre, first at the stage door, then backstage. After a day of cadging scrap, he'd go down to the York and watch the vaudeville acts. He was enthralled with the gritty romance of show business. The audience saw only the charisma of the performer, but Louis was as fascinated with the backstage grind as he was by the magic of performance.

There is a local legend to the effect that, when Jacob was picking up some fabric scraps at a Germain Street tailor shop, the tailor began lamenting the problems he was having with one of his sons. "I have one like that, too," said Jacob. "All he wants to do is hang around that new Opera House every chance he gets."

Louis had to get out, and get out he did.

He would always speak of his debt to John Wilson and pay lip service to Saint John ("No matter what part of the world I am in—in France, England or the United States—it is always a matter of pride with me to be able to say I am from Saint John, New Brunswick."), but the truth was that Saint John mainly reminded him of how poor and unhappy he had been. Mayer would never be a generous man where Saint John was concerned, although he was made a Freeman of Saint John and received an honorary Ph.D. from the Provincial University. In 1949, he contributed money to the construction of a chapel to the memory of his mother and the mother of his cousin Nathan Cummings. But it would be left to the foundation he would fund after his death to endow a memorial scholarship in his name at the University of New Brunswick.

Louis Mayer was nineteen when he left Saint John. He had attained his full height of five feet seven inches, but little else. No matter. Poor and unhappy was a state of being he meant to put behind him. He was sure of it.

On January 3, 1904, Louis took a train from Saint John to Boston and rented a room at 17 Rochester Street in the South End. It was a neighborhood like the one he had just left: tenements and stores, pushcarts and yarmulkes. "I hadn't the price of a sandwich," he remembered. His landlord was distantly acquainted with his mother, and had promised to keep an eye on Sarah's boy. First he got a job with a local scrap metal merchant in Chelsea, then he found the woman who would become his wife.

Across the street from 17 Rochester Street was a kosher butcher at No. 14. The butcher—Hyman Shenberg by name—and his family lived above the store. Shenberg was also the cantor of the Emerald Street Synagogue.

"He met Margaret Shenberg through a picture," said Helen Sandler, Margaret's niece. The person holding the picture appears to have been Margaret's Aunt Annie. Aunt Annie recognized that the young man was serious, mature, and unafraid of success.

" 'Who is that beautiful girl?' Louis asked. 'Could I meet her?' He was a homely little man, but Margaret's mother liked him, so [Margaret] did what her mother wanted her to do and married him. I think, at the time, she loved someone else, actually, but she was an obedient girl."

If Margaret had ever loved anybody else, he was immediately forgotten. She became devoted to Mayer, or, as Helen Sandler remembered, "hypnotized. Everything was 'L.B., L.B.' She worshipped him, and he worshipped her. She was his Margie."

Louis B. Mayer and Margaret Shenberg were married on June 14, 1904, in Boston. He listed his age as twenty-two, and his occupation as merchant—two pieces of wishful thinking.

Mayer had married a sweet, supportive woman with artistic ability, and one who was accustomed to basking in the reflected glory of a domineering man— her father, Hyman Shenberg, was known as the Golden One for his voice, his bearing, and his beauty—a blue-eyed blond who demanded that his homely wife, Rachel, walk several steps behind him in public.

Margaret painted, and, remembered her niece, "could do a room in the most artistic taste. She could play the piano. She played a little golf, but not that great. But Margaret always did a lot of good for a lot of people." She had a generous spirit and was always giving or serving one of the endless roster of relatives that landed on her doorstep. Her daughter Irene would say of her mother, with a brutal honesty, "My mother was the sweetest, purest, kindest person, but no one ever accused her of being bright."

In the manner of newlyweds everywhere, Mayer had married Margie's entire family, and he was regarded with a mixture of love and respect. "I loved him, and he loved me," remembered Helen Sandler, the daughter of Margaret's sister Lillian. When Helen's father walked her to school, Louis would walk alongside them, a second Daddy. "He was always very generous and very loving with us."

Louis and Margaret moved into the Shenbergs' five-room Boston apartment. Their first child, Edith, was born on August 13, 1905, and soon afterward, Louis moved his little family to Brooklyn, New York, to 101 Russell Street, Greenpoint, where he sold junk. On April 2, 1907, Louis and Margaret had another girl, Irene, who looked so much like her mother that Louis called her "Little Margaret."

By the summer of 1907, the Mayers had moved back to Boston, again to the Shenberg apartment. Mayer was basically broke and absolutely depressed; he told friends that if he had to declare bankruptcy, he'd kill himself. It was nothing more than rhetoric from a moment of weakness; actually, he was in the process of tying a knot at the bottom of his rope.

Chapter
TWO

LOUIS RAN INTO a friend named Joseph Mack, who owned a nickelodeon on Dover Street. Mayer had attended Mack's theater, and occasionally had even taken tickets and worked the box office. Mack told him of a burlesque house that was for sale in Haverhill, on the north bank of the Merrimack River.

Then and now, Haverhill is a blue-collar, working-class town situated about thirty miles from the ocean. It was a thriving mill town by the time of the Civil War, when it manufactured uniforms for the Union army. The Merrimack River, which drops with enough force to generate considerable power, made the town perfect for manufacturing. By 1893, there were more than thirty shoe factories in Haverhill.

The town had a population of 45,000 people in need of cheap entertainment. Of course, those who labored in the mills worked fifty- and sixty-hour weeks, not leaving them a lot of leisure time. But they did have some, and they also had $9 or $10 in their pockets every week. Fishing was a popular pastime, but not appealing to everyone. Some of them were bound to do other things, such as going to the movies, or to the theater.

Not many of them, however, went to the Gem, at 8 Essex Street, just off Washington Square, the theater that Mayer's friend told him about. It was a six-hundred-seat, run-down, vacant burlesque house, generally considered so disreputable that one longtime Haverhill theater man said that no woman would go within a block of the place. The people of Haverhill also called it "The Garlic Box," evidently referring to a preponderance of Italian customers.

Stories about the Gem were numerous, usually very funny, such as the night the announcer proclaimed "Miss Blanche Fernandez will now sing 'White Wings.' "

"Blanche Fernandez is a whore!" yelled someone in the audience.

"Nevertheless, Miss Blanche Fernandez will now sing 'White Wings.' "

"What I saw in front of me wasn't that dingy theater," Mayer told a friend thirty years later. "I saw what it could become, and I convinced Margaret that I knew what I was doing. I got the owner down to about half what he was asking, and gave him a hundred dollar bill as a binding down payment."

Undoubtedly aided by family funds—Haverhill historians believe that investors also included Joe Mack and the Miles Brothers, a film distribution firm that wanted a Haverhill outlet—Mayer took a lease on the place, although he waited until 9:00 P.M. on the day his option expired to put down the rest of the money, which varies between $300 and $600 in the telling. The money bought him six months' rent in advance. In August 1907, Mayer moved his family to Haverhill, converting the theater manager's office into a small apartment, and began to work. (The jury-rigged apartment is probably the reason Mayer doesn't show up in the town directory until 1909—"Mayer, Louis B. Mngr." at 21 Temple Street. Certainly, a daily commute from Boston, nearly sixty miles round-trip, would have been unworkable.)

He recalled that it took about three months of labor before the theater was ready for the public. "Our only assistant was a lumberyard foreman, a skilled carpenter, who volunteered his services for nothing. He had already given us all the wood we needed with no more security than our word that we would pay the bill when the theater was a success."

With the help of his brothers, Jerry and Rudolph, and a couple of local painters, he cleaned up the place. While lugging and painting, Mayer would keep a careful eye on a diamond ring he had acquired in his Saint John days. He had cut up a lot of iron with this ring on, he would say, and he had never taken it off nor had it been damaged by flying scrap. Just before the theater opened, he took an employee named Charles Shute on a tour around the theater, radiating pride. He had made this place shine, and he had done it himself.

A new name was mandatory for the old theater, so, on the advice of Joe Mack, Louis called it the Orpheum, which would be devoted to "high-class films . . . the home of refined amusement devoted to . . . moving pictures and illustrated songs."

Mayer took the radical step of raising prices from 5 cents to 10 and 15 cents and of making the theater's orchestra section for ladies only, to, as he put it, "attract other ladies" because "you tell me how one makes a success in any business without attracting the ladies."

He couldn't afford a band, not even a small one, but he wanted something better than a piano, so he compromised with an organ. He hired neighborhood kids to deliver flyers to every house in town, inviting people to come look at the new Orpheum. He hired three women to help Margaret bake cookies for each of the first three days of the open house, and everybody that came was given a pass for the opening week's film.

The newly reconstituted theater opened on Thanksgiving Day, November 28, 1907. The Orpheum was a hit. The *Haverhill Evening Gazette* reported that "Throughout the day, a large number of patrons attended, welcoming the change and assuring the new management of a generous support in its new field . . . The program will be frequently changed as the new reels are received and it is planned to conduct the theater along the same lines as those practiced in the best houses . . . in the country." The first feature to be shown at the Orpheum was *The Passion Play*, at Christmastime, accompanied by religious slides with the organist playing hymns.

Mayer was cautious at first; for a time, he paid the organist and ticket-taker in installments. One employee, a former New York policeman named John "Bodger" Flynn, came right out of *The Last Hurrah*. Flynn was five feet eight, weighed about 285 pounds, had a shoe shop in Haverhill, and moonlighted as the Orpheum's bouncer/ticket-taker. If Flynn had a good week at the shoe shop, he'd let his pay for work at the theater slide for a few days.

Haverhill natives soon grew used to seeing the long lines waiting to get into the new cinema. "Many a . . . girl took the afternoon off from the factory to go to the Orpheum," remembered Charles Shute. Mayer soon began to show hints of his showman's personality, the motto for which seemed to be, Always Bigger, Always Better. Less than a year after the Orpheum reopened, he embarked on a major remodeling, and in September 1908, the New Orpheum opened.

The local newspaper reported, "A grand piece of work has been accomplished of which the city as well as Manager Mayer may justly feel proud. It is not a moving picture house enlarged, but an actual theater. . . . No expense has been spared in making for Haverhill theatergoers a model playhouse. . . . Louis B. Mayer, prominently identified with local theatrical enterprises, will offer a new and up-to-date line of entertainments of such a class as will speak for itself, no expense to be spared in securing for patrons exactly what they want."

Around the same time, the Mayers moved to 21 Temple Street, then, after a year, to 8 Merrimack Street. The girls finally had a yard to play in.

When other films didn't repeat the success of *The Passion Play*, Louis had to do what he did best: convince people. He spoke to every Jewish group in Haverhill, telling them that he had two children of his own and would never show anything at the Orpheum that he would be ashamed to show Edie and Irene. Not only that, he said, but the movies were a good way for new arrivals from Europe to learn American ways, and reading the intertitles could help anyone master English. He pledged money to the Beth Jacob Synagogue, where the Ashkenazi Jews prayed, as well as to the Ahavas Synagogue, where the Sephardic Jews worshipped.

Speaking to a Gentile audience, he explained that the criticism of movies emanated largely from those involved with the legitimate theater, who wanted to drive out the competition. If the people of Haverhill would just give him a chance, he would prove that the movies were an occasion for delight, not danger.

Louis was becoming an A-list celebrity in Haverhill. George C. Elliott, a wealthy bachelor known for his philanthropy and long days at the country club, invited the Mayers to his showplace home. "The day my mother first walked through the door of that house, she thought she'd arrived," said Irene Mayer Selznick. "This was the top—she never expected to see anything better."

Mayer was invited to take over the management of the competing New Bijou. "Manager Mayer," reported the *Haverhill Record*, "has gained number-less friends since his appearance here a year ago, and those who are acquainted with the New Orpheum have watched its progress from practically nothing to one of the finest playhouses in New England. Everything possible will be done to make the Scenic Temple [Mayer's name for the New Bijou] as great a suc-cess as the New Orpheum."

"We knew we had to spend money to make money," said L.B., so he went to Boston and New York looking for touring legitimate shows. The Boston Light Opera came for two weeks; Maude Adams played *Peter Pan* there, and told her friend William Farnum about the fine time she had had with young Mr. Mayer. As a result, Farnum brought his company of *The Littlest Rebel* to the Scenic Temple.

Mayer treated actors like visiting royalty and habitually rolled out the red carpet. He brought in Mary Pickford and her delinquent brother, Jack, for a personal appearance. "Mary was a darling," he remembered. "Everything we asked, she did. . . . We won't talk about Jack." The most cooperative star of them all was Florence Lawrence, the beloved Biograph Girl. She sat in the lobby for hours signing autographs, shaking hands, kissing babies. "A beautiful lady," said Mayer, who remembered her kindness to a struggling provincial theater manager, and later repaid it many times over.

Actors returned to New York singing the praises of this amazing man, Mayer. He invested his profits in a hotel, where the visiting shows were billeted, thereby getting a piece of all the travel traffic he was creating. He devised theme shows, getting director Sidney Olcott to send him all the films Olcott made on one of his location trips to Ireland, and running nothing else for two weeks. He invested in another theater, then another. Soon there was a chain of six Mayer theaters, each with a specific identity—one might concentrate on westerns, another love stories. Mayer was creating the kind of specific, branded identity that would have to wait eighty years to be widely replicated on cable television.

By 1910, Mayer was looking to do something grander. He enlisted some investors (George Elliott and C. Howard Poor), put together $100,000, and built the Colonial Theater on Emerson Street. Construction began in March 1911, and the new theater opened on December 11. There was a ninety-five-foot lobby finished with old rose and green frescoes, decorated with pictures of the great stars of the day, and boasting a marble staircase. The auditorium held 1,500 patrons and had a thirty-six-foot proscenium arch. Louis was so fond of a painting of a reclining lion that he gave it the place of honor, hanging it over the lobby's fireplace. Near the entrance was an oil painting of the man who had made it all possible: Louis B. Mayer. The policy was movies and vaudeville, 25 cents a seat.

The Colonial became Haverhill's showplace, and at the opening ceremonies, Mayer told the first-nighters that "The Colonial is the zenith of my ambition." Over the years, such future luminaries as Milton Berle, George Burns, and Jack Benny would play the Colonial, not to mention "Hardeen, the Handcuff King."

On February 11, 1911, just before construction began on the Colonial, Mayer sat down and filled out his "Declaration of Intention," the first step toward becoming an American citizen. In his flowing, accessible script, he averred that his name was Louis Bert Mayer, that he was twenty-four years old and a theatrical manager. He was five feet seven, weighed 160 pounds, had brown hair and eyes, and had been born in Dumier, Russia, on July 4, 1885. Residing at 21 Temple Street in Haverhill, he renounced all allegiance and fidelity to Edward VII, King of Great Britain, "my father having been a naturalized subject of Great Britain." Allowing for the slight evasion on his birth date, and the matter of his middle name, it was an accurate petition. (Around the time he arrived in Haverhill he began using the middle name Bert, sometimes spelled Burt, which later became Burton—possibly deriving from a Saint John lawyer named Burton who handled legal matters relating to the Mayer scrap operation. The euphony of the middle name indicates the extent to which respectability was a primary need for Mayer from the very beginning of his career. He would always tell people he liked that they could call him "L.B.")

On June 24, 1912, Louis Bert Mayer, residing at 2 1/2 Merrimac Street in Haverhill, a married man with two children, occupation listed as "Manager," became a citizen of the United States of America, sealing a fervent love affair that would never die.

The New Orpheum remained his pet, the one that played the best films he could get, with new stage shows every second or third week. Soon, Mayer was telling people how remarkable he was.

"Mr. Louis B. Mayer," announced the program for the Colonial Theater for November 21, 1912, "whose inspiration and ambition it was to make grand opera in his home city a possibility, and through whose energy tonight's performance was made possible, is undoubtedly as well known in Haverhill and its suburbs as any man in public life." The program went on to extoll Mayer for being "on a plane equal with the most successful of theater men in New England; and Haverhill can boast, among other things, of having a citizen who is to be depended upon for those things which are necessary to enjoyment, with an assurance that everything is of the best."

The occasion for all this hyperbole was Mayer's importation of the Boston Opera, the first manifestation of a passion for bringing classical music and operetta to the masses.

Louis wanted success and he was getting it; he wanted class and he would get that too. George Elliott, one of Mayer's investors, would remember "Louis was a worker. He never sleeps, you know, and he was always scheming up something." Daniel Shea, who worked for him, noted, "He would spend a dollar anytime if he thought he could get $1.10 back." By this time, he had the theater business in his bones; he was that rarity, a natural.

Haverhill was a wonderful town, but it seemed to enclose Mayer as he grew more successful. He was already talking about making movies. You could shoot exteriors around Haverhill, he explained, and interiors could be shot right on the stage of the Colonial, with sets his crew could build. When he explained his idea, people looked at him as if he'd lost his mind.

Mayer's was a family operation as much as possible. His brother Jerry was the manager of the New Orpheum, and Margaret's brother was the projectionist at the Colonial. Louis's burgeoning success meant he was able to buy another house, at 27 Hamilton Avenue, formerly a home for nurses.

At the end of 1912, Mayer converted the New Orpheum into a legitimate theater, where he began running a stock company. With backing from investors, he built the Broadway Theater in Lawrence, Massachusetts. The opening was by invitation only, and the millworkers with their dimes got nowhere as the carriage trade swept past them with their invitations. The millworkers got mad and didn't come back, and neither did the carriage trade. One local businessman said that Louis lost $80,000 on the theater. It was one of the few failures he had during this period, which included opening theaters in Lynn, Brockton, Manchester, and Lowell. There were also trips back north to visit family and friends and tend whatever business interests he still had there.

An old Saint John chum named David Perkins became the juvenile for the Mayer stock company for the 1913–14 season at the New Orpheum. This was the golden era of theater, at least in terms of density—there were dozens of road shows touring every year, and about 250 resident stock companies. Mayer invariably secured the best plays as soon as they were available for stock, and that winter of 1913–14, the opening play of the Mayer stock company was David Belasco's *The Charity Ball.*

Irene and Edie were regular attendees of the stock company performances, always at Saturday matinees. Margaret Mayer used to come to the Colonial once or twice a week and check the box office statements. She always came in the evening, and she would always call the sitter at home, usually inquiring, "How are my babies?"

That winter, David Perkins caught pneumonia, and Mayer had the receipts for Christmas Day given to him. Perkins never forgot the gesture, and when he was an old man he remembered, "That shows the caliber of Mayer. He stood by his friends. . . . When he gave his friendship, he did so with no strings. As an executive administrator, he was a genius."

The Mayer stock company was run on the highest level of the trade. "The scenery was of the best for each play, done by a very capable scenic artist, while the players were experienced actors with reputations," Perkins remembered many years later. "Many a Broadway play of today in production values fails to surpass those of the resident winter stocks of 1900 to 1915."

Salaries were small—Mayer paid Perkins $45 for the entire season, but that was enough for him to support his wife and two children back home in Portland, Maine, as well as put $5 to $10 aside for his savings.

A Broadway producer named Jack Welch developed a lucrative trade in road companies of Broadway shows, although his troupes were too high-priced for Mayer. But Welch liked Mayer and made a practice of allowing him to book his companies into Haverhill at the end of a tour for a cut price, so Louis could make some money.

Years later, Welch fell on hard times and found a sinecure at MGM, where Mayer gave him a position in the production department, a job that involved Welch reading the *Racing Form*. Still later, Welch's son, also named Jack, got a stock acting contract.

It was often said that Louis B. Mayer never forgave a slight; it could also be said that he never forgot a kindness.

Success agreed with Mayer, enabling him to live up to his own idea of himself. Besides his activities in New England, in 1913 Mayer formed the Louis B. Mayer Company of Pennsylvania for the purpose of "establishing and maintaining theater and opera houses." His partners were Samuel Johns, Nan Haley, and Edgar Pershing, all residents of Pennsylvania. Mayer himself was still residing in Haverhill, and he held thirty of the forty shares of preferred stock issued by the company. The capitalization was only $5,000, so it's possible that the operation was more speculative than actual.

He also incorporated the Louis B. Mayer Co. in New York in January 1913, "to conduct general amusement business in New York City, U.S. and Canada . . . purchase, lease, license, sell, produce, manage, operate and exhibit plays, dramas, operas, musicals." The initial capitalization for this company was only $2,000. The capitalization would be increased to $25,000, then, in November 1922, to $500,000, as the company's producing activities solidified around movies, and the offices moved from the Fitzgerald Building at 1482 Broadway to the Longacre Building at 1470 Broadway. (The company's name would be changed to Louis B. Mayer Productions, Inc., as of November 1920, before it was dissolved in June 1926.)

Mayer's daughter Edith would remember accompanying him on a business trip to New York around this time. "He wasn't like Little Father [her nickname for him] any more. He sounded tougher, he was doing business and I'd never seen him like that . . . I guess I saw him get more sure of himself, and I guess I realized overnight that he's a very important man."

Sarah Mayer had made at least one visit to Haverhill, so had an opportunity to see what a success her son Louis was making of his life. Brother Rudy—or Ruby, as he was known in Saint John—was briefly part of the expanding operation, but Rudy wasn't like his brother; he was flashier, more concerned with the quick score than the carefully constructed foundation, and always carried the slight odor of the disreputable around with him. Rudy was quickly hustled out of the way.

In the second week of October 1913, Mayer was informed that his mother's health was failing. She had been suffering from gall bladder disease. Mayer hired a private railroad car to get the family to Saint John, bringing with him his own doctor as well as a Montreal surgeon. Surgery was performed, but there were complications. Ida Mayer's daughter, Ruth, remembered the dying woman saying in Yiddish, "I shall be crossing a great sea. And I shall never come back."

"Do not grieve, Louis," she told him. "We must all die sooner or later. Now it's my turn. I wish I could have stayed a little longer, so I could see you do the big things I know you are capable of doing. But I will watch over you. I will know all about you and your work. And I will wait for you."

That, at least, was what Mayer would tell people Sarah Mayer told him as she lay dying. That belief and the vision it outlined—the primacy of blood relations, the dead watching over the living—would inform his belief system and many of the films he would oversee.

Sarah Mayer died on October 14 and was buried in the Jewish cemetery of Saint John. Years later, after her son had relocated to California, he inquired about having her body exhumed and sent to California so the family could be united, at least in death, but the conservative congregation refused, angering Mayer. After that, he generally refused to contribute to the Saint John Temple, although he subsidized a considerable marker for his mother's grave.

Sarah Meltzer Mayer was buried beneath a large monument that reads:

Sarah
Wife of Jacob Mayer
Born Nov. 14, 1851
Died Oct. 14, 1913
Rest in Peace O Mother
Sleep Within Our Hearts

Louis was completely devastated. If anybody asked about his mother, Mayer would say, "Only God was more important to me than her." "No kind of emotion in his life ever matched the grief he felt at her death," said his daughter Irene. "Every victory of his brought with it a pang that she was not there to share it, and that his money had come too late to save her."

For the rest of his life, a portrait of Sarah Mayer hung over her son's bed; for the rest of his life, Louis invested great religious power in her memory, and in her image. Irene Mayer believed that, had her grandmother lived a full life, long enough to see her boy become the emperor of Hollywood, his emotional development would have been considerably different. Had Louis been nine, say, rather than twenty-nine when his mother died, she undoubtedly would have been right, but he was a grown man, married with children; L. B. Mayer's character was formed long before Sarah Mayer's death.

The loss of Sarah increased his devotion to Margaret. His beloved mother had once knelt on the floor and kissed the hem of Margaret's dress. The torch, you might say, had been passed. To the role of wife and mother of their children was now added the role of mother of her husband. "I do things in a day that maybe aren't right," he would say. "I make mistakes. I come home tired. I look in her eyes. Whatever I think of myself, it comes out all right. I am forgiven everything. I start fresh. I am cleansed. If she loves me, I'm a good man. It's not that she's smart; I don't know what it is. Can you have intuition without being smart? It's her intuition that counts."

Mayer knew that the true entrepreneur never stops with an initial success; momentum needs to be encouraged, and if others aren't willing to do the grunt work, you have to do it yourself. Charles Shute remembered that one day at a Mayer theater, the projectionist didn't show up. The manager put in an SOS call, and in about five minutes, L.B. walked in, went up to the booth, and ran the entire afternoon show himself without ever telling the manager he was there.

The Colonial continued to prosper; Fred and Adele Astaire would perform there, as did the great Bill Robinson. But L.B. still had a sense that the movies were his future; he gingerly stuck his toe in the movie business and formed the American Feature Film Company. Mayer was pyramiding companies at this point, expanding in all directions. In Saint John he had bought and sold wholesale, and now in America he was discovering that he had a knack for retail as well. Louis B. Mayer was learning firsthand that what he wanted to sell, the public also wanted to buy—a reciprocal bond that would form the foundation of an empire.

The American Feature Film Company bought the New England rights to the first six pictures produced by a new outfit called the Jesse L. Lasky Feature Play Company. *The Squaw Man,* their first film, was co-directed by an enterprising young actor named Cecil B. DeMille. "I guaranteed quality, wholesome films," said Mayer. "And I gave them what I promised." It was one more immersion in learning what people actually paid to see—not what they said they wanted, but what they actually wanted—a discipline in putting bodies into seats that served as an invaluable training for all the early moguls.

Charles Shute remembered the night Mayer ran *The Squaw Man* for the first time. It was after hours, and the vaudeville performers and stagehands were invited to sit down and watch the reputedly splendid new picture. "We all gave it the ahs and gee whizz'es because none of us had ever seen anything like it before," remembered Shute. "Mrs. Mayer commented several times regarding the photography. Mr. Mayer said, 'They say this is the coming form of entertainment.' "

Mayer paid $4,000 for the New England rights; until the day he died, Sam Goldwyn, treasurer and sales manager of the Lasky Company, swore that Mayer only paid half of the money he had promised to pay, the beginning of a lifelong enmity between the two men. Also contributing was a tactless remark Mayer had made when Jesse Lasky asked what he thought of the impending marriage between Goldwyn and Lasky's sister, Blanche. "I would rather attend your sister's funeral than her marriage to that so and so," Mayer replied.

The Squaw Man did well for Mayer and his partners, but George Elliott remembered that it was another DeMille picture, *Brewster's Millions,* that was the real gold mine. It played for several weeks at the Colonial, with sub-runs at other theaters. The Lasky pictures made a handsome profit for Louis and his partners.

Throughout this period, the extended Mayer family was mostly out of sight, although Mayer's employees would see an occasional visitor from Saint John. Rudy would come down and widen everybody's eyes when he went out of his way to flash a roll that consisted of better than $2,000—several years' salary for that period. By 1913, the Mayer boys were doing well enough to enable their father to retire.

L.B.'s usual uniform consisted of a dark suit, a knee-length black coat with silk lapels, and a derby hat. But he still thought economically whenever possible. When he went to New York for meetings and deals, he liked to pass out good cigars. The price was usually 10 cents, or three for a quarter, but occasionally they'd go on sale for 5 cents, and when that happened L.B. would send his employees out to canvas all the drugstores in the area and buy as many as they could find. That way, he could take an entire box of cigars with him to New York.

The beginnings of L. B. Mayer's wealth derived from his purchase of the New England rights to *The Birth of a Nation*. D. W. Griffith's masterpiece was distributed in a haphazard fashion that involved subleasing the film in neighborhoods while the film's producers and primary distributors, the Epoch Corporation, would roadshow the film at the same time, sometimes in the same town. Why? Because Epoch received 60 percent of revenues from the road show and only 33 1/3 percent from conventional distribution.

"Not only was this insane, it was probably illegal," says Griffith scholar Russell Merritt. "What saved the situation was that there was so much money being made nobody cared." Just from the road shows, from March 1915 to July 1916, *The Birth of a Nation* earned receipts of nearly $3 million, with a net profit of $1.449 million. The Aitken brothers, Harry and Roy, the film's producers, also pocketed $237,000 from the sale of state's rights to Mayer and a few other entrepreneurs. Griffith's 37 percent royalty amounted to $485,182 for this period, while author Thomas Dixon made $438,137.

Harry Aitken was a dervish of deals, and he couldn't keep his figures straight. At various times, he reported that Mayer had paid either $25,000 plus 10 percent of the gross, or $50,000 plus half the net. Associate producer Roy Aitken reported that Mayer, in concert with one Daniel Stoneham, offered $50,000 for the New England rights to the picture, half up front, with a 50-50 profit split once his costs had been recouped. He was consistent about one thing only—Mayer never sent him a dime of any percentage monies.

Mayer's own version of the deal, as he recalled it ten years later for Lillian Gish, was that "I pawned everything I owned—my house, my insurance, even my wife's wedding ring—just to get the New England states' rights. Since then, everything's been very pleasant. If it hadn't been for D. W. Griffith, *The Birth* and you, I'd still be in Haverhill." The figure he remembered paying was $55,000.

Actually, the deal seems to have been far more clear-cut than the Aitkens claimed. Mayer formed a company called Master Photoplays—he owned 25 percent of it and paid $50,000 down against 10 percent of the net after Mayer paid off his investment. Boston was excluded from Mayer's territory until September 12, as the Aitkens had that area for themselves until then.

In his first year of handling the film, Mayer sent Epoch $15,000 for their 10 percent of the profits. The year after that, he paid only $1,500. Mayer always said that his company made a million dollars off the picture, 25 percent of which was his, indicating he radically underpaid Epoch. However much Mayer ended up with, it was the foundation of his fortune — and his future.

Chapter
THREE

IN 1914, Al Lichtman, former sales manager of Adolph Zukor's Famous Players, had organized Alco Films, dividing ownership among various local film exchanges in the country, among them Richard Rowland in Pittsburgh and Louis B. Mayer in Boston. Lichtman's plan was to tie up the leading theaters in every key city—the same idea that would be brought to fruition after World War I by the formation of the First National Exhibitor's Circuit.

As was typical of that time—the show business equivalent of the Wild West—Alco started with flourishes and high hopes. Among its films were Mack Sennett's *Tillie's Punctured Romance*, *Michael Strogoff* with Jacob Adler, and Olga Petrova in *The Vampire*.

By the end of the year, however, the receiver was at the door—Walter Seely, Alco's managing partner, had drained off cash reserves into companies set up to avoid the new income tax. Alco failed, but the group had meshed. Besides that, they now had an effective distribution and exhibition group, lacking only a mechanism to supply product. They decided to stay together.

In January 1915, in a meeting in Parlor B at the Claridge Hotel in New York City, the shareholders reorganized as the Metro Pictures Corporation. Richard Rowland, a lurid fashion plate who favored green gabardine, purple socks and shoes, diamonds and sapphires, was chosen as president, Mayer was secretary, and the counsel was J. Robert Rubin, who was representing the creditors of Alco. Capitalization was $300,000. Metro subcontracted with independent producers for their supply of motion pictures. Metro's plan was to release one feature per week costing between $15,000 and $20,000. The company's first picture, *Satan Sanderson*, was released in May.

Of all of Mayer's associates in Metro, it was J. Robert Rubin who would play the most critical role in his life. Rubin was born in 1882, attended Syracuse University and Law School, after which he became an assistant district attorney, then went to work in the New York police department. A friend was appointed a receiver for Alco, and he hired Rubin to do some legal work on the bankruptcy. It was there that he met Mayer, and as Mayer's professional activities increased, Rubin became his lawyer.

Rubin was the sort of Jew that Mayer admired: tall, handsome, elegant—everything, in short, that Mayer was not. "Mayer looked up to him and vastly respected him," said Mayer's secretary. Rubin became Mayer's lifelong partner, and the man who gave him entrée to the most crucial alliance of his life.

Mayer knew that *The Birth of a Nation* was its own star, but he also knew that the movie had made a couple of stars, and that the business was changing. When L.B. had bought the Gem, people had gone to movies without knowing who was in them, more or less on the basis of the title, or the story, or just because they liked to watch the pictures moving on the screen.

But Mayer and Adolph Zukor were among the first to realize that a picture could be sold—or, even better, presold—on the basis of the star who was appearing in it. Zukor had begun the Famous Players Film Corporation in 1912 and had a great success with Sarah Bernhardt's *Queen Elizabeth*, which led him to sign Mary Pickford and set up an entire company (Artcraft) solely for the release of her pictures. Zukor always had expansionist instincts, and soon merged Famous Players with the Jesse L. Lasky Feature Film Company, the equal partners behind what would become Paramount Pictures.

"If we had a popular star we made a little money and we could build the star up by making more and more pictures," was the way L.B. later described the phenomenon. "The real business of making movies . . . became the business of making idols for the public to love and worship and to identify with. Everything else was secondary."

Metro's most valuable star was probably Francis X. Bushman, a barrel-chested matinee idol of the old school who was slotted to make one feature a month. A few months after signing Bushman, the studio also signed Beverly Bayne, Bushman's mistress and co-star at Essanay. The pair set to work, but soon grew dissatisfied with the quality of the scripts they were getting; at one point, late in 1915, Bushman was advertising in *The Moving Picture World* magazine for "scenarios for Francis X. Bushman. . . . Good, strong subjects as vehicles for the greatest star of the screen. Stories of romance and stories of adventure are especially desired. . . . Subject and treatment must be clean and wholesome."

Metro sought to put Bushman's complaints about material to rest by producing a lavish adaptation of *Romeo and Juliet*. It proved popular, but then Metro undercut the duo's prestige by announcing that the succeeding Bushman-Bayne project would be a serial called *The Great Secret*.

Shortly thereafter, Bushman triumphantly committed career suicide when he announced that he was leaving his wife and five children to marry Bayne. By August 1918, *Variety* reported that "The Mall and Alhambra theaters in Cleveland, Ohio, announced that they would no longer run pictures in which Bushman and Bayne appeared, clearly implying the recent marriage of the two was the reason for the decision."

The primary Metro studio was on 61st and Broadway, a cavernous, two-hundred-foot-long space over a garage. The stage was in the middle of the room, while offices circled the walls. Mayer's office was on West 45th, and Edie Mayer remembered that her father would storm the sixteen blocks to the studio as if embarking on a military campaign, ignoring traffic lights at the risk of his life and exhausting anybody who was walking with him.

Mayer's primary business partner at this time was Nathan Gordon, with whom he had a number of things in common. Gordon was also a native of Russia, who came to America at the age of seventeen. Although he was Jewish, he was notably unobservant. As his son, William, would remember, "It came as a complete surprise to me that I was Jewish. My father and Mayer could avoid Temple together, if you know what I mean."

Gordon and Mayer formed the Gordon-Mayer Theatrical Company, which booked vaudeville talent for Gordon's theaters and distributed Metro's pictures in New England. Gordon was one of the largest exhibitors in the Northeast, and he had been forced into production by the fact that there weren't enough top-of-the-line movies being made. But he didn't like the people production forced him to deal with.

"My father was a typical bourgeois," remembered William Gordon. "The theater business wasn't formal enough for him. Some people he admired on the screen, but couldn't do business with. Chaplin, for instance; he couldn't stand him personally. Father was a banker; the sooner he could put on banking clothes, the more relaxed he was. Louis he regarded as perhaps overenthusiastic but an honorable man, far more than most of the people in the business."

Nate and Louis were also bound together by the fact that their wives became close friends. Gordon's wife liked Mayer, even though she would often parody his melodramatic responses to events. They were a happy foursome professionally and socially; Nate Gordon was puritanical, emphatically not one of the boys, and would never have overlooked dalliances on the part of his partner.

"He and my father made a lot of deals on the phone," remembered William Gordon. "I'd be there, listening to the call. They could always decide things without writing or lawyers, even major expenditures involving corporations. A deal was a deal, and they trusted each other. It was always 'Nate' and 'Louis.'"

The men became even closer when Nate Gordon's wife, Sally, began a drive to build a Jewish hospital in Boston. For Louis, this was a chance to alleviate some of the guilt over the death of his mother, who had died in a non-Jewish hospital. L.B. pledged money to Sally Gordon's project and became a director in 1915. On the same board he met Colman Levin, a carpet manufacturer who would often take vacations with Mayer in Palm Beach and invested funds in some of L.B.'s early enterprises.

People in the business didn't know what to make of this bumptious, inquisitive young man. He would hover around the New York office of Universal, asking pointed questions. One day, Universal's sales manager told Vice President Robert Cochrane he was vaguely disturbed about Mayer's questions, that he was fairly sure he was sniffing around because he was planning to go into production and wanted to steal some actors. Cochrane said to give Mayer the salaries of people they didn't want to keep, suggesting that perhaps he might even want to exaggerate their earnings.

Mayer and his family relocated to Boston, at 501 Boylston Street, in the Brookline district, close to the John D. Runkle school. As with all the other homes they lived in, the girls shared a single room and, until their teens, a single bed. L.B. wanted his girls to be friendly but aloof, not to trust anyone outside the clan. Above all, they were to tell their mother everything: "It is a sin," Margaret told her girls, "to keep a secret from your mother."

Edie was not a pretty girl—she would get better-looking as she aged. She had a sharp face, small eyes, and thin lips. Irene was far more attractive, overtly resembling her mother. Edie was willful and vain, and her father took her at her own lofty valuation: dainty and feminine, where Irene was more of an aloof tomboy. L.B. called Edie "Edi-La" throughout his life.

Mayer was an attentive father. He taught his girls how to row a boat, how to fish, how to drive a buggy. They were given the *Book of Knowledge* and the

Golden Treasury, but anything other than these and a few other sanctioned texts drew disapproval. When he went to New York on business, he would make sure to bring back some of the deep chocolate ice cream the girls loved.

What he wanted was girls who would be useful to themselves and the men in their lives; he showed Irene how to play pinochle, and how to change a flat tire, but he drew the line at summer camp. Why go to a camp full of strangers and germs when they could stay at home, safe and surrounded by love? As for school, the occasional B was met by frowns. Expectations were high and achievement had to equal expectation. Once he took Irene to the World Series. Irene didn't understand the game, and L.B. hadn't taken the time to explain it to her beforehand. He grew irritated. Where was what he called her "instant grasp"?

Despite the enforced proximity, Irene and Edie were essentially incompatible. Edie liked clothes and makeup and romance; for her future, she had designs on acting or interior decoration. Irene was serious about art and literature and wanted to go to Wellesley and become a doctor or scientist.

"They were such different people," remembered Budd Schulberg, who knew the girls as adolescents. "Irene was forceful, almost mannish. She did everything well. For instance, she was a big, strong tennis player. Edith was just the opposite, a little hothouse flower, sweet and soft and delicate. They had nothing in common, could not have been more different. Even as children, they didn't relate to each other very much, although I don't remember the enmity that developed later."

A friend who knew both girls and their father in later years believed that Mayer "handled Irene and Edie the same way he handled everybody else: divide and conquer." Each girl was particularly cognizant of the other, and of the ever-present question of who would be Dad's favorite. Most people believed it was Edi-La. "He worshipped the ground she walked on," said Jack Cummings, Mayer's nephew. Others believed that the question was moot, because, as they saw it, the only person L.B. ever really loved, beside his mother, was himself.

At home, Margaret would relax by playing the piano, picking out a tune from sheet music one finger at a time and singing softly to herself. "She had the same kind of serenity I beheld when she blessed the candles at sunset each Friday night," remembered Irene. While Maggie played the piano, L.B. would read the newspapers (he had no patience for fiction). He was partial to Hearst's *Boston American* because of columnist Arthur Brisbane, who Mayer thought was superb and beyond criticism.

For Margaret, Louis was her Lord and Master. For Louis, Margaret was his

Maggie, the woman he put on a pedestal. In every sense, it was a successful Victorian marriage—each put the other first within their respective domains, each backed the other completely.

The entire house was geared to L.B. What would his mood be? What had happened at the office? Had he talked to any stars? L.B. always brought the office home with him, pouring out his successes and frustrations so that his family could better appreciate his struggles, his acumen. Although he was a young man, his demeanor was oracular; he talked a lot about just rewards, sowing and reaping. Maggie and the girls were expected to sit in reverent, appreciative silence; spontaneous conversation was not encouraged.

Occasionally, he even brought home an authentic movie star, as when Francis X. Bushman magically appeared at their front door. Bushman tended to strike poses rather than act, but he was a smiling *grand seigneur* all the same. "He was the very first movie star I ever met," remembered Irene Mayer Selznick. "What a *magnanimous* man he seemed—so big, with an enormous amethyst ring on his little finger. I recall thinking, 'My husband shall wear an enormous amethyst.' "

Metro's pictures were popular for a time, but Louis was already becoming impatient with helping to run somebody else's company. His primary quality, even then, was intensity, the enthusiasm that was the flip side of his temper. Mayer would come to credit the purgative function of his short fuse for his general health and boundless energy. He held nothing back, saved nothing for himself—what you saw was what you got.

Show business, he had come to believe, could not be a question of the lowest common denominator. It should be a diversion, of course, but also a potent force, a profound moral influence—if only the people in charge would treat it that way. And if show business and the movies were important, the idea of America was even more important. Americans, he said, took their riches for granted. They should be as proud of their country as he was.

It was all exhilarating and also exhausting. Even when he relaxed, it was with a driving singleness of purpose. "I'm not sure I always liked my father," remembered Irene, "but I admired him and loved him. And I wanted desperately to please him."

There was dissension within Metro. As Robert Rubin would recall, "Mayer's idea was that the so-called 'program pictures' produced by the members of the Metro group for about $15,000 each were on the way out and that the future was for so-called 'specials.' Rowland, who was president of Metro from the start, opposed this idea, and upon this point he and Mayer broke."

In 1917, a group of exhibitors, infuriated by the block-booking practices of Famous Players-Lasky, formed their own production and distribution company, which they dubbed First National. For subscribing a given amount, each franchise holder got the rights to the First National pictures in their designated territory. The only way for the company to survive was to make a big splash in a hurry, and that they did, signing Mary Pickford and Charlie Chaplin, thus achieving instant credibility.

Mayer and Nate Gordon, under the name of the Gordon-Mayer Film Corp., with offices at 35 Piedmont Street in Boston, became the franchise holder in their area, handling First National films such as *Shoulder Arms* and *Daddy Long Legs*, not to mention less prestigious titles such as *Kiss or Kill* and *Unpainted Woman*.

There was a process of consolidation and filtering going on. The early movie studios—Vitagraph, Biograph—had often been run by WASPs who lacked the entrepreneurial spirit. Griffith had to leave Biograph to fulfill his expansive, grandiloquent vision, and Vitagraph never employed a top-notch filmmaker. The studios that would define and dominate the future of American movies were run by men named Zukor, Goldwyn, Mayer, and Fox (né Fuchs)—all Jews from Eastern Europe, all brilliant at expanding manufacturing and distribution. Because of their background, and their immigrant's adoration of America, which would give them fame and riches, each of them believed in elemental values that needed only to be beautifully costumed. And they knew that people are mostly interested in other people, especially if they are beautiful, especially if they are stars.

For a few months in 1917, Mayer also distributed the product of L. J. Selznick's Select Pictures in New England, but Select was failing, weighed down by more than a quarter-million dollars of debt. Mayer didn't like Selznick's gambling, he didn't like Selznick's drinking, and he didn't like the way Selznick slept around and neglected his family, including his sons, David and Myron. Mayer got out of the distribution deal, and blamed Selznick for the failure of his company. "Watch what I say," he said, "watch and see what happens to him. There is no firm foundation. Things must be built stone by stone."

By this time, Mayer and his associates were familiarly known as "the pawnbrokers," indicating their perceived lowly status, their hard-driving ways, and the pervasive anti-Semitism that surrounded them. If Mayer knew of the contemptuous epithet—and he almost certainly did, for nothing escaped him—it would only have caused him to redouble his efforts. Distributing and exhibiting other people's films only put a small percentage of the proceeds in his pocket. Distribution was safe, but production was where the glory—and the money—really were.

He would show them. He would show them all.

Anita Stewart began acting at Vitagraph while still a student at Brooklyn's Erasmus High School. Stewart's patrician quality soon made her Vitagraph's most profitable acting property, and she became the idol of millions of young girls, including Irene and Edie Mayer, who cut out the Anita Stewart paper dolls that were published in *Ladies' World* magazine.

Sniffing around for a star on which he could hang his projected Louis B. Mayer Productions, Louis settled on Stewart, whose contract with Vitagraph was due to expire at the end of January 1918. With that sense of an opening that would never fail him, Mayer was introduced to Stewart by a man she remembered only as "Toby the Hunchback," a newspaper boy who was her most ardent fan. Toby would beg pictures from Stewart's secretary and give them away at large public gatherings, the better to spread the gospel of his adored star.

At some point, Toby became one of Mayer's circle, and made it a point to meet Mayer at the train every time he came to New York from Boston. Stewart seems to have been a genuinely kind woman with a trusting nature, and the fact that Toby had admiration and confidence in Mayer carried a great deal of weight. (Years later, when Toby died of pneumonia, Mayer paid for his funeral.)

When Mayer returned from his first meeting with Stewart in Atlantic City, he was exuberant. "I met her, I met her!" he yelled. "And I danced with her, too! She was a princess! She carried a wand in her hand! You should have seen us! What a picture! Everybody was talking about me."

"You know what they were saying?" asked his secretary, playing the Eve Arden part.

"What were they saying?"

"They were saying, 'Who's the funny little kike with Anita Stewart?'"

In the summer of 1917, Stewart began to be regularly indisposed, and Vitagraph's production of her films slowed, then stopped entirely. On September 15, it was announced in the trade papers that "Louis B. Mayer of Boston" had signed Stewart to a long-term contract. Anita Stewart Productions, Inc., was incorporated on September 1, with capital stock worth $1 million, and a board of directors including L. B. Mayer, Rudolph Cameron (Stewart's husband), J. Robert Rubin, and Nate Gordon as chairman.

Louis knew that, when it comes to seducing actors, money was not always enough; vanity had to be appealed to. Anita Stewart Productions, Inc. was too much for the actress to resist. The new company would put Stewart on the same plateau as Pickford and Norma Talmadge.

But Vitagraph sued over the work slowdown, charging that Stewart had shortchanged them under her old contract, and that Mayer had tried to "induce Anita Stewart to break her contract." The judge ruled that every day lost because of the legal battle over Stewart would be added to the end of her Vitagraph contract, which pushed the expiration of her deal to September 1918. Stewart returned to Vitagraph to knock off two more pictures, while Mayer began scouting around for suitable story material.

According to a Vitagraph financial statement, Stewart was no commercial prize. A 1917 release entitled *The Girl Philippa* lost nearly $20,000, which would indicate that either Vitagraph was foolishly trying to keep a money-losing star, or it was cooking the books.

Mayer's signing of Stewart displeased Richard Rowland, the head of Metro. Rowland was sick of Mayer's agitating for bigger and better movies, for spending more money. And now Mayer had gone and signed a big movie star for himself, not for the company he was a part of. As a result, Mayer resigned from Metro.

Mayer and Vitagraph finally came to a settlement under which Mayer paid off Vitagraph—Robert Rubin's memory was $75,000—and took over the uncompleted pictures Stewart had started, in order to be rid of her old contract. To point up the family-quarrel aspect of the early film business, Stewart didn't actually start filming for Anita Stewart Productions until August of 1918, and when she did, it was in a studio Mayer rented from Vitagraph!

The Mayers were gathering momentum and gaining status. L.B. spent $2,500 for another house in Brookline, one that was on the edge of the high-priced neighborhood. Back home in Canada, Rudolph had relocated to Montreal and was running a steel company, a wrecking company, and a railway company, with Jerry as his partner. Ida, Louis's favorite sister—whose temperament was nearly as effusive as his—was in Boston, married to a dull man Mayer didn't like.

In Europe, World War I had been raging for some time. When, by mid-1918, most of the scripts L.B. was reading were war stories, he became nervous; he had a feeling the war wouldn't last much longer, and he didn't want to be stuck with an inventory of war pictures when the public suddenly tired of the genre.

As Robert Rubin would remember, "Everybody told Mayer that now that he had a great star for his own picture, he didn't have to bother with a story or production, but he paid a sizable sum [about $15,000] for a magazine story by Owen Johnson called 'Virtuous Wives.' "

Mayer hired George Loane Tucker to direct, and the excellent Ernest Palmer to photograph. In support of Anita Stewart were Conway Tearle and a character actress named Hedda Hopper. "When he was finished," said Rubin, "he put on a phenomenal advertising campaign, taking a solid block of thirty-six pages of advertising in one trade paper. People in the business thought he was mad and that he would surely go broke right off."

But Louis felt sure he was right—his model would be bread-and-butter program pictures, sold as if they were *The Birth of a Nation*. "Don't worry, Bob, you'll see," he told Rubin. "This is going to pay off."

"Mayer," said Bob Rubin, "had foresight and courage, the essentials of a good showman." L. B. Mayer had found the thing he was put on earth to do. *Virtuous Wives*, Mayer's first personal production, opened at the Strand Theater in New York on December 29, 1918.

The printed program provided to patrons offered this encomium: "Mr. Louis Mayer presents Miss Anita Stewart in a series of new productions designed for the better theaters. Miss Anita Stewart and her company will interpret only famous plays or widely read stories by well-known contemporary authors. Each subject's title will have a box office appeal at the better theaters second only to that of the star's name." The reviews for *Virtuous Wives* weren't great, but they weren't awful either, and business was good. Louis had guessed right, as he usually did.

In the trade press, Stewart's salary had been announced as $1,000 a week plus 10 percent of the profits, but that was a diversion. Her deal with Mayer was actually considerably richer than that, but not impossibly so—Stewart was to be paid $80,000 per picture plus a percentage for the first six pictures, with an option for six more at $100,000 and a percentage. The contract was for three years, with an option for another two years.

The honeymoon didn't last long. "I was completely happy at the Vitagraph," Stewart would remember, "and have often felt that I made my best pictures there, but Mr. Mayer promised me better parts, better directors, more money—really the moon. . . . I have often wondered since if it would not have been better if I had remained with Vitagraph in dear old Brooklyn.

"Working for Mr. Mayer was not like working at the Vitagraph. There we were like one big happy family. Here, it was all work and no play and I guess I was a little spoiled and found it difficult to accept the strenuous routine."

Stewart's feelings of nostalgia were understandable but pointless; by the end of World War I, the business was steadily heading west, and Vitagraph would slowly asphyxiate. From the vantage point of the early 1950s, Stewart damned Mayer with faint praise: "Although we did have some differences of opinion, I have always had the greatest respect for his foresight and ability."

During 1918, Edie Mayer came down with the deadly Spanish flu that was sweeping the world, but she gradually recovered. As a result, Mayer wanted to get his family to a healthier environment. *Virtuous Wives* had been made in New York, but he couldn't supervise a sustainable flow of productions commuting from Boston to his office on West 45th Street. There was only one solution: go West, young man.

"It is with a tinge of regret that I am leaving the East this time, for it means taking my very home with me," he told the *Exhibitor's Herald.* "It is because I have set a standard of motion picture production so high that I am afraid to trust the reaching of that standard entirely to others. . . . I have stinted on nothing— money, time nor energy. . . . I have consistently held to my policy of combining the great star, great play, great director and great cast."

L.B. announced that he was forming Louis B. Mayer Productions in Los Angeles, with the highly doubtful capitalization of $5 million, and he was planning to sell off his theaters in New England in order to consolidate—and raise money for—his production activities. (In association with Nate Gordon, Mayer now owned pieces of about fifty theaters throughout the area, including several in Boston.)

In the annual industry yearbook, there was a feature depicting the hobbies of major industry figures. There were caricatures of such people as William Fox (golfing), Cecil B. DeMille (flying), and Jesse Lasky (boxing). Louis B. Mayer is depicted standing firmly, holding tiny little movie stars in each hand, while at his feet, another one waits to be picked up.

(For eighty-odd years, it's been thought that at the same time L.B. was making a respectable series of features with a major star, he was double-dipping in exploitation by making a cheapjack version of *Dr. Jekyll and Mr. Hyde* with the character actor Sheldon Lewis, competing with Paramount's lavish John Barrymore version. But the historian Richard Roberts has discovered that the Sheldon Lewis version was produced by a man named Louis Meyer, the head of

Virginia Pearson Photoplays. He produced two films with Pearson in 1919, and when they failed, he produced the quickie version of *Jekyll and Hyde* with Lewis, who was married to Pearson. The confusion stemmed from two articles in the *Moving Picture World* in 1920 that listed J. Charles Haydon, the director of the Sheldon Lewis film, as Charles J. Hayden and Louis Meyer as Louis Mayer—film history distorted by a typo.)

Beneath the tussling vaudeville, Louis was engaged in climbing a very slippery slope with a remarkable degree of sure-handed skill. "He made his first success as a theater owner," said his nephew Gerald Mayer. "Then he became a distributor, and then he realized that if you made your own product, you were in a better position than someone who didn't. This is very rational thinking; beneath the turbulent surface emotions he was an extremely rational man."

In 1918 Hollywood was nothing more than a village. There were no parking meters, and very little smog (the Indians referred to the San Fernando Valley as the "valley of smoke" long before the arrival of the automobile). It was provincial and charming, and virtually every day you could see all the way to Santa Catalina Island. The corner of Hollywood and Vine was marked by a large orange grove, and one block down was the Lasky Studio, with its front entrance lined by a row of pepper trees. At the corner of Hollywood and Highland was the Hollywood Hotel, a glorified theatrical boarding house, with a large veranda that held rows of rocking chairs. In the early days, it was the town's nerve center.

It felt like a small town that had been invaded by a genial carnival. Working actors walked down the streets in greasepaint makeup, and actors who weren't working did the same thing, trying to create the impression that they were employed.

On Sundays, people would dine at a restaurant called Victor Hugo's, then go to the Orpheum in Los Angeles to see the weekly vaudeville show. Likewise, the Mason Opera House was always crowded, and the visits of the D'Oyly Carte company brought out every Englishman within a hundred miles to luxuriate in Gilbert and Sullivan.

The William Selig Studio had been constructed in Edendale, at Glendale Boulevard and Clifford Street, in 1909. In 1911, Selig began moving the entire studio to thirty-two acres off Mission Road in Lincoln Park—a narrow, winding, semirural neighborhood. The studio was seven hundred by six hundred feet, shaped like a wedge, and was actually only half a studio; the other half held the remnants of the Selig Zoo. The animals were used in Selig's films and were available for rent to other filmmakers—elephants cost $200 a day, monkeys $25 to $50 a day. By 1915, the Selig Zoo held seven hundred different species, but many of the animals died in a severe storm that washed over the zoo. By the early 1920s, most of the zoo was liquidated, and the ones that were left were donated to the city—the birth of the Los Angeles Zoo.

The north end of the studio had small offices, wooden buildings that were only marginally less crude than the administration office at the northeast corner. There was a skating rink and dance pavilion, septic tanks for sewage, and a single star dressing room that was only twelve feet long. Every activity at the studio was accompanied by the cackling, cawing cacaphony of the zoo, increased by two neighboring animal attractions.

"Across the street from the studio was an ostrich farm and an alligator farm," remembered Budd Schulberg. "It was kind of like a tropical tourist attraction, but it was in open country. The studio itself only had two stages."

A few years later, Mayer would move into a custom-built administration building on the Selig property, a structure that resembled the château at Chenonceaux. In addition to offices, it also had four stages and actual dressing room/bungalows for several stars. But at the moment, the primary decorations at the Mission Road studio were the stone lions and elephants that Selig had commissioned from a sculptor named Carlo Romanelli. Mayer rented the stages, enough room on the back lot for outdoor sets, and a eucalyptus grove of several acres that could be used for a variety of outdoor scenes.

L.B. wasn't too sure about automobiles, so initially he took a house close enough to the studio to walk to work. By his own tally, he worked "seven days a week, fifty-two weeks a year. My days sometimes started at five in the morning and ended at midnight." He built a rabbit hutch at the studio for Irene, and, rather strangely, bought her a pet lamb, mostly because the image of the animal trailing after his daughter struck him as irresistible.

Mayer and the family went everywhere and saw everything—San Juan Capistrano, San Diego. As far as Mayer was concerned, California was the Garden of Eden. No flu, no sinus infections, no frigid winter weather. The hell with Boston. He took particular care of his daughters' diet; the menus for the house usually featured chicken, beef or lamb chops, or fish. In restaurants, the girls would tell their father what they wanted to eat and he would order for them as if they hadn't spoken.

Margaret hovered solicitously, constructing a kitchen at the studio and personally cooking L.B.'s meals. The actors and technicians began asking her to make their lunches too, so Margaret expanded, hiring a cook and two girls to wait on people. The result was one of the first studio commissaries, and, Mayer was proud to say, "it made a profit, which Margaret put in a separate account of her own." When L.B. felt the concern was sufficiently stable, he convinced his brother Jerry to leave the salvage business in Canada and come to work as the Mission Road studio manager.

L.B. began gathering a nucleus of talent. The first director he hired had been the estimable George Loane Tucker, and soon he hired the innovative woman director Lois Weber. "THANKS FOR EXPRESSION OF SATISFACTION WITH OUR BUSINESS RELATIONS," Mayer wired Weber. "IT IS MUTUAL, REGARDING MY IDEA OF LEADING MAN, IT IS THE SAME AS MY IDEAS OF THE PLAY AND CAST, NAMELY THE BEST. MY UNCHANGING POLICY WILL BE GREAT STAR, GREAT DIREC-TOR, GREAT PLAY, GREAT CAST. YOU ARE AUTHORIZED TO GET THESE WITHOUT STINT OR LIMIT. SPARE NOTHING, NEITHER EXPENSE, TIME, NOR EFFORT. RE-SULTS ONLY ARE WHAT I AM AFTER. SIMPLY SEND ME THE BILLS AND I WILL OK THEM. BEST WISHES."

Mayer began laying siege to Marshall Neilan, and hired John M. Stahl when Edward Small, Stahl's agent, asked, "There are no Jewish directors in this business; why don't you give a job to one?" A young girl named Margaret Booth, the sister of the late Griffith actor Elmer Booth, began working at Mayer's studio assembling film. Stahl taught her how to edit, explaining how and why he was doing what he was doing. Every once in a while, remembered Booth, "an older man [would] come in. It was Mr. Mayer. 'Oh, you're working for Mr. Stahl.' . . . He used to come by the cutting room and say, 'How's every-thing?' "

L.B. believed in organization and in discipline, and he didn't stint on either with his daughters. One suitcase for both girls was sufficient. (They learned to travel light.) If they had to go somewhere, the girls were in the front hall, ready to go, purses in hand when their parents came down. L.B. was first out the door, then Margaret, then Irene and Edie. If they were supposed to go someplace with him and they were late, he left without them. (They learned to be punc-tual.)

In the mornings, L.B. and Irene would go riding, out to the Hillcrest Coun-try Club for breakfast, then back. One morning at the stable, L.B. gestured for Irene to get on a horse with blue eyes, a black tail, and a white coat. The horse could dance and kneel. "Get on," said Mayer. "Her name is Marcheta. She's five-gaited. She's yours." A year later, he gave her a saddle horse with a gorgeous gait named Dixie.

L.B. and Irene would take car rides up over the Cahuenga Pass to Universal

City, or through Hollywood's Poverty Row, the area around Gower and Sunset, where Harry Cohn and the Christie brothers made shorts and westerns. Occasionally, Louis would park on Santa Monica Boulevard, where Mary Pickford and Douglas Fairbanks made their movies in full view, enclosed only by a wire fence. "I'll bet you'd be surprised if I became head of a studio like this someday," he said, thinking out loud.

In most respects, his daughters turned out the way he wanted them to, but he was grievously upset by their refusal to learn to cook. "You can't run a house if you don't know how to cook," he asserted. "Your cook will have no respect for you." It didn't work. For years, whenever he would get angry with them for some perceived insufficiency, his parting shot to everyone in the room would be, "What's more, they don't know how to cook."

Mayer hired his secretary, Florence Browning, away from an attorney named Edwin Loeb. "That's the kind of person I want working for me," he told Loeb. "I want high-class people."

Browning remembered that she "couldn't have worked in more awful conditions. Mayer's office was a little hole off in one corner of the large barnlike place, and I was in a larger room outside it, where the cameramen kept their cameras, the cowboys kept their saddles, etc. It was awful, but I loved it."

Browning had never met anybody like Mayer before, but then nobody else had either. He was, she remembered, a "funny little man riding around in a Ford telling everyone confidently that he was going to be the greatest man in the picture-making business. He seemed to have absolutely no reticence, no inhibitions, no sense of embarrassment at his evident manifestations of conceit."

Mayer was tireless in familiarizing himself with all of the crafts and techniques that go into moviemaking. He spent most days on the back lot, finding out how the carpenters built the sets, how the electricians wired the lights, how a cameraman lit a set. He was innately vigorous and invariably impetuous. When he answered his mail, he would bluster and fume. "Tell him to go to hell!" he would snap at Browning about a letter demanding overdue payment. "Give this son of a bitch a nasty answer!" was another frequent order, which Browning would translate into a diplomatic response.

Occasionally, Browning would use a word in a letter that Mayer didn't know, and he would call her into his office and demand a definition. A few days later, she would notice that he would use the word in conversation, and always correctly.

He learned fast, he did everything he could to charm and captivate, and he never lacked for nerve. When Browning would go to their bank, she would be asked, "What sort of person is this fellow? Is he crazy? He owes us money and still he calls up and demands that we come out to see him! If he wants to see us, let *him* come *here!*"

Beneath the imperious exterior, Mayer was petrified. Everything was riding on him—his family's future, his mother's hopes, his own lofty expectations. The actress Carmel Myers remembered that, left to his own devices, in those early days, "Mayer was very shy and speechless." Florence Browning grew used to displays of emotional uneasiness and instability. Before meeting someone he regarded as "big," Browning would go into his office to find him crying help-lessly, an inconsolable child. She would get him a glass of water, and he would sniffle and wipe his eyes. A few minutes later, when Browning showed the guest in, Mayer would greet his visitor with complete assurance, just like an actor beset with a panic attack who pulled himself together before he walked on stage.

"I recognized his faults and loved him," said Browning. "I didn't like—I couldn't stand—to have people make fun of him, and many did." Once, Browning requested a raise, and Mayer ignored her. A few days later, she was planning to go to Catalina for a weekend, but missed the trolley ride from the studio. Damning the expense, she hailed a cab, which passed Mayer's own car.

On Monday, he asked her what she was doing taking an expensive taxi. After she told him, he said, "Who'd have thought a nice, careful Baptist like you would spend money on a taxi!" A few days later, he called her in and told her, "If you're going to ride around in taxicabs you can't afford, I guess you'll have to have a raise."

In its early days, Louis B. Mayer Productions was scraping by, with each picture earning just enough to make the next picture. Once, a small fire broke out at the studio, and someone rushed to the phone to call the fire department. "Don't," said Mayer as he quietly watched the blaze. "Let it burn."

He subleased some space to the former journalist and publicist B. P. Schul-berg, who was beginning independent production. Mayer then went east on a money hunt. While he was away, Schulberg erected a sign that proclaimed "B. P. Schulberg Studio." When Browning told him about it a few days later, Mayer was nonchalant. "We need the money," he said. "What do we care what sort of sign he puts up?"

With both Mayer and Schulberg attempting to use the small studio, a de-gree of cooperation was necessary. "The business managers had to work to-gether," remembered Schulberg's son Budd. "They'd decide, 'Well, we'll use that set until Thursday,' and then very often Louis or my father would use the same set, just slightly altered, slightly differently decorated, and shoot some other movie virtually in the same set."

Mayer and Schulberg shared a reception office, guards and cleanup men, carpentry and paint shops. Each was doing the other a favor, each was saving the other money in overhead, and in the picture business, a dollar saved was a dollar earned. The Schulberg and Mayer families became close and would alternate Sunday brunches. Ad Schulberg, B.P.'s wife, and Margaret Mayer would drive down to the Jewish quarter around Temple Street and load up on lox, whitefish, cream cheese, bagels, and onion rolls. Margaret kept kosher until Louis demanded as a symbolic gesture of assimilation that she get rid of the extra dishes required.

By this time, the Mayers were "holiday Jews," observing Rosh Hashanah and Yom Kippur but little else. "Sunday was a sturgeon and salmon and whitefish day," said Schulberg. "They were very close friends and they were talking about the films that they were making, and there was a good deal of rivalry and cooperation." The families became intertwined, and Ad Schulberg became almost like a second mother to Irene and Edith. L.B. felt so comfortable with the Schulbergs that he would even reminisce about the old days, when he was courting Margaret from his junk wagon, driving out from South Boston for a picnic in the country.

Mayer signed director Marshall Neilan to make two pictures with Anita Stewart, to see if Neilan's humorous, whimsical directorial touch could do for her what it had done for Mary Pickford. The first Neilan picture, *Her Kingdom of Dreams*, was shot while Mayer was still back east, with what Neilan claimed as "my own organization, as Mayer had none," and was followed by *In Old Kentucky*. But the relationship nearly ground to a halt over Mayer's continual presence on the set of *Kentucky*.

Neilan's response to Mayer's hovering was, first, sarcasm, then venom. "My difficulties with Mayer in the early stages was simply the man was going to the school of HOW ARE MOTION PICTURES MADE, and this was a 24 hr. way of living with the man. He would come on the set and ask, 'WHY are you doing that—it's not in the scenario?' This would call for a complete stop, and arguments would follow. After a few days of this, I put a quick stop to it. When he came on the set, I would stop work, set down by him and politely say, 'Well, my little student, what lesson shall I give you today? Your interference yesterday cost you a lot of MONEY, KID.' Then I would make a long study of my wristwatch. He would look at me dumbfounded, at the cast, at the workers standing by doing NOTHING, and then he would wipe the sweat off his brow and wend his way back to the front office WHERE HE BELONGED."

Mayer seethed, but Neilan had talent and was a name. Even after Neilan's humiliations, Mayer kept hounding him to merge his company with Mayer's, a deal Neilan bluntly refused. Eventually, Mayer got the hint, and Neilan realized it "had to come to the point where he said to himself, 'That SOB Neilan must not like me . . .' " It was also at this point that Mayer remembered never to forget.

Eventually, Neilan reverted to his old habit of disappearing for days or weeks at a time in pursuit of booze and good times. Alfred E. Green ended up directing large portions of the film, which might be why Mayer never paid Neilan the $5,000 bonus he was promised for bringing both pictures in under budget.

A little over a year after signing Anita Stewart, Louis agreed to pay Mildred Harris Chaplin, estranged wife of the great comedian, $50,000 apiece plus a percentage for six pictures. Harris had been a child actress, but had little public profile beyond her brief marriage to Charlie Chaplin; hiring her was exploitation pure and simple, and as close as Louis would ever come to bottom feeding.

Naturally enough, Charlie Chaplin was outraged. Robert Rubin was a witness to the famous fight between Mayer and Chaplin in the Alexandria Hotel. The two men ran into each other in the corridor leading to the men's room. "You can't use my name in your pictures," snapped Chaplin. "What are you going to do about it?" asked Mayer. "I'll show you what I'm going to do about it," said Chaplin, and lunged at Mayer, who, according to Rubin, conveniently stuck out his fist just in time for Chaplin to run into it.

Mayer's almost feral belligerence would always be a large component of his personality, one he undoubtedly regarded as necessary. He had no advantages of birth, money, or looks. He had to make his own breaks, and woe to anyone who got between Mayer and something he wanted.

Within two years of arriving in Hollywood, L.B. was running a successful, if small-scale operation, making predominantly melodramatic films with titles like *The Dangerous Age*, *Women Who Give*, and *The Child Thou Gavest Me*. Work fed home and vice versa. Louis admired Hedda Hopper's flair with clothes and asked her, as a personal favor, if she would take Margaret shopping and get her "some decent clothes." It wasn't easy; Margaret had grown up without money and it felt unnatural to her to spend huge sums on clothes. About all

Hopper could do was induce her to buy some nice underwear, "But only because she already had it on!"

At that point, Mayer's star roster was fairly undernourished—besides Anita Stewart and Mildred Harris Chaplin, there would be a skinny young girl from Canada named Norma Shearer. But his directors were all solid craftsmen: Reginald Barker, John Stahl, Fred Niblo.

Most of the Louis B. Mayer productions of this era haven't survived, but the ones that have are instructive. Several reels of *Virtuous Wives*, the first Mayer production, feature well-appointed sets and costumes, spacious locations offering compositions full of light and air, and a dynamically edited motorboat chase that confirms the gift of director George Loane Tucker—as well as Mayer's ever-present eye for talent.

Sowing the Wind, a 1921 Anita Stewart vehicle, is insanely moralistic—not content with a Sins of the Fathers plot, it also throws in the Sins of the Mothers, with Stewart playing "A lonely little convent girl" who becomes a Broadway star. "*She* never deserted me," she tells an old roué who happens to be her father, "and if her sins be as scarlet—she was my mother and I owe her reverence."

But the film is very well produced, with excellent sets, good photography (by René Guissart) and direction (John Stahl), and effectively showcases the rather sedate charms of Anita Stewart. It's conventional, but not negligible, and, script aside, is far better than equivalent pictures being made by other independent producers of the period.

The same can be said of *One Clear Call*, a 1922 John Stahl picture starring Milton Sills, Claire Windsor, and Henry B. Walthall, the Little Colonel from Griffith's *The Birth of a Nation*. As Kevin Brownlow says, *One Clear Call* is "high hokum of Mother Love and Great Sacrifice, despite the title at the front which insists it's about real people. It is very watchable—something big seems to be happening all the time, including a Ride of the Klan—and it out De-Milles DeMille."

One Clear Call signaled a transition in Mayer's work. He realized he had to do more than Anita Stewart movies—Mildred Harris Chaplin was discarded early in 1921—so he began making all-star movies, using three or more popular players instead of just one big star. For the next several years, Mayer's productions would feature solid second-stringers like Frank Keenan, Anna Q. Nillson, Matt Moore, Enid Bennett, and Wallace Beery, as well as some attractive juveniles: Shearer, Ramon Novarro, and Renée Adorée.

At the end of 1920, for $1,000 down on a purchase price of $10,000, Mayer bought a house at 1834 North Kenmore, south of Franklin Avenue in the Los Feliz district of Los Angeles. It was a block or two from the house of William de Mille, C.B.'s brother, and L.B. added a sleeping porch for his girls.

He decreed that his daughters wouldn't go to college. His girls work for a living? Under no circumstances. Of course, college also meant a loss of parental control. Irene and Edie might develop ideas that were . . . different. "Those [other] girls *have* to go to college," he told his daughters. "They don't have your advantages."

Despite Mayer's dislike for his father, he brought Jacob to be close to him — first to America in 1915, then to California in 1918. Jacob Mayer's conversation was heavily spiced with Talmudic wisdom, and he would make regular pleas for money for relatives, especially Ida and her clan, whom he obviously favored. "Louis," he would say, "God made you the treasurer. Every family has one and that is why He gave you the brains and the strength. It is to earn money for the family."

"He was a very cagey fellow, always looking for an opening, feigning benevolence, careful to be on his best behavior in front of Dad," remembered his granddaughter Irene. Louis had evidently decided the cost of putting up with the father's conniving *mishegas* was less onerous than the guilt he would feel by exiling him.

When interviewing writers and directors, Mayer gave them chapter and verse about what he expected for his money. He would talk with such enthusiasm about making pictures that "at any moment I expected him to burst at the seams," said screenwriter Frances Marion. He would point to framed photographs on his desk and explain that his little Edie and his little Irene would never be embarrassed by anything they saw in their father's pictures — Mayer productions would be clean and wholesome. "I worship good women, honorable men, and saintly mothers," he would intone. At the same time, he would let them know he was slightly embarrassed about his quarters, and regarded them as temporary.

If a writer brought back a script that pleased him, he would be enthusiastic — in his own way. "I like your scenario very much. So does Mama — that's my wife. It hit me here," and then he would deliver a mighty punch to his own stomach. "If a story makes me cry, I know it's good. I like humanity. In fact, I'm a sucker for humanity."

He was relentless in his pursuit of talent. One day, director Raoul Walsh looked out the window to see Louis coming up the walk to his front door. Louis had been after Walsh for some time, but Walsh wasn't interested. "He's always over-anxious to make himself agreeable," he had written his wife. "I'm not keen on tying up with him."

Walsh told his wife to go downstairs and get rid of him. She told Louis they were just about to leave for New York and they were too busy to see him. Louis persisted, telling Walsh's wife that he had Anita Stewart and he needed more directors of talent. "He kept saying how much he could do for Raoul and me," remembered Miriam Cooper Walsh. "He didn't say how much we could do for him.

"I kept backing away from him. He was short and fat, with squinty eyes and a big nose and the worst case of halitosis I'd ever been this close to. The odor really made me sick. There was green stuff on his teeth, like moss. The more I retreated, the more he came on. He backed me all the way from the front door to the backyard."

Some details of this account are highly doubtful, if not anti-Semitic. Fully aware of his own homeliness, Mayer was always immaculately groomed. But the pit-bull aggressiveness mixed with a placating neediness—that's Louis B. Mayer.

There is no question that L.B.'s reputation was dubious, and there is no doubt that he knew it and craved respectability. He implored Hedda Hopper to help Irene and Edith get admitted to a private school that didn't accept Jews. Hopper said it was impossible. "Can't you tell the headmistress how important I am?" he asked her.

Irene and Edith ended up attending the Hollywood School for Girls, with Douglas Fairbanks Jr.—despite the name, it was coed—who remembered that they had "as many loyal friends as their father had devout enemies. And *that* is saying a great deal." Photos of a school theatrical production show Irene adapting to stage posture very successfully in a scene from *The Forest Ring* with two other children who would go on to considerable careers of their own: Agnes de Mille and Ben Alexander.

Irene Mayer remembered that invitations to the home of William de Mille were cherished occasions, both because of the inherent quality of the people, and the contrast to her own house. "Their intellectual and cultural standards were new to me. They had more books than I had ever seen in one house in my life. I liked the simplicity of their house, their food. At the table, the girls and I were treated like thinking people. It was a bracing climate."

The sex and drug scandals of 1921–22 (Fatty Arbuckle, William Desmond Taylor, Wallace Reid) only confirmed Mayer's distrust of Hollywood values. "If you have the right values, the dignity, none of this will touch you," he told his daughters.

Adolph Zukor, whose Paramount studio was the home to all the people involved in the scandals, needed cover, and he got it from Will Hays, a rat-faced politician from the Harding administration. Hays set up a censorship board that would, in theory, police Hollywood production so state censor boards and the federal government wouldn't have to.

Mayer was and always would be terrified of an angry, moralistic populace rising in a wave somewhere in Indiana, gaining momentum as they passed through Kansas, smashing into California and obliterating the movies. "If this keeps up, there won't be any more film business," L.B. told director King Vidor.

In his personal life, Mayer would always be a man of his place and time, crudely paternalistic in his dealings with his daughters. "When I was 18," remembered Edie, "I had an opportunity to audition in New York. I remember going to see Dad and telling him I wanted to go. I'll never forget his answer. He said to me, 'You're the best goddamn actress of 'em all. But you need it for living.'"

Neither of the girls wanted to make him angry. "He was a forceful, powerful man," Edie would remember. "He'd just shout. The resonance of that voice! 'God damn you!' That's it. I'd hear it and I'd run."

This was the same man who would surround himself with smart women on whom he depended—at the office. He hired woman directors, gave women like Kate Corbaley, Frances Marion, Ida Koverman, and Margaret Booth privileged positions at MGM, and entrusted his life to one of the rare women doctors of her time, Dr. Jessie Marmorston. But at home, he wanted women to remain dependent, hence subservient.

Mayer had been distributing his pictures through First National, but then Robert Rubin once again lent Mayer a hand and arranged a Metro release for four additional Mayer productions per year. The little man in the little studio on Mission Road was slowly but inexorably moving into the big time.

These weren't great releasing deals for Mayer. First National gave him 50 percent of the gross after it recouped the money advanced for production costs, which was $125,000 per picture. But Mayer's desire for quality meant that he was often spending more than that, so he was always gambling that his share of the profits would exceed the extra money he was spending. Still, he was beginning to do well. *Thy Name Is Woman*, one of Louis's independent productions for Metro, earned domestic rentals of $388,000. Presuming a production cost of around $175,000—more than his average budget but not terribly more—Mayer should have cleared about $100,000 on the picture, which doesn't even take into account foreign receipts.

Louis quickly devised a masterly technique for avoiding bill collectors for those times when money ran short. "He would suddenly pitch forward and pass out," remembered Budd Schulberg, "and the secretary would rush in and say, 'Oh, my God, Mr. Mayer is having a heart attack,' and they would be putting cold compresses on his forehead. My mother, who was always fonder of Louis than her children were, remembered these almost ritual heart attacks that Louis Mayer would have on Fridays." During one of these fits, Budd's mother, Ad, knelt down beside L.B. and tried to soothe him by stroking his forehead. "Oh, that feels so good—like the hand of my mother," Mayer moaned.

With the trouble at hand forestalled by an apparently lethal cardiac episode—Mayer somehow contrived a means of turning pale to render these attacks even more convincing—the problem would have to wait at least until Monday. Like a thwarted child threatening to hold his breath until he passes out, in years to come Mayer would encore the phony heart attack routine whenever he was faced with someone he regarded as potentially gullible, often a recalcitrant actor.

Ad Schulberg believed that Louis's collapses were not put-ons, that they were authentic manifestations of a personality forever perched on the edge of an anxiety attack. "He was a very emotional man," she would tell her son, "so intense that he might be described as on the borderline of insanity. Well, maybe that's too extreme, but L.B. was always very strange. Absolutely the worst hypochondriac I ever met. He was paranoid about his health, as if the whole world was conspiring to give him a heart attack, or double pneumonia, or whatever disease was fashionable at the time. . . . He was always an extremist."

The only security that had ever meant anything to Mayer was his mother. Without her, he felt that life was an elongated episode of either seduction or smash-and-grab: inner fear thinly covered by a shell of courage and bravado.

He began taking Edie for long drives during which he would talk to her about business. Edith would mostly just listen, which is all he wanted her to do. He would tell his girls that he was glad he had them, because "If I had a son and he disappointed me, I couldn't live through it. I couldn't live with the shame."

He left nothing about the girls' upbringing to chance. He ordered them always to smile when meeting someone, saying that it would draw people to them and show they weren't snobs. He bought them golf lessons, because it was a sport they would be able to play with their husbands. When it was time for the girls to be educated about sex, he gave them all five volumes of Havelock Ellis, told them to read all of it and write down any questions, after which the family doctor was invited over to clear up any gray areas. "Be smart, but never show it," he told them.

At night, sleeping was a problem, and he fought a nervous rash. He was afraid that everything he had earned could be taken away, afraid that his need to belong to a more powerful tribe than that of poor Jews would never succeed.

If Mayer's anxieties were increasing, it might have been because his responsibilities were growing as well. His sister Ida, her son, Jack, and two daughters moved to Los Angeles in 1923, and depended on Louis for most of their income.

Although Louis B. Mayer Productions was successful, Louis knew he had problems. For one thing, his operation was too small, manufacturing films one or two at a time, while Paramount had already shown the industry that Henry Ford had been right—mass production was the wave of the American future. Louis hated to see actors and crew idle and drawing salaries just because he didn't have scripts or stage space for them. He would often comment that it would be much better to have fifty stars instead of five, twenty stages instead of three.

Make it, he believed, and the audience would come.

In those days, Mayer endured great distress from the directors who deigned to work for him, and the remainder of his career can be viewed as an extended revenge fantasy in which no director ever got the upper hand again.

John Stahl, Mayer's most prestigious employee, was very much the director as ham, a master thespian full of affectation. He would wear his coat over his shoulders as if it were a cloak, and habitually carried a cane, the crook of which he would put around the neck of the person he wanted to talk to, drawing them toward him. "He was trying to imitate David Belasco," the screenwriter Sheridan Gibney said. "He thought he was a magician—hypnotizing everybody. . . . He amused people. But he did have a way of getting what he wanted."

"John Stahl made *The Dangerous Age* over and over again," said screenwriter Carey Wilson. "Stahl's costs were less than [Fred] Niblo's and [the] profits more. Mayer loved his pictures, the moral thing—a guy starts to leave home and then returns, brought together [with his wife] by the little baby."

Stahl would stay with Mayer for years, and Margaret Booth remembered that the director was "a hard task-master. He was a perfectionist; he kept doing things over and over again. He shot every sequence so it could be cut in many different ways." Stahl's method of making the movie, not on the stage but in the cutting room, was a method that Mayer would come to believe was the only way to run an industrial operation like a movie studio.

Even now, nearly seventy years after his death, the legend of Irving Thalberg remains. He was a small man, slender, delicate, with what one writer remembered as "a striking Italianate face." He carried the aura of a Renaissance prince, and "was as fragile as alabaster," according to producer/director Sidney Franklin. He almost never raised his voice, had to play with something while he was talking or listening, and when he was surprised or pleased his right eyebrow would go up above his left, which gave him a severe appearance at odds with his basically pleasant, soft-spoken manner.

"He had a boyish quality, yet his demeanor was serious," remembered Franklin. "He had a sense of humor, but there was very little wasting of time with Irving. It was all business—at times I thought too much so. . . . He worked at a pace that gave me indigestion. I worried about the pace he kept. Many a time, he would stay at the studio until eight or nine in the evening."

"When you were shown into his office," remembered the screenwriter Lenore Coffee, "he was invariably standing behind his desk, looking at a letter or fiddling with various objects with an abstracted air, as if he were quite unconscious of your presence. After a good moment he would look up as if startled to find you there. . . . He had enormous dignity; I can't imagine anyone taking a liberty with him, either in business or in his personal life."

Thalberg allowed writers to contribute ideas about casting, and gave them some veto power. "You know your own brain children," he said. "If so-and-so doesn't fit the character you've created, find someone else. Bad casting can destroy the unity of every scene in your script." On the other hand, Thalberg believed that writers had to be correctly cast, like actors. Some writers were better at plot than dialogue, some better at comedy than love scenes. Thalberg's aim was the best script, not the happiest writer, and he thought nothing of shuffling or removing writers at will—his.

Years later, someone asked Coffee what the difference was between Thalberg and all the rest of the producers. "If you were going to have a knife stuck in your back," she replied, "Thalberg would not only hold the knife correctly but would use it with a certain elegance."

Irving Grant Thalberg was born in 1899 in the attic of his father's home at 19 Woodbine Street in Brooklyn, and retained traces of his hometown's accent all his life. He attended P.S. 85 and Boy's High School, intending to go into law, but he was struck by rheumatic fever, which damaged his heart. "Irving was an invalid," remembered MGM story editor Sam Marx, who knew Thalberg when they were both young men about town in New York. "He spent most of his early school days in bed. He was an avid reader, with a dominating mother." After six months of recovery, he learned shorthand and typing, becoming expert at both; years later, at MGM, he walked out of his office and noticed three secretaries banging away at their typewriters. "Hold everything!" he said, and sat down for an impromptu speed-typing contest. He beat all the professional secretaries.

He was visiting his grandmother's cottage at Edgemere, Long Island, when he met Carl Laemmle, founder and president of Universal Pictures, who was visiting next door. Laemmle was impressed by the boy's quiet demeanor and aura of command, and hired him, first as his secretary, later as general manager and eventual production chief of Universal.

Thalberg impressed everybody. Robert Cochrane, general manager of Universal, would remember that "he was a keen observer and would make suggestions to Laemmle that were very helpful and valuable. He had a good business mind, as well as a good artist's mind. . . . Everyone had confidence in Thalberg . . . but no one was notably struck by his genius at that point. His pictures were not extraordinary." Of course, he was limited by the talent at Universal, which also wasn't extraordinary.

After a couple of years running production at Universal, Thalberg was restless, and with good reason. Laemmle was subjecting him to the death of a thousand cuts. In a letter to Thalberg dated December 5, 1922, Laemmle expressed disappointment about the Lon Chaney vehicle *The Shock*, had only faint praise for *The Storm*, complained about cost overruns and Thalberg's taste in writers and directors, and predicted that Wallace Worsley was going to turn *The Hunchback of Notre Dame* into another "flivver." "Irving," he implored his production chief, "turn over a new leaf, do business along conservative lines, and be cocksure you are right before you go ahead with anything."

Laemmle's nagging was mostly just sublimated anger over Thalberg's refusal to marry his daughter, Rosabelle. In any case, Thalberg was only making $400 a week. One of Thalberg's favorite dictums was "Never remain in a job when you have everything from it you can get." It was time to go.

In November of 1922, Thalberg met Louis B. Mayer for the first time, at the studio on Mission Road. Mayer was looking for someone to upgrade his production, take charge of the day-to-day details. L.B. immediately sensed that this was a man with whom he could do business; more importantly, this was a man he could trust. In part, his reaction was a function of class—Mayer had the Russian Jew's automatic respect for the more learned and aristocratic German

Jew—and partly it was in recognition of Thalberg's very real accomplishments. Wasn't this young man making *The Hunchback of Notre Dame?* Wasn't that a classy picture?

They also saw most aspects of the movie business the same way. "It is hard to . . . explain the whole motion picture situation to a banker," Thalberg once noted. "It is a creative business dependent, as almost no other business is, on the emotional reaction of its customers. It should be conducted with budgets and cost sheets, but it cannot be conducted with blueprints and graphs."

Mayer's innate enthusiasm led him to talk about giving Thalberg a piece of the company—his own unit and 20 percent of the profits. Robert Rubin counseled his client to calm down and see if the boy worked out. "Wait a while," he said. "Try him on straight salary for six months."

The next day Mayer called Edwin Loeb, Thalberg's attorney. "Tell him if he comes to work for me, I'll look after him like my own son." Two Momma's boys, one in need of a son, another in need of a father, both ambitious, both believing in class melded with efficiency—a dynamic relationship that always carried the potential for an explosion. On February 15, 1923, Thalberg went to work for Louis B. Mayer Productions at a salary of $500 a week. (It has always been stated that Thalberg was making $600 a week working for Mayer, but there is at least one surviving canceled check made out to Thalberg drawn on the Louis B. Mayer Studios Inc. account in the amount of $500—for example, a check dated November 10 for services ending November 7, 1923. It is possible that Thalberg was deferring $100 a week, but it's more likely that the $600 figure involved paycheck hyperbole.) Apparently, Laemmle didn't bother to counter-offer.

It was something of a shock for Universal—Thalberg's production of *The Hunchback of Notre Dame* was only half-completed—but the really surprising thing was not that he was leaving, but where he was going.

Mayer handed Thalberg the pursestrings. When Thalberg sent Hedda Hopper out to buy a hat for a picture, she found a sale and bought three hats for the price he had allotted. But Thalberg had only wanted one hat, and sent Hopper back to return the other two.

Mayer remained frugal, but out of instinct more than necessity. Once, someone asked him why he drove a Ford to the Mission Road studio. He gestured out the window. "See that line of imported cars down there? Well, not a week passes that the sheriff doesn't come and take at least one of them away from its owner. I'm not going to buy one until I can afford two!"

Mayer and Thalberg would rarely socialize. But they were bound together by mutual respect. Both wanted the same things from the movies—beautiful pictures of beautiful people, strong but decorous melodramas, increased standing for the business they had chosen and, not coincidentally, for themselves. In 1923, and for years afterward, they would complement each other beautifully. Mayer would always speak of Thalberg in familial terms; if it wasn't father and son, they were "brothers under the skin," although, as one woman said, "we would hate to have them skinned to find out."

Around the Mission Road lot, the change was immediately noticeable, as Mayer let his young prize make the movies. "Mayer backed out and let [Thalberg] do it," said Margaret Booth. "We didn't see Mayer like [we did] before." Booth had more time to notice the overall environment at the studio, such as a little girl who used to sit in front of her cutting room. She was working for B. P. Schulberg and had a tendency to quarrel with people—"a common, ordinary girl," according to Booth, named Clara Bow.

Another young actress who was working for Mayer was Norma Shearer, and, remembered Florence Browning, she was "determined to get Irving from the day he first walked into our studio. . . . She used to sit in my office, pretending to talk with me, but actually waiting to see him and be seen by him. She once told me that she got him by watching Rosabelle [Laemmle] and avoiding doing the things that Rosabelle did wrong. Irving never knew he was being caught. After he was married, he said to me, 'You never thought I'd get her, did you, Florence?' "

Thalberg was running production, but Mayer was no absentee boss. Thalberg hired the special effects artist Norman Dawn to do the glass paintings for a picture called *Master of Women*, with exteriors to be shot around Great Slave Lake in Canada. One day on location, Dawn was astonished to see a dog team approaching. Seated in the sled, wrapped in fur, was Mayer.

Mayer and Dawn hit it off, and the producer asked to see the local sights. Dawn took him to see a herd of buffalo, but the animals were nervous and began to stampede. Dawn and Mayer had to jump a five-foot plank fence to get out of the way. Mayer may have been shaped like a dumpling, but he was agile and made the leap with no trouble whatever. "You're not the only jackrabbit around here," he told Dawn.

For Mayer, all the pieces were now in place. He had been successful in the junk business, he had been successful in the theater business, and now he was successful in the producing business. Soon he would be successful in the mogul business, beyond his or anybody else's wildest dreams.

By the end of 1923, Frank Godsol of the Goldwyn Company had a sick company on his hands, and wasn't feeling too great himself. As he would admit, he didn't know much about movies and was strictly a businessman.

Originally built in 1916 as the headquarters of the Triangle Film Company, the twelve-acre studio in Culver City was leased to Sam Goldwyn in November 1918. Goldwyn ended up buying the lot as well as another twenty-three acres.

Goldwyn's production efforts quickly ran into trouble with a less-than-stellar star lineup. He then formed Eminent Authors, a group of best-selling commercial novelists such as Rex Beach, Mary Roberts Rinehart, and Gertrude Atherton, who sold their stories exclusively to Goldwyn. But movies are about stars, not writers, and Eminent Authors failed to stem the tide of red ink.

Goldwyn took the Shubert brothers and Al Woods in as partners in July 1919. Du Pont money was also invested in the organization, which enabled Goldwyn to refurbish the Culver City lot and make some good hires. A young art director named Cedric Gibbons came on board in 1918, and Howard Dietz started working for Goldwyn in 1919. It was Dietz who devised the trademark of a lion and the slogan *Ars Gratia Artis* as the trademark for Goldwyn pictures.

By the middle of 1920, Goldwyn was having another financial crisis. The company went to the du Pont interests for more money, but they would ante up only if Goldwyn were removed. Goldwyn found some new investors on his own, so he retained his position. He also imported *The Cabinet of Dr. Caligari*, hoping that it would kick off a series of mutually supportive relationships with European producers. But 1921 was a bad year for the movie business as costs rose and attendance slipped, and in March 1922, Sam Goldwyn was fired from the corporation bearing his name. He was given $600,000 for his stock and used that money to form the independent company where he would be remarkably successful for the next thirty-odd years.

Frank Godsol replaced Goldwyn and hired June Mathis to head up the studio story department and supervise production. In February 1923, the Goldwyn Company formed an alliance with William Randolph Hearst's Cosmopolitan Productions, and began distributing the films of Marion Davies. Then Godsol bought the screen rights to *Ben-Hur*, which June Mathis thought would be a worthy successor to *The Four Horsemen of the Apocalypse*, which she had written for Metro.

But the Goldwyn Company continued to deteriorate commercially. Only seven films went before the cameras in 1922, while 1923 saw fifteen films produced—still an insufficient number for an organization of Goldwyn's size, one that had a roster of some of the best directors in the business, including Marshall Neilan, King Vidor, and Erich von Stroheim. The studio was running into production catastrophes with two runaway productions at the same time: von Stroheim's *Greed* as well as *Ben-Hur*, indicating serious problems with central management. Goldwyn stock, which had been selling for 22 in June of 1923, was down to 8 1/4 by the end of the year.

During a vacation in Palm Beach in January 1924, Godsol approached Marcus Loew about buying the Goldwyn Company. "Prior to the purchase of Metro Pictures, Marcus Loew had given little consideration to going into the production end of motion pictures," said Loew's associate Nick Schenck. Lee Shubert said that he was the one who talked Loew into the deal, and that's probably the case. Shubert had been a friend of Loew's since the early nickelodeon days, when Shubert had rented him legitimate theaters for film shows.

"Loew wanted to know what would be gained by combining with a company that was in worse condition than his own," remembered Shubert. "I explained that the Goldwyn company had certain assets which if handled properly would prove of great value, one of which was . . . *Ben-Hur*."

Also proving a healthy incentive was the forty-acre Goldwyn lot in Culver City; Metro had only a tiny lot, and if the new company was to compete with Zukor and Fox, it needed a bigger studio.

There had been considerable discussion within Loew's company about either building up production facilities or getting out entirely. Metro had had one smash hit with *The Four Horsemen of the Apocalypse*, but, despite acquiring Jackie Coogan and Buster Keaton, had been unable to repeat the success of the Rex Ingram–directed Valentino film.

Loew went back to New York and proposed the deal to Bob Rubin and Nick Schenck. Schenck remembered that "We thought that the Goldwyn product showed great possibilities, and were inclined to think that properly managed they would turn out . . . hit pictures. The studio facilities were very good. Also, from a sales and distribution point of view, it was quite important to have a volume of product in order to get adequate playing time."

The key phrase, of course, was "properly managed." Creatively, Goldwyn was under the loose supervision of June Mathis, who was behind the remarkably sophisticated, if lamentably uncommercial, production schedule that included *Ben-Hur* and von Stroheim's *Greed*.

Loew, Schenck, and Rubin were all theater and distribution men, and knew nothing about production. Nick Schenck asked Rubin if he thought his client Mayer would be interested in running the prospective consortium. Interested? Mayer was ravenous. Like a man who feels compelled to straighten pictures other people have hung crookedly, Mayer was offended by the hap-hazard way Goldwyn was being run and wanted to show everybody how it should be done. Finally, he could be the *macher* he had always felt himself to be. Mayer came to New York for a meeting with Schenck and Loew. Yes, he said, he would be very interested.

Marcus Loew was born in 1870 in New York at 173 Fourth Street, right off Av-enue B; his father, Hermann Loew, was a Viennese waiter. Max, the family's name for Marcus, sold newspapers and lemons—not always distinguishable commodities—and his mother used the unsold papers for tablecloths. "I was poor," he remembered, "but so was everyone around me. . . . It's an advantage to be poor in one sense. That's why so many successes come from the [Lower] East Side."

Loew was not particularly religious—his son David remembered him going to Temple only when his sons were bar mitzvahed—and he spoke neither German nor Yiddish. He didn't gamble, although he occasionally played pinochle or bridge, always for low stakes.

"He was a very enterprising man who started in life selling fur pieces from door to door," remembered his great-niece, the novelist Doris Grumbach. He was a diminutive man with thick-lensed glasses and a raspy voice, like a "nut-meg grater," as one friend said. He carried a look of suspicion and habitual dis-trust, but it didn't carry over into his personality. Predominantly good-natured but superstitious, Loew wouldn't sign a contract on a Friday, wouldn't walk under ladders, was suspicious of certain doctors and most surgical procedures.

Loew left school at the age of nine and worked in a map-printing plant, pulling out the freshly printed maps from the large presses ten hours a day, six days a week. From there, he tried a small printing business of his own, which failed. Then came a furniture store, then a fur factory, where, at the age of twelve he worked eleven and a half hours a day.

Six years later, he was bankrupt, owing his creditors $1,800. He promised to repay in full, and did. Loew's combination of aggressiveness mixed with honor made him a particularly likely bet; he had the assurance of the hustler who knew he had more to offer than mere effort. Notwithstanding the early bank-ruptcy, Loew had a gift for the fur business and managed to make a success the second time around.

Married to Caroline Rosenheim in 1894, Loew's work in the fur business brought him into contact with Adolph Zukor, who became a friend. In 1903

Loew bought his way into a penny arcade company Zukor had started, with Loew developing New York locations. But the two men found they couldn't get along working in the same office—Zukor was quiet and cold, while Loew was friendly and *gemütlich*—and soon there were open hostilities; Loew would amuse himself at meetings by flicking matchsticks at Zukor. When the company moved into new offices, Loew made sure that Zukor, the company's treasurer, was not allotted a desk and had to examine accounts standing up.

With a penny arcade still running in New York, Loew opened another one in Cincinnati. He heard about a man in Covington, Kentucky, just across the Ohio River, who had opened a theater in his house. For the box office, he had used a large packing crate with holes cut in it. The feature ran only sixty feet, but the Covington house was full of patrons, and Loew realized that public exhibition could make much more money than penny arcades. He went back to Cincinnati, rented the floor above his arcade, and made a deal with the Vitagraph Company for projectors and films. "That was on Tuesday," remembered Loew, "and we proposed to open on the following Saturday. I had no idea what the picture would be, and was not much concerned about it. We borrowed chairs and charged 5 cents admission, and on the day we opened we played to a few less than 5,000 persons."

In January 1908, he converted the Cozy Corner Burlesque Theater in Brooklyn into the Royal Theater. The Royal was soon the premier theater in Brooklyn, playing a combination of vaudeville and movies. Loew's penny arcades on 23rd and 125th Streets were soon converted into movie theaters.

While Loew was still in the fur business, Joe Schenck and his brother Nicholas had emigrated from Russia in 1893. According to their naturalization registrations, Nick Schenck was born in Russia on November 18, 1880, Joe on December 25, 1876, both in Rybinsk, where their father supplied wood fuel for the steamers plying the Volga.

Contrary to the stories in the history books asserting that Nick became a pharmacist, it was his brother Louis who became one. Nick and Joe slept on the floor of a drugstore in the Bowery, where the pharmacist allowed them to stay after the store was closed. During the day, the brothers would do any kind of job they could get—odd jobs, delivering newspapers, and so on. They eventually owned the pharmacy, as well as another one at Third Avenue and 110th Street.

In 1908, Joe raised enough capital to refurbish a decrepit dance hall in Fort George, in Upper Manhattan, as a getaway destination for working-class families. A year later, Nick and Joe acquired an adjacent parcel, built a Ferris wheel, a scenic railway, and other rides, and called the establishment Paradise Park.

One of their employees was a woman named Mary Gish, who ran a candy stand. Her two daughters, Lillian and Dorothy, learned to ride horses at Paradise Park. Years later, Lillian Gish would become one of the signature stars of the company L. B. Mayer would run for Marcus Loew and Nick Schenck.

In 1910, the Schenck brothers purchased Palisades Park in New Jersey, across the Hudson from Upper Manhattan, where Nick built an elaborate roller coaster called the Red Devil. After it was constructed, nobody wanted to go on it because it was thought to be unsafe, so Nick went on it himself, and the ride became one of the most popular at the park.

The Schencks struck a promotional pact with the Hearst organization that helped cement their growing status as amusement kingpins. In one chapter of *The Perils of Pauline*, the heavy is plotting with an employee of an amusement park, and the camera lingers on the sign advertising "THE SCHENCK BROS.—PALISADES AMUSEMENT PARK."

All the histories claim that in 1909, Marcus Loew leased the concessions stand at Paradise Park from Joe and Nick, and soon afterward, the brothers joined Loew's operation as managers. But the relationship predated that. Nick and Joe Schenck signed a note dated October 30, 1906, depositing $7,500 worth of stock in the Fort George Amusement Company as security for a loan, "which is to revert to . . . Marcus Loew in case of accident of any kind, whereby said note is not met by the undersigned."

Nick Schenck's memory—quite precise in most cases—was that after the 1907–08 season, Loew suggested that the Schenck brothers join his organization. Nick wanted to tend to Paradise Park, but Joe joined Loew and, after a time, so did Nick. "When I joined the company I had no specific job," remembered Nick Schenck. "In fact, I worked for a time without salary because it was a question [as to] whether I'd like it or not."

Loew issued $200,000 worth of new stock to finance expansion, most of which was bought by the Shubert organization. Within a year he had a string of twelve theaters and by 1910 he was expanding into other cities. Unlike some of his competitors, Loew adopted a go-slow, conservative business plan that would be the hallmark of the corporation for the next half-century.

Marcus Loew understood that theaters were a sort of convenience business, that people wouldn't go far out of their way to attend one. Although he had a warmer personality than most of the founding generation of moguls, he shared their drive and sense of drama. "You must want a big success and then beat it into submission," he said. "You must be as ravenous to reach it as the wolf who licks his teeth behind a fleeing rabbit; you must be as mad to win as the man who, with one hand growing cold on the revolver in his pocket, with the other hand pushes his last gold piece on the 'Double O' at Monte Carlo."

By the end of World War I, Loew offered his patrons a 50-50 mix of vaudeville and movies in luxurious thousand-seat theaters in good neighborhoods. He owned 112 theaters, employed ten thousand people, and owned a corporation worth $25 million. Loew believed in the movies, but, even more, he believed in people's need to be entertained. "We sell tickets to theaters, not movies," he once said.

Nick Schenck would always be a company man, but Joe Schenck proved to be a wildcatter. He converted an old warehouse on East 48th Street in Manhattan into a movie studio, where he made films starring sisters Constance and Norma Talmadge, the latter of whom he married. Norma's films were made on the first floor, Connie's on the second floor, and Fatty Arbuckle and Buster Keaton made two-reel comedies on the third floor. At the end of the summer of 1921, Joe decided to follow the sun and move his operation to Los Angeles.

By the beginning of that decade, Marcus Loew owned thirty-four theaters in New York City alone, a total of 119 in the United States and Canada. Compared to Adolph Zukor's operation, that wasn't a lot, but Loew's theaters were the best theaters on the best corners. The stronger Loew grew in exhibition, the more dependent he became on the films that would fill the seats. He needed what every merchandiser needs—a guaranteed supply of standardized product, made for a price that ensured a profit.

So it was that Marcus Loew bought Metro Pictures in a deal announced on January 3, 1920. The terms of the deal were simple—Loew paid $3.1 million for Metro, including the new Metro studio at Cahuenga and Romaine in Hollywood. Of the purchase price, $1.5 million was paid in newly issued Loew's stock, $1.6 million through some of the profits from foreign sales of Metro pictures. In other words, the purchase didn't cost Loew any cash.

Each side had something to gain—Metro would get guaranteed playtime for its pictures, and Loew would have a steady flow of films for his theaters. It was the beginning of a period of expansion for Loew; a little more than a year after buying Metro, he opened the Loew's State Building at the corner of 45th and Broadway. The Loew's State Theater on the ground floor seated 3,500; above that were fifteen floors of offices from which Loew ran his empire. Loew's plans dwarfed Mayer and the little studio on Mission Road.

Mayer was producing reasonably profitable melodramas whose commercial strength lay not in the big cities, but in the provinces, where people knew what they liked and were willing to pay for it. An alliance with Marcus Loew would boost L. B. Mayer from Double-A ball to the major leagues.

Marcus Loew made a trip to California and Robert Rubin drove him out to the Mission Road studio for a guided tour. Mayer was in the middle of shooting *Thy Name Is Woman,* directed by Fred Niblo, with Barbara La Marr and Ramon Novarro. Loew arrived at Mayer's studio to find the crew setting up a complicated glass shot—a miniature of a whaling ship was mounted in front of the camera, while a glass painting created an Arctic sky with an aurora borealis above it. Loew looked through the camera to see the completed effect and was visibly impressed.

Addressing his remarks to Bob Rubin but really to Loew, Louis pointed out that he was manufacturing commercial pictures on a budget, with major, if not quite top-line, stars. "When you stop to think about it, Rubin, all producers use the same raw stock, same make of camera, same textures in the sets, same textiles in costumes, same lighting equipment. It's all the same. There's only one way a producer can be different . . ." Mayer tapped his head. "Brains!"

Marcus Loew knew that the movies were all a gigantic gamble. So much of it—the appeal of an actor, the power of a story—is subjective. But real estate, theaters, they were tangible, and they were what Marcus Loew believed in. What he needed was someone with an understanding of the great dream who could fill those theaters with other dreamers, and keep one eye on the bottom line. "Well, come on, Louis, let's go up to the office," said Loew. "We got a lot to talk about."

It was clear that Loew needed someone to run an efficient operation and put the newly amalgamated companies on a solid business footing. If they could rein in *Ben-Hur* and von Stroheim, so much the better. But, Loew thought, this Thalberg fellow seemed awfully young. Besides, he wanted his son Arthur to take charge of production.

Mayer adamantly refused to sell out his newly adopted partner-son. "Thalberg can do the job better than anyone. If you don't take him, I'm not interested in joining you."

There was also the question of the percentage agreement the prospective management team was insisting on. Arthur Loew, Marcus's son, remembered his father wasn't crazy about granting the Mayer group a percentage, but "we had a producing company on our hands and no management and we were losing money and [we] were trying to find someone who could operate profitably for us. . . . [My father] was pretty soon convinced that a percentage of the profits was better than a losing proposition."

Finally, it was decided. Marcus Loew invited L.B. and his partners, Thalberg and Rubin, to come into the new organization with a three-year contract. Mayer and Thalberg clearly had no faith in the commercial potential of the two problem children Goldwyn currently had in production. Loew sent out a separate memo that said, "To set your percentage consideration on films in production, it is understood that *Ben-Hur* and *Greed* will not be included in this agreement."

On May 16, 1924, Loew merged his shaky Metro with an even shakier Goldwyn Company and Mayer's small but stable company. Loew purchased Goldwyn for $4.7 million, and Louis B. Mayer Productions for $76,500. Goldwyn may have been rudderless and in trouble, but it had forty acres of studio lot as good as anything in Hollywood. Goldwyn was capitalized at $20 million, Metro at $3.1 million, and the stock of Loew's was worth $26 million.

Metro and Goldwyn . . . sure. But Louis B. Mayer? His company had capital stock worth only $500,000, and that valuation sounded high to a lot of people. True, Irving Thalberg was smart, but audiences didn't pay to see Irving Thalberg. Mayer had . . . what else? Clearly, the company's primary assets were management skills, not property.

Included in the purchase was the distribution contract with Hearst's Cosmopolitan Pictures, the contracts of some directors and actors, and the Goldwyn theaters and exchanges, which included the Capitol Theater in New York, the largest in the country. The latter was a particularly enticing part of the deal; Bob Rubin considered the theater to be about half the value of the Goldwyn deal. Along with the purchase of the company, Loew's acquired a half-interest in the theater, half the profits, and control of its management.

As far as Louis B. Mayer Productions, in addition to the studio management team, what Loew was buying for the bargain-basement price was a roster of story properties that had cost Mayer $43,964 and included titles like "Flames of the Blue Ridge," "Foolish Youth," and—perhaps the least enticing title in the history of motion picture properties—"Volunteer Organist."

Mayer had contracts with directors Fred Niblo (five pictures), and John Stahl, among others, writer Elinor Glyn, as well as commitments with secondtier actors such as Norma Shearer, Hedda Hopper, and Renée Adorée, and a one-picture commitment with a rising character actor named Lon Chaney, whom Thalberg had chosen to star in *The Hunchback of Notre Dame* at Universal. L.B. was named vice president and general manager of Metro-Goldwyn at a salary of $1,500 a week; Thalberg became second vice president and supervisor of production at $650, and Robert Rubin was secretary at $600.

What made the deal potentially rich for L.B. and his partners was the profit incentive. The three men would divide 20 percent of all company profits, with Mayer getting 53 percent of that share, Rubin 27 percent, and Thalberg 20 percent. (A picture's profits were calculated to kick in after all production and distribution costs were recouped and sufficient monies had been withheld to pay an annual dividend of $2 per share of common stock.) The group was obligated to deliver a minimum of only fifteen pictures a year, indicating that Loew was indeed starved for product.

The contract stipulated that Mayer's name be "prominently displayed" on prints and advertising. L.B. had the option of putting "A Louis B. Mayer Production" on any picture made by the company.

In the five years since he had begun independent production, Mayer had made more than thirty pictures. He had signed stars to exclusive contracts, he had hired them on a per-picture basis, and he had even discovered a couple of nascent stars—Norma Shearer and Renée Adorée. Beneath the surface doubt, he was certain that he was ready for the great responsibility that Marcus Loew was dumping in his lap.

On May 16, 1924, Thalberg was sitting in a story conference with Fred Niblo and a couple of other people. The subject at hand was a dialogue title: "I am in a mood for dalliance."

A buzzer on Thalberg's desk went off. Thalberg disappeared into Mayer's office. He was gone a long time, then came back and stood in the door. "Ladies and gentlemen," he announced, "I have the pleasure to announce to you that the merger is now an accomplished fact.

"I think we'll do no more work today. I find myself in a mood for dalliance."

PART TWO

"Organization is responsible for the success of motion pictures exactly as machinery is responsible for the successful running of a ship."

—LOUIS B. MAYER

Mayer in his dark, cramped office at MGM in 1925,
soon to be replaced by something more impressive.

Chapter
FOUR

FOR MANY in the American movie industry, the merger that created Metro-Goldwyn-Mayer didn't make sense. As somebody said, "Three failures put together to make one success?" Marcus Loew compared the amalgamation to the combine of the Union Pacific, Southern Pacific, Central Pacific, and Illinois Central railroads, insisting that each of the companies would retain its own particular production character. But nobody believed that the "efficiency and economy" that Loew spoke of could be accomplished without centralizing everything.

With hindsight, it can be seen that Marcus Loew had a remarkable eye for talent, for Mayer would prove to be, as Richard Griffith would call him, "the keystone of the arch."

Carey Wilson, who was a writer at Goldwyn and spent the rest of his career at MGM, remembered that at the time there was no sense that show business history was being made. "While Mayer was ambitious, I had no feeling he had a pattern laid out. He was a young man, although he was never really young. He always gave you the impression of being ten years older than he was. Mayer contributed a reasonable optimism, tremendous vitality, *salesmanship* . . . devotion of his time and shrewd judgment of character. He was gutter-smart."

Each of the companies brought a roster of stars and directors to the table. Mayer and Thalberg were solid on mainstream directors such as Niblo and Stahl, while Metro contributed stars Jackie Coogan, Buster Keaton, and Monte Blue, as well as directors Rex Ingram and Victor Schertzinger. Goldwyn offered Mae Murray, Conrad Nagel, Blanche Sweet, John Gilbert, William Haines, and, via Hearst's Cosmopolitan, Marion Davies, while its roster of directors included King Vidor, Marshall Neilan, Erich von Stroheim, Robert Z. Leonard, Charles Brabin, and Victor Seastrom.

Among the films in various stages of production at the time of the merger were Goldwyn's *Ben-Hur*, consuming large quantities of money in Italy; von Stroheim's *Greed*, consuming large quantities of time in editing after the Goldwyn executives had insanely approved a 330-page script; and Marshall Neilan's *Tess of the D'Urbervilles*.

Metro had only a few pictures in production, but they included Keaton's *The Navigator*, Rex Ingram's *The Arab*, and Jackie Coogan's *Little Robinson Crusoe*. Of the three companies, Mayer had the most pictures underway, none major.

Mayer moved most of his own equipment over within a week of the contract signing. The amalgamation in Culver City left B. P. Schulberg holding the bag on Mission Road. L.B. had kept all the negotiations secret and hadn't even told Schulberg that he might want to scout around for a new co-tenant. "Without warning, he was left with responsibility for the entire rent of the Selig lot," remembered Budd Schulberg. With his overhead doubled almost overnight, B.P. was suddenly in a precarious financial position. This precipitated a quarrel that became a feud that became a lifelong loathing. At the end of his life, Schulberg told his son that he wanted his ashes placed in a box and delivered by messenger to L.B.'s office. "Then," he said, "when the messenger gets to Louis's desk, I want him to open the box and blow the ashes in the bastard's face."

Thalberg and the Goldwyn production manager, Joe Cohn, went over the payroll, picking the best person for each job from the three organizations. Most of the people who would be in charge of the physical operation came from Goldwyn. Cohn would remember that it was "not a difficult transition. . . . It was a marvelous thing for [Mayer's people] to be able to walk into a studio with standing sets, which they didn't have on Mission Road. That was a fourth- or eighth-rate studio. . . . There was no indecision. Right off the bat, no question about it—they were in charge. . . . It was a different kind of management completely. It was a wishy-washy management before that, you see. They weren't real picture-makers. They were a much firmer and stronger company with Thalberg and Mayer."

At the dedication ceremony for the new company, newly signed producer Harry Rapf sat on the dais with L.B. and Thalberg. Facing them were the stars of the studio. The admiral in charge of the Pacific Fleet was there, a shower of roses was dropped from an airplane, telegrams of congratulations were read from President Calvin Coolidge and Secretary of Commerce Herbert Hoover. A giant key inscribed "Success" was handed to Mayer.

"I have been warned that this new company starts off with a handicap," he announced from the dais. "That its pictures will bear a name that can never become easy to say—A Metro-Goldwyn-Mayer picture . . . that we should have a short name, one crisp with which the public is familiar, like other studios. I can only tell you, fellow-workers, this—if we all do our jobs, as I know we will, within a year wherever you go, when someone asks where you work, you can simply say, not three long words, but three short letters—MGM! and everyone will know you're connected with the foremost movie studio in the world." (These remarks were quoted in Spencer Tracy's eulogy for Mayer, undoubtedly recalled by Carey Wilson, who was there at the opening ceremonies and who co-authored the eulogy. The mention of MGM is probably false—Mayer's name wouldn't be added to the firm's for nearly a year after the merger—but the resolute, optimistic sentiment and the hortatory phrasing sound authentic.)

"I hope that it is given to me to live up to this great trust. It has been my argument and practice that each picture should teach a lesson, should have a reason for existence. With 17 of the great directors in the industry now calling this great institution their home, I feel that this aim will be carried out."

At that point, there was a disturbance in the audience. Marshall Neilan stood up, pushed back his folding chair, and called out to his cast and crew, "OK gang, let's get back to the set." With much rumbling and shuffling of chairs, Neilan and his people left Mayer in mid-speech.

Neilan later justified his calculated rudeness by saying, "I knew the speeches were going to last all day. I had dough in the picture, besides I wanted to finish that day thusly getting rid of a lot of actors so . . . my gang were called to work causing quite a lot of laughter and confusion." The speech, Neilan explained, had been written by Pete Smith, who had worked as Neilan's publicity man. Neilan had already read it and could tell Mayer was running long.

Startled for a moment, Louis pulled himself together and finished his speech. "I fully realize what a great moment this is for me. I accept this solemn trust and pledge the best that I have to give."

The first office L.B. moved into wasn't large enough, didn't provide the proper stage he needed. Then, remembered his daughter Irene, "he got a big office in which he could do a proper act for the people of the studio. That was his very conscious purpose—to convey to them [his ideas] and inspire them."

L.B.'s new world didn't appreciably change things at home. He kept a very sharp eye on the girls, and would let them out of the house only if they were chaperoned by someone he both liked and trusted, such as his nephew Jack Cummings. Safe for him, a trifle dull for the girls. Until the day they got married, they had a 1:00 A.M. curfew — 2:00 A.M. on New Year's Eve.

When L.B. entertained, he instructed his daughters on how to behave. They were not to talk to people they liked, or the biggest stars, but to people who were sitting in a corner by themselves. They received no special credit if they did this, but they got lectures if they didn't.

He told them what to think as well as what not to say and what not to do. And one other thing — be discreet, i.e., shut up. Even if you know more than the other person, you don't have to let them know it. People, he believed with a good deal of evidence, talk too much. The more Mayer found out about the lives of young actresses, the more horrified he became, and the more Irene and Edie had to labor beneath the burden of his alarmed oratory. "He was a very unsophisticated man threatened by a sea of iniquity," remembered Irene.

Despite the restrictions, the diaries Irene kept as a teenager in 1924 and 1925 document a charmed life. There is the self-conscious drama expected from teenagers ("When I ride on a train I am always reminded of relentless fate."), but only a few outbursts from the worried father ("Dad was shocked to find me up at 11:15!! Shame! For I had been keeping much later hours than that — just doing nothing — idling along. I must reform.). . . . (Dad on rampage against clothes — was very unreasonable but later saw my point of view.").

Mostly, though, the diaries are a golden procession through young adulthood: "Met von Stroheim — fascinating but makes me nervous. Alice Terry beautiful but home-made gown. . . . Went over to Norma Talmadge's for a barbecue lunch (for Nick Schenck) the same old crowd — Norma perfectly oblivious of everyone — is that a pose? It makes me furious — she'll snap out of it yet. . . . Fatty Arbuckle was the cook — Marion Davies was there — Charlie Chaplin and about 30 others — awfully cold — everybody was drinking and eating rare beef steaks with their hands."

"I think Constance [Talmadge] is back with Irving [Thalberg]. Glamour very much gone — she seems rather tawdry and secondhand — her looks seem to be leaving her — not her old self — clothes messy. . . . Norma Shearer is getting to be a regular vamp — quite a shame because she's an *adorable* girl."

The nights out were often followed by days at the studio: "Big von Stroheim set — he cursed terribly — met Madge Tyrone, Pat O'Malley, King Vidor,

Eleanor [Boardman], Mrs. [Elinor] Glyn, R. Adoree, the Prince, and hosts of others . . . met von Sternberg & saw a couple of reels from his new picture— unusual but can't judge yet—he has [a] charming personality . . . we all went to the studio in the P.M.—big [Maxim's] set of von Stroheim marvelous—naughty costumes! Chatted with Mae Murray—she seemed very effected [sic] (as tho she were trying to hide her irritation) very conceited—how she hates Von!!"

Mayer took his family to Washington, where a starstruck Irene met President Coolidge ("Dad did most of the talking"), and to New York, where she immediately felt at home. "[I] think I'd love to live here. [California] is great for the poor, the sick, the indifferent, the very old and the very young. . . . New York is so exhilarating and exciting. It's all I expected and more. . . ."

"All of us went for ride in Packard limousine to Coney Island—family was charming—was thoroughly relaxed and had a good time. Saw my birth-town pretty well. Also the ghetto—it was unbelievable. How much I have to be thankful for!!!"

There was a unity between work and home, as Mayer would bring people for dinner without much warning: "E[die] phoned that Dad was bringing home Irving (we expected neither) and only had sliced cold chicken and 30 min. notice—Panic! I rushed Mom to Heinie's and she paid a fortune for a little cold turkey—not so bad."

She approvingly quotes her father about boys: "Don't rush things, it'll come," and concludes by saying, "I think he is the most brilliant man of the age. Is that conceit, pride or filial love?" Irene worshipped her father and always would: "Dad is *so* R-I-G-H-T (almost to a divine degree!!)"

She notes only a few unpleasant character traits: "Last night . . . Dad snubbed [Sol?] Lesser until Mother reminded him. I wonder what Dad would say if I informed him how many people he has cut almost dead. However, I won't."

L.B. and Margaret are happy and in love: "Dad pulled in about one— slightly damp and lonesome. He wasn't *very* glad to see Mom!!—And she was just transfigured." Later, she notes, "Dad and Mom went for an automobile ride together to-nite after dinner. Cute parents!!!"

Mayer occasionally collapsed under the weight of the same hyperbole he freely distributed at the studio: "Dad didn't get home until 8:30 for dinner. He was very tired and had a heart attack. . . . Dad very tired—so we didn't see [Cecil B. DeMille's] 'Golden Bed'—he has been snoring loudly since 8:45!"

Irene demonstrates the clarity and intelligence that would make her so stimulating—and occasionally such a trial—all her life: "Saw *Romola*—liked it very much (contrary to everyone's opinion) galley fight 'cheesy'—D. Gish marvellous—L. Gish good as always but didn't make the most of her opportunities—leading male part should not have been the villain—not enough love interest."

Most surprisingly, there is none of the tension and sniping between the two sisters that would occupy them in later life. "E. drew Mom's portrait tonight—Mom perfectly adorable. I consider Edith very talented, capable of great and diversified work."

But Mayer was struggling with Edie, nominally the passive, obedient daughter. According to Edie, she had auditioned for a show while on the trip to New York with the family and had been accepted. When she told her father of her plans, he looked at her appraisingly. How, L.B. asked, would she make the trip? By train, she said. And how would she pay for the fare? She assumed that he would give her the money.

He would do no such thing. He wouldn't have any of his children perform. "[You] would be wasted on the stage."

"Why did you let me take all those singing lessons?"

"Because it kept you busy. It gave you something to do when I wouldn't let you go to college."

Not only did neither of Mayer's daughters go to college, neither was allowed to pursue a career. Fifty years later, Irene and Edie were still upset about this.

On the old Goldwyn lot, the sets and cast had been prepared for a Victor Seastrom picture called *The Tree of the Garden*. But on the Saturday before the picture was to start shooting, Seastrom was called into a meeting with Mayer, Thalberg, and Harry Rapf. Thalberg wanted to read the script before going ahead with the picture.

On Monday, Thalberg canceled the picture—he didn't like the script and thought it unfit "for a director of your caliber." He would, he promised, find something better for Seastrom. A couple of days later, Thalberg sent him Leonid Andreyev's play *He Who Gets Slapped*, and Seastrom responded enthusiastically. He went ahead and wrote a script in Swedish while Carey Wilson wrote one in English and the two were combined, a system that would be followed for all of Seastrom's MGM pictures.

He Who Gets Slapped would be the first picture produced as well as released by the new company, debuting six months after the merger. It started things off on a high note. The critics were impressed both by its cultural pedigree, by Seastrom's artful execution, and by the strong cast headed by Lon Chaney, John Gilbert, and Norma Shearer. Produced for a modest $172,000, it made a profit of $349,000.

He Who Gets Slapped would be released as "A Metro Goldwyn Picture, Produced by Louis B. Mayer." But the prospects of Louis receiving a producing credit for every picture the new company made must have seemed too unwieldy. By 1925 and the Buster Keaton picture *Go West*, the credit was "A Metro-Goldwyn-Mayer Picture." Mayer was immensely proud of the new hyphenate, and when he heard a telephone operator slip and answer a call "Hello, Metro-Goldwyn," he snapped, "It's Metro-Goldwyn-Mayer, and the next time you forget it, you won't have a job."

"They were amazingly farsighted," remembered Joe Cohn. "Mayer was a builder. [His] policy [from] the beginning was not to grab the quick dollar. He wanted to build an organization with the principal viewpoint being producers—good producers—then good directors. . . . Principally, editorial things, what I call the making of the picture, he left to Thalberg, but he added into it. In terms of day-to-day preparation, in production and post-production, the plumbing so to speak, Mayer didn't get involved. But he did with overall policy."

Louis was omnipresent around the lot. "If the first set was opened at six, he was there," said Douglas Shearer, Norma's brother. "If the last lights were shut off at midnight, he was there. . . . He never asked anyone to do anything he wouldn't do himself."

He hired and fired, made all the business arrangements—duties that played to his primary executive strengths: a knack for picking talent and the confidence to delegate.

Frances Marion, a screenwriter and ardent Thalberg acolyte, remembered that Mayer "kept an active finger in the pie. He never let a story be made under his banner unless he had weighed it well, analyzed his own emotions in relation to it, and considered how interesting it would be to the general public. Calling himself an 'average American citizen,' he figured that if the story moved him or made him laugh, it would react upon the masses in much the same way. . . . Therein lay his greatest asset as a producer; keeping his fingers on the pulse of the public. 'Let us pose as worldly men and women,' he argued, 'try to hide our emotions like the British, call ourselves hard-boiled; but just scratch the surface and you'll find a human being reacting as any normal human being should react. We're all sentimentalists at heart, no matter how hard we try to deny it.'

"In spite of [his] idiosyncrasies, we liked to write for him, especially in the old days; he was our sounding board, a sort of one-man preview."

Mayer played a revolving series of parts that encompassed emotional variations on the roles of rabbi, good cop, bad cop, and CEO. To those he liked he would freely share portions of his lunch, perhaps some of the chicken soup made from his mother's recipe that would soon become legendary, or potato latkas. (Mayer always asked the commissary to prepare his matzoh balls grilled crisp, like potato pancakes. He would then eat them separately from the soup itself.) Along the way, he would dispense investment advice: buy land in Beverly Hills or Palm Springs.

With all his soul, he believed in alliances, taking care of those who take care of you. The studio's first still photographer was Ruth Harriet Louise, who happened to be the niece of Rabbi Israel Myers, the founder of the Reform synagogue in Beverly Hills that Louis occasionally attended, who in turn was the father of Carmel Myers, one of the early MGM stars. Not only that, but Anna Myers, the Rabbi's wife, was English-born and served as an unofficial social coach for Margaret.

Family.

Favors.

Taking care of your own.

In the manner of many men who admire qualities in others that they themselves don't possess, Mayer revered Thalberg's gentleness. "Just be charming, Irving," he once said. "I'll be the prick."

He wasn't kidding. For a man who could cultivate a reputation for paternal sweetness with obedient stars, it didn't take much to make Mayer crack the whip. Illness, for example. When a prominent leading lady would have to spend a week or two in bed, Mayer would often suspend her salary and add the time to the back end of her contract.

A display of temperament could bring a severe response. When Norma Shearer bridled at the direction of action director Reginald Barker, Mayer inquired if she was "yellow." That got her back up, which was the response that Mayer wanted. (Later, he would have to be more circumspect with Shearer.)

Because of his hyper-emotionalism, Mayer was attuned to fear—his own as well as that of others. Because there is nowhere to hide on a movie screen, any actor's primary fear is humiliation. When Eleanor Boardman refused a part, Mayer told her he would intentionally cast her in a bad film with a bad director and ruin her. A panicked Boardman told King Vidor about Mayer's threat, and he sensibly pointed out that Mayer was not about to spend money to make an intentionally bad film. Nevertheless, Boardman nursed a lifelong loathing for Mayer, whom she usually characterized as "a real son of a bitch."

On the MGM lot the offices were small, shabby, and jury-rigged. The writers' building, unaffectionately dubbed the Triangle Shirtwaist Factory, was infested with mice, and one writer sourly characterized his quarters as a "worm-eaten desk, two gumwood chairs and a spavined divan. It was a pity . . . that the studio's prodigality did not extend to its decor." The center of the studio was a large green lawn, ringed by glass-roofed stages, offices, and dressing rooms. The executive building was right next to the gate, and Thalberg and producer Harry Rapf had adjacent offices on the second floor. There was a metal staircase on the outside of the building that went up to a balcony that opened onto two rooms, then a corridor that led to producer Hunt Stromberg's office on the third floor. Mayer was across the way, on the second floor of the wardrobe building, with a metal walkway connecting that building to Thalberg's and Rapf's offices.

Everything was piled on top of everything else, with no particular logic. The portrait studio was three rooms on the third floor of the editing building, and could only be reached by another exterior iron staircase; even the grandest stars had to lug their own costumes up the stairs for sittings. Nearby was a fig tree, and Maurice Rapf, Harry's son, and his pal Budd Schulberg would occasionally hide in the tree and assault passersby with fruit.

Thalberg didn't care about the physical appointments. What mattered to him were talent and stories—material. The first thing Thalberg did in his new position was organize Saturday morning meetings. During those Saturday meetings, the discussions centered around films—what movies had everybody seen during the week? What pictures were doing business and why? Thalberg made it clear that everybody was expected to see every MGM preview—a favorite theater was the Alexander (later the Alex) in Glendale. Thalberg had a Pacific Electric Red Car spur cut right into the studio; a chartered car—at $400 a night—picked up executives and a print of the film to be previewed, and delivered them to a spot near the theater, where limousines would finish the trip. "It would take an hour on the Red Car," remembered Robert Vogel. "Champagne and caviar and [we'd] play bridge on the way out and back."

"We previewed in Highland Park, San Bernardino, Pasadena," remembered Margaret Booth. "We were always previewing. You'd preview two, three, four times until you got it right . . . Mayer would go to the first preview. If you had two after that, he might not go."

The rationale behind these screenings was that if people looked at enough film, if they talked enough with each other, perhaps the studio would be able to tune in to the audience's frequency, find out why some movies connected and others didn't. And when movies connected, Thalberg meant for the vast majority of them to be MGM pictures.

Despite his youth, Thalberg had a way of assuming a parental role for even those much older than he. Cedric Gibbons said that "Thalberg was an intuitive person. He had an insight into almost everything. Emotionally, he was almost always correct."

Partly, Thalberg's power came from the fact that writers and actors tend to be needy personalities, and Thalberg withheld approval. When one screenwriter did Thalberg a favor by producing a scene overnight, he was shocked by Thalberg's reaction to his efforts: contempt. When the scene was rewritten, he frowned and shook his head, but at least there was no more contempt. On the third try, Thalberg nodded and mumbled "not bad."

The *gravitas* was partially a function of his rheumatic heart—once, Lenore Coffee came into his office and Thalberg was rolling down his sleeve after an insurance examination. "I'm 25," he said, "and I have to pay the premium of a man 40 years old." Another time he remarked, "I'd settle for another ten years." He allocated his time grudgingly, and didn't do things he didn't want to do, such as answering mail.

Also contributing to his aura was an essential lack of humor. While he appreciated wit, his own was infrequent, and, when it did appear, dryly biting. Sam Marx said that in all the years he knew him, he never knew Thalberg to laugh out loud.

Thalberg's instructions to a director could be snappish, specific, and not conducive to debate: "I don't like the seduction scene and I don't like the retake of the scene between Gilbert and Young," he would tell even so respected a talent as Victor Seastrom. "Prefer fading out to the mirror shot." A week later, he would tell Seastrom to stage a retake "close to the back wall of the set" for a better effect.

At a party, Thalberg would be charming, but he also exuded the unmistakable aura of a man who would rather be someplace else. "He was an extremely complex personality," remembered Lenore Coffee. "He had an enormous sense of guarding a kind of inner privacy, even from his friends. . . . He had the gift of inspiring great friendship, among men. He had men friends who really and truly loved him, and for whom I think he himself had great affection. . . . But I don't believe he ever had a woman *friend* in the whole of his life. Although we did not know the term in those days, he had what is now called a 'love-hate' feeling towards women. And he had precisely the same thing towards writers, for . . . he was himself a frustrated writer. He knew he needed writers, but that very need irritated him. He once said to me with ill-concealed contempt, 'What's all this business of being a writer? Just putting one word after another.' My reply was, 'Pardon me, Mr. Thalberg—putting one *right* word after another.' "

Thalberg could be cold. When a writer told him she wanted to come to MGM, he tested her ardor by asking if she wanted to work at home or on the lot. When she replied that whatever suited Thalberg was fine with her, he smiled, said he would prefer an office at the studio, and added, "So you've become organization-minded?"—a very high compliment in the MGM value system, perhaps the highest.

Whether consciously or not, Thalberg became the remote, hard-to-please professor that all the students kill themselves trying to please. Everyone tried to execute Thalberg's instructions, thereby earning praise from the distant father figure. For New York writers, Thalberg was a throwback to their publishers—assertive but soft-spoken, with passive body language that made him nonthreatening. "Anita Loos thought Thalberg was a genius, which he was," said her niece, screenwriter Mary Loos. "She felt like a gentle lady working with a gentle man."

A very reserved gentle man. "He was thoughtful when he thought of you, but he rarely thought of you unless you were useful to a picture project," remembered Howard Dietz. "I never had a conversation with him about anything except movies."

The historical importance of MGM has usually been characterized as its strict adherence to—and dependence on—the star system. Industrially this is true, but culturally it doesn't get close to what Mayer and Thalberg were about to achieve. Their genius was in recognizing that there was a niche waiting to be filled: classy films for the growing middle class. Paramount's Adolph Zukor had instituted assembly-line production for the masses, to feed his ever-growing chain of theaters, but much of that output was disposable B movies that needed the prestigious extravaganzas of DeMille and, later, Lubitsch and von Sternberg to anchor them.

L.B. and Thalberg were taking production in a different direction: mini-mize B films, bring up the overall level—and trust that the audience would follow.

The equation was entirely different than it had been at the little studio on Mission Road. Mayer no longer had the luxury of making a handful of pictures every year. Marcus Loew expected MGM to compete with Paramount, which meant that the studio would be engaged in mass production, and mass produc-tion cannot work unless a format is devised, a pattern is imposed. Both Mayer and Thalberg were emotionally drawn to the idea of order, and worked to find similar-minded people.

By the spring of 1925, the transformation was well underway. There was "en-thusiasm everywhere," noted one screenwriter who had done time on the lot when it was Goldwyn's. "It's a modern version of the Sleeping Beauty's Court coming to life." New buildings were being thrown together nearly every month; the writers were now herded together in a wing that had been added onto the old Goldwyn publicity building.

Joe Cohn was there with Goldwyn when Will Rogers and Big Boy Williams lassoed goats every afternoon on the lot, he was there when Marcus Loew merged with Mayer, he was there all the days of L. B. Mayer and many days thereafter. Joe Cohn was still in Hollywood in the 1990s, hale, if not quite as hearty as he had been when he was a youngster.

"We weren't a penny ante outfit," remembered Cohn in 1993. "If the assis-tant director or the director needed 20 people, we didn't say, 'Can't you get along with 18? . . . ' We didn't go on the basis of cheating on the picture; the pic-ture was important."

The preferred production method was an early version of creative tension. For instance, when titling a picture, the producer would read out a proposed title to the continuity writer and a few others. If one person didn't like it, the title writer had the unpleasant duty of watching the others fall on it like hungry wolves. Then a half-hour or more might go by while the committee haggled over improvements.

This was definitely a new regime, one that was determined to find and grasp success, with a new generation of stars, a new style of filmmaking.

The first year of operations can be gauged by the campaign book prepared for exhibitors. "Metro Goldwyn Presents: Metro and Goldwyn have been two of the greatest of our industry's Producers and Distributors. Louis B. Mayer has been an outstanding showman and producer. The three, now combined, make the Greatest all around Motion Picture organization today—*bar none*."

The book calls Mayer "First, last and every time—a Showman. And a showman whose vision, whose uncanny sense of picture values, and long record of striking successes have combined to make Louis B. Mayer a dominating figure in the film industry today. No producer enjoys greater confidence and respect among exhibitors, for Mr. Mayer was originally an exhibitor himself."

The roster of films listed in the book included Rex Ingram's *The Arab*, von Stroheim's *Greed*, Fred Niblo's *The Red Lily*, Keaton's *The Navigator*, King Vidor's *The Wife of the Centaur* and *His Hour*, Mae Murray and John Gilbert in *The Merry Widow*, and Marion Davies in *Yolanda* and *Janice Meredith*. Other pictures included *Tess of the D'Urbervilles*, *He Who Gets Slapped*, and *The Sporting Venus*.

As a group of pictures, it was strong, but the lineup was weak on stars, and if they were to make a profit, the company had to be run far more efficiently than either Metro or Goldwyn had been run.

"There are no waits," Mayer told a trade paper. "As soon as one picture has finished with the stage another is ready to take its place; production dovetails so that we are able to keep far ahead of our schedule and still not sacrifice one iota of quality for the sake of speed, for if there is one thing that I insist upon it is quality. There will be no production on the . . . releasing schedule this season that is not the finest that can be made in every way, shape and manner . . .

"Let me cite one instance to illustrate this point. An outdoor set was erected for a production by a . . . director at a cost of $10,000. This cost was thought to be unwarrantedly extravagant for the picture that was being made, but that set, with slight alterations, was used for half a dozen succeeding productions! . . .

"We intend to give 'em something to shoot at, to make a record of consistent production that will not be broken for years to come."

One day, Louis called his directors to a projection room, where he ran a reel of film consisting of clips excised from MGM pictures. Prominently featured was a love scene from King Vidor's *His Hour*, an Elinor Glyn story with John Gilbert and Aileen Pringle. "His arm was under her robe, and there was just a tremendous amount of energy while he was working her over," remembered Vidor, speaking of the deleted scene. This, said Louis to his directorial brain trust, was why MGM was happy to cooperate with the Hays Office. The message was clear: don't bother shooting this kind of footage, because it won't get released.

In the company's first months Mayer and Thalberg had their authority tested several times by their most prestigious directors. They lost one test, and won the rest. The temporary victor was the great pictorialist Rex Ingram, who had one of the great successes of the silent era with *The Four Horsemen of the Apocalypse* for Metro in 1921 and was beginning his love affair with North Africa by making *The Arab* at the time of the merger.

The studio clearly regarded Ingram as a primary building block of the company, as indicated by its effusive advertising: "Rex Ingram Productions Are Aristocrats of the Screen Art." But Ingram informed Loew and Nick Schenck that he refused to submit to anyone's authority in the matter of his movies. It wasn't personal—Ingram had never met Mayer—but professional. "My sympathies are all with those directors who stand or fall on their own merits," Ingram said. "I have too often seen a good picture, and the career of a promising director, ruined by supervision. I believe that the box office should be the artist's last consideration."

Ingram's bluntness wouldn't have endeared him to Mayer, but his prestige, not to mention his critical and financial track record, tipped the scales in his favor; "We felt he was of great value to the company," said Nick Schenck, "and we made a deal whereby I supervised him independent of the studio." A studio was outfitted for Ingram at Nice, where he made a series of exotic romances free of studio oversight.

Mayer tried to heal the breach; when he screened Ingram's *Mare Nostrum*, he cabled that "It's a travelogue, take out a thousand feet and you have a swell picture."

"Mayer was right," Michael Powell, Ingram's assistant, would say, and Ingram must have thought so too, because the cuts were made.

Around this time, *Photoplay* printed Marshall Neilan's vicious crack that "An empty taxicab drove up at the studio today and Louis B. Mayer got out." Shortly afterward, Neilan was giving the comedy producer Jack White a ride when they passed MGM. "When we came to Culver City," remembered White, "he stepped on the gas and yelled back 'Hey Mayer, you Jew sonofabitch!' I never had anything to do with him for years after that. He didn't know I was a Jew."

L.B. and Thalberg wanted team players, preferably ones who weren't anti-Semitic. Mayer took a look at Neilan's version of *Tess of the D'Urbervilles* and ordered a happy ending. Tess would no longer go to the gallows for murdering the man who seduced her, she would be pardoned and return to the man she loved. Neilan exploded and castigated Mayer in front of Harry Rapf, among others.

"My argument was that they wouldn't stand for [a happy ending] in England," remembered Neilan. "The outcome was I shot a happy ending myself, the picture was then tried out in New York and San Francisco and the verdict of the public was the original ending. . . . After this I could see that there would never be a happy union between Mayer and his gang [and me]. But still he talked me into two more pictures but there was constant bickering . . . and I at long last quit cold." For the rest of his life, Neilan told people that the initials L.B. stood for "Lousy Bastard."

Neilan came from the era of the director, roughly 1915 to 1921, the period of Griffith and his followers, when the director, not the corporation, was the primary creative component of filmmaking, the period whose death knell had been announced by Thalberg's firing of von Stroheim from *Merry-Go-Round* when they were at Universal in 1922—probably *the* major event in the early corporate history of Hollywood.

Neilan, however, was not going to change his ways for anybody, let alone people he didn't respect. He was used to getting his way despite his sharp tongue, his alcoholism, his spendthrift ways. And he liked reading about himself, liked trade paper headlines that said "Errant Marshall Neilan Pulls Rabbit Out of Hat Again," but the day was inevitably going to come when the rabbit wouldn't make an appearance.

Erich von Stroheim, without a strong commercial track record or friendship with Marcus Loew, had an equally rough time. Irene Mayer was one of the few who saw von Stroheim's complete cut of *Greed*, and she remembered that going into it she was prepared to do battle for the picture. Then she saw the movie. "Ten hours in a concrete box in MGM. I wish everyone who talks about a ruined masterpiece could be condemned to spend ten hours in a concrete box watching it. It was masterful in ways, and parts of it were riveting, but it was an exhausting experience; the film in conception was a considerable exercise in self-indulgence, and a testament to the incompetence of the previous regime."

Aside from the fact that *Greed* represented the antithesis of what Mayer and—let's be honest—most of the world regarded as entertainment, the film was an early example of an orphan movie, a film with no one to defend it after the executives who commissioned it had quit or been fired while the movie was still in production.

Thalberg had already fired von Stroheim once, and he had no compunctions about doing it again. The odd thing was that both Mayer and Thalberg acknowledged von Stroheim's immense talent. In June 1925, Mayer named von Stroheim one of "the towers of strength" in the industry, along with Victor

Seastrom, Rex Ingram, King Vidor, Marshall Neilan, and Frank Borzage. But they couldn't abide the fact that he wasn't a professional filmmaker, that he functioned more as a novelist or a painter than a filmmaker working with other people's money in a commercial environment.

Greed had been shot between March and October of 1923, and by March of 1924, the Goldwyn company was investigating the legal basis for firing von Stroheim from the picture. He had gone far over budget, shot for eighty-three days past the scheduled 115, and was refusing to cut the film to anything less than twenty-two reels, in spite of the fact that his contract specified twelve reels. The merger dumped the film in the lap of Mayer and Thalberg, and it would be released in a heavily edited version as "A Metro-Goldwyn Picture, Produced by Louis B. Mayer," which must have galled von Stroheim and Mayer in nearly equal degrees.

As if *Greed* hadn't been enough, von Stroheim had another picture on his contract. During pre-production on *The Merry Widow*, he went to see Mayer about rumors that he would be pulled from the project in favor of Robert Z. Leonard (husband of Mae Murray, the picture's star). There was a confrontation between the two men in which von Stroheim called Mae Murray's character "a whore."

That, to Mayer, was the ugliest word in the English language; whores had no place at his studio. He erupted, slugging von Stroheim, then throwing him out of his office. *Variety* reported that von Stroheim "contemplated swearing out a warrant for the arrest of Mayer on a charge of assault and battery," but, for perhaps the only time in his life, he thought of the big picture first. Nothing came of the episode.

The Merry Widow began shooting under von Stroheim on December 1, 1924. The production was a nonstop succession of tantrums from the film's divas—the star and the director. At one point, Mayer replaced von Stroheim with Monta Bell for a few days, and personally escorted von Stroheim to the studio gates. Production ground to a halt because of intransigent crew and extras. Mayer and von Stroheim patched things up, but Joe Cohn still had to turn off the generators at midnight to keep the obsessive-compulsive von Stroheim from working through the night. After fourteen weeks, the film was completed, with von Stroheim being billed $78,000 for excess charges, as per his contract.

The film was previewed in June in Pasadena, at a screening attended by Mayer and Thalberg. In the middle of a suggestive scene, the lights went up and the executives were invited to meet the local police, who threatened to throw them both in jail for showing an obscene movie.

Mayer was at his best in situations where other men would freeze, and he immediately launched a brilliant counteroffensive. "We knew you had the strictest censorship in this community and that is why we chose Pasadena for this preview. This fellow von Stroheim is a genius, but he often goes too far. We wanted your opinion on how far he is to go. Thank you for your action. I will come back to this town after the film is released, and we will see it together and you will agree with me about its high artistic quality." The screening continued, the scenes were trimmed, and *The Merry Widow* made a profit of $758,000.

With very few exceptions, MGM would never be a comfortable place for artists with uncompromising visual or dramatic styles—director Josef von Sternberg would wash out twice. The flip side to Thalberg's intense supervision and a strictly observed house style was that very ordinary directors could make far more stylish movies than they could ever have under other circumstances, examples being Fred Niblo and *The Mysterious Lady*, John S. Robertson and *Annie Laurie*, among others.

The chaos of *Ben-Hur* began early, as soon as the Goldwyn company purchased the property in June of 1922, and absurdly agreed to pay Klaw and Erlanger, the theatrical producers, 50 percent of the gross. Production manager Joe Cohn went to Italy to scout locations. "I came back," said Cohn, "and said there are only two ways: make it in Vienna or some such place for $300,000–$400,000 or make it [in Hollywood] for $1.2 million," a figure that appalled everybody. Major Edward Bowes, who was an assistant to Goldwyn's Frank Godsol, made another trip to Europe without Cohn and came back to tell his boss that he could make the picture in Italy for $300,000–$400,000. As Cohn would say, "the die was cast."

Godsol began casting directors. King Vidor? Alan Crosland? Marshall Neilan? Allan Dwan? Henry King? Victor Seastrom? Sidney Olcott? Charles Brabin? All were considered, but only Brabin was hired, for what he remembered as "$25,000 and boat fare." By January 1924, Goldwyn had spent more than $100,000 just for the rights and "editorial expenses." By April 1924, shortly after the picture began shooting, the production had already eaten $167,307 of a budget that had been raised to $750,000.

Dozens of actors, including Valentino, were considered for the title role, and eleven actors (Ben Lyon, Forrest Stanley, Robert Frazer, Edmund Lowe, George Walsh, William Desmond, George O'Brien, Antonio Moreno, John Bowers, McKay Morris, and J. Warren Kerrigan) were actually tested. June Mathis gave the part to George Walsh.

By the time the company arrived in Italy, there was no finished script, just an outline, but three thousand costumes were on order. There was a visit to North Africa to buy camels and make arrangements to shoot the footage of the Three Wise Men in the Tunis desert. Some of these scenes were actually shot, and Brabin had to resort to building fires under the camels to get the animals to move, only to have them sit down on the fires and put them out.

It was all very exotic and very chaotic. Mathis arrived with her script and insisted on being on the set every day, as she had done with Rex Ingram. Brabin objected to Mathis's presence, but Edward Bowes and other production people talked him into putting up with her.

But the footage was terrible. On May 2, 1924, Joe Schenck, acting at Mayer's behest, sent Marcus Loew a come-to-Jesus wire demanding immediate action. "YOUR PRESENT ARRANGEMENT WITH MATHIS DOMINATING ENTIRE PRODUCTION SITUATION IN ROME GEORGE WALSH LEADING MAN AND EVEN BRABIN DIRECTOR WILL SPELL EITHER ABSOLUTE FAILURE OR AT BEST TREMENDOUS WASTE OF MONEY RUNNING INTO AT LEAST HALF OR THREE QUARTERS OF A MILLION STOP YOUR SCENARIO IS SEVENTEEN HUNDRED SCENES WHICH WILL MAKE PICTURE OF AT LEAST TWENTY FIVE REELS AND THAT IS MOST CONSERVATIVE . . . REMEMBER ALL THIS EXPENSE YOU CAN ONLY GET BACK FROM FIFTY PERCENT OF GROSS AND THAT ERLANGER DOES NOT OBJECT TO YOU SPENDING HUGE SUMS WHETHER NECESSARY OR UNNECESSARY AS HE IS NOT INTERESTED THAT PHASE . . . THE PROPER TIME TO SAVE IT IS NOW RUBINS IDEA TO SEND FRED NIBLO OVER TO ROME WITH AN OFFICER OF NEW COMPANY LIKE BOB RUBIN WHO WOULD REMAIN THERE LONG ENOUGH TO SUPPORT NIBLO IN GETTING SITUATION QUIET . . . I AM NOT TRYING TO UNDERMINE MATHIS BUT JUST TO POINT OUT TO YOU NECESSITY OF IMMEDIATE ACTION."

Irene Mayer saw some of Brabin's footage and described it to writer and film historian Kevin Brownlow as "terrible. They'd got huge sets over there, but you never saw them on the film. What did appear, looked cheesy. The make-up was awful, the wigs terrible. They'd lost contact with their own taste. The atmosphere was fraught, people were getting hurt and a great deal of money was being wasted."

Thalberg was furious. "It is almost beyond my conception that such stuff could have been passed by people of even moderate intelligence," he wrote. "That anyone could have tolerated for one single day the ill-fitting costumes, the incongruous action, the almost silly and typical European movements of the people; not in my wildest imagination could I have pictured anything that broad."

The responsibility for the entire production was dumped in Mayer's lap; all the surviving correspondence from Fred Niblo, Carey Wilson, and the production managers is addressed directly to him.

On Sunday, June 8, 1924, shortly after taking control of the studio, Thalberg called the handsome Mexican actor Ramon Novarro to his office and told him he was being sent to Italy to play Ben-Hur. There were two conditions. First, Novarro had to make a test. Second, he had to waive his contract for the three months they believed shooting would take. He would also have to pay his own living expenses while on location. Novarro refused to make a test, but agreed to the rest.

Mayer approached Fred Niblo about directing. Niblo had proven himself capable and—at least as important—loyal. Moreover, according to Carey Wilson, who wrote the final shooting script, "Niblo had been a pet of Erlanger's [during his theater career] so it was easy to get him to replace Brabin. I don't think Mayer was much sold on Niblo at the time."

Niblo read the script and knew trouble when he saw it: "Personally, I will be more than pleased if you will count me out entirely. It is not too big a job for me but if I can't do it right I don't want to do it at all." Niblo called Mathis's script, "an impossibly long story and twice as long a continuity as it should be." He went on to call the cast, with a single exception that he didn't specify, "the most uninteresting and colorless that I have ever seen in a big picture. . . . I believe *Ben-Hur* should be recast almost entirely."

There were directorial alternatives, good ones, but with complicating factors. Rex Ingram had always been desperate to make the picture, but there was no possibility of that happening, given his and Mayer's history of mutual distrust. Fred Niblo wanted the job, but on his terms. He got them. As of June 9, Niblo was on salary to direct *Ben-Hur* at $2,500 a week. He was also given a couple of second unit directors (Christy Cabanne and Al Raboch), in hopes of speeding up the production. In Rome, Brabin was called in to production manager Harry Edington's office and asked for his resignation.

Replacing the cast cost a lot of money; Ramon Novarro was getting a weekly salary of $1,000, compared to George Walsh's $400. The only economy was in hiring Carey Wilson ($700) to write a new script to replace the prolix effort of June Mathis ($1,000). At this point, Mayer and company knew they were in for a long haul, but they could have had no idea of just how long the haul would be. *Ben-Hur* would be in production for the next year and a half and would stand as the most expensive movie made until *Gone With the Wind*.

L.B. was now heavily invested in proving to Marcus Loew and his lieutenants that hiring him had been a prescient decision, and that his ideas and methods were better than those of his predecessors. Mayer suggested they bring the picture back to Hollywood, but Loew flatly refused: "If our company cannot maintain the distinction of producing this great film in Italy, then we had better shut up shop."

The mandate was clear. Loew intended *Ben-Hur* to be the primary test of his new management team. *They* couldn't; *we* can.

Niblo arrived in Rome on June 21 and was immediately plunged into a maelstrom that was the template for every budgetary disaster in film history—a distant location, a shifting script, an underprepared production, and an indecisive director. On July 1, Niblo wired Mayer that "conditions here generally most deplorable; organization splendid overcoming obstacles; start shooting about two weeks . . . don't worry all well." The primary location was seven miles outside Rome, with no water. A couple of wells were dug, but they were insufficient to meet the needs of the cast and crew. Eventually, every drop was trucked in from Rome.

Three days later, all wasn't well, and Niblo was giving a very good impression of a man in total panic. "Condition serious must rush work before November rain; no sets or lights available before August 1st. 200 reels film wasted; bad photography terrible action."

On July 5, L.B. cabled Harry Edington: "Keep me completely informed progress conditions Niblo cabled photography and action terrible film already taken . . . will consider your cables strictly confidential depend my full support your usual competent business administration; Niblo likes battle he knows value of argument; my directors have respect for management you are my business representative; go over everything with Niblo; give me your opinion which part you agree with him which part you don't; be frank above board with him."

Two days later, Mayer cabled J. Robert Rubin, who had also been on site in Rome, that there was plenty to worry about: "Inform me constantly your whereabouts; cannot understand your leaving Rome so soon; Niblo cabled oblige destroy 200 reels film taken bad photography and action; asking practically new organization; can you get back there."

While Carey Wilson was banging out a new script to replace the June Mathis version, Mayer was trying to put together a new cast. Claire McDowell had been requested for the part of Ben-Hur's mother, but Mayer seemed appalled by her demand for a ten-week guarantee for a small part; Niblo, who must have sensed that ten weeks would result in just about enough footage for the trailer, responded that the ten-week guarantee for McDowell would be okay and she should be in Rome by August 4.

In a long, confidential letter to Mayer on July 21, Niblo unloaded: "Imagine a company of Americans coming to Italy with the announcement that they were going to spend millions of dollars—expense meant nothing and then following it up by calling the Italians lazy idiots and fools." Niblo went on to say that Brabin and Mathis had fallen out as soon as they arrived in Italy, and the company fell into warring factions. Not only that, but there was no clear narrative line. "They were weeks and weeks in North Africa making a few feet of desert stuff that took up thirty or forty reels of film but cannot be used. Am sending you a print of everything they shot so far, so you can see for yourself."

Over a month had been spent on the galley sequence, "but very few feet of the shots can be used. . . . Regarding the studio itself, one can only say that it will be fine when it is finished . . . the [studio] floor is so shaky that it is impossible to use it until it is completely braced from underneath . . . so far we have no juice as the generator plant is still unfinished, therefore up to now it has been impossible to use any of the stages. They promise me juice in a week."

Niblo sent long letters to Mayer detailing his unhappiness with his camera crew, especially von Stroheim alumnus Ben Reynolds, terming his efforts "horribly disappointing." He was staggered by the expense, both before he arrived and afterward. "For the life of me I can't understand where the money goes," strongly implying that material and cash were both going out the back door.

Production manager Al Aronson was appalled by Niblo's temper, biting sarcasm, and indecisiveness, which led him to spend days shooting a sequence only to slowly come to the opinion that the light was wrong, the photography was wrong, and maybe the set was wrong too. The set would then be altered and the lighting changed, and Niblo would remake scenes he had already shot once, sometimes twice.

Niblo would only lay out about one day's work in advance, placing the production department in a rushed, reactive position, and seemed to want to shoot about 70 percent of the picture himself, leaving second unit directors Cabanne and Raboch little to do. Al Aronson strongly suggested that Mayer fire Niblo and get somebody else, which must have led Mayer to wonder what he had ever done to be punished like this. Firing one director is bad enough, but firing two, and starting from scratch yet again?

All this must have made a control freak like Thalberg frantic. Clearly, Niblo alone was not the solution. The director was Mayer's appointee, so Mayer had little choice but to go to Italy and take the situation in hand. L.B. and family arrived in Rome on October 12, 1924: the general coming to inspect the battlefield and the condition of his troops. It became a publicity-filled opportunity to improve his stature with his employers, his employees, and his family.

When Mayer arrived, Niblo was reshooting the sea battle, which quickly got out of hand; some extras had been designated to jump in the water, but in the excitement and panic of the burning timbers, some men outfitted in armor also jumped into the sea.

"I heard their cries for help," said Francis X. Bushman, who was playing Messala. "I said to Niblo, 'My God, Fred, they're drowning, I tell you.' "

"I can't help it," yelled Niblo, "those ships cost me $40,000 apiece." Editor Basil Wrangell believed some extras almost certainly drowned, but Ramon Novarro doubted it. Others pointed out that the hostile atmosphere would certainly have boiled over had there been dead Italians mixed into the already poisonous brew.

As the pressure mounted, Louis began to feel the effects. On October 20, Carey Wilson sent a wire to Thalberg saying that he was "terribly worried" about Mayer's physical condition; that he had had four teeth pulled, was having jaw trouble, and that he was a "mental and physical wreck." Someone else from the studio, Harry Edington or Thalberg himself, was going to have to spell L.B.

In the pre-antibiotic era, abscessed teeth were a serious matter. A spreading dental infection could easily prove fatal. Thalberg responded that he was "paralyzed with fear" about Mayer falling seriously ill. He should get out of Rome and go to a spa someplace else in Europe and get back on his feet. More teeth were pulled, then more still, until Mayer had every tooth in his head removed.

He hung on, working through the pain, trying to ramrod the production into some reasonable pace. Reading the telegrams that were flying back and forth between Culver City and Rome, it's hard not to believe that the new company was teetering on the brink, buffeted by the massive cost overruns that were taxing its financial and creative resources.

Still, Louis was not so harried that he wasn't able to do some talent scouting. He made a quick side trip to Berlin, and had Basil Wrangell, who had been functioning as his interpreter, run him all the best new European pictures and translate the titles as they went. One of the pictures was Mauritz Stiller's *The Atonement of Gösta Berling* which had premiered in Berlin in September 1924.

The screening was on a Sunday in November. Irene Mayer didn't find the film very interesting, but her father's reaction was unusually intense, even for him.

"Look at that girl! There's no physical resemblance, but she reminds me of Norma Talmadge—her eyes. The thing that makes Talmadge a star is the look in her eyes." He kept up a steady stream of chatter during the screening. "Stiller's fine, but the girl, look at the girl!" If he had to choose, he said, he'd go for the girl. "I'll take her without him, or I'll take them both [but] number one is the girl."

"He was hell-bent," remembered Irene. "He said it had not to do with beauty, 'It's what she conveys and the expression emanating from her eyes.' He wanted to meet her that day, and a meeting was arranged for our hotel." Stiller's young protégée, Greta Garbo by name, signed a letter of intent to come to Culver City and work for MGM on a five-year contract starting at $400 a week. Stiller was signed as well.

Louis finally left Rome on the 21st of November and went to London, where he took Thalberg's advice and decompressed at the Savoy. The wires from Rome continued on a regular basis; the *Ben-Hur* company was shooting seven days a week and holding conferences and script readings at night "to keep everyone imbued with the story." One of the production managers wrote Mayer that whenever a problem arose, he would ask himself, "What would Louis B. say?"

A week later, Mayer was back home. In Rome the chaos continued. Early December saw heavy rain, so the production tried to work on interior sets, only to find that they didn't have enough power trucks to operate three interior units; in fact, they barely had enough power for Niblo's unit. The best they could hope for in the case of bad weather was the equivalent of one and a half units shooting at the same time, with everybody else sitting around waiting for the sun—not a frequent occurrence in Rome in December.

"Frankly, I want to say to you that the quicker we leave this country the better," wrote Al Aronson to Mayer. Aronson enclosed a list of scenes that he thought could be shifted from Rome to California. On the day after Christmas 1924, Aronson wrote that he believed the problems were far too critical to be healed by anything except radical surgery, that everybody just wanted to go home, and that Niblo completely lacked the diplomacy needed to soothe ruffled feathers. Even Niblo, he said, had admitted that "he was not sure we could ever make the *Ben-Hur* you want over here."

On January 2, Niblo, Al Aronson, and Carey Wilson sent Mayer a telegram stating that they had shot only 187 scenes out of 774, that because of inadequate lighting they would be unable to shoot the chariot race on the nearly completed Circus set until April or May. They proposed sending Niblo home to shoot interiors in Culver City and leaving Cabanne and Raboch in Rome for pickup shots. After Niblo completed most of the film in Hollywood, he could then come back and shoot the chariot race in the summer.

Mayer went them one better; on Saturday, January 3, he told Irene that he was ordering the picture home; two days later, he sent the necessary wires to Italy, and the production began to fold its many tents.

Francis X. Bushman, harried by alimony payments, chose this moment to demand a raise of $1,000 a week. He knew that there was no way the studio could recast Messala at this point. Mayer was livid. "If he quits *Ben-Hur*, that is [the] finish of him in [the] theatrical world, theater as well as pictures," he thundered to Al Aronson, but he managed to forestall disaster by making Bushman a personal loan. This extortionate demand for money would result in Bushman's being blackballed for years.

Aronson went on to tell Mayer that, in his carefully considered opinion, unless Niblo had an entirely different perspective in California than he had in Italy, Mayer would be forced to take him off the picture in fourteen days. For just its last three months of shooting, from September through December, the money pit known as *Ben-Hur* amassed costs of $648,028. Add in the abortive Brabin period, and MGM was well over a million dollars in the hole, with the end nowhere in sight. (MGM A pictures of the period would generally cost anywhere from $300,000 to $500,000, although occasional super-spectaculars made by other studios—Douglas Fairbanks, Cecil B. DeMille—might run slightly higher than $1 million for a finished picture.)

On February 11, 1925, Aronson reported to Mayer that film editor Lloyd Nosler and the Brabin negative were on their way home, but that was unacceptable to Mayer. "Brabin negative and positive worthless destroy," he wired Harry Edington. The negative was finally burned in April.

Niblo and Nosler brought back twenty-three reels of Italian footage with which they were reasonably happy. Production began on the American shoot of *Ben-Hur* on February 18, 1925. Besides having to make nearly 600 of the 774 scenes called for in the script, the cast and crew also had to remake a considerable portion of the material shot in Italy. Under the line for "Production Days Allotted" on the daily production report, there was only a blank space, the same blank space that occupied the space for "Days Ahead" and "Days Behind." Once again there were three directors working. To take one day at random— March 2, 1925—Niblo was directing the Calvary sequence on Stage 8, Cabanne was directing yet more scenes on the rebuilt Joppa Gate set, and Al Raboch was shooting the Last Supper on Stage 6.

Juggling scenes and rebuilding sets meant that actors were often not working, so all the principals were slotted into other pictures during their downtime. Novarro made a programmer called *The Midshipman*, Bushman was put in *The Masked Bride*, and leading lady May McAvoy was loaned to Warners for *Lady Windermere's Fan.*

Mayer clearly was not thrilled by Niblo's rushes. On March 22, L.B. wired Nick Schenck that he wanted to fire Niblo and replace him with Ernst Lubitsch(!): "This picture has cost so much that we feel unless it is greatest picture ever made no chance of getting our money back or even great part of it and Niblo apparently has lost himself. . . . Actors like Novarro and McAvoy not Barrymores and Gishes and need great help which Niblo doesn't seem able to give them consequently performances ordinary where should be inspired."

Both Jack Warner, to whom the director was under contract, and Lubitsch were fine with the offer, and as Lubitsch was between pictures, scheduling would not have been a problem, but both men wanted Harry Warner to sign off on the loan-out. For some reason, the tantalizing possibility of Ernst Lubitsch directing a biblical spectacle never came to pass. Fred Niblo continued on his stolid, unimaginative way.

In July, Niblo had a brainstorm: "After having a long talk with Miss Lillian Gish, and showing her the MARY and JOSEPH episode on the screen, I am sure that she could be induced to play MARY if you would care to do this entire episode over again. It would not take over two weeks because we could still use the long shots that we have and put her in the close-ups."

Mayer and company decided, just this once, to simplify their lives. The footage of Betty Bronson as Mary was retained.

The studio bought a lot on Venice Boulevard and Brice Road (now La Cienega Boulevard) and built part of the vast Colosseum set for the chariot race. "Only the left side was built," remembered Maurice Rapf. "It was a Hippodrome kind of thing, but only half of it. It held about a thousand extras, who were paid $2 a day. But the studio made sure to install some slot machines so that they could get the money back!"

Since the studio had thrown out so much of the initial production, they decided to throw out the original design for the Circus Maximus that had been built in Rome by Horace Jackson. He redesigned it on a more massive scale, and increased by a factor of four the stature of the crouching giants that anchored the spina.

The fact that only one side of the structure was actually constructed was disguised with camera angles, and the brilliant use of a hanging miniature, a construction mounted right in front of the camera that blended in imperceptibly with the full-sized half-set in the distance. "The miniature had all these little dolls with round heads," remembered Maurice Rapf. "They wore togas and their hands went up and down." The hanging miniature gave the impression that the studio had constructed the vast set to full scale.

MGM set the opening of *Ben-Hur* for Christmas 1925, blithely assuming that the chariot race, which had yet to be shot, would be suitably spectacular. By late August, Niblo was lathered with flop sweat. He sent a memo to Mayer reminding him that they had only sixteen weeks till the premiere, that the chariot race would take at least a month by itself, the miniatures for the galley sequence hadn't been completed, while other big sets weren't built yet. Finally, he concluded "The Bethlehem star is still missing [and] the Wisemen and camels on the desert and the shepherds and their flocks are waiting on the star . . . FOUR MONTHS FROM TODAY IS CHRISTMAS." The implication seemed to be that Mayer should grab a hammer and build sets.

While all this was going on, Marcus Loew was attempting to set up a merger of MGM with United Artists. It would have united the Schenck brothers and brought Mary Pickford, Douglas Fairbanks, and Charlie Chaplin together with the MGM roster—in effect, all of the greatest stars in the movies would have been under one roof. But the proposed merger fell apart because Chaplin wouldn't go along. There was the antagonism between him and Mayer, for one thing, but there was also the fact that he would lose his hard-won autonomy.

The big day for *Ben-Hur* was October 3, when the crowd scenes for the chariot race were shot. The studio filled the vast—but nowhere near as vast as it looked—set with celebrities, including Douglas Fairbanks and Mary Pickford, John and Lionel Barrymore, and Sam Goldwyn, as well as Hearst columnist Arthur Brisbane.

For weeks afterward, the crew worked on getting close-ups for the chariot race, and devising a massive crash scene for dramatic punctuation that killed numerous horses, while Thalberg supervised editing. In spite of the studio's publicity line that the crash was an accident that the cameras just happened to catch, Joe Cohn would admit clearing out the stadium so no extras would be witnesses and report the studio to the SPCA. (Later, when the film premiered, Fred Niblo would utter baldfaced lies that not only was it all an accident but

that "every horse and every man who figured in this accident was employed fifteen minutes later.")

Mayer approved the final billing sheets for the advertising on December 23,
then sat back and waited. *Ben-Hur* was a smash hit from its opening day. On
December 31, 1925, Nicholas Schenck cabled exultant congratulations to Thal-
berg. "WELL, KID YOU WERE REPAID LAST NIGHT FOR ALL THE HARD WORK YOU
PUT IN ON BEN HUR STOP IT WAS THE MOST MAGNIFICENT OPENING I EVER WIT-
NESSED STOP THERE WAS CONTINUAL APPLAUSE RIGHT THROUGH THE PICTURE
STOP THE ONLY TIME I REMEMBER GETTING AS BIG A THRILL AS I DID DURING THE
CHARIOT RACE WAS AT THE DEMPSEY FIRPO FIGHT . . . THINK OF IT IRVING WE
NOW HAVE THREE PICTURES RUNNING AT TWO DOLLARS ON BROADWAY TO SELL-
OUT BUSINESS."

Pointedly omitted was any mention of Louis B. Mayer.

The studio carried the final cost of the picture as $3.96 million. (The Cul-
ver City end of the production cost $1.86 million all by itself.) *Ben-Hur* grossed
a massive $9.3 million worldwide, but because of the contract that paid Klaw
and Erlanger 50 percent of the gross, MGM still lost nearly $700,000 on the ini-
tial release, although it would finally go into profit on a 1930 sound reissue. No
matter; the entire affair was a learning experience.

As for Niblo's Italian footage, little of it was actually used in the final print.
"Of the 300,000 feet of Roman negative," wrote editor Lloyd Nosler, "we used
5,000 feet for our three negative copies of *Ben-Hur*." In other words, slightly
more than a reel and a half of Rome negative, twelve to fifteen minutes' worth,
was used for each of the three negatives, meaning it took eight months to shoot
what, under ordinary circumstances, would have taken little more than a week.

The Rome adventure seemed to be a sort of bizarre selling point, assuming
mindless extravagance was your idea of a come-on—as it often is in the movie
business. "It seemed impressive at the time that a picture should have been
made in Rome," said Irene Mayer Selznick. "Nobody ever mentioned that almost everything in *Ben-Hur* was actually shot in Culver City."

Clearly, this story couldn't be the version presented to the public. Fred
Niblo told *Motion Picture Director* magazine that "everything that we photographed in Italy is in the picture. . . . I should say that one-third of the picture
was made in Italy, the balance in Culver City."

Ben-Hur was a crucible for the young company, draining resources and
money, straining creativity. It was the sort of picture that would ever afterward
be anathema to Mayer and Thalberg; when they undertook a massive spectacle

in the future, they made sure to shoot it within a day or two's distance from the Culver City lot. There was only one exception: *Trader Horn*, in production on and off for a full year and a half, seven months of it in Africa. But even with all the production mishaps, *Trader Horn* cost only $1.3 million, a third of what was spent on *Ben-Hur*, and made nearly a million dollars in profit.

The 1925 *Ben-Hur* is better than the 1959 remake, if only because it's an hour shorter. Even in 1925 it was a fusty old warhorse in dire need of all the showmanship MGM lavished on it: Technicolor scenes, splendid matte work and elaborate hanging miniatures, a great sea battle with predominantly full-sized ships, a hellacious chariot race. But sometimes the exhaustion shows: there are a surprising number of interiors that take place in front of nothing but hanging draperies.

Otherwise, they might still be shooting.

Chapter
FIVE

MAYER AND THALBERG were an unprecedented combination, a brilliant team working in complete cohesion. Each relied on the other, neither operated unilaterally. Together they were creating a primary moment in the history of Hollywood. The telegram Mayer had sent to Lois Weber years before ("Spare nothing, neither expense, time, nor effort. Results only are what I am after.") was not just puffery, it was what L.B. and Thalberg really believed. Additional monies were spent, not to try to save a picture that was on a morphine drip—the usual case then and now—but to convert a fine picture into a great one.

Exhibitor J. J. McCarthy was at Culver City to look at footage from *Ben-Hur* when he saw some sequences for *The Big Parade*. Renée Adorée's farewell to her lover as he leaves for battle convinced McCarthy that MGM had a possible road show epic. McCarthy's opinion, combined with King Vidor's lobbying, convinced Thalberg to put the picture back into production. Mayer boarded a train to New York with a print of the film. He showed the picture to the Loew's executives, then gave an emotional oration about how additional scenes would enhance the picture by enlarging the scale. The executives, who were perfectly content with what was, after all, a completed John Gilbert picture, nevertheless authorized money for new scenes. Vidor was sent to Texas to restage the mobilization sequence and George Hill directed a night battle scene. Because Mayer felt the sequences with Gilbert's parents could be stronger, the actors were recast and the beginning and ending were reshot. The film, originally slated to cost around $250,000, ended up costing $382,000.

After the picture was finally finished, Mayer went to Vidor. Perhaps the director would be interested in selling his percentage of the movie back to the studio in return for straight cash? Mayer had gauged his man perfectly. "My father was funny about money," said his daughter Suzanne Vidor Parry. "You might say he was very, uh . . . *frugal*. Mayer sensed that and offered him a lump sum and my father bit like a fish on a line."

The Big Parade was one of two monster hits of the silent era. (The other was *The Birth of a Nation*.) Vidor's film played reserved seat engagements for twenty-two months, grossing $6 million, more than $1 million of that coming from a ninety-six-week run at the Astor Theater in New York. The $6 million gross was more than one-third the entire industry's earnings for 1925. Even with the heavy overhead of the reserved seat engagements, the film cleared $3.4 million in profits.

The Big Parade made the reputation of both King Vidor and the studio, also giving Metro-Goldwyn-Mayer a rock-solid financial footing that would last for more than twenty years. It confirmed to Thalberg and Mayer that their theories of filmmaking were correct, that a film wasn't finished until they thought it was, and that spending money on the right things was a good way to make more money.

In October 1925, the Mayer group renegotiated their contract with Loew's, Inc. The studio had gone from strength to strength in little more than a year, and the new contract mandated that the Mayer group agree to deliver at least forty-four pictures a year to Loew's. In return they were guaranteed a minimum bonus of $500,000, and a new salary scale. Mayer's weekly pay went from $1,500 to $2,500, Thalberg's from $650 to $2,000, and Rubin's from $600 to $1,000. The Mayer group's percentage was expanded to include profits from the money earned by Loew's theaters, not just MGM films.

As for King Vidor's lost profit percentage, the one that would have made him wealthy? Vidor was never overjoyed about having signed it over, but he was never bitter either.

During 1925–26, the first full year of operation, MGM made forty movies. As of August 1925, the studio showed a net profit of $4.7 million, only $1 million less than longtime industry leader Paramount. Mayer and Thalberg had quickly ramped up a production line that had taken Paramount more than ten years to build. In 1925, MGM had three massive hits: *Ben-Hur*, *The Big Parade*, and *The*

Merry Widow. Soon, *Flesh and the Devil, Love, La Boheme,* and a string of extremely profitable Lon Chaney pictures would fill the company coffers.

Finding and developing stars like Garbo and Shearer, Gilbert and Chaney, the success of *The Big Parade,* getting out alive on *Ben-Hur,* put MGM on a lofty level. Within a few years, to be at MGM was a common goal for everybody in show business, and everybody at MGM knew it. "[We were] the crème de la crème," said William Haines. "None of them [compared] except . . . United Artists. But all the rest of them, no matter who . . . [we] always looked down [our] noses at the other actors. . . . We were snobs. We believed our publicity."

Mayer was indefatigable in building up his roster. Clarence Brown, a director who had been Maurice Tourneur's assistant and possessed a similarly luxuriant pictorialism but a stronger sense of narrative rhythm, had made Valentino's successful penultimate film *The Eagle* at United Artists, and was hired by Joe Schenck to make Belasco's *Kiki* as a vehicle for his wife, Norma Talmadge.

But *Kiki* fell flat at a studio screening, and the normally placid Schenck excoriated Brown. "What do you mean lighting Norma like that? Do you realize we're going to have to reshoot half the picture?"

Brown decided his future wasn't with Joe Schenck and First National, so he signed a contract with Paramount. But when *Kiki* was previewed to see which parts needed reshooting, an audience brought it roaring to life. Schenck had the picture previewed again, and it drew an even stronger response than the first time.

Schenck, realizing he had made a serious mistake, went to Brown to get him to renew his contract. "When I told him I'd signed with Paramount, I think he thought briefly of exploding, but he tried a different tack," remembered Brown.

Schenck invited Brown to lunch with Mayer, who was even more effusive than usual, telling Brown he was the greatest director since Griffith. Brown said that was all well and good, but he had signed a deal with B. P. Schulberg, who was now running production at Paramount. That, said Louis, was not a problem.

"He simply called up Schulberg," remembered Brown, "mentioned a few things, and talked him into canceling my contract. Louis had something on him and used it for leverage. I wasn't working for Joe Schenck directly, but I was still in the family, and that was the main thing. And that's how I went to work at MGM."

Brown stayed with MGM for the next twenty-five years, directing many of the Garbo films like *Flesh and the Devil* and such studio classics as *National Velvet, The Human Comedy,* and *The Yearling,* as well as some lovely, too little known pictures such as *Of Human Hearts.* Along with King Vidor, Brown was the best, most personal director on the lot. He would also become one of Mayer's closest friends.

By mid-1927, the Mayer-Thalberg system was a smoothly functioning assembly line. There were seventy-seven stories in various stages of development and ten pictures in actual production, with seven completed and ready for release. Of the twenty-five directors under contract, twenty-three were working, indicating that people weren't allowed to hang around on salary for long. The dominating principal of the seventy-seven projects in development was the star slated to headline each prospective picture. Thalberg supervised about a third of the pictures, with other supervisors splitting up the remainder.

Mayer and Thalberg tried everything. In spite of their focus on glossy, A-level productions, they noticed that Rin Tin Tin was pulling big audiences for Warner Bros. MGM would try a dog star as well, but none had the glowering personality of Rin Tin Tin. Mayer's search for a dog star was delayed until the spectacular success of Lassie during World War II.

The studio even tried B westerns, with cowboy star Tim McCoy making sixteen for MGM between 1926 and 1929, films that were economically but ingeniously produced. An assistant named David Selznick came up with the idea of sending a director out on location with two casts and two scripts, and shooting all the long shots and action sequences for two pictures at once. The result was that two pictures could be made for about the cost of one and a half.

MGM had a stellar roster of directors, but none was as important as a star or a producer, especially if the producer was named William Randolph Hearst, who through Cosmopolitan had an independent production deal at MGM, primarily for films starring his mistress, Marion Davies. Mayer had a lifelong aversion to independent producers, but the situation with Hearst was different.

Hearst's deal was a gold mine for him, wildly expensive for MGM. MGM financed all Cosmopolitan pictures and Hearst got a third of the profits. Hearst also got 40 percent of the profits from any MGM pictures made from stories in his *Cosmopolitan* magazine, in addition to being paid for the rights to the stories. Davies's salary was set at $10,000 a week, $6,000 of it paid by the studio, $4,000 paid by Hearst. In the real world, this is known as a sweetheart deal, and Hearst embraced it.

In return, Metro had complete run of the Hearst press to publicize its motion pictures. "They were mentioned at every turn," remembered William

Haines. "Mr. Mayer, being a very bright man and a good businessman and could see a good thing when he saw it, always saw to it . . . that this association was kept alive." That "complete run" meant that MGM stars and pictures would be kept front and center in Hearst's twenty-two daily newspapers, fifteen Sunday papers, and seven American and two British magazines, with a total circulation of about nine million. All in all, it was a more equitable arrangement than it might have appeared.

Beyond that, L.B., who had voraciously ingested Hearst's Boston paper for years, was now an intimate of the great press lord himself. In moments of special emphasis, Hearst would affectionately put his hands on Mayer's head and call him "son."

The two men had a lot in common, as Clarence Brown would note: "When Hearst got his first newspapers, he wasn't an editor or a reporter, and he didn't know shit about the newspaper business. But he had ideas and this inborn sense of what the American public wanted to read. He was also smart enough to know that there were some things he didn't know, so he hired the best newspaper corps in America, stole them away from other papers. Mayer did exactly the same thing. . . . Like Hearst and Henry Ford, he was an executive genius."

Hearst required a great deal of special handling, which Mayer and Thalberg split between them, although there was a strong element of mutual ingratiation between the two older men. Arthur Brisbane, Hearst's columnist, wrote his boss that "I would suggest that nothing could be more important than to please the wife and daughters of my friend Mr. Mayer. . . . They are extremely presentable, ten times more real than most picture people. To do anything to bring them into a good 'gentile' atmosphere would be extremely wise."

In October 1927, Mayer wired Hearst about a business proposal: "Believe we should discuss further when you return New York. Don't believe you and I far apart, but needs clarifying. Hope you are well. Girls wish to be remembered to Uncle William. . . . Look forward to seeing you in New York. All will be well in our happy family."

A week later, Hearst was returning the favor, suggesting Mayer build a bungalow on the MGM lot that would suit his position as studio head. "Gosh man don't you realize that you are one of the big fellows of the country making a product that more people are interested in than in anything else presented to the public. Everybody of distinction from all over the world comes to Los Angeles and everybody who comes wants to see the studio and they all want to meet you and do meet you so put on [a] few airs son and provide the atmosphere." The letter was signed "Uncle William."

When the Loew and Mayer families vacationed in Palm Beach in 1927, Hearst instructed his syndicate to "please send out good pictures and pleasant stories about them to our papers, morning and evening, with instructions to print." Conversely, when Mayer was indicted in an investment matter, Hearst kept the story out of his papers until the indictment was dismissed, at which point the papers were instructed to run an announcement of the dismissal in "a conspicuous position . . . and through all editions." Since MGM had no news-reel operation, Hearst volunteered to start one. "The news reels should be built on the same lines as tabloid newspapers," he instructed Eddie Hatrick, his man in Hollywood. "All stuff brief, bright, and newsy."

L.B. was impressed by Hearst's patrician *noblesse oblige*, his aura of power and authority. Hearst was a big, strapping, powerful Westerner, more American than apple pie. Hearst was what Mayer wanted to be.

Although Marion Davies was a delightful comedian, she was never a potent box office star. Davies made twenty pictures at MGM; nine would be profitable, with cumulative profits of $937,000; the losses of the other eleven totaled $1.76 million. But for Mayer and Thalberg, $800,000 in losses was a small price to pay for the publicity the Hearst papers lavished on MGM during their alliance.

The tie-up with Hearst encouraged others to follow suit. In 1926, Eugene Brewster, publisher of various popular movie magazines, sent out a letter to his editors: "This is to notify you of a very important business arrangement I have just made.

"I, President, Editor-In-Chief, and sole stockholder of Brewster Publications, have entered into a business arrangement with Metro-Goldwyn-Mayer studios, the details of which are too lengthy to explain here, but the part that concerns you follows:

"From now on, for a period of one year at least, Metro-Goldwyn-Mayer are to be our best friends among the producers, and we are to be their best friend. We are to favor them in every way possible in the way of covers, galley pictures, interviews, etc., etc., and when it comes to expressing views on their stars and criticising their pictures we are to be as favorable as possible . . . If we cannot say anything favorable, we won't say anything at all — at any rate we will leave out the bad things. Wherever you can serve their interests in any of our pages, please remember you are serving your own . . . MGM are our friends, and in a way part of our organization. Of course, you must do this in such a way that it will not reflect discredit upon our magazines, and it must not be obvious publicity."

The co-opting of the press, presumably by hefty advertising from Loew's, Inc., was essential if the image that Louis and Thalberg wished to project was to succeed.

In January 1927, Mayer was idly playing solitaire while actor Conrad Nagel and some others were discussing the advisability of different branches of the industry getting together in an organization for everybody's mutual welfare. L.B. looked up and said, "Why don't you get together, then, and try it out?"

Invitations were issued to thirty-six of the industry's leaders for a dinner at the Biltmore, paid for by Mayer. The initial charter of the Academy of Motion Picture Arts and Sciences was vaguely worded, but Mayer's own need for status and validation would have enthusiastically embraced the entire concept of awards to honor artistic accomplishment. In any case, 80 percent of the paperwork in the first years of the Academy concerned the issues of standardization of the many competing formats that derived from the early years of sound; the awards themselves were very much a left-handed endeavor.

Aside from honoring the year's best movies, Mayer and his confreres intended the Academy to arbitrate contracts between the studios and the various craft guilds. Although it was technically an intermediary organization, not a company union, the fact that it was totally a creation of the studios meant that it could hardly be impartial in negotiations and could easily serve as a means of combating legitimate unionization. As a result, the Academy delayed serious labor negotiations in the movie industry for years.

As a creation of the studios, the voting for awards by the Academy was capable of being swayed by the wishes of the most powerful of those studios, which led to such out-and-out absurdities as MGM's *The Great Ziegfeld* being named Best Picture of 1936, beating out *Dodsworth* and *Mr. Deeds Goes to Town*, not to mention *Modern Times*, which wasn't even nominated.

As far as L.B. was concerned, the Academy was about manipulation, but for immediate, MGM-related goals rather than distant, generic Hollywood goals. "I found that the best way to handle [moviemakers] was to hang medals all over them," Mayer would say. "If I got them cups and awards they'd kill themselves to produce what I wanted. That's why the Academy Award was created."

This was made explicit in a letter Cecil B. DeMille wrote to Mayer. DeMille informed him that film editors were being courted for a union, as were the cameramen and actors: "You should explain the situation to the Producers there and let them know the seriousness of the situation and explain to them that if the actors are to be kept out of the mess, the Academy must be supported

financially and substantially without delay." Mayer's response to union orga-
nizers was a scribbled sentence on a notepad: "We are splitting their ranks—it
is natural that they should try to split ours."

The industry's prevailing anti-labor stance was supported by the right-wing
Republicanism of the administration of the city of Los Angeles, led by Harry
Chandler, the publisher of the *Los Angeles Times*, whose motto was "Keep Out
the Unions!" The LAPD contained a cadre known as the Red Squad, whose
primary purpose was to gather information on labor leaders, smear them, break
up any meetings they managed to organize, and run them out of town.

Mayer's and Thalberg's method of operating the studio was to establish an
MGM star with a spectacular picture—John Gilbert in *The Big Parade*, Ramon
Novarro in *Ben-Hur*—then put him in three or four medium-budget vehicles
for every high-budget picture. Novarro may have been given Lubitsch and a
no-expense spared *The Student Prince in Old Heidelberg*, but he was also more
or less wasted in economical programmers such as *Across to Singapore* and *The
Flying Fleet*. If the audience stayed loyal through the programmers, then
MGM had a star.

Mayer was the general and Thalberg was the field commander, sending out
memos to producers, charging Hunt Stromberg with four sophisticated comedies, Harry Rapf with three tear-jerkers, and so forth. Besides Thalberg, there
were only three producers in charge of MGM product: Stromberg, Rapf, and
Bernard Hyman.

Few people liked or respected Rapf, but Hyman and Stromberg were a different matter. Hyman was from West Virginia, had studied at Yale, then found
his way as a reader to Universal, where he met Thalberg. Hyman was good-
natured, quiet, and reserved—a lot like his mentor, who brought him over to
MGM. He is undeservedly forgotten today—he died young, in 1942—but he
produced such films as *A Free Soul*, *Tarzan the Ape Man*, and *San Francisco*.

Donald Ogden Stewart remembered that Hunt Stromberg always strode
back and forth in his office, brandishing a riding crop—a prop Billy Wilder
would later favor—saying, "I like it. I think it's a fine scene. But how about that
dumb Scranton miner? Would *he* understand it?"

Stromberg's references to the dumb Scranton miner became so incessant
that writer Charles MacArthur once tried to have a Scranton miner sent to the
studio for an elaborate practical joke, but, he claimed, he couldn't find one stupid enough.

Beneath the blue-collar affectations, Stromberg was a very effective commercial producer. "Hunt Stromberg was the best producer I ever worked for," said screenwriter Irving Brecher. "He was helpful and knowledgeable. He was the only one who understood writing; you could sit and talk about lines and get intelligent reactions from Stromberg. He had been a journalist and understood language. You could not get that from the other producers."

Another of Thalberg's bright young men was Albert Lewin, a tiny but twinkly intellectual who had graduated Phi Beta Kappa from NYU and gotten his master's in English literature from Harvard. Lewin had just graduated to screenwriting at Metro when the merger occurred, and Thalberg quickly learned to rely on Lewin's instincts for quality, using him as a sort of cultural advisor. Lewin graduated to production supervisor, then associate producer under Thalberg. Lewin would occasionally make noises about wanting to direct, and every time he appeared at Thalberg's door with a project, Thalberg would say, "No, no, Albert, you don't want to do that. You're a great producer. I'll give you a raise in salary instead."

Also maintaining a hefty balance of power was Harry Rapf, producer of the program pictures. "Harry Rapf came from Warner Brothers, where they chiseled," grumbled Joe Cohn. "Everybody hated my father," remembered his son Maurice. "He was fussy and never gave writers any credit; he always expected people to do better than they did. He thought writers stunk, although he was wrong. Most of my friends were writers and they hated him and I knew that.

"Thalberg and my father had a lot of arguments and didn't get along. Thalberg was actually a nice guy, and not only that, he had gold-tipped Melachrino cigarettes. His office was right next to my father's and I stole handfuls of cigarettes from his office."

Despite Mayer's delegation of the charm to Thalberg and the muscle to himself, he could and did go out of his way to be considerate of others. "I was with Joe Cohn as an office boy," remembered the director Joseph Newman, who went to work at MGM in 1925. "Joe wanted to take L.B. to show him some sets that had just been finished, but L.B. was waiting for a phone call from Marcus Loew. So they took me along with them so I could be near the phone that was on every stage. When Loew's call came in, I was to tell Mr. Mayer, and he would leave and take the call.

"The call finally came in, I told Mr. Mayer, and he got in his car and started up. Then, suddenly, the car stopped, and he waved me to get in. He told his driver to hold the car until I could get to the car, then he picked me up and took me back to the office, so I wouldn't be stranded on the back lot. That shows you the consideration he had for people, even office boys. It was the same with me the entire time I worked for him, and past that time.

"There was truly a family feeling around the studio," continued Newman. "I can't stress that enough, that it was a family-oriented institution. Mayer and Thalberg complemented each other. Thalberg had a great story mind, and Mayer had a great business ability. They were a great combination, although they were nothing alike. Thalberg at first would be distant; sometimes it would take years for him to warm up to people. He would hardly notice you, but Mayer was a much warmer personality, a Jewish papa. But they were alike in their guiding philosophy, which was to make good pictures, the best motion pictures they could, even if they had to reshoot the entire picture."

Within the industry, Thalberg was already being held up as the quintessential producer, a man who loved movies and would do anything to make them as good as possible. Part of Thalberg's greatness was occasionally making pictures he knew wouldn't make money—perhaps one that would break new ground in art direction or costume design, alter the way a story could be told with a movie camera, or even a film that would be a glorified vanity production for a valued employee. *The Crowd* or *Man, Woman and Sin* were films made for prestige, not profit, and they gave MGM the aura of being a class act.

The MGM silents are often knockout combinations of lush art direction and spectacular camera work bespeaking a radiant self-confidence. The difference between a Metro picture made before the merger, say Rex Ingram's 1922 *Prisoner of Zenda*, and these later films is instructive. Ingram's picture is shot with a hard focus and his typical stately, methodical story progression. The style is all in the compositions, which means his pictures can feel slightly static. But MGM silents have more romantic photography, a brisker, more assured story-telling rhythm.

Sidney Franklin's adaptation of *Quality Street* opens with a long, complicated tracking shot, then calms down to produce a quietly jubilant combination of cast, art direction, and story working in unison. Even when the picture is less than distinguished—Edmund Goulding's *Love*, a middling adaptation of *Anna Karenina*—MGM offers a little something extra, in this case, the characteristic rhapsody of cameraman William Daniels's immersion in Garbo's face.

In *Our Dancing Daughters*, the something extra is eye-popping sets—one living room is approximately the size of the entry hall at San Simeon; in Monta Bell's *Upstage*, it's a bittersweet feel for the milieu and reality of vaudeville life; in Fred Niblo's *Mysterious Lady*, there's a stunning moment when Garbo lights candles in a dark room that slowly illuminate her face; in King Vidor's *Show*

People, we get an expert send-up of the semaphoric performance styles of low-end silent movie acting, as well as a guided tour of Hollywood in the 1920s, a sunlit enchantment that's the flip side of *Sunset Boulevard*—the nightmare that carries the bite of truth.

It doesn't matter whether the directors are first- or second-string, the MGM silents radiate professionalism and panache in the form of vigor and polish and a sensual presentation compensating for those inevitable occasions when the stories are weak.

"You're looking at a company that felt they had a responsibility to bring quality to the public," says film historian Joe Yranski. "Not every film would be an art film, not every film would be successful, but MGM played to the suburban middle class; Warners, especially after sound, played to a tenement mentality. A lot of MGM stories were geared to upwardly mobile audiences. There's something to be said for the gloss, there's something to be said for that communal idea of filmmaking, the pleasure quotient of those films."

The gold-plated aura of MGM was so pronounced that it leaked into real estate. In 1928 a developer in San Luis Obispo built a subdivision called Morro Strand in which every street was—and still is—named for someone at MGM. Not only were streets named after Norma Shearer and Ramon Novarro, but they were also named after Louis B. Mayer, Harry Rapf, and Lon Chaney. The intersections include Thalberg and Shearer Avenues, and (John) Gilbert and (Renée) Adorée Drives. That didn't happen with Fox or Paramount or any other studio.

For the most part, Mayer and Thalberg didn't like consciously artistic directors, but they made an exception for Victor Seastrom, probably because he could deliver beautifully realized movies on a budget.

"My father was mad about Seastrom," Irene Selznick remembered. "Simplicity, dignity, charming European gentleman, big reputation and unspoiled, no show biz about him. He had talent and poise and my father believed every word he said."

Mayer called Seastrom into his office and told him how happy everybody was about his work. It was good to have a director who could do things properly. Moreover, the studio wanted to correct his old contract, which Mayer thought hopelessly unfavorable to Seastrom. Everything about the percentage of net profits was impossible for Seastrom to check. MGM was going to tear up Seastrom's old contract and give him a new one. Seastrom's price per picture was raised to $20,000, and the studio gave him a surprise bonus of $5,000 that was repeated on every picture. (MGM kept a slush fund of $100,000 for bonuses to actors, writers, and directors through the calendar year.)

There was nothing in the new deal about a percentage of the profits, but Seastrom had never seen a dime on his percentage of the pictures he had made for Goldwyn, so he was perfectly happy to settle for more money per picture plus a bonus in lieu of an imaginary profit percentage.

Seastrom subsequently directed the Lon Chaney–Norma Shearer vehicle *The Tower of Lies*. Mayer tore up the revised agreement a month before *Lies* premiered and signed Seastrom to yet another contract. Around the studio, Mayer began referring to Seastrom as "Christ," because of his miraculous ways with actors and a camera, and his unassuming yet spiritual manner. The studio also agreed to finance a trip home for Seastrom and his family so that he could "study European production methods, gathering ideas for pictures."

For his part, Seastrom called Thalberg a "genius," and said of Mayer, "I . . . regarded him and still regard him as an especially and sincere good friend." Seastrom seems to have liked everything about MGM except the story conferences Thalberg mandated.

"I can still feel agony sneaking upon my chest when I think of them. One in particular outstanding. It was a script based upon a play. The only thing finally left of the play was the title. Absolutely nothing else. As far as I can remember seven different scripts were written, one after another, by seven different writers. At the last conference four or five other people (so-called readers) were called in to Mr. Thalberg's office to give their opinion on the final script. Each of them had suggestions. Many suggestions. . . . The conference lasted all day—Irving Thalberg had hardly said anything, I said nothing. Finally, he dismissed the experts. He himself was evidently very confounded, told me, 'Well, you have now heard what they have said, try to get it into the script, some way, if you feel so.' I went to my office, sat down, very bewildered to say the least. I had in fact not understood at all what had been said. So after trying to think a while, I decided that I did not 'feel so.' "

In 1929, Seastrom was alarmed to realize that his two young daughters were becoming distressingly American—they spoke almost no Swedish. "So I told L. B. Mayer that we wanted to go back although I had another two pictures to do according to my contract. He thought it over for a couple of weeks, could not understand me but said finally, 'We don't want to compel you to stay here, do as you wish, you are always welcome back here.' So we went home. I still don't know if it was wise. I do know that we spent the happiest years of our lives in California."

Other émigrés weren't such a smooth fit. Benjamin Christensen was hired after Mayer saw Christensen's hair-raising *Häxan,* more commonly known as *Witchcraft Through the Ages.* "Is that man crazy or a genius?" Mayer asked Seastrom. Assured that it was the latter, Mayer brought Christensen on board, but Christensen never quite found his sea legs at MGM. He managed to complete two pictures, notably *Mockery,* a rather heavy Lon Chaney vehicle, but Christensen would remember that, "during the silent film period, every time one proposed to the studio powers a film subject of some worth, one invariably received the answer: 'Do you think the American farmer would like a picture of that kind?' "

The studio was exploding with production. The six glass-walled stages were in constant use. There were twenty-seven writers, thirty-two film editors, eighteen publicists creating stories about twenty-five individual departments, including the costume department headed by the Russian Romain de Tirtoff, better known as Erté. Mayer had never seen a gay man as flamboyant as Erté, but he was intrigued. Mayer gave him a Packard car as a gift and had his studio in Sevres, France, photographed and duplicated. Erté was too temperamental to adapt his style to the equally urgent needs of actresses and scripts, but his hiring certainly spoke well for the ambitions of Mayer and Thalberg.

Success did not appreciably change the relationship between the two men. They were friendly, but not quite friends. For one thing, Thalberg lacked Mayer's emotionalism. For Thalberg, moviemaking was a kind of science; for Mayer, a mysterious alchemy. Still, they enjoyed the success they were creating, and they enjoyed the feeling of *esprit de corps* fostered by success. They instituted Sunday morning softball games, Mayer pitching for one team, Thalberg for the other, with a truck arriving to transport the players to the diamond on the back lot. The game was open to anyone who wanted to play, with electricians sliding into bases covered by executives.

Despite the camaraderie, the famous—or, depending on your point of view, infamous—MGM bureaucracy was in place early. "Everything is done in conference," complained writer Katherine Hilliker. "They'll give three different continuity men the same story. Then call a conference on the three continuities which they then whittle down and combine into one, and I give you my word I have yet to read a continuity here which is not as full of holes as a Swiss cheese."

Hilliker wrote that she had never seen "so many second-rate writers on one lot before . . . There's a Miss Powell, a Mr. Doyle, a Mr. Faye, Marian Ainsley, Albert Le Vino, Joe Farnum, Wid Gunning, Howard Hawks. . . . Agnes Christine Johnson, Hope Loring & Louis Lighton, a Mr. Ibsen (grandson of the great Henrik) and the Lord knows how many more; no list of course complete without the great Mr. Carey Wilson's name attached."

Because of the profusion of talent, there was a certain lack of urgency for people in the middle and bottom of the pack. As one writer would remember, "Metro—you might as well be out in the middle of the desert. Nobody even knew you were there. You could sit there for four weeks and draw your pay and not say anything and you never heard from anybody."

Mayer wasn't in creative competition with writers, as Thalberg, in some sense, was. One of L.B.'s few dictums about writers was that no original author of a play or novel should be hired to adapt that property into a movie, because they would be too rigid. But writers are by nature spiky and often disreputable, which drove Mayer crazy. "Some of these writers are getting drunk," he complained to Thalberg, "and they have three-hour lunches in the Derby. We ought to put our foot down!"

"No, Louis, they're signed for 52 weeks," he replied. "If I get 42 weeks a year out of them, that's fine with me. It's worth it. Let them alone, they're doing fine."

Lillian Gish was welcomed to the studio with a banner across Washington Boulevard that proclaimed LILLIAN GISH IS NOW AN MGM STAR. Bands played, flowers were strewn, beaming executives welcomed her. Gish was going to be paid a great deal of money—$800,000 for six pictures, with an option for a seventh. Mayer granted her consultation rights on stories, directors, and cast. There was no morals clause, nor were there any requirements for publicity or promotional appearances.

For *La Boheme*, Gish's first MGM picture, she was given the studio's hottest leading man, John Gilbert, fresh from the smash hit of *The Big Parade*. King Vidor did his usual dramatically subtle but visually dynamic job and the picture showed a profit of $377,000.

When Gish told Mayer she wanted to make *The Scarlet Letter* as her second MGM picture, Mayer leapt to his feet and responded with a virtuoso monologue that Gish could still recall fifty years later with perfect pitch and inflection.

"You? You? You? In a story like that? Miss Gish, would you feel comfortable making a motion picture about such a woman like Hester? How are we going to show that on the screen without running into the censors? We can't show you and that minister just holding hands and staring into each other's eyes. This isn't *Way Down East!* Motion pictures have grown up. This is the twenties, not D. W. Griffith! Audiences have grown up! They want a real love scene, especially since they know the book, as you say. They know a baby's going to come of this lovemaking! How do you propose to show that?"

Gish suggested that titles might come in handy for touchy transitions, but Mayer wasn't having any.

"Titles? They can get words from the book. We make pictures, not titles. Today's crowd wants women to act like women, not like little innocent school girls. How do you think the churches are going to take this film? Do you think they'll recommend it? They'll think that Lillian Gish has betrayed their trust!"

Gish asked if Mayer would let her make it if she could get around the obviously dicey story problems, and Mayer said yes. In due time, Gish received cautious approvals, so the talk turned to who could play Dimmesdale. Gish told her biographer Albert Bigelow Paine that by this time, "I had faith" in Mayer. "I think I have found the minister for your *Scarlet Letter*," he told her one day. He told Gish to go into one of the projection rooms and look at *Gösta Berling*. There was a young actor named Lars Hanson in the film, and Mayer thought he might be right for Dimmesdale. "If you like Hanson for the part, we'll bring him over," he concluded. She did; they did. Thalberg selected Victor Seastrom to direct.

The Scarlet Letter flowed; Seastrom shot the film in less than two months. Lars Hanson didn't speak English and played all his scenes in Swedish while Gish and Henry B. Walthall spoke only English, but Hanson's emotional power and sense of character overcame the language difference. At the end of one dramatic scene, the crew spontaneously applauded; when the picture was completed, Thalberg said, "We have done a good job," which was about as emotional as he ever got. Seastrom was given a bonus—not the usual $5,000, but $10,000.

Seastrom's *The Scarlet Letter* remains the best screen version of the novel. The acting is so intense you can practically hear the voices, and Hendrik Sartov's camera gives the story a lyricism all the other versions lack. In spite of the stark, still ending, *The Scarlet Letter* made a profit of $296,000, but sniper fire erupted from magazines like *Photoplay*, which said "Lillian Gish wears the red letter of sin with her stock virginal sweetness." Aileen Pringle, who was starring at MGM contemporaneously with Gish, believed that Mayer was un-happy with Gish's choices in material and was using *Photoplay* editor James Quirk as a surrogate.

"Mayer didn't get the returns he thought Lillian Gish was capable of bring-ing in," Pringle told Stuart Oderman. "But he didn't want to look like the evil man. He let *Photoplay* do the job. Then he could call in Lillian and show her what was being written about her. Movies have always been about money."

The lot was humming in Culver City, the machine smoothly emitting product each and every week. When British comedian Beatrice Lillie showed up to make a delightful comedy called *Exit Smiling*, she was bewildered by the speed and the lack of any apparent effort. "I was used to working for months to perfect a gesture or a piece of business," she remembered. "Here, we were due to finish in five weeks, and it is hard to believe that these disconnected scenes could pos-sibly be patched together to make a movie with any kind of plot. . . . When [di-rector] Sam Taylor announced that the shooting was over, I couldn't believe that we'd completed a picture."

The mood was upbeat and familial. Jacob Mayer would occasionally arrive at the studio in a chauffeur-driven Model T, radiating a grand air and giving or-ders right and left. L.B. was visibly embarrassed, but he didn't say a word. In spite of the fact that Mayer, according to his new secretary, Margaret Wills, "never really liked his father and blamed him for everything . . . outwardly he was a dutiful son." ("Blamed him for everything" is an intriguing phrase, but Wills didn't elaborate. Mayer could have reasonably blamed his father for being a poor provider and helping to make him homely and short. Could he also have blamed his father for his mother's premature death?)

But the delicate, perfectly calibrated balance of MGM changed perma-nently on September 5, 1927, when Marcus Loew died. The funeral services were held at Pembroke, Loew's forty-six-acre estate jutting out into Long Island Sound. Two thousand mourners were admitted to the red-stone palace with thirty-five rooms, twelve baths, and Tiffany stained glass. There were Japanese gardens and wrought iron bridges, a garage that held twenty cars. Loew's yacht *Caroline* was docked at the landing with the flag at half-staff. All very impres-sive, all of no more interest to the small man who was laid out in the marble re-ception hall. Marcus Loew was only fifty-seven years old.

At the time of his death, Marcus Loew had amassed an estate worth around $30 million. He left 400,000 shares of Loew's Inc., one-third of the outstanding shares, to his wife and sons.

Mayer had been Loew's choice to run MGM; Loew's replacement would be Nicholas Schenck. It was a shotgun marriage neither partner would ever be comfortable with.

Nick and Joe Schenck had a strong fraternal resemblance—broad, homely faces, large noses, high foreheads that got higher with every passing year, noticeable Russian accents. They were, remembered Howard Dietz, "continually solicitous about each other." Joe would become president of United Artists and 20th Century-Fox; Nick would control Loew's, Inc. Between them, they maintained more power than anybody else in Hollywood.

Howard Dietz would believe that, of the two men, Nick was the sounder because he was more levelheaded than Joe. But it was Joe who would come to be regarded as the Godfather of the movies, the wise man other wise men went to when they had a problem. As producer David Brown would recall, "Schenck . . . was not only the catalyst. He put things together. . . . He was a godfather, an elder statesman, a problem solver when costs got out of line. Uncle Joe was totally loyal—a crony loyalty. You could go to him with a problem and he'd solve it."

"Joe's personality was that of a wonderful Jewish uncle," remembered his goddaughter Mary Ellin Barrett, the daughter of Irving Berlin. "He was enormously generous, in terms of the presents he gave and the favors he did and the endless troubles he took for his friends. When I was fourteen, he would come to New York and I would put on my best dress and he would take me to dinner at the Colony, a place I normally wasn't allowed to go. We always had a million things to talk about. He was curious about what I was up to. He was a very good friend."

In contrast with the expansive Joe, nobody outside his immediate family got close to Nick Schenck. "Nick was a very strange man," said Mickey Rooney, and Herbert Swope Jr., the son of the famous editor of the *New York World* whose house was a few doors down from Schenck's on Sands Point Boulevard on Long Island, remembered, "He was a quiet man, who smiled a good deal but not warmly. He was a very good family man. We would go over to their house for dinner; their house was right next to Simon Guggenheim's." Most of his family played cutthroat games of croquet at the Swope house, but Nick preferred to watch.

The house on Sands Point was a gracious place of unobtrusive luxury that resembled an English country house. There was only one odd detail, a set of large brass cuspidors in the bar that were labeled "Great Expectorations." The house had a yacht and a speedboat, the latter used for the commute between Nick's house and his office in Manhattan.

Besides the business of Loew's, Inc., Nick's focus stayed resolutely on his family, especially his wife. "He adored my mother," said his daughter Nicola. "It was quite wonderful to see. He would say, 'You know your daddy loves you, but this is the one,' and he'd point to her. He was as straight as a ramrod. He loved his work and worked seven days a week—people were always coming to the house on weekends for meetings."

"His brother Joe was a bon vivant," said Herbert Swope, Jr., "a very pleasant man, always at the racetrack and beloved, really. Nick was too cold to be well liked. They were very different men." Where Nick was monogamous, Joe, after Norma Talmadge divorced him, was quite the opposite. David Brown says that "Some disappointed girl is reputed to have said to Joe, 'You told me you loved me!' And Joe said, 'I didn't say I loved you. I said I loved *it.*' "

But despite the many differences between the two brothers, they were extraordinarily close. "They spoke three times a day at least," remembered Nick Schenck's daughter Nicola. "And they invented their own languages, two of them, so that nobody could understand what they were saying to each other. One was a variation on pig Latin. I don't think either one of them ever made a deal without checking with the other one."

Nick Schenck was successful with the horses, owning a champion named Dangerous Age and eventually going into breeding. "He would sit there handicapping races and take me with him so people wouldn't interrupt him," remembered Nicola. "I would talk to the people that came up to us while he would sit and work the numbers. Out of eight races, he would only bet four or five, but he always won those four or five. I never understood how he did it."

Nick was not without his pretensions. He liked to be called the General, even though he wasn't a general of anything—"a bullshit title," snorted the director George Sidney. And he was a hard man, as became obvious when he showed a visiting MGM executive a chicken coop on his property. One of the roosters had been attacked by the others, and was in bad shape. "You look at that," said Schenck, "and you realize that this is the way you must behave in the world. . . . You must not let others pick you to pieces."

He was, in other words, a worthy opponent for Mayer, one armored by the coldness he could switch on at a moment's notice, and the accouterments of power contained in the Loew's Building at 1640 Broadway.

Anybody that knew Nick Schenck sensed that he was not a man to be crossed—one executive called him "the smiler with the knife." Thalberg regarded him with open scorn, thinking him small-minded: "He thinks we're a bunch of bad boys who make bad pictures just to annoy him, and he wants us to stop."

Although Nick Schenck would give L.B. a vast amount of freedom to run his operation, although they were both Russian Jews, *landsmen*, they would never be truly friendly. Mayer could never quite varnish over his lack of education, his plainspoken way of speaking—or screaming. Nick Schenck, on the other hand, was a smooth operator—quiet, almost imperturbable.

There are differing theories about the bad feeling that existed between the two men, varying from the eternal conflict between East and West, Hollywood and New York, to those who believe that each man was jealous of the other—Mayer because Schenck had control over what he did, Schenck because the name of the movie company was Metro-Goldwyn-Mayer, not Metro-Goldwyn-Schenck.

Mayer and Nick Schenck clashed as early as 1925, when Schenck was running the company while Marcus Loew was ill. Mayer began to suspect that Schenck had approved a plan to sell MGM films to Loew's theaters for rates that were below market price. This meant that the pictures would gross less, and the profit participants would make less. To Mayer, this was like sacrificing one child to feed another. Schenck vehemently denied he had done any such thing, but Mayer told Robert Rubin to keep a careful eye on the books.

The two men never reached any kind of rapprochement after that. "They had *huge* arguments," remembered Nicola Schenck. "I would hear my father on the phone raising his voice, which was very unusual. Louis would come to visit us periodically; my father would issue the order, 'Come east.'

"The funny thing is, for all their fights, my father was a fan of Louis B. He always said, 'Louis is a brilliant studio chief.' The only way he ever talked about him was in the most flattering terms, which is not to say that they ever fooled each other into thinking they were friends. Louis B. was very aggressive and dominating, and maybe that might have offended Dad. But truly, whenever he spoke of Louis B., it was always in terms that he thought he was brilliant. They had bitter telephone conversations, terrible business quarrels, but those never seemed to lower his opinion of Louis B."

But there was no question as to who had ultimate power. Nicola remembered that whenever L.B. visited Schenck's house, his hands and face were notably sweaty. "He would always bend over to kiss you, and it was not pleasant."

In Culver City, Louis surrounded himself with men he could trust. There was Eddie Mannix, who had a gravelly voice, the face of a bulldog, and a bearing to match. The legend about Mannix, spread largely by Mannix, was that he had worked construction at Palisades Amusement Park, until he landed a job as a bodyguard for Nicholas Schenck. When his defenses were down, he provided a less dramatic version: he was working at Palisades Park because he knew the gang members and was hired to keep order, not as a bouncer exactly, just as someone the tough guys would respect. Although Schenck had essentially sent Mannix to spy on Mayer, Mannix was quickly turned and became part of the inner circle of MGM.

"I came out," he would say in his New Jersey accent, "and I coulda gone with the numbers game, but I went straight." Born in 1891 in Fort Lee, Mannix entered the movie business in 1916, managing Joe Schenck's New York studio. Sent to California by Nick Schenck in November 1924 as a comptroller, Mannix agreed to come out for three months and handle administration while Mayer was in Europe struggling with *Ben-Hur*.

Mannix soon became a valuable force in handling grievances and departmental rifts and was named general manager. He was married to a nice woman named Bernice, but didn't see any reason to curtail either his appreciation of other women or his fondness for gambling. California was made for Mannix, and vice versa.

Beneath the surface geniality, Mannix had a temper. Mannix also drank, and the intersection of those two could be ugly. One of his mistresses, the notorious actress Mary Nolan—her real name, which the Hays Office wouldn't allow her to use because of her reputation in New York, was Imogene Wilson—reputedly endured fifteen abdominal surgeries after his beatings.

When Bernice Mannix was killed in a traffic accident, Mannix's mistress, who had been stashed at the Sunset Towers, the town's favorite residence for kept women, promptly showed up at his house on Linden Drive, announced that she had "squatter's rights," and married Eddie. Nobody liked Toni Mannix—she was loud and demanding, with the demeanor of a Broadway moll—but people put up with her because of her husband.

Mannix, remembered screenwriter Millard Kaufman, "had teeth like a horse and a wife with the greatest legs of any woman I've ever seen in my life, although she was a pain in the ass. Eddie had the manners of a police chief—superficially jovial, but turn around and he could put a bullet in your ass. He was phenomenal in making the most of any situation. He had power, and the remarkable physicality that went with it. He wasn't Hollywood tough, he was Jersey tough—authentic."

Mannix became the designated negotiator with unions, and, remembered Maurice Rapf, who became a writer at MGM and union firebrand, "was a decent guy. Straight." If Mannix felt that a loyal employee had signed a contract that paid him less than he was worth, Mannix would tell them to pick up an extra $100 for expenses from the cashier's office every week. Nothing was ever put on paper about such arrangements; they were just Mannix's way of doing business.

Benny Thau was a booker for the Loew's vaudeville circuit who gave Mayer such good advice that he made Thau part of the casting office in Culver City; he quickly rose to become one of the most important members of the front office.

Thau's essential job was as a liaison between the front office and the talent, and he was generally regarded as a kind and appealing man; many MGM people remember him with great affection. But Thau and Mannix and the rest of the inner circle were powerful men at MGM, and many of the would-be female stars attempted to attach themselves to them in order to ensure access to good parts. Greer Garson was Thau's mistress for the first years of her stay on the Culver City lot, until she was a big enough star that she didn't need him anymore; likewise, Joan Crawford served as Harry Rapf's mistress until she had some hit movies under her belt, and deemed herself ready to marry Douglas Fairbanks Jr.

"These were solid, hardworking guys who came from the fringes of New York," said Mary Loos, the niece of Anita Loos and an old Hollywood hand. "They could have run a casino. They were tough, but not outside the line."

The end result of all this variance between the personal, paternal, sexualized atmosphere of the West Coast and the more corporate manner of the East Coast was an emotional and psychological rift. Nick Schenck's men disliked and distrusted Mayer, and Mayer's men viewed Schenck and his minions as soulless bean-counters who didn't understand the creative process. Nevertheless, everybody knew that the power resided in New York—where the power has always been.

The death of Marcus Loew made it easy to get rid of the great pictorialist Rex Ingram, whose three pictures made in Nice had produced a modest profit. But Ingram had refused to have Mayer's name on his pictures, thus making an enemy of a man who was a good hater. When Ingram was finishing up *The Garden of Allah*, Mayer asked him to give the farewell scene between the two lovers more of a kick. "They wanted to see a big scene," griped Ingram, "much weeping and gnashing of teeth, and . . . a chance for the orchestra to play William Tell." In other words, the studio wanted Ingram to emulate the farewell scene between John Gilbert and Renée Adorée in King Vidor's *The Big Parade*.

"Needless to say, I did not change the sequence," said Ingram. Needless to say, Ingram never worked for MGM again. Howard Strickling, who loved both Mayer and Ingram, believed that he could have been the bridge that could have brought the two of them together, except for the unpleasant fact that their pride wouldn't allow either of them to make the first move. Ingram would not ask, and Mayer would not entreat.

The fact that Ingram was a prestigious filmmaker whose films didn't really cost the company anything meant little to L.B. Ingram had made it personal. Ingram made two more movies—visually impressive, dramatically stiff—both financially unsuccessful. There were offers, but Ingram's demands were so imperious he scared everyone off.

Obviously, Mayer and Thalberg could band together at a moment's notice when they needed to. When MGM was negotiating with Ramon Novarro for a new contract, Mayer invited the actor in to look over the draft. Novarro should read the contract quickly, said Mayer, as he had to leave for New York in a half hour. Thalberg walked in and began playing with his keychain. While Novarro was reading, Mayer peppered the actor with fatherly questions about his family.

The distractions didn't work; Novarro noticed a clause that forbade him participating in non-MGM undertakings such as stage work or recordings. "Does this also include farting?" he asked Mayer. "How can I do anything if I am not allowed to advertise me, or what I can do besides act? No, Mr. Mayer, you just go to New York and have a good time. This contract needs revising and I am sure that Mr. Thalberg and I will get together in your absence." For good measure, Novarro demanded a $100,000 bonus for spending more than a year on *Ben-Hur* working for $1,000 a week. He settled for $50,000, and got the publicity clause he wanted.

In the late 1920s, Louis's main areas of conflict were with freewheeling actors like John Gilbert and William Haines. Both indulged themselves sexually, Gilbert with women, Haines with men when he could get them, boys other times. Mayer's feelings about sex were similar to those of Alice Roosevelt Longworth, who made the famous remark about not caring what people did as long as they "didn't scare the horses." He didn't really want to know.

But Billy Haines not only scared the horses, he terrified their riders. Although Mayer did not have a particularly tolerant personality, he was pragmatic. Discreet gay men like Ramon Novarro or George Cukor could have long and satisfactory careers at MGM, but Haines was at the outer edge of gay behavior for that period. He and his lover, Jimmy Shields, could be seen cruising Hollywood Boulevard in a touring car in broad daylight, Shields with his arm around a young man, Haines in the back, sandwiched between two sailors.

After Haines was dropped by MGM, he made two more pictures, both for the Poverty Row studio Mascot. But after that, there was no more work in the movies for the man who just a few years earlier had been a major box office star. Clearly, there was some sort of loose, reciprocal arrangement between the Mayers and Zukors and Warners about people whose behavior was considered beyond the pale.

Haines would always be unrepentant about the life he led; in many respects, he was ahead of his time. "I was blind when you talk about Thalberg," Haines told writer Fred Lawrence Guiles. "He was a great fellow, but Mayer— I remember everything that's nasty about him."

As for John Gilbert, his daughter, Leatrice, would remark, "Father was the way he was. He smoked too much, drank too much, and took Thalberg to brothels where a nice Jewish boy shouldn't go. He did everything that Mayer wholly disapproved of. The word Mayer used in the highest approbation was 'wholesome,' and Jack wasn't wholesome. He had barely finished seventh grade, but he was sophisticated, and he read books, and Mayer hated people who were sophisticated."

Irene Mayer Selznick said that the family could always tell when L.B. had seen Gilbert, because he would come home furious. "Just the sight of him made him angry," she would remember. "Those two should never have been on the same planet, let alone the same studio."

The relationship would come to a head on September 8, 1926, when Gilbert was supposed to marry Greta Garbo in tandem with King Vidor's marriage to Eleanor Boardman. Garbo never showed up, but Vidor and Boardman got married anyway. Mayer supposedly told Gilbert he should be satisfied with sleeping with Garbo. Gilbert decked him, breaking his glasses, after which Mayer said that he would destroy Gilbert if it cost him a million dollars.

Some people have disputed this story, which derives from Eleanor Boardman, who told it to both Kevin Brownlow and Leatrice Gilbert Fountain. Irene Mayer, who was a guest at the wedding, insisted it was "whole cloth," while Joe Cohn strongly doubted it, for the simple reason that "If Gilbert would have hit

Mayer, Mayer would have killed him. Mayer was a brutally strong man." The wedding took place only a month after shooting had begun on *Flesh and the Devil*, which starred Gilbert and Garbo, making their rapid courtship and engagement a matter of days—improbable for a pathologically shy and cautious personality such as Garbo. Yet, as Kevin Brownlow points out, "You only have to look at *Flesh and the Devil*, the most authentically erotic of all silent films, to see what Garbo felt about Gilbert; I can quite believe the impulsive nature of Garbo's decision, and then her withdrawing in panic."

That a smart, sophisticated woman like Boardman would fantasize such a remarkable event from her wedding day seems strange. On the other hand, Boardman also claimed that Charlie Chaplin offered her $100,000 for her first child.

In 1926, L.B. decided it was safe to build a house in California. Because Margaret had always dreamed of living at the beach, Mayer purchased a lot at 625 Pacific Coast Highway in Santa Monica. The house on North Kenmore was sold for $20,000, and the family moved to a rented house while the Santa Monica sale went through. Mayer told Cedric Gibbons to build the house in a hurry. Floodlights were set up, and three shifts worked around the clock, seven days a week. Mayer thought beach houses looked and often were flimsy, so he had thirty feet of pilings driven into the sand to support the walls. The twenty-room villa was completed in six weeks at a cost of $28,000.

Louis and Margaret ended up with a Spanish house with a red-tile roof that was impressive without being ostentatious, and had, as the real estate ads say, a stunning ocean view. There were four bedrooms, and onyx and marble bathrooms. The floors and beams were dark wood, and, as insulation against the summer heat, the white stucco walls were a foot thick. For Margaret, there was a wrought iron balcony overlooking the Pacific. The den had a pegged oak floor and a large fireplace. There was a private projection room, and a gatekeeper's apartment where L.B. installed his father.

"The house was very nice," remembered Mayer's nephew Jerry, "but not extraordinary, not a mansion by any means."

"It was a typical beach house," remembered Maurice Rapf. "The living room fronted on the swimming pool, and in those days the ocean came into the pool during a storm. . . . Margaret was a good hostess and did most of the work; she would import sturgeon and Jewish deli food from Barney Greengrass in New York."

Thalberg's house was on the same road as Mayer's, but the Thalberg home replicated a vaguely French-Norman style as opposed to L.B.'s Spanish.

L.B. was proud of his home, but only opened it up to outsiders on Sundays, when he hosted what amounted to an open house. There would be a buffet supper, drinks, and, for those who hung around long enough, a movie. One Sunday, even Garbo showed up. Irene Mayer remembered that she had on a black velvet suit with rhinestone buttons. Garbo was accompanied by Eddie Mannix; they had a few drinks, made some small talk, and were gone in twenty minutes. "She'd never been in our house before, and she never came again," said Irene.

Anita Loos lived a few doors down from Mayer in Santa Monica, and her niece Mary grew friendly with Irene and Edie. "I liked them. They were in a tough spot—everybody wanted them on account of their father. I was doing publicity in New York and I became friends with Lucius Beebe, who gave me a Christmas present of a beautiful robe monogrammed with his initials, so I'd remember where I got it. When I went back to Los Angeles, I took it with me, and I was wearing it while I was leaning over the fence talking to the girls. I saw them making this horrified face. I followed their eyes and looked at the pocket and saw the monogram: L.B. So I had to explain to them that it came from Lucius Beebe, not their father!"

While Mayer played the Daddy for his crew of actors and actresses, there could be no mistaking the distinct difference in status between them and his family. Irene and Edie remembered seeing Joan Crawford jogging past their house in shorts and a blouse with no bra. They invited her in for lunch. When Mayer came home and heard the story he exploded. "How dare you socialize with an *actress?*" he yelled. Edie came right back at him: "Why don't you lock me up in a convent and throw away the key if you want me to be the Virgin Mary?"

L.B. was doing a fair amount of investment wheeling and dealing. Mayer, Thalberg, and Thalberg's father, William, were partners in a real estate operation called the Melvil Hall Corporation that paid $171,875 for 625 acres in Glendale. Mayer, Thalberg, Harry Rapf, Joe Schenck, Norma Talmadge, and Doug Fairbanks and Mary Pickford were part of another operation called Title Guarantee and Trust Company that bought and sold dozens of lots in and around Los Angeles, sometimes for as much as $500,000 a transaction.

Mayer, however, endured a financial and public relations nightmare in a

1927 scandal involving the Julian Petroleum Company. C. C. Julian was a Canadian con artist who ran a large-scale Ponzi scheme in the Los Angeles area from 1922 to 1927, fronted by some remarkably effective newspaper ads ("Julian Refuses to Accept Your Money Unless You Can Afford to Lose! Widows and Orphans, This Is No Investment for You!"). The ads brought in money, and the investors brought in more investors. By the end of 1922, Julian had sucked in $11 million.

Julian produced some oil, but mostly he produced stock certificates, far more than any actual assets were worth. In 1924, Julian sold the operation, and his successors were even more flagrant. Before the scheme blew up, there were 3.7 million shares of Julian Petroleum floating around, paying out huge dividends from the river of money that came in from the new investors eager to be a part of the gravy train. When the scheme fell apart, forty thousand Los Angeles investors lost $150 million.

By mid-1927, indictments were flying. District Attorney Asa Keyes suspected that some of the money had gone into the pocket of *Los Angeles Times* publisher Harry Chandler—who had promoted Julian's activities in his paper—and his friends: Mayer, C. B. DeMille, banker Motley Flint. As it turned out, around $100,000 of the Julian money seems to have landed in the pocket of Asa Keyes, which, given the public aggressiveness with which he pursued the case, made him one of the stupider district attorneys in history.

Dozens of people were indicted, including Mayer, several bank presidents, former judges, and current attorneys. Mayer and DeMille were both charged with usury for being part of a scheme in which allegedly excessive rates of interest were charged for loans in Julian's stock pools. (DeMille supposedly loaned the corporation $62,000 for forty-five days at 20 percent, collecting about $12,000 in interest.) About $18 million was collected in usurious interest charges.

It was revealed that Mayer flew into a snit over being shorted $39.50 in a stock transaction involving thousands. He ended up returning $53,709 in allegedly illegal gains, and the complaint was dismissed. Ultimately, the jury acquitted the Julian Petroleum Company's two principal officers, then explained that the case was too complicated for them to come to a verdict about anybody else. The indictments were thrown out, but Asa Keyes spent two years in jail for taking payoffs to throw the case.

Mayer was introduced to the lofty heights of Republican politics through Ida Koverman, the executive secretary of the Republican Party of Southern California. Born in Cincinnati as Ida Brockway, Koverman—there was an early marriage to the mysterious Mr. Koverman—was introduced to power when she met Herbert Hoover while working for the Consolidated Gold Fields in South Africa. In 1924, Hoover named her executive secretary for Calvin Coolidge's presidential campaign and she came to Southern California in 1926 to begin organizing Republican women. She was serving as executive secretary for the Hoover campaign in 1928 when she met Mayer and introduced him to Hoover. Sensing a valuable alliance just waiting to be made, Mayer hired her as his executive secretary, where she quickly became one of the most formidable women in Hollywood.

Koverman was one of the invisible power centers in both MGM and the city of Los Angeles. She served as a director or officer for organizations such as the Opera Guild, the St. John's Hospital Guild, the Municipal Art Commission, the Los Angeles and Hollywood Chambers of Commerce, the Hollywood Bowl, and a dozen or so others. Her networking was impeccable, and she served as Mayer's eyes and ears in the community at large. She reorganized the MGM accounting system and served as a mother figure to special favorites; because she was used to power, ego trips and tantrums left her unmoved; because she shared Mayer's values and politics, she could serve as a surrogate in matters of conduct and behavior, as well as a talent scout without portfolio. L.B. would look to her for cues on everything from the proper greeting to the Japanese ambassador to when to wind down a speech.

And, of course, there were her political connections. She was worth a lot more to the company than her $250 weekly salary would indicate, but she was happy in her various roles, supplemented her income with the odd real estate deal, and spent the rest of her life at MGM.

It was a small hire, but a powerfully metaphorical one. Men like Mayer and Thalberg and Loew and Zukor all shared a generalized instinct—primarily, that in a market where the public was clamoring for movies, power accrued to those who could supply a large amount of reliable product. But it was Mayer alone who instinctively understood that, while Hollywood sold itself as a self-sufficient, magnificently innocent toy store that caused the rest of the world to press its nose against the glass in wonderment, it was in fact a prototypical American industry. It had a power and influence that could only grow, one, moreover, that was becoming increasingly politicized and increasingly dependent on the goodwill of bankers, politicians, and other members of the Eastern establishment—people Koverman had entrée to, and L.B. would spend the next twenty years cultivating.

Another of the women L.B. depended upon was Kate Corbaley, a Stanford graduate and librarian married to a construction engineer. Corbaley was a compulsive reader who went home each night with a stack of books and returned in the morning having read and digested each of them. Every day a synopsis of possible material would be sent to MGM executives, and every week there would be a story meeting at which Corbaley and the story editor would tell Mayer, Thalberg, and the other producers the stories they were particularly high on. Much of Corbaley's job consisted of narrating potential story purchases to Mayer. Corbaley was known as "Mayer's Scheherazade," because with her telling a story, Mayer could visualize the settings as well as the stars. Years later, at Corbaley's funeral, Mayer leaned over to his neighbor in the church pew and said, "I would rather have lost any star than this woman."

Because MGM was in Culver City, nine miles from Hollywood, there was a sense of isolation from the rest of the town, which fed the elitist feeling that Louis and Thalberg were trying to inculcate. "You didn't mingle," said screenwriter Frederica Maas. "If you worked at MGM, you didn't know what was going on at Paramount or First National." For that matter, because of Thalberg's preferred habit of pitting writers against one another, moving them in and out of assignments, the writers never had the fraternal feeling they did at, for instance, Warners. "The writers on the lot didn't congregate, didn't talk to each other," said Maas. "Everyone tended to his or her own knitting. They were suspicious of other writers. Writers are not kind people. Never trust a writer."

Just a few years after *The Big Parade*, the top-down MGM system of heavy supervision was already in place. Thalberg decided to let King Vidor make *The Crowd*, a very personal—and very great—picture that was far removed from the emerging MGM ethos.

The Crowd was the most flamboyant make-good imaginable for Vidor signing over his profits from *The Big Parade*. But Mayer hated the picture—in one shot, Vidor showed a toilet, which sent Mayer through the roof—and campaigned against it at the nascent Academy Awards in 1928. According to Vidor, the voting for Best Picture was essentially in the hands of Mary Pickford, Douglas Fairbanks, Joe Schenck, exhibitor Sid Grauman, and Mayer. Grauman called Vidor early one morning and said he had held out all night for *The Crowd*, but finally gave in—Mayer adamantly refused to vote for it and in fact voted for another picture, *Two Arabian Nights*, rather than the actual winner, *Wings*. Mayer hated *The Crowd* for the rest of his life, often using it as an example of everything that was wrong with "artistic" filmmaking.

He was similarly uneasy about Victor Seastrom's *The Wind*, with Lillian Gish killing a would-be rapist. Seastrom shot the picture in the spring of 1927, at his usual efficient pace, on location in the Mojave Desert.

Seastrom remembered a particularly grim preview of the picture. When it was over, none of the MGM officials said a word to him beyond, "Good night, Victor." To the end of his life, Seastrom remembered the horrible feeling of this experience. "It comes sometimes still to me in the middle of the night."

As Gish recalled, Thalberg told her, "We have a very artistic film," which she knew was a criticism. In Gish's telling, Thalberg explained that a preview audience hadn't liked the ending, in which Gish's character was driven insane by the omnipresent winds and wandered out into the storm to die.

"Mr. Mayer heard about the reactions and he rushed us into a happy ending," Gish said years later. "Mr. Thalberg kept saying how artistic the film was, and Mr. Mayer kept shaking his head, repeating over and over like a broken record, 'Change the ending. Change the ending. Change the ending.' "

That, at least, was Gish's version; the historical record says something quite different. In fact, Gish was reciting the ending of the novel, which was never in any version of the script and was never shot.

The studio clearly was nervous about the picture, not releasing it for a full year, in November of 1928. By that time, sound was a roaring freight train obliterating the softer music of silent movies, and *The Wind* was an orphan film. The provisionally happy ending didn't help—the film lost $87,000, anyway.

Lillian Gish had made *The Scarlet Letter*, *La Boheme*, *Annie Laurie*, *The Enemy*, and *The Wind* for MGM. The cumulative result for the five pictures— three financial successes and two failures (*Annie Laurie* and *The Wind*)—was $418,000 in profits. But after the successive failures of *Annie Laurie* and *The Wind*, the relationship between Gish and the studio cooled off. They had a serious argument over time off, then Thalberg asked her to cut her salary, offering her 15 percent of the gross after the studio had recouped its costs in an attempt to placate her. As always, MGM played hardball: "They all point to the harm they could do me by putting me out in bad pictures," Gish wrote to her lawyer, "which, of course, is only too true. They also tell me that it would do them no harm, as they are so organized that they would go on just the same, but that I would suffer irreparable loss."

By October 1927, with *The Wind* finished but the studio postponing its release, Gish was writing that "I hardly think that I will continue with Metro. Theirs is such a large organization that I feel they haven't the room or the time for me." Shortly afterward, MGM let the greatest film actress of her generation go—not because her films didn't make money, but because they didn't make enough. Gish was "difficult" and single-minded about her work, which was more important to her than the MGM method.

In the formal manner of Victorian men, Mayer and Herbert Hoover addressed each other as Mr. Mayer and Mr. Hoover. L.B. usually played the sycophant, initially sending Hoover little letters full of strenuous apple polishing. "I cannot help but express to you the keen enjoyment I had in the little chat we had together while you were my guest at the studio," he wrote. "I wish the responsible citizens of our glorious country could know you intimately as you deserve to be known, as I am sure you would create the same impression on them as you have on me."

In return, Hoover responded with friendly but never buddy-buddy notes. "Glad to see you any time on 24 hours notice," is typical. Other times, there was more of a quid pro quo, as in the matter of a proposed Hearst radio station.

"GET BUSY WITH [HOOVER]," Mayer wired Ida Koverman. "SEE WHAT HIS ATTITUDE IS AND WHAT CAN BE DONE STOP THIS VERY IMPORTANT AS WILL GIVE ME JUST THE AMMUNITION I NEED TO ENLIST THEIR SUPPORT AND FRIENDSHIP."

Hoover replied: "Strictly confidential to yourself. In accordance with my promise I am now working on a plan to arrange a satisfactory wave length for your proposed station in a general readjustment. Do I correctly understand that this is a joint license for yourself and the Hearst interests?"

After much string pulling, Hoover told Mayer that "Pending the construction of your station and assuming its completion within a reasonable time this wave length will not be assigned to any other Los Angeles station but will be held for your use when ready."

The men exchanged autographed pictures, and Mayer sent Hoover a pass for Loew's theaters on an annual basis. When Hoover was nominated for President in 1928, Mayer wired him that "when you are finally elected President of the United States it will be the crowning event of our country's history." Some of Hoover's campaign pictures were taken by MGM portrait photographer Ruth Harriet Louise.

Hoover's election in November 1928 must have seemed like final proof that God was on L. B. Mayer's side. Mayer responded to the election with an effusive telegram: "While I never had any doubt of outcome because our people are thinking people and as such could come to no other conclusion nevertheless am glad suspense is over. . . . Anyone who has been fortunate enough to know you or has studied your record and career realizes that there can be no

doubt that history will record you as one of the great presidents of all time."
Little Louie Mayer from Saint John was a friend of the President of the
United States.

Mayer began acting as the White House's man in Los Angeles, arranging
letters of introduction for C. B. DeMille's trip to Europe, and gently requesting
presidential time for him. He began a series of recommendations about presidential appointments. He campaigned for a specific collector of internal revenue in Los Angeles, an appointment for a federal judge in Los Angeles, an
assistant U.S. attorney general in Washington, and nominees for the Federal
Home Loan Bank Board in several cities. All of these appointments came
through.

When Hoover wasn't facilitating Mayer's private affairs, the relationship
was primarily one of Louis's enthusiasm and Hoover's pleased acquiescence.
Rumors began to circulate that Hoover would make L.B. an ambassador someplace, perhaps Turkey. Hoover's final word on the matter was, "Mr. Mayer decided he could not leave his responsibilities and declined to have his name
submitted to the Turkish government."

For all of his intimacy with various Republican power brokers, there is a
strong sense that Mayer was more interested in proximity to power than he was
in actual policy. The Republican financier Louis Lurie remembered that
"[Mayer] was never a large contributor and never did any work on the organization level. [Ida Koverman, Raymond Benjamin, and Mendel Silberberg]
were instrumental in making him Chairman of the Republican State Central
Committee. But, unfortunately, L.B. did no work."

Politicians knew how valuable Mayer could be. When Hoover failed to respond immediately to an invitation to Louis and Margaret's twenty-fifth wedding anniversary, a New Jersey congressman sent a snappish letter to Hoover's
secretary, saying, "He most certainly should send some type of message or all
will be lost."

Hoover came through: "I understand that you will celebrate your twenty-
fifth wedding anniversary on June 15. Mrs. Hoover and I wish to add our felici-
tations to those you will receive from many other of your sincere friends and I
am in hopes we shall be able to send you a similar message twenty-five years
hence."

The true bond seems to have been between Hoover and Ida Koverman. To
Hoover, Mayer was "Mr. Mayer," until they had known each other for fifteen
years, but Koverman was always "My Dear Ida" or "My Dear Friend." No detail
about Hoover was too small for Koverman to attend to. After a Hoover radio

speech in October 1932, she noticed the rattling of paper, and promptly sent a batch of heavy blotting paper to the White House. "We mount the speech on these heavy sheets and it is then absolutely noiseless," she wrote the President's secretary.

For Louis, all this political gladhanding reassured him that he was "Somebody," as well as making sure that the house odds stayed on his side of the house. Ida Koverman appraised her new boss with instinctive accuracy: "This is another small boy," she wrote about Mayer, "new at the game [of politics] and used to a great deal of attention." Mayer's immediate line to his temper—the petulance, the willingness and the ability to seduce, the tendency to always need as well as want more—all were traceable to his emotional identity as the child who never got enough.

While Mayer's instincts were excellent, they weren't infallible. Frances Marion enjoyed telling the story of a time in mid-1928 when she summoned Mayer to a projection room with Margaret Booth, Victor Fleming, and George Hill to watch a cartoon on offer from a young animator. A squeaking mouse came on the screen, and Mayer immediately shouted, "God damn it. Stop that film! Stop it at once." He launched into a tirade about something so obviously offensive to at least half the audience. "Every woman is scared of a mouse, admit it. And here you are thinking they're going to laugh at a mouse on the screen that's ten feet tall, admit it. I'm nobody's fool."

He exited the screening room with a slammed door as punctuation. Leaning against the back wall of the projection room, Walt Disney realized he'd have to look for distribution someplace else.

As the most culturally conservative of studios, MGM took the longest to commit to sound. When Buster Keaton went into production on *Spite Marriage* at the end of 1928, the studio refused his request to make the film with some dialogue and sound; it needed its sound equipment for musicals and dramas, not comedies. As late as May of 1929, Nick Schenck was saying that "I believe [silents] will continue to be a very positive factor in motion picture production . . . my personal opinion is that the silent film will never be eliminated, since certain stories are naturally suited for silent treatment."

MGM's strategy was to let the other studios tussle with the technology and find out what worked and what didn't, at which point MGM could saunter onto the battlefield, shoot the wounded, and make off with the spoils. This cost the studio profits because the public was storming theaters that had sound pictures, even bad ones, but Mayer didn't care. As he wrote Thalberg in October 1929,

"MGM is still behind the other studios in sound production, but quantity is not important. . . . What matters is that MGM becomes identified with the *quality* talking picture" (emphasis added).

More or less because nobody knew any more than he did, Mayer and Thalberg made Norma Shearer's brother Douglas head of the sound department. MGM's preparations for sound were somewhat frantic; by the late spring of 1929, twenty-two soundstages were in various stages of construction. Grass was ripped up, magnolias and willow trees chopped down. Where there had been flowers, there was now asphalt. A sylvan atmosphere was converted into something industrial.

For two years, Marcus Loew's widow held her 400,000 shares of stock, close to a third of the company. The industry knew that Loew's was in play; beginning in January 1929, trade paper headlines told the story: "SCHENCK AGAIN DE-NIES LOEW-FOX DEAL REPORT . . . NO DEAL FOR SALE OF LOEW TO WARNERS, SCHENCK SAYS . . . DEPARTMENT OF JUSTICE DE-CLARED SCANNING FOX-LOEW REPORT . . . WARNER OR FOX DEAL FOR LOEW READY SOON IS COAST BELIEF."

Both Fox and Warners were in a cash-rich position from being on the leading edge of sound. The wild card was William Fox, a misanthropic lone wolf who, his niece said, "invited enemies. He would boast that if he died, all the executives of his company put together couldn't run the business." He was probably right. Allied with no one, fighting everyone, plagued by rampaging paranoia, Fox worked alone and meant to control the movies alone.

The tip-off came in a phone call from Eddie Hatrick, supervisor at Cosmopolitan Pictures, to Florence Browning, Mayer's old secretary, who was now working for Loew's in New York. "Florence," yelled Hatrick, "they're over at the bank right now, signing papers to sell the company to Fox." Browning called Robert Rubin, then Mayer. His initial reaction was stunned silence. Then he said, "Well, Schenck is president of the company. He can do what he wants with it!"

The purchase was carried out under absolute secrecy; Robert Rubin had only heard rumors. On February 28, 1929, William Fox delivered $15 million that he had borrowed from AT&T and a few investment houses. That day, Loew's stock closed at 84. It was estimated that Nick Schenck and Loew's treasurer, David Bernstein, split a profit somewhere in the vicinity of $20 million.

Besides two motion picture companies—his and Metro-Goldwyn-Mayer— Fox also took control of Loew's theaters throughout the country. The combined assets of the company would exceed $225 million. In addition to the Loew's stock, Fox also bought the shares held by Nick Schenck. Fox said that the officials, executives, and production policies of MGM at Culver City would remain the same. It was essentially the same statement that the new management of MGM had issued after the 1924 merger, just before the new broom of Mayer and Thalberg swept the declining fortunes of Metro and Goldwyn out the door.

When the news broke, L.B. knew that his days as chief operating officer at Culver City were numbered. Mayer was traveling with his family to the White House to be overnight guests of President Hoover at the inauguration on March 4 when word of the merger reached him in New Orleans. He went to New York, as did Thalberg, where they confronted Schenck. He had sold them—and the company—down the river.

Meanwhile, Fox began what seems to have been a fruitless attempt to seduce Mayer into being his friend. Mayer told people that there was every chance that the Justice Department, directed by his friend President Hoover, would be very interested in the antitrust implications of such a purchase.

Fox then went even further, purchasing another 260,000 shares of Loew's stock on the open market by June 1, 1929, all under various names, most of it on margin. He was now on the line for $70 million worth of the company's stock.

The longer they had to think about it, the angrier Mayer and Rubin got. Loew's had expanded from a gross income of $19.5 million in 1923 to $116.2 million in 1929, almost completely because of the efforts of Mayer, Thalberg, and their team.

What would have elevated their blood pressure even more was the fact that William Randolph Hearst, who had publicly pledged his support to the Mayer faction, was secretly negotiating with Fox. Hearst knew that Fox would need help to navigate the antitrust minefield, and he knew that Fox had the sound-on-film patents that Hearst would need if he was to convert his newsreels to sound. Hearst ended up buying a stake in Fox's Movietone Corporation.

What made the situation even more galling was the fact that the Mayer group had taken most of their profits in straight cash; they owned little Loew's stock. Nick Schenck had offered to give Mayer and Thalberg Loew's stock as payment in full of their annual bonuses, but Mayer had advised Thalberg to take the cash. For one thing, their share of the profits would be watered down if they started taking shares. Mayer was right, but he was also shortsighted—the cash just increased their tax burden, whereas shares might not have.

According to William Fox's account, Mayer, Thalberg, and Rubin felt that they were entitled to part of the money Fox was paying. Fox and, presumably,

Schenck, disagreed. "What they would have liked to do was to buy some of these shares on the market, and sell them for more than twice as much as they bought them for," Fox told Upton Sinclair, his official biographer. "I told them that they hadn't expressed any faith in their company, by the mere fact that they had not seen fit to invest any of their money in the stock of that company. . . . As a result, I incurred their animosity in these conferences."

At this point, rumors were rife that Nick Schenck planned to ease Mayer out and install his brother Joe as head of the studio. According to both Mayer and Robert Rubin, Nick Schenck gave Thalberg a $250,000 bonus as a make-good for the Fox debacle. Mayer said that Schenck offered him $100,000 but he refused. Despite Thalberg's promises to share any bonus money he got from Fox, nobody else at the studio saw a dime of that $250,000. "His only weakness was love of money," said Mayer, by way of summing up his partner's personality.

The need for money would indeed become the dominating theme of Thalberg's life. "He wanted as much as L.B. was getting and that touched off the rivalry between them," said Eddie Mannix. "Irving was after the big money then, and L.B. began to think of the day he would produce the pictures. It changed them both and it never should have happened. Irving was a sweet guy, but he could piss ice water."

Still, Mayer was closer to Thalberg than he was to Nick Schenck, so he used his influence with the new Hoover administration to clear up Thalberg's IRS problem. In an effort to lower his tax burden, Thalberg had given some Loew's shares to his mother. He was also employing his sister, Sylvia, as a screenwriter, personally paying her salary and deducting it from his taxes. All this got Thalberg into trouble with the Internal Revenue Service, which in mid-1929 accused him of fraudulent deductions. Now, thanks to Mayer's insider status with the Hoover administration, the government settled for $100,000 of Thalberg's bonus and let the matter drop. In other words, Loew's stockholders paid for Thalberg's illegal deductions.

Mayer would later tell William Fox that he "moved heaven and earth" to prevent the consolidation of Fox and MGM, which could only mean one thing: Hoover's Justice Department. Hoover, however, would never admit to any influences: "All the important leaders of the motion picture industry brought the problems of the industry to the President," wrote Hoover's secretary. "It is quite possible that Mr. Mayer protested against the actions of Mr. Fox, but Mr. Hoover has no recollection of the matter."

According to Fox's own account, he enlisted Mayer as an intermediary and offered him and his associates $2 million for his help in smoothing things with the administration. Mayer would always deny having entered into an agreement with Fox, but John Lord O'Brian, Hoover's assistant attorney general in charge of antitrust investigations, said that Mayer came to see him shortly after he was appointed and said he was not opposed to the Fox deal. O'Brian was surprised—his predecessor had told him Mayer was strongly opposed. O'Brian was convinced that the merger was a blatant violation of antitrust laws, and he continued moving the case to trial.

But Fox's luck was about to run out. In July 1929, he was involved in a bad auto accident that laid him up for months, and in October the stock market crashed, precipitating the worldwide Depression. Fox Theaters shares dropped from 25 7/8 to 15 1/8; Fox Film dropped from 101 to 71; Loew's dropped from 64 1/4 to 49 5/8. (By May 1932, Loew's would be selling for 16 and Fox Film for 1 1/8.) Fox owned more than 660,000 shares of Loew's, for which he had paid slightly more than $73 million, a third of it on margin. Bankers began calling in Fox's notes, and the house of cards tumbled. Fox lost control, not merely of his Loew's shares, but of his own companies.

As the result of something close to divine intervention, Louis and the rest of his group survived. The entire experience was invaluable if only because it taught Mayer one thing: Nick Schenck could never be trusted; money was more important to Schenck than MGM or Loew's, while nothing was more important to Louis than MGM. "Mayer *cared* about MGM," remembered Maurice Rapf. "It bore his name."

From now on, despite their public amity, despite the daily phone calls, L.B. knew who his enemy was. From now on, he would always refer to Nick Schenck as "Nick Skunk."

Chapter
SIX

DESPITE THE PRESSURES of running a production schedule that was complicated by all the problems of early sound, Thalberg remained calm and often considerate. The young editor Ralph Winters was running a picture with Thalberg, and when the executive would give him cutting notes, he would stop the picture every once in a while and ask quietly if Winters was getting everything down. "What a doll that man was," remembered Winters.

"There's a slight misapprehension about Thalberg," said Winters, "that he could take a film apart cut by cut. He didn't do that. I worked with him on a Norma Shearer–Robert Montgomery picture, running it with Shearer and Eddie Mannix, and he worked in broad strokes. He'd stop the film once in a while and give me a note—'We need a close-up there,' or something like that. But that was all."

That said, Winters remembered him as "a humble man with talent. He was a gentleman, very nice and helpful to me, and I was just a kid that he didn't have to be nice to. Whatever situation you were trying to solve, he could put in a little something that helped."

Sound would make stars, and it would break stars, and the most famous star that it broke was John Gilbert. Gilbert's situation was complicated by the fact that the studio had signed him to a $250,000-per-picture contract at the end of 1928. It was the richest deal for a contract actor in Hollywood, and the studio had been forced into it because Gilbert had gone so far as to outline a draft contract with United Artists in August of that year.

Gilbert was far too chaotic a personality to successfully produce, but MGM couldn't very well stand by and lose its most popular leading man, so it anted up. It's entirely possible that in its haste to re-sign Gilbert, MGM ignored a voice test for the actor.

After his first couple of abysmal talkies tanked, poor Gilbert soon grew paranoid. "Gilbert always drove a convertible with the top down," remembered Howard Strickling. "But he started driving it with the top up because he thought people were laughing at him. [He developed a] persecution complex."

Assuming for the sake of argument that the legend of Gilbert's and Mayer's 1926 fistfight and the ensuing vendetta is true—that Mayer did indeed sabotage Gilbert—the conspiracy theory falls apart over the question of why Gilbert's friends Thalberg and Nick Schenck would stand idly by and watch their pal— and primary corporate asset—be ruined. As Joe Cohn pointed out, "No matter how much Mayer may have wanted to bury [Gilbert], Nick Schenck never would have stood for it." Gilbert's daughter Leatrice had no answer for that, nor does anybody else.

In any case, Gilbert was rendered expendable by the rapid rise of a young actor named Clark Gable. Gable was born in Cadiz, Ohio, in 1901, the son of an oil driller. His mother died before he was one year old. He left school at seventeen to work on his father's newly purchased farm, but that didn't last long. After some paternal push-pull, he left home and began working in Akron rubber plants. Akron was where he saw his first play, loving it and the entire experience. The stagestruck young man was then hauled to Oklahoma by his father to work in the oil fields.

At the age of twenty-one, he began acting in itinerant stock companies, filling in the cracks between acting jobs with lumberjacking and sales. He married an older actress named Josephine Dillon in 1924 and landed in Hollywood, where he got extra work in Lubitsch's *Forbidden Paradise* and von Stroheim's *The Merry Widow.*

Gable could get no further in the movies than jobs as an extra at this point, and went back to the theater. His marriage broke up, but he was slowly rising in his profession. By 1930 he was playing the lead role of a tough convict in the Los Angeles company of *The Last Mile.* That got him the role of a heavy in a western at Pathé, and soon afterward, the agent Minna Wallis got him a contract at MGM.

Gable was a different actor for a different era, an MGM equivalent of Warners' James Cagney, except with sex appeal. The most popular silent era leading men like Valentino and John Gilbert tended toward the ardent and exotic — they could be French or Spanish, American or Italian.

Gable was brusque, overtly masculine, and implicitly American, with an aura that indicated he was as likely to slap a woman as kiss her.

Thalberg had initially dropped Gable into 1931's *The Easiest Way*, a Constance Bennett vehicle, and when the picture was previewed, he took his staff to the theater in Glendale.

"Mayer had a marvelous eye for talent," remembered Sam Marx. "Thalberg didn't, but he could develop talent. And at that preview, every time Gable came on screen, the audience was interested. In the lobby, Thalberg was stopping people and asking them what they thought of that actor. So then we put Gable opposite Garbo, opposite Crawford, opposite Shearer — a rising personality against people who were already established."

By the end of the year, Gable had appeared in nine MGM pictures, and had been loaned out to Warner Bros. for two others. He had been paired with strong men and strong women and had held the screen with all of them. Thalberg's gamble paid off; MGM now had a masculine young stud to replace the fading John Gilbert and complement the genteel young Robert Montgomery.

This was classic MGM: take care of the most obvious physical defects (teeth, eyebrows, hairline), then throw the talent into a half-dozen different kinds of parts. If and when they seemed to hit a nerve, and the public agreed, leap to exploit it. Writers constructed scripts to emphasize those qualities that seemed to mesh with the actor's talents, and publicists sweated and strained to promote the same image that appeared on screen.

And, for God's sake, show the public what they were paying for. When a young MGM director shot some close-ups of his leading lady shaded by leaves, Mayer called him on the carpet. The director was "startled by the older man's vehemence, by his notions, by his odd possessive insistence. It was a deep personal involvement with Mr. Mayer, a seemingly life and death concern."

The movies weren't just a business with Mayer, they were the vehicle for the projection of his own fantasies of social mobility and sexual attractiveness. He took the fantasies seriously, he took the audience seriously, and he took the movies seriously.

In each period of Mayer's MGM, the studio had a secret commercial weapon: one or two stars that often flew beneath the critical radar but still guaranteed grosses that dwarfed those of far more prestigious stars. In the silent era, it was

Lon Chaney. The chameleonic actor made a long series of B films whose sole distinction was their overriding overtone of the grotesque and arabesque, and the charisma of their star. Costing between $200,000 and $300,000 apiece, the films each reliably netted an equivalent amount. Since Chaney made four pictures a year, MGM was making a minimum profit of a million dollars a year on him.

By early 1929, Chaney was earning $3,750 a week. When sound came rolling in, Chaney wanted a $150,000 cash bonus—his contract said nothing about talking pictures. MGM refused to pay a bonus, any bonus, until Chaney took a voice test. He was an experienced stage actor so he passed with flying colors. After offers and counteroffers the negotiations stalled at Chaney's demand for a $50,000 bonus and L.B.'s offer of $25,000. At this point, Chaney was adamant: no deal. Mayer's petty avarice was—and is—bewildering. In essence, the studio was haggling about $25,000 ($500 a week) for a star who was bringing them a million dollars a year and was likely to bring them far more in the future.

Just at the point where Chaney and Mayer were in a standoff, Thalberg entered the negotiations and began mediating the deal, a highly unusual occurrence, for Louis negotiated nearly all studio contracts. Ultimately, Thalberg gave Chaney everything he wanted, and Louis signed off on the deal. He had little choice—lack of contractual boilerplate about sound films forced them to renegotiate a lot of deals—and Chaney got his $50,000 bonus, not to mention an equal amount if and when the studio picked up the next of his yearly options.

But all the wrangling was for nothing, for Chaney had throat cancer. He struggled through his first sound film, a remake of his silent hit *The Unholy Three*, shot in a little more than three weeks. The film finished shooting in late April of 1930, and in July, the studio took him off payroll because he was unable to work. On August 26, Chaney died at the age of forty-seven.

The next day, Mayer issued a statement to all the studio's employees: "To honor the memory of our beloved friend Lon Chaney, whose untimely passing has been a severe blow to us all, this studio will observe a period of silence tomorrow, Thursday, at three o'clock."

A few weeks later, Mayer was in deep consultation with studio lawyers to see if MGM had any legal recourse to recover the $50,000 bonus. The attorneys regretfully informed Mayer that the money belonged to the actor's estate.

In Jacob Mayer's final years, he radiated pride about his son. "My Louis was always my best son," he told the lawyer Fanny Holtzmann. "The oldest boy,

Rudy, was smarter, but he gave me trouble; from Louis I had only *naches* [dividends of pride]. He worked hard, he was reliable." He would remember how movie-struck Louis had been, how Louis was out all day and night scavenging metal along the shore, while Rudy spent his time talking about real estate deals that never came off.

Whatever grudges L.B. held against Jacob, he took pride in treating him as a good son treats his father—with respect. Margaret planned two menus each day, a kosher one for Jacob and another for everybody else. Whoever came to the Santa Monica house saw Jacob, yarmulke on his head, in the honored position at the table.

Jacob had been afflicted with chronic myocarditis for several years and had left his son's house for Glendale Sanitarium in mid-March of 1930. On April 18, he fell, fractured his left femur, and died suddenly, probably from heart failure, at the age of what the death certificate estimated as "about eighty-three years." Jacob was buried at Beth Israel Cemetery beneath a stone that read—in Yiddish—"A wonderful man, exceptionally versed in learning experience through the Talmud, and greatly beloved."

Jacob left an estate of $10,000, and instructions for modest bequests to many charities: a Hebrew Home for the aged, an orthopedic hospital, a Jewish orphans' home, a half-dozen other places. What was left was to be divided among his five children.

Now Louis was the titular, as well as practical head of the family. Yetta Mayer was operating a ladies' clothing store in Montreal, Jerry was working at MGM, Ida was raising her family in Los Angeles. Rudy remained the charismatic black sheep, indulging in fantastically obvious real estate scams, accumulating mistresses and arrests, and forever being bailed out by his brother until his death in an apartment fire in 1951.

Thalberg noted the great success of Universal's 1931 *Dracula* and *Frankenstein* and reasoned that MGM should get in on the horror genre. He decided to commission something even more horrible. He got it. *Freaks*, as directed by Tod Browning and starring a cast of actual circus freaks, was much more than a horror film. Rather, it was an inquiry into the nature of deformity, with a climax that achieves the texture and imagery of a screaming nightmare.

Mayer was appalled by the project, and even more appalled by the rushes. On the other hand, the freaks were allowed to eat in the MGM commissary— live and let live. But then, Mayer's lifelong approach was to state his objections loudly and clearly and then let his people do what they wanted to do.

When *Freaks* was released in 1932, it was a critical and commercial disaster, losing $164,000 of its modest $316,000 cost. MGM was so mortified by the film that it leased it out for years to sub-distributors, so that the film wouldn't be traced to MGM. The studio would make only a few more horror films (*Mark of the Vampire* and *The Devil Doll*, both also by Browning) and Mayer must have regarded the genre with undisguised loathing—even westerns were more respectable. It would take thirty years for *Freaks* to be recognized as the perverse masterpiece it is.

Because of Nick Schenck's distrust of debt, Loew's was particularly well suited to survive the constraints of the Depression. At the depth of the Depression, Loew's had only $32 million in notes and bonds outstanding, because they had fewer than two hundred theaters nationwide, compared with Paramount's 1,600 and Fox's 1,000. Of Loew's theaters, a little fewer than half were in New York City—five alone in Times Square.

Because Loew's theaters were mostly in big cities, MGM's proportion of urban-oriented A pictures was far above that of most studios. All this meant that in the summer of 1931, when Paramount reported a quarterly loss of $5.9 million, a then-record for the movie business, MGM, unburdened by a massive debt load of real estate that couldn't return enough revenue to cover mortgage costs, proceeded more or less as it always had, even though their average picture cost of slightly more than $400,000 was still more than other companies were spending. "MGM happens to be the corporation which has gone through the Depression with less corporate trouble than any other in the industry," reported *Fortune* magazine.

For the industry at large, MGM was an amazement. There were twenty-two soundstages, $2 million worth of antique furniture, twenty-two projection rooms, sixteen company limousines, and a commissary that charged 50 cents for a lunch of Long Island oysters. The largest of 124 subsidiaries of Loew's, Inc., it had a weekly payroll of $250,000, of which $40,000 a week went for its staff of sixty-two writers and $25,000 went for eighteen directors.

The ascendance of MGM was crystallized by an article in *Fortune* magazine in December of 1932. The problem, aside from the piece's stunningly pervasive anti-Semitism (Thalberg was "a small, finely-made Jew"; Sam Marx "an intelligent Hebrew with a Neanderthal forehead"), was that Mayer was relegated to the status of a "commercial diplomat."

The Thalberg legend that reached its apotheosis in F. Scott Fitzgerald's novel about Hollywood, *The Last Tycoon*, began with the story in *Fortune*. He was, wrote Henry Luce's anonymous but reliably stentorian writers and rewriters, "changeable as the chameleon industry in which he labors. He is five and one half feet tall, and weighs 122 pounds after a good night's sleep. This lightness, in calm moments, is all feline grace and poise. . . . His brain is the camera which photographs dozens of scripts in a week and decides which of them, if any, shall be turned over to MGM's twenty-seven departments to be made into a moving picture."

The article reverently described his office, "flanked by a fire escape that leads onto a viaduct to his private projection room (with three desks, two pianos and twenty-seven velvet armchairs)."

The product of the studio was carefully—and accurately—appraised. "It is easier to state what [it] is *not* than what it *is*. It is not innovation. MGM was the last of the big companies to adopt sound. . . . It is not superior direction. Probably no MGM director is as gifted as Ernst Lubitsch or Josef von Sternberg . . . both of whom work for Paramount. It is not superior writing. MGM has the largest literary staff in Hollywood—its superiority, however, is debatable."

After paying tribute to MGM's nonpareil roster of stars, the article fell back on "a general finish and glossiness which characterizes MGM pictures and in which they excel. Irving Thalberg subscribes heartily to what the perfume trade might call the law of packaging—that a mediocre scent in a sleek *flacon* is a better commodity than the perfumes of India in a tin can."

And L. B. Mayer? He brings up the rear of the piece, after art director Cedric Gibbons and costume designer Adrian ("the tall, twittering hunchback") and even Kate Corbaley ("a plump, ruddy lady who looks like a good character actress made up to resemble a county dowager").

Mayer was described as "probably the most dignified personage in Hollywood . . . the diplomat, the man of connections" apparently most valuable for the maintenance of the connection with William Randolph Hearst. "By obliging Mr. Hearst in the matter of Miss Davies, Mr. Mayer is not only insuring Hearst support for his own productions but also preserving the rest of the industry from the indignation which the Hearst press would doubtless extend to the cinema as a whole if Miss Davies were to suffer some indignity."

It was a viciously slighting article, and Mayer was hurt. Frances Marion compared his response to "an injured lion lashing out blindly and furiously." First Nick Schenck had tried to snatch the company Mayer had built; now Thalberg was taking a good portion of the credit that Mayer felt belonged to him.

The truth was something else entirely, as Walter Wanger found out when he was brought to MGM at a salary of $2,000 a week. Mayer let Wanger in on his plans. "I'm going to build up the biggest collection of talent so that this studio can't fail. I want you to help me. If you come across any actor, director or writer who looks promising, let me know and I'll sign 'em up."

Mayer wasn't kidding. "If there was anybody in this business who was any good, Mayer never rested until he got them," said Joe Vogel. "My God, the money we spent on people! With a little more care and management, we could have made much more money."

The Dartmouth-educated Wanger had the usual mixture of wariness and amusement about Mayer. Wanger's first MGM picture was *Gabriel Over the White House*, a fable about the disappearance of democracy under economic duress, which is revived only by the actions of a President who becomes a dictator. Wanger was worried about the politics of making such a picture at MGM, specifically Mayer's politics. "Don't pay any attention to him," advised Thalberg.

For insulation, Wanger enlisted the support of William Randolph Hearst, who even contributed a speech or two for Walter Huston, playing the President. Mayer didn't like the picture; after a preview, he told Eddie Mannix to "Put that picture in its can, take it back to the studio and lock it up!" Retakes and recutting—some of it suggested by Mayer, some by Motion Picture code administrator Will Hays, and some by President Franklin Roosevelt—fixed most of the political problems, and the film was released to considerable success in spite of its fascist sympathies.

Hearst remained unhappy. "There were a lot of alterations in the picture which were not requested by the government and which in my humble opinion were in no way necessary," he wrote to Mayer on March 25, a couple of days before the film opened. "You have been afraid to say the things which I wrote and which I say daily in my newspapers and which you commend me for saying, but still do not sufficiently approve to put in your film."

Mayer and Thalberg must have felt fairly confident about their man—they ignored him. Obviously, there was a clear business understanding: Hearst was free to run his newspapers as he saw fit and L.B. and Irving were free to run MGM as they saw fit.

Wanger's diary is full of annotations attesting to Mayer's hands-on running of MGM. Some examples: "L.B. phones re appt. to close deal." (Jan. 3); "L.B. re deal." (Jan. 4); "Afternoon see L.B. long session . . . close deal." (Jan. 6); "Looked at 5 reels with L.B." (Jan. 13); "L.B. and Harry R. until 7:45 p.m. re general situation." (Jan. 14); and, spectacularly, "L.B.'s tirade and frenzy" followed by "Garbo sermon cont'd" and "L.B. ill" (April 22).

The notations drift away in the latter part of the year, but it's clear that Mayer took a very aggressive supervisory position regarding the incendiary *Gabriel Over the White House*, less so about Wanger's production of *Queen Christina*, indicating that contemporary politics were more important to him than sexual politics.

Thalberg was something of an autodidact; because he liked writers, writers liked him, hence *The Last Tycoon* and thousands of reverent anecdotes—mostly told by writers. For Mayer and, to a lesser extent, Thalberg, the most important components of filmmaking were, first, the star, second, the producer, third, the script, and, bringing up the rear, the director.

"L. B. Mayer had a theory that if one writer could do a good job, then five writers could do five times the job," recalled the writer-director George Seaton. "So you would have constructionists and idea men. As an example, Bob Hopkins was an idea man. He didn't even have an office. He would just walk around and get ideas for pictures. He couldn't write a script, but he had ideas." (In an oral history recorded for the Culver City Historical Society, Sam Marx left a hilarious record of the way Bob Hopkins worked. "Hoppy was a great character, a landmark of that studio; he was so well-ensconced he could insult producers. He would walk around the lot with a cup of black coffee and a pointed finger. 'Got a marvelous idea. San Francisco. Get it? Get it? You stupid son of a bitch! Gable! Tracy! *Earthquake!!*' ")

"Then you had a constructionist like [James Kevin] McGuinness followed by a continuity writer and he would be followed by somebody who could polish a script. George Oppenheimer, for instance, was often put on as a polish man. He was sort of the local Noel Coward when it came to comedies. He was always used for sophisticated dialogue."

A movie called *China Seas* is applicable. Thalberg began work on the picture late in 1930, and simultaneously assigned three different writers to write three different treatments. By the fall of 1931, Thalberg had settled on a single story line, and the next four years were occupied by processing the best efforts of two dozen writers, half a dozen directors, and three supervisors before the picture finally went into production in early 1935 with Clark Gable and Jean Harlow. This was a ridiculously complicated, calculatedly extravagant approach to making movies, but it usually worked. Even with the dozens of writers coming and going over the years, *China Seas'* costs were high but not unrealistic—$1.1 million—and it grossed $2.8 million worldwide, with a profit of $653,000.

The MGM record for writers seems to have been a Harry Rapf mess called *Broadway to Hollywood,* consisting mostly of a lot of revue acts that had originally been shot for an abandoned picture called *The March of Time.* Thirty-six writers worked on it, off and on—mostly on—between 1930 and 1933.

"Sometimes writers worked in succession," said Irene Mayer Selznick. "Sometimes they worked in teams—or several writers worked separately on the same script, and each one thought he was alone on it. Sometimes one writer did the outline, someone else did the synopsis, someone did the dialogue, someone did the revision, someone did a complete rewrite. Who the hell knows who wrote anything?"

The producer, that's who.

"Looking back, I can see that at MGM the producer was the chain belt in the factory," said screenwriter Robert Lees. "He got the writers, he got the script, he gave it to the director, he took the film from the director and gave it to the cutter. He kept the writers writing, the directors directing, and the cutters cutting. Nobody ever got together and talked to each other. The only unifying factor was the producer."

And yet, some fine writers put up with the MGM system—at one point MGM had on the lot Philip Barry, Robert Benchley, Marc Connelly, Oscar Hammerstein, George S. Kaufman, Anita Loos, and S. N. Behrman.

The MGM scripting process was begun by the readers, fifteen in New York and ten in California, who covered twenty thousand novels, stories, and original scripts a year. The story editor plowed through this mass of coverage. If a story seemed appropriate for one of the MGM stars, the story editor would take it to one of the producers responsible for said star. The purchase made, the story editor and the producer cast the writer(s) just as they would actors.

When it came to apportioning credits, the system was haphazard. Often, it was no more systematic than having each writer's contribution typed on a different color paper. When the rainbow script was completed, it was tabulated, with the writer with the largest number of a specific color of pages getting the credit.

Other times, the Old Boy Network came into play. One time, producer Paul Bern informed a couple of writers that he was putting Carey Wilson's name alongside theirs on *Arsene Lupin* because "Carey needs the credit."

"Well, that's a very nice warm overcoat you're wearing," said Lenore Coffee, "and my chauffeur badly needs one. Would you mind taking it off and giving it to me?"

Thalberg's preference for tag teams of writers resulted in a particular kind of screenplay, films that are stronger in individual scenes than they are as a dramatic whole. As the historian Tom Stempel pointed out, Thalberg's essential goal was to "find scenes that worked, that played. Sometimes there are connections between the scenes and sometimes there are not. Often moments built up to either never appear or else go by very quickly."

From Thalberg's point of view, he was involved in the business of creating vehicles for stars, not creating intrinsically magnificent scripts; his orientation was essentially the same as a nineteenth-century impresario like David Belasco or a twentieth-century playwright like S. N. Behrman.

There are some indelibly great scenes in MGM films of the 1930s— Harlow and Gable cracking wise in *Red Dust*, William Powell shooting Christmas ornaments in *The Thin Man*, Jean Harlow and Marie Dressler going to dinner at the end of *Dinner at Eight*, Charles Laughton bearing down in *The Barretts of Wimpole Street* and *Mutiny on the Bounty*, Garbo's tour of the bedroom in *Queen Christina*, her death scene in *Camille*, and so on—but they're peaks amidst a lot of flatlands.

Mayer's theory was that if the producer had the right script with the right cast, any competent director could make a successful, if not distinguished film. And, within the limitations imposed by assembly-line production of forty or fifty films a year, Mayer was right.

At MGM, the director was, with some exceptions—King Vidor, Clarence Brown, George Cukor—a craftsman who moved actors and cameras around, a technician whose job was to effectively stage a scene that the producer and writers had already agreed on. When Groucho Marx asked Thalberg why on earth Sam Wood was chosen to direct *A Night at the Opera*, Thalberg replied that "If he shoots a scene and I don't like it I can call Wood into my office and say, 'Sam, shoot that scene again. I didn't like the way you handled it,' and he will do it."

MGM's directorial pride and joy was W. S. "Woody" Van Dyke II, a hard-drinking, quirky character who made the breezily charming *The Thin Man*, among many others, and who was, according to Joe Cohn, "the most underrated director in Hollywood." Van Dyke broke into the business when the actor Walter Long, an old friend from stock company days, got him a job on *Intoler-*

ance. "I was really just one of Griffith's 10,000 messenger boys," he would remember. "My salary was $3 a day, some days. But I was working under Griffith and that meant everything."

"Woody was the speed king," remembered George Sidney. "His mottos were 'Don't waste time; don't take any bullshit.' He was an amazing guy. He would get up at four in the morning and go to a Turkish bath and work out his day. Then he'd show up at the studio, say, 'Put the camera here, then put it here, then put it over there,' and everybody thought he was a genius. They didn't know he'd already been up for four hours.

"Everything was military with Woody. If he figured a close-up would only run for three feet, that's all he shot. He knew cutting. He would get on the second rung of a ladder and stand there, looking over the set, making everyone look up at him. I was there one day when they were ready to start work. Joan Crawford came on the set at 8:29, and Woody lined up a shot looking over her shoulder onto the other actor.

" 'Cut, print,' he called, 'Over here.'

" 'What about *my* close-up?' Crawford wanted to know.

" 'I only make close-ups of people who are on time,' he said."

Van Dyke's own estimation of his talent was spot on: "I resent simpering idiots who babble about the Artistic Urge in a director's job—a director's job like mine, anyway. . . . They try to build me up at MGM as a great artist—they flute melodiously about artistry inherent in me as a director—when THEY know—and I know—that I'm a darned good commercial director." Mostly, he insisted, "It's just a technical job. You have to possess some power of visualization, imagination, but that's not genius."

Van Dyke's own rationale for his obsession with speed was a pragmatic adherence to the Big Picture, when it was probably just a low threshold of boredom and little patience. "The trouble with most movie people is that they take the whole thing too seriously," he told one reporter. "It's no great matter of life and death about a picture. The public isn't going to stop buying theater tickets if the length of an extra's dress isn't just right or a set has a little too much shadow in it."

Nevertheless, a man who could ram an A picture with major stars to completion in three weeks was someone to be prized. Van Dyke used a specially constructed small crane, which could move the camera from floor level to a height of seven feet, and minimized the number of setups, hence lighting time. He also used his own crew, who were utterly loyal to him.

Because of his addiction to work, and an all-purpose style that could be applied to any genre, Van Dyke was often called in to take over from other directors if they got sick or the studio didn't like the early rushes. He also doctored without credit various sequences in a dozen other pictures on and off the MGM lot, as, for instance, Selznick's 1937 *Prisoner of Zenda*, for which he shot the duel scene between Ronald Colman and Douglas Fairbanks Jr.

The end result of a studio attitude that viewed the director as a glorified mechanic was that, for the next quarter-century, with the exceptions of Vincente Minnelli and Fred Zinnemann, no important director was launched by MGM. Mayer and Thalberg employed great directors, but they all were well out of their developmental stage by the time they arrived in Culver City. Stars would be created by the dozens, but under Mayer the business of MGM was to buy established writing and directing talent that could work within the MGM system.

For all of Louis's conservatism and horror of the current Russian political experiment, MGM was the very essence of a collective, where the group took precedence over any individual. Even A list directors would happily step in and shoot second unit footage for less distinguished talent, as William Wellman did on *China Seas* and *Tarzan Escapes*, as Victor Fleming did for Richard Thorpe on *The Crowd Roars*.

It's clear that the rise of the auteur theory and director-oriented criticism, when even mediocre or barely competent directors without a trace of personal style claimed possessory or vanity credits was a reaction against the Mayer-Thalberg ethos.

Thalberg justified this attitude toward directors with a canned speech he would often deliver to a director who was working at Metro for the first time. "I consider the director is on the set to communicate what I expect of my actors. It's my experience that many directors only realize 75% of our scenarios, and while audiences never know how much they missed, I do. You . . . have [an] individualistic style and I respect [that]. It's one of the principal reasons we want you here. But if you can't conform to my system, it would be wiser not to start your film at all."

MGM directors usually shot entire scenes in long shots, then would restage the same scene for each separate angle and close-up, giving the editing department a vast amount of material to play with. Van Dyke was so sure of himself that he would shoot only the beginning and ending dialogue of a long shot, then pick up close-ups as he planned to use them. He always got what he wanted; if a powerful department head didn't give him what he wanted, Van Dyke would dismiss his company for the day.

Editor Ralph Winters remembered, "He knew where each shot went. He would do the coverage, but not as much as other directors. And he would only print one take."

Beginning in 1932, the directors' ranks would be filled out by the remarkably underrated Victor Fleming. "Vic was very positive, very serious," said George Sidney. "No jokes. He wore gray suits, nothing but gray suits. He had a closet full of gray suits. Once, at a funeral, he showed up in a dark blue suit, and we were all shocked."

"Vic had gray hair and was about six foot three inches. All man. And when he got ready to make a picture, he'd always get a little sick to his stomach. 'I don't feel well,' he'd tell me. 'Would you go check these locations for me?' I did a lot of little things like that for him. I was doing a test of a young actress named Edythe Marrener for a part in Vic's *Dr. Jekyll and Mr. Hyde*. He was watching and he came over to her. 'Do you understand this scene? This boy has come back to you, and what he's brought you is not expensive, but it's special—a bottle filled with water from all the seven seas. Do you understand?'

"So she said yes, and Vic said, 'Okay, George, take over.'

"And then she came over to me and said, 'What the fuck did I agree that I understood?'

"That was so like Vic; he wasn't like George Cukor, who would talk to an actor for four minutes before a scene. Edythe Marrener didn't get the part, but she changed her name to Susan Hayward."

Beneath a tough, masculine exterior, Fleming was extremely empathetic. "Fleming was directing an added scene for *The Crowd Roars*, which Richard Thorpe had directed," remembered Gene Reynolds. "I'm playing Robert Taylor as a boy, and I'm in a saloon with my old man, played by Frank Morgan. A telegram falls out of his pocket. I pick it up and it's the news that my mother has died, and I had to cry.

"I had difficulty with it. And Fleming said to me, simply, 'Pick it up, and look at it, and . . . you cry!' And *he* began to cry! I could see it coming over him. And I went along with him, with his sensitivity, and *I* cried."

"Vic was a very shy man," remembered Ralph Winters. "He backed away from fame. He stuttered you know; whenever he had a tough scene, he would have trouble explaining what he wanted, but he always got it."

Fleming may have been awkward with actors, but he was extremely assertive with his employers. For eight years, he refused to sign a long-term contract, accepting only one-picture deals for prices that began at $40,000 a picture. (*Red Dust* would earn him an additional $5,000 if he shot it within eighteen days.) In February 1934, he signed a one-year contract for $2,500 a week; he didn't sign a multiyear contract until 1939, the annus mirabilis during which he directed most of both *Gone With the Wind* and *The Wizard of Oz*.

When he finally did sign a term deal, Fleming banished the hated morality clause, and included a provision that no producer could be credited on a Fleming picture without his permission. When Sam Zimbalist asked for a producer credit on *Tortilla Flat*, Fleming said okay, but only if he, Fleming, got three months' paid vacation.

As Irene and Edie became adults, their relationship with their father grew stormy. The obstinacy that was such a large part of the father had showed up in the character of his children. By the time the girls graduated from high school, they had begun the three-sided battle of wills that would continue for the rest of their lives.

Mayer wasn't comfortable with them dating—the sphere of influence again—but, on the other hand, it would reflect badly on him if his daughters became old maids. "Isn't it enough that I'm Louis B. Mayer," he shouted irrationally at Edie. "Can't you get yourself a husband?"

A few months later, she did. She fell in love with an aspiring producer named William Goetz. "On our first date," she once said, "I laughed more than I'd laughed in my entire life." Mayer wasn't thrilled—Mayer wouldn't have been thrilled by his daughters marrying anybody outside the House of Rothschild—but Goetz was at least presentable. "He's a very nice young man," he told Edie. "But what's with the jokes?"

Edie and Bill wanted a small wedding, but Mayer overrode their objections by saying, "The wedding isn't for you. It's for *me*." A man in his position had an obligation to show the community that he could marry his daughter off in style. Edie began to cry and rushed out. Mayer tried to make amends through Margaret—he generally said he was sorry through a third party—and the mother spent several days working on the daughter's sympathy.

One morning, Mayer appeared in his daughter's doorway and fell onto his knees. He crawled over to her, grabbed her hands, held them to his face and started to sob. Anything she wanted, she could have. Anything at all, just as long as she would always be his beloved Edi-La. Edie also began to cry. She would do anything to make him happy, she said. "You say you love this boy? Then how you get married shouldn't matter. You should have only eyes for him!"

And so, on March 30, 1930, Edith Mayer married William Goetz at the Biltmore Hotel in a gown by Adrian, with seven hundred guests and more stars in attendance than there were in heaven, let alone at other girls' weddings.

As far as Irene was concerned, her father had bought Edie a husband, and she resented the fact that her father forbade her to marry until Edie was married, simply because Edie was the elder. L.B. was initially appalled by Irene's growing love for David Selznick; he hadn't liked or respected Lewis Selznick when he'd distributed his pictures during the New England days. "Keep away from that schnook," Mayer yelled. "He'll be a bum, just like his father." But Irene wasn't L.B.'s daughter for nothing. She had the same indomitable will, and she also had her father's instincts without the rampant emotionalism.

After Edie married Bill Goetz, David and Irene figured the coast was clear, and David went to Mayer's office to ask for his daughter's hand. The date needed to be late April, so Selznick could set the fall production schedule at Paramount and take his wife on a leisurely honeymoon.

Mayer exploded. "You've made travel plans?" Was David asking for Irene or telling him he was taking her? "Let's be practical. We just finished the biggest wedding that ever happened in this town. What do I look like, I give another one like that?" He asked them to wait for another six weeks, mid-June. In fact, how about June 14, the day he had married Margaret?

Selznick refused. Not only did he want his own wedding, on his own anniversary, but his own urgent physical needs took precedence over pleasing his father-in-law. Mayer found the mention of his future son-in-law's sexual desires—and by extension his own daughter's—offensive. Selznick stormed out. Irene stayed, and told her father that she had been an obedient and loving daughter and intended to stay that way.

But.

She loved David Selznick, was going to marry him, and after the marriage she fully intended to put his interests ahead of her father's. The argument went on. Irene finally pulled a tactic out of her father's repertoire, and fainted. That night, Margaret Mayer took up the battle on her daughter's behalf; it was the only time Irene ever heard her mother raise her voice.

That ferocious meeting in Mayer's office was never mentioned again by either L.B. or Irene. He let it go, and so did she. "Nevertheless," she remembered, "that day in Dad's office cost him a certain latitude with me . . . I must add, though, that from that day on he never again tried to run my life."

On April 29, 1930, Irene married David Selznick at a comparatively simple ceremony at Mayer's house. The ceremony was late; Mayer took his prospective son-in-law into the library and locked the door behind them. For forty-five minutes, the two men engaged in heated conversation while Irene grew increasingly frantic. Finally, L.B. emerged and curtly told his daughter, "You may start the wedding." Photographs of the wedding show grim faces on the bride and her father.

L. B. Mayer had finally run up against someone he couldn't bluff, seduce, outmaneuver, or overwhelm. That it was his own daughter must have filled him with a mixture of horror and grudging respect. As for Selznick, he began addressing Mayer as "Dad," although, in later years, as he became more successful, "Dad" was gradually replaced by "L.B."

Mayer's wedding gift to his daughters was a house of their choice. Edie and Bill chose a Wallace Neff Normandy house in Bel Air, while Irene chose a Roland Coates Georgian mansion across the street from Pickfair. In August of 1932, Irene gave birth to Jeffrey Selznick, L.B.'s first grandchild. "Dear little mother of my grandson miss you," L.B. wired from Washington, where he was consulting with Hoover about the upcoming election. "Miss you David and Jeff very much. . . . President delighted your happiness. Will hustle to return soon."

Selznick and Mayer would become very close, but Mayer initially erected barriers for his son-in-law to jump over. A year after the marriage, when Selznick was making some exploratory moves toward independent production, Mayer made it clear to other major distributors that any such plan would result in a stampede of producers and directors toward independent production, inevitably leading to the breakup of the major studios. Without a releasing agreement, Selznick couldn't get his company off the ground, and that was the end of that.

Still, it seemed like a good idea to Selznick. He would keep it in mind.

Part of the perennial level of anxiety that afflicted the moguls was the fact that Mayer and his brethren were isolated from the other monied Jews of Los Angeles. "They were men who made all that money and realized they were still a bunch of Goddamned Jews," said Rabbi Edgar Magnin. "So they looked for other ways to cover it up."

The impetus behind Mayer's climb, however, was not the bumptious optimism he prominently displayed, but fear—of failure, of being passed over, of having to return to Saint John. That's why any kind of confrontation was an even-money bet to end with him raising his fists or bursting into tears—extreme behavior calculated to get him what he wanted. But Louis couldn't, wouldn't channel that same aggression into the films of Metro-Goldwyn-Mayer. Instead, fear would be transmuted into optimism, into parables of an honest striving bereft of insecurity or racial prejudice. He would be sunny, effusive L. B. Mayer, the man who would tell his associates that his studio had greatness "because our people are bound together by love. We have no hate here, we have love. I love Irving. I love everybody"—and here he thought for a moment— "except John Gilbert, Sam Goldwyn, and Charlie Chaplin."

Before he had been unceremoniously removed from his own company, Sam Goldwyn had been unceremoniously removed from Famous Players-Lasky: he was just impossible to work with.

No matter; the third time would be the charm. Goldwyn took $600,000 for his stock in the Goldwyn Company, and negotiated a production loan for $200,000 from the Commercial National Bank with the help of bank director Cecil B. DeMille, who okayed the loan in spite of the fact that the professional bankers were leery.

Samuel Goldwyn, Inc., began in 1923 and, over the next thirty-six years, made such distinguished pictures as *Stella Dallas* (both 1925 and 1937 versions), *Dodsworth*, *Wuthering Heights*, *The Little Foxes*, *Pride of the Yankees*, *The Best Years of Our Lives*, and *Guys and Dolls*.

The equivalent successes of Goldwyn and Mayer didn't change either man's opinion of the other; when they would meet at industry functions, they would either ignore each other or exchange curt nods.

MGM's adherence to two main themes—great personalities the audience loved and stories that showcased the personalities' most attractive characteristics—carried them through every difficulty. The MGM system was in full flower, and the studio's prevailing ethos had taken hold, but at a fearsome cost. The incessant responsibilities of the studio ramped up Mayer's persistent hypochondria; he was always getting examined for one complaint or another. But the pressures were real as well as imagined; one day, he fainted on the third tee of the Hillcrest Country Club.

Worried about his own health, L.B. also guarded Thalberg's. When an agent bypassed the bureaucracy and gave Thalberg a story directly, causing him to be up all night reading, Mayer called the agent on the carpet. "He's not a well man and he had to sit up all night reading your book," Mayer said, then broke down into grief-stricken sobs. The alarmed agent said that nobody had ever told him that the chain of command at MGM couldn't be violated. Mayer told him not to let it happen again.

In January 1928, producer Joe Schenck, Buster Keaton's brother-in-law, had sold Keaton's contract to MGM. The comedian was to get $3,000 a week for two pictures a year, with his production company receiving 25 percent of the net profits, and Keaton getting 25 percent of the production company's 25 percent. This made Keaton the third-highest-paid actor on the lot. Of all the stars in the MGM stable, there were none that could be considered a star comedian, a designated slot that Keaton was clearly supposed to fill. Charlie Chaplin, among many others, told him not to acquiesce. "They'll ruin you helping you. They'll warp your judgment. You'll get tired of arguing for things you know are right." Keaton went along anyway. It was, he remembered, "the worst mistake of my career."

Keaton believed that his trump card was his friendship with Irving Thalberg, who had courted Constance Talmadge, Keaton's sister-in-law, and who occasionally played cards with Keaton. For a time, even Mayer was friendly. But friendship was one thing, and MGM another. Before long, Keaton's crew was absorbed into the machine and was busy on other people's pictures. Keaton always insisted that MGM assigned him a plethora of writers instead of the three or four gag men he was used to; Keaton remembered twenty-two writers working on *The Cameraman*, but studio records indicate only five: no more burdensome a group than Keaton was used to. Still, there is no doubt Keaton was overwhelmed by a studio bureaucracy intent on housebreaking him into making, not Keaton movies, but MGM movies.

Other than *The Cameraman*, Keaton's MGM pictures would never be more than mediocre, and most of them were appalling, but he was helpless to do anything about it; contractually, he only had consultation rights about story and direction, and the decision of the producer was final.

Yet Keaton's MGM films all tended to make good profits, something that his silent masterpieces hadn't always accomplished. Keaton had been making great films for a small audience, but at MGM he found a mass audience—and made inferior films. Keaton's sense of what was good and bad must have been shaken. His drinking was spiraling out of control, and the delays caused by his absences were costing the company money. Thalberg, his erstwhile friend, was firing off telegrams reminding him that his unprofessional behavior was costing the company a "considerable loss."

Mayer had different ways of handling different people. When Jackie Cooper began acting like the child he was and held up production, he was brought to Mayer's office. Mayer sat the boy down in his lap, then began to sob.

"Jackie, the whole studio is resting on your shoulders!" he gasped through his tears, thoroughly terrifying the child.

But an adult alcoholic was not so easily reached. The company tried everything except making good Keaton pictures. They teamed him up with Jimmy Durante, rendering two brilliant comedians equally ineffective because of impossible chemistry. They assigned him material derived from plot-heavy Broadway farces.

Mayer gave him a $10,000 bonus and a three-month, all-expenses-paid European vacation. Nothing seemed to help. Then the studio was embarrassed when one of Keaton's girlfriends got into a brawl with him in his dressing room. Shortly afterward, his wife filed for divorce. Mayer and Thalberg tried to hammer out a reasonable explanation for the public, then just told Keaton to pay off the girlfriend. By the time Keaton's next picture, *Speak Easily,* was completed, the studio figured that his absences had cost them eleven shooting days, or about $33,000.

Louis was a very light drinker himself ("Maybe half a dozen times a year he would have a Dubonnet, but that was the most he ever drank," remembered Irene), so he was not terribly sympathetic to Keaton's problem. Then there was the fact that he ran the studio on a tight rein. "If they wanted to save you, they tried to solve your problem," remembered Maurice Rapf, "but for somebody they wanted to get rid of, they wouldn't bother."

By early 1932, Keaton wasn't showing up at the studio, and Mayer was sending threatening telegrams and registered letters ordering him to appear at such and such a place on such and such a date. Typically, Keaton ignored the telegrams; typically, Mayer would suspend Keaton's salary for not showing up. Keaton countered by refusing to cash checks MGM had issued for weeks he had shown up. All this only served to enrage Mayer.

After *What! No Beer?* was finished, Mayer took weeks to consider what to do about Keaton. Finally, he came to a decision: "You are hereby notified that for good and sufficient cause we hereby terminate the contract with you dated October 5, 1932," read Mayer's memo. Keaton was completely taken aback. He blamed Mayer—for the rest of his life, Mayer would usually be referred to as "that SOB."

When Thalberg heard about the termination, he was upset. "Go ahead, argue with me," said Mayer. "Show me where I'm wrong." Thalberg did his best, arguing that Keaton's marital problems and divorce had been the root cause of his problems, and probably adding that he was still good box office (*The Passionate Plumber* had made a profit of $186,000; *What! No Beer?* had come out in the black by $132,000). Mayer relented, and Thalberg put out feelers about Keaton's return. With all the delusional grandiosity of the drunk, Keaton refused to come back unless Mayer apologized. That was that.

Thalberg liked Keaton, and he brought the Marx Brothers over to MGM when they washed out of Paramount. But no one remembered him laughing at any of them.

Sound brought the music of the Broadway revue to the movies, and gave it a worldwide audience. L.B. liked operetta and opera, in the form of heartrending arias, and was intent on transmitting his enthusiasm to the mass audience. He brought Metropolitan Opera star Lawrence Tibbett to the studio for some films that proved unsuccessful, but as always, once an idea lodged in his head, he'd keep circling it until another opportunity presented itself. He tried Jeanette MacDonald and Maurice Chevalier, tried Jeanette MacDonald and Ramon Novarro, then tried Ramon Novarro and Evelyn Laye.

Mayer's determination to revive the operetta, a genre that was dying on Broadway, finally bore fruit with Nelson Eddy, a special favorite of Ida Koverman's, who prodded Mayer into signing him so the studio would have somebody to pair with Jeanette MacDonald. Years later, Mayer himself would take the lead in signing a far more talented singer named Mario Lanza.

MacDonald has suffered more than any other star of her generation for the unpardonable sin of going out of style, which obliterated her delicious sensuality in the films she made for Lubitsch at Paramount, as well as her more prim but by no means negligible charm at MGM, where she basically had to play two parts—carrying the dialogue of the terrible actor she was working with as well as her own by slightly overplaying in response to his presence in an attempt to make him seem more compelling than he actually was.

The Eddy-MacDonald operettas were a breakthrough commercially—*Naughty Marietta* made more than $400,000 profit, while *Rose Marie* exploded and returned profits of nearly $1.5 million. Add *San Francisco*, with a clear profit of $2.3 million, and L.B. had a major female star on his hands. And Jeanette MacDonald knew it too.

Sam Marx remembered sitting outside L.B.'s office for an appointment, only to have MacDonald vault in front of him when the door opened, saying, "Sam, I promise not to be more than half an hour." MacDonald, not Garbo, was the true diva of the lot.

Mayer—and Ida Koverman—indulged most of her whims; on the first day of every new film, she would get dressed in her lucky costume, an Old Mother

Hubbard cloak with a hood, and burst into his office, asking for his blessing. Others may have rolled their eyes at MacDonald's coy affectations on and off screen, but she was the first of Mayer's *shiksa* goddesses to spell "class," and for years she could do no wrong.

For Jeanette, behavior that would have brought other actresses a blast of rage, if not outright exile, were countenanced. MacDonald basked in her power, while making sure to specify that her presence was "studio-requested," so she could deduct the costs of her clothes from her personal appearances.

MacDonald and Eddy burned out fairly quickly—the stock of likely costume operettas with marketable titles and scores was limited, and the films seemed awfully stodgy next to the Arthur Freed musicals the studio began making as World War II heated up. But for a time they, and the musicals of the amazing tap dancer Eleanor Powell, constituted a triumphant vindication of one of L.B.'s hunches.

Mayer had now attained a level of respectability he cherished, and the Los Angeles papers were full of honors bestowed. He was elected to the executive committee of the American Jewish Committee; duly noted. He was presented a life membership with the San Francisco Shriners at the Palace Hotel; duly noted. Throughout the 1930s and 1940s, he would be available for charity lunches, to head up one fund-raising campaign or another, and would be happy to accept the awards of recognition that inevitably come to those who head up fund-raising campaigns.

When he lunched with Hoover at the White House early in 1932, it was worth ten inches of copy, in which he indulged in sports metaphors to explain the Depression: "I have observed that when Babe Ruth strikes out he is a bum, but when he hits the ball for a home run he is a hero. Being President of the United States is much like being in that situation."

He engaged in political punditry: "I believe when November comes around you will find that the people will not want to make a change in the White House. A man who has studied the situation for four years is the man to cure the depression . . . it will only delay recovery to put a new man in."

At times, these occasions would tempt Mayer to speak without preparing his remarks, usually a bad idea. "The last words spoken on earth by Jesus Christ were 'Love one another,'" he told one enclave, proving that he was no Bible scholar.

Mayer went all-out for Hoover in 1932. He campaigned for him; he—or, more likely, MGM—paid for the lighting, the balloons, and dictated the songs the bands and the organ played during demonstrations at the Republican convention in Chicago.

Mayer tried to sway William Randolph Hearst to throw his support to Hoover, but Hearst was appalled at the suggestion: "Dear Louis: I am sorry but I cannot conscientiously support that man. He is selfish and stupid. He injects himself into the present situation for his own advantage. He will harm his own party, handicap the whole conservative movement, and strengthen the hands of the radicals. . . . If you don't suppress this hoodoo, your party will lose its chance, too, of electing a Congress as well as a President. His name is an anathema to the American public."

Mayer's efforts on behalf of his party attracted the notice of *Variety*, which ran a shamelessly flattering editorial headlined "Louis B. Mayer a National Figure." "Show business owns in Mayer an international statesman. . . . For Mayer's advice [is] sought on the domestic and foreign problems of state. One gets nothing of this by speaking to Mayer. If [talking to] a showman, he talks show business only, probably believing anything else would be wasted on a showman. Yet one of the biggest problems of the show business is where Louis Mayer picked up his statesmanship? Where did he find time or opportunity to grow so intimately familiar with politics over here or over there, that he can converse with the world's leaders on that subject? Mayer hasn't been abroad for years. Yet there he is, Louis B. Mayer, a national figure, of politics and the show business, the only American holding that dual honor."

At the studio, L.B. called an employee meeting where he told everyone to vote for his man and to wear Hoover buttons. Neither his oratory nor his position of power helped: the day after Mayer's speech, all the members of the production crews showed up wearing FDR buttons, as did the vast majority of the electorate.

Even after Hoover's loss in a landslide to Roosevelt in the 1932 election, L.B. and the former President stayed in close touch, often getting together whenever Hoover passed through Los Angeles.

Despite Mayer's strenuously maintained respectability, MGM in the early 1930s was no paradise for prudes. "There was an opium den on the lot," remembered Maurice Rapf. "It was in the building next to the gate that led to the area that's now the Thalberg Building. I went there with Edgar Allan Woolf, who worked a lot with Florence Ryerson. Woolf was a homosexual and a dope addict. He wanted me to try the opium. It was lunchtime and the place was mostly full of writers, with Woolf as the leader of the group."

For either booze or betting, the center of operations was the studio barber-shop. Saturday mornings were entirely devoted to placing bets on college foot-ball games. If they weren't actually in production, directors, writers, and actors would usually be found at the barbershop placing bets, then going to the USC football game. Thalberg knew about the gambling because he used to make bets himself.

Like the mayor of a well-run city, Mayer cut himself in for a taste of some of the illegitimate activities. Set decorator Edwin Willis had an antiques business on Santa Monica Boulevard that was stocked with a lot of the furniture pur-chased for the MGM movies—Mayer had a cut. One friend of Mayer crony Frank Orsatti was the studio's designated bootlegger; after Prohibition, he opened a liquor store around the corner from the studio—Mayer had a cut.

Tabs were kept on who was moonlighting or having an affair by the studio's branch of Western Union, and anything of a scandalous nature landed on Mayer's desk.

Around Hollywood, everybody else was either going broke or narrowly avoiding going broke—by early 1933, three studios (Paramount, Fox, and RKO) were in bankruptcy or receivership—but MGM was holding its market value and continued to turn a profit. While the market value of the other major stu-dios plummeted because of the decline in the value of their theatrical real es-tate (Paramount went from $300 million to $117 million in three years), Metro's assets held steady at $130 million.

L.B.'s primary problem in this period was his partner, Irving Thalberg. Nineteen thirty-two would prove to be a momentous year in their relationship. The death under suspicious circumstances of his friend Paul Bern and the ac-cumulated exhaustion had worn Thalberg down. He began making loud noises about wanting out of his job. "The boy is getting spoiled," Mayer told Nick Schenck. "People are telling him how good he is. I believe it is turning his head a little. There are all kinds of offers."

In September 1932, the three men gathered for a meeting and Thalberg let them have it: he wanted out of MGM—a year's leave of absence.

"Irving, that is silly," said Schenck. "You have a contract up till 1937. I have no right to release you. I don't own the company. You are a valuable man."

"I don't feel well. The responsibility is too great. I would like to go away and come back and then see what I want to do." Out of the question, said Schenck.

Talk continued, tempers grew frayed, voices were raised. "What in hell do you do with all your money?" yelled Schenck. It was 1932, for God's sake; $400,000 a year in salary and bonuses wasn't enough?

"I was watching Schenck," said Mayer later. "His fingernails were purple as he held on to the side of his chair. Irving was riding him terribly hard and driving him. He told Schenck he didn't give a damn; that he [Schenck] was cold as ice, that he wasn't even human just as long as we made lots of money for the company. Oh, it was just fierce! And Schenck kept yelling back, 'Damn it, I've been decent and right with you! This is a corporation! I've got legal responsibilities!' Oh, it was hell!"

Mayer's recollection of the confrontation came in a 1938 deposition. "Because income taxes were swallowing [Thalberg's income] up and he felt, considering the strain he had gone under during three years, he wasn't a strong fellow. . . . He would rather quit and retire and not work in pictures unless there was some way . . . for him and his family in the event anything happened to him and he got played out. . . .

"I wouldn't take what Schenck took. . . . But Irving fought a hard battle and nothing could convince him that he ought to go on and discharge his obligations. He said that we had built plenty of millions: that he didn't have any scruples. . . . It was hell. It went on for a long time."

Finally, Schenck threatened to sue. Thalberg laughed and walked out of the room. The solution was unpleasant, but obvious. Only one thing had worked with Thalberg before and they all knew it would probably work again: money.

Thalberg's percentage of the profits had been continually bumped upward. In December 1929, his cut of the profits had been raised from 20 to 30 percent, the additional 10 percent coming directly out of Mayer's own percentage of the profits. In April of 1932, Mayer had again given up money, deducting another 2.5 percent of his profits so that both he and Irving were receiving 37.5 percent of the group profits.

Schenck refused to diminish company profits any more than he already had by giving the Mayer group more than 20 percent of the overall corporate profits. Thalberg's actual options were limited; he was under contract and the courts wouldn't have let him go to another studio, especially not if Mayer got on the phone to the senators and judges he counted as his friends. But MGM was making money, and nobody—not Schenck, not Mayer, not the board of directors—wanted the gravy train to stop running. So Thalberg's bluff wasn't called.

Mayer wasn't about to give up any more money, and Schenck wasn't about to give Thalberg more salary. What about stock? Thalberg said he would consider it if he could buy several hundred thousand shares at $10 apiece (they were currently selling at about $60). Schenck had to placate him somehow. It was finally agreed that if the Mayer group extended their contracts to December 3, 1938, they could have options to buy stock at $30 to $40 a share. Thalberg could buy up to 100,000, Mayer 80,000, and Rubin 50,000.

This contretemps was the beginning of the breach. Twice Mayer had taken money out of his own pocket and presented it to Thalberg, who accepted it as his due. At the same time, the cult of Thalberg was spreading, whose central doctrine was that Irving was a creative genius and Mayer was a glad-handing pencil-pusher—a theology Irving implicitly believed. Alone, neither man could have accomplished half of what they had accomplished together, but Hollywood has always believed in heroes and villains, off screen as well as on. Physically and emotionally, Mayer was typecast for the role of a bad guy.

Now, the studio not only had to contend with the divide between Hollywood and New York—that was normal—but it also had to contend with a divide in its Culver City management. The atmosphere in Culver City gradually grew so poisonous that when Howard Strickling would come to Thalberg with some ordinary question, Thalberg would eye him suspiciously and say, "Did Louie tell you to say this?"

L.B. was genuinely angry, and stayed that way. As screenwriter, novelist, and film biographer Gavin Lambert wrote, "Mayer never denied Thalberg's value to MGM and he was infuriated when Thalberg seemed to be denying MGM's value to himself." This time he wouldn't forgive and forget. Thalberg's relentless acquisitiveness, and the fact that placating him was taking money out of everybody else's pocket, completely alienated Mayer. Hadn't he plucked the boy from the penny-ante clutches of Carl Laemmle? Hadn't he been like a father to the boy? Was all of Loew's Inc. to be consecrated to satisfying his bottomless greed? *What about me? What about L.B.?*

There were no friends among the upper echelon at MGM, only shifting alliances based on self-interest. Irving took to calling Schenck "the All Highest," which did not amuse Schenck, who much preferred "The General." A few years later, at Thalberg's funeral, Schenck would bad-mouth the deceased in front of his widow, until Robert Rubin shushed him.

On Christmas Eve 1932, Thalberg went home from the annual studio party. Two days later, he was laboring with a bad case of the flu. On December 28, he was struck with severe pains in his arm and chest, lasting for about twenty minutes. An electrocardiogram confirmed that he had had a heart attack.

Later that week, Thalberg announced that he was going to take six months off for a vacation at Bad Nauheim, Germany. He went to the trouble of getting a letter from his doctor attesting to the fact that he had actually had a heart attack, presumably to present to Messrs. Mayer and Schenck as the equivalent of a note from his mother.

Thalberg needed to be replaced, at least temporarily. Mayer's first choice was Darryl Zanuck, but he was making plans with Joe Schenck to take over the moribund Fox organization. Mayer then approached David Selznick, who had been quite successful as production chief at RKO. Selznick agreed to a two-year contract.

Although Selznick's own achievements would in time dwarf Thalberg's, neither Mayer nor Schenck thought he was as yet up to running the entire production slate. Mayer came up with the idea of spreading Irving's power among a board of executives that would run the studio while Irving recuperated: Walter Wanger, Harry Rapf, Eddie Mannix, Hunt Stromberg, and Mayer. A month later, Bernard Hyman and Selznick were added to the roster.

For the rest of Mayer's time at MGM, this board would be the ruling body of the studio. People came and went—death took Bernie Hyman; Stromberg and Wanger left to go independent—but Mayer and his trusted lieutenant Mannix stayed put.

Mayer went to Thalberg's house at 707 Ocean Front, a few doors from his own, to tell him about hiring Selznick. The conversation lasted about fifteen loud, contentious minutes, after which Mayer hurriedly left the house. As a blusterer whose temper quickly escalated and was often just as quickly forgotten, he must have been shocked by the frigid force of Thalberg's infrequent anger.

Sometime between Thalberg's heart attack at Christmas and his vacation in March, Nick Schenck wrote him about the changes he wanted to make at MGM. From the issues Thalberg takes up in a twelve-page memo dated February 2, 1933, which was as close as he ever came to writing a manifesto, Schenck's ideas could be summarized thusly: institute a unit system involving other managers besides Thalberg; remake MGM more along the lines of other studios, especially Warners and Paramount; squeeze more out of the stars and producers; lower overhead.

It was all very curious. Since 1924, Loew's had shown constantly increasing revenue from its MGM subsidiary and a vast array of talent had been assembled. Alone of all the movie companies, MGM was making good profits in the teeth of a terrible international financial crisis. MGM wasn't even close to being broken, but Schenck wanted to fix it anyway.

Summoning all the considerable eloquence of which he was capable, Thalberg responded at length. Without stars, he explained to Schenck, rather as if his superior was unlikely to be mistaken as the brightest executive in the business, a company is in the position of having to start over again each year. A star is not a matter of publicity. Otherwise, what would account for the box office drop in such "splendid" actors as Lew Ayres, Will Rogers, Janet Gaynor, Ruth Chatterton, William Powell, Richard Barthelmess, Chevalier, Colman, and Jolson?

Then Thalberg went on to judge the competition. Paramount? They had never had any idealism in the organization. It was a plant run for the purpose of making money, one year making expensive pictures and the next year making cheaper pictures.

Warner Bros.? He was irrevocably opposed to any policy that would pay short-term profits, but which tended to destroy the industry. He thought many of their pictures were crude and distasteful, appealing only to urban markets and often possessing little entertainment value.

He went on to assert that the movie business could survive only by producing real entertainment, glamour, and stars in good taste. Without these it would emulate vaudeville and die. If Schenck wanted to mimic Warners, Thalberg said, MGM might as well get rid of its high-priced stars and directors, because the down-market scripts that would cut costs would be ridiculous for the kind of talent MGM had carefully assembled.

Thalberg then asserted that for fifteen years he had been reading bad scripts with good ideas, that he had "inspired" the boys into making good scripts with better ideas. He took credit for rescuing specific, recent MGM pictures such as *Mata Hari* and *The Champ*.

Thalberg closed by asserting that there was only one way, the traditional MGM way—his way. The alternative was disaster: he wrote that if Schenck's plan was implemented, within six to eighteen months some of the MGM actors would be commercially annihilated, not to mention the company's prestige and profits. He was, he said, personally humiliated by some of the provisions in the contract that had been given David Selznick ($4,000 a week and no supervision). He was afraid that Selznick's hiring would provoke a breakdown of discipline and stimulate a lot of office politics from people desperately trying to ingratiate themselves with either Thalberg or Selznick.

There are several things clear from this document. One, Schenck and Mayer's plan to decentralize production was already well underway long before

Thalberg left on his vacation in March—he wasn't stabbed in the back by a telegram while on vacation in Europe, as Norma Shearer later claimed.

Two, Thalberg was highly analytical, supremely self-confident, and well considered about stars and other studios—a definitive example of a man capable of encompassing the big picture. Part of what he's doing in the letter is defending his business model, but he's completely unable to imagine a different model—in the movie business, hubris is a basic personality trait.

Third, the letter encapsulates the difference between the East Coast and the West Coast, the exhibitor mentality (Schenck) versus the producer mentality (Thalberg). Thalberg is talking about story values and putting stars and characters across—the things he habitually worried about—and is arguing far over the head of Schenck, who just wanted more pictures at lower costs.

Thalberg's arrogance—"More than any single person in Hollywood," he proclaimed to the writer Allen Rivkin, "I have my finger on the pulse of America"—led him to believe that there was only one kind of moviemaking—his own.

Obviously, Thalberg's letter didn't work. On February 8, he sent Schenck a one-paragraph note saying that he did not consent or acquiesce to the changes that were underway, and upon his return from his trip intended to protect his legal rights.

On February 23, 1933, a few weeks after their argument over the arrival of David Selznick, L.B. sat down and wrote an extraordinary letter to Thalberg:

> Dear Irving,
>   I cannot permit you to go away to Europe without expressing to you my regret that our last conference had to end in a loss of temper, particularly on my part. It has always been my desire to make things as comfortable and pleasant for you as I know how, and I stayed away from you while you were ill because I knew that if I saw you it was inevitable that we would touch on business, and this I did not want to do until you were strong again. . . .
>   It is unfortunate that the so-called friends of yours and mine should be only too glad to create ill feeling, and attempt to disrupt a friendship and association that has existed for about ten years. Up to this time they have been unsuccessful, but they have always been envious of our close contact and regard for each other.

If you will stop and think, you cannot mention a single motive or reason why I should cease to love you or entertain anything but a feeling of real sincerity and friendship for you. During your absence from the studio I was confronted with what seems to me to be a Herculean task, but the old saying still goes—"the show must go on." Certainly we [Mayer and Schenck] could not permit the company to go out of existence just because the active head of production was taken ill and likely to be away from business for a considerable length of time. I consider it my duty and legal obligation under our contract to take up the burden anew where you left off, and to carry on to the best of my ability. I believe I have done so, without prejudice or partiality to anyone in the studio. My only concern has been to organize things so that we will make the very best pictures possible.

I have felt your absence from the Studio very keenly, and have never consciously done anything that might reflect on you, and this I repeat regardless of what anyone may tell you. Of course, I cannot guard myself every moment as to what I say, and which remarks may be misconstrued by malicious scandalmongers and gossipers who thrive on other people's unhappiness.

I regret very much that when I last went to see you to talk things over I did not find you in a receptive mood to treat me as your loyal partner and friend. I felt an air of suspicion on your part towards me, and want you to know if I was correct in my interpretation of your feeling, that it was entirely undeserved. When I went to see you I was wearied down with the problems I have been carrying, which problems have been multiplied because of the fact that the partner who has borne the major portion of them on his shoulders, was not here. Instead of appreciating the fact that I have cheerfully taken on your work, as well as my own, and have carried on to the best of my ability, you chose to bitingly and sarcastically accuse me of many things, by innuendo which I am supposed to have done to you and your friends. Being a man of temperament, I could not restrain myself any longer, and lost my temper. Even when I did so I regretted it, because I thought it might hurt you physically.

Regardless of how I felt, or what my nervous condition was, I am big enough to apologize to you, for you were ill and I should have controlled my feelings.

I am doing everything possible for the best interest of yourself, Bob [Rubin], myself and the Company, and I want you to know just how I feel towards you; and if possible, I want you to divest yourself of all suspicion, and believe me to be your real friend, and to know that when I tell you I have the greatest possible affection and sincere friendship for you, I am telling you the truth.

I hope this trip you are about to take will restore you to even greater vigor than you have ever before enjoyed, and will bring you back so that we may work together as we have done for the past ten years.

And let me now philosophize for a moment: Anyone who has said that I have a feeling of wrong towards you will eventually have cause to regret their treachery, because that is exactly what it would be, and what it would be on my part if I had any feeling other than what I have expressed in this letter towards you. I assure you I will go on loving you to the end.

I am going to take the liberty of quoting a bit of philosophy from Lincoln. This is a quotation which I have on my desk, and one which I value highly:

"I do the very best I know how, and the very best I can, and I mean to keep doing so until the end. If the end brings me out right, what is said against me won't amount to anything. If the end brings me out wrong, ten angels swearing I was right will make no difference."

I assure you, Irving, you will never have the opportunity of looking me in the eye and justly accusing me of disloyalty or of doing anything but what a good friend and an earnest associate would do for your interest, and for your comfort.

If this letter makes the impression on you that I hope it does, I should be awfully glad to see you before you go, and to bid you Bon Voyage. If it does not, I shall be sorry, and will pray for your speedy recovery to strength and good health.

With love and regards, believe me Faithfully yours . . .

Two days later, Thalberg responded:

I was deeply and sincerely appreciative of the fact that you wrote me a letter, as I should have been very unhappy to have left the city without seeing you. I was indeed sorry that the words between us should have caused on your part a desire not to see me, as I assure you frankly and honestly they did not have that effect on me. We have debated and disagreed many times before, and I hope we shall many times again. For any words that I may have used that aroused bitterness in you, I am truly sorry and I apologize.

I'm very sorry that I have been unable to make clear that it has not been the actions or the words of any—as you so properly call them—so-called friends, whose libelous statements were bound to occur that have in any way influenced me. If our friendship and association could be severed by so weak a force, I am sure it would long ago have been ruptured by that source.

There are, however, loyalties that are greater than the loyalties of friendship. There are the loyalties to ideals, the loyalties to principles without which friendship loses character and real meaning—for a friend who deliberately permits the other to go wrong without sacrificing all— even friendship—has not reached the truest sense of that ideal. Furthermore the ideals and principles were ones that we had all agreed upon again and again in our association, and every partner shared equally in the success that attended the carrying out of those principles.

I had hoped that the defense of these principles would be made by my three closest friends. I say this not in criticism, but in explanation of the depths of the emotions aroused in me, and in the hope that you will understand. . . .

Please come to see me as soon as it is convenient for you to do so, as nothing would make me happier than to feel we had parted at least as good personal friends, if not better, than ever before. As ever . . .

Pretty words. But the fact that two men who had been talking incessantly since 1922 now had to communicate by letter was an indication of how badly the relationship had broken down.

L.B. had tried salary cuts before, as in an August 1932 letter to all MGM con-tract employees asking for "loyalty and devotion to this organization." It hadn't worked. Ramon Novarro said he hadn't been paid for most of the past year be-cause the studio hadn't assigned him to pictures; Walter Huston said he had only made $80,000 under his MGM contract, compared to $200,000 the year before; Jean Harlow said no, and even Jackie Cooper refused. Also contributing to the bogus aroma of the request was the fact that MGM was, after all, making money.

For the executive staff, the pain was real—Mayer, Thalberg, and Robert Rubin took 35 percent pay cuts effective July 13, 1932, for one calendar year. And, when FDR closed the banks in March 1933, that lent momentum to the cost-cutting impetus and air of national emergency. Columbia and United Artists shut down, Universal suspended all contracts, and Fox announced that nobody would be paid until the banks reopened. Mayer asked for a "voluntary" 50 percent pay cut to keep MGM open, a move that the Academy of Motion Picture Arts and Sciences recommended be implemented throughout the industry.

Merian Cooper of RKO and Harry Cohn of Columbia were adamantly opposed to asking anybody making less than $50 a week to take a cut, while Mayer and Harry Warner argued that the cut had to be unilateral. Joe Schenck, Sidney Kent at Fox, and Sam Goldwyn were in the middle, recommending that all studio employees earning over $50 a week take an immediate cut of 50 percent and those receiving less take a 25 percent cut, said measures to last for at least eight weeks.

On Wednesday, March 8, 1933, Mayer walked into the largest projection room in the studio. His eyes were red, he hadn't shaved, and his expression was bereft. "My friends," he began, with an accompanying gesture of supplication. He stopped, overcome with emotion.

"Don't worry, L.B.," called out Lionel Barrymore. "We all know why you're here. We're with you." Mayer announced that every studio in Hollywood was on the verge of closing its doors if the cut was not accepted; he spoke of a world without soundstages, without movie stars, *without movies!* He spoke of the thousands of innocent little people—clerks, extras—who would be thrown out of work. He said that he wouldn't put the cuts into operation unless the stars, directors, the writers and department chiefs—the people who could most afford to take the losses—signaled their approval.

Barrymore announced that he proposed to accept the cut immediately, and that if everybody followed his lead it would be "for the good of MGM, of Hollywood, and of the country." Ernest Vajda, a screenwriter, stood up and objected, running through a list of MGM's recent hits, wondering why a company that was doing so well would need to enforce salary cuts.

Barrymore drew himself up and announced, "Sir, you are acting like a man on his way to the guillotine who wants to stop for a manicure." There was laughter, some applause, and Mayer smiled. Encouraged, Barrymore began to belabor the metaphor: "The tumbrels are rolling; the guillotine is waiting outside and we're haggling over pennies!" Barrymore and Mayer carried the day. "No more than eight weeks," Mayer promised. "I, Louis B. Mayer, will work to see that you get back every penny when this terrible emergency is over."

After the meeting, Mayer and Ben Thau were crossing an iron bridge from the projection room to the executive office building, when Mayer turned to Thau. "How did I do?" he asked.

"Oh, that L. B. Mayer," said screenwriter Albert Hackett. "He created more communists than Karl Marx."

Merian Cooper and Harry Cohn won their point—no one making $50 or less had to take a cut. Actually, the cuts were in effect for only a brief time—Sam Marx remembered six weeks, others said eight—but none of the money was ever returned. As the screenwriter Frances Goodrich would remember, "Most of us had never had so much money anyway, and we preferred a few tough weeks rather than coming to the end of the pastures of plenty."

It was a truly remarkable display, on both sides. MGM stayed in fine fettle; the forty films it released in the 1932–33 season returned a profit well in excess of $4 million, and in the 1933–34 season, the profit would be $5.7 million.

It's been estimated that the studio saved up to $800,000 through the temporary salary cuts, which went into the general fund of Loew's, Inc., becoming part of the year's profits. In other words, the only people who benefited were those who had a piece of Loew's profits: Mayer, Thalberg, Schenck, and Rubin. Thalberg had been against the pay cuts, feeling the damage they would do to morale would exceed the value of the savings, but he didn't return the percentage of his profit payoff that derived from the pay cuts.

The cuts led directly to the actors and writers breaking away from the half-hearted guidance of the Academy and moving to form their own bargaining unions. Darryl Zanuck resigned from Warner Bros. because he felt that Jack and Harry were being dishonorable, and he needed to get out from under a family business where he wasn't family.

Zanuck hooked up with Joe Schenck to form 20th Century Pictures. Schenck brought to the table an initial investment of $375,000 from none other than L. B. Mayer, with a matching amount from Joe's brother Nick. All Mayer asked was that his son-in-law Bill Goetz come in as a partner, which came to pass. Mayer proceeded to up the ante by lending out a couple of the prime MGM stars (Clark Gable, Wallace Beery) to help the company get started. Mayer would eventually invest somewhere between $1.2 million and $1.4 million in 20th Century. It was maneuvering on an Olympian scale, and typical of Mayer in that it brought another studio into MGM's sphere of influence, rather than the other way around, as Nick Schenck had intended with his aborted amalgamation with United Artists.

Eventually, Mayer deeded 12.5 percent of his 20th Century (later 20th Century-Fox) holdings each to Edie and Bill, and Irene and David. Selznick refused his share, trying hard to avoid any kind of emotional or practical indebtedness to his father-in-law. (Early in the marriage, he had told Irene to send back a diamond necklace her father gave her, saying, "When I want my wife to have presents like that, I'll buy them.")

Selznick's share was divided between Edie and Bill Goetz, but Irene cast a pall on a fairly simple case of paternal largesse when she agreed to take the stock but asked her father to pay the gift tax, and to reduce her share in order to compensate for the tax. L.B. grumbled but did the deal. "You have a very good character," he told his daughter, "but you are not flexible. I'm not sure I want to do business with you in the future."

Mayer was, of course, buying a place for Bill Goetz. For a man of Mayer's orthodox, patriarchal sensibilities, Edie deserved an equivalent standing with Irene, and if her husband couldn't earn it, then he, L.B., would have to buy it. While Bill was an engaging, amiable man, nobody had as yet detected a burning creative fire residing within him. ("Goetz wouldn't recognize a good script from a roll of toilet paper," snarled Zanuck. "[But] so long as he keeps his father-in-law's money in our company, he can work for me as long as he likes.") No longer would Goetz be a *tummler* at the banquet; now, Bill Goetz would be a player, worthy of his wife and, more to the point, worthy of his father-in-law.

Louis would be as sensitive to a slight directed at Goetz as he would be to one directed at himself. When Zanuck took off to Europe for a two-month vacation, he left screenwriter Harry Joe Brown, not Goetz, in charge. When he returned, Mayer asked him to drop by his Santa Monica beach house, where Zanuck found him in a state of frothing rage that was predicated on one basic sentence: "How could you humiliate my son-in-law?" Zanuck managed to placate him—"Bill is a born thumbtack," he told Mayer. "He doesn't function when the thumb is missing"—but he never revised his opinion of Bill Goetz. "He was a very good assistant. He had a banker's kind of mind, which was far away from me. . . . I never thought of him as a creative producer." Later, when Zanuck went off to World War II, he did leave Goetz in charge.

Mayer and Schenck's new production system made it clear that Mayer had coldly, if brilliantly, effected a palace coup by consolidating power in his own office. From Mayer's point of view, he had made a hard, pragmatic choice because of Thalberg's dicey health and future. No one knew when he would be coming back from his trip to Europe. The studio had movies to make, and somebody had to be in charge, preferably someone who had not already exceeded his life expectancy.

There were, of course, other factors as well; as Mayer would grumble to Sam Katz, "It got so I couldn't hire an office boy without Thalberg's consent."

Finally, L.B. had reasserted his primacy. Irving was a great producer and would continue to be just that. But there could be no more question in anybody's mind about who ran Metro-Goldwyn-Mayer.

When Thalberg finally returned to America in early August 1933, he went to Nick Schenck's house on Long Island for a conference about his future. Schenck tried to placate him, telling him that power had to be spread around to protect the stockholders in case, God forbid, anything happened. Besides, hadn't Irving talked for years about wanting to cut back and not take on the full responsibility for the production program? Well, now was his chance.

They had him and he knew it. Thalberg agreed to run what amounted to an independent unit, with a staggering 37.5 percent of the profits coming to him on pictures he personally produced. Thalberg's unit would have first call on a group of select MGM stars and no supervision from anybody but Schenck. Soon, Cecil B. DeMille's old Spanish bungalow was refitted for Thalberg, re-decorated in white, with a fireplace and massive leather chairs.

Thalberg got back to Culver City on August 19. Al Lewin told Thalberg that the impetus for removing him had actually come from Schenck, and that Mayer had embraced it.

Thalberg remained peevish, and began writing Schenck letters detailing a multitude of slights. He couldn't get the writers he wanted. He couldn't get the directors he wanted. Mayer wouldn't let him take over Franchot Tone, who Thalberg believed was a potential star being misused by the company.

Thalberg came to the unpleasant conclusion that there was no point in try-ing to build up his own roster of stars since it would mean additional grief for him, and only the company—which would presumably put up a fight at being proved wrong about specific actors—would benefit.

Not only that, but, he believed, the studio was demoralized and uninspired. Standards had slipped. When he offered helpful comments and criticisms about MGM pictures, he found they were treated as criticisms of policy or spe-cific producers, and thus resented. Everywhere he looked, he wrote Schenck, he saw incompetence and antagonism.

But he was doing all he could to balance impending corporate doom. Since returning from Europe, Irving had accomplished the following: a script called *Riptide*; a complete story outline on *Marie Antoinette*, "the finest stuff I have ever had since I have been in motion pictures"; a remake of *The Green Hat*, hampered because he could only get the writer he wanted (John Meehan) for a week; a complete continuity for *The Good Earth*; *China Seas*; and S. N. Behrman's *Biography*.

He assured Schenck that, in spite of the multitude of difficulties he was in the process of rising above, he loved the new independent unit he was running and wouldn't go back to supervising the entire studio output for anything.

Such whining from a normally composed, self-possessed personality is startling, but it shows the extent to which even extraordinarily powerful men on the West Coast had to curry favor with their bosses on the East Coast.

Thalberg and Selznick liked each other and were alike in all kinds of ways, starting with taste in material, and continuing through their primary identity as Americans, not Jews, which enabled them to make movies entirely about the *goyim*. (When Edward VIII abdicated, Selznick began sobbing because "it'll wreck the Empire.") Selznick quickly proved himself to be the most gifted producer of his generation. His first MGM picture was *Dinner at Eight*, and was followed in the next two years by *Manhattan Melodrama, Dancing Lady, David Copperfield*, and *A Tale of Two Cities*.

Mayer gave his son-in-law a free hand, and his productions for MGM combined the MGM polish with a melodramatic snap unusual for the studio. When Selznick and George Cukor wanted to make *David Copperfield*, Mayer suggested making it a vehicle for Jackie Cooper—people under contract had to be used, whether they were casting perfection or not—but both Selznick and Cukor bridled and insisted that it had to be an English child. "We argued and won him over," said Cukor. "That was one great strength of Mayer's; he would listen to intelligent reasoning and if he had confidence in you, he could be swayed."

"Thalberg and Selznick were both very smart and very neurotic," remembered Maurice Rapf. "I was with them both in projection rooms, and they would show off. Thalberg would spot something, a spot on a shirt, and he'd make a big fuss about it. 'We've got to reshoot it.' What the hell for? Nobody will see it except you. And Selznick was the same way, sitting in the projection room seeing all kinds of things nobody else saw."

Selznick's respect for Mayer was growing. When Selznick showed him his production of *Night Flight*, Mayer turned to him and said, "It's a thrilling picture, but what the devil are they flying for?"

"What?" said Selznick.

"What are they flying for? You have terrific heroics, death and sacrifice and not a thing that will justify all this suspense and danger in the minds of audiences. Never ask an audience to sympathize with characters that are acting like fools, David." In September 1933, months after the bulk of the picture was shot,

Selznick put the picture back into production for some retakes involving serum being rushed across the Andes to stop an epidemic of infantile paralysis.

Of course, Selznick also came with his full share of human failings. Gambling, for instance, an extension of the essential psychology of the movie producer, but a trait that he would take to a disfiguring level. "David used to place $1,000 as a nominal bet on the roulette wheel," recalled Louise Steiner Elian, the wife of composer Max Steiner. "I saw him lose $10,000 in five minutes. And he acted like it was nothing."

Selznick's favorite place was the Clover Club on Sunset, near Ciro's, a private supper club with exquisite food and a miniature casino next to the dining room. The rumors were that Billy Wilkerson, of the *Hollywood Reporter*, had a large piece of the Clover Club; Wilkerson was also a serious gambler and had come to the not unreasonable conclusion that the only way a gambler could beat the house odds was to own the house.

And now, Nick Schenck began maneuvering yet again, going to Selznick to ask, not if he would be interested in replacing Irving, but if he would be interested in replacing L.B. The approach was made through Joe Schenck. David told his wife, and of course Irene eventually told her father. One night at Sands Point, when L.B. and Irene were Nick's guests, she went into her father's bedroom and told him of the Schencks' plot.

David wrote an angry letter to Nick Schenck, but L.B. refused to let him send it, instead stockpiling the incident as yet another sample of Schenck's perfidy. Meanwhile, he and everyone else at Loew's tried to get Selznick to renew his contract—Mayer, Bob Rubin, and even Thalberg were going to open up the limited profit pool, diminish their own shares, and let David into the inner circle. But Selznick wanted to go it alone and try independent production.

L.B. had to try the direct approach: he showed up unannounced at the Summit Drive house he had bought for Irene and David and walked in talking. "We talk to that boy every day," he announced to Irene, who was standing, thunderstruck, on the stairs. "He listens, he's interested. The next morning we have to begin again. Something happens overnight. Is this where my opposition is, right here in my own family? I happen to know you people are broke. Are you in a position to turn down a million dollars a year?"

Despite the fact that the Selznicks were indeed broke, Selznick went out on his own, and made a triumphant success of it. L.B. responded with fatherly pride.

Mayer felt that he couldn't really relax with his peers; they were all angling for something—an advantage, for one thing. Other than the agent Frank Orsatti, there were few people he could relax with. One was Fanny Holtzmann, another of the strong women he liked in his professional life. Holtzmann was the attorney for Edmund Goulding, Noel Coward, Clifton Webb, and, at one time, John Gilbert. Mayer admired her acumen, as well as the fact that the two of them could relax in the kitchen with some of Margaret's pot roast. Holtzmann knew better than to come on like an intellectual lawyer—she pitched her conversation on the level of one tough pro talking to another, with Yiddish seasoning, something Mayer usually avoided around the family.

When word of the current crack about the true meaning of MGM ("*Mayer's ganze mishpocheh*," i.e., Mayer's whole family) reached him, he told Holtzmann he was proud it was true. "Sure, my nieces and nephews work here, and all my wife's relatives, too. Why shouldn't those with *mazel* [luck] in a family help out the others? It's not as if I tried to pad the payroll with *nudniks* [pests]. They have to make good, or out they go."

Holtzmann saw Mayer as essentially a provincial old-country Jew, with a Talmudist for a father and a kosher butcher for a father-in-law. When Fanny was in Hollywood on the High Holy Days, Mayer would give her tickets to the elegant Reform temple on Wilshire. He wouldn't be there, he told her, but would be praying downtown at the Orthodox Temple Israel his father had liked. "There I put on a *tallis*," he told her. "I stand with other Jews as my people have done for thousands of years—and I feel closer to God."

Mayer genuinely believed in the moral attitudes that accompanied such worship. He was like a real-life Jakie Rabinowitz, the lead character in *The Jazz Singer*, torn between the religion of his father and the fact that he was in a business antithetical to that religion, and sincerely embracing them both. "I don't care what DeMille does, with his naked slave girls," he muttered one day. "No Mayer picture will have bedroom scenes, even where couples are married."

During their occasional kitchen conferences, Louis would present current problems and implicitly ask Fanny for her advice. He bewailed the problem people—drunks, actors who couldn't keep their pants—or panties—on: the people who drove him crazy. Louis was surrounding such people with spies and "publicists" who kept an eye peeled and worked to minimize embarrassments. When Mayer was contemplating firing John Gilbert for earning $250,000 a picture when his pictures weren't grossing much more than that, Holtzmann talked him out of it.

"You don't spit in the soup you have to eat," she told him. "You still own thousands of feet of Gilbert footage usable in many parts of the world. You can keep sending out stills, preserve the illusion in those places. Why throw away the assets in your vaults? Then there's the public relations aspect. How do you think movie fans would feel about Louis Mayer throwing out the former idol who did so much for him?"

"Ha!" snorted Mayer. "He did so much for me, that *shikker*, if I have an ulcer he should get the pill!"

"So leave him alone and maybe he'll drink himself to death. Or let him take a swing at somebody in public, and you'll have legal cause."

Mayer relented, called her a "female Solomon," and let Gilbert work out his contract, after which he did indeed drink himself to death.

Mayer took over as a binding arbitrator, approving budgets, refereeing disputes and turf wars between writers, producers, and directors. Kate Corbaley and Sam Marx stopped weekly story meetings and began taking stories directly to producers they thought most likely to be interested.

If MGM was to be a full-service studio, it needed a program of shorts as a supplement to the MGM features. Initially, L.B. made overtures to Jack White, whose Educational Comedies were responsible for about twenty-four two-reelers annually—most prominently with the odd, interesting Lloyd Hamilton—and another twenty-six one-reelers. White told Mayer he'd need $50,000 per picture, take it or leave it.

"Mayer didn't even look up from a desk drawer he was opening," remembered White. " 'I'll leave it,' he growled. 'I don't want anyone with a goddamned Napoleon complex.' " Nicholas Schenck stepped in and signed a releasing agreement with Hal Roach for all of his films—most importantly Laurel and Hardy and Our Gang. Roach had been a good friend of Marcus Loew's, who was godfather to Roach's son. Although Mayer could have no complaint about the quality of Roach's films, it bothered him that Schenck had presented this to him as a fait accompli, and Roach always believed that Mayer held it against him. "Louis Mayer and I were friendly for years, but he never forgave me for not coming to him first and making the deal with him," said Roach.

Roach always dealt directly with Schenck, discussing the number of films he would provide in the coming year. Then the two men would settle on a budget, almost all of which was provided by Loew's. For MGM, the Roach films were fillers and B pictures, but they were a necessary component of the studio system. Mayer's mania for quality meant that the most menial MGM B movie looked like an MGM movie, and was better than the best effort of Mono-gram or Republic.

Success had given Mayer's always expansive, bossy temperament an even firmer foundation. "I only knew him away from the office," said Maurice Rapf, "and he was just as authoritarian as everybody said he was at the studio. I didn't like him at all. He always seemed to be throwing his weight around about some-thing. And as a matter of fact, he did know a lot, but I didn't realize it. What he knew was how to run a studio, how to pick stars, and, in some respects, how to pick stories."

For all of his spasms of self-approbation, Mayer was extremely vulnerable to slights. One night, Thalberg and his entourage departed on the railroad car for a preview, leaving Mayer to go home for the night. He spotted a new employee, Fred Wilcox, the brother of Nick Schenck's wife, Pansy, and offered to drive him home. After a few minutes, Mayer started to sniffle, then cry, then sob as if his heart was breaking. Wilcox was alarmed and asked what was the matter, if there was anything he could do.

Mayer grabbed Wilcox's hand for support. "They all went off and left me!" he said through his tears. *"They didn't ask me to go along!"* Inside, he would al-ways be the short, ugly little Jew from Saint John.

The MGM commissary sat 225 people and had been designed by Cedric Gib-bons in chrome and green. L.B. had the passion for food of someone who had grown up without enough of it. As he would say, "If [we] were lucky enough to get a roast on a Sunday, you had it in hash for the next ten days." His standard instructions to the commissary manager were: "Try not to lose more than $20,000 a year." That proved to be an impossibility, but even when losses climbed to $50,000 a year, Mayer figured he was saving a lot of money by keep-ing people within the studio grounds.

The commissary, of course, was famous for its chicken soup. Mayer had the head chef spend a couple of weeks at his house, watching Margaret cook, so he could reproduce her recipes. The famous chicken soup was made by taking nine fat two-year-old kosher hens for every three gallons of liquid, stewing them overnight, then separating the broth from the chicken. Add chunks of chicken and delicate matzoh balls, and it was heaven at 35 cents a bowl. "Mr. Mayer wanted everything right, you know," Margaret Booth would say. "There was no reason to go off the lot because you couldn't get better food."

"It was the best chicken soup I've ever had," said Gene Reynolds. "It had big chunks of chicken and noodles. It was delicious, almost a lunch in itself."

The studio catered to the idiosyncrasies of its stars at table just as it did everyplace else. Lionel Barrymore had a special brand of bacon reserved for his exclusive use, and his fried eggs had to be timed to the second; John Barrymore would only drink a special brand of coffee.

As for L.B., aside from chicken soup, he liked beefsteak tomatoes, wanted his beef—usually giant prime steaks—either roasted or broiled rare, and liked whole wheat bread. For dessert, he liked strawberries, sometimes an entire quart, with honey poured over them.

To foster the feeling of one big happy family, L.B. insisted on elaborate, studio-wide decorations at Christmas, complete with numerous trees and plenty of gifts. Likewise, the Fourth of July was devoted to a celebration of his birthday, including a supposed surprise party in the commissary. All the employees would gather, and the MGM orchestra would strike up "Happy Birthday" as Mayer walked in. L.B. would invariably clasp his hand to his heart and say, in a voice choked with emotion, "Oh, how nice! How lovely!" For twenty-five years, he always managed to look surprised.

In the commissary there was a bulletin board that announced all the studio activities such as golf tournaments. The commissary had two tables reserved for specific clienteles, directors and writers, who usually had varying political orientations. The directors' table attracted department heads and some other favored members of other departments, or some writers considered particularly loyal company men (John Lee Mahin, James Kevin McGuinness), while the writers' table was for people who were more interested in a union than they were in MGM. Also reliably holding down a seat at the directors' table was Cedric Gibbons, who always wore a blue suit with a dark red tie, ordered a minute steak, and told wild stories of his sexual exploits with women, with himself as the butt of the joke.

Mayer exercised power not merely for himself, but for the industry. When gossip columnist Louella Parsons threatened to become a little too powerful, he and Ida Koverman took the fading character actress Hedda Hopper and helped promote her until she was given a daily column in the *Los Angeles Times* and a dozen other papers. By 1939, she had achieved parity with Parsons, and could be counted on to give good mentions to Mayer and his extended family.

Mayer liked—no, relished—power, even more than he relished its perquisites. Once, he was in New York and asked an officer of the Dramatists

Guild to explain the way the organization worked. Mayer was given a talk about the guild's history, its insistence on a minimum basic contract, the rights of the author, and other matters, when Mayer exploded.

"Let 'em get fresh with me," he said. "I'll knock 'em down!"

"It isn't one man, Mr. Mayer. This is a group of several hundred people."

Mayer smiled. "Once in a while you've got to show 'em the badge," he said, and turned back his lapel, taking the cuff of his sleeve and rubbing it across an imaginary badge—just like a police chief in one of his own movies.

MGM's influence was so pervasive that a studio like Warners basically defined itself as the antithesis of MGM. "I remember distinctly being called in once," said Warners writer-producer Jerry Wald, "and [being told] that we could not compete with Metro and their tremendous stable of stars, so we had to go after the stories, topical ones, not typical ones. The stories became the stars. . . . We used to say 'T-T-T: timely, topical, not typical.' "

While MGM films weren't as racy as Warner Bros.—nobody's films were as racy as Warners—they weren't all tuxedos and moonlight either. Thalberg productions such as *Riptide* were racy acknowledgments of a woman's right to sexual fulfillment, as was Clarence Brown's *Possessed*. Violence held sway in *The Beast of the City* and *The Secret Six*. John Gilbert, his star descending, starred in *Downstairs* and *Fast Workers*, a couple of knowingly adult films. *Bombshell*, *Dancing Lady*, and *Hollywood Party* had tussles with the Production Code.

MGM's major battle with the Hays Office centered on *Tarzan and His Mate*, which featured a lovely, erotic bathing sequence in which a double for Maureen O'Sullivan was completely nude. The Hays Office rejected the film for its obvious violation of the prohibition against nudity. MGM appealed; appearing for the studio were Mayer, Thalberg, Eddie Mannix, and Bernie Hyman, while the jury consisted of Carl Laemmle Jr., B. B. Kahane, and Winfield Sheehan.

MGM's main argument was that films such as *White Shadows in the South Seas* and *The Common Law* had already featured nudity. Joe Breen of the Hays Office responded that it was "suggestive nudity," not actual and obvious nudity. "After a rather animated discussion between the jurors, the representatives of Metro, and Mr. Breen," stated a Hays Office memo, "the verdict of this office was sustained by the jury." It was the first time that an appeal had been upheld against one of the major studios, and it meant that the Production Code had been suddenly supplied with a gleaming set of teeth.

It's entirely possible that the entire nude sequence was a sort of bargaining chip; that the studio fully expected to have to make changes that they gauged would buy them leeway to keep Johnny Weissmuller and Maureen O'Sullivan in their skimpy animal skins. In any case, the nude sequence continued to be featured in the film's trailer and, evidently, in some circulating prints, and it survives in existing prints today.

Despite their tussle over the *Tarzan* sequel, as far as Mayer was concerned, Joe Breen—the Code enforcer—was someone who could be dealt with. As the producer Val Lewton once described him, "Mr. Breen goes to the bathroom every morning. He does not deny that he does so or that there is such a place as the bathroom, but he feels that neither his actions nor the bathroom are fit subjects for screen entertainment. This is the essence of the Hays Office attitude . . . at least as Joe told it to me in somewhat cruder language."

All very interesting, especially as Mayer was fond of using precisely the same metaphor to make precisely the same point.

When not negotiating with the Hays Office, L.B. was riding herd on his obstreperous crew of filmmakers. Rouben Mamoulian certainly had his hands full on *Queen Christina*. To begin with, there had been Garbo's preference for no rehearsal and the first take, which resulted in a difficult period of adjustment—for Garbo. Then there had been the firing of Laurence Olivier in favor of John Gilbert, Garbo's choice. Gilbert's self-confidence was shot, he was drinking, and he was far from a steadying influence.

Just before production ended, Mamoulian was summoned to Mayer's office, where he was informed that L.B. and everybody else had concluded that the ending was too unhappy. Something else would have to be devised. Mamoulian asked a perfectly sensible question about why nobody had noticed that until now. It had been overlooked, said Mayer, but he was certain that audiences would be depressed. Look at the plot: Christina's lover was dead, and Christina is marooned on the prow of the ship taking her away from her beloved country. That's not sad?

Mamoulian asked if Mayer knew Greek tragedy.

Yes, said Mayer, he knew Greek tragedy.

"Well, it usually has an unhappy ending, but it never depresses the audience. It exhilarates them. . . . I would like to shoot it just the way it is, and if it depresses the [preview] audience, if they walk away miserable, then I'll do something about it [in just] three days of retakes."

That seemed fair to Mayer, but he wanted Mamoulian to explain how the ending could be made exhilarating. "I can't describe it because it's mostly visual imagery. There are sails, there is Garbo, practically no dialogue. But I'll guarantee you will not be depressed."

On the set, Mamoulian instructed Garbo to show no emotion whatever. "Just be completely passive . . . express nothing, and preferably don't even blink your eyes. Just be a mask, and then the audience will write in whatever emotion they feel should be there."

Weeks later, Mayer, Thalberg, and Nick Schenck gathered in a screening room to watch *Queen Christina*. "They all walked out on cloud nine," said Mamoulian. "Not a word was spoken—they didn't even wait for a preview. But I must give [Mayer] his due—once he saw it he was quite satisfied that it was all right. It didn't depress him."

In the early 1930s, MGM's biggest female star was not Garbo, not Crawford, not Shearer, but an old woman with the face of a bag lady. Some random samples of the commercial clout of Marie Dressler: *Min and Bill* made a profit of $731,000, *Emma* made a profit of $898,000, and *Tugboat Annie* made a profit of $1.1 million. Dressler had come to enduring movie stardom late, had no pretensions, and a delightful sense of humor. Once, visiting San Simeon, William Randolph Hearst's fabled California palace, one of Hearst's monkeys pelted her with some of his excrement. "Oh, a critic!" she exclaimed.

Howard Strickling remembered that while Dressler wasn't exactly scared of Mayer, she was in awe of him. It was Mayer who suggested that she get a thorough examination when she complained of feeling run-down. The doctors found incurable cancer. They didn't tell her, but they told Mayer, who took charge. When Dressler wanted to go to New York to attend a charity affair, Mayer wouldn't let her. "That man's trying to run my life," she said. "She was angry as all hell," said Strickling.

Mayer took personal charge of her medical care. He told Dressler's companion Claire Dubrey that Marie had cancer, but still didn't tell her. Dressler didn't learn of her true condition until nearly six months after some experimental medical treatment. When she was able to go back to work, Mayer enforced special conditions—she could only work three hours a day, stand-ins were used for all lighting and blocking rehearsals. He promised her a $100,000 bonus if she could complete three pictures in 1933. (In the January 1933 exhibitors poll in the *Motion Picture Herald*, Dressler was the number one box-office star, above Janet Gaynor, Crawford, Garbo, Shearer, and Will Rogers.)

With the bonus as impetus, Dressler managed to squeeze in two starring pictures and a small part in *Dinner at Eight*. The bonus check duly arrived. It was for $10,000, not the $100,000 Dressler believed she had been promised. Finally, Dressler had to be hospitalized up in Santa Barbara and Mayer made the trek to visit her every week.

Dressler died on July 28, 1934, without ever getting the other $90,000. This story, if true—it was reported by Dubrey, in an unpublished memoir—is among the most damning things ever reported about Mayer. It also flies in the face of many who insisted that, whatever his faults, Mayer was a man of his word, that a Mayer promise would always be kept.

MGM was spreading in all directions. Fire was now a very real fear, because the lot had been overbuilt to such an extent that it was impossible to get fire trucks very far into the property. Also spreading was L.B.'s sense of self-approbation, his ability to overwhelm dissent by the force of his own will.

Howard Dietz was a Schenck man, and spent most of his time on the East Coast, where he moonlighted as a successful lyricist ("Dancing in the Dark," "I Guess I'll Have to Change My Plans," "That's Entertainment").

When Mayer showed *Dinner at Eight* to Dietz, the publicity chief was underwhelmed. "With all those names in the cast, we'll put it over," said Dietz. Mayer was furious. "This is one of the biggest pictures ever made. No wonder we have so many flops with you handling them. Your opinions aren't worth a damn!"

Mayer was throwing a party that Saturday, and told Ida Koverman to tell Dietz that he wanted him to come, but also wanted him to apologize for his lack of critical acumen. Dietz didn't feel he had done anything to warrant an apology. Koverman suggested that Dietz could just tell her he was sorry and she would tell Mayer and everybody would be happy. No dice.

Dietz was invited to the party anyway, and when he showed up at the door of the Santa Monica house, Mayer threw his arms around him. "This fellow is no softie," he announced to the assembled guests. "He saw *Dinner at Eight* and thinks it's a great picture." Dietz could only smile and shrug. What could you do with such a man?

Chapter
SEVEN

THE ONSET of Mayer's sexual restlessness is impossible to determine with precision, but Sam Marx observed that "Mayer had a reputation for being a relentless womanizer long before he deserved it. . . . He was the most circumspect man in his studio; he knew that revelations of an affair between him and a leading lady could lead to a devastating scandal that would probably ruin both of them."

As with every other studio, at MGM there was a supply of what were known as "six-month-option girls" to be passed around the executive offices. Hardly any of them went on to any sort of career at all — most could be seen passing behind a star in a hotel lobby scene, for example. But Mayer would never be the kind of man that, say Cohn or Zanuck was, both notorious womanizers. (Charles Brackett, dismayed over an egregious miscasting that had been visited upon one of his films, once confided to a young producer, "Dear Boy, you must realize one thing: every time Darryl takes a girl to bed, a star is born.")

Still, Mayer's roving eye was certainly evident by the early 1930s. Margaret was beginning to have some serious health problems. In September 1933, she underwent what the papers called a "major operation." It was actually a hysterectomy. In those days, it was thought that women who had hysterectomies had to abstain from intercourse, which was problem enough; beyond that, Mayer told Eddie Mannix that because of the state of Margaret's internal organs, the thought of making love to her was repugnant to him. He had never had sex with another woman since his marriage day, but as he confided to friend Frank Orsatti, "I'm just as virile today as when my mother said I should make love only to have babies."

He tried to seduce the beautiful young starlet Anita Page, but she refused—she knew and liked Margaret—so he attempted to bully her: "I can make you the biggest star in the world in three pictures," he said snapping his fingers, "and I can kill Garbo in three pictures."

"But Mr. Mayer, I'm already a star," said Page.

"I could make you bigger," he replied. "We could handle things discreetly." Page respected Mayer for his executive abilities and liked him for the personal kindness he was capable of, but she wouldn't go to bed with him. "I was very happy to be working with him," Page remembered, "but I would not play any games. He wanted to play romantic games and I simply was not going to! I liked him as a boss but that's where it ended."

At MGM, Page had been working with Robert Montgomery and Marie Dressler, but beginning in 1933, she suddenly was loaned to Columbia, Universal, Monogram, and Chesterfield. She was out of the movie business by 1936.

More compliant was Ad Schulberg, the estranged wife of B. P. Schulberg, and Charlie Feldman's second-in-command. Mayer had liked and respected Ad since the Mission Road partnership with her husband. Mayer began a summer 1932 meeting with her in his office by commiserating with her about the public scandal of her husband's affair with Sylvia Sidney, which evolved into an admission that he and Margaret too had moved apart, that Margaret was, in fact, in terrible condition. They had stopped sleeping together, Mayer told her. B.P. was a fool not to realize what a gem he had in his wife, and he went further, declaring that the two of them together, L.B. and Ad, could rule Hollywood. He began to cry, and soon Mayer and Ad Schulberg were lovers. For both partners, it seems to have been a matter of sexual relief and mutual comfort, both of them revenging themselves on their spouses—B. P. Schulberg for his sins of infidelity and irresponsibility, Margaret for her sins of being dull and depressed. L.B. and Ad were asserting their independence through sex.

Perhaps living in the candy store was getting to Mayer; perhaps it was male menopause; perhaps it was all of those things or none of them. His niece Helen Sandler believes that there were several factors, and she confirms the stories of Margaret's difficulties. "Margaret had a hard time with the change; they didn't have hormones in those days. And after the girls got married, things changed."

Mayer wouldn't have been the first man catapulted into sexual panic by slamming into his fifties. Even if his daughters were married, he was at the top of his game, with all of his youthful vigor. He began to develop a bipolar sex life—moony crushes that often went nowhere, followed by quick, acquisitive, purely sexual affairs. It must have caused him some private discomfort—the man who had raged against John Gilbert and Buster Keaton for their loose morals would have known he was being a hypocrite.

Friend Frank Orsatti tried to set up assignations for Mayer with willing girls, but his resolve would fail him and nothing happened. He couldn't have sex, he told Orsatti, unless he liked the girl very much. "He couldn't get laid in a whorehouse," said one friend. "Mayer was a Puritan," said Walter Wanger, who thought his onetime boss was authentically naive about sexual matters. "He was like a bashful boy." "Mayer thought *that* [a gesture toward the crotch] was for making babies or going to the bathroom," said Howard Strickling. "It wasn't until after he was 50 that he realized it was for fun, too."

Those who remember Frank Orsatti describe him as a mildly charming Damon Runyon character who ran speakeasies in San Francisco during Prohibition. From there, he moved down to Los Angeles, where he began supplying the movie colony with booze smuggled in from Mexico on his sailboat. Supposedly, Mayer used his pull to keep members of Orsatti's clan out of jail, when he finally suggested that his friend might want to consider a line of work with less damaging consequences. Mayer recommended Orsatti become an agent; he would guarantee him entrée to MGM, which would in turn guarantee him a steady stream of clients.

Orsatti invited his brothers Vic, Al, and Ernie—the last a former St. Louis Cardinals outfielder—into the business. Orsatti would ask Mayer to his Bel Air house for dinner parties where no other agents would be present, only other agents' clients—presumably women clients. If Orsatti noticed that Mayer showed more than passing interest in one of the guests, he would enter negotiations to split commissions with her agent, or, in the event of an MGM deal, an outright buyout of the contract so that Orsatti would have exclusive representation. It was the movie equivalent of the protection racket. To many, Mayer's alliance with Orsatti was inexplicable for a man with a fetish for propriety, but it's probable that Mayer thought of the girls that Orsatti supplied as his designated weakness.

Jean Howard was a beautiful young actress who was having a nominal career at MGM in small parts in films like *The Prizefighter and the Lady*. Louis began taking what one writer nicely called "an intense personal interest in her welfare." Mayer began openly squiring Howard around Hollywood nightspots, indulging his newly discovered love for dancing.

When Mayer and Margaret went to Paris in the summer of 1934, Howard and a friend of hers were also on the ship. Traveling with a prospective mistress as well as a wife was certainly an indication of a different L. B. Mayer. He was clearly head over heels about Howard, and she would later report that he had offered her money if she would marry him. As it happened, she had fallen in love with the rakishly handsome agent Charles Feldman. When Howard told Mayer that she was going to marry Feldman, the response, according to Howard, was a full-tilt tantrum, which ended with Mayer trying to hurl himself out the window of the Ritz Hotel.

Howard Strickling, who accompanied Mayer to Paris, denied that any such thing happened. Mayer, he said, was in an emotionally violent state, but did not threaten suicide, and never tried to jump out of a window. "We just did a lot of walking around the streets of Paris late at night," said Strickling. "Mayer was big about it; that was the way he felt a rejected suitor should be."

Howard would claim that she was never Mayer's mistress. "As God hears me, that fellow never kissed me on the lips. I mean, I never knew that he was in love with me. I had no idea he felt that way about me. He never tried to grab me or kiss me passionately. I'm sure I would have gone to bed with him if he had asked me," she told Sam Marx.

Few who knew Jean Howard believe that version. She was a woman of considerable erotic needs and accomplishments, was living a life independently of Feldman shortly after they were married, and was perfectly capable of sustaining multiple relationships. The enclaves of Palm Beach and Beverly Hills are still home to elderly men who grow moony at memories of Jean Howard in bed. "My God, what a woman!" exclaimed one.

If not Anita Page or—supposedly—Jean Howard, perhaps another beautiful blond *shiksa*. The silent screen star Esther Ralston had been cast adrift by talkies, so the $750-a-week contract MGM offered her in 1934 was a lifesaver. Mayer told her he had big plans for her. She would be working with Clark Gable.

Soon after the contract was signed, Mayer invited her to go with him to a preview. After the show, they went to the Colony Club. Mayer was constantly touching Ralston during the evening and it began to dawn on her that he wanted more than company—an appalling prospect as far as Ralston was concerned. When Mayer whispered in her ear that he wanted to leave, Ralston excused herself and approached Randolph Scott, who was at the club that evening with Claire Trevor. Would Scott let her take him and Trevor home . . . right now!

"You think the old man's got ideas?" said Scott.

Ralston collected Mayer, and when he saw Scott and Trevor sitting in the back of their car, his face grew red. He climbed in, but didn't say a word on the way home. The next day, Ralston was called in to his office. "Think you're pretty smart, eh? Think you fooled me? Let me tell you, I can have any woman on this lot—Joan Crawford and—"

Ralston interrupted the tirade by saying he couldn't have her.

Pacing up and down furiously, Mayer continued his diatribe. "You sing your psalms, young lady, and see where you get! I'll blackball you in every studio in Hollywood, and what's more, you'll get nothing here!" Clarence Brown ignored Mayer's blackball and used Ralston in *Sadie McKee*, but after that she was farmed out to Universal and B movies until MGM let her contract lapse.

One has an overwhelming sense that Mayer was much younger sexually than his chronological age. His passes were clumsy, and Howard Strickling said that Mayer never really understood anything about homosexuality. Once or twice, some of his associates would attempt to explain the mechanics, but Mayer would be both amazed and appalled. "Don't tell me people do such things!" he said. He couldn't and wouldn't believe it of anyone, let alone anyone who worked at MGM, and would end the conversation.

Mayer would tell intimate friends that besides being depressed, the post-hysterectomy Margaret was delusional and psychologically damaged. Others think that Mayer constructed this scenario to justify his own sexual wanderings.

"The reason Mayer always disliked me was not because I was a Communist, although that was part of it," said Maurice Rapf. "It was because I liked his wife a lot. When I went to Paris in 1934, I went to see her. She was in this kind of asylum because he had pretended she was nutty. She wasn't nutty at all. He had put her there, and he never forgave me for going to see her.

"She talked about him. She loved him, and she loved her two daughters. She was a straitlaced, very nice woman, who looked a lot like Irene. Back in New York and Hollywood, Mayer was chasing everybody. Jean Howard, who always claimed she wasn't Mayer's mistress, but was. Later, it was Ann Miller."

As if a rough menopause and a restless husband weren't enough trouble, Margaret was further depressed when, in July 1935, her father died. To Margaret, it must have seemed as if the walls were closing in.

Sweet and dowdy Margaret was typecast for the role of the First Wife, and even people who might have been expected to feel loyalty to her seemed to take L.B.'s side. "Margaret was very sweet and very nice," said Kitty Carlisle Hart, "but she didn't have much of a role in Hollywood."

"He married her when he was very young," said Mayer's nephew Gerald Mayer. "He grew. She didn't. She was a perfectly pleasant woman, but as time went on, she was in over her head."

Even when things were in an uproar, Mayer's focus was undiminished. While he was in Paris dealing with Jean Howard, he decided to do his usual talent search and, as usual, brought them back alive. He liked the melodies of a young songwriter named Bronislau Kaper, and signed him. He visited Max Reinhardt at the Schloss Leopoldskron, his baronial castle outside Salzburg that was soon to be confiscated by the Nazis as "Jewish property." Reinhardt took Mayer to a performance of his venerated production of *Everyman*. Reinhardt knew that the play about the life and death of a rich man and the pointlessness of earthly vanities was bound to affect Mayer, but he didn't know how much. For an hour and a half, Mayer gripped Reinhardt with such force that the director couldn't use his arm for days.

Mayer always remained friendly and considerate, in a strictly gentlemanly way, toward Jean Howard. Charles Feldman, however, was something else. For starters, Mayer called every studio in town and told them not to do business with Feldman. Since Feldman's clients included such major stars as Claudette Colbert and Joan Bennett, this wasn't entirely practical. Mayer induced Frank Orsatti to make offers involving multiple picture deals to the most desirable of Feldman's clients.

Various attempts by intermediaries like Harry Cohn and Joe Schenck to smooth over the breach usually ended in punches and profanity. Right around this time, MGM needed someone to play Napoleon opposite Garbo in *Conquest*. There were a lot of character actors who could have played the part, but they needed a leading man; they needed Charles Boyer. Boyer was under contract to MGM alumnus Walter Wanger, who had been Feldman's best man when he married Jean Howard. Wanger said Feldman could handle the loan-out deal for Boyer.

Feldman went into a meeting with Thalberg, who asked how much money Boyer was getting. "Walter is paying him $25,000 a picture," said Feldman. Thalberg did what Thalberg always did whenever negotiations involved anybody besides himself—get the price down: "That's a lot of money for an actor to expect, when he has an opportunity to play Napoleon opposite Garbo."

"I didn't say that's what we expect from you," replied Feldman. "I said that's what Wanger has been paying him. As a matter of fact, what we expect from you is $125,000."

After the storm had passed, after the broken windows had been repaired and the papers put back on Thalberg's desk, Boyer got his $125,000, with an equal amount to be paid for any French version, as well as an overtime provision, all of which combined to force the studio to pay Boyer what Feldman remembered as close to $450,000 for a picture that was heavily reshot and eventually ran up the very high cost of $2.7 million.

Shortly after this, Wanger went to Mayer with a request to borrow Myrna Loy. "Why should I loan *you* Myrna Loy?" Mayer asked rhetorically. "Because I loaned you Boyer when you needed him," said Wanger. Mayer erupted from behind his desk and went for Wanger, with the two men falling to the floor in a flailing ball. "Get out! Get out!" screamed Mayer. Wanger got out.

Eventually, Mayer developed a healthy respect for Feldman, trying to recruit him as a producer several times, and, after Mayer left the studio, to work with Mayer as an independent producer. What is stranger still is that Feldman respected Mayer. "L.B. was the czar," remembered Feldman, "in control of the studio and all the great talent. He was also the ablest administrator we had out there. Talent would work for MGM for half of what they would anyplace else because they knew MGM would put them in classy pictures with good directors and good casts. Mayer's strength was in the fact that he controlled the largest pool of talent in Hollywood and thus in the world — talent that other studios were virtually compelled to seek from time to time. And the authority to dispense the use of this talent was possessed entirely by Mayer. Thus he was in a position to ruin another studio, with respect to the making of a picture that depended entirely on MGM stars.

"Working for MGM was like working for the *New York Times* — you couldn't do any better. This was one of the strong factors that Mayer developed, and that was a source of his power."

Hollywood and the surrounding communities had evolved from the barely settled farmlands that filmmakers found when they began arriving twenty years earlier. Beverly Hills, which had been practically uninhabited in the 1910s, increased in population during the 1920s by 2,500 percent. There was still vacant land between Hollywood and downtown Los Angeles, still a profusion of palm trees and Spanish stucco houses with bougainvillea and orange trumpet flowers, but the elysian fields were very much reduced.

Another sign of the burgeoning movie industry was a propensity for odd, surreal, attention-grabbing sights such as a restaurant built in the shape of a gigantic brown derby, or the tall radio towers that advertised Aimee Semple McPherson's Angelus Temple, close to L.B.'s old Mission Road studio.

Within Hollywood, the citrus and bean fields had been pushed to the fringes of the town, replaced by a profusion of mostly Spanish-style buildings that were only a few stories high because of the fear of earthquakes. Everything looked fresh and new, a stark contrast with the dismal gray that had settled over New York and the East in this, the pit of the Depression.

But beneath the sunlit bowl of blue California sky, trouble was brewing.

In the spring of 1934, the novelist Upton Sinclair declared for the governorship of California. Although he was a Socialist, Sinclair registered as a Democrat and vowed he would win the party's nomination. Running on a program he called EPIC (End Poverty in California), Sinclair defeated eight other primary opponents in a landslide and won the nomination.

The EPIC program proposed two different economic systems in California. One would be private enterprise, which would continue more or less the way it always had, while the other would be a state-run system of cooperative farms and factories, which would be acquired through eminent domain or tax revenues. The state's new businesses would put the unemployed to work producing for use, not profit.

The details were fuzzy, but it was the quintessential desperate time that seemed to call for desperate measures; thousands of liberals, progressives, and Communists began working for Sinclair. A few well-known industry figures— Charlie Chaplin and Dudley Nichols—even endorsed his candidacy.

Early polls showed Sinclair with a two-to-one lead over Republican Frank Merriam. Respected film industry leaders such as Joe Schenck and Douglas Fairbanks Sr. responded by saying that the movie business would relocate to Florida if Sinclair was elected. Schenck and Fairbanks backed up their words with a reconnaissance trip to Miami in the first week of October. Would MGM relocate as well? "That," said L.B., "is something to be considered if and when the time comes."

Relocation was almost certainly an empty threat—Florida would have required tens of millions of dollars for new studios.

But it was clear that Frank Merriam was going to need all the help he could get, and if it was extracurricular, so be it. A well-funded apparatus, an early version of a political action committee, was formed, headed by Harry Chandler of the Los Angeles Times, Asa Call, vice president of Pacific Mutual, Mendel Silberberg (Mayer's attorney), and a few others. Their goal was to raise $500,000 to fight Sinclair.

The leaders of the anti-Sinclair forces were William Randolph Hearst, L. B. Mayer, and, bringing up the rear, Irving Thalberg. Once, a writer asked

Thalberg why he was so conservative, so opposed to Socialism, from which a man as gifted as he would have nothing to fear.

Thalberg stared at the man as if he had lost his mind, then began relating the activities of an average day in his life, from ten in the morning till eleven at night. There were the rushes of films that were shooting, story conferences, there were the meetings with directors, producers, the art department, the telephone calls about second unit photography, about hiring and firing actors, the endless troubleshooting and putting out of fires. "All that I should do for five hundred dollars a week?" he asked.

L.B. didn't like Socialism for purely practical reasons. As he explained in a fatherly talk to one young leftist, what he was doing was bad for the Jews, because they were frequently identified with Communist causes. Turning Communist would strengthen the view that Jews and Communists were synonymous. His argument, not strong to begin with, was considerably weakened by the fact that he was sitting beneath an autographed picture of Benito Mussolini, who had a considerable vogue in Hollywood in the early 1930s, said picture driving every centrist or left-wing person on the lot straight up the wall.

Thalberg ordered Carey Wilson and Felix Feist Jr. to start production on a series of fake newsreels that would deliver a death blow to Upton Sinclair. To maintain plausible deniability, the fake newsreels were made by an independent unit, using rental cameras and trucks. Even the lab work was done off the MGM lot. "Mayer had nothing to do with instigating or carrying out this project," said Wilson.

Two of the shorts were more or less simple man-in-the-street interviews that featured little old ladies in gingham dresses ("I am voting for Governor Merriam . . . because I want to have my little home. It is all I have left in the world.") and stalwart businessmen proclaiming their support for Frank Merriam. Those supporting Sinclair were shown as being either confused or intimidating, as with a man who says, "Upton St. Clair is the author of the Russian government. And it worked out very well there, and I think it should do so here."

The third short used extras to play the parts of diseased-looking anarchists and bums that were supposedly making their way to California where the citizens would be forced to take care of them ("I am foting for Seenclair . . . Vell, his system vorked vell in Russia, vy can't it vork here?"). When the shorts triggered fights in theaters, the studios blamed EPIC supporters.

Hearst and the *Los Angeles Times* turned the full power of their papers against Sinclair, printing a relentless stream of negative news about him—the

Times printed a regular box on the front page containing various quotations from Sinclair's writings, which were edited to make him sound like a raving lunatic. When Turner Catledge of the *New York Times* had dinner with the *Los Angeles Times*'s famously manipulative political editor, Kyle Palmer, he asked why Palmer didn't print any actual news of Sinclair's campaign.

"We don't go in for that kind of crap that you have back in New York of being obliged to print both sides," snapped Palmer. "We're going to beat this son of a bitch Sinclair any way we can. We're going to kill him."

Mayer mobilized the advertising and publicity departments of MGM to produce scurrilous newspaper, billboard, and radio ads (written by Joe Mankiewicz) that demonized Sinclair. One billboard, on Wilshire, utilized imagery from the Hate-the-Germans propaganda of World War I: Sinclair was depicted as a hairy apelike creature with blood dripping from his teeth as he grasped a bomb in one hand and a knife in the other. Opposing him was Governor Merriam, posed in a protective stance, as he stood over a frightened, cowering mother and her children.

The studios began extorting money to fund anti-Sinclair publicity. Warner Bros. deducted $100 from the paychecks of high-salaried employees, while Mayer and Harry Cohn asked that each employee contribute one day's pay. Accounting issued everybody a check made out for one day of their salary; all they had to do was sign it and turn it in. Implicit was the suggestion that if you didn't send in your check you could be met with an unpleasant surprise when option time rolled around.

"Nothing happened if you didn't [contribute]," said screenwriter Alvin Josephy. "I've never voted for a Republican, and I certainly wasn't going to give money to one. At MGM, contributing was almost a monthly part of the job. Someone was always coming around to get what you could afford for some cause. Mostly, it was nonpolitical, but contributing was considered to be part of your job."

MGM story editor Sam Marx was a Sinclair man and refused to be coerced, sending his day's pay to Sinclair instead of Merriam. Nor was Marx bothered by the nearly unanimous support for Merriam among studio executives. Standing in line with L.B. one day to register to vote, Marx said to his boss, "You know we're just going to cancel each other out, so why don't we just leave and go back to the office!"

Mayer's response wasn't recorded, but a thin smile sounds about right. He intended to put EPIC in its grave. It was widely thought that if anybody could save Frank Merriam's career, it was Mayer because, as one studio wag said, "He knows how to salvage junk."

The propaganda began to have an effect. "Before Louis Mayer, Irving Thalberg . . . and Carey Wilson stepped into this political battle," editorialized Billy Wilkerson of the *Hollywood Reporter* in late October, "the whole Republican Party seemed to have been sunk by the insane promises of Mr. Sinclair. With that group in the war, and it has been a WAR, things took a different turn. . . . Sinclair is not defeated yet, but indications point to it, and California should stand up and sing hosannas for their greatest STATE industry, MOTION PICTURES."

Merriam won the election by 200,000 votes, a far greater margin of victory than polls had suggested just a few weeks earlier. L.B. threw an election night party at the Trocadero, where guests included Thalberg, Carey Wilson, Sam Goldwyn, Harry Cohn, Howard Hughes, Clark Gable, Helen Hayes, Ernst Lubitsch, Gloria Swanson, and Groucho Marx. There were even a few Sinclair supporters invited, such as Dorothy Parker and Sam Marx. Frank Merriam sent a telegram extending his best wishes to "my good friends in the motion picture industry," and offered special congratulations to Louis B. Mayer. L.B. basked in a political triumph that must have absorbed a good deal of any residual sting he felt from the 1932 presidential debacle.

Mayer's consistent conservatism may seem confusing or perverse; succeeding generations of movie moguls have, with few exceptions, been liberal Democrats, and even Jack Warner, the most craven of all the moguls during the Red Scare, flirted with progressive ideas, most notably in the early 1930s when production at Warner Bros. was being guided by Darryl Zanuck.

But it should be remembered that Mayer had emerged from an environment that defined instability: a Jew in tsarist Russia lived with perpetual anxiety deriving from the fact that what lurked around the next corner was not prosperity, but a pogrom. The remarkable political and social stability of America stood out in stark contrast, and was to be cherished. What could threaten that stability? Bolsheviks. Wobblies. Unions. For Mayer, keeping his nose clean and his profile low, doing nothing to inflame people outside the movie industry and doing his best not to remind anyone that he was a Jew, became articles of faith.

Besides that, Mayer was a man whose life was a testament to the American Dream. For him, the myth was fact. It was proper to tell stories of success and its importance, so others could achieve what he had achieved. As a Russian Jew who had made it in America, Mayer knew firsthand that America was indeed the land of opportunity, and he was the proof. All his life, L.B. would vouch for establishment verities.

Nephew Gerald Mayer said that "It's funny that my father [who became the studio manager] and my uncle were both Republicans, and everybody else in the family and the business were Democrats. I've thought about that, and I think that one reason they were Republicans were the unions, which were incredibly corrupt and constantly agitating with the studios."

There was a limit to Mayer's conservatism, however, and that involved the Nazis—not in Europe, but in America, specifically Los Angeles, where in 1934 the German-American Bund was already broadcasting and issuing broadsides against the Jews of Hollywood. In March of that year, Mendel Silberberg called a meeting of his friends at the Hillcrest Country Club. Mayer took the floor and said he wasn't going to take the Bund lying down. What was needed, he said, was money and direction. This meeting resulted in the Community Relations Committee, a political organization of wealthy Los Angeles Jews who monitored Nazi sympathizers and issued broadsides of their own. Mayer contributed enough money to publish a newspaper on anti-Semitism.

A few years later, as anti-Semitism was on the march throughout Europe and America, Mayer would be more tentative about the militant stance recommended by younger writers and executives. As Neal Gabler observed, Mayer and his peers felt "they had to balance their roles as businessmen with their roles as prominent Jews."

The industry's tactics may have cost Sinclair the gubernatorial election, but they had a series of unintended consequences. Mainly, the blatant attempt by the studios to control the lives and political beliefs of employees left every liberal and many moderates in the business muttering, "Never again." The enormous chips on the shoulders of actors and writers worked to the advantage of the mobilization effort for the Writers Guild and other unions.

"Thalberg, not Mayer, was the toughest and most ruthless man in the industry," said Robert Montgomery. "He was nothing of the dreamer. He was money-mad. He was a shrewd, tough, hard, cold operator, with a complete ruthlessness towards people."

The most public exhibition of Thalberg's propensity for emotional surgery without anesthesia was the movement toward unionization. "I was there when the Writers Guild was organized," remembered Maurice Rapf. "There was a meeting in Thalberg's projection room that was connected to his office. All the writers were brought in—there must have been a hundred guys crowded in, some that Thalberg had never even seen before. Then Irving came in with Mannix and Thau.

"He said that we all owed a lot to him and to MGM, and that if we voted for amalgamation with the Authors League, he wouldn't forget it. 'You've all gotten a great deal out of this industry,' said Thalberg. 'It's been good to you, and what you're proposing to do is give it away and turn it over to outside interests, and we are not going to tolerate it. We have a lot to protect here and we are going to protect it with everything we've got.'

"It was exactly like a gangster coming in with the assistants that actually did the shooting," said Rapf. "It was a real threat and he behaved very badly. Usually, Thalberg was kind of a lovable guy, but not that day."

After Thalberg, Mayer said his piece. He referred to the Authors League as "those foreigners," and asked, "Why have anything to do with them when you can always come and talk to me?" Then he began to cry.

The idea that writers would need protection and a bargaining agent was anathema to Thalberg, who saw them as traitors to their class. "Those writers are living like kings," he said. "Why on earth would they want to join a union, like coal miners or plumbers?"

Thalberg had promised to make the smart, anti-Semitic James Kevin McGuinness a producer—if McGuinness helped break up the Writers Guild. McGuinness did his best, helping to form a company union, the Screen Playwrights, but the Writers Guild took hold anyway. Suddenly, Thalberg relieved McGuinness as the producer of *Maytime*, which led McGuinness to an office tirade: "I'll show that Jew bastard that loyalty is not a one-way street," he screamed. Listening through the walls was Maurice Rapf.

Ironically, one of the determining factors in getting a legitimate writers union was the lowly MGM shorts department, which employed around forty writers. When the Wagner Act was passed by Congress in 1935, it altered the equation from a standoff, and the Screen Playwrights tried to adjust. "They came down to the shorts department with brandy and cigars," remembered Robert Lees. "It was like we were pledging a fraternity. 'We have the best agents and we can always talk to Mayer,' they said. 'Join us.' "

"The pressure at MGM was relentless," remembered Frances Goodrich. "[The studio had influential people] around all the time, day after day, talking to writers, particularly the young writers, the ones who were just starting. . . . So we proselytized too. We walked around [the] lot, and so did Lilly Hellman, and we talked to the young kids . . . but only on our lunch hour, so that no one could ever say we had used studio time for union activities. And we couldn't do our proselytizing on the phone, of course, because [the studio] boys were always listening in."

The younger writers in the Shorts department tipped the balance. "We said, in effect, 'Screw you,' " remembered Robert Lees, "and there were forty or fifty votes for the Writers Guild." Occasionally, one of the liberals would walk by the Screen Playwrights table in the commissary and be taunted: "You better get out of that Commie organization or you won't be here long."

This resulted in Thalberg calling in George Seaton and Robert Pirosh, two recently arrived liberals who had been threatened. Thalberg told them that he disagreed with their choice, but, "If anybody tries to threaten you, to tell you your job is in danger, you come and tell me."

These divisions were lifelong; S. J. Perelman demanded that Bennett Cerf delete a piece of his from an anthology when he learned that a piece by James Kevin McGuinness was also to be included. "I have no intention of singing in the same choir as this distinguished fugleman of . . . Mr. Thalberg."

Roosevelt's New Deal had been dubbed the Raw Deal by Hearst because of the higher income tax rates that had pushed the publisher's always shaky finances to the brink. Throughout the 1920s, top-bracket income tax rates were reduced by Republican administrations and Congress from over 75 percent to slightly more than 20 percent. Roosevelt jacked them up again, mostly through something called the Wealth Recovery Tax. The rates rose until they were at 80 percent by 1940, and peaked at 90 percent by 1945. Added to that was a California state tax that could run as high as 15 percent. In 1937, Louis would earn $1.296 million in salary and bonuses, the highest salary paid to any American that year. He paid $1.1 million in federal and state taxes, leaving him a net income of $188,151. No wonder Hearst and Mayer regarded Roosevelt with personal animus.

One of L.B.'s new producer hires was Edwin Knopf, the brother of the New York book publisher and a resolute New Deal Democrat. "He was tolerated," remembered Alvin Josephy, Knopf's nephew. "Knopf had a strange complex about Mayer. He looked on him as a benevolent father figure. And Mayer saw him as a cultured guy, with a background and a celebrated brother in a related field. Mayer treated him with kid gloves and would come over to his house for dinner."

Among the old-timers, Harry Rapf was still producing major successes for the studio, but he was widely regarded as a figure of derision. "He was pathetic," said Alvin Josephy. "I knew his sons, Matt and Maurice, and they were not dopes, they were good guys, but Harry . . . Harry had this huge nose, and there were all kinds of stories about it. I knew a writer who came out of a meeting with Harry crestfallen. He had to get another job, he said. During the meeting with Rapf about a script, he'd opened his mouth and said, 'Why, it's as clear as the nose on your face,' without thinking."

By the mid-1930s, MGM was the ultimate studio and Louis B. Mayer was recognized as the ultimate studio head. Sam Marx, ostensibly a Thalberg loyalist, would write that "Mayer was a brilliant individual and an unparalleled administrator." The latter quality was defined simply by L.B. in a frequently enunciated precept: "I hire people for their brains and I'm not such a fool that I don't let them use them."

Mayer had set up the studio so that things had to be handled through channels. Rosalind Russell remembered that Benny Thau, presented with a problem or complaint, would say, "I'll take it up with Mannix." Mannix would say, "I'll take it up with Mayer." Mayer would say, "Well, Rosalind, that New England girl again, the one that always wears tweeds. I'll have to take it up with Nick." And Nick was always someplace remote, like Tibet. Worst of all was when he was on the train coming west, because then the problem wouldn't get to him until he got back to New York, if then.

If the layers of management didn't defeat a recalcitrant actor, there were other means. Each star was generally presented with another actor further down the pecking order who could, at least theoretically, supplant them. Garbo first had to confront Luise Rainer, then Hedy Lamarr; Robert Montgomery kept a weather eye on Franchot Tone, and Myrna Loy's competition was Rosalind Russell.

The California papers regularly covered Mayer's comings and goings in a manner that was rarely extended to other movie moguls. He proffered his views on movie technology, saying that neither color, wide screen nor television would ever revolutionize the movies as sound had. Color, he explained, distracted the audience from the story being told, and was best used for short travelogues. He addressed a course in movie distribution at the University of Southern California, and told the students that "You can't shout 'colossal,' 'stupendous' and similar expansive superlatives about mediocre products. Tell the truth, but make it attractive; sell your product, but don't oversell it."

Increasingly, the public grew to know Mayer, as remote broadcasts from prestigious premieres would feature an "impromptu" moment at the microphone from L.B., invariably introduced as "your friend and mine." Other moguls listened when he spoke, even the terrible-tempered Harry Cohn. As always, Mayer knew just how to reduce somebody else to a subtly secondary position. In Cohn's case, it was by addressing him as "Herschel." "Whenever Mayer sneezed, Cohn took aspirin," wrote Frank Capra. As George Jessel noted, "Most of the [other moguls] were terribly jealous [of Mayer] and went out of their way to condemn him all through the hours of the day."

The studio's Tiffany status was further solidified by its treatment of sequels. When MGM had a hit, it didn't rush out a cheater in order to skim as much money as quickly as possible, as, for instance, RKO did with *Son of Kong*, which was in theaters the same year as *King Kong*. MGM sequels were crafted with the same care as the original, often cost more, and were usually released at two-year intervals.

When the studio had an enormous hit with their 1932 *Tarzan the Ape Man*, the studio went to work on a sequel, but it didn't appear until 1934. Likewise, the sequels to *The Thin Man*, which, while never erotic—William Powell's energy tended to top out with the shaking of a pitcher of martinis—did contain a quietly gleeful irresponsibility, as well as suggesting that a male-female relationship could be more than June/moon idealization; marriage between two intelligent people could be a lot of fun, providing both parties held on to their sense of humor.

By the mid-1930s, the studio's success mandated a round of building and refurbishing. The old star dressing rooms were a sort of coed bungalow, with men downstairs and women up, with open verandas running along the front, and everybody passing each other on the way to the communal bathrooms. But now the studio erected a two-story wing of dressing rooms for its women stars, with another one for the men. There were three suites upstairs and three down, and Tony Mendoza, the studio gardener, would plant gardens for each star with her favorite flowers. Joan Crawford got roses and gardenias, Garbo had French heather, and Norma Shearer—who had her own bungalow—got lilies.

Six years of Thalberg's agitating for more money meant that, by 1935, Mayer and Thalberg were barely speaking. Mayer explained the situation as stemming from the conflict created by Thalberg's demands for the premium talents on the lot—which increased after he returned from his recuperation vacation in 1933—and Mayer's need to keep his eye on the big picture. "I wouldn't yield and Irving wouldn't yield. Thalberg wanted first call on all and every artist on the lot. I told him, 'I will have to throw up my hands! Irving, you ought to be fair. You are going to place me in a position that I am going to flop. . . . I will give you every darned thing you want, as if you were my own son, but I've got to run that plant successfully.'

"He didn't want to stay there at all."

Others saw that the failing relationship was due less to specifics than an emotional misalliance and jealousy over their shared dependence. "Each of them wanted what the other had," remembered MGM screenwriter Dore Schary. "Mayer, Thalberg's creative style and mind; Thalberg, Mayer's money and lusty power."

Part of the reason the studio could run so effectively in spite of a shooting war between its executives was a series of very strong department heads. Each area of the studio was handled by someone who had a great deal of power within the hierarchy. Cumulatively, this group of strong department heads supplied what Ralph Winters would call "the quality of work beneath the film."

Other than Mayer and Thalberg, Cedric Gibbons was the most powerful arbiter of style at the studio. From 1924 until his retirement in 1956, Gibbons supervised the look of more than one thousand MGM movies—every MGM picture carried his name. Gibbons was born in Brooklyn in 1890; the son and grandson of architects, he studied painting at the Art Students League in New York and was working under Hugo Ballin at Edison by 1915.

Gibbons was an innovator, getting rid of painted scenery, insisting on three-dimensional constructions. When Gibbons designed a 1921 Will Rogers comedy called *Doubling for Romeo*, he designed a Verona that could have served splendidly for a straight version of Shakespeare. By the age of twenty-five, he was head of the art department for the Goldwyn company and came aboard during the merger.

Gibbons was a major exponent of what one writer would term "MGM Grand Bourgeois." Billy Wilder was more specific, referring to the "white satin decor" Gibbons favored. Gibbons's most momentous design influence came from a visit to the 1925 Paris Exposition des Arts Décoratifs. After that, many MGM films featured stunning moderne designs, especially *Our Dancing Daughters*, *The Kiss*, and the spectacularly beautiful *Grand Hotel*: polished black floors, fluted arches, and jagged wall reliefs. The moderne style was also apparent in the design for the Academy Award statuette that was executed by Gibbons.

The years flowed past, stars came and went, tastes changed, the studio would go through one upheaval after another, but Cedric Gibbons stayed. Gibbons arrived every day in his Duesenberg, wearing a gray homburg and gloves. Six feet tall, handsome, charming, and apparently wealthy, "Gibbons always had on a suit and a double-breasted vest," remembered Maurice Rapf. "He was very sharp-looking, and could have been an actor. I always thought he looked like Warner Baxter." Other people saw the immaculately turned out gentleman and saw "a fop. He wore an ascot, for God's sake!"

Although Gibbons instituted something of a cult of personality, and could be considered a credit hog, he was held in high regard by everybody who knew him. "You never worked for this man," said art director Preston Ames. "You always worked with him."

Gibbons ran his department with remarkable efficiency. Like Mayer, he gave his people a great deal of support and, within limits, freedom. One of the department no-nos was combining red and green—the Christmas colors. Those, Gibbons believed, should never go together.

There was a formality to Gibbons—a sketch artist could work at the department for months and never be introduced. It was like working as a draftsman for a famous architect—access was limited. Still, throughout the two-hundred-person department, "nothing, absolutely nothing, went through unless Gibbons had okayed it," said Preston Ames. Gibbons personally designed almost nothing outside of the statuette for the Academy Awards, but controlled every set at MGM and much else besides.

Gibbons set up a series of brilliantly managed sub-departments—the model shop; the prop department; the scenic artists shop, where artists like Ben Carré painted backdrops on hundred-foot paint frames; Arnold Gillespie's special effects department; Warren Newcombe's matte painting department.

Although Gibbons's taste would come to seem rigid and stultifying in later years, it is important to remember his daring in the late 1920s and early 1930s. His own house, exquisitely designed in the moderne style, attested to his sincerity when it came to bold designs, and much of the MGM art direction in this period is far in advance of anything being built concurrently in America.

Gibbons imposed a rich, upholstered look on the Metro sets; he wanted them overlit, and since he hated wallpaper and liked clean white walls, the sets at MGM had a strong tendency toward a rich, soft, grayish white, so that the superb finishes could show. The tone was almost the polar opposite of the sooty look of Warner Bros. As Preston Ames would put it, "Cedric Gibbons believed that the case had to be worthy of the jewel."

Art Deco segued into the longer-lasting era of the Big White Set, most notably *Dinner at Eight*. Gibbons would sometimes insist that a BWS be inserted into a film even if it had no place for one, as with the Garbo film *Conquest*, which is largely authentically designed with appropriate details for the

Napoleonic era, except for an anachronistic white ballroom. (Gibbons would always strenuously resist dark, looming expressionist shadows; he wouldn't allow the great designer William Cameron Menzies on the MGM lot.)

Gibbons's method was to read the script for a film, then give it to one of four—in the early 1930s—unit art directors, who then actually designed the film. The sketches and designs would be passed back to Gibbons for his approval. A model for each set, no matter how insignificant, would be built. Gibbons would send the designs back to the unit man, who would then send them out to be converted to blueprints for the construction department, after which Gibbons would have to approve them yet again. If the producer or director disagreed with Gibbons's choices, he had to deal with Gibbons. This constant supervisory checking took large amounts of both money and time, one of the reasons MGM's budgets were the highest in the business.

Each of the forty or fifty pictures MGM released required somewhere between thirty-five to fifty sets, so Gibbons was responsible for a vast assembly line that supplied somewhere around 2,300 sets for the dream factory every year. On screen, the only art director credited would be Gibbons, under the theory that he was head of the department, even though, as he once told a young art director, "I haven't held a pencil in my hand in fifteen years."

Gibbons's comparatively monochrome sensibilities limited the possibilities for any kind of customized look for any single picture. "Whether it fitted the story or not, he was going to have his sets paramount," complained Mitchell Leisen. Leisen directed a picture at Metro that had scenes in both a country club and a bookie joint. The country club looked like the most elaborate country club in America, and the bookie joint, said Leisen, "looked like something out of *House and Garden.* . . . That was the MGM style, and that's what you got."

If Gibbons defined the MGM look, then Douglas Shearer of the sound department and Herbert Stothart of the music department defined its sound. Shearer was brilliant, but slightly pedantic, given to professorial remarks like "The behavior of a molecule under excitement is always interesting, whether in a piccolo or a power line." When the studio made a dog picture called *The Voice of Bugle Ann,* they needed a very distinctive "voice" for the dog. Just the normal bay seemed insufficient, so they mixed in the sound of a French horn and got exactly what Shearer was looking for.

Although Mayer prided himself on having the best departments of any studio in the business, there were those who felt that Shearer was the weak link. "Their sound system wasn't that good," remembered Kathryn Grayson, who rose to moderate stardom at MGM in the 1940s and 1950s. "I found that out when I went to Warners, where they had a fantastic sound system. MGM's mixer was named Mike Laughlin, and he'd turn up soft notes and stifle high notes. But Warners had Dave Forrest, who could read music and scores. He let a big note be a big note."

Herbert Stothart was born in 1885 and had been a professor of music at the University of Wisconsin. Eventually, he became a music director for Arthur Hammerstein, then began contributing songs, which led to writing entire shows—including *Rose Marie*—with such collaborators as Rudolf Friml, Oscar Hammerstein II, and Otto Harbach.

The coming of sound brought Stothart to Hollywood in the spring of 1929. His first assignment was to compose and conduct the score for the operetta *The Rogue Song*, but he was writing dramatic scores by 1931. Soon, Stothart was the studio's premier musical composer, far more highly regarded then than now, but reliably dominating the studio's most prestigious scoring assignments.

Stothart was the de facto head of the music department, in spite of the fact that he had no administrative duties. "He was God at MGM," remembered the composer Bronislau Kaper, "because he was blonde, had blue eyes, and, in the eyes of the executives, he was a showman. They said, 'Maybe he doesn't know music that well, but he is a showman.' " Stothart, said Kaper, had tremendous influence and was "full of intrigue. When he wanted a movie, he got it." In keeping with the hierarchichal nature of the studio, nobody in the music department could be paid more than the $1,000 a week paid Stothart; if somebody's option would boost him to $1,250, he would be informed he could stay, but at no more than $1,000.

Stothart's philosophy of film scoring was largely impressionistic, with shimmering strings—listen to the title music for *The Wizard of Oz*—with Ravel and Debussy as primary influences. His writings about the film business are awash in phrases like "tone poems" and "impressions," and he was clearly concerned that the music work at an almost subliminal level, "at such a level as to permit the audience to be conscious of the music without its being heard so strongly as to intrude on the drama itself." He also had a strong ego, singling out the "masterful" scores for *David Copperfield* and *A Tale of Two Cities* as possessing "a true symphonic quality"—both written by Herbert Stothart.

Unlike the splendid thunder of Max Steiner and Erich Wolfgang Korngold, Stothart's music never reached out and grabbed you, because the composer didn't want to distract from the overall effect of the film. Stothart's music worked in a subtle, psychological way.

Besides Stothart's strings, the other primary characteristic of MGM music was its low level of dubbing, largely because Douglas Shearer hated music. "You can pour just so much milk into a quart bottle and then it spills over," was Shearer's favorite dubbing metaphor. The composer David Raksin had a slightly more acerbic metaphor, saying that the music at MGM sounded the way it did because the tracks all went through a booth where a little man covered them in peanut butter.

It was rare for a woman to be head of a studio department in the 1930s. In fact, it was rare for a woman to be anything but a writer, but L.B. liked women and gave them a good deal of power within the organization. Besides Ida Koverman, there was Margaret Booth, the head of editorial. Once, a newly arrived producer asked a (male) editor on the lot why Booth was head of the editing department. "Because she's *better*," was the reply. "She knows how every cut affects the entire picture."

With a director the studio was unsure of, Booth would be assigned to oversee each day's shooting. The director would rehearse the actors, then the cameraman would indicate where they should stand, and where the camera should be. During a take, the director would be on one side of the camera, Booth on the other. By this time, most directors would be so intimidated they wouldn't actually watch their actors, only Booth. If Booth smiled, the director would say, "Cut. Print," but a slight frown would bring, "Let's do it again."

In time, Booth would be elevated into an executive position, with the responsibility of looking at every foot of film shot at MGM and reporting any problems to Mayer. "Booth had access that no one else did," said editor Ralph Winters. "She had a very strong personality, and she'd raise hell with the most feared producers and directors on the lot. 'You don't know what you're talking about,' she'd snap, and they'd take it because they knew she knew."

Booth was a perfectionist, and her refusal to countenance anything less than a polished perfection dovetailed with Mayer's own sensibilities. "I can't count the number of times Margaret sent me away to do something over," remembered Winters, who began at MGM in 1928 and left in 1961. " 'Fix it,' she'd say. 'It doesn't look good.' And I can guarantee you that ninety-nine out of a hundred people would never have noticed it. Socially, Margaret was a lot of fun, but her work was her life."

The costume designer Adrian—real name Adrian Adolph Greenburg— had studied design in Paris, then was hired by Irving Berlin and Hassard Short to work on *The Music Box Revue of 1921*. By the 1923 edition, he was designing the bulk of the show. Natacha Rambova, the wife of Rudolph Valentino, saw the 1923 show and hired Adrian to design costumes for her husband. He then was offered a job in the DeMille unit by Mitchell Leisen. Adrian designed twenty-six films at the DeMille studio, including *King of Kings* and *The Volga Boatman*. When DeMille moved to MGM in the summer of 1928, he took his entire unit with him. DeMille soon left MGM, but Adrian stayed for the next thirteen years.

Until the advent of Edith Head, Adrian was the most influential designer in Hollywood. He avoided the middle range of grays and liked stark contrast—black and white, with straight, almost severe, lines. Even Adrian's sketches were in the same blacks, whites, and grays they would be in the finished films. Because of MGM's frequent use of close-ups, he tried to keep necklines clean while keeping the important details of a costume above the waist and below the neck.

"Adrian always played down the designs for the big scene," remembered Joan Crawford, the primary beneficiary of his theatrical genius. "For the lighter scene he'd create a 'big' dress. His theory, of course, was that an absolutely stunning outfit would distract the viewer from the highly emotional thing that was going on. There should be just the actress, her face registering her emotions, the body moving to express her reactions—the dress is only the background. But in the next scene, where she goes to the races and cheers for her horse, the costume would be just absolutely smashing."

Adrian was a fiend for work; even on mammoth productions like *The Wizard of Oz* and *Marie Antoinette*, he would design everything, no matter how insignificant, tossing off a sketch in a few minutes, more than seventy-five drawings in a single day. Beneath him was a large department made up of ten or more head cutters and fitters, each with his or her own staff. There were specialists for modern clothes, period clothes, men's and women's clothes.

Like all the costume designers who worked in films, Adrian was expert at diverting attention from various figure problems; the famous shoulder pads he installed on Joan Crawford were devised so that her hips would seem narrow by comparison.

Most people around the lot believed Adrian to be a quiet loner, but he delighted in entertaining people he felt comfortable with, Hedda Hopper and Mercedes de Acosta among them. He was particularly renowned for his Christmas parties and Easter brunches. Although he was widely presumed to be homosexual (*Fortune*'s "twittering hunchback" crack), Luise Rainer remembered him coming into her dressing room to breathlessly tell her he had fallen in love.

"That's wonderful, darling. Who is it?"

Main Street in Saint John, New Brunswick, circa 1890. One of the buildings on the left was the Mayer home (on the upper floors) and junk shop (street level). (Harold E. Wright, Heritage Resources)

Saint John, circa 1900: a teenaged Louis Mayer (top row, third from left, with his arm around another man) supervises the salvaging of a ship in Saint John harbor. Rough work, but not work to be done roughly; there is a watch chain and charm in Mayer's vest.

(Harold B. Lee Library, Brigham Young University)

Mr. and Mrs. Louis B. Mayer of Haverhill, Massachusetts, going for a Sunday drive, circa 1911.

(Bison Archives)

On March 15, 1911, a prosperous Louis Mayer (front, third from left) has his picture taken at an exhibitors' convention. Next to Mayer, in the white cap, is Vitagraph president Albert E. Smith. The slightly blurred figure directly to the left of Mayer is his partner Nate Gordon.

(Harold B. Lee Library, Brigham Young University)

The Orpheum Theater in Haverhill in 1914 when L.B. was running it. (Haverhill Public Library)

The signing of Anita Stewart to star in Louis B. Mayer Productions gave the young company instant credibility. Here, in 1918, Mayer greets Stewart at the Los Angeles train station, along with director Marshall Neilan (with glasses, right).
(Bison Archives)

Signing Anita Stewart proved to be a good idea, but signing Mildred Harris Chaplin, Charlie's estranged wife, was anything but. Here Mayer and Mildred look over prospective story material.
(Harold B. Lee Library, Brigham Young University)

The opening day of the amalgamation of Metro, Goldwyn, and Mayer. Here, Mayer addresses the crowd in front of the glass-walled shooting stage, while M.C. Fred Niblo waits his turn.

Before the Moderne remodeling, Mayer's office resembled an oak-paneled clubroom. Here, he and Irving Thalberg discuss MGM production matters.

(Harold B. Lee Library, Brigham Young University)

During the bleeding wound that was the production of *Ben-Hur*, Mayer went to Italy to inspect the troops. Here, director Fred Niblo demonstrates his mastery of the sea battle for Mayer, who is standing next to Margaret, Irene, and Edie Mayer. Screenwriter Carey Wilson is standing behind and between Margaret and Irene. (Museum of Modern Art/Film Stills Archive)

Fred Niblo (left) and Mayer meeting with Marcus Loew.

(BFI Films: Stills, Posters and Designs)

Ben-Hur was a crucible for the young company, but also a triumph of showmanship, with a splendid sense of spectacle, mainly because of expert special effects. All that the studio actually built was the track itself, the wall around it, and the spina in the center, and only half of that. The galleries above the track are entirely a hanging miniature, filled with hundreds of little puppet people who gave a seamless impression of throngs of humanity.

The Thalberg-Shearer wedding in 1927. Left to right are Jack Conway, unidentified bridesmaid, Douglas Shearer, Marion Davies, Norma Shearer and Irving Thalberg, unidentified woman, L. B. Mayer, Edie and Irene Mayer, and King Vidor.
(BFI Films: Stills, Posters and Designs)

Mayer with William Randolph Hearst (far left),
Monta Bell (to the right of Mayer), and an
unidentified man inspecting set construction at
MGM circa 1928.

(Harold B. Lee Library, Brigham Young University)

Mayer and his friend Herbert Hoover.

(Harold B. Lee Library, Brigham Young University)

Jacob Mayer, L.B.'s father, with his daughter-in-law, Margaret (to his left), and his granddaughters, Irene (left) and Edie (far right).

(Bison Archives)

Mayer's daughters caught for what may have been the last time in an attitude of open affection. Irene (left) and Edie Mayer, 1929.

(Bison Archives)

April 29, 1930: Irene marries the young producer David Selznick. The expressions on Mayer's and his wife's faces indicate the tensions caused by the marriage.

(Harold B. Lee Library, Brigham Young University)

In front of Marion Davies's bungalow at the MGM studio, Buster
Keaton poses with the MGM brain trust. From left: Keaton,
Harry Rapf, Irving Thalberg, Nicholas Schenck, Mrs. Schenck,
Mayer, Eddie Mannix, and Hunt Stromberg. (Bison Archives)

The Barrymore brothers, Lionel (left) and John (right) in
Arsene Lupin (1932). Lionel signed with MGM in 1926, but
when Mayer signed John and Ethel in 1932, MGM was the
home of the entire Royal Family of Broadway.

In the early years of MGM, Mayer and
Thalberg captained opposing baseball
teams that played on the weekend.
Here, Mayer shows a good
semi-pro form.

(Harold B. Lee Library, Brigham Young University)

Of the hundreds of people responsible for
the look of MGM films and MGM
actors, none were more important than
chief art director Cedric Gibbons (above)
and fashion designer Adrian.

(BFI Films: Stills, Posters and Designs)

Two shots of the MGM cafeteria, the first dating from about 1932; visible on the left are Marie Dressler and Philips Holmes, while in the middle distance are Warner Baxter and Myrna Loy talking to W. S. Van Dyke II. The second shot shows the Moderne remodeling of the same facility in the mid-1940s.

(BFI Films: Stills, Posters and Designs)

In March 1933, George Bernard Shaw and Marion Davies get in between Mayer and his old adversary, Charlie Chaplin, at what must have been an uncomfortable lunch.

(Bison Archives)

The distinguished director Clarence Brown was an MGM stalwart for twenty-five years and Mayer's closest friend, during the MGM years and after.

After his 1932 heart attack and recovery in Europe, which resulted in some much-needed weight gain, Thalberg and Norma Shearer return to Mayer and MGM.

L.B. and Margaret in 1937 at a party at Marion Davies's beach house. The marriage was already under pressure from Margaret's emotional distress deriving from a hysterectomy, and L.B.'s wandering eye.
(Bison Archives)

Mayer rehearsing an appearance on the MGM/Maxwell House "Good News of 1938." On the left are music director Meredith Willson and Judy Garland; on the right is director Bill Bocher.
(Museum of Modern Art/Film Stills Archive)

One of the few photos showing Mayer and Nick Schenck enjoying each other's company. On the right, Clarence Brown pretends not to notice anything unusual.

(Harold B. Lee Library, Brigham Young University)

Busby Berkeley, Mickey Rooney, Mayer, and Judy Garland enjoy themselves while shooting *Girl Crazy*.

The stars of *The Women*: (from left) Norma Shearer, Joan Crawford, and Rosalind Russell all loathed each other and drove director George Cukor crazy, but the picture was a great critical and commercial hit.

In late middle age, Mayer grew entranced by the trappings of the horse world and built a major racing stable.

(Harold B. Lee Library, Brigham Young University)

The Hardy family, (from left) Mickey Rooney, Lewis Stone, Fay Holden, Cecilia Parker, and Sara Haden, represented Mayer's ideal American family, as well as one of the most successful movie series ever made.

Louis B. Mayer and the MGM star roster (minus Clark Gable), circa 1944.
(BFI Films: Stills, Posters and Designs)

Mayer with Ann Miller at the Mocambo in 1945. Many at MGM believed
Miller was Mayer's mistress, although Miller always denied it, saying they were
just good friends. She did claim he asked her to marry him.
(Museum of Modern Art/Film Stills Archive)

An unusual shot of Mayer without his glasses and with a big smile, dancing with Irene Dunne at his birthday party at the Mocambo in 1946.

(Museum of Modern Art/Film Stills Archive)

Lorena Mayer was everything Margaret Mayer wasn't: young, gentile, exuberantly social, and outgoing.

(Harold B. Lee Library, Brigham Young University)

Mayer's movie studio was built for and around stars. Here, a succession of the charismatic people that spelled MGM to audiences of the 1930s and '40s:

Marie Dressler

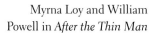

Jean Harlow in
Dinner at Eight

Myrna Loy and William
Powell in *After the Thin Man*

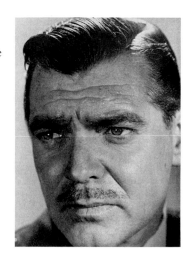

Clark Gable

Walter Pidgeon and Greer Garson
in *Mrs. Miniver*

Spencer Tracy and
Katharine Hepburn in
Woman of the Year

Garbo

Gene Kelly

Fred Astaire with
Eleanor Powell
in *The Broadway
Melody of 1940*

First among equals were Judy Garland and Mickey Rooney—vibrant and overwhelmingly talented, Mayer's embodiment of American youth.

What hath L.B. wrought? The Goldwyn lot in Culver City, circa 1923 (top); the MGM lot twenty-five years later. The block is the same, the street is the same, the town is the same. Everything else had changed. (BFI Films: Stills, Posters and Designs)

The L. B. Mayer few people ever saw: with his grandson, Daniel Selznick; trying to get a dog to obey (with son-in-law William Goetz); relaxing with his wife, Lorena, at Edie Mayer Goetz's house.
(Daniel Selznick Collection)

Mayer poses with Lorena just a week or so before he resigned from MGM in 1951. He is standing on the step above hers so he looks taller.
(Bison Archives)

A sentimental journey: Mayer stands in front of the old Orpheum, the now-derelict Lafayette, in Haverhill, in April 1954.
(Haverhill Public Library)

After leaving MGM, Mayer wandered around Hollywood and the world, seldom looking happy. Here he is in the mid-1950s, surrounded by Clarence Brown (left), an unidentified woman, Lorena Mayer, and Mrs. Brown.
(Bison Archives)

Toward the end, Mayer seemed to get smaller. Here, in January 1957, he stands uncertainly with his arm through Mike Todd's, with Lorena Mayer next to Todd.

L.B.'s coffin is carried out after the services, with Clarence Brown (left of coffin) as chief pallbearer.

(Harold B. Lee Library, Brigham Young University)

"It's . . . a woman!" he exclaimed.

The woman was Janet Gaynor, whom he eventually married and had a son with. There were those who believe that Adrian married Gaynor to give her cover for a long-term affair with actress Margaret Lindsay. Adrian was probably bisexual, but he remained married to Gaynor for the rest of his life. In an era of don't ask, don't tell, he was usually accepted at face value.

Then there was Howard Strickling, the head of publicity, the keeper of the secrets. Strickling was a native of L.A., a high school dropout who had worked as a sportswriter. Because he had worked as a reporter, he knew that journalists were usually easy to co-opt, often by something as easy to arrange as access. Strickling was a kind and considerate man who was, remembered one of the people who worked for him, "one of the most loved people in the publicity business." Strickling's job was to ensure that there were never scandals, that things were worked out. The job of publicity was not merely publicity, but to make life for their performers as comfortable as it could possibly be, to protect them from unpleasantries of all kinds.

If Clark Gable sent a message through Strickling that L.B. could shove it up his ass, Strickling's translation would be, "Clark thinks it's a great idea, but he wants some time to mull it over." And if Mayer snarled that he had made Gable and could, by God, break him, Strickling's translation was that Mayer would be personally indebted if Gable would do him this one favor. To the end of Strickling's life, L. B. Mayer could never be wrong, just misunderstood.

For stars who presented considerable challenges, like the man Strickling referred to as "the multiple-problem . . . [violent alcoholic Spencer] Tracy, we devised an . . . elaborate technique. We kept an official-looking ambulance on call at the studio. Every bar owner and hotel manager in the area knew what to do if Tracy showed up drunk and began causing a problem. They'd phone me, and I'd phone [MGM police chief] Whitey [Hendry], and the ambulance would take off with a couple of our security men dressed as paramedics. They'd go to the scene, strap Tracy to a stretcher, and then rush him away in the ambulance before too many people would recognize Tracy as the trouble-maker."

When an MGM star got in some kind of jam, one of the men that the studio kept on its payroll in every local police department—any policeman from any town in America was always welcome at MGM and given tours and honorary MGM police badges—would tip off Hendry, who often got to the scene before the official police. While Hendry worked the police, publicist Ralph Wheelwright took care of the press. This system worked like a charm—

newspapers would never print stories for fear of losing access to the MGM stable of stars.

"Whitey Hendry was a pretty good guy," remembered Culver City fireman Ray Moselle. "Could he throw his weight around? Yes, he could. If anybody got a traffic ticket, Whitey would fix it. He cultivated a lot of friendships with police and fire chiefs throughout the area. When we'd throw fund-raising dances, Whitey would always buy tickets for the studio. He'd see to it that fire and policemen would get hired on a standby basis at MGM. And if you did Whitey a favor, he'd do you one in return.

"That said, they didn't try to run roughshod over everybody, or get special preference."

Of course, they didn't really need to. "We controlled the fan magazines," said MGM publicist Esme Chandlee. "When a star did an interview with a fan magazine, that story was submitted to us, and we took out whatever we wanted. If a situation was bad enough, Whitey Hendry would be called. He had a lot of influence downtown. Maybe it wouldn't hit the papers at all, or if it did, it would be minor, or a blind item for (gossip columnist) Harrison Carroll."

Contributing to the insulation was a close relationship between Mayer and Los Angeles district attorney Buron Fitts; MGM was the top contributor to his election campaign.

"I always thought of Hollywood as a principality of its own," remembered Budd Schulberg. "It was like a sort of a Luxembourg or a Liechtenstein. And the people who ran it really had that attitude. They weren't only running a studio, they were running a whole little world. Their power was absolutely enormous, and it wasn't only the power to make movies or to anoint someone or make someone a movie star or pick an unknown director and make him famous overnight. They could cover up a murder. You could literally have someone killed, and it wouldn't be in the papers. They ran this place.

"Louis Mayer was a supreme organizer, very well set-up to run a major studio operation. But in many ways he was overbearing, running things in a very high-handed dictatorial way, and the studio was almost like a little fascist state."

Strickling assigned a publicist as a sort of elder brother or sister to every major MGM star. Besides serving as a publicist, the person could, depending on the star, also be a procurer, a lover, or a snitch. "They liked you to be friendly with the stars, so you could go to their homes and get pictures you wouldn't ordinarily get," said the MGM publicist Berdie Abrams.

Strickling's office was a model of efficiency. Forty people attended Monday morning meetings, and the publicity angles flowed out to cover the town. If

Mayer was the Closer, Strickling was the Fixer. Abortions were magically transformed into "appendectomies," alcoholism into "exhaustion." Strickling only had a few inviolable rules for his staff: no publicist's name should ever appear in print; no MGM performer should ever be pictured with a drink in his or her hand. "To this day," said publicist Esme Chandlee, "I reach out and take a drink out of a client's hands whenever a camera shows up."

Strickling was masterful at fostering loyalty. When a story needed to be written for a magazine, say something about a star's house for *House and Garden*, it would be handed to a junior publicist, who would get the necessary quotes without delay, then keep the freelance check for $400—a lot more than their weekly salary.

The upside to all this, for blue-collar and white-collar employees alike, was a sense of true security, the feeling of the corporation functioning as a strong, beneficent safety net that indemnified people from outside reality. The sense of uniformity, of studio style, was even present in the company's coming attractions, which for over twenty years were narrated by a staff publicist named Frank Whitbeck. Whitbeck's middle-aged, phlegmatic voice was as far from radio-style slickness as could be imagined, and seemed an odd fit with the glamorous MGM style, but Mayer and Strickling liked him.

"They exercised this fantastic control," said Robert Young. "The whole studio. From the top straight down. Which in one way mitigated to your . . . benefit; in another way it's horribly restricting. You're not supposed to get married, and if you get married, you're not supposed to have any children, or at least if you have children don't take photographs or don't allow photographs to be taken of your children, lest they be printed and the public sees that and says, 'Oh, well, he's married, he has children, he's in a sense unavailable, he's out of circulation.' "

All this could lead to a crippling dependency. As one star put it, "MGM created a certain name, but they didn't prepare you for life. I mean, what do you say when Howard Strickling wasn't around and you had to get an abortion?"

Actually, Mayer drew the line at a staff abortionist; that was the province of "Docky" Martin, the husband of Louella Parsons, who was employed at Fox to take care of the unplanned pregnancies of the actresses, as well as keep the favorable mentions of Fox pictures coming in the Hearst press.

In the 1930s, the studio barbershop was the social center, especially in the late afternoon, when Mayer would go in for a shave, trim, or manicure. The shoeshine stand next door was run by a black man known as Slickum, who doubled in all sorts of jobs. He would recruit black extras when needed, and he would supply prostitutes for certain executives.

The studio bookie was named Rudi, tiny (five feet) and very friendly. Rudi had free access to the lot and was the only bookie allowed—most people on the lot believed Mayer got a percentage of Rudi's take—coming in every day at nine and leaving the scratch sheets for all the major tracks at the shoeshine stand and barbershop. After taking care of his small bets, Rudi would visit the executive offices and take care of the big bettors.

Mostly the studio was all business, except during the annual Christmas parties. Early on Christmas Eve, the first few hours were spent delivering gifts—agents to department heads, producers, and other important types. Menial employees would be given generous tips as a Christmas bonus. By 11:00 A.M., each department had a bar going. Around this time, Mayer would make an appearance, mount a rostrum, and promise another great year like the one just passed. And then he would leave the studio. Like the parent leaving the house, it was the signal for the kids' party to kick into high gear. The projection room in the sound department began running stag films, and by the early afternoon, remembered Wallace Worsley Jr., the proceedings had evolved into "an orgy that would have made Caligula feel at home."

People began passing out in the late afternoon and most of it was over by evening. Sam Marx believed that Mayer's absence was a function of his knowledge of human nature; that while he didn't necessarily approve of the debauchery, he realized that the celebration was a way of letting the staff blow off steam, not to mention a cheap way of maintaining high morale. The Christmas parties were merely part of the social aspect of the studio.

"You never left the studio for anything," said Joseph L. Mankiewicz. "When you were at the studio, you were not only safe from the outside world, you could participate in any part of the outside world that you wanted to. If you wanted to register to vote or renew your driver's license, they came on the lot. At Christmas time, the department stores used to bring stuff over to your office to show you.

"I used to wander around the studio at night. That's when the sets were built. There was all this activity, lights blazing. It was fantastic. The commissary was open 24 hours a day. Every day at 5 o'clock, the barber shop was locked and only executives could use it. You went in if you were one of the privileged."

Between Mayer and Thalberg, it was nearly impossible to get anything remotely progressive politically into production at MGM, which didn't stop people from trying. Two junior writers, Robert Lees and Fred Rinaldo, who had developed a specialty in Robert Benchley and Pete Smith shorts, wrote a feature script called *Tomorrow Never Comes*, which was more or less *The Grapes of Wrath* in an urban setting. "Mayer read the script," remembered Lees, "and said it wasn't politically proper for Metro-Goldwyn-Mayer to do this kind of thing, and they wouldn't handle it."

"There was real tumult going on socially," remembered Alvin Josephy, a writer at the studio in two crucial periods: the Depression and just after World War II. "There were strikes and threats of strikes. The general tenor at the studio was that Franklin D. Roosevelt was popular, even among some of the business types. Even at MGM, if you were a Roosevelt man, you were in the majority.

"But in the movies, the most valued writers are the guys who can write formula. I always wanted to be fresh and say something, but you couldn't do that. Mayer would say, 'No messages.' "

Fury began as a story about a lynching by Norman Krasna in collaboration with Joseph L. Mankiewicz. The script was constructed by Leonard Praskins, Bartlett Cormack, Mankiewicz, and director Fritz Lang, who had been requested by Mankiewicz, and who had been biding his time at the studio for a year without anything coming to fruition.

Mayer loathed the script, but he liked Mankiewicz so he used the film as a test case. "I've got to prove to you right away the facts of this business," he said. "I'm not only going to let you make *Fury*, but I promise, in writing, that every penny that Irving spends on *Romeo and Juliet*, I will spend exploiting *Fury*. It will get great reviews, and it will go on its ass."

"He kept his word," remembered Mankiewicz. "He had skywriting over New York promoting *Fury*. And his prediction came true. It got great reviews and it went on its ass."

Actually, it did no such thing. *Fury* showed a clear profit of $248,000, more than Selznick's vaunted *A Tale of Two Cities*, and more than the first Andy Hardy film, *A Family Affair*. But Mayer's attitude toward socially conscious filmmaking with a literary bent would be revealed by a story illustrator Al Hirschfeld liked to tell. A friend of Hirschfeld's once asked Mayer why so many movies were so terrible, so dopey. Mayer gazed at the man and said, "We do make a good picture occasionally, you will admit that?"

Yes, yes, of course, said Hirschfeld's friend.

"Well, we don't have to," said Mayer.

Stars were the coin of Mayer's realm, and nothing was too good for them. "It was wonderful," remembered the singer Frances Langford, who was under contract to the studio in the middle 1930s. "They did things for you. Your dressing room was customized for you. There were fresh flowers, changed every day. And when Mayer would come on the set, it was lovely, like the family being visited by the father. RKO and Paramount were nice, but they weren't that way. They weren't Metro."

For L.B., good enough wasn't good enough. The prop furniture had to be real—for *Marie Antoinette*, there were authentic, very valuable antique pieces on the sets. That belief in the intrinsic value of premium goods filtered down and gave the imprimatur of quality to everything and everyone on the lot, whether they deserved it or not.

The Metro stars were types. There were blue-collar types (Wallace Beery, Spencer Tracy, Joan Crawford) and there were white-collar types (William Powell, Robert Montgomery, Myrna Loy).

Above everyone else was Garbo—not in her box office, which was decent but not overwhelming—but in her aura, which concealed a rather ordinary, pinched woman.

"Garbo would never go to bat for anybody, especially for money," said Peter Viertel, the son of Garbo's friend and screenwriter Salka Viertel. "She was very cowardly, a narcissist. Charming, certainly beautiful, but not all that great a friend. Actually, she used my mother more than my mother used her, which sounds funny, because she was a star and my mother was an oarsman in the galley."

It was widely understood that Clark Gable was the rock upon which MGM was built. He was first among equals; Gable got six weeks off after every movie; he never had to go on a publicity tour; he was protected by everybody at all costs. "The secret of Clark's surviving his own fame," reported director Richard Lang, the son of Carole Lombard's best friend, Fieldsie Lang, "was that he was protected by the people around him. If a building was falling, for whatever reason, they would throw themselves over him."

None of this tender loving care would have made the least difference if Gable wasn't Gable, if he wasn't one of those rare men that men want to be and women want to be with. Eddie Mannix's secretary, June Caldwell, remembered Gable coming into her office unexpectedly, with a big smile on his face. "I'd never seen anything like it. He was just the most beautiful man. He opened the door with that smile and I lost my voice."

Gable's attitude toward Louis B. Mayer would never be more than grudging; he had the creation's resentment toward the creator; he resented lectures about morality from a man who was having affairs, and he would mightily resent MGM making a fortune off his unwilling participation in *Gone With the Wind*. He was, he told a friend, looking forward to the day he could walk down Washington Boulevard, take out his false teeth, and heave them through L. B. Mayer's window.

"Gable was a presence," remembered Ann Rutherford. "The important thing in the movie business is whether or not the crew likes you. Clark would know most of the names of the men on the crew. He was not above straddling a carpenter's horse, pulling out a deck of cards and playing a couple of hands. He was a very nice man; he had been where the crew members had been, and never thought he was any better than they were."

"He was the most professional actor alive," remembered Ricardo Montalban. "The camera loved him, the moment loved him. He was always the first one on the set, made up and ready to go. He knew his lines backward and forward. But at five o'clock, he was gone. 'Clark, we need just one more shot . . .' 'No, sorry, that's it.'

"Personally, he was an unassuming, sweet guy, but a little dull. You expected the Gable of the screen, and he was not that. He was only interested in motorcycles, cars, and hunting. Outside of that, it was yes, or no. I didn't want to be a pest, but once I asked him a question about *It Happened One Night*.

" 'Did you really not want to do that picture?' I asked.

" 'No, I really didn't,' he said. And that's all he said. That was it."

The woman the world knew as Jean Harlow was actually Harlean Harlow Carpenter, born in Kansas City in 1911. Of all the MGM stars, she probably had the steepest learning curve. She worked her way up through the extra ranks (she's somewhere in the nightclub scene in Chaplin's *City Lights* and can be glimpsed in some Laurel and Hardy two-reelers). In her initial speaking parts, as in 1930's *Hell's Angels*, she is a rank amateur whose only distinction is her spectacular figure, which is flagrantly displayed by her lack of underwear.

But after just a few years at MGM, Harlow had risen to be a wonderfully brash comedian with a specialty in good-hearted floozies, and at least a competent actress. This was partially a result of the experience of working with first-rate directors like George Cukor and of having to raise the level of her game to compete with her co-stars, who were all polished pros.

Harlow was universally beloved by her co-workers; she was fun, unpretentious, and invariably thoughtful of other people. Her Achilles' heel was her disastrous taste in men, which ran from the much older cameraman Hal Rosson to the MGM producer Paul Bern, who may or may not have been homosexual and who may or may not have committed suicide after a few months of marriage to Harlow. Douglas Fairbanks Jr. told a harrowing anecdote of a lunch at which his friend Bern was proudly telling him about their engagement, while Harlow was playing footsie with Fairbanks under the table.

Bern's mysterious death, officially ruled a suicide, was accepted as such by most of his friends. Edward Bernays, the father of modern public relations and an early mentor of Bern's, accepted the official verdict because he believed Bern to be "so much in love with his mother that he felt that any relationship with a woman that ended in marriage, psychologically had the effect on him of an incestuous relationship."

Harlow was an unspoiled, unsophisticated woman. When she was being fitted at Magnin's for her wedding gown for the ceremony with Bern, she couldn't make up her mind and decided to buy three different dresses. The problem arose because, as was well known, she refused to wear underwear, and her pubic hair showed under all three choices. The fitter at Magnin's felt compelled to point this out, but Harlow waved her objections away. "Don't worry about that, honey. I'll just put 'Stay-Comb' on it."

When Howard Hawks checked onto the Metro lot to make *Viva Villa!* he and Harlow struck sparks, and he asked the screenwriter John Lee Mahin for an introduction. Hawks and Harlow were soon in deep conversation and went home together. The next day, Mahin sidled up to Hawks. "Well?" he asked. Hawks proceeded to tell Mahin that she was all right, but that he had been disconcerted by the moisture she secreted during sex. Mahin tried to tell his friend that that was normal, but Hawks wouldn't hear of it.

Since Hawks was married to the sister of Norma Shearer at the time, and was brother-in-law to Irving Thalberg, the story is indicative not merely of sexual ignorance, but of professional foolhardiness. It might explain why Hawks's MGM career was so brief. Tragically, Harlow died of kidney failure at the age of twenty-six.

Wallace Beery was the roughneck, the kind of man who, Luc Santé wrote, "broke chairs over . . . heads in pre–Volstead Act saloons, died at Vera Cruz and on the Marne, ran Florida real estate swindles . . . populated hobo jungles before the CCC trucked them off."

He was a bulbous, upstaging ham who wouldn't rehearse and stopped acting around the time of *Viva Villa!*, content with playing the lovable slob. He was also a grumpy, miserable miser who would park his station wagon by the stage door and use his lunch hour to steal material and props that weren't being used, then move his station wagon elsewhere. Once the prop man caught on to what was happening to his disappearing stock, he would cruise the lot until he found Beery's car, jimmy the door, and unload the booty.

Personally, Beery was, as Robert Young remembered, "a shitty person," scratching his crotch, never bothering to learn his lines, choosing instead to approximate them and resenting any kind of correction, often using the other actor's dialogue as well as his. When prompting for another actor's close-up, he would intentionally read the wrong lines, so the other actor had to respond in a vacuum.

Beery was loathed by everybody, and happily oblivious. When he had lunch at the commissary, he wouldn't leave a tip. Questioned about it, he would explain that a tip was for special service, and since he was a famous movie star, he automatically got special service. Therefore, a tip was a waste of money. Once, Beery invited the twelve-year-old Darryl Hickman to go to lunch with him. They ordered hamburgers, and when it was time to go, Hickman said, "Gee, thanks, Mr. Beery."

"Okay, kid," replied Beery, "you owe me 75 cents."

Beery met his match only once, when he worked with Marie Dressler on *Tugboat Annie* and *Min and Bill.* "She was really lovely," remembered Robert Young, "a wonderful person. She'd come the long, hard way, and she was very, very grateful. And she wouldn't take any nonsense from this baboon. She straightened him out the first day. 'Look you silly shit, you pull one more thing like that on me and I'll have your head. On a platter. And not an expensive platter. A little, cheap, lousy, wooden platter. Like John the Baptist. With a personal note to L. B. Mayer.' "

Everybody waited for the explosion, but it never happened. "He got very cowed," said Young, "and then he was like a little boy being very careful that Mommy didn't catch him with his hand in the cookie jar."

When Howard Strickling went to Mayer to complain about Beery, Mayer listened and sighed. Finally, he said, "Yes, Howard, Beery's a son of a bitch. But he's *our* son of a bitch."

For years, the biggest star on the lot was a miniature force of nature named Mickey Rooney, whose star had been in the ascendancy since arriving at MGM in 1934, culminating in a performance in *The Devil Is a Sissy* that blew fellow child star Jackie Cooper off the screen, then off the lot.

Rooney was born Joe Yule Jr., in Brooklyn in 1920, the son of vaudevillian parents. He was on stage at fifteen months and became part of the family act.

He learned to sing, dance, act, and project his ineffable personality by the time he was eight, when he had already been in the movies for two years. His father's alcoholism broke up the marriage, so Rooney had to earn a living. Between 1927 and 1930, he starred in a series of comedy shorts named after a comic strip character called Mickey McGuire, a tough little street urchin with a taste for cheap cigars.

To watch Rooney in those films is to see a butterfly in chrysalis form: you can clearly make out the actor's primary colors—his bumptiousness and boyish charm—but he lacks smoothness, polish. That came gradually, as Rooney worked and worked.

By the time MGM signed him, at the insistence of David Selznick, they had a fourteen-year-old show business whirlwind who could do absolutely anything that might be asked of him, including playing Clark Gable as a child in *Manhattan Melodrama*. Mayer, who had been initially unimpressed, was soon won over and the young actor became one of his favorites, a vehicle for projecting Mayer's vision of young America: endless exuberance mixed with a good heart, needing only the seasoning of wisdom to complete his personality.

MGM always featured more juveniles than any other studio in Hollywood. (In the ten years from 1933 to 1943, MGM films starred Cooper, Rooney, Judy Garland, Freddie Bartholomew, Margaret O'Brien, Butch Jenkins, Elizabeth Taylor, and Roddy McDowall—and those were just the actors who were notably successful.)

"You weren't going to work, you were going to have fun," Rooney said. "It was home, everybody was cohesive; it was family. One year I made nine pictures; I had to go from one set to another. It was like I was on a conveyer belt. You did not read a script and say, 'I guess I'll do it.' *You did it.* They had people that knew the kind of stories that were suited to you. It was a conveyer belt that made motion pictures.

"Everybody at MGM had an eye for talent. They reached out; they were sybarites for talent, they wanted only the best. And they had, not a lax, but an elastic hand for people who made motion pictures."

As far as MGM was concerned, nothing was too good for these men and women. "If you went to New York, you stayed at the Waldorf Towers in the MGM suite," said Evie Johnson. "If you traveled to London, Paris, or Rome, the studio would have someone there to meet you and shepherd you around. You were completely catered to; your slightest wish was their command—as long as you were big at the box office."

Mayer and Thalberg cast their directors the same way they cast their actors.

There were blue-collar directors (Victor Fleming, W. S. Van Dyke) and white-collar (Robert Z. Leonard, George Cukor). Fleming directed with his genitals, Cukor with his mind, Clarence Brown with his heart, and Woody Van Dyke and Robert Z. Leonard directed with slightly calloused hands.

In the same way that young actors of the same type would be groomed as possible replacements for an established star, so young directors would be groomed. Metro plucked Richard Thorpe from Poverty Row in 1935 and brought him along as an unpretentious all-arounder, a young Woody Van Dyke. It didn't work out; Van Dyke had energy, and sometimes a surprising grace, but Thorpe was hardly ever anything but a by-the-numbers director, albeit a busy one: sixty-six films for MGM in thirty years. Metro tended to use Thorpe for maintenance work on ongoing series—four Tarzan films, two Lassies, a late *Thin Man*, a dozen musicals for Joe Pasternak, but never one for Arthur Freed. But he lasted longer than anybody at the studio, directing his last MGM film in 1967.

The success of *The Barretts of Wimpole Street* showed Irving Thalberg his wife's future: she would be the screen equivalent of Katherine Cornell or Lynn Fontanne. In Thalberg's mind, Norma Shearer's career would ascend toward *Romeo and Juliet* and *Marie Antoinette*, and then she would retire. "Too many stars stay on camera too long," Thalberg said in May of 1935. "I want her to bow out at her highest point."

Although she was the boss's wife, Shearer didn't throw her weight around in any obvious way. "She always smiled," recalled Robert Young. "And it wasn't a false smile, it was a lovely, sweet, gentle smile. They would ask her something, 'Miss Shearer,' or 'Mrs. Thalberg,' and she would just smile and she'd say 'No.' And that was it. . . . She just smiled, and, 'No.' And that was it. Bingo. Took care of the whole thing."

Romeo and Juliet and *Marie Antoinette* were planned as spectaculars, but Mayer was particularly worried about Shakespeare, which he regarded as uncommercial. Thalberg went directly to Nick Schenck, who approved the film so long as the budget didn't exceed $1 million, a figure Thalberg must have known was absurd, given the scope of the film he was planning. (The film ended up costing a little more than $2 million, and lost nearly $1 million.)

Romeo and Juliet widened the breach between the two men even further; Thalberg believed that Mayer cared too much about making money and not enough about making quality films, while Mayer believed that Thalberg was indulging himself with overtly uncommercial vanity productions. "When a producer tells me he has a prestige picture, I know we're going to lose money," Mayer said.

Thalberg had always been cavalier about production schedules. He indulged King Vidor with plenty of time—*The Crowd* had taken ninety-seven days, longer than far more lavish productions such as *The Merry Widow* and *Mutiny on the Bounty*, which took eighty-eight days apiece. A fairly small-scale Thalberg picture like *China Seas* had taken fifty-three days, even though Woody Van Dyke was able to push a spectacle like *San Francisco* through in fifty-two days.

But as Thalberg moved on to the testimonial phase of his career, he slowed down even more; *Romeo and Juliet* was in production for an unconscionable 108 days. Thalberg hovered around the set, ordered Herbert Stothart to rewrite his music, supervised Douglas Shearer's dubbing. This was not only Norma's monument, it was his.

Mayer thought Thalberg's plans for *The Good Earth* were insane—he snapped that he didn't even want a picture about American farmers, and here Irving was making one about *Chinese* farmers! Screenwriters wrote multiple drafts—four writers ended up getting credit—and directors came and went: George Hill, Victor Fleming, Sidney Franklin, and even Fred Niblo all shot footage for the picture, but only Franklin received credit. *The Good Earth* took 120 days for principal photography, and many more months for special effects and second unit work.

With Thalberg focusing only on his own productions, the studio came to rely more on Mayer, and Mayer came to rely more on Kate Corbaley and the story department. Mayer knew few writers and even less about current stories. Sam Marx remembered that L.B. had a few favorite books from his childhood and would often mention how he would enjoy seeing them on film, but the issue was never pressed and Mayer didn't object to his executives' indifference to his preferences.

Mayer's habit of holding a grudge came to the fore with Lenore Coffee, who had worked for him at the Mission Road studio. She had developed a specialty in women's stories, and had a new original for which she wanted $5,000, but Mayer thought it was too much money. Mayer called her into his office and told her she would accept $2,500 for it or "get the hell out of this studio!"

From there, Mayer escalated into a personal attack. "You're what I always thought you were: a cold, selfish, mercenary, unscrupulous woman!" and he finished his tirade by threatening to put her out of the movie business: "You'll never earn another penny in it as long as you live!" This was all a rather drastic way of negotiating the price down. Instead Coffee left the studio. As was also typical, she later returned and was greeted by Mayer with literal open arms and a warm greeting of "So you had to come back home!"

In 1934, William Randolph Hearst packed up Cosmopolitan and Marion Davies and decamped for Warner Bros. The relationship between Hearst and Mayer had been touchy for some time, and the two men had also diverged politically. The breaking point was reached when MGM denied Marion Davies the starring role in *The Barretts of Wimpole Street* and *Marie Antoinette*, both of which went to Norma Shearer for obvious reasons.

Marion Davies claimed that Thalberg relented and said she could have *Marie Antoinette*, but that Mayer had intervened, telling Hearst that Marion could make the film only if Hearst paid for it. What actually happened is that Thalberg simply decided not to waste his energy and handed off the delivery of the bad news to Mayer. Hearst was fighting a rearguard action against the Depression and mountains of debt that would overwhelm him; there was no way he could pay for an expensive film, and Mayer knew it.

Hearst had no one to blame but himself. He adamantly refused to add sex appeal to Marion's films, and refused to let her do sophisticated or slapstick comedy. At the same time, age and alcohol were beginning to make Davies's face puff up; she could no longer play pretty young things—in *Going Hollywood*, made when Marion was thirty-seven, she played a college girl.

"When King Vidor had made Davies's films," said historian David Nasaw, "he kept the costs down. But everyone else went way over budget because Hearst was continually demanding rewrites. Everything, scripts, rushes, rough cuts, was being sent to him at San Simeon. And by that time, Thalberg was paying less attention, and Thalberg was the only one who could rein him in. The overruns were incredible, and after a point, MGM just gave up." Hearst took Marion and her bungalow and left for Burbank. But Hearst soon found out that power in Hollywood is fed only by success. The Hearst papers were now on the run from the Depression, their vindictive editorial treatment of Roosevelt, and the owner's profligate lifestyle. On top of that, Marion's unexceptional box office was faltering even further. She made two mediocre films at Warners before retirement.

Although the business relationship had become untenable, the friendship between Mayer and Hearst—whom L.B. called "Pops"—continued. Mayer visited the lovers at their astonishing Bavarian retreat at Wyntoon, and he would attend Hearst's funeral.

By the mid-1930s, L.B. was regarded as a seductive man with an eye on the big picture. "Louis had been after me for many years," remembered producer Pandro Berman. "He was a very farsighted man. He was the kind of man who would call you up and say, 'I want you to go to work for me.' Once I said to him, 'I'd certainly like to do that, Mr. Mayer, but unfortunately I just signed a five-year contract with [RKO]. He said, 'I didn't say when, did I? I want you to go to work when you're through there.' Not many men were thinking that far in advance in those days, and I doubt if they are now." Berman finally signed with MGM and stayed for twenty-five years.

When Mayer launched a full-court press, few could resist, not even the FBI. When an agent stopped by his office in June 1936, to ask about an anonymous letter he had received that reported some scurrilous remarks of Walter Winchell's, Mayer had no interest in talking about Winchell or the letter, but instead wanted to talk about the FBI. He wanted to know the qualifications needed for agents, he wanted to know about the salaries, he wanted to know J. Edgar Hoover.

The public didn't appreciate what it had in the FBI, he said, and he instructed his secretary to get Mr. Hearst on the phone, so the publisher could commission a series of articles that would result in greater congressional appropriations for the bureau. When Hearst proved unavailable, he left a message for Hearst to call him back. The thunderstruck agent called the visit "pleasant and interesting." Hoover noted on the memo that resulted from the meeting, "Place Louis B. Mayer on mailing list."

Under the terms of his agreement with Loew's for the I. G. Thalberg Corporation, Thalberg could automatically get any five or six MGM stars for his films, with the exception of Gable and Garbo, who would require special dispensation. He asked that Norma, Charles Laughton, and the Marx Brothers be considered his personal property, and that was all fine with the home office. But Mayer was still worried about trying to run a studio where Irving would skim off the cream for his couple of pictures a year. Here was the ultimate proof that it wasn't about MGM—it was all about Thalberg.

In 1935, Thalberg contributed *Mutiny on the Bounty, A Night at the Opera,* and *China Seas. The Good Earth* was in production, as was *Camille.* Other Thalberg projects included *Pride and Prejudice, Marie Antoinette,* another Marx Brothers picture, *Goodbye, Mr. Chips,* and *The Forty Days of Musa Dagh.* It was a very ambitious roster—the only picture that didn't present considerable production problems was *Pride and Prejudice*—and all the pictures were scheduled to be made in the next three years.

By 1936, the turf war was felt throughout the lot. The studio was divided between the Mayer camp and the Thalberg camp, with each side quietly denigrating the other's slate of pictures. For much of 1936, besides Garbo's *Camille* and *The Good Earth*, Thalberg was working on a MacDonald-Eddy picture called *Maytime*. "Edmund Goulding had started it," remembered Joseph Newman, "even though we didn't have a script, but Thalberg let him go ahead anyway. Goulding would write it every night at home, and I would take it over to Thalberg's home in Santa Monica, where he would read it over."

By now, Thalberg had warmed up to Newman, who had worked as an assistant director on a number of Thalberg productions, including *The Merry Widow* and *China Seas*. "Thalberg was down on the set all the time, but not with Lubitsch and *The Merry Widow*; he gave Lubitsch, a wonderful picturemaker, a free hand. Thalberg had a very astute story mind, and I think he could have been a great writer. When we had some trouble with the script on the set of *China Seas*, he would come down to the set many times and rewrite the scenes himself, right there on the set. Sometimes he'd dictate the changes so you could write them down, sometimes he'd do it himself with a pencil."

The first floor of Thalberg's bungalow contained his office, a long, wood-paneled room with a huge desk near the windows. Chairs and couches took up space around the perimeter.

Upstairs were quarters for the writers. On the third floor was a kitchen, a pantry, and a dining room. In the afternoon a butler would make the rounds to inquire if anyone wanted tea or a highball.

In January 1936, Mayer took a three-week vacation trip to Panama, announcing on his return that Roosevelt's veto of the veterans' bonus would have ramifications in that year's presidential elections. A year and a half earlier, he had taken Margaret with him to Paris, but now they were taking separate vacations. It was a sign to one and all that the marriage was on the rocks.

Mayer and Thalberg had to make some decisions together, so on occasion a steely outward amity was maintained. On June 2, 1936, they gathered to listen to Cole Porter play his score for the Eleanor Powell vehicle *Born to Dance*. According to Porter, Thalberg was "looking more dead than alive, and [was] obviously angry at being disturbed to hear this score." But after a couple of numbers, Mayer rose and "began jumping around the room," and soon Thalberg loosened up and cracked a smile. When Porter was finished, Thalberg grabbed

Porter's hand and told him, "I think it's one of the finest scores I have ever heard." L.B. was more effusive, hugging Porter and asking him to sign a new contract.

Porter signed a three-year deal with MGM, and worked on the score for *Rosalie,* the title song of which went through seven versions until Mayer was satisfied. On the other hand, Mayer was instantly delighted by Porter's "In the Still of the Night," bursting into tears the first time he heard it. Nelson Eddy told Porter it was impossible to sing, but the composer went to Mayer, who ordered Eddy to quit bellyaching and sing the song.

Behind closed doors L.B. and Nick Schenck could have screaming fights, but between L.B. and Thalberg there was just a frigid contempt.

One day Thalberg was in a story conference with Lenore Coffee, when Mayer came storming in, upset about something or another.

"Would you mind leaving the room, Miss Coffee," said Thalberg, "while I put Mr. Mayer in his place?"

At this point, Thalberg didn't care whether he offended Mayer or not, because he knew that as long as he had Nick Schenck he didn't need L.B. In setting up an independent company, Thalberg was kicking back, while Mayer, as Howard Strickling observed, "never backed up, always moved forward."

In the first week of September 1936, Mayer returned to Saint John to be feted in a series of local-boy-makes-good banquets. He visited his mother's grave, he paid a visit to a woman who had taught him in grade school. He tried some of the raspberry jams and jellies he had seldom been able to afford as a boy, proclaimed that you couldn't get flavor like that in warm climates, and ordered nine cases—three for him, and three each for Edie and Irene.

At a banquet, a friend of his childhood toasted him as "a poor boy endowed only with intellectual worth, moral steadfastness and tenacity of purpose." In response, Louis quoted John Wilson's favorite maxim: "When you come to the end of your rope, tie a knot and hang on." He expounded on his philosophy of movies, citing innovations such as the MacDonald-Eddy operettas and literary adaptations like *David Copperfield* and *Captains Courageous* as exemplars of his strategy. "MGM has been trying nicer, better, finer things, gradually to raise the taste of the public, which is one of the finer things pictures can do, for they are *the* popular entertainment." The company's primary purpose in making *Romeo and Juliet* was not financial profit, he said, but to encourage other companies to take chances on better things. He even managed to utter a few sentences in praise of Nick Schenck for his courage in permitting expensive productions that might negatively impact the bottom line of Loew's, Inc.

Thalberg was still a workaholic, finding enough tasks to fill up his usual twelve-hour days. He saw *Tudor Rose*, a new picture made by Gaumont-British and liked it. Michael Balcon, head of Gaumont, wrote to thank him for his kind words and Thalberg responded on July 1, 1936, by writing that he had been hoping to get away for a vacation, but didn't know exactly when he was going to be able to do it. The signature was the indecipherable scrawl of a dying man.

There is a perceptible sense of Thalberg as a man weary of having to cope with people he clearly regarded as his intellectual inferiors. Around this time, Thalberg sat down and dictated what amounted to a long position paper about the causes of the Depression, and the strengths and weaknesses of the American political system in the aftermath of Roosevelt. It's well reasoned, professorially articulate, a little dry. But professors couldn't make hundreds of thousands of dollars a year, so Thalberg remained yoked to the movie business.

As the fall of 1936 approached, Thalberg was comfortably ensconced in his baronial office—the Tudor fireplace, leather chairs, bookcases, and large wooden tables of a prosperous club room. He arrived at his office by 10:30 in the morning, his poker face already in place. Every few minutes a secretary would appear to announce another visitor.

Thalberg had a meeting with Sidney Franklin, Al Lewin, Basil Wrangell, and [editor] Margaret Booth about last-minute tweaking of *The Good Earth*. He had offered Franklin the chair at the head of his conference table, but Franklin refused.

"You're the director," said Thalberg. "You sit here."

But Franklin knew who was really the chief and insisted that Thalberg take the chair. After an hour, Thalberg excused himself and explained that he was going away to Pebble Beach in Monterey for a few days of golf and relaxation.

A few days later, news spread through the studio that Thalberg had caught a bad cold and returned home. Joe Newman kept bringing the pages of Edmund Goulding's script for *Maytime* to Thalberg's house, even though he could see that the producer was feverish, laboring and was "pretty ill."

On the night of September 13, Thalberg fell into a coma. The next morning, September 14, 1936, at 10:16 in the morning, Irving Thalberg died at his home at 707 Ocean Front Avenue. When Norma Shearer called him with the news of Thalberg's death, Mayer went at once to Thalberg's house, where he and Shearer both broke down.

As the stunning news spread across MGM, people couldn't believe it. Executives huddled together in offices. Sidney Franklin came upon Al Lewin, standing at his window, staring out at the lot, tears rolling down his face. Mayer issued a statement whose windy generalities bore the hallmarks of Howard Strickling. "I have lost my associate of the past fourteen years and the finest friend a man could ever have. There is so very much to be said about Irving Thalberg, but there are so few words with which to say it and the shock is too great. He was the guiding inspiration behind the artistic progress of the screen. His brilliant leadership, his idealism, his warm, human qualities made him the foremost figure in the advancement of the high standards and the appreciation that has marked milestones in film history. He was a creator, a man with vision who believed sincerely in the mission of motion pictures; a man to whom no effort nor sacrifice was too great if it served a purpose toward attainment of artistic achievement. My heart goes out in this sorrow to his fine, gifted wife, Norma Shearer, whose unfailing devotion and courage knew no bounds. Irving Thalberg was a simple man, a man whose greatest tribute is having achieved in so short a life so towering a monument of affection."

The funeral was the Hollywood equivalent of a state occasion. The ushers included Clark Gable, Fredric March, Douglas Fairbanks Sr., Woody Van Dyke, Sam Wood, Carey Wilson, Sidney Franklin, Cedric Gibbons, and Harry Carey. The Barrymore brothers attended, as did the Marx Brothers. Chaplin, Disney, Lombard, Gary Cooper, and even Erich von Stroheim came to pay their respects. Every studio observed five minutes of silence, and MGM suspended operations for the day.

During the service, an MGM executive leaned over to his companion and said, "They won't miss him today or tomorrow or six months from now or a year from now. But two years from now they'll begin to feel the squeeze."

Sitting in the car on the way to the funeral with Eddie Mannix and his wife, Mayer looked out the window, contemplating his life. "Isn't God good to me?" he said. That night, he went dancing on the Sunset Strip.

That, at least was the story told by Toni Mannix. But Norma Shearer told friends that Mayer spent that night at his own Santa Monica house a few doors from Thalberg's, thinking about the good days they had together, at Mission Road and Culver City, when Irving had been like a son and he a loving father. Shearer told L.B. that as Thalberg had weakened in his last few days, he told her that the loss of Mayer's friendship was high on his list of regrets.

Around MGM, there was the general feeling that the great times that had lifted the studio to the pinnacle of the profession were now past. In Mayer's mind, there was sadness, but also an innate security. He was a starmaker, wasn't he? What he understood that others didn't was that one of the stars he had made was Irving Thalberg. If he had done it once, he could do it again. But others weren't so sure.

"The studio," said Joseph Newman, "started to change when Thalberg died. For the worse."

PART THREE

"Mayer didn't dislike Nick Schenck. He *hated* Nick Schenck. It was the old story, The Tale of Two Cities: Los Angeles and New York."

—GEORGE SIDNEY

Mayer and the glowing Jean Harlow at an industry function circa 1935.

Chapter
EIGHT

L.B. SPREAD THE WORD to the people finishing Thalberg's last pictures: "If anything can be done to make them better, do it, no matter what the expense." Bernie Hyman was given the responsibility of completing *The Good Earth* and *Camille, Maytime* was handed to Hunt Stromberg, and *A Day at the Races* was left to the tender mercies of Sam Wood. Mayer ordered that *The Good Earth* carry an on-screen dedication written by John Lee Mahin: "TO THE MEMORY OF IRVING GRANT THALBERG WE DEDICATE THIS PICTURE—HIS LAST GREAT ACHIEVEMENT."

Thalberg left behind a wife, two children, and $4.49 million—before taxes. Another legacy was a studio in very fine shape. In 1935, the studio's profits ($7.5 million) had been more than that of all the other studios combined.

L.B. knew what all this meant: "Every son of a bitch in Hollywood is waiting for me to fall on my ass." Then there was the specter of Nick Schenck, also waiting for him to fall on his ass. Disagreements between the two were now met by Mayer saying, "I will debate you on this point and be willing to pay $1 million to charity if I lose. You can pick the judges." Schenck would repeat the challenge to friends and say, "How can I debate with a guy who talks the way Louis does?"

Schenck sent exhibitor Sam Katz, co-founder of Balaban & Katz, out from New York to help L.B. with his administrative tasks.

"He'll be like another arm to you, Louis," said Schenck.

"I don't need another arm," Mayer grunted.

Frank Orsatti told Mayer he thought Katz had died. "Dead or alive, he's a son of a bitch," snapped Mayer. Katz was a smiling glad-hander, always upbeat. "Nobody can be as happy to see anybody as Sam Katz is to see everybody," observed Joe Mankiewicz.

Mayer knew that Katz was there to be Nick Schenck's eyes in Culver City, and, if possible, usurp his authority. It didn't matter. He had to prove himself all over again? Very well. He would be the soul of graciousness to a man he loathed. His door was always open to Katz; he never once acknowledged that Katz's presence was a pebble in his shoe. "He was a truly positive thinker," remembered Sam Marx. But every once in a while, the strain showed. Once, Mayer was passing the cutting rooms when an assistant editor came by whistling. Mayer asked him why.

"I'm happy, Mr. Mayer," the assistant said.

"I wish I could say the same," Mayer replied, hurrying on his way.

The word went out to the MGM staff on both coasts: "If you come across any actor, director or writer, who looks promising, let me know and I'll sign them up. I'm going to fool them. I'm going to build up the biggest collection of talent so that this studio can't fail." Now began the full flowering of what L.B. would call "strength in depth."

"There was a pall around the place after Thalberg died," remembered Ralph Winters. "It was really a big shock. But it didn't affect production much, because Thalberg had cut back to just making three or four pictures a year at that point. He didn't wield the influence he once had."

The death of Thalberg meant that the reorganization begun when he was given his own independent unit would be speeded up. Hunt Stromberg looked at the Technicolor footage of *Maytime* and hated it. As assistant director Joseph Newman remembered, "Thalberg envisioned a romantic comedy with music such as had never been done before. [Director Edmund] Goulding was aiming for a British music hall style of movie. It was a terrible mess." Stromberg decided to scrap everything—at a cost of $800,000—and begin again with a new script and with Robert Z. Leonard directing, in black and white, so costs could be contained.

Some of Thalberg's associates weren't going to wait around for the reshuffling. Al Lewin still had two years to go on his contract, but wanted out. "Mr. Mayer was infuriated with me," he remembered. "Actually, what I thought and never got a chance to explain was that since I had worked so closely with Irving, it was not fair to compel them to keep me for two more years. . . . Instead Mr.

Mayer was affronted, misinterpreted the cancellation, and wouldn't even talk to me for quite a long time."

It was generally felt that something palpable was needed to memorialize Thalberg, so the front office was consolidated in an elegant new four-story Art Deco building built near the studio entrance in 1938 and christened the Thalberg Building. The building quickly became known as the Iron Lung for reasons both psychological and physical.

The first floor and part of the second were for writers, while Mayer, Mannix, and Thau occupied offices on the third floor, which also held the executive dining room, where twelve to sixteen of the elite ate for free every day. Under them—literally, on the second floor—were the producers with the most power: Edwin Knopf, Sam Zimbalist, Larry Weingarten, Carey Wilson, Sidney Franklin, Pandro Berman, Arthur Freed, Joe Pasternak, and Jack Cummings.

The Thalberg Building had an early version of central air-conditioning, so none of the windows opened. "Fred Rinaldo and I moved into the building just as it was finished," said screenwriter Robert Lees, "and you couldn't open the goddamn windows. We finally got one open and five minutes later a bunch of engineers came in and said, 'Ah, this is where all our air is going.' "

The studios' prolonged anti-labor stance had an unintended consequence when the International Alliance of Theatrical Stage Employees (projectionists, art directors, makeup men, gaffers, and other technicians) fell into the hands of Willie Bioff and George Browne, two racketeers from Chicago. After shaking down the Balaban & Katz theater chain in Chicago with a series of projection mishaps that led to payoffs, Bioff and Browne moved to Hollywood where they convinced labor leaders that one union, IATSE, could be a more efficient bargaining agent than a dozen unions competing for attention. They promised a 10 percent pay hike within the first year. Bioff threatened to shut down every studio in the business by calling projectionists' strikes across the country, and got his promised pay increases. He also squelched independent unions by calling in goons to bust heads, then blamed management.

In the early part of 1936, Bioff and Browne had a private session with Nick Schenck and Leo Spitz, who was in charge of RKO. The men walked out having committed each of the four major studios (MGM, Paramount, Warners, and Fox) to pay the labor racketeers $50,000 each per year to keep wages down and prevent strikes. The smaller studios (RKO and Columbia) agreed to pay $20,000 apiece.

With the payoffs as leverage, Bioff and Browne stepped up their strong-arm tactics. Loew's had been buying its raw film through Jules Brulatour and Eastman Kodak. The DuPont corporation wanted Loew's business, and Nick Schenck suggested that DuPont could have it if a way could be found for Bioff to share in the commission. Mayer protested; what was he supposed to say to his friend, the salesman from Kodak?

"Just handle it, Louis," said Schenck. "I want you to give that DuPont commission to a friend of Willie Bioff's. Because he can make us plenty of trouble. But I don't want you to argue. Just do it."

Bioff, Browne, and the Chicago syndicate made $236,474 in commissions in just two years. As a result, Bioff and Browne were even more well disposed toward Loew's than they had been. The intersection of the movie business and organized crime got a little more congested. The Mob had helped finance Columbia Pictures, and Budd Schulberg remembered that Columbia boss Harry Cohn always had a soft spot for his bankrollers. "He liked the feeling of it, the proximity to real power."

For the studios, it was good business, for the pennies paid to the racketeers saved them dollars that could have been paid out to studio and theater workers. John Cogley's *Report on Blacklisting* reported that the producers could have saved nearly $14 million through the payoffs to Bioff and Browne.

At one negotiating session at Mayer's Santa Monica house, Screen Actors Guild leader Robert Montgomery arrived to find Willie Bioff among the negotiators. Montgomery announced that he would return to the meeting after the "hoodlums" had left.

Cutting deals with Bioff didn't sit well with Mayer, and he hired some private investigators to look under Chicago rocks. He found that Bioff had served time for perjury and procuring. When Bioff found out that Mayer was having him investigated, threats were made. "There is no room for both of us in this world," Bioff supposedly said, "and I will be the one who stays here." A shaken Mayer realized Bioff's record had to be made public and fast. He spilled everything to *Daily Variety*. The Illinois state attorney's office realized that Bioff had only served eight days of a six-month jail term and he was called back to finish serving his time.

On May 9, 1937, Robert Montgomery, Kenneth Thomson, and Franchot Tone, representing the nascent Screen Actors Guild, showed up at L.B.'s house during a brunch. Mayer and Joe Schenck were in the middle of a bridge game, and were told that if the committee didn't have something in writing to take to their members that night, a complaint would be filed under the Wagner Act and a strike would close down the studios. It was no idle threat; MGM stars such as Garbo, Crawford, and Harlow had already thrown in their lot with the Guild.

Mayer was petulant, while Schenck said it was impossible to get all the studio heads together on a Sunday. Schenck called Harry Cohn, who was playing the horses at Agua Caliente. Cohn said that whatever was good enough for Schenck was good enough for him. Mayer refused to call a stenographer, claiming he had two hundred guests to take care of. So Kenneth Thomson wrote out an agreement in longhand mandating an actors union, and Mayer and Schenck signed. Always a realist when it came to business, Mayer understood that there was nothing more to be done. It was a great moment for Montgomery and Franchot Tone, who remembered Thalberg vowing that an actors union would be allowed at MGM over his dead body.

The continuing fight against Bioff was led by the unofficial *Daily Variety* and the quasi-official Robert Montgomery, who leaked the result of investigations to journalist Westbrook Pegler, who won a Pulitzer Prize for his exposé. When investigators discovered a $100,000 check made out to Bioff by Joe Schenck—a "loan" used by Bioff to buy a ranch—they had what they wanted.

The investigation widened, and Bioff and Browne went to prison for extortion; Joe Schenck, after testifying under oath that the money was a loan, was found guilty of perjury and income tax fraud. The 1940 trial resulted in a conviction carrying a sentence of three years in prison and a $20,000 fine, but he served only four months and five days because he gave evidence that helped convict Bioff. "We had about 20 percent of Hollywood when we got in trouble," Bioff would say. "If we hadn't got loused up we'd of had 50 percent."

Joe Schenck, who hadn't done anything other people hadn't done, and had done considerably less than his brother, took the fall for everybody. "He took the rap," said his goddaughter Mary Ellin Barrett. "Since he didn't have children, he felt that was the way to go."

After serving his sentence, Joe returned to Hollywood and his job at Fox, bringing with him a couple of prison guards who had been particularly kind to him. They were given producer contracts and proved successful at their new occupation. Harry Truman gave Joe Schenck a full pardon in 1945.

Mayer didn't deemphasize any of Thalberg's stars, but some stars were more equal than others. Jeanette MacDonald for instance. "Mayer was always around during the making of her pictures," remembered Joseph Newman. "And that was very unusual for him, because he didn't hang around sets. I think he was very attracted to her, but I don't think there was any reciprocation on her part."

There's a delicious story, impossible to confirm, involving MacDonald and Mayer. It seems that one day MacDonald came to her Christian Scientist practitioner, a woman named Genevieve Smith, and handed her a small box containing some jewels. "I want you to hold on to these for me," she said. Smith didn't ask any questions and put them away. Time went by, and Jeanette came back for the box, then told her the backstory. It seemed that Mayer had called her to his office and given her the jewels as a token of the studio's gratitude for all of her hard work. A little while later, Mayer thought it would be nice if MacDonald reciprocated, one way or the other. MacDonald said no, whereupon there was an attempted burglary at her house. Realizing that Mayer wanted his jewels back, she took them to Smith for safekeeping. Her house was broken into and thoroughly searched. After the burglars had come up empty, she took the jewels back home. The story, which was told by Genevieve Smith to Leatrice Joy, also a Christian Scientist and the mother of Leatrice Gilbert Fountain, has a few problems—Mayer regularly dispensed bonuses, but this is the only episode involving anything other than a nice fat check. Besides that, whatever happened to safety deposit boxes?—but it also has a nice aura of deviousness and gamesmanship that makes it not out of the question.

In spite of her status as one of Mayer's pets, MacDonald didn't press her advantage on the set; Newman remembers that she "wasn't difficult. She'd have her tantrums, but mostly they happened in makeup or hairdressing. On the set, she was even-tempered."

But even MacDonald overplayed her hand with her incessant maneuvering for money. Unlike Nelson Eddy, she refused to sign a long-term contract, preferring deals that ran for nine months and covered the making of two films. As a result, MGM refused to give her the time off it gave Eddy, which resulted in him making as much as $200,000 a year in recitals.

By the spring of 1939, Mayer was running out of patience with MacDonald. The manipulative singer had gone over his head to Nick Schenck, and was writing kittenish letters to Howard Strickling: "I understand Mr. L.B. had a close call [Mayer had just gotten over a bout with pneumonia]. Do you suppose it will make him more, or less, tolerant and understanding?

"Sometime . . . you and I must have a long serious talk, as I have heard from a couple of sources some things about you that have warmed me considerably."

For her new contract, MacDonald wanted $10,000 a week, with a guaran-

tee of two pictures a year, with fifteen weeks scheduled per picture. She asked
for sole above-the-title billing, and demanded Technicolor, Adrian, cinematographer Oliver Marsh, Herbert Stothart, and mixer Mike McLaughlin, as well as
veto power over the studio's choice of a co-star. These were privileges Mayer
wouldn't have ceded to Clark Gable, let alone MacDonald, whose negotiating
position was hampered by the fact that there weren't any other studios
equipped to make her pictures.

Her attitude struck Mayer as ungrateful. When her attorney was in Mayer's
office for a negotiating session and declared himself her "confidant, guide, and
father-confessor," Mayer exploded. He sprang up from his chair, slammed his
fist down on the desk, and yelled, "*I* am her father-confessor! *I* am the one she
confides in, not you! Get out of my office!"

"I could feel the temperature falling," she would write in her unpublished
memoirs. "L.B. still gave me his good wishes when I went in to see him on the
first day's shooting, but something had gone wrong between us."

Also running into a wall was Luise Rainer, winner of back-to-back Oscars,
for *The Great Ziegfeld* and *The Good Earth*. But according to Rainer, the death
of Thalberg was the death of her career. "I made eight films in three and a half
years, and . . . I had to shoot *The Great Waltz* twice, because Louis B. Mayer
did not like the director's first cut."

Yet, unsure of herself and insecure about her marriage to Clifford Odets,
Rainer was soon appearing in less prestigious pictures—*Dramatic School, The
Toy Wife*. Around the lot, she was regarded as a prima donna—"Luise Rainer
. . . fainted a great deal whenever she disagreed with the director or something
in the script," sniffed Ann Rutherford. Finally, Rainer aborted Odets's child
and announced to her makeup woman that she didn't want to make movies
anymore.

She was promptly summoned to Mayer's office. "Mr. Mayer, I cannot work
anymore," she said. "It simply is that my source has dried out. I have to go away,
I have to rest."

"What do you need a source for?" Louis asked. "Don't you have a director?"

Rainer asked to void her contract or, at the very least, get a leave of absence.
Mayer refused, the argument escalated. "Luise," said Mayer, "we've made you
and we're going to kill you." Rainer stormed out and broke her contract, effectively blacklisting herself.

In the first week of December 1936, a few months after Thalberg died, L.B. and
Nick Schenck engaged in another semipublic wrestling match over what was

vaguely termed a "conflict over studio policies." It was a power play by Schenck, who was undoubtedly assuming that with Thalberg gone, he had one less opponent.

L.B.'s response was instant and severe: he threatened to resign. He had some time left on his contract, but there were other places he could go—Paramount, for one, treading water with Emanuel Cohen; RKO for another. Al Lichtman, the head of sales, said that Schenck seriously considered letting Mayer go. Schenck undoubtedly thought that, given the organization set up by Mayer and Thalberg, anybody could run MGM. But when Schenck arrived in Culver City for a showdown, the other executives warned him that it would be difficult, if not impossible, to keep the heavyweight talent together if Mayer left. With Thalberg dead, Mayer was now even more vital to the continuity and success of MGM. When L.B. began making noises about being sick and tired of the constant competition—perhaps it was time to retire?—Schenck knew it was time to bite the bullet.

"I owe you a duty," said Schenck. "I want to tell you that you are absolutely wrong. You are making a mistake in resigning. You are going to regret it. I don't think you will live six months or a year."

Mayer was startled and asked Schenck to elaborate. "You love [this] kind of thing. Maybe I could do without it, because I know how to live outside of work. But not you. All you live for is work. That is what you love. That is what you need and that is what your nature demands."

Mayer, of course, had no serious intention of resigning a job that made him the highest paid man in America. He just wanted to be wined and dined, and he was, as was shown by the contract he signed at the end of 1937, which took effect January 1, 1939, and continued for four years. His base pay was set at a minor $3,000 a week, but he was also entitled to an undivided 6.77 percent of the annual net of Loew's, Inc., and "all companies, subsidiaries and ventures in which Loew's shall have any direct or indirect interest by stock ownership or otherwise," said percentage to kick in after the company amassed $2.6 million of profits per year. (Nick Schenck and his men in the East took their cuts from first dollar net.) As of 1941, Schenck's compensation was pegged at $2,500 a week plus 2.5 percent of net corporate profits; Robert Rubin was getting $2,000 a week plus 1.25 percent of net corporate profits.

Mayer was entitled to four weeks of vacation and "required" to spend at least three months of each year on a European trip, with an assistant and a valet also included in the expenses to be covered. Finally, and most remarkably, he was awarded 10 percent of all the net profits from continuing distribution of all

MGM films made since April 7, 1924, "so long as there shall be receipts there-from." Because of this provision, Mayer also had a 10 percent piece of any re-leased films whose stories might be remade or sold to another studio.

It was a very rich contract, especially in regard to the percentage of profits from Loew's subsidiaries, including the Robbins Corporation, a major pub-lisher of sheet music from the musicals that L.B. was shortly to begin making, to his and the corporation's benefit.

There were only two niggling provisions: "In the performance of his duties and obligations as . . . managing director of production Mayer shall at all times be subject to the direction and control of the President of Loew's. The term 'managing director' shall not be construed to imply any obligation on the part of Loew's to elect Mayer as a member of its board of directors or as a member of the board of directors of any of its subsidiaries."

In other words, he was still under Nick Schenck's thumb. Louis B. Mayer was a very cosseted salaried employee, but nothing more. Once again, Schenck retreated across the Mississippi; once again, Schenck had to bide his time.

A loose confederation known as the Executive Committee—or, more colloqui-ally, the College of Cardinals—was formed, with Mayer as the Pope. There were nine members: Mayer, Mannix, Thau, Sam Katz, now executive pro-ducer in charge of Mayer's beloved musicals (and, according to Joe Cohn, "a master double-crossing son of a bitch"), Al Lichtman, Harry Rapf, Hunt Stromberg, Bernie Hyman, and Lawrence Weingarten.

All of the men on the committee were brought into the profit-sharing agree-ment, with the largest profit percentages (1.5 percent apiece) going to Mannix and Lichtman. Larry Weingarten was getting $156,000 plus .35 percent of Loew's net, with a raise effective to $169,000 as of the end of 1940. Hunt Stromberg, befitting his position as first among equals, was drawing $260,000 plus 1.05 percent of the Loew's net.

Each top MGM executive producer—such as Hyman and Stromberg—was given what amounted to his own unit where he was in charge of a group of lesser producers. As chief executive, Mayer interested himself in issues that . . . interested him. "What this meant," remembered Ralph Winters, "was that Mayer had about six guys reporting to him instead of about twenty. It was actu-ally a hell of a good system." But beneath Mayer, the system created a heavy bureaucracy. Unlike Warner Bros., where there were basically only three exec-utives (Jack Warner and Hal Wallis, plus Bryan Foy, who didn't report to Wal-lis) in charge of production, at MGM there were, at the bare minimum, nine.

Mayer cut back on the time that could be spent on any film; musicals like *Babes in Arms* were finished in forty-four days—*Broadway Melody of 1940* took only thirty-one!—while location-heavy pictures such as *Northwest Passage* would be shot in fifty-nine days.

The B pictures were usually scheduled for eighteen days of stringently maintained production, and a picture was finished on the eighteenth day even if everyone had to work till midnight. But even Bs like the Dr. Kildare or Nick Carter pictures looked good; as Mayer told cameraman Hal Rosson, "If it's an MGM film, it has to look like an MGM film."

Because L.B. did not micromanage, there was a good deal of power to be derived from being in a secondary or even tertiary position. Mayer was an early proponent of creative tension, which meant that he tended to choose cardinals who loathed one another—for instance, Katz hated Lichtman because he knew that Lichtman wanted Mayer's job every bit as much as he did. Mayer, a believer in the old adage that you have to keep your enemies closer than your friends, enjoyed the maneuvering of the scorpions.

Subtle, and sometimes not-so-subtle, disparagement of Thalberg began to be common. "Mayer was less involved in downgrading Thalberg than were the others," remembered producer David Lewis. Now that Thalberg was dead, he was vulnerable, and Bernie Hyman and Hunt Stromberg meant to keep it that way. At one meeting, as Lewis finished up explaining the problems with *Maytime*, Sam Katz exclaimed, "It's a good thing Irving died when he did. He would have ruined MGM."

An appalled Lewis stared at Katz, whereupon Mayer took Lewis out of the room. "You wait here," he said, then returned to the office to deal with Katz. After a bit, he came out again and told Lewis, "Nobody will ever speak badly of Irving in your presence again. Never."

Nobody ever did, but, like a whipped dog, Sam Katz hated David Lewis with a passion from then on. Mayer took Lewis under his wing—for a time. "[Mayer] was not only a fascinator of people," remembered Lewis, "he could be equally fascinated himself. He could also become unfascinated—he was a moving object, a UFO. . . . In ordinary times, he spoke very softly, although he could out-roar and out-bellow anyone. Through all his gentleness to me I could sense his enormous power over himself and others. His magnetism could not be missed. He was a spellbinder and a hypnotist."

Lewis's memory of his intensive immersion in the Gospel According to Mayer was of hearing the story of his life many times, which segued to a discussion of the top executives at the studio, none of whom he respected. "He had no morality of any sort, apart from his goody-goody feelings about mothers and family. . . . A rattlesnake was tame compared to Mayer."

Lewis made an inadvertent but fatal blunder when he walked into the studio dentist's office to discover Mayer sitting there with his false teeth out. "He looked a little like the caves of Capri," remembered Lewis. "Mayer stared at me in horror. He was a vain man and this was simply too much."

Suddenly, the daily calls and conversations ceased, and Lewis realized he had become persona non grata. He was all alone in the old Thalberg bungalow and the phone wasn't ringing. The message couldn't have been clearer. Lewis soon went over to Warner Bros., where he produced *Dark Victory* and *Kings Row*, among other pictures. At the end of his life, he remembered Mayer as "a fascinating figure: brilliant, seductive, unprincipled, but all in all a man of genius."

L.B. didn't have many highs and lows, and worked mostly in very smooth gear, but occasionally would be struck by a brainstorm. After Edward VIII abdicated, Mayer called in story editor William Fadiman and asked, "What's he doing?"

"I don't know what he's doing," replied Fadiman. "He was just King of England."

"What do you think he gets?"

"I don't know, but he's a very rich man, Mr. Mayer. I don't think it's a question of getting him."

"Cable him."

"Cable him what?"

"He was King of England, wasn't he? I want him to be the head of our European offices. I don't want him to do a goddamn thing. I just want him to be the head of the offices. How does that strike you?"

Everybody *said* that it was a brilliant idea, everybody *thought* it was a ridiculous idea, and they managed to talk him out of it.

In November of 1937, MGM began to broaden its brand name when it went on the NBC radio network with a program called *Good News of 1938*. It was billed as the most spectacular radio show ever produced, costing sponsor Maxwell House $25,000 a week. The program was under the creative control of MGM, with every star on the lot except Garbo available for appearances. Promising talent such as James Stewart, Robert Taylor, and Robert Young all served regular stints as host, and one of the featured vocalists was the young Mary Martin.

Each week a new MGM film would be dramatized, with the original stars. One feature, "Backstage at the Movies," let listeners hear what were billed as executive conferences at MGM, and audio tours of stars' dressing rooms were also given.

In essence, the show was a sixty-minute infomercial. The initial broadcast (Thursday, November 4, 1937) pulled out all the stops, featuring Robert Z. Leonard, Douglas Shearer, Eleanor Powell, George Murphy, Buddy Ebsen, Ilona Massey, Judy Garland, Sophie Tucker, among many others, with the featured film *The Firefly*. The guest of honor was none other than L. B. Mayer himself.

"Our business, of course, is to make motion pictures," said L.B. in remarks addressed to C. M. Chester, chairman of General Foods, which owned Maxwell House. "We have tried to make good pictures, and your response has been both generous and satisfying. . . . Let me welcome . . . the radio audience tonight, not only to the MGM lot, but into the MGM family. And in token of that welcome, let me present you with this master key to the big gate of our studios—which I know you'll hold as custodian for the listening public, and which will bring them all our facilities—all our talent of every kind—let them see and *know* Hollywood as it really is."

Mayer turned the proceedings over to Robert Z. Leonard, who introduced *The Firefly* with the throbbing scene setting familiar to all who loved silent films: "The year is 1808. The scene is Europe. War clouds over every nation! Over every capital, the dread shadow of Napoleon! Spain is facing a national crisis—threatened daily with possible invasion! French troops massing on the border—and yet, for a moment, the people of Madrid forget their cares and surrender the city to a gala celebration!"

After a few weeks, Fannie Brice was added to the cast and introduced her Baby Snooks character, thereby giving herself a whole new career. The interesting thing about the shows was the simultaneous projection of Mayer as a powerful man ("the production chief of our studio, the man who made the appearances of these stars possible"), and as a fuzzy grandpa who wanted his stars to be loved as they loved him, "the head of this big Hollywood family."

On one episode, most of the show was given over to a celebration of Lionel Barrymore's birthday, which, host Robert Taylor reported, took place on Stage 2, which had been transformed "into the magnificence of a gay banquet hall . . . a thrilling spectacle of red, white and blue. From the towering walls hang festoons of patriotic satins while floral designers repeat the red, white and blue on the rows of tables at which are seen scores of faces familiar to the motion picture screen."

After some coy round-robin greetings ("With friendship sincere and affection that's true, we wish every happiness, dear Lionel, to you," said Clark Gable), the affair was turned over to "the head of this big Hollywood family, Mr. Louis B. Mayer."

On another show, Mayer is "surprised" with a birthday cake and a chorus of "Happy Birthday": "Our major purpose in entering radio was to have you know our fine artists better . . . to have you enjoy the warmth of their personalities within the intimacy of your own homes. We wanted you to feel that when you went into a theater to see your favorite stars you would not just be going to see actors, but going to visit friends."

Mayer even evinced a sense of humor about his tendency toward the long-winded, as on a show when Robert Young announced that there would be no long speeches and cut off Spencer Tracy and Mickey Rooney, while Mayer was allowed to ramble on, much to Rooney's displeasure.

L.B. was comfortable in front of a microphone and made appearances on various other shows over the years, such as a guest spot on Louella Parsons's show that made full use of Mayer's own mythology. Mayer made sure to present the proper amount of modesty in the face of flagrant flattery: "I don't discover stars, Louella," claimed Mayer. "I am only the talent scout who brings to the public talent presented in what I think is the proper manner. It's the public that pays its money, chooses, and makes the star."

This canny positioning of Mayer by Mayer raised his public profile, and made him, along with Cecil B. DeMille, who took over the *Lux Radio Theatre* program in 1936, one of the handful of behind-the-scene powers who became synonymous in the public mind with Hollywood.

MGM under Mayer was subtly different from MGM under Mayer and Thalberg. For one thing, exteriors were deemphasized; the occasional flavor of the city streets that had seeped through in *The Secret Six* or *Hold Your Man*, or even the modest location jaunt to Catalina for *Mutiny on the Bounty*, became increasingly rare. The MGM movie now was localized to the back lot or to one of Cedric Gibbons's plush interiors.

L.B. was now the uncontested front man for the American movie industry. He began to be honored, to be a spokesman, to accept awards. There were banquets to attend with his peers among the ruling elite of California—judges, district attorneys, mayors, governors, lieutenant governors, sheriffs, archbishops, rabbis, newspaper publishers, university chancellors.

He accepted the Order of the White Lion from Czechoslovakia, he wrote a check for $20,000 for a new wing at UCLA, he was awarded the French Legion of Honor, he accepted leadership of an effort to remove between 100,000 and 200,000 Jews from Europe and relocate them to Cuba.

People such as Norma Shearer paid him rich tribute at these events: "The lives of Louis and dear Irving and my own have been so beautifully associated. Louis' friendship has been so full and so rich. It has reached out to me when I needed it most."

But for all the public friendship, the struggle for control between L.B. and Thalberg was now transferred to his widow. As always, it was about money. Mayer and Robert Rubin's contention was that Thalberg's percentage of the profits of MGM movies ended with his death; Shearer's that his contract, which wasn't due to expire until 1938, continued in full force.

Nick Schenck came out to Hollywood for a conference with Mayer and Edwin Loeb, the West Coast attorney for the company, who was also the personal attorney for Mayer as well as Thalberg. (Nothing like conflicts of interest.) Loeb mentioned that he thought it only proper to emphasize that he was also representing Thalberg's estate. Mayer's response was to turn to Schenck and say, "Nick, I think we should ask Edwin to tell us how much money he is getting to represent Irving's estate and then pay him that much and have him give up that case."

Schenck seemed shocked and dismissed the suggestion, but a week later, Norma Shearer telephoned Loeb and told him she thought she needed completely independent counsel in the matter. Norma hired other lawyers, but more importantly, she hired public relations men. The widow played out a scenario implying impending impoverishment. In fact, Thalberg had left, after taxes and probate, around $3 million, of which Norma's trust was slightly over $1 million, a pleasant enough nest egg in the late 1930s, which didn't even take into account the money she had earned herself.

Her first move was to send a letter quitting MGM; her second demanded Irving's percentage of the films he had been preparing when he died: *Camille*, *The Good Earth*, and so on. She explained to Louella Parsons that she was under the financial gun, that "I must go back to work or face the poorhouse."

For a studio that prized its image above all, this was a debacle. The studio backed down and granted the Thalberg estate all its profits from MGM movies made and released between April 1924 and December 1938. In the twenty years after Thalberg died, the estate received more than $1.5 million in percentage payments. "Norma is brilliant," L.B. admiringly told MGM hairstylist Sydney Guilaroff. "She should have been an attorney." In addition, Shearer's contract was renewed for six pictures at $150,000 each; like Garbo, Norma Shearer would never work for any studio but MGM.

In 1928, the United Kingdom Board of Trade had passed the Cinematograph Act, which mandated that all foreign studios releasing films in England had to subsidize English film production, or at least produce films utilizing local talent. This led to the rise of the dreaded "quota quickies," dismal B pictures made to burn off the obligation as inexpensively as possible. Mayer had no intention of financing 20 percent of English film production, but there was a nugget of an idea buried in the Cinematograph Act. Why not open MGM British, a full-service studio that could cross-pollinate American stars with English stories and personnel?

Louis believed in expansion, in the spreading of the gospel. In 1936, a flush MGM, along with 20th Century-Fox, purchased one-fifth of Gaumont-British. This deal gave the two studios access to those British films they felt could be successfully distributed in America. Far more important, it enabled Loew's to distribute its films in the U.K. at a lower cost than would otherwise have been possible.

"He was the only American to understand that one could not take everything from a country and put nothing back in return," said the English director Victor Saville. By November 1936, MGM British was ready to roll. The capitalization was £250,000, and Loew's leased the Denham Studios, north of London, that Alexander Korda had built before his London Films empire began to totter. Denham was the most lavish studio in England: 165 acres with seven soundstages, eighteen cutting rooms, the largest electrical generating plant in England, and its own film laboratory equipped for Technicolor. Mayer was very actively involved. The offices in London were outfitted with a sixty-five-seat private theater on Tower Street, behind the Ambassador Theatre.

Mayer arrived to inspect the new facility, accompanied by Nick Schenck, Benny Thau, casting official Robert Ritchie, and Ad Schulberg. Schulberg suggested that they attend a performance of a play called *Old Music*. Assuming that the show was a Viennese musical, Mayer agreed, but when they trooped into the St. James Theatre, he was disgruntled to find that the play was a melodrama, not a musical. He was, however, entranced by the leading lady, a radiant redhead named Greer Garson.

At intermission, Mayer told Ritchie to send a note to Garson's dressing room inviting her to dinner at the Savoy Grill. He was not disappointed. She was indeed beautiful in a patrician manner, and spoke glowingly of her mother. So far, so good.

The next day he continued his full-court press, appearing at her apartment. When Garson shied away, he turned his attentions to her mother, who managed Garson's career. MGM, he told her, was a family that worked together to make the best movies in the world. He invited the young actress to take a tour of the new Denham lot and make a screen test.

Garson proved to have a face that wasn't easy to photograph, but Mayer persisted; this woman had something. He offered her a contract starting at $500 a week, a sum indicative of his confidence in her. Garson's confidence in herself—she was only making £65 in *Old Music*—led her to demand $1,000 a week. Mayer bridled and went away for a few days, but eventually relented— the determining factor may have been the fact that she was divorced, and the sole support of her mother.

Garson was his idea of a beautiful woman—reserved, British, *classy*—and he would always be crazy about her. He assigned her to a ration of pummeling, massage, dieting, and makeup tests, then had Sidney Franklin direct an elaborate screen test of several reels. "MGM spent more money making [the test] than I had spent making some of my films," observed Victor Saville sourly. For her MGM debut, Garson was assigned the part of Mrs. Chips in *Goodbye, Mr. Chips*, and was off on a ten-year run as queen of the lot.

It would be a productive trip; besides Garson, Mayer also signed directors Victor Saville and Julian Duvivier, actress Hedy Kiesler—later Hedy Lamarr— and writer Walter Reisch, among others.

The trip back to America proved torturous for everybody but L.B. The *Normandie* lost a propeller somewhere between Le Havre and Southampton and remained in port for three days. When the voyage finally got underway, the ship ran into a terrible storm, which made everybody ill except Mayer. To pass the time, he called Walter Reisch to his cabin and asked him to tell him a couple of stories that might become movies.

Reisch managed to pull himself together and come up with a few likely possibilities. Mayer was making notes, oblivious to the ship's violent swaying. Years later, when Reisch told Mayer how seasick he had been during the story conference, Mayer was surprised; he had thought Reisch's greenish pallor had just been nervousness at being called to Mayer's cabin.

It was on this trip that Mayer met a Viennese lawyer named Paul Koretz, who negotiated contracts for Luise Rainer and Hedy Kiesler. Those trouble-some women became a running joke between the two men, as Mayer would often chastise Koretz for "putting these crazy women in my life." Koretz was a gifted diplomat who came to America in 1940 and became an early expert in copyright law, doing much work for Mayer and MGM.

Mayer had been keeping an eye on Michael Balcon, the enterprising young English producer who was successfully running Gaumont-British. The two had developed an occasional correspondence involving Balcon as the po-lite supplicant and Mayer as the lordly bestower of favors. L.B. hired Balcon to run MGM British, and brought him to Hollywood for six months of indoctri-nation in the MGM ethos. Balcon found the Culver City lot to be a highly effi-cient film factory, and he was clearly Mayer's new favorite. "I was given every consideration," he wrote in his memoirs. "The legendary L.B. himself con-sulted me about the suitability of stories and subjects for the British market." But Balcon noticed with some dismay that Mayer's slightest wish was taken as a command.

Balcon found that L. B. Mayer liked being L. B. Mayer, and took full ad-vantage of it. One night Balcon had a dinner date with Frances Marion, but Mayer decided that Balcon would eat with him. He telephoned Marion and peremptorily told her Balcon wouldn't be coming to dinner after all.

Balcon then set about staffing his studio. He tentatively offered Alfred Hitchcock $165,000 for four pictures over two years (although Hitchcock wanted to go to Hollywood, not Denham), but the offer was withdrawn. Ac-cording to Benny Thau, the studio didn't want Hitchcock "under any circum-stances or at any price." To add insult to injury, they regarded George B. Seitz as "a much better director than Hitchcock."

Mayer was uneasy about the operation in Denham, closely supervising Balcon's stories, budgets, and schedules. He was also unhappy about Balcon's casting of the second lead in A Yank at Oxford. The girl was a promising young starlet named Vivien Leigh, but Mayer felt the picture needed a bigger name. Casting official Bob Ritchie, who had been Jeanette MacDonald's lover for years, suggested a different actress. Balcon responded to Ritchie's suggestion by saying, "Don't be a bloody fool," and that opened the floodgates.

Balcon should not speak to his men like that, Mayer said, walking over to throw open the office window. He went on and on, thoroughly working Balcon over at an ever-increasing volume, positioning himself so the entire office and the immediate studio could hear Balcon being reamed.

In the animal kingdom, this is known as marking your territory. Balcon was mortally offended. Even though *A Yank at Oxford* was a smooth production and a successful picture, Balcon's relationship with the home office was never the same. Mayer's attitude became formal, and Balcon got the distinct impression that "each time I went to the lavatory it was being reported to L.B. in Culver City. . . . I soon sensed that there was a movement afoot for [Victor] Saville to take over production generally and replace me in due time."

By the time *A Yank at Oxford* had moved to the editing stage, Balcon found he had nothing to do besides read scripts and synopses. Suddenly, nobody was interested in his opinions about anything. He had the unmistakable look of the well-groomed corporate leper. Balcon eventually resigned, and generally referred to his former boss as "the unspeakable Mayer." For the rest of his life, Balcon received a Christmas card from Mayer every year, an unintentional running joke that could only have reminded Balcon of how much he hated the man who had humiliated him.

MGM British had considerable success. Besides *A Yank at Oxford*, it also produced *Pygmalion*, *The Citadel*, and *Goodbye, Mr. Chips*. But by 1939, with the obviously dicey situation in Europe, MGM British would be closed down, not to be reactivated until after the war.

Ring Lardner, Jr., remembered that story editor William Fadiman vowed not to let Lardner in the studio because he had fought the Screen Playwrights in favor of the Screen Writers Guild. But the divisions of the Guild battles only deepened, eventually splitting into the crevasses of the McCarthy period. Donald Ogden Stewart, returning to the studio after some time off to write a play, was cut dead by the Screen Playwrights' John Lee Mahin, who had been friendly with Stewart since he doctored the script of *Red Dust* for Mahin without credit.

There were factors other than politics at work in the schism, factors that had to do with the role of screenwriters and the way they were controlled. It was common for screenwriters who worked for a specific actor or actress not only never to meet them, but never even to talk to them on the phone. This wasn't a permutation of divide and conquer, it was just a heavily compartmentalized system. "A successful writer, at that time, was already on his next assignment when they were casting and building the sets for the last script he had done," said Devery Freeman. "You were far away, sometimes at another studio. There was no meaning attached to it. You worked for the producer, not the star."

Beyond that, "screen credits were given at the will or the whim of the studio. Now, I didn't mind. I figured I was getting paid for writing and I took it for granted that they had the option to do what they wanted.

"John Mahin was a great guy, a big name, a powerful writer at the studio. He could easily get a credit. The Screen Playwrights were the guys that worked all the time and they didn't want anybody rocking their boat. They had it made and they intended to keep it that way."

Even people who had no particular portfolio wielded power. Ida Koverman made it her job to actively promote the careers of musical talents like Nelson Eddy, Judy Garland, and, later, Mario Lanza, while other special favorites included Mickey Rooney, Clark Gable, and Robert Taylor. "She was the middleman between talent and the opportunity to showcase it," said her friend Hedda Hopper. Esther Williams said that Koverman "was the wise lady of the studio. She knew everything that was going on. Her musical tastes ran to José Iturbi, but L.B. respected her matronly qualities. She'd tell you all sorts of things. 'You're not here to make swimming movies,' she told me once. 'You're here to be one of Sam Katz's girls.' All those men had a woman on the payroll—Katz had Ilona Massey, Benny Thau had Frances Gifford. 'I'm telling you this because I think you can handle it,' she said."

Sidney Franklin had spent more than a year preparing *Marie Antoinette* as a vehicle for Norma Shearer. The preproduction costs were considerable—Thalberg's studio overhead at the end of his life had amounted to $11,597 a week, and the roster of writers who had worked on the script was staggering: Ernest Vajda, Carey Wilson, Robert Sherwood, Donald Ogden Stewart, Talbot Jennings, Vajda again, George S. Kaufman, Jacques Thiery, Sam Hoffenstein, Zoë Akins, and Bruno Frank.

The prospective budget made any possibility of profit highly problematic. The vast production entailed ninety-eight sets, and Edwin Willis, the head of the prop department, had spent three months in France buying furnishings, paintings, statues, scrolls, objets d'art, and even original letters—supposedly the largest single consignment of antiques ever received at Los Angeles Customs. Franklin wanted to shoot the moon; when he proposed shooting the film in Technicolor, Hunt Stromberg replied that the cost would be prohibitive. "We have a great story and star and do not need the incentive color MIGHT [provide]."

At the end of December 1937, Franklin was called into a meeting with Mayer and Mannix and asked to accept a shorter schedule, which would have meant pruning the script. Franklin refused. On New Year's Eve, he was called into another meeting with Mayer, Mannix, Nick Schenck, and Hunt Stromberg, who had taken over producing duties. It was four against one, and the four again asked the director to cut a month off the schedule. Franklin refused, saying the movie couldn't be made properly in sixty days.

Mayer and company then revealed that they had gone behind Franklin's back and asked Woody Van Dyke if he could direct it in sixty days. Van Dyke, who probably thought he could shoot it in forty days, naturally said yes. There was a pregnant pause, then Franklin broke the silence. "If he says he can shoot the picture in sixty days then give it to him." (Actually, as of December 22, the picture was scheduled for eighty days of shooting.)

Angry, bitter, and ready to leave MGM, Franklin struggled home to an evening he remembered as the worst New Year's Eve of his life. Both he and Norma Shearer regarded the experience as the biggest missed opportunity of their careers. "If only I had had the courage that day when I was called into Mr. Mayer's office and he gave me the sad news," Norma Shearer would write in later years, "if only I had had the confidence to say I wouldn't accept a compromise. But no, I thought I had to *conform*—because there were so many skeptics waiting for me to be difficult."

A few days later, Mayer began a seduction designed to make Franklin forget his anger, offering him such premier properties as *Goodbye, Mr. Chips, Boys Town, Northwest Passage, Madame Curie,* and something called *Ninotchka.* By the time he was through, Mayer had convinced Franklin to produce full-time. It was a superb decision, as the precise, erudite Franklin would be responsible for some of the best, as well as most profitable, MGM dramas of the next ten years—*Waterloo Bridge, Mrs. Miniver, Random Harvest, The Yearling.*

But a message had been sent. If Norma Shearer was not immune from the front office, no one was. Mayer's MGM would be a studio for the stars, not by the stars. The era of vanity projects was at an end; the era of Louis B. Mayer had begun.

Van Dyke took more than seventy days to shoot *Marie Antoinette,* not counting the inevitable retakes, and was able to shoot it that quickly only because Julian Duvivier directed at night, after Van Dyke went home at 6:00 P.M. "His [Duvivier's] name is not to be mentioned on screen," instructed a memo from Eddie Mannix, "or in connection with paid advertising or publicity." Few other economies were in effect. Actor Robert Morley remembered that limousines waited outside the stage door all day to take the actors a hundred yards to their dressing rooms. A small orchestra, a remnant of the silent days, was on the set to while away time between takes because Shearer felt she worked better with music around her.

Shearer and the other actors were amused by Van Dyke's unvarying routine: Every night at six, an assistant would bring Van Dyke a glass with a slug of gin in it, and shortly thereafter he would leave the set, even if they were in the middle of a take. Shearer knew what she had to cope with; she wrote a note to Hunt Stromberg on March 15, saying she was confident that Van Dyke hadn't covered one scene properly, and when did Stromberg want to schedule retakes? Even with the economies Mayer imposed, *Marie Antoinette* cost $2.9 million, and lost $767,000. As one columnist wrote, "the trouble with Marie Antoinette is that she lived 45 minutes too long."

Cedric Gibbons always regarded his work in *Marie Antoinette* as the height of his career, and took pride in how he made the ceiling moldings much heavier than they actually were at Versailles in order to show up on camera. The end result was that he got a letter from the Beaux Arts school in Paris commending him on his accuracy, and no Oscar for Best Art Direction, which went instead to *The Adventures of Robin Hood.* "I always got my Oscars for pictures I didn't deserve, and never got one for the pictures I did deserve," Gibbons said glumly.

"You're doing *Marie Antoinette*, aren't you?" Mayer asked Robert Morley when they met. "Not your fault, but God how I hate epics."

In the fall of 1937, L.B. opened negotiations with Mervyn LeRoy. LeRoy was an institution at Warner Bros., but what made the deal particularly audacious was that LeRoy was married to Harry Warner's daughter, Doris. Mayer had liked LeRoy since he had been loaned to MGM to make *Tugboat Annie*, which had made a clear profit of $1.2 million, more money than *Grand Hotel*, more profit than any MGM picture that year. In mid-December, LeRoy called in Lana Turner and Irving Brecher, a writer he had recently signed for $650 a week, and told them he was taking them with him to MGM.

"I was kind of startled," said Brecher. "I didn't understand all the implications. On January 1, 1938, we went to MGM. One of the reasons that Mayer went after LeRoy was that he and Jack Warner hated each other. Mayer wanted to outpoint Warner, so he gave LeRoy a contract that was unheard of: $6,000 a week! *Clark Gable* didn't make that much; *Garbo* didn't make that much. It was a gotcha. Fuck Jack Warner!"

While Mayer was paying LeRoy $6,000 a week, plus .7 percent of the Loew's net, he announced it as $3,000 a week, so as not to enrage the other producers. But it was obvious that LeRoy was now first among equals; he was given an office on the third floor next to Benny Thau and Eddie Mannix, consulted with the Executive Committee on MGM's entire program, and was handed four top assignments including the studio's biggest production for 1938–39, a project very close to Mayer's heart: *The Wizard of Oz.* "Mayer wanted him to make good, so he gave him this big-deal project," said Irving Brecher. "LeRoy did the casting and he said to me, 'We got a script, and you're not doing anything. The three comedians aren't funny enough. Do something about their scenes.' So I wrote some stuff for them without credit."

LeRoy was the second man to temporarily inhabit the part Mayer would spend the rest of his career searching for—a creative executive who could also do duty as a surrogate son, a successor to Thalberg.

Metro-Goldwyn-Mayer could have had *Gone With the Wind* before David Selznick. The New York office had been leaked a copy of Margaret Mitchell's unedited manuscript, and William Fadiman devoured as much as he could, finally preparing a fifty-page synopsis. The problem with the story was that it would be large, formidable, and very expensive. Because of the high cost of buying the novel, Mayer told Fadiman to see Nick Schenck. Fadiman made an appointment at Schenck's mansion on Long Island and arrived to find the chairman of Loew's battling a bad cold. Pansy Schenck was bringing him relay servings of orange juice, and Schenck was not really in the mood to talk about a Civil War story.

"You got a story to tell me?" he asked Fadiman.

"Yes."

"Tell."

Much later, Fadiman finished the story of *Gone With the Wind.* "Young man, *Gone With the Wind* is a title?" asked Schenck. "*Gone With the Wind?* What does this mean? It's about what . . . a war? Who needs war? Everybody dies?"

"Well, some do."

"Everybody dies. It's sad. You tell Louis, 'No.' "

After David Selznick bought the property for $50,000, and the book became the best-selling novel of its time, Mayer began circling. His son-in-law had two serious problems. The first was cost—*Gone With the Wind* would be extremely expensive, certainly $3 million, maybe more, too much money for Selznick's thinly capitalized independent company. The second was that the short list for Rhett Butler was too short: Gary Cooper, Errol Flynn, Ronald Colman, and Gable. Colman was too old and reserved, Flynn wasn't a good enough actor, and Cooper couldn't be freed from Sam Goldwyn's clutches. That left Gable, everybody's favorite for the part anyway. And Gable belonged to MGM.

Mayer's initial offer was for a complete buyout of the property, which would include a generous profit for Selznick. Under this deal, Selznick would produce the picture with MGM money, cast, and facilities on the MGM lot.

This would solve all the obvious problems, but create a more serious psychological one — *Gone With the Wind* would inevitably become an MGM picture, just as *Dinner at Eight* and *A Tale of Two Cities* were MGM pictures, despite the fact that they had been produced by David O. Selznick. Selznick wanted this to be a *Selznick* picture, not an MGM picture. Maybe Flynn could act it after all . . .

While Selznick vacillated, L.B. moved in. On January 10, 1938, there was a meeting with L.B., David Selznick and his agent brother Myron, Eddie Mannix, and Al Lichtman. At the end of March, Selznick was conferring with L.B. about possible directors — Mayer wanted Woody Van Dyke, not Selznick's choice of George Cukor. In early May, Selznick went down Washington Boulevard to MGM four times in seven days.

The deal that was finally struck involved MGM contributing Gable and $1.25 million. In return it would receive 50 percent of the profits, on top of which Loew's, Inc. would take 15 percent of the gross to distribute the picture. Selznick had to pay Gable's salary of $4,500 a week, plus a bonus of $16,666, a third of the $50,000 bonus MGM gave Gable for agreeing to make the picture, which he used as a settlement for his second wife so he could marry Carole Lombard.

It was a brutal, almost usurious deal, far inferior to the one Warners had offered with Flynn and Bette Davis. Selznick didn't absolutely need Loew's distribution, although it could do a much more comprehensive job than United Artists, Selznick's usual distributor. Selznick didn't absolutely need the $1.25 million either. But he did absolutely need Gable. He had to take the deal.

As the picture moved toward production, L.B. kept up the pressure on the matter of George Cukor. A few days after the burning of Atlanta was filmed by William Cameron Menzies — Selznick opted not to accept William Wellman's offer to shoot the action sequences for free — L.B. and Selznick were talking on the phone about Ernst Lubitsch, who was coming over to Metro to make *Ninotchka* and *The Shop Around the Corner*. "During the same conversation," Selznick wrote to his wife, "your father made another stab at getting George off of *Gone With the Wind*. Incidentally, so far I am very happy with George on this job."

L.B. lent John Lee Mahin to Selznick for last-minute script patching, as well as some quiet reconnaisance. "What's going on, John?" Mayer inquired after a couple of days. "Is he in trouble?"

"I don't know," said Mahin. The script needed work, he said, but there was nothing drastically wrong. The picture was, however, definitely going to be very long. Mahin told his boss that the script he was rewriting would mean a movie of about four hours.

"They'd stone Christ if he came back and spoke for four hours," said Mayer. L.B. was worried; Gable was the MGM franchise and David Selznick was the MGM son-in-law.

After a couple of weeks of production under Cukor that resulted in footage Irene Selznick appraised as "No magic. And fussy detail," Selznick took him off the picture. Cukor was immediately assigned to *The Women*. Mayer yanked Victor Fleming off *The Wizard of Oz*, threw him onto the set of Tara, and had King Vidor finish *Oz*. Everybody at the dance had changed partners, and Mayer finally had what he wanted.

"I loved Fleming, that son of a bitch," said Rand Brooks, who was playing Charles Hamilton, Scarlett O'Hara's ill-fated first husband. "I wanted to play it a little more lustfully, but Vic said, 'Goddamnit, I want this guy so in love it's sickening, and I'm gonna be here until I get it.' So I gave it to him—I don't think we ever went more than two takes per shot—and made the character a complete ass, which ended up hurting my career."

Later, L.B. moved Sam Wood over to cover for Fleming when he had a temporary breakdown. After Fleming returned, Wood stayed to direct what amounted to a second unit.

Although there was a considerable MGM presence on the picture, Rand Brooks remembered it as "completely a Selznick operation. You didn't see Mayer or Eddie Mannix around. Selznick ran that show."

When it came to actually looking at the movie at an early screening, L.B. had to get up a few times to go to the bathroom, but he loved the film, and, along with the other executives, was euphoric about the commercial prospects, and justifiably so. For $1.25 million and a couple of loan-outs, MGM had a half-interest in the greatest financial success of the movies' first seventy-five years.

At the end of 1940 and the film's road show release, before *Gone With the Wind* went to the neighborhood theaters, the film had grossed $20 million. Metro's distribution fee alone amounted to $3 million, in addition to a clear profit of $8 million to split evenly with Selznick. A few years later, Selznick sold his interest in the picture to Jock Whitney, his financier, for $400,000. Whitney turned around and sold the picture to MGM for $2.4 million.

So much for giving your son-in-law a break.

David Selznick had made *the* Hollywood touchstone, something the vaunted Thalberg had never managed to do, and it increased his stature in Mayer's dynastic mind. The relationship deepened.

David Selznick's home movies—shot, unlike most people's home movies, in 35mm sound—feature special guest appearances by L.B., as he instructs his grandson Jeffrey on how to pick a tulip, then picks him up, cradling and swinging the boy. In other scenes, he comes walking into the frame to say hello to his grandsons, Jeffrey and Daniel, then pushes them along in a miniature fire truck, or prompts helpfully from off camera: "How old is Jeffrey?" When Margaret makes an appearance, she looks more like Irene's sister than her mother—the same haircut helps.

Although Mayer is dressed in a suit and tie in these home movies, he's far more relaxed and demonstrative than usual. But then, he was always an indulgent grandfather. For birthdays or Christmas, Mayer's gifts were generous, but never consisted of cash—"Mother would not have approved," remembered grandson Dan Selznick. "He had a wonderful physical presence," Jeffrey—who often referred to L.B. as "The Old Man"—would remember. "He was kind of a rough-and-tumble physical man. He could be gruff, but you knew he didn't really mean it. . . . I liked Grandpa a lot. I always wanted to see him more than I was allowed to. He was very tactile. He loved to hug, kiss, hold me, rub my hair. The only thing that was disagreeable with him, I usually got a lecture, often centered on my father, about what a fool he was, that he could be the most important man in Hollywood but he wouldn't listen."

A belief in discipline, in the proper management of one's core gifts, was one of the similarities between L.B. and his younger daughter, Irene. Nothing could anger them more than profligacy, than carelessness. Or disloyalty—very broadly defined. Once, Jeffrey disliked an MGM film he saw at a preview, and he wasn't invited to another preview for months. "My mother said that if Grandpa ever really became angry at me, he might never forgive me," said Jeffrey. "Maybe she was exaggerating, but I wasn't going to find out."

By 1939, the bonuses for an elite fourteen Loew's executives spread between both coasts averaged about 20 percent of the company net. Mayer's total take from Loew's for the year was $688,369. Of that, $541,119 derived from his share of the profits. Wallace Beery had made $355,000 and Hunt Stromberg took home $328,818, including $68,000 in profit sharing. That year, Nick Schenck received a comparatively minor $145,543.

L.B. was worth the money he earned. In 1939–40, MGM spent over $37 million for its productions, an average of $777,283 per picture. Those pictures amassed more than $68 million in total earnings, with an average profit per picture of $142,667. Compare that to RKO, which spent $14 million, or $340,666 per film, bringing in slightly more than $22 million, for an average per-picture loss of $13,286. Both studios owned or controlled approximately the same number of theaters and released about the same number of pictures each year.

There were 16,250 movie theaters in America, and only 125 of them were owned by Loew's. In a good year, those 125 Loew's theaters grossed around $40 million. But those 125 theaters alone couldn't supply enough money for MGM pictures to turn a profit, so it was incumbent on all the major studios to play each other's pictures.

By itself, this would have tended to disprove the government's allegations of a trust, but the organization of the theater chains owned by the majors was a little too neat. Loew's was concentrated in New York state, Paramount covered Canada, New England, and the South, Warners was strongest in Pennsylvania and New Jersey, and Fox predominated on the West Coast. In other words, there were clearly gentleman's agreements in effect to complement rather than compete, and not to poach on each other's designated territories.

From an exhibitor's point of view, MGM was the best because they made your job so easy. "Paramount had Hope, Crosby, and, a little later, Alan Ladd, and that was about it," remembered David Friedman, exhibitor, publicist, and later producer. "Every second year, you'd have a *Road* picture and every third year you'd have a DeMille picture. And that was about it; Paramount's main problem was that they were very light on female stars.

"Loew's had one great ace: MGM pictures. Look, Columbia would only come out a few times a year with a picture you could actually play, and Paramount had limitations, but MGM was making forty or fifty pictures! Two Gables, two Crawfords, the great musicals, and so on down the line. Stars that people *loved*, presented the way they wanted to see them. And they had a lot of women stars. Any theater manager playing the Loew's product knew a year in advance what he was going to be playing. He could start putting up his posters a year ahead of time."

Actors liked Mayer because he believed in them—the entire MGM star system was an implicit tribute to Mayer's faith in them, which was usually reciprocated. But he could be hilariously peremptory with actors, especially young ones. "Grow a mustache," he ordered one young talent, "and don't come on this lot without it."

"But why, Mr. Mayer?" asked the young actor.

"With that mouth and those teeth? You need a mustache!"

If an actor contradicted him, and continued to do so, his temper would be unleashed. "His face turned almost purple," remembered Esther Williams, "and he began pounding the desk and screaming at the top of his voice, spewing spittle. 'How dare you question my authority? . . . I'm the head of the greatest motion picture studio in the world, [bang!] and you . . . [bang!] work [bang!] for me!' " If the tirade didn't achieve the desired results, Mayer would escalate into a full-scale tantrum, hurling himself to the floor, and rolling around on the rug. The resemblance to a brattish six-year-old was either amusing or horrifying, depending on your tolerance for juvenile misbehavior.

The aftermath of such a set-to would be a freezing over of relations—curt nods or grunts with, perhaps, a touch of respect in his eyes. "Louis B. Mayer had an enormous ego," said Williams, "but underneath all that was the smart little Russian Jewish immigrant with a lot of chutzpah who had built his reputation by knowing when to say yes and when to say no." The key to battling him was to possess similar qualities and be impervious to his remarkably varied methods of persuasion.

The singer Kathryn Grayson became one of Mayer's designated brats, someone who was allowed to argue with him without consequences, perhaps because they had adjacent boxes at the Hollywood Bowl, where they would enthuse over classical music. "I wanted to do stories that required acting, because everybody said I was going to be a great actress. But he would say, 'How can I have great stories with great music? The public likes you the way you are.' The Met wanted me for *Lucia*, I wanted to do it, and Ida Koverman wanted me to do it. I went around and around with him about it, and he said, 'Listen, if you do that opera, regular people will think you're an opera star, and you will have a short movie career. And if you make movies, you'll be a movie star for the rest of your life.' And was he ever right! I thank him every day of my life for that. He had by far the greatest instincts of any man I've ever known."

But most writers were antagonized by L.B.'s paternalism and preference for producers and stars. As S. J. Perelman once snarled, "Louis B. Mayer just went by the window, Hedy Lamarr on one arm and leprosy on the other."

"We don't want you to stay a writer," Mayer told one fair-haired young talent. "We want you to become a producer. We have a little ceremony when this happens where I break your pencil."

Many writers refused to have their pencils broken, which usually led L.B. to up the ante and tell them that they reminded him of Irving Thalberg. It was a comment that struck terror in the hearts of anybody who had any memory at all because, as one agent commented, "He hated Irving Thalberg!"

L.B.'s preference for the producer over the writer drove away some good talent. Anita Loos hung around for a few years after Thalberg died, writing films like *The Women* and *Blossoms in the Dust,* but finally left. "I started out to be a writer," she told her niece, "but now I'm a story doctor. They stop me on the set and ask me to think of a better line. And I cannot work with L.B." For Loos and most of the other New York contingent, Mayer lacked culture and any appreciation of the literary point of view. He wasn't interested in classics—he never would have made *Romeo and Juliet*—but in best-sellers.

At the same time, Adrian was growing restless. When he designed a dress with a bare midriff for Joan Crawford in *The Women,* Mayer went crazy. Calling Adrian and Hunt Stromberg to his office, he told them the outfit was in "very poor taste" and demanded it be altered. Adrian told Stromberg he had no intention of changing the dress, but finally came up with a halfhearted substitute that nobody liked. Finally, Crawford, Adrian, Stromberg, and George Cukor ganged up on Mayer. He capitulated and Crawford's stomach was indeed visible in the final film. But Adrian was furious at having to waste energy on an all-out fight when he had been right all along. He had to go through a similar struggle over the pantsuit he designed for Katharine Hepburn in *The Philadelphia Story,* which struck Mayer as yet another example of "permissiveness." It took a personal pitch by Hepburn to convince Mayer that the republic could withstand the sight of an MGM heroine in pants. Adrian would leave the studio in 1941, after *Marie Antoinette* and *The Wizard of Oz,* the films he regarded as his greatest accomplishments.

In May 1939, Mayer returned to New Brunswick for three days to accept an honorary Doctor of Laws degree from the University of New Brunswick for "cultural advancement of the moving pictures." He was given a luncheon by New Brunswick Premier A. A. Dysart and his entire cabinet, and given the freedom of the city of Saint John by the mayor.

"Refuse to be discouraged," he told a crowd. "Sweat and sweat some more, work and work some more. If you have anything at all you're bound to get there.

I have a great investment in Saint John. My mother lies buried in Saint John. I'm coming home to mother. I am sentimental enough to feel she knows I am being honored by my home folks. I believe she knows and is smiling. My heart is overflowing."

He promised that he would visit the University of New Brunswick every year as a way of paying back the honor of the LLD they were conferring on him, go fishing, and tell the world "what a grand and glorious land this is." But this was apparently the last time Mayer would travel to New Brunswick.

The Jewish community of the city expected Mayer to contribute as much as $50,000 to the university, but he contented himself with a check for $5,000, and never did set up the scholarship he had promised. The community also wanted him to donate a sizable sum to improve the Jewish portion of the cemetery where his mother was buried, but he donated just enough to refurbish her grave.

The studio could make a star like Gable, or could pick up an actor who was believed to be on the downhill slide, as with William Powell, who was let go by Warner Bros. and emerged a much bigger success than he ever could have been at that rough-and-tumble playground.

"I can't prove this," said Clarence Brown, "but I think Mayer had set up a spy system—certain employees at other studios were paid to tell him when an actor was being dropped. And if he was interested, he'd get in there and start negotiations before even the agent knew his client was about to be out of a job."

Being under contract at MGM meant that you were on call six days a week, forty weeks a year. Contracts mandated a twelve-week layoff period, in effect a three-month vacation without pay, but all the salaries were amortized so that there was a paycheck every week year-round.

For Mayer, new stars usually evolved out of old stars, either in a similar look, niche appeal, chemistry, or in their ability to hold their own with a contemporary star. As Howard Strickling said, "Along comes a Clark Gable. You put him first with a Joan Crawford, then with Norma Shearer, then Greta Garbo. Along comes a Bob Taylor. You put him with a Garbo, and then with Irene Dunne and you've got a star. Along comes Myrna Loy, and you put her with a Tracy or Gable, and *she's* a star."

Mayer knew how nebulous the whole process was, how much it depended on intangibles, chemistry between a personality, an image, and the audience. In L.B.'s mind, he was the sculptor modeling the clay, which is probably why there was a fairly strict rule that the credit for the discovery of every MGM star had to go to Mayer and to no one else. Only once did he come clean and de-lineate the process he went through in creating a star.

"The idea of a star being born is bush-wah," he snapped. "A star is made, created; carefully and cold-bloodedly built up from nothing, from nobody.

"All I ever looked for was a face. If someone looked good to me, I'd have him tested. If a person looked good on film, if he photographed well, we could do the rest. Age, beauty, talent, least of all talent—had nothing to do with it.

"Once I saw a face that I liked . . . once I had the face, we could do the rest. It didn't have to be a pretty face, nor even a handsome face. If it were a face that I liked, I knew that the American people would like it too."

And how would this be done?

"We hired geniuses at make-up, hair dressing, surgeons to slice away a bulge here and there, rubbers to rub away the blubber, clothes designers, light-ing experts, coaches in everything—fencing, dancing, walking, talking, sitting and spitting. . . . We could make silk purses out of sows' ears every day of the week. . . .

"If we want a man to be a lover—if we want the women in the audience to love him—we have the women in the picture love him. The audience identi-fies him with the women in the picture and winds up loving the guy.

"With a male star the secret is to get physical-looking men. Get all the women wanting to make love to an actor and you've got a new leading man, and a big one at that.

"Unfortunately, not all women want to make love with the same type man. That's why we had William Powell and Clark Gable both. Powell was cold, a gentleman. Gable was hot, a virile roughneck. Each appealed, primarily, to a different type of woman, but Gable's appeal was more universal, that's why he was a bigger star than Powell."

Mayer believed that, of all his stars, only three were great actors—Spencer Tracy, Garbo, and Marie Dressler—and he took special pride in Tracy. "Fox had him playing villains and he probably would never have been anything more than a good character actor if I hadn't seen something wonderful about his face—something more important than his acting ability.

"We signed him, found just the right stories for him and he became Spencer Tracy, the star, not Spencer Tracy, the actor. We did that, no drama school did. We did it with the stories we picked for him, with cameras and lights and music and a hundred tricks."

This is L.B. in vintage form, a monologue in which mistakes are banished and successes seized and personalized. It is also, in many respects, the truth.

Under the MGM system, writers and directors had little power, so Mayer lacked respect for most writers and directors. When Sam Marx came to him and said he wanted to quit being the story editor and do some writing of his own, Mayer thought it was ridiculous. "If you're going to be a writer, you'll have a producer who'll be your boss. Why don't you be a producer and be a boss?"

Mayer became fond of the ceaselessly energetic young writer Joseph L. Mankiewicz. "We need your *manpower*," he told Mankiewicz. But Mankiewicz wanted to direct. "No!" shouted Mayer. "You will produce. You've got to crawl before you walk." Mankiewicz said that was the best description of a producer he'd ever heard, but he became one anyway.

"Mankiewicz was not a warm, fuzzy guy," remembered John Waxman, the son of composer Franz Waxman. "There was no subject—sports, politics, anything—that he didn't know everything about. Or think he knew everything about. He was the sort of man with a vast collection of miscellaneous knowledge who's great at parlor games."

Mayer liked the young man's intelligence and wit, but he was chagrined when Mankiewicz brought him a musical project that spanned three generations of scandalous love affairs.

"So you think that's a very clever idea for a musical?" asked Mayer.

"Yes, L.B., I think it's new, different, enchanting."

"New, different, enchanting," repeated Mayer mockingly. "Young man, let me tell you what I want from you. I want *43rd Street, 44th Street, 45th Street . . .*" As Mayer moved out from behind his desk and began to yell, Mankiewicz beat a hasty retreat. Behind him, he could hear Mayer's voice: "Don't come to me with anything new. Give me *46th Street, 47th Street . . .*"

"He hated writers and he particularly hated directors," said Mankiewicz, "because they were the fellows who got out there on the sets and gave him the most trouble. He used to say, 'Give me a great producer and a great star and you can fuck your directors.'" Ultimately, Mankiewicz would also fail to be the son Mayer was looking for. At some point, the father has to cede power and authority to the son, and this was something L.B. could never manage. Before him, Culver City had been a virtual desert, and he would always believe that without him it would return to its natural state.

Chapter
NINE

IN F. SCOTT FITZGERALD's *The Last Tycoon*, a character contemplates the strange affection the Hollywood Jews developed for horses: "The Jews had taken over the worship of horses as a symbol—for years it had been the Cossacks mounted and the Jews on foot. Now the Jews had horses and it gave them a sense of extraordinary well-being and power."

The dormant racing scene in Southern California was revitalized by the 1934 reopening of the Santa Anita racetrack in Arcadia, a bedroom town northeast of Los Angeles. But Santa Anita was very much a WASP bastion, and Jews were not welcome. Just as barriers to Jews at the Los Angeles Country Club impelled the Jews to form Hillcrest Country Club, they reacted to the restrictions at Santa Anita by forming Hollywood Park. And L. B. Mayer found a new obsession. "He was told to get a hobby," remembered George Sidney, the son of MGM executive L. K. Sidney. "So he did. Yachting bored him. Golf was all right, but he couldn't do it all the time. But he could go to Saratoga and drop $78,000 on yearlings. He wasn't a show-off about it at all. He just got the best, the same tactics he used in the movie business."

Within ten years, Mayer would accomplish the unprecedented feat of building one of the finest racing stables in the country, almost singlehandedly raising the standards of the California racing business to a point where the Eastern thoroughbred establishment had to pay attention.

First, he spent $600,000 for a ranch covering 320 acres in Calabasas. He hired a trainer named Don Cameron, and went into the market for brood mares and a first-class stallion. And he had somebody—perhaps Cedric Gibbons—design livery for his jockeys and horses: predominantly blue, with pink belts, blue caps, and hoops on the sleeves.

Since the studio was a smoothly operating machine, and Mayer was not notably insecure about his position, he began delegating more of his duties to Sam Katz, who made sure everyone knew that he might be considered the de facto studio head, a position he was more than willing to make de jure. Soon, a code developed; if someone said of Mayer that "He's on Lot 14" or "He's on Lot 15," he was really at Santa Anita or Hollywood Park, respectively.

Katz had grown to respect Mayer, and admired him for his instinctive sense of the application of power—the way, for instance, he had of summoning someone to see *him*, never the other way around . . . except, of course, for Nick Schenck. "He [was] prosperous because of extravagant thinking," Katz would remember. "He was an inspiration. . . . *He was the boss* . . . a great showman who believed in glitter and glamour. . . . Mayer's integrity was above reproach. I never saw him make a decision in which he stopped to think, 'Is this good for me?' He always thought of the company.

"He was adroit by keeping himself removed. He would not talk to people. He would have his secondaries do that and say, 'Well, I'm not sure whether Mr. Mayer will go for this.' Thus, when Mayer did come into the situation, and being a good talker, making a fine front and so forth, he was . . . strong and commanding, [everything] his people represented him to be. . . .

"Mayer applied to horse breeding the experience of buying well and cultivating it. He had a keen sense of public relations in the right places. He was adroit at bringing any discussion—foreign policy, politics, whatever—around to the picture business in which he was *the big man*."

Horses would not be a hands-off hobby for a slow weekend; according to Jack Baker, his chief veterinarian, he had a comprehensive grasp of the day-to-day operations of his stable, and knew all the details, from track records to the proper grain mix in the horses' feed. When he was at the farm, Mayer would walk around with a large wax paper bag full of lump sugar, which he'd hold in the palm of his hand so the horses could lick it off.

Mayer's grandson Dan would remember, "As he had his own specially developed relationship with each secretary on the lot or a certain chef on the lot or a chauffeur, so he had a relationship with certain horse trainers, certain jockeys and the individual horse. He had a sort of playful dialogue that he entered into with each of his horses that I believe he improvised just for us. It was as if different members of his family were being introduced to one another. He would say . . . 'You know my grandson, Daniel Selznick' or 'You know my grandson, Jeffrey Selznick.' "

While Louis was steady and focused in the movie business, he seemed far more mercurial when it came to racing. He fired trainers right and left until he got the results he wanted, buying horses until he got some that could win. Shortly after spending $100,000 for young horses, he announced he was folding up his operation in California and moving his stable to the East, predominantly Kentucky. But after going to a lot of trouble to relocate to Kentucky, he reversed himself and moved twenty-seven brood mares to Deep Cliff Farm at Cupertino, near San Francisco. By this time, he owned fifty-two horses, twenty of them yearlings, with thirty-two horses stabled at Santa Anita alone.

Harry Warner helped build Hollywood Park, but was helpless when it came to building a successful stable. In fact, no one went in for racing as intensively as Mayer, and nobody was so successful. He offered $1 million for Man o'War and failed, tried to get the famous English horse Hyperion and also failed, but did buy one of Hyperion's sons, named Alibhai, and a famous thirteen-year-old stallion named Beau Pere.

Then he bought 504 acres in Perris, California, seventy-five miles south of Los Angeles, at the base of the San Jacinto Mountains, where, with a million dollars of his own money he built one of the most modern, beautiful horse farms in America.

The Mayer Stock Farm had two thirty-six-stall training barns, two eight-stall foaling barns, one twelve-stall isolation barn, and a beautiful six-stall stallion barn for the cream of Mayer's crop. There was a five-acre plot for the growing of various experimental grasses, and water was provided by seven deep wells. There were bungalows, a commissary, and a men's dormitory among the trees. Mayer had his own small bungalow, no more elaborate than anybody else's.

For three years in a row he would be the country's leading breeder of stakes winners. The similarities to the movie business struck him as obvious. "In the movies, a man likes to develop stars. In racing it is very much the same way. You take a horse and train him and bring him along and watch him develop. You get a lot of satisfaction watching them blossom out."

Mayer's bloodlines turned up in such legendary horses as Swaps, largely the result of two horses—Alibhai and Beau Pere. At the time, it was believed that Mayer's $100,000 was a considerable overpayment for Beau Pere—he had been a mediocre racer—but he was a remarkable stud. He sired 125 foals in North America alone; of the mares, a full 50 percent were stakes producers—an amazing ratio.

The next step was assembling a supply of brood mares, and Mayer ended up with about seventy-five of them, among them a horse named Busher. Busher had been owned by the Palm Beach sportsman and gambler E. R. Bradley, until attorney Neil McCarthy bought her for Mayer for $50,000. McCarthy told Mayer that he thought he could get the price down to $40,000, but Mayer had replied, "If Colonel Bradley wants $50,000, that's a good price. Pay it." Within a year of her purchase, Busher had won ten of thirteen starts and over $273,000. She ended up becoming the horse of the year, and the greatest money-winning filly up to that point.

Busher's sire was War Admiral, the 1937 Triple Crown winner, and her grandfather was Man o' War. In 1945, L.B. was the leading money-winning horse owner in America, earning $533,150. Ten percent went to his jockeys and 10 percent to his trainer, but Mayer's investment was still paying off in a big way. In the years L.B. had an active stable, he earned purses of about $1.7 million, a feat racing experts termed "phenomenal."

L.B.'s brother Jerry also had a ranch at Perris and needed to do something to keep up with his brother. Horses were too expensive, so he decided to collect birds. Soon, Jerry's ranch looked like an avian Noah's Ark. Jerry wanted to add some white-crested Chinese pheasants to his collection, and asked Robert Vogel if he could use his international contacts to find him some. Vogel cabled his man in China and found that white-crested pheasants were hard to come by even in China. Nevertheless, a pair was procured for Jerry, but when they arrived at the studio, they were sent to the prop department. Props hadn't ordered any live pheasants, so they were sent over to the commissary, where they were promptly slaughtered and served. An enraged Jerry told his brother, who was equally enraged. The head of the commissary, who had been there for years, was fired.

L.B. gave a couple of horses to Jerry, one of whom, On Trust, finished third in the Kentucky Derby. On occasion, he would even give a horse to an actor instead of a bonus, as when he gave Elizabeth Taylor King Charles, the horse she rode in National Velvet.

"His horses were like movie stars to him," remembered Ann Miller. "He loved the fact that they were beautiful. And if they ran fast enough, they were stars. He loved the thrill of it. The funny thing was, he never bet very much on the races, never more than $2. It wasn't the gambling that appealed to him, it was the thrill of winning."

By the late 1930s, the MGM shorts department contained such directorial talents-in-waiting as Fred Zinnemann, George Sidney, Jules Dassin, and

Jacques Tourneur, who all learned to cope with the strictures of the form: one-reelers were shot silent, because they were all narrated, but two-reelers were shot as conventional sound films. In either case, moving the camera was verboten because lighting the set for a tracking shot took too long.

For directors like Zinnemann, it was invaluable training; he remembered that for a scene outside a hospital, he had to make ten extras look like a crowd. Zinnemann dressed one of the extras as a policeman and had him push the remaining nine bodies backward, toward the camera, giving the impression that dozens of people were milling around. Beyond that, the precision mandated by the shorts would prove invaluable when Zinnemann later had to shoot *High Noon* in thirty-two days, and *From Here to Eternity* in forty-one.

The shorts department became a studio within a studio, with its own staff of fifty, including writers, directors, editors, and supervisors. The shorts had the same pearly sheen that the A features did, and L.B. thought of them as a valuable training ground. Judy Garland, James Stewart, and Robert Taylor all got their first chances in MGM shorts.

"We made about seventy shorts a year in different series," remembered Richard Goldstone, who began as a writer and gradually worked his way up to head of the department. "Mayer was very good at delegating, once he was satisfied. If a unit was cooking successfully, he was pretty much hands-off. He was delighted with the product as a whole. As long as the machinery was working, and there were Oscars every year—that was important to him—then you were left alone."

The shorts even developed their own star system with droll series that starred Robert Benchley and Pete Smith, who used to be a studio publicity executive but whose shorts became ubiquitous on MGM bills. Smith's sarcastic, nasal delivery about the misadventures of an all-American klutz usually played by Dave O'Brien were the mid-century version of *The Simpsons*.

"Robert Benchley always considered himself to be first and foremost a critic of the New York stage," said screenwriter Robert Lees. "He'd say, 'I wanna go back to New York for the fall. If you want any shorts done, send the boys and we'll shoot a couple at Astoria.' So Fred [Rinaldo, Lees's writing partner] and I would go to New York, to a suite at the Algonquin. The Royalton, where Benchley lived, was across the street. We were given carte blanche to see anything that Pete Smith or any of the other producers could use, and we saw wonderful plays like *Pins and Needles*, all at Metro's expense."

Benchley was a charming man, a great procrastinator, and a serious alcoholic. "Most alcoholics specialize," said Robert Lees. "Benchley drank anything. He would drink aperitifs during and after dinner. I remember going into his apartment at the Royalton. I came through the door and he threw something at me and I caught it. It was a dildo! My God, I was holding a rubber prick! I threw it right back."

Most of the MGM shorts are boilerplate, but there are some very interesting ones as well. *Important News* with Chic Sale and a practically adolescent James Stewart involves a small-town newspaper editor who witnesses a wanted criminal shot down on the street by the FBI, then refuses to put the story on the front page, where it would bump a story about a frost warning. His readers, he explains, need the news of the frost warning more than they need the news of a crook's death, which goes on the obit page. The editor is laughed at until his judgment is ratified by a journalism award. The short points up the extent to which MGM's values skewed rural and were made palatable to the widest audience by the studio's stars, who skewed urban.

For animation, the studio had subcontracted its work to Hugh Harman and Rudolf Ising, who worked in a very Disneyesque mode. In 1937, as part of L.B.'s expansionist instincts, the studio decided to develop its own animation unit and installed Fred Quimby, one of the company's top salesmen, as executive. To house the operation, the studio used a run-down bungalow behind Lot 2, whose bare furnishings made it seem even more forlorn than it actually was.

The operation was given focus by the activities of a pair of young animators named William Hanna and Joe Barbera. "Why don't we do a cartoon of our own?" asked Barbera one day. "One where we don't have to explain the characters." Barbera came up with the idea of a cat and a mouse tormenting each other, and he and Hanna created the first Tom and Jerry cartoon.

Soon, Tom and Jerry were the profit centers for the entire MGM animation department. The unit was eventually housed in a two-story corner building that employed 150 artists and technicians making only eighteen cartoons a year. In 1941, and continuing for fourteen years and sixty-seven shorts, Hanna and Barbera were joined by the great Tex Avery, whose violent, fragmented, frenetically paced fantasias on paranoia, survival, and movies themselves have become accepted as the model for postwar animation. Avery's counterpart to Tom and Jerry was a deadpan bassett hound named Droopy, an imperturbable, waddling understatement in total control of Avery's hyperbolic valley of exaggeration.

"Mayer never came through the animation building, not once," said Joe Barbera. "His brother Jerry, who was in charge of operations, yes, but L.B., never."

The budgets for MGM cartoons would settle at between $25,000 and $30,000 apiece, above the industry average. "MGM was a country club operation," said Hanna. "We put the same quality into the shorts that we did into our feature animation. [The Hanna-Barbera unit] did six or seven, or at the most eight cartoons a year. Years later, when we went into TV, we did more animation in a week than we had turned out in a year at MGM."

The expensive, beautifully upholstered MGM animation made the explosive, parodic violence palatable, and somehow less surreal. Beginning in 1943, Hanna and Barbera's Tom and Jerry cartoons won seven Oscars ever nine years.

Mayer's strictures were as important in the shorts department as they were in features: "Don't forget that the audience is twelve years old. Tell them everything three times: before it happens, when it's happening and after it has happened." And "The star's face must always be seen, even if it's midnight in a tunnel."

The shorts would be among the studio's most moralistic products. After MGM took over the Our Gang shorts from Hal Roach in 1938, it turned the series, which had always been more or less realistic movies about kids' problems—getting an ice cream cone was a sufficient plot—into tedious ten-minute morality plays that focused on issues only adults cared about: pedestrian safety, for instance.

For eleven years, the Roach shorts had buttressed the Loew's releasing program and made money, although not a lot. In 1929–30, Laurel and Hardy films had made a profit of $143, 678. For the two years after that, the films lost money.

This perfectly satisfactory relationship with Roach came to an end in the late 1930s, at least partially because of Roach's ill-advised business alliance with Benito Mussolini. Roach had been traveling through Europe when Mussolini asked to see him and proposed a joint business venture involving the recently completed Italian film production complex, Cinecittà. Although Roach said he didn't want to do anything if there were sanctions against Jews, Mussolini assured him that was not the case, and the two men announced the formation of RAM (Roach and Mussolini) Productions.

In September 1937, Mussolini's son Vittorio accompanied Roach to Hollywood, where the producer threw a lavish party for the boy's twenty-first birthday. By this time, the increasingly anti-Semitic tone of Italy's militaristic pronouncements had alarmed everybody. "The industry as a whole let Roach know, but fast, that they weren't happy," said Roach special effects man Roy Seawright. "But Roach could be stubborn; he used to be a truck driver and he ran his business the way he did a truck. He saw a road to take, and he was going to go down that road come hell or high water."

The upshot of all this was that an appalled Nick Schenck pulled Loew's distribution out from under Roach. His last MGM release was the Laurel and Hardy feature *Blockheads*, after which, in May of 1938, he began releasing through United Artists. For Loew's, it was a decision of moral principle that had the potential of negatively affecting their corporate bottom line—but not by much.

Roach had no apparent regrets; as an old man living in Beverly Hills, one of the prominent features of his house was a warmly autographed portrait of Benito Mussolini.

Nick Schenck's decision about Roach was in contrast to what was going on over a picture called *Three Comrades*. MGM's relationship with Nazi Germany had always been somewhat ambiguous; as early as 1935, a reporter from *Film-Kurier* had taken a tour of the lot and written a story whose central point was that the secret of MGM's success was the systematic application of the *Führerprinzip*—the leadership principle. It was a comment that contained, even at the time, an unpleasant implication that Mayer would not have wished to hear.

The Erich Maria Remarque novel had been the subject of blatant pressure tactics from George Gyssling, the Nazi consul in Los Angeles, as soon as it was published. As early as September 1936, Gyssling was writing the Hays Office's Joseph Breen about production plans for the Remarque book. Gyssling had been emboldened by MGM's canceling of a film based on Sinclair Lewis's controversial novel *It Can't Happen Here* a few months earlier. The studio had been no more than a week away from going into production when the film was suddenly shelved.

The studio blamed a high budget, but Lewis claimed that Will Hays, worried about a threatened boycott from Germany and Italy, had told MGM to cease and desist. By the early part of 1937, MGM was still moving forward with the Remarque story, and Gyssling was "a little concerned."

"As this book deals with conditions as they allegedly existed in Germany after the war and during the 'inflation period,'" Gyssling wrote, "I would be grateful to you, if you would give this matter your attention, so that future difficulties might be avoided."

Gyssling did this more or less reflexively with any picture with a tinge of anti-Fascism, or any film based on a Remarque novel. (When word of Chaplin's plans to make *The Great Dictator* leaked in October of 1938—a month after Czechoslovakia was annexed—Gyssling fired off a letter to Joe Breen that referred to "serious troubles and complications" if the picture burlesqued Hitler. But Chaplin financed his own movies and answered to no one; he ignored the threats and made his picture anyway. *The Great Dictator* wasn't exhibited in Germany until 1958.

"Future difficulties" were ambiguous but also obvious. The Germans could slap a boycott on MGM pictures or, for that matter, on the pictures of every studio in Hollywood. The economic implications of a German boycott were serious. At this point, the major Hollywood studios received between 30 and 40 percent of their income from overseas distribution.

When the first draft script of *Three Comrades* was completed in May 1937, Breen found only one speech that might offend the Germans. But Gyssling was not mollified, and Breen tried to convince Mayer to cancel the picture. The story, Breen wrote, is "a serious indictment of the German nation and people and is certain to be violently resented by the present government in that country."

According to Joe Mankiewicz, who was producing the picture, Breen also suggested making the political agitators in the film Communists rather than Nazis, and Mayer was willing to go along with that until Mankiewicz threatened to walk off the picture.

On January 19, 1938, a clearly worried Breen wrote Mayer that, while the completed script fit the criteria of the Production Code it also presented "enormous difficulties from the standpoint of your company's distribution business in Germany and from the general standpoint of industry 'good and welfare' as a whole. Because of this we suggest, respectfully, that you give serious thought to all this, before putting this picture into production."

To its credit, MGM went ahead with the picture; to its discredit, it gelded the script. By the end of January 1938, after conferences including Mayer, Breen, Mannix, Sam Katz, Benny Thau, and Joe Mankiewicz, it was agreed that all references to the Nazi government would be deleted from the script, as well as scenes of book burning and names such as "Blumenthal" and "Mendelsohn." All references to democracy were cut, and the story was moved to a couple of years immediately after the Armistice of 1918. Most, if not all, political or social content was systematically drained from the script.

A couple of weeks later, *New Masses*, which apparently had good sources within MGM, wrote, "Persecuted German Jews and Catholics will be interested to know that Mayer and Breen have collaborated in authorizing a script denuded of any suggestion that Jews and Catholics are not wholly comfortable in Naziland, and in which the storm troopers have been reduced to a barely discernible minimum."

By mid-May of 1938, the picture was completed and previewed for Breen and Gyssling. And still the placating went on, as Breen wrote to the Nazi consul to assure him that "the shot showing the drums at the head of the parade will be deleted from all prints put into circulation. In addition, the scenes of the rioting have been materially shortened. So, too, has the scene of the fist-fight over the crushed automobile."

F. Scott Fitzgerald always blamed Joseph Mankiewicz for watering down the picture, not to mention rewriting his (overwritten) script, while Mankiewicz passed the buck to Mayer, saying that the studio head was nervous about a backlash from the German government if the picture exposed Nazism as an evil force. His version is entirely possible; Mayer once told screenwriter George Oppenheimer that Oppenheimer worried too much about Fascism. From September 15, 1939, to January 1940, the production of films that could be considered anti-Nazi was explicitly banned by the Hays Officer.

"Warner Bros. had guts," said Mankiewicz. "They hated the Nazis more than they cared for the German grosses. MGM did not. It kept on releasing its films in Nazi Germany until Hitler finally threw them out." By 1940, only MGM, Fox, and Paramount could export films to Germany, and they were finally refused access that September.

Three Comrades was a sizable success, grossing over $2 million, netting $472,000, but Mayer's attitude toward Nazism was problematic; in his worldview, things were either good or bad for Metro-Goldwyn-Mayer and were judged accordingly; the larger picture tended to elude him. "Louis Mayer was only thinking of motion pictures," said Loew's executive Robert Vogel. "He didn't think of anything else."

But even before Pearl Harbor, Mayer was enthusiastic about the shorts department being used for propaganda purposes. "We began inserting doctrine into films," said Richard Goldstone. "Carey Wilson's Miniature series had been doing shorts about Nostradamus, and all of a sudden Nostradamus was predicting the rise of Nazism. And L.B. was really involved in all this, as he was in some of the pictures, like *Joe Smith, American. Very* involved. Another project involved going to the High Sierras to make seven full-length films for the Ski Patrol, because the War Department had determined that there was going to be fighting in Scandinavia. It was one of Mayer's sources of pride that we were doing this for the government."

There was much worry at the studio over what was happening in Europe.

Mayer's own feelings about the situation were crystallized in a speech he gave in San Francisco on Saint Patrick's Day 1938: "I am a Jew, and I try to be a good one. In some lands, an increasing number, you are persecuted if you are a Jew; you cannot own anything, may not vote; you can be driven from your home, torn from the arms of your loved ones because . . . of how [you] worship. . . .

"Tyrannies dictate what shall, and what shall not a man hold sacred. Never in all history, not even in the grim pages of the blackest inquisitions, has the world been so beset by religious intolerance. Birthright becomes a bondage, divine worship a crime, in this maelstrom of prejudice which is attacking the very foundations of a civilization built upon the teachings of Christ."

Mayer knew a pogrom when he saw one, but subtle gradations eluded him. In July 1939, Mayer hosted a lunch at the studio for Dr. Frank Buchman, the founder of the Oxford Group, later renamed Moral Rearmament, largely regarded as an anti-Semitic, pro-Nazi front. Whether or not Mayer knew about the philosophy of Buchman's group, or whether he was just seduced by the phrase "Moral Rearmament," is unclear. On screen, however, all was sweetness and light in the accustomed MGM manner.

MGM's hesitation about condemning Fascism was finally abandoned after World War II erupted in Europe. Mayer authorized the production of two anti-Nazi films: *The Mortal Storm* and *Escape.*

The Mortal Storm was a creative failure that cruelly revealed the limitations of MGM's worldview. The script didn't specify that the events were happening in Germany, even though it was clear that's where the story was set. One day, the set was visited by a functionary of the Swiss consulate—by this time the Germans relayed all their information through the Swiss—who announced that *The Mortal Storm* and Warners' *Confessions of a Nazi Spy* would be remembered by Germany when—not if—they won the war.

"I didn't give a goddamn about what they were going to remember," recalled Robert Stack, who was playing a Nazi in the picture, "and that was the attitude of Jimmy [Stewart], Maggie [Sullavan], the director [Frank] Borzage, and most everybody else. But Bob Young was very affected by this little announcement and he kept asking me, 'What about my children? What about my kids?' I'm not saying he was wrong, because Warners ended up having to assign guards to the family of Edward G. Robinson after *Confessions of a Nazi Spy.* Maybe I was just too young and dumb to worry about it. . . . But except for Bob Young, nobody had the brains to take what the Swiss guy said seriously." According to Stack, the Germans also threatened Mayer with a boycott of all MGM films.

The film eked out a profit of $108,000, but the response of Hollywood to the Fascist threat revealed the primary weakness of the studio system: it groomed and installed house talents on assembly-line projects developed strictly for their ability to house those talents, rather than for any expression of passion for an individual film. Because MGM was the incarnation of the dream factory, approximating political or social reality was a contradiction in terms and in practice.

In the long year of 1940, Mayer was nervous, therefore MGM was nervous. "Never was back-slapping harder, cordiality louder, mistrust greater," wrote Christopher Isherwood. "Rumor travels the corridors on roller skates." The preferred social attitude was guarded optimism, which thinly masked the low-grade panic of courtiers everywhere.

In mid-July 1940, Mayer called a mass meeting on Stage 30 to aid the American Red Cross. The stage was decorated with flags and crammed with four thousand employees, everybody from actors in full makeup to carpenters. It looked, wrote Christopher Isherwood, like "Democracy's Nuremberg Rally."

Jeanette MacDonald sang "The Star-Spangled Banner," and Robert Montgomery, just back from France, addressed the crowd. After the selected short subjects came the main feature: Mayer made one of his rambling, sentimental speeches.

Salka Viertel had been through these moments before; she described the speech as "Capitalism licking Labor's Ass."

With Thalberg dead, and Nick Schenck in New York, Louis was at last able to exercise his will in regard to the entire MGM output. Thalberg favorites such as the Marx Brothers would be allowed to work out their contracts and depart, although nobody was sorry about that because every Marx Brothers picture after *A Night at the Opera* lost money, except for *The Big Store*, which eked out a $33,000 profit.

In 1940, Buster Keaton approached Eddie Mannix for a job. The actor was more or less sober, had recently entered into a new marriage that would prove lasting, and was sick of making cheap two-reelers at Columbia. Keaton asked Mannix if he could be put on the payroll as a gag man and comedy constructionist. Mannix gave him a job that started at $100 a week. Keaton stayed for the next nine years, his pay rising consistently, the studio always giving him time off for any acting jobs that came up.

Mayer never talked about Keaton being welcomed back in a menial position, similar to that which had been given Erich von Stroheim in the mid-1930s. It's probable that it simultaneously satisfied that part of him that enjoyed humbling those who had fought with him, as well as his sense of noblesse oblige.

MGM was the worst place for any comedian with a bent for physical slapstick, but Mayer's own prissiness has been overstated. At the preview of *The Big Store*, the Marxes got into a row with producer L. K. Sidney over an exchange between Groucho and Margaret Dumont:

Dumont: "I'm afraid after we've been married awhile, a beautiful girl will come along and you'll forget all about me."

Groucho: "Nonsense! I'll write you twice a week."

Sidney wanted the lines out. As Mayer came up to the group after the preview, Harpo explained the argument. "Greatest line in the picture," said Mayer as he exited. The line stayed.

One of L.B.'s favorite dictums was, "Motion pictures are nothing more than beautiful photographs that move." He might have interjected "of beautiful people," after "photographs," but the point had been made nevertheless. He allowed no one to deviate from that central premise.

When cinematographer James Wong Howe suggested mussing Myrna Loy's hair and subtly deglamorizing her for a scene calling for her to roll out of bed, Loy thought it was a good idea. The next day, Howe was called on the carpet. "What do you mean by shooting that kind of stuff of Loy? Here we've spent a couple of million bucks building her up as a glamour girl and you knock the whole thing for a loop with one shot." A retake was made, in which Loy woke up looking as if she'd just emerged from Max Factor's.

Even an ardent Mayer loyalist like Clarence Brown acknowledged there were problems at MGM, which were brought home when he was loaned out to Fox. Brown had grown used to the MGM system, where each craftsman was more beholden to his powerful department head than to the director. At MGM, if a corner was not perfectly lit, a cameraman could be criticized by his chief, or by Cedric Gibbons, so he would take as long as he wanted to get the lighting exactly right, overlooking the fact that no picture ever became a smash because of the stunning lighting or wonderful sets.

"Working with Zanuck at Fox was the happiest experience of my career," said Brown. "Everybody at Fox worked, and for the benefit of the story, not like at Metro. . . . Technically, Fox was way ahead of Metro. If [a director] wanted action at MGM, you had to shoot it in front of a process screen or use a second unit. Well, I don't like second units or back projection. Zanuck let me do most of my own action stuff; he was a dream producer for me. At Metro, I got what I wanted but I had to fight for it. At Fox, I didn't have to fight, just ask."

If a Metro stalwart like Brown had to use all his leverage to get what he needed, there was very little hope for directors who were lower on the totem pole, which included nearly everybody else on the lot. "Original thinking or original approach to storytelling scared the daylights out of studio executives at practically any level," concurred Victor Saville. Yet, Brown stayed put, because he loved Mayer.

"To me, Louis Mayer was a god," said Brown. "He was a strangely dependent man; we traveled a lot together, and if I told him to wait for me while I went to the bathroom or something, he took it very literally. 'Clarence told me to wait here and I'm waiting right here until he comes back,' he'd say.

"People hated him out of simple envy. He was a great filmmaker and a great executive. . . . Schenck handled the money and Mayer handled the talent. That's why MGM was the greatest studio. When that changed, MGM began to fall apart."

By 1940, Irving Thalberg had been dead for three years, and the prophet at his funeral who had predicted a squeeze in two years' time was proven wrong. MGM's list of pictures in 1939–40 included *The Wizard of Oz, Waterloo Bridge, The Shop Around the Corner, Ninotchka, The Philadelphia Story, Strike Up the Band,* and *The Women,* none of which Thalberg had anything to do with.

L.B. admired and respected doctors, but Margaret was afraid of them. As a result, she either pretended she was healthy (which was far from the case), medicated herself, or went to faddist quacks. This tendency drove Mayer crazy. He pleaded with her to go to proper doctors, but Margaret was obstinate. Her hysterectomy had precipitated a depression that the medicine of that era, long before hormone therapy, was helpless to ameliorate. From being afraid of doctors, she became a hypochondriac. Mayer's response to this was a kind of continuing helplessness. Where was his Maggie?

"In their thirty years together," their daughter Irene remembered, "he had spent very few nights apart from my mother. [Now] he wandered around brooding, homeless and bereft. . . . For ten years he was neither married nor unmarried, had neither his freedom nor a home."

Margaret's nephew Stanley Hoffman spent nearly every weekend at the Santa Monica house and grew very fond of his uncle. "He was particularly nice to our family financially. They knew our circumstances, and every month he made it much easier to go to sleep at night. He was very responsive to me and to those around him. He wasn't demonstrative particularly, but he would always smile when he saw me. He had a good smile.

"Every Sunday night, they had dinner parties. My family didn't have spit, but they invited us just the same. He was always very neat and formal; I can honestly say I never saw him in swimming trunks. At dinner, he sat at one end of the table, Margaret sat at the other end. After dinner, they'd show a movie, and if he didn't like it, he'd leave the room, just get up and leave and go to bed.

"He never talked about the past, his childhood in Canada, any of that. And I never saw the temper. But I heard about it."

Helen Sandler, Hoffman's sister, said that L.B. was imposing by dint of his position and his attitude. "It was always, 'Here comes L.B.' 'What will L.B. say?' It was intimidating. I just loved him, but I was in awe of him too. Even though I had lived at their house, even when I was grown up and married, I was always a little afraid of him. He had an office that was the length of a football field, and by the time I crossed it and sat down and he said, 'How are you, Helen?' I was practically crying. It wasn't anything he said or did. He was kind and good. It was what he represented."

Chapter
TEN

"WHO WAS L.B. MAYER?"

The question hung in the air as former MGM star Esther Williams pondered it, seated by her pool on one of the highest mountaintops in Los Angeles. Finally, she had an answer.

"He was God."

God rose early—he rarely slept very well—and was on the phone to New York by 8:00 A.M. Sometimes he would ride the exercycle in his bedroom—he was ahead of his time in believing in daily exercise—and sometimes he would head out to the golf course for a brisk round played at a dog trot; he took considerable satisfaction in being able to get in eighteen holes within forty-five minutes, which meant he couldn't possibly have been putting the ball in every hole. Often, he played a nine-ball onesome at Hillcrest, hitting balls from every tee and running after each shot from tee to green. He never bothered to keep score.

He had mellowed slightly; in his younger days, he had regularly invited associates to his house for breakfast at 6:00 A.M., then accompanied them to the studio at breakneck speed. Now in the full splendor of his middle age, Mayer was at his desk by 9:30, plowing straight ahead. After dinner, there was always a movie, sometimes two, and he often went to nightclubs, where he was known to dance with his designated female companion for two hours straight, with an annoyed look crossing his face when the band took a break.

On Sunday mornings, he would call for his grandchildren and take them to a pony ride on Pico Boulevard, leading the horses by the bridle, towing them and their precious cargo. Even when relaxing around the house, he smelled perceptibly of witch hazel aftershave and was always impeccably dressed, in silk sport shirts with French cuffs monogrammed "LBM."

As might be expected, no one needed an early warning system to know when he was around. His arrival at the studio would be announced by the loud slam of his car door, then the sound of him striding briskly down the hall, the bang of his office door, then a series of buzzers going off as he began his day. He rarely sat, but strode around the room, orating, thinking, acting.

The office was designed in Australian hardwood, with modern lighting and furniture. It had wall-to-wall white carpeting and the desk was on a platform, so any visitor was slightly below Mayer's eye level. Once a day, he would gaze at a picture of his mother and say a silent prayer to her memory. He believed she was observing him at all times.

He sat behind his white kidney-shaped desk "damn near as big as a pool table," said director William Wellman, in an office with white leather walls and a piano. (He didn't play, but producers and songwriters might come in to audition a song, and he wanted to be ready.) There was a side room and a bathroom with a shower, a refrigerator, a daybed, and a private elevator that went from his office down to the first floor. There were no scripts. "The whole huge room was money," remembered Wellman.

He worked furiously, decisively, without much of a schedule—he was impatient with paperwork—occasionally darting into a soundproof booth for telephone calls to Nick Schenck or Bob Rubin in New York, which weren't routed through the studio switchboard. His secretaries would never get used to his explosive energy. Nobody could keep up with him. The day went until 8:30 or 9:30 P.M., the last two hours reserved for watching rushes in his private projection room.

Everybody knew about his temper, but everybody also knew that the anger faded quickly. He was patient and preferred to leave department heads alone, but would fire executives if they failed to produce time after time. He didn't like to fire those on lower echelons. "Maybe we *could* get somebody better," he would say. "Still, he has been with us a long time. Give him another chance."

He never panicked over a bad picture. If somebody suggested canceling a movie that seemed to be floundering in production, Mayer would almost always refuse. "This isn't a piker business. Get the best writers you can hire. Do another script. Get other actors if you want them. Keep at it. It's a good story. It'll make a good picture."

Among the roles Mayer played was that of a *yenta*; he would anxiously take over anybody's life, telling someone where to shop, what to order at which restaurant, what doctor to see, always suggesting ways others could take care of themselves. If someone had a pimple, he'd say, "What about the doctor? What does he say it is? Has he given you anything for it—some salve, maybe? Does he know what is causing it? Any trouble with your skin? Has he got to the core of it?"

There were those who thought this was a manifestation of his will to power, his urge to dominate, and that was undoubtedly part of it, but his concern was sincere. To work at MGM in these years was to have a sense of security unparalleled in the movie industry—many employees were like enlightened Moonies, spouting a cult of MGM. The studio newspaper is full of golf tournaments and picnics, carpenters and secretaries who got their names in the paper and who had the added consolation of working on movies like *The Wizard of Oz* and *The Philadelphia Story*.

"He was stubborn, hardheaded, ruthless, sentimental, occasionally explosive, although such outbursts were often hammed deliberately," remembered story analyst Ross Willis. "He rarely appeared on the lot, and when he did he wasted no time patting anybody on the head but moved, head down, briskly to his destination. If you spoke to him in passing, he'd give you a quick nod or mumbled greeting and you weren't sure he recognized you, although he was not unpleasant. He seemed always, and rather belligerently, absorbed in some problem. Indeed, he usually proceeded with the air of a man on his way to give somebody hell."

Walter Seltzer went to work as a publicist for Howard Strickling in 1935 and soon became aware of the root cause of the studio's superiority complex. "Mayer was terribly egocentric. The world revolved around him and his comfort, and Howard contributed a lot to that. It was interesting—Howard had a terrible stammer, and it was amazing that he was able to be at Mayer's right hand, because Mayer was an impatient man. But they had total trust between them, and great camaraderie.

"I must have covered forty film openings. Howard never sat down; he stood two paces behind Mayer, and saw to it that Mayer's chair was there and there were no distractions. Nobody could approach him. It was like Mayer was the President of the United States and Howard was the Secret Service."

Seltzer seemed to be headed for great things until he committed a mortal sin. "The way I got canned was illustrative of the studio. When they needed to give VIP tours, they would be conducted by kids in the mailroom. One day on the lot, I saw a friend of mine named Bobby Schultz conducting a tour, giving the standard spiel. The guide would walk backward and say, 'And on the right is Stage 3, the largest soundstage in the world . . .'

"As I walked by him I said, very quietly, so nobody else could have heard me, 'You're full of shit, there's a bigger one at Warners.'

"A half hour later I had a call to see Strickling. I came in and fire was shooting out of his eyes. 'Where were you a half-hour ago?'

" 'On the lot.'

" 'Did you see a tour being conducted?'

"At this point I knew the jig was up. Bobby Schultz had gone back to the mailroom and told the story and got a laugh, but he didn't know that the head of the mailroom was a stoolie.

"So I got a half-hour lecture about the studio that had been so good to me, that had given me a $5 raise. The fact that I lacked pride in the organization was a cause of great concern to him. A week later, they had an economy drive, and the only person to get canned was me, a $50-a-week press agent. Now, I had been there four years at this point, and Howard and I were friends. I had the top job in that department, and Howard trusted me to fill the water tumbler on his desk with gin every day."

Seltzer went over to Warners, where he soon hooked up with Hal Wallis, and the difference between the studio heads was instructive. "Warners was much more relaxed, with a looser attitude. Jack Warner was a buffoon; he'd make rules and everybody would laugh at them. For instance, people would clock in, then go over to the drugstore for an hour and have coffee. One day, Warner had [head of studio police] Blainie Matthews posted by the drugstore taking names of all the Warner employees who were having coffee at the drugstore. Nobody paid any attention to it. They just kept clocking in and going over to the drugstore.

"That never would have happened with Mayer. He was no buffoon. In fact, in my experience with him, he was cold and autocratic. But there was a little bit of awe within the industry about how that studio ran. *It worked.* It was unified under him, and it was indeed the Tiffany's of the business."

Everybody on the lot respected Mayer, and most held him in some affection, if only because wearing the MGM label meant you were a marketable property—even if you were fired for incompetence, you'd been at MGM and that meant you could always get another job. As Ross Willis remembered, "L.B.'s eventual, settled policy came to be: hire good people, or see that they were hired, and let them alone. Every other studio went through numerous upheavals or reorganizations, but not his. He kept the place stable and sound, and jobs were secure; there was a comparative minimum of whimsical firing, and so long as an employee did a reasonably good job, he was let alone, given a considerable area of freedom."

"MGM had a caste system, just like India," remembered actor Turhan Bey. "At Universal, everybody sat at the same table and everybody chatted. Not at MGM. If you were an associate producer, you didn't eat with Pandro Berman. On the outside, everything was lovey-dovey, but there was—not a military thing—but everybody had their position, and that position was important and it was also important that you realized your position."

If you weren't already aware of your position, Ida Koverman would remind you; before you got into Mayer's office, you had to pass Koverman's inspection. "We called her Mount Ida," remembered Evie Johnson. "How to explain her? She was Margaret Thatcher, but much worse. She was dictatorial, unbending and unyielding. She was *not* a nice old grandmother."

Past the ferocious gatekeeper, the seduction began.

Confronted with anger or frustration, Mayer would listen sympathetically and let the aggrieved person get it out of their system. Then he would "proceed to show them they are right insofar as they know the facts. I show them the other side of the question and they usually change their opinion." Part of the way he diffused anger was to disclaim interest in anything but the person's welfare.

His manner was often impeccable. "L.B. wasn't crude at all," said Esther Williams. "Super-intelligent people might have found him common or crass, but he was trying to be the kind of executive that Lew Stone or Walter Pidgeon would play. He may have been an immigrant with a good suit of clothes, but never forget that this was a man working hard to be an American." Because of this, Mayer almost never spoke Yiddish at the office. "He spoke Yiddish only with some of the poor relatives," said Irene Mayer Selznick, "or very rarely to my mother so the children wouldn't understand."

Despite his grade school education, his warm voice was as commanding as his sharp eyes—like "very dark maple syrup," remembered his grandson Daniel Selznick. There was no trace of either a Canadian or New England accent; if anything, there was a touch of the Midwest.

On his home turf, L.B. demonstrated his remarkable grasp of the overall, the big picture. So much of the job was exercising an innate practicality. There's a problem—here's a solution. There's another problem—here's another solution. Don't dawdle. Be decisive. He knew that sometimes he would be right and sometimes he would be wrong, but that first impulses were vital.

Weren't impulses what made the audience decide whether or not to see a particular movie? Surely, the same thing applied in making those movies. This, he knew, was what he had been born to do.

When meeting a prospective talent he wanted, Louis would rise from his desk, shake hands and say, "Welcome to MGM." On his desk would be a still—if he was talking to an actor—or, if the talent was a writer, a copy of his book or play. "Will you trust yourself to MGM?" he would ask. "I don't need a test," he might say to an assistant in the room, although there had almost certainly been a test made. "I can sense stardom. She has it. I have only felt like this with two other people. One was Greer Garson. The other was Mickey Rooney."

He would then move in and ask the prospect to sign a contract with the studio, for either three or seven years, with six-month options. The talent would ask for a day or two to think it over, and Louis would smile and say, "Of course. I know what you'll decide." The studio was the most successful, the money was usually the highest; most people signed.

If there was a girl he was trying to impress, he would first bring casting director Billy Grady into his office, then get the girl on her feet. He would adjust her hair into several makeshift styles. Perhaps a Veronica Lake look? No? Then how about a psyche knot on top of her head? Um, better.

The girl would stand in front of a window, where Mayer would observe her profile in the light, then she'd be moved to more normal lighting where the profile would be examined again. Then came the inspection of her legs, and Mayer began circling her like a sculptor observing the raw marble from which the masterpiece would be hewn. Grady, who went through this routine untold numbers of times, would do his best to avoid yawning.

If he was in a mood for economizing, Mayer's negotiating tactics could get personal. When Irene Hervey, the wife of Allan Jones, came in to ask for a raise, Mayer listened carefully, then said, "I have the best mouthwash in Hollywood." Hervey was flustered and embarrassed. Mayer led her to his bathroom, poured some of the mouthwash into a glass, gargled with it, then handed it to her. She tried it, nodded her approval. "Now go out and buy that gargle!" he told her. The ostensible subject of the meeting was forgotten, and Hervey was too embarrassed ever to try again.

With executives, Mayer was cooler, more professional. "Mayer respected brains, respected talent," said Joe Cohn. "One time he said to me, 'Never be afraid of hiring a fellow smarter than you are. You'll only learn from them.'"

"Mayer prided himself on picking people," said Robert Vogel, director of international publicity for MGM. "Mayer's involvement with individuals was always the same. He put an individual into a job because his judgment was that this fellow was ideal for the job, and after that he didn't interfere with them. It didn't matter whether he was a producer or a department head or a janitor. He was left entirely to his own devices."

Vogel recalled a time when Paramount fired its entire publicity department, leaving some good people available. He told Mayer that MGM could use some of them. "You want to put them on here?" asked Mayer. "You know better than to come to me with that. You're running the publicity department. If you want them, take them. [It's] none of my business."

The powerful personality, the perennial certitude about nearly everything, swayed weaker personalities. As Walter Seltzer observed, "Clark Gable was a staunch Republican, as was Robert Taylor, who did everything Gable did. Neither of those people had politics before they got to Metro. Some people retained their independence. Gable, politics aside, was his own man, and I loved Joan Crawford. She was brutal with her children, but I always found her a forthright, basically honest lady."

The Sunday brunches at his house featured guests that might include a visiting statesman, Cardinal Spellman from New York, or a former President of the United States. Ernst Lubitsch, for whom Mayer had the greatest respect, would drop by to contribute to the conversation, which tended toward movies and L. B. Mayer's likes and dislikes. One of Mayer's ambitions, he would tell people, was to own a country newspaper where he could write daily front page editorials, just like Hearst or Arthur Brisbane. "I'd rather be nicer than richer," was a frequent utterance.

If an employee was quiet and obedient and in need of a father figure, he would never see any side of Mayer other than the benign papa, a role Mayer could always slip into with alacrity. He would slip his arm through an actor's arm, escort him to lunch or dinner, asking questions about his family and level of contentment, asking only to make the actor happy. Many MGM contractees heard the stories of the other Mayer—the sobbing, the rages—but they never saw that Mayer.

"Mr. Mayer was to me like a father," said Ricardo Montalban. "Seriously. He was very nice to me, very nice. Of course, his nephew, Jack Cummings, had discovered me, and took me to lunch in the private dining room, where Mr. Mayer insisted on the best—steaks from New York, the matzoh ball soup, the fish, the pies, everything absolutely A-1.

"But I was brought up in a certain way, to be a gentleman. My nails were clean, my manners were good, and I was shy. Mr. Mayer liked all that. He really thought of the people under contract as his boys and girls."

June Allyson had a two-tier relationship with her boss. If she wanted to see him, the advantage was always with her. He would listen to her problem and lecture her and tell her what she needed to do. If he wanted to see her, it was trouble, usually because she was seeing someone he didn't approve of. She recounted a conversation she had with him:

"Is it true that you are going out with David Rose?"

"Yes sir, he's very nice and I'm learning a lot about music from him."

"Buy a book. If you care about your reputation, you cannot be seen with a married man—a twice-married man—no matter what he's teaching you about music . . . this must stop immediately."

It did.

When Allyson began dating Dick Powell, also divorced, also much older, Mayer again ordered her to stop seeing him. This time she refused. Then, in a tactical master stroke, Allyson asked Mayer to give her away at her wedding. He was struck dumb by the effrontery, but gathered himself together, and, presumably amused at having been outmaneuvered, said, "I'd be happy to."

There was a general ritual of everybody standing up when Mayer passed through the cafeteria on the way to his private dining room. The unquestioning deference usually continued when Mayer would ask a star to make a personal appearance. Once he woke up the child star Margaret O'Brien with a request for her to come down and recite the Gettysburg Address for Douglas MacArthur, Chester Nimitz, and some other military notables that were visiting the studio. O'Brien's mother got her dressed and drove her to the studio so she could perform.

He was a familiar sight on the streets of MGM. "He went chugging along with his head down, not saying hello to anyone," remembered screenwriter Devery Freeman. "There was a writer named Jerry Davis, who had been saying hello to him for years, and Mayer would always go right past him. And one day Mayer looked up, saw Jerry and said, 'Hello, Mr. Davis.' Davis hadn't said a thing and was ten feet past him when he realized what had happened, and he turned on his heel and followed him, saying 'Good morning, Mr. Mayer, good morning, Mr. Mayer . . . ' all the way down the alley.

"Mayer was cordial when he wanted to be, or had to be. He was regarded with both fear and respect; he could be tyrannical, although I never encountered it. But I must tell you that the proudest moment of my career there came when my option came up and Mayer said, 'We have plenty of work for that young man.' "

Mayer's paternalism was no joke; the studio devised the Dr. Kildare series as a way to keep an ailing Lionel Barrymore on the job. (Over the years, a great many conflicting stories about the reasons for Barrymore's gradual invalidism have been spread, ranging from a twice-broken hip to syphilis. According to Gene Reynolds, who worked with Barrymore, it was just arthritis. "You could see it was arthritis from his hands; the knuckles were enlarged and the fingers were kind of gnarled, half-curled. He'd come to and from the set in his wheelchair. He could stand, but not for very long. He didn't seem to be in pain. In fact, he was a fine, nice man, not grumpy at all.") Likewise, when a messenger boy named Herbert Wrench broke his leg, the studio kept him on salary for the six weeks it took his leg to heal.

"L. B. Mayer was a great romantic," asserted Robert Young, who spent fourteen years at MGM. "Nobody thinks of him that way, [but] he was. . . . You show him a . . . picture with a little baby, he cries all over the place." Actually, a baby of any species could move him. One day at his Perris ranch, Ann Miller watched Mayer observe the birth of a foal, and saw tears streaming down Mayer's face as the pony struggled to its feet.

But for the echelon of actors beneath the elite, MGM could be a scary place, with the studio holding the whip and using it in subtle ways. Options were often not picked up until five minutes before the midnight when they were due to expire, when a Special Delivery letter would arrive at the employee's house. Once an actor asked Benny Thau about this overtly cruel policy—the studio must have made up its mind a week or two beforehand, why keep people hanging? Between that time and option time, explained Thau, the actor could be caught using drugs or having sex in Griffith Park, which would make him unsalable to the exhibitors.

This rationale, of course, was gibberish, used only on those actors who the studio felt were more or less expendable. To take just one minor example at random, MGM picked up Tim McCoy's option two months early in mid-November 1927, and it's a safe bet that was more or less normal procedure for talent that was valued or might be in demand elsewhere. On the other hand, even a featured player at MGM was treated as someone special. "They took care of you," said Rand Brooks. "They had gyms, they had singing teachers, they had dancing teachers, they had fencing teachers. They would do anything to take whatever ability you had and develop it, build you up."

Turhan Bey, who showed up on the lot to appear in *Dragon Seed*—the cast

soon renamed the picture *Draggin' Seed*—was familiar with Mayer from parties. "He was a charming, wonderful, perfect host," said Bey. "When we were
making the picture, they came to me and said they wanted to include me in a
picture that was being taken of all the stars on the lot. I said no. And the man
grew pale. 'Turhan, you don't know what you're saying.'

" 'Nobody can force me to have my picture taken.'

"And then the man said, 'Turhan, I must tell you frankly, I know you're a
man who likes to go your own way. But this time, do not go your own way.'

"So I had one of my brighter moments and went and had my picture taken.
But I'm not sure that the story didn't get back to Mayer. I was at a party after
that, and he was just as nice as ever, but I noticed a coolness about him. *Everything* on that lot came back to him."

One of Mayer's pet projects for a movie was an omnibus film about a window washer who spends his life going up and down the facade of an office
building, observing the vignettes of life and drama that occurred in the offices
and apartments. Mayer thought this was a crackerjack idea, and for years tried
unsuccessfully to sell it to producers and writers. L.B.'s window washer got to be
something of a joke around the studio. They were presumably more enthusiastic when Hitchcock adapted a similar idea and called it *Rear Window*.

L.B.'s personality and desire for social acceptance meant that the studio had
an eye for class and gloss, but little for the snap and irreverence necessary for
comedy. Paramount had Bob Hope, Goldwyn had Danny Kaye, but after the
Marx Brothers, MGM made do with recycled Buster Keaton vehicles for the
oafish Red Skelton. A gifted comedy director like George Cukor made only two
real comedies at MGM between 1940 and 1949. (*The Philadelphia Story* and
Adam's Rib.) The rest of the time, Cukor was coaxing drama from divas and
helping to bury Garbo and Norma Shearer.

In certain ways, it was like the Renaissance—the finest craftsmen in the
world under one roof, a guild containing the best of the best. It was for all these
reasons that decades after Mayer was dead, people who had worked with him
would demur about telling a particular story because "Mr. Mayer wouldn't approve."

Then there were the times when he had to confront what he felt were obvious flaws in his actors. Robert Young remembered being called to the boss's office one day. "Well, he wants to see you, it means one of two things, either he's
gonna tell you you're doing a great job, which is very, very unlikely—they don't
bother to send for you to tell you that—or you were gonna get fired, or there's
something wrong, you're gonna face a cut, or something."

By the time he got to Mayer's office, the insecure Young had worked himself into a state of fear and trembling. "Bob," said Mayer, "I've been thinking about you, and watching your work. A couple of things I think that you should do. For your career."

Young, always eager to learn, always wanting to improve, came to the edge of his chair.

Then Mayer imparted his suggestions: "Put on a little weight and get more sex."

Young stared. Get more sex?

"You live at home, don't you?" asked Mayer. "With your mother? I think you should have your own apartment. And then I think you should get yourself a valet."

"What the hell's a valet?"

"A houseboy. Japanese, preferably. White coat, black trousers." The valet, Mayer explained, could greet people at the door and serve drinks.

Young said that none of this would help him gain weight, which Mayer had to agree was true, but it would serve as an image-builder, a front, something for Hedda and Louella to write about. And if Young would start going out to Ciro's or the Mocambo, with a different girl each night, it would be even better.

"We've got a whole stable of girls here," Mayer continued. "The publicists pick it up; the columnists pick it up. And the inference, the implication, is, you know, a very very sexy guy, you got a different girl every night . . ."

Young did as Mayer suggested and rented an apartment with a Japanese houseboy and told his girlfriend he wouldn't be able to see her for a while because he was going to be going out to nightclubs. After six weeks, the exhausted Young realized he missed his girlfriend, who later became his wife, and settled down for forty years of a very comfortable second-tier career playing solid middle Americans.

Mayer's power, and his fearlessness in using it, naturally earned him mingled responses of respect and fear. With people who were resistant, the hammer could come down, as when Jules Dassin went on suspension rather than direct any more films he hated. After what Dassin remembered as a year without work, but still being kept on salary—Mayer kept sending the paychecks to Dassin's agent—the director finally caved in and appeared in Mayer's office.

Mayer began a long monologue, addressed more to the Executive Committee, who had been assembled to witness the return of the Prodigal Son. "Son," Mayer began, "I'm glad to have you back in the family." And then he told a long story about one of his horses whose will to run had suddenly dried up when he turned three. The horse would fly away from the gate, then end up quitting.

One day the trainer came rushing in. "L.B., I just found out why Pater quit all the time. That horse has developed the biggest balls I've ever seen on any horse. And after a furlong or so, they bang so hard against him he has to stop."

At this, Mayer paused, looked at the Executive Committee, then at Dassin. "So, my son, I gelded him. And he's winning races again."

"Not my balls, you son of a bitch," said Dassin.

"Get out of here, you dirty Red," replied Mayer.

The man who had had jags of insecure sobbing on Mission Road was long gone. He once explained that he had never wanted to be a director of the corporation. "I just want to be a plain doughboy, just an employee of the company. I don't want to be a director or an officer . . . or anything like that." Why? "Take the greatest company that was ever built—it is a romance." To become a corporate lackey, that would take the passion out of it. That was for New York.

When he was displeased, he moved with dispatch. Once, after hearing of some problems with a picture called *Journey for Margaret*, Mayer sat down to look at the first week's rushes. When the lights came up, he turned to Benny Thau and said, "Close it down." People started talking about how to save the picture, but Mayer snapped, "Shut up, all of you. You people don't know what you're doing."

"And then," remembered William Ludwig, who witnessed the episode, "he began to tell them everything that was wrong. 'How could you let Laraine Day have that hairdo?' Everything! Every little detail, and nothing escaped him. And he was right on everything, things we hadn't even seen." Although *Journey for Margaret* was a modest little tearjerker, Mayer wanted it to be all that it could be.

The splendor of MGM—the way a shopgirl's apartment in an MGM movie looked like a suite at the Waldorf—was Mayer's revenge on his benighted youth, on his beginnings in the movie business when he had existed on the fringes and people laughed at him for his clothes and his bad teeth.

The combination of his paternal attentiveness—whether real or fake—and aura of power made him attractive to many women. Elizabeth Taylor's mother, Sara, was very enamored of him, and, believed Ava Gardner, would have happily left her husband for Mayer if he had returned her interest. This drove her daughter, who didn't like Mayer at all, up the wall.

He was the sort of self-made man who needed to let everybody know that he was self-made and that he was the intimate of the rich and powerful, hence rich and powerful himself. Once, when the financier C. V. "Sonny" Whitney had just left his house, Mayer turned to his butler and told him, "George, that man is one of the richest men in the country." This kind of behavior led Barbara Stanwyck to call MGM "a pompous studio run by a pompous man."

When meeting an established star coming to MGM for the first time, Mayer would invite them to sit and chat. He would welcome them to the family of MGM. If they were liberals, he would never mention their politics. Rather, he would segue to a discussion of the difficulties of their business, the making of movies. People, he would say with a sigh, were unpredictable and sometimes emotions ran strong. If interests conflicted, a compromise would have to be reached, and he, Mayer, was the great compromiser. Never be afraid to come to him for help, or a sympathetic ear—that was always his message.

Only the reflexively cynical would fail to be swayed. A smart, sophisticated man like Edward G. Robinson would have his guard up as he walked through the door, but be charmed and convinced by the time he left. "Not for an instant," remembered Robinson, "did I discern hypocrisy or untruth in what he was saying. He meant every word, and . . . I found him to be a man of truth. . . . Behind his gutta-percha face and roly-poly figure (contained in some of the best tailoring I've ever seen) it was evident there was a man of steel—but well-mannered steel, the very best quality steel, which meant the hardest and most impenetrable steel."

Mayer could be more peremptory with writers, but again politics never came into it. The screenwriter Marguerite Roberts had radical sympathies that eventually got her blacklisted, but was happy at MGM for thirteen years. "If you delivered for them, they treated you magnificently," she remembered.

Always there was the pungent wisdom of a hustling immigrant, a man who knew value as well as price, a man who could cut to the chase. When contract actress Audrey Totter was pressured to dye her hair black for a part, she went to Mayer for advice. It was the first and only time she had been in his office. "I asked him what he thought, and he said, 'Stay blonde.' " Totter began to be invited to his parties, and she found him to be "a charming man. He ran the studio well, and he took care of his people. You could borrow any of the clothes in wardrobe that you wanted. It was great." For his part, Mayer was impressed by Totter's refusal to sleep around in order to better her career. The first time Mayer met her doctor husband, he snapped, "Congratulations. You married the one girl in Hollywood without any stink on her!"

Mayer's belief in success as an intrinsic validation could turn boorish. Once, he was trying to get writer S. N. Behrman to do some work for him and invited him to his suite at the Waldorf. Gofers were rushing in and out—the screening was prepared, the steaks were on the dining cart, everything was ready. Mayer turned to Behrman and said, "You don't like this, eh? It doesn't interest you? It's not to your taste?" Mayer had sensed Behrman's intellectual disdain for the captain-of-industry trappings he thrived on and, with the combative childishness that was always lurking beneath the surface, was determined to confront it.

When frustrated or angry, he could explode in a cataract of profanity, and if the person he was excoriating happened to be Jewish, the phrase "kike bastard" could be heard. When he moved in a more elevated world, with people named Hoover or Spellman, he could easily match his own excellent mind with theirs and morph into a much smoother personality. He liked to listen to scientific explanations, the joining of elements to make something else, the world of catalytic agents—which is how he regarded himself.

"In our family, all the basic decisions were made by him," remembered his nephew Gerald Mayer. "He was the giant. If we were to go to dinner, he would decide on the place. He gave his sister Ida a comfortable allowance so she could live well, but I would describe him as an attentive rather than warm relative. Were we afraid of him? Jesus Christ, yes! We were afraid we might say something that would annoy him. He didn't have much humor, he didn't tell jokes or anything like that, and disagreeing with him would set him off."

"My grandfather," said Dan Selznick, "represented a certain lifestyle which was, by its very definition, grander. Even though my father was known to be a very extravagant man, he was, by personality, so funny and warm and human and accessible—emotionally accessible—that I never put him on a pedestal, nor did my brother. My grandfather put himself on his own pedestal. It was not that he was less human, but that he had a little bit of the . . . czar?"

Every once in a while, Daniel and Jeffrey would visit MGM, and L.B. would take them out to a field within walking distance of the studio to buy some corn. He would peel the ears down to check on the kernels and choose them one by one, then pull his money clip out and buy ten for himself and another half-dozen for Frank—his Hispanic driver and favorite employee—to take home to his family.

At home, he would sit there waiting for the family to eat the corn he had picked for them. "How do you like it?" he would ask. "Is it really wonderful? How does it compare to the corn from a week ago?"

His favorite pastime was going to the Hollywood Bowl, especially the annual John Philip Sousa concert. He would quietly sing along with his favorite marches, until the orchestra swung into "The Stars and Stripes Forever," and then he would levitate out of his seat. The surging music melded with his pride in America, and he would be stoked with extra exuberance for days afterward.

Ida Mayer Cummings was proving herself to be nearly a peer of her brother with her activities on behalf of the Jewish Home for the Aged in Los Angeles. Ida was a natural executive—a bright, gracious hustler.

Mayer helped his sister's endless fund-raising with yearly lunches featuring MGM stars recruited for marquee value. "Everybody knew Ida," remembered Herbert Brin, a *Los Angeles Times* reporter who covered the Home and would eventually come to live there. "Busy, busy, busy. This home is really Ida's; she and Mary Pickford and Louis B. got everybody in Hollywood to help the Home. Ida had street intelligence; she knew what had to be done. Would Louis B. have come along without her? Probably not. But he was the one who made a lot of the decisions for the Home, and the Home didn't know it. He had many wonderful attributes."

L.B.'s activities for the Jewish Home for the Aged also cemented his friendship with Edgar Magnin, the powerful rabbi at the Wilshire Temple. "Edgar and Louis B. virtually built that temple," said Herbert Brin. "Louis B. put a lot of money into that temple, and when they needed big bucks to swing deals for the home, it was always Ida and her brother.

"But Magnin's and Louis B.'s personalities never really meshed. Magnin was a tough guy on the outside, but a gentle soul within. A poet, really. Louis B. needed that kind of spiritual setting, needed the spiritual values that only a Magnin could deliver.

"Was Louis B. spiritual? I think he was, but I couldn't swear to it. Ida was."

Mayer's primary areas of vulnerability remained Irene, Edie, and Margaret. Jack Cummings remembered Mayer coming all the way to New York to talk to him about problems he was having with one of the girls. It was trouble that he blamed himself for, and Cummings, whom Mayer called *macher* (Yiddish for a "big shot"), got him out of the hotel for a long walk in Central Park. "Finally," said Cummings, "after hours of walking, he said, 'You know, I think you're right. I'm glad I came to New York.' The point is, the great Louis B. Mayer was human. He had a heart, and he could be hurt." And the great Louis B. Mayer evidently had no one in the entire state of California he could talk to about family troubles.

Mayer had an open-door policy for his employees. "I could go up to his office anytime and see him," said the editor Ralph Winters. "But if you were an executive, you needed an appointment." When one of his people came to him, he would listen with absolute focused attention, never interrupting. Then he would get up, come around from his desk and put his arm around the person. "That's no problem," he would say. If he thought the situation needed fixing, he would say "We can fix that," but if he was perfectly happy with the status quo, he would explain why things were going to stay the same.

When Mayer was presented with a proposition, he would listen attentively, then pause. He would take off his glasses, puff on them, pull out a handkerchief and wipe them off. Then he would mop his forehead and stand up and walk around for a minute or two. If he liked the idea, he'd make the deal then and there; if he didn't, he'd say that the idea had merit but that he had to discuss it with others before he could make his decision. And then a week or two would go by and the eager supplicant would call Ida Koverman, who would tell him that Mayer wouldn't be calling him back.

L.B. exulted in his job, loved doing it, but occasionally he would at least pretend to grow snappish about his duties. Once, when Esther Williams came to him with a complaint, he held up his hand and said, "Don't! I had to spend the day talking to Katharine Hepburn about wearing a red dress to a rally and telling Jeanette MacDonald she had a low ass and a flat chest."

He attended nearly every public preview of a Metro picture. "That's where the audience is!" he would say, "and that's where I want to see the picture— with them!" Howard Strickling remembered that Mayer made no effort to be diplomatic. If he lingered in the lobby and chatted, studio personnel could relax; if he walked away from the theater without saying anything, trouble was sure to follow.

But if he really liked the movie, his joy was contagious. "I would sit next to him at sneak preview after sneak preview," remembered Dan Selznick. "He had that quality of somebody who knows what's going to happen: 'Now watch this—yes!' He was watching the audience for confirmation of his own taste. . . . He adored movies with a relish that, I suspect, may have been unique. I mean, I wonder whether Jack Warner or Harry Cohn loved movies the way Mayer loved movies. You talk about people who love restaurants or love eating—the incredible relish with which they anticipate each dish on the menu, the relish taken in each bite. [That was] the incredible pleasure he took in the movies he'd made."

That same exuberance was on view at his parties. At one gathering, he announced to his guests that "you're going to see something you'll remember the rest of your lives." He snapped his fingers, the band started playing, and Judy Garland and Gene Kelly came out and began entertaining the crowd. Mayer didn't watch them, but kept his eyes on the audience, gauging their pleasure, deriving his happiness from theirs.

In spite of L.B.'s poisonous dislike of Nick Schenck, they had to pretend at least to tolerate each other. Mayer was voluble in his feelings about Schenck, but when Mayer's name was brought up to Schenck, he would usually throw up his arms and say, "Goddammit, I don't want to talk about him!"

Every Tuesday morning, Mayer would call Schenck in New York, and Schenck would give him the company's gross for the previous week, as well as the net—the complete trade balance from Loew's worldwide activities.

Mayer regularly attended ballet and opera and never missed the annual Los Angeles concerts of Heifetz and Rubinstein. He had a large Capehart phonograph at home that tended to be stacked with Russian romantics. When his grandchildren were old enough for school, he bought them recordings of *La Bohème*, *Aida*, and *Carmen* and would tell people at the studio about their progress in music appreciation.

He drank almost no alcohol and cared nothing for haute cuisine, but if he had to head back east, he didn't board the *Super Chief* until his own steaks were put on the dining car, and he was equally picky about fish and chicken. His table manners were lusty, sometimes a little too lusty for Nick Schenck. Confronted with hard rolls, Mayer would tear the soft bread out of the middle and pop it into his mouth.

Sometimes a sycophant would proclaim that L.B. was the greatest showman in the world, but Mayer demurred. He only believed he had a sense of talent, and thought a lot of his success stemmed from identifying with his audience. "If 75 percent of the American people didn't feel as I do about the American family, we wouldn't be here," he said.

"He was a good gambler," observed actor Buddy Ebsen. "He liked family entertainment. His theaters in New England had guided him to the importance and success of catering to families, and he never strayed very far from that. I didn't like him at the time, but as the years have gone by, I've seen his many good points. I was inexperienced in the ways of the world. He wasn't. One time when he wanted me to sign a contract with him, he said to me, 'Ebsen, never turn your back on enthusiasm. We're enthusiastic about you. Sign the contract!' "

He didn't read stories, but would have them told to him by Kate Corbaley, the longest serving of what George Oppenheimer called "the lady storytellers, the Metro troubadors." Mayer loved to listen to her read because she reminded him of his mother telling him stories. When she died in 1938, she was replaced by Lillie Messinger and a round-robin of other women.

"Mayer would look up into space while Kate was reading," remembered George Sidney. " 'Who's that?' he would say. 'That's Clark,' she would say. And then he would tell her to stop and start over again. And after she'd read for a while, he'd say, 'It's not Clark, it's Bob Taylor. And the girl is Myrna.' He'd cast it in his mind while he was listening. He'd fine-tune it."

S. N. Behrman remembered that Mayer would ask fundamentally alert and interested questions about a script. Why did Queen Christina wear men's clothes? What was she after? What was the significance of eating the grapes?

What he didn't like in a story were brutality and killing; making gangster or horror pictures entailed a number of people making a considerable effort to overcome Mayer's prejudices. The result was that the studio didn't make a lot of those pictures.

When Lillie Messinger told Mayer the story of Meet Me in St. Louis, all of her creativity didn't help. Thau, Mannix, and the rest of the men around the table hated it. There was no plot, no conflict, no action. Somebody asserted that the villain was New York, the evil metropolis that would take the family away from hearth and home, but that only infuriated the men.

Finally, Mayer put a stop to it. "What's the matter with you guys? I think the story is very exciting, there's a lot of action! And what about those girls who have to leave their home and their sweethearts? I tell you, it broke my heart!"

"Mayer had wonderful intuition," said Esther Williams. "He worked purely from instinct. He didn't read, he couldn't really create from scratch, but give him the framework, and he could assemble the pieces like his life depended on it, which it did."

Even in late middle age, he retained his immense reserves of animal energy. "I used to say he owed his success to his feet," remembered George Sidney. "I would take walks with him through the studio, and he'd walk until my feet felt like they were falling off, and he was thirty years older than I was."

Gambling made him nervous—he didn't shoot craps or play roulette—so he only played penny-ante card games. He preferred two-handed games—gin rummy, pinochle—usually with Frank Orsatti holding down the other chair. At Hillcrest, surrounded by his landsmen, he relaxed to a great degree, letting down his scrupulous sense of formal dress and demeanor to the extent that he appeared in shirtsleeves and told jokes that were often interrupted by kibitzers.

"Of all the picture executives I have known, L.B. was the best listener," remembered Victor Saville. "He wanted to know. He was the devil's advocate. He would prod you and question you and suck you dry of any knowledge that you might have, and then he would store it away in his computer-like mind."

Movie stars, Mayer knew, are verbs, not nouns. Once, when asking a writer to construct something for Clark Gable, he explained, "Don't put one thought in his head. Write the story from the neck down. Action only. Keep him doing something. When he talks, all they've got to do is hear his voice. He doesn't have to say anything that means anything."

Because Mayer thought in the broad strokes of emotions, his instructions on how to deal with a finished picture that turned out to be unfinished could be less than concrete, more metaphorical. Ben Hecht remembered that after one ugly preview, Mayer called the creators responsible for the picture into a room. "Mr. Mayer looked at us for about three minutes in silence," remembered Hecht. "Mr. Mayer then walked over to his grand piano where there stood a single rose in a vase. It was sort of in the dark. He lifted the rose out and brought it to his desk where it was light and put it in another vase. And then he said, 'That's what I want you to do with the movie.' "

Writers tended not to like him, although there were exceptions. "I liked him immensely, but generally, he was feared," said Irving Brecher. "It certainly wasn't love. He ruled by respect. People recognized that if you crossed him, you were in trouble. But that's true of any big executive. He didn't hit anybody, he was not as rough on people as Harry Cohn."

Mayer developed a liking for Brecher and would take him and Mervyn LeRoy out to the horse farm in Perris. "We'd go out and look at the yearlings," said Brecher. "He'd talk a lot, but I didn't find him pompous. He was earthy and kind of pleasant. But he was not a funny man, although he appreciated humor somewhat.

"I got the feeling that he didn't do the racing stable because he loved horses, but because it gave him a sense of stature, or perhaps publicity. I don't know that he had a lot of friends. He had confidants, but I have no recollection of friends."

His temper could be aroused if he thought someone was trying to roll him. When Walter Pidgeon arrived for an interview about a prospective MGM contract, Mayer's first question involved his birthplace.

"Saint John, New Brunswick," replied Pidgeon.

Mayer leaped from his chair. "Who told you to say that? How dare you claim to come from my hometown? Get out of my office! We don't want frauds at MGM."

Pidgeon stood his ground and told Mayer he had actually been born in Saint John.

"Tell me two of the principal streets," demanded Mayer.

"Queen Street and Duke Street," replied Pidgeon.

"That's no proof. Every town has one of those. Spell it, spell Saint John, you phony."

Pidgeon spelled it out, not abbreviating it as an outsider would. Suddenly, L.B. was smiling. "You really do come from Saint John, don't you? I was just testing you. Tell me about Saint John."

The two natives conferred for two hours about their hometown. Mayer finally ended the interview by calling Ida Koverman. "Ida, prepare a contract for this man from Saint John, he will tell you his name. And add another $50 a week on the contract for a good Canadian."

As Pidgeon turned to leave, Mayer had one more question. "You do act, don't you?" he said hopefully.

On those occasions when someone crossed him, his reaction would be swift. The screenwriter Noel Langley was visiting a set when he cracked, "Every time Mayer smiles at me, I feel a snake has crawled over my foot." Mayer wasn't there, but the temperature on the soundstage plunged anyway.

"Even the extras moved away," remembered Langley. "In two minutes, I was alone on that whole goddamned soundstage. And that was the end of me." The freeze came down and Langley couldn't get another job anywhere until Mayer called off the blacklisting in 1942 and MGM hired him again for $1,000 a week.

When people had problems, he would be the sounding board, the diminutive tower of strength. Standing by the cafeteria one day, Mervyn LeRoy was moaning about various crises he was encountering. "Lean on me, Mervyn," Mayer said. "That's what my shoulders are for."

He was the arbiter, the broker. After a few days of shooting on *Ninotchka*, there was a meeting with Billy Wilder, Charles Brackett, Ernst Lubitsch, Victor Saville, Bernie Hyman, and Mayer. The first day's rushes were run, then the lights came up. The concern was the ill-fitting nature of Garbo's commissar wardrobe. Was it too clunky? The conversation went back and forth, until Mayer piped up. "She may look an ill-dressed, unfashionable female, but gentlemen, aren't we forgetting that she's Greta Garbo?" There was a pause, and Lubitsch leaped up. "Come on, boys, let's go," he said. "End of problem!"

It was more important that he respect an employee than like him. "Louis B. Mayer never really liked me," George Cukor mused near the end of his life. Cukor's friend and biographer Gavin Lambert believes this was partly because Cukor had been brought to MGM by David Selznick, with whom Mayer had a father-son competitive feeling, and partly because Mayer regarded Cukor as "a smart-ass New Yorker."

Cukor's sexuality probably didn't enter into the equation at all; Metro traditionally employed more homosexuals than any other studio in town, including powerful department heads such as Adrian. "Thalberg had not been homophobic in the least," said Gavin Lambert, "and if Mayer was homophobic he kept it to himself."

His primary need was for the pictures that went out with his name on them to be the best they could be. "We took at least three months to do the animation of Jerry the Mouse dancing with Gene Kelly in *Anchors Aweigh*," remembered Joe Barbera, "and then we had to do it over because Jerry didn't have a reflection in the floor and Gene Kelly did. Nobody cared about the cost, just that it be done right."

Actress Audrey Totter remembered being at an MGM preview that went very well and afterward the producer and some of his staff were gathered under the marquee talking about changes. Mayer listened, then put his foot down. "We're not going to change a thing," he snapped. "The people liked it; that's all that counts."

Mayer always tended toward the dramatic, but with actors who hadn't been warned, the performance could be overwhelming. The French leading man Jean-Pierre Aumont, who was resisting Metro's standard seven-year deal, was called in for a meeting. He noted that Mayer had the "dimpled hands of a cardinal," and then received the full-court press.

"Don't sit over there, young fellow. Come close to me, near the foot of this map of the world. It's placed here to remind us all how insignificant we really are. Come, come closer. Don't be impressed by my legend. I'm a man just like everybody else . . . a little better, perhaps, but a *very* little and if God chose me for this post, it was because he wanted a man who's just like everybody else."

God provided the keynote of the conversation, and Aumont began to grow confused by the verbiage and the accompanying emotionalism. "I was all the more confused because of the tone of voice, which was unctuous and monotonous, like a priest's. He was crying. Then I was crying, too. Finally, he held out his pen for me to sign the contract.

" 'Use my pen, young fellow. It will bring you luck. And keep it as a souvenir of this moment.' I fell on my knees and signed."

Assignment in Brittany, Aumont's first film for MGM, was a success, and it looked as if he had a future at MGM as a more adaptive Jean Gabin. Then Aumont did the unforgivable: he went and joined the Free French Army. Mayer was not happy, but Aumont attempted to convince him that something positive would result: his English was sure to improve in the next couple of years. Mayer turned pale. "Whatever you do, don't do that!" he said. "I'd rather see you come back without a leg than without your accent!"

Mayer's insularity when the war began, his maneuvering at a time of national peril, is startling. He tried to talk James Stewart out of enlisting—which the actor did nine months before Pearl Harbor—and also unsuccessfully exerted pressure on the Culver City draft board to keep Mickey Rooney out of uniform.

And when Lew Ayres, Dr. Kildare himself, announced that he was a conscientious objector and couldn't serve as a soldier, the Balaban & Katz chain announced it would refuse to play pictures featuring Ayres. *Variety* editorialized that Ayres was "a disgrace to the industry," and Nick Schenck said that Ayres was "washed up with this studio," although he later took an ad in the *Hollywood Reporter* denying these remarks. Even Erich Maria Remarque, the author of *All Quiet on the Western Front*, the film that made Ayres a star, issued a statement saying he was sorry that Ayres had taken such a step.

Ayres had been a pacifist for years and had told Mayer of his beliefs two years before Pearl Harbor, but the issue was moot until America was involved in the war. Ayres's problem was that he wasn't a member of any recognized pacifist sect, as were most of the 42,000 conscientious objectors—Quakers, Jehovah's Witnesses, among others. His primary influences were the New Testament, Romain Rolland, and Leo Tolstoy.

Mayer hurriedly recalled a picture that was about to be released and had all of Ayres's scenes reshot with Philip Dorn, then retitled the film *Calling Dr. Gillespie*—after the crusty mentor played by Lionel Barrymore. Ayres was granted 4-E status and eventually served as a medic for several years at beachhead invasions at Leyte—where he commandeered a Catholic church for use as a hospital—Luzon, and Hollandia.

Mayer didn't want actors to be soldiers because that took them away from the studio; he didn't want them to be noncombatants because that lowered their value to the studio.

When the government thought of enlisting Mayer to do some war work, it pulled out some FBI interviews that had been done on him. The report was devastating.

Harry Warner reported that Mayer was "money-mad" and wanted to be the leader in anything he was involved with. Walter Wanger told the FBI that Mayer was the most powerful man in Hollywood, highly opinionated, a man who always got the job done, but who would not be "above putting to his personal or company's profit anything of knowledge he might obtain through a connection with the federal government."

Warner went on to tell the agent that Mayer loved publicity and that if he thought he could get his picture in the paper he would assist any community effort. Warner had, he said, sought charity donations from Mayer, who never gave more than $3,000, even though he was "well able to give $25,000." When Warner pressed him to give more, Mayer demurred, saying "I just can't make myself give any more."

Paramount's Frank Freeman agreed that Mayer was money-mad and vindictive, but, he pointed out, so were most other executives in the industry. Robert Montgomery said that Mayer had the majority of people in the movie business frightened, that he had placed state judges on the bench for his personal profit, that he was a shrewd, ruthless, and unprincipled man who confined his war efforts to bringing racehorses over from England. Montgomery also said that although Harry Warner "hates Mayer's guts," he would probably give him a good reference because "the Jews are sticking together during these times."

Richard Day, the great art director of *Foolish Wives* and *How Green Was My Valley*, said that Mayer was a four-flusher and would cut anybody's throat, but was unquestionably a loyal patriot. Loyd Wright, president of the California Bar, and a prominent attorney for the movie colony, said that Mayer was immoral and unprincipled, was closely associated with the Orsatti brothers, who had been bootleggers during Prohibition and were evidently now dabbling in narcotics. Wright believed that the very idea of Mayer working for the government was terrible. As an example of Mayer's unprincipled ethics, Wright revealed that he donated money to both Republican and Democratic candidates.

The government decided to let Mayer remain under the exclusive employ of Loew's, Inc. The FBI file is a fascinating series of documents, revealing the fear and loathing in which Mayer was held in the business, as well as the extent to which business morality has altered over the years. Mayer's donations to both political parties, his essential belief that he and, by implication, his company,

were entitled to special treatment from a government that he regarded as subservient to the will of corporations, made him stand out in 1941. But in the
twenty-first century, these things are just business as usual.

As for his dreadful reputation among his peers, it filtered down to the lower
echelons and greatly affected his standing, both at the time and subsequently,
despite his many generous acts. A friend of Mayer's had firsthand experience of
this when he was talking to two men in the business. One of the other men
mentioned he was working at MGM, and the other said, "I wouldn't work for
that bastard Mayer for all the money in the world."

"What did he do to you?" inquired Mayer's friend.

"Nothing. I've never met him. But I've heard all the stories."

"*Everybody* heard the stories," remembered Mayer's friend. "The bad stories. But nobody heard the good stories because he didn't really want them to
be heard."

Chapter
ELEVEN

ON JUNE 26, 1942, Louis was lying in bed when the mail was brought in. Addressed to "Lewis" B. Mayer, 625 Oceanfront Avenue in Santa Monica, was a letter that began, "MR. MAYER, IS YOUR <u>LIFE</u> WORTH $250,000 TO YOU BECAUSE IF IT ISN'T—<u>YOU WILL BE A VERY DEAD MAN</u> INSIDE OF TWO SHORT WEEKS!"

The letter went on for three rambling pages to tell of a group of six who wanted Mayer dead but could be bought off for a quarter-million dollars. Enclosed was a clipping from the *L.A. Times* about a recent unsolved murder, at the top of which had been written "THIS MAN THOUGHT WE WERE KIDDING."

A week later, Mayer got a postcard that repeated the demand and outlined instructions for payment. The money was to be left at the Ambassador Hotel for one "Robert Sexton." On July 13, 1942, two men called for the parcel and were promptly arrested by the FBI. They were thirty-nine-year-old Meyer Philip Grace, a former welterweight boxer turned songwriter, and twenty-five-year-old Channing Drexel Lipton, a gas station attendant who was the son of former MGM writer Lew Lipton.

The case went to trial on January 5, 1943. Mayer's own testimony was brief, and mainly involved a recitation of how he received the extortion letter. The defense attorney asked if Louis B. Mayer was really his name. "As far as I know," he replied.

"Were you born and christened Louis B. Mayer?"

"As far as I know—I don't really remember."

The FBI kept close tabs on the prosecution and background of the case. FBI background documents and the court testimony reveal that Lew Lipton and his son had a "persecution complex" about Mayer. The defense never denied that Channing Lipton committed the crime, but asserted that Lipton's parents had continual conversations over the years about Mayer blacklisting the elder Lipton, and that Mayer had at least one episode of "becoming familiar" with Mrs. Lipton, offering to put her up in an apartment as his mistress.

This, in essence, was the defense's version: Until 1931, Lew Lipton had been a happy employee of Louis B. Mayer, earning $1,000 a week, living in a sixteen-room house in Brentwood. After a rift, Lipton couldn't find work anyplace else, and had to gradually divest himself of his home and possessions in order to stay afloat.

"Am I going to be Monte Katterjohn?" Lipton would ask rhetorically, referring to a screenwriter who had written for Mayer in the Mission Road days, before seeing his career peter out in talkies, supposedly because of a blacklist. Producer Paul Bern hadn't committed suicide, Lipton told his son, but had been "taken care of" by Mayer. John Monk Saunders had also been blacklisted by Mayer, he told his son, and also committed suicide.

It was alleged that Mrs. Lipton had gone to Mayer's office in 1939, pleading with him to let her husband go back to work. Mayer had refused, but while taking her downstairs in his private elevator, had patted her in "familiar places" and told her that she was putting on weight, thereby losing the appeal she had always had for him. She should get rid of Lipton, he told her, change the children's name so they could get work, and he would take care of her and the children.

The judge charged the jury, saying that Mayer was not on trial, and that the truth or falsity of the various accusations in the Liptons' conversation were not an issue, and that those things had only been entered because of the effect that they might have had on the boy's mental condition.

The jury came back with verdicts of not guilty on both counts for Meyer Grace—who went to pick up the package because Lipton had promised him $5,000—and not guilty on the first count for Lipton, with the jury deadlocking on the second count before finally giving up. And that was the end of that. Whatever the extent of Mayer's grip on the police of Southern California, he didn't have much control of the papers; most of the accusations against him were reported in the daily coverage of the trial.

The judge thanked the jury, but not before revealing that Francis X. Bushman had sent him a letter corroborating Mayer's penchant for blacklisting. "It is about time some of Louie B. Mayer's chickens came home to roost," wrote Bushman. "He deserved this scare. Perhaps it may have some salutary effect. While I know in my heart he has kept me from the Major Studios since 1925, I have no proof—there were no witnesses to our conversation.

"In my case it was an imaginary slight given by a new valet. He was an educated Mulatto who knew nobody in pictures. Had been here but 24 hours. Before a very large gathering of picture people, he told Mayer I was busy and had no time to see him. Mrs. M. and the daughters were along, so it looked like a planned public snub. It blasted my name and fame." Bushman closed by begging the judge not to release his letter, as he feared Mayer would blackball him from radio.

Judge Leon Yankwich wasn't having any of it. He released the letter to the media. Bushman, he said from the bench, was guilty of "un-American, idiotic" behavior because he was "wrapped in his conceit." The actor, he said, was probably guilty of contempt of court; the judge turned the letter over to the U.S. attorney for possible action. There the matter died.

What to make of this episode? The extortion attempt itself was patently childish and not to be taken seriously. As for Lew Lipton's blacklisting, he had ten credits after supposedly being cast into outer darkness in 1931, including uncredited work on such A pictures as *Follow the Fleet* at RKO and *You Can't Cheat an Honest Man* at Universal. As late as November 1934, he was working for MGM, doing touch-up work on the script of *Mutiny on the Bounty*. John Monk Saunders was an alcoholic, and worked more or less consistently in the film business until a year or two before he committed suicide in 1940.

Oddly, none of these facts, which might at the very least have mitigated some of Lipton's more irrational charges, came out at the trial. The probability is that MGM wanted the matter behind it more than it wanted a conviction. There was always the chance that real dirty laundry might be exhibited.

Still, some of the details—Mayer's awkward pass in the private elevator that echoes his seduction of Ad Schulberg, his vindictiveness when he thought he had been crossed—carry the same ring of truth years later that they did to Francis X. Bushman, who, of course, didn't mention his extortionate demand for more money when he was making *Ben-Hur* as a contributing factor for Mayer's anger.

Men like Mayer are seldom reflective, because they're born with the desire to outrun their past. To spend time contemplating where you were from and why you had to get out could take energy needed to keep adding miles between then and now.

When a young movie-struck Royal Canadian Air Force pilot named Charles Foster came to Hollywood in July of 1943, he was told to call the retired silent film director Sidney Olcott, who was always happy to stand a Canadian soldier to a meal and a bed. Foster and Olcott hit it off, which led Olcott to introduce him to Mary Pickford. When she asked about his favorite studio, Foster invoked MGM. She promptly picked up the phone and called L.B., who was also happy to meet a fellow Canadian, one, moreover, who was from New Brunswick.

"Mary's driver took me through the gates, and I saw this little man come running down the steps of the Thalberg Building. I thought, 'Oh, he's sent a man to greet me.' And I got out of the car, and this man threw his arms around me and said, 'Welcome to my studio!' "

When Foster told him that he had an appointment with Mr. Mayer, the little man said, "I am Mr. Mayer. And don't call me Mr. Mayer. My name is Louis. Now, what would you like to see first?"

With that, they were off on a personally guided tour of the lot.

"Everybody waved to him, and he waved back. He spoke to people and knew them by name. I was shocked. 'I make it a point to know people,' he said. It was always, 'They work with me,' never, 'They work for me.' "

Mayer took the young man onto sets, even if a red light was on outside the door. On one stage, a director was arguing with an actor about pronunciation of a word. Mayer stood there listening, then said, "Here's a man who can tell you how it should sound. He's British." Foster offered his idea of the correct pronunciation. Mayer looked at the director and said, "Do it." In an occasional relationship that would last until Mayer died, it was the only peremptory moment Foster would observe.

"He asked me a lot of questions about myself. How did I get in the air force without a high school education? Had I ever been to Saint John?"

"Canada," Mayer told him, "taught me that if you worked hard, you can do anything. And America took me in hand and showed me I was right."

The two men ended up back in Mayer's office, where they continued talking. "It was like he was the father I never knew. I felt somehow he was interested in me, and I didn't know why. He seemed totally genuine, and I felt completely safe and secure. He didn't seem to be either Canadian nor American; he was the most important man in Hollywood, and he was interested in me.

"There was a big dictionary in his office. He told me that he would open it at random and run a finger down the page until he found the word for the day. He never used the words himself, but he wanted to know what they meant if someone else used them."

Mayer had his driver take Foster back to Olcott's house, and called him that night, inviting him back to the studio the next day for lunch. Foster arrived to find that Mayer had convened every Canadian in Hollywood to meet the young flier. Fay Wray, Walter Pidgeon, Jack Carson, Rod Cameron, Deanna Durbin, Walter Huston, Ann Rutherford, and even the despised Jack Warner were all there. Mayer later told Foster it was the first time he had sat down with Warner in ten years without getting into an argument.

Foster spent three weeks in Los Angeles. When the time came for him to go back to Canada, Mayer called and asked him to come in for a half-hour. "I just want to wish you luck," he told Foster with one of his rare big smiles. "When this war is over, if you want to come back here, I'll find a job for you."

Whatever Mayer's failings, and whatever his peers thought of him, the system that he had built functioned immaculately. "They picked you up off the street and put you in front of a camera," said Esther Williams. "You could be green and lost and it didn't matter. The day you signed your contract was the day you met your publicist. By the first time you had been photographed, you had been to Jeanette Bates, who taught you how to walk and move so you weren't clumsy; you had been to Harriet Lee to find out if you could sing; you had been to Lillian Burns, who taught you how to act. Or tried to. Mayer let you think and do and feel and if you had any talent, it would show itself. And the message of all this was to get very smart very fast."

"They outdid everybody in terms of patience," said Irving Brecher. "When they thought somebody had talent or the potential to score—writers, actors, anybody—they would stick with them all the way. They operated in a way that was far different than the other studios. At MGM, nobody ever said, 'You gotta finish this script on Tuesday.' When the script was finished was when you went into production."

George Sidney began working at the studio in 1930 and observed Mayer in many different guises. "Psychiatry wasn't around much in those days," he said, "but he knew exactly what to say to someone to get the desired result. He knew how to play people."

There were so many ways for Mayer to get what he wanted, even indirectly. Say there was a star with the usual retinue of useless relatives. Put a stepfather or a brother or sister on the MGM payroll for a nominal sum, and come option time, L.B. would be able to say how much he loved the star and his family, but couldn't he see his way clear to stay on at the old salary instead of the new salary? After all, Didn't I do you a favor by hiring your stepfather/brother/ sister?

The result of all this was not necessarily the saving of money over the contractual figures; it was to maintain the house odds, to foster a complete, almost canine devotion on the part of the talent toward the benevolent despot known as the studio, in the guise of L. B. Mayer—He from whom all blessings flowed.

To accommodate his high public profile, Mayer hired the Reverend William Briegleb, a retired pastor from the Westlake Presbyterian Church, to write speeches for him. When he addressed the studio personnel his clique would be led by Frances Edwards, who managed the commissary. If Mayer said something sad, she would weep loudly; if he said something funny, she would laugh even more loudly, with all of her waitresses following suit.

Occasionally, Mayer would get carried away by emotion while delivering a speech and the lines between his brain and his mouth would short-circuit. During one War Bond rally on the lot, he began by speaking about imperiled France, which led to him saying, "My friends, can you imagine what happens to the women in a town of 40,000 people when 400,000 soldiers go down on them?"

He took care of his family, somewhat grudgingly. Mayers were scattered throughout the studio in various middle-management positions, but the Shenbergs, his wife's family, were found only in more menial positions—a guard for the process stage, say.

Socially, at a party, he could be immensely gracious. "Mayer's parties were done by the book," said Esther Williams. "They were wonderful, fantastic! There would be an orchestra, there was dancing in the living room, and Gable, Walter Pidgeon, Cary Grant, Gary Cooper, and George Burns would be there. Colbert. Dietrich. Not just Metro people, but the elite from the entire town. You learned about who mattered."

He was a very good dancer, with rather exuberant, almost boyish manners— he would escort a dance partner to her chair and bow in thanks. He once looked straight into the eyes of an actress he was twirling around the floor and announced, "You're only dancing with me because I'm Louis B. Mayer," simultaneously a rueful proclamation of his homeliness and his status. More often, though, he wouldn't watch his partner, but would pay attention to the ringsiders, in the hope that they would notice his vitality and dancing ability.

For longtime Mayer co-workers, the nightclub years were disconcerting. They all agreed that Mayer's religion had been a vital part of his makeup in the early days, and now he was out doing the rhumba with young girls. Mayer must have been aware of the talk, because one day he told Carey Wilson, "Everybody says I'm a fool because I'm out dancing every night with cheap little floozies. I asked Joe Schenck about it one time and he said, 'I do it to keep young.' He took me out with him one time to try it out and I liked it. I assure you this has no relation to anything else."

Wilson believed that Mayer felt life was passing him by, and that the dancing signaled the final breach between Mayer and Margaret. "He wanted to wear something on his arm," said Wilson. "He wanted a lovely Mrs. Mayer, and he got her."

The war gave Margaret a reason to get out of the house. Mary Loos would pick her up and take her down to the USO in San Pedro, where she would put on a cap and apron and talk to the soldiers over coffee. "Margaret was gentle and nice," recalled Loos. "She didn't receive as a hostess an awful lot. She was really something of a misfit in society here. On the weekend, the men would go over to the house in Santa Monica to play poker, and she would sit around until someone would insinuate that it would be better for her to go someplace else. So one of the women there would take her out to sit out on the patio. I used her as a character in one of my novels—the Hollywood wife who's neglected while her husband goes out with the secretary."

L.B. and his wife had entered marriage's death spiral—mutual recriminations. Margaret blamed L.B. for her condition, saying, "This came on because I dieted. Louis likes slim girls, and it's left me like this." Mayer blamed Margaret for allowing herself to become dowdy, which he felt compromised his eminence.

In truth, L.B. had finally overwhelmed Margaret; she had weakened with age, and he had grown stronger, more willful. The only woman he could really talk to was Irene, and she had marital problems of her own. At one point, Mayer, among the least introspective men of his generation, even consulted a psychiatrist—Dr. May Romm, who was also the therapist for his daughter and son-in-law. There was nothing to do but shed Margaret; like tens of thousands of bored husbands, Mayer had to construct a scenario that gave him leave to do what he wanted to do. "I am leaving Margaret," he told one friend, "because she is too good for me."

In June 1944, Louis left 625 Ocean Front. He moved in with Howard Strickling temporarily, then rented a house at 910 Benedict Canyon from William Randolph Hearst. One headline read "Louis B. Mayer Breaks Up Home After 40 Years."

Dan Selznick remembered that there was something sad about the little man rambling around in a big house with enormous ceilings. "I was just very aware of his loneliness and his need for companionship in that particular period. . . . He needed someone to enjoy the pleasure and pain of life with. He needed an audience."

There was something even more poignant about Margaret, alone in the house on the beach. "I went down to see her in Santa Monica," said Budd Schulberg. "Margaret had almost lost her mind. Louis was living somewhere else, but she had set the dinner table for him. And she talked about him as if he was still living with her. 'He's always late,' that sort of thing. As if nothing had changed. It was out of a Russian play. But she was sweet with me, sentimental about the old days on Mission Road. Margaret was a very simple soul, raised in a very simple, conservative way. She wasn't really ever ready for Hollywood. My mother, our whole family, felt sorry for Margaret."

A year after L.B. left Margaret, Irene left David Selznick. She tried to explain the situation to her father, but he cut her off: "Enough, enough. Don't make it too complicated. It went to his head." An oversimplification, but not by much. Besides, it takes one to know one. He promised his daughter he wouldn't see David for a time, but that promise was broken, and at great length, as Selznick spent hours in Mayer's office at MGM.

There was a kind of reciprocal bond between the two men, each presenting the other with roads not taken. For David, L.B. was the sort of man he believed he should have been — focused. For L.B., David's chaotic lifestyle — degenerate gambling, a multiplicity of women culminating in a destructive affair — represented a subliminally attractive irresponsibility.

While L.B. was encountering turbulence, Nick Schenck was cruising. He now spent much of the winter at Miami Beach, where he had a house at 5369 Collins Avenue, down the street from the Firestone estate. Schenck's house was three stories, built around a courtyard, with full-grown coconut palms shading the center of the house. His daughters loved the area, and developed a business walking the dogs of all the other corporate executives in the neighborhood.

Edwin Knopf, then the head of the story department, came to Mayer with a story he thought ideal for Robert Taylor. Mayer listened and reported back to Knopf that he had decided against it — the India setting would require extensive and expensive second unit shooting overseas, and he didn't think it was worth the money. Knopf shrugged; if that was the decision, that was the decision.

A few days later, Knopf and his family—a wife, three children, and a dog— left for a vacation at Lake Tahoe. Shortly after their arrival, a motorboat arrived and the driver told Knopf that Mr. Mayer wanted Knopf back in the office at nine in the morning for an important conference. Knopf packed up the wife, three kids, and dog and returned to Los Angeles.

At nine in the morning, Knopf was ushered into Mayer's office. "Eddie," said Mayer, "I've reviewed that story again that you wanted for Bob Taylor. I've thought about it from every angle. I believe my first decision was the correct one. It's not for us."

Knopf exploded. "You dragged me and my family back from vacation to tell me something you already told me?" The conversation grew in volume. Epithets of a deeply personal nature were exchanged, and Knopf stormed out of the office. Knopf went home and told his wife, Mildred, "My career is over. I've had the most terrible fight with Mr. Mayer and we called each other names."

The next day, Knopf went back to the office to face the firing squad. He was sitting in the executive lunch room when he was told to report to Mayer's private dining room. Mayer was alone. "Come in, Eddie, sit down." Mayer came over and put a hand on Knopf's shoulder. "Eddie, I want to tell you something. Never, ever, as long as you live, talk to anybody the way I talked to you yesterday." And with that, Knopf was enjoined to go back to his lunch and his career at MGM. He enjoyed telling that story for the rest of his life as a way of explaining both the maddening and charming aspects of the man he worked for.

Most of the time, for the men on the second and third floors of the Thalberg Building, things were calm. Arthur Hornblow's chauffeur came in every day at noon with a hamper full of Hornblow's personal linens and silver, and a bottle of wine chilled to the perfect temperature. After lunch every day, Sidney Franklin would lie down on his office couch and take a nap, with his loyal secretary covering him with an afghan. A producer with the Perelmanesque name of O. O. Dull was nicknamed "Bunny" because he looked like one.

"The atmosphere was professional," said June Caldwell, Eddie Mannix's secretary. "L.B. was very animated. He'd yell for his staff, or his secretary, he needed this, he needed that. He was not a quiet individual; he was kind of theatrical, actually. Bombastic, colorful. I never heard him use nasty language. He had a great loyalty to everybody, and everybody respected him. And he would listen. He wasn't like the Warners or [Harry] Cohn. You could work with him. I never saw any sign that he was impossible to deal with at all.

"There was nothing about affairs, and I never saw him do anything indiscreet, although there was an unwritten law that you never sent anybody's wife into their office without calling in first. We had a door buzzer that let people in and I would have to announce them. With certain people, it was not advisable to let wives in unannounced."

There were, of course, some people who were less family-minded than others. June Caldwell remembered being invited into an executive party on Christmas Eve for a glass of champagne, only to be met by a withering glare from Ida Koverman. "It made me very uneasy. I wasn't to be included, like she was. None of the men minded, but I definitely got the cold shoulder from her."

For everybody who swore that Mayer kept his hands off the company property, there was somebody else swearing that he used the contract list for his private harem. He met Ilona Massey at Max Reinhardt's castle in Salzburg and brought her back to Hollywood at the same time as Hedy Lamarr and Rose Stradner (later to marry Joe Mankiewicz). The three women were set up at a house in Los Angeles, and many, Gottfried Reinhardt among them, believed them to be Mayer's property.

"Mayer often saw to it that someone he could trust went ahead of him with a girl," said Reinhardt, "just so the dame could never claim he had corrupted her. It was his way of putting them in the position of whores. Yet he had violently attacked John Gilbert and von Stroheim for saying all women were whores."

A lot of the stories were probably urban legends, but not all. Some surviving MGM employees in a position to know believe that Ilona Massey's Hollywood career was blighted when, as one put it, "she couldn't quite see Mr. Mayer." Pandro Berman, among others, believed that the actress Beatrice Roberts served as Mayer's mistress for years; although she never got leads or even major supporting parts at MGM, she was a frequent presence in small parts at Universal and other studios.

Word of Mayer's hypocrisy was even alluded to in left-of-center publications such as New Theater: "When a man who controls the greatest medium for moulding the popular imagination steps out occasionally with the ladies, that is his private affair; but when he poses as a champion of 'good,' 'clean' pictures extolling the old-fashioned virtues, that is hypocrisy—which in the case of a public man is a public vice." Marilyn Maxwell was also thought to have bartered her services to Mayer before she became one of Bob Hope's primary mistresses. "If you were a lady, you were treated like a lady," said Kathryn Grayson. "If you weren't, you weren't."

Mayer's inability to allow anybody to become emotionally intimate with him meant a certain continuing loneliness. Moderation was never L.B.'s strong point, so all this meant that the only answer was marriage. Although he was technically still married to Margaret, he began throwing wedding proposals around like contracts.

Ginny Simms, the singer for Kay Kyser's orchestra, was a Texas girl with the dark, glossy look that Mayer liked. She was brought to MGM for a musical entitled *Broadway Rhythm,* and Mayer began squiring her and her mother around to nightclubs. He would come down to the set and gaze at her with obvious affection.

People who knew Simms didn't think she wanted to be his mistress and doubt that she was. Gerald Mayer, L.B.'s nephew, remembered a party where Simms was at the bar, talking in a loud voice and making fun of the older man who had fallen in love with her. "He'd been courting her—and 'courting' is the right word—and here she was demeaning him in public."

L.B. proposed, and Simms turned him down, causing a reaction that Ann Miller remembered as "brokenhearted . . . he wept for days."

Screenwriter Dorothy Kingsley became the target of his attentions shortly after the Ginny Simms episode and would remember that Mayer's sexual attitudes were simple to decipher: if a woman was unmarried, that meant she was a virgin and to be treated beautifully; but if she was divorced, she wasn't a virgin and was therefore fair game.

Kingsley was divorced, and Mayer began asking her out. Since she was under contract to MGM, she was in an awkward position, but she turned him down anyway. Finally, L.B. had his secretary call Kingsley's secretary and tell her that she was to attend a screening at his house. Assuming there would be other people there, Kingsley's heart sank when she walked in and realized the screening was for two. Mayer held her hand during the movie, and when it was over, made his move.

Thinking fast, Kingsley told him that she was flattered but, unfortunately, she was already engaged. (As a matter of fact, she had just met the man she would marry but they had barely begun dating.) Upon hearing the word "engaged," Mayer backed off.

In 1944, Ann Miller, the daughter of a criminal lawyer, was hovering on the fringes of a career at Columbia when she became a client of Frank and Vic Orsatti, who put her on the fast track. Frank Orsatti gave a dinner party at his home that introduced Miller and her mother to L.B. After dinner, Mayer came over and said, "I have enjoyed your dancing on the screen so much, Miss Miller. Perhaps you would give me the pleasure of permitting me to take you out to dinner—and dancing?" Miller, who was barely twenty-one to Mayer's sixty, shot a questioning look at Vic Orsatti, who said that it would be all right to bring her mother. "Of course, I meant your mother would come with us. She is a very beautiful and charming woman."

So the nights on the town began. "He was a superb dancer," remembered Miller. "He had feet of gold and he loved to fly around the dance floor." Although Mayer could never be considered handsome, Miller felt that "he was brilliant and he had compassion and he was kind. He was virile and strong, with a big neck, broad shoulders, and the muscular build of a man half his age. I must say he looked and acted much younger than he actually was. . . . He had energy, he was vital, and he had a commanding presence. When he walked into a room, you knew it. . . . I never knew him to be anything but utterly gracious, charming, attentive, and solicitous of the comforts of others around him."

Miller always called him "L.B.," and found that his idea of a good time was to gather up some of his friends—the Orsattis, his brother Jerry, Miller and her mother—and head out to the Mocambo for dinner and dancing. If the dinner party was at Mayer's house on Benedict Canyon, two tables would be combined to make a long banquet table, with Mayer presiding in high style. When dinner was over, it was off to the Mocambo, or to the projection room to watch a new movie or some screen tests. Miller remembered that sometimes the phone would ring and it would be one of the MGM ladies wanting to come over to discuss playing a part in a new film. The quid pro quo was obvious, but Mayer turned to Miller and said, "You see, Ann, this is why I like you. You would never do anything like that. This is the ugly side of Hollywood."

Occasionally, Mayer would come over to the Miller house for dinner— roast beef, spinach, chocolate soufflés. Sometimes they would listen to the radio. Miller realized he was lonely and wanted badly to have someone he could call his own, someone he could trust. Gifts began to accumulate at the Miller house—a topaz ring at Christmas, a diamond and ruby bracelet watch for her twenty-second birthday. And Mayer asked Miller's mother for permission to marry her.

At the same time, Miller was seeing other men. "Go ahead and have your fun, child," Mayer would say, "but you'll come back to me. I'll wait." She ended up marrying a nonentity mainly to get out of marrying Mayer. When she called to tell him that she was engaged, there was a long pause, then she heard him begin to sob and choke. Miller begged him to stop, but after a time, Mayer hung up the phone without having said a word.

Miller's marriage lasted less than a year. When Vic Orsatti suggested she call L.B. about a part in an upcoming musical, Mayer was polite, but no more. He agreed to talk to a producer about giving Miller a shot at the part. "I'll see that you get the test," he said. "But if you don't do well in it, I can't help you any further." Miller got the part and an MGM contract, although any off-screen relationship was impossible. L.B. had found someone else, someone who looked a lot like Ann Miller, someone a bit better at playing her cards.

That at least was Miller's version of the relationship, promulgated with remarkable consistency in her autobiography and in interviews.

The tone Mayer adopted in meetings was fatherly but authoritative; the person sitting in front of the desk was Andy Hardy; the person behind the desk was Lewis Stone. Underneath the various poses, there was a weary practicality. When Arthur Hornblow Jr. was having trouble casting the female lead in a picture, Mayer impatiently asked him, "What is it you want?"

"Another Hepburn," replied Hornblow.

"Well," replied Mayer, "get one with breasts!"

"We all thought he owned Metro," said the screenwriter Philip Yordan. "Nobody ever questioned his position. He was the one that maintained the aura about MGM." But Mayer was taking most of his compensation in the form of cash, not in stock. There were those in Hollywood who believed this to be shortsighted. "He's stupid," snarled Jack Warner to anybody who would listen. "They could get him out one day." But everybody knew Jack Warner hated and envied Mayer; everybody assumed Jack was talking through his homburg.

Chapter
TWELVE

THE TONE of post-Thalberg MGM gradually altered to one that was more genteel than in previous years. If the studio's perfect marriage had been the nimble teasing and subtle sexuality of William Powell and Myrna Loy, it was now far more domesticated—and middle-aged—as seen in Greer Garson and Walter Pidgeon.

At the peak of his power and influence, L.B. figured he could take a risk or two. The studio signed the gorgeous, copper-colored Lena Horne for *Cabin in the Sky*, an all-black musical in the planning stages. On the cast's first day on the lot, Jerry Mayer refused to allow them to eat in the commissary. L.B. promptly invited them to eat in his private dining room, and the next day the commissary was open to everybody on the lot—white or black. L.B. issued a memo to the MGM department heads stating, "All colored performers and other employees of MGM will, in future, have the same access as white performers and employees to all the facilities of this studio."

So far Mayer could go, but no further; he tried to forbid Horne to date the white musical director Lennie Hayton because he was concerned about publicity about an interracial romance. Roger Edens arranged for them to meet at his house.

Mayer was mildly responsive to the nascent civil rights movement. In late 1941, he met Walter White, president of the NAACP, at the home of Walter Wanger and Joan Bennett. White expressed concern about *Tennessee Johnson*, a screen biography of President Andrew Johnson that MGM was making. He asked to see the script and requested changes, and Mayer had some scenes reshot. "I live and breathe the air of freedom, and I want it for others as well as myself," Mayer wrote to White.

Although *Cabin in the Sky* was a hit ($587,000 profit), there was no real follow-up; Horne was relegated to specialty numbers in other people's vehicles, "pasted to a pillar to sing my song," as she put it. Although they had a potentially breakout performer who was probably *soignée* even in the shower, L.B. was too much a creature of the status quo to take advantage of it.

Horne's sensual style—nostril flaring was a temptation to which she always yielded—may have presented many opportunities, but it also presented an equal number of problems, especially for theaters below the Mason-Dixon line. It is hard to replicate the sense of erotic danger that a woman like Horne represented to the immigrant Jews who had founded Hollywood. When Horne was loaned out to Fox to make *Stormy Weather*, she was summoned to Joe Schenck's office for a series of lunch invitations. Schenck, one of the most profligate cocksmen in the industry, could only sit staring at Horne, who kept up a nervous chatter until she ran out of chitchat. After a week or so, the invitations stopped without a pass having been made.

Mayer liked Horne. He would smile and pat her on the back and say, "Good girl," whenever he saw her, and once asked her to privately record one of his favorite wartime songs, "I'll Get By," just for him. She worked out her seven-year contract doing one or two pictures a year, spending most of her time in nightclubs and personal appearances in Loew's theaters.

"He was the most honest man I ever met in Hollywood," said Katharine Hepburn. "L.B. had a sense of romance about the movie business and the studio system. . . . He knew more without any formal education than most. He had a sense of smell for the business. He was a real entrepreneur in the old-fashioned sense. He understood that the artist was something sacred. He understood that Judy Garland had something that he didn't entirely comprehend.

"Although Mayer was very conservative politically, he wasn't at all that way as far as the business was concerned. . . .

"He was a romantic. He *believed*."

For his part, Mayer believed that Hepburn was proof that one could have talent without temperament. She was not one of the bawling children that surrounded him at the studio; she was an adult. As with Nate Gordon, between two honorable people who understood and respected each other, a handshake was enough.

After the first preview of her film *Woman of the Year,* Hepburn ran into Mayer outside the Thalberg Building. He congratulated her on the picture; she said that she thought the ending was terribly weak.

"Well, we can always fix that," said Mayer. "Come up with an idea for a new ending and we'll shoot it."

"I think that was a remarkable thing for him to do," Hepburn would say. "It meant spending a *lot* of money—sets had to be rebuilt, the crew reassembled, but when we did come up with a better ending, he approved it without hesitation. That's one of the reasons I found him such a satisfactory person to deal with. He *adored* the business and he understood it."

Mayer was a romantic, but he also understood the cruel, Darwinian nature of show business and of Hollywood, perhaps because he embodied many of the same contradictory elements within himself. "Look out for yourself," he told a friend, "or they'll pee on your grave."

There were no rebels at MGM, no James Cagney or Bette Davis to infuriate the front office (Garbo's indifference might leave them stunned, but not infuriated). He understood actors, viewing them as vulnerable people who respond to security. As a result, "You lived in a velvet cocoon," said Betsy Blair, the wife of Gene Kelly. "The studio took care of everything. If you were disembarking at Le Havre, there were three cars to meet you. When we bought a house, the studio lined up three housekeepers for us. They had already checked all their references, all we had to do was choose the one we wanted. They didn't just give you all that money, they took care of you as well." Of course, this also kept the minds of the talent on the job at hand; they didn't pay Gene Kelly to fret about a housekeeper.

But a lot of actors also understood his needs. "I had been to his hometown," said Ann Rutherford. "I knew from whence he sprang. He taught himself grammar. He taught himself manners. If anybody on earth ever created himself, Louis B. Mayer did."

Everybody knew that a verbal commitment from Mayer or one of his lieutenants was as good as a written one. "If Mayer thought we ever tried to get around an actor with some sneak clause which they didn't understand," said MGM legal head Floyd Hendrickson, "we would have been fired."

"What he would say was, 'We have big plans for you, but things aren't going well, so we have to keep you on at the same salary," remembered Ann Rutherford. "I had started at $350 a week, a lot of money for a kid back then. And when I heard this about Mayer, I began taking my bankbook to work every single day, and riding the bus to Culver City.

My option was due to be picked up, and I got the call from Ida Koverman: 'Mr. Mayer says we can't raise you to $500 a week.' 'Oh, Mrs. Koverman, I need the money.' "

The next step was a meeting between Mayer and Rutherford—he wouldn't call her agent, just her, assuming she could be intimidated. "So we had a meeting in Mr. Mayer's office, and I said the magic words: 'My grandmother lives with my mother and me, and I want to buy my grandmother a house.' Tears welled up in his eyes. Suddenly I was a good girl. Had I tried his chicken soup in the commissary? He never tried to talk me out of the raise. And I kept taking the bus to work, even when I was making $500! I bought the house for $18,500, a Georgian two-story in Bel Air. It's still there, worth several million."

"There have been things written and said about Mr. Mayer that were not kind, that he was a tyrant, etc.," said Mickey Rooney. "Not so. He was the Daddy of everybody and vitally interested in everybody. He was genuinely brokenhearted when Harlow died. They always talk badly about Mayer, but he was really a wonderful guy. Everybody butted heads with him, but he listened and you listened. And then you'd come to an agreement you could both live with.

"He visited the sets, he gave people talks. . . . Creative? Yes! He had ideas, and he would have scripts changed to fit his ideas. What he wanted was something that was *American*, presented in a cosmopolitan manner."

But Mayer made others very nervous. It wasn't just the power he held; it was his vigor, his strength of mind, his absolute certitude about nearly everything.

Salka Viertel, who was on staff mainly to write for Greta Garbo, was once drunkenly expounding to Christopher Isherwood about the battle of the sexes. "If a man wants a woman enough, he can have her," she said. "Absolutely. It's only a question of time and place." Somebody asked Viertel if she was serious, and if that applied to her as well. "Certainly I do," said Viertel. "*Any* man. Any man on *earth!*" And then she paused for a moment and added, "Except Louis B. Mayer."

MGM had bought a 1928 play by Aurania Rouverol entitled *Skidding* about a judge and his young son named Andy. "My mother," remembered Jean Rouverol Butler, "had observed that Fox had done a sequel or two to the Jones Family films they were making, so she had her nephew, who was her lawyer, hold on to sequel rights."

MGM only paid Rouverol $2,500 for each Andy Hardy film—proverbial peanuts, but still more peanuts than most writers were getting for sequels. Not only that, they guaranteed her two films a year. "That money was what she raised us on," said Jean Rouverol Butler. "It kept us in food, clothing, and rent money. And they also signed her to a writing contract for a while. They gave her a gangster picture to write, among others. Poor mother, I remember she had to write an orgy, and her notion of an orgy was to have ladies in teddies diving into the pool. She knew nothing from orgies."

The first Hardy film was titled A *Family Affair*, and it was very much a B movie. The series began to pick up steam with *Judge Hardy's Children*, which opened in Chicago while the previous installment was still playing. "You can visit the Hardys one night at one theater," wrote one critic, "and call back again for a second visit the next night at another theater—just as you'd want to do if they lived next door!" J. Robert Rubin in New York cabled Mayer that the Capitol Theater's premiere booking of *Judge Hardy's Children* had done $5,363 on Saturday and $5,136 on Sunday, excellent box office for the time. The floodgates were now open.

The success of the Hardy films seemed an obvious case of a need being filled, but, like any great hit, was actually anything but. The chemistry could have been altered at any number of points, from the character of a grandfather that was removed from the first film, partly because of the death of Chic Sale, to Lewis Stone replacing Lionel Barrymore as the Judge. (Thomas Mitchell actually tested for the part in the second Hardy, *You're Only Young Once*.)

The Hardy films captured the way America saw itself—"typical, average American family," is a phrase that recurs obsessively in the press coverage, which is to say a typical audience bludgeoned by years of the Depression and frightened of what was going on in Europe. The Hardy films were a comforting placebo about life in a medium-sized American town that is neither an ominously threatening city nor a bucolic dale. Mayer was recapturing the small-town, provincial world he remembered from Saint John, with Jacob Mayer transformed into a more kindly Lewis Stone, and his sainted mother transformed into warm Fay Holden, bestowing unconditional love on her brood—a nineteenth-century Russian Jewish family seamlessly converted into twentieth-century WASPs.

Even Damon Runyon was charmed: "This picture is quiet, and gentle, and as plain as an old shoe, and Hollywood will not heave any of those bronze statuettes at it, but we hope it makes money for the producers."

That it did; that they all did. The Hardy films were a cash cow for MGM. The first film in the series, A *Family Affair*, cost $178,000 and had a worldwide gross of $502,000, for a profit of $153,000. By the time of *Love Finds Andy Hardy* in 1938, the shooting schedule was still a modest nineteen days and the cost an equally moderate $212,000. After the "book" portion of the film was completed on June 20, co-star Judy Garland spent a couple of days recording some songs for the film, with director George Seitz shooting the scenes to playback the day after they were recorded. On June 25, the lab was kept open late so cutting and dubbing could go on all day Sunday in time for a Monday preview, with yet another preview to follow—remarkably painstaking procedures for a B picture, but typical for MGM.

The film exploded. When *Love Finds Andy Hardy* opened in July, a couple of weeks after it was previewed, Howard Dietz cabled Culver City that Loew's State had to schedule extra screenings in order to take care of the crowds that had gathered. The gross was $2.2 million worldwide, $1.6 million of that domestic, with a net profit of $1.3 million, a fairly typical profit for the pictures that would be made through World War II.

For Mayer, the Hardy films were a triumphant vindication of his belief system, and he hovered over them like a doting parent. "The best pictures (I) ever made—the only pictures I really ever took an active hand in—were the Andy Hardy series," he asserted late in his life. "They were good and wholesome. They had heart. You can't imagine how much good they did for America. I saw them in Turkey and Egypt, all over the world."

Mayer told producer Carey Wilson to be especially careful about the relationship between Judge Hardy and his son—the son had to be respectful of his father at all times. "A boy may hate his father, but he always *respects* him," Mayer told Wilson in one of his more unintentionally revealing remarks.

Once, watching the rushes, he was horrified to see a distracted Andy brusquely refuse his mother's cooking at dinner. "I am sorry for you, my friend," he told Carey Wilson. "I didn't know you never had a mother."

Undoubtedly hearing the ice cracking beneath him, Wilson volunteered that he did indeed have a mother. "Did you ever throw your own mother's food back at her?" Mayer exploded. "Did you ever tell her 'Take this junk away?' What kind of unnatural son would do that to his mother?" The scene was reshot so that Andy was apologetic about his lack of appetite.

The screenwriter William Ludwig developed a specialty in the Hardy films, and hit upon a formula of parallel problems for the Judge and his son. "You gave Mickey a problem," he remembered, "and he found his solution in the case that the Judge was working on. Or the Judge would have a case that had him baffled, and the way Mickey would work out his problem would give the Judge an idea for the case. The two were integrated in the end."

Most of the Hardy pictures were directed by a quietly talented man named

George B. Seitz, who had made some very good films in the silent era, such as *The Vanishing American*. "George B. Seitz was a big huggy bear of a man who had tremendous wisdom," said Ann Rutherford. "He listened to Mickey Rooney. Once, when the pictures were making so much money they were practically supporting the studio, they put Woody Van Dyke on one. Woody would print the first take if you got half the words right. But he had never worked with a Hardy film, and when they saw the rushes, it wasn't a Hardy picture. And they called back George Seitz.

"Mayer would say, 'If you get a better director, you won't have as good a picture. Please don't make better pictures.' "

Seitz was open to the happy accident, which A picture directors often weren't. "After Seitz directed a scene," said Ann Rutherford, "and would say, 'Print It,' Mickey would twist his sleeve and say, 'I have an idea, could we just try it?' And George would say, 'Sure, kid.' And Mickey would direct Lewis and Fay and me and that was invariably the shot that ended up in the picture."

Mayer was always worried about Rooney's mugging ruining the reality of the picture. On one picture, Seitz let Rooney break from a kiss and throw up his arms and legs while yelling, "Woo, woo, woo!" as if he were the wolf in a Tex Avery cartoon.

Mayer called Seitz in and said, "George, if you want to get a sex laugh, I can tell you a better one. Let Andy kiss her, then turn around and unzip his fly and take out his prick. That'll get you a wow!" Seitz could take a hint, and when Mayer saw the reshot scene, he said to Carey Wilson, "I hope you'll notice Mickey didn't even reach for his fly."

For the 1938–39 season, MGM made three Hardy pictures, costing about $300,000 apiece—slightly more than the Dr. Kildare films, but still B picture budgets. Each had clear profits of more than $1.2 million—nearly $4 million in profits in a year when the studio's entire profits were $9.3 million. There was as much hyperbole in the movie business then as there is now, but the Hardy films really were an enormous contributor to MGM's financial health.

Such success meant that extra care had to be taken with the cast. Carey Wilson, the old MGM hand in charge of the Hardy films, made it a practice to pump the young actors for their experiences as teenagers. "I remember complaining about a boyfriend who paid more attention to his secondhand car than he did to me," said Ann Rutherford. "Carey blew it up and made a movie out of it. Carey would give us monthly dinner parties. Black tie. We'd play charades. And we'd tell about our experiences that would be made into a film. It also helped maintain the feeling of a family."

Once, William Ludwig pitched Carey Wilson an idea for an Andy Hardy picture. A few days later, another writer told Ludwig about a great idea that Wilson had for an Andy Hardy picture. When she told him about it, it was identical to Ludwig's story. Ludwig snatched the story Wilson's secretary was busily typing up, told Wilson he would never work for him again, and stalked out of the office.

When the inevitable call to Mayer's office came, Ludwig explained what had happened. "Sure he stole your story," said Mayer. "He gets a $5,000 bonus for any original story he comes up with." This tic of Wilson's was well known to everybody but Ludwig, and had shown up as early as the mid-1920s, when one MGM writer called him a "writer vampire."

Mayer agreed that Ludwig would never work directly for Wilson again. When they needed Ludwig for a Hardy picture, Ludwig didn't have to have any meetings with Wilson, and his scenes were shot as written.

The junior-writer program, begun a couple of years before Irving Thalberg died, picked up steam under Mayer. Over the years, writers such as Robert Lees, Waldo Salt, Hugo Butler, George Seaton, and many others would emerge from the program. "It was a wonderful system, a very constructive thing," remembered Jean Rouverol Butler, who was a member of the program in 1940–41, and whose husband, Hugo Butler, had been part of the class of 1936–37.

The system was structured more or less on the mentor system, with the program being headed by Richard Schayer, an amiable writer left over from the silent days who acted as a surrogate father. The group could encompass as many as twelve or as few as five or six writers per year. They shared offices, ate together, looked at movies, and were given old scripts to read, usually scripts that hadn't been made, on the off chance that a fresh young mind might be able to come up with a solution to the problems that had stifled production.

The problem was that the movie business has always measured status by the size of a paycheck. "We discovered," remembered William Ludwig, "that no matter how much we wrote, nobody was reading anything we wrote. It wasn't taken seriously."

But that began to change when Ludwig was discovered to have a knack for writing the Andy Hardy films, or when Hugo Butler was assigned to write *Lassie, Come Home* for his contract salary of $35 a week.

Arthur Freed was born in Charleston, South Carolina, in 1894, and became a successful lyricist in tandem with Nacio Herb Brown. He had been at MGM since shortly after the coming of sound, and he and Mayer began their friendship early in 1933. By the late 1930s, Freed had a standing invitation for breakfast at Mayer's house.

"Freed was not the typical Hollywood party person," said his biographer, Hugh Fordin. "He was glued to Ira Gershwin's hip, and Oscar and Dorothy Hammerstein's. But he believed Mayer to be a highly creative man; he thought a lot more of Mayer than he did of Thalberg."

Freed wanted to make *The Wizard of Oz*, but Mayer assigned Mervyn LeRoy to serve as senior producer. Freed would later claim that he was responsible for bringing the property to the studio, that he cast it, hired Harold Arlen, E. Y. "Yip" Harburg, and Victor Fleming, and that "Mervyn LeRoy has got the biggest false credit on that that was ever given." And it was Freed who fought the battle for "Over the Rainbow." "Yip" Harburg remembered that when some thought was given to cutting the number to speed up the pace of the picture, Freed threatened to quit the studio first.

"Don't get overly dramatic," advised Mayer. The scene stayed.

The Wizard of Oz is one of the primary arguments for Mayer's system. "The thing that astounded me," said Ray Bolger, who appeared in the film as the Scarecrow, "was that they bought people. It was like you would go into a grocery store and say, 'Give me four comics and three toe dancers, and I want five girls and five male singers. I want nineteen character actors, and I want some unique personalities.' You buy them and then put them on the shelf. We would never have been able to make *The Wizard of Oz* if they hadn't had all those geniuses on the shelf."

After *Oz*, Freed and Mayer were having breakfast when Freed began raving about Judy Garland. "I'd put my bet on her if I were a producer," said Freed.

"Well, Arthur, now is the time. Find a property and make a picture."

Freed's first picture as a producer was *Babes in Arms*, a Garland-Rooney vehicle that was rehearsed, recorded, and shot in sixty-six days in the middle of 1939, at a cost of just $745,341. It grossed $3.3 million, making it one of the top ten hits of that remarkable year.

Freed's follow-up was supposed to be the collegiate musical *Good News*, but when the script came in, nobody liked it. Mayer suggested that Freed do an original musical built around the Gershwin song "Strike Up the Band." "It sounds so patriotic," he said. It was one of his vague, move-the-flower-from-the-darkness-into-the-light remarks, but Freed knew what he meant, and another great hit was born.

"Freed and Mayer were cut from the same cloth," said John Waxman, the son of film composer Franz Waxman. "They knew how to operate: Hire the best people. Leave them alone."

"Arthur would go and do everything," said Cyd Charisse. "I don't know that L.B. knew what [Freed] was doing. Arthur was the one who put me under contract. They needed a dancer and heard that I had come from a ballet company. I went over and auditioned, and Arthur and I talked for a few minutes and he said, 'How would you like a seven-year contract?' I said, 'I don't know.' Arthur said, 'Get an agent.' So I got one—Nat Goldstone—and came back and signed the contract.

"Up to that point, I never saw L.B. at all. Then Nat Goldstone said we were going out to dinner, and my dinner partner was L.B.—he was very sweet and charming, but I hadn't known we were having dinner! He looked me over pretty good, as he did with all the ladies. He was very cute. I had no problems with him at all.

"That's the way Arthur worked. Irving Berlin would show up on the lot and L.B. would say, 'Irving! How good to see you!' and you could tell he was surprised. Arthur wouldn't talk about what he was going to do, he would just go do it. From lighting to scenery to music to performers, Arthur knew what to do, and he built a group that knew what to do. When they wanted to do a musical, everything was right there, completely self-contained. To pull a group like that together to do just one musical is impossible."

"Arthur only had four words in his vocabulary," remembered Leslie Caron. " 'Terrific,' 'terrible,' 'yeah,' and 'naaaaaahh.' It was like that. He couldn't put a sentence together, but he was a very shy, tender, affectionate person."

"Freed's talent," said the vocal arranger Lela Simone, "was that he knew what was good and he knew what was bad. Period. He couldn't have told you why. But he had an infallible instinct [for] what was good and what was bad or what was insufficient, artistically and otherwise."

Cyd Charisse put it best: "He was an artist."

Freed's unit was a corner suite on the second floor of the Thalberg Building overlooking a mortuary, the subject of much gallows humor over the years. His position within the company was indicated by the private bath with shower, an amenity only vouchsafed to the most favored employees. Freed's office featured a generous selection of the orchids he raised and the paintings he loved— Roualt, Dufy, Utrillo, and Leger—interspersed with ashtrays that were always full of cigarette stubs.

The mood in the Freed unit was light and amusing, and nobody stood on ceremony. Shortly after Sally Benson came out from New York to work on early drafts of *Meet Me in St. Louis,* she sent a memo to Freed: "I have gone shopping. All items will be charged to your accounts at Saks Fifth Avenue, Bullocks Wilshire, etc. Also, please don't come around begging me for money all the time. You just spend it all on drink, and I am on to you."

Mayer nurtured and believed in Freed's instincts. When the producer cast a young dancer named Gene Kelly in his first picture opposite Judy Garland, all the kibitzers at the studio told him he was crazy. "He's the wrong kind of Irishman," Eddie Mannix grumbled. At lunch one day Freed told Mayer that everybody was telling him he was wrong about Kelly.

"How do you feel?" asked Mayer.

"I love him," said Freed.

"Well, then, don't listen to all those schmucks."

Likewise, when Freed thought he had a likely director in Vincente Minnelli, nobody else agreed. Minnelli was obviously effeminate and hopelessly inarticulate. Freed even tried to place him with the B movie unit, but they wouldn't give him a picture. "The only way to start him was to buy him a property," remembered Freed, so he purchased *Cabin in the Sky.*

Sometimes Freed's friendship with Mayer bore fruit in unexpected ways. When Freed went to the Plaza Hotel for a business meeting with the legendary Broadway star George M. Cohan, he was startled at Cohan's opening remark: "You know—I haven't seen Louie Mayer in years, but he was awful nice to my mother . . . he always took care of her and got her theater seats." Cohan ended up selling Freed *Little Nellie Kelly* for the bargain basement price of $35,000.

Freed had several idiosyncrasies. Personally, he went beyond messy to being something of a slob. "The back of his car was full of delicatessen wrappers," said Betsy Blair. "The first time I went to his house, I thought, 'This man shouldn't be allowed to have French Impressionist paintings!' " When Judy Garland would see him coming, she would say, "Here comes the tank!"

But Freed's musicals had a quality all their own, a sense of zest and history that derived from the theatrical royalty L.B. had worshipped as a young man in Saint John and Haverhill. By embracing the legacy of Florenz Ziegfeld in movies like *The Great Ziegfeld, Ziegfeld Girl,* and *Ziegfeld Follies,* the studio was claiming its place as the great showman's successor.

In Freed's *Babes on Broadway,* Mickey Rooney and Judy Garland explore an old theater. "Every theater is a haunted house," says Rooney. "Think of all the shows that have been in this theater. Flops, successes, bad shows, great shows. It's all around us right now. Laughter, applause, cheers." Mickey and Judy then proceed to re-create Richard Mansfield and Sarah Bernhardt, Fay Templeton and George M. Cohan. As Faulkner said, the past isn't dead, it isn't even past.

Freed relied a great deal on people like Roger Edens to handle the administrative duties, and other men, like Conrad Salinger, to devise the specific orchestral feel of MGM musicals, which one composer characterized as "a very *sexy* horn line wandering through perhaps a big haze of strings . . . a way of surrounding the voice."

"One day I was in a meeting with Freed and a writer," remembered George Sidney. "The writer and I were arguing, and at one point, Arthur said to us, 'Please carry on; I have something to do.' Ten minutes go by, twenty minutes go by. He never came back to the meeting. On my way out, I pass the commissary, and there's Arthur Freed sitting by himself with a cup of coffee! He didn't want to be the big *macher*; he wanted the talent to beat themselves up."

The result was a string of musicals that have defined the form for sixty years. "We all felt consciously superior to Fox or Warner Brothers," remembered Betsy Blair. "We were at the best studio for musicals and we knew it. We were incredibly snobbish. When Betty [Comden] and Adolph [Green] and I would see some Fox musical, we looked at it as if it was from a different planet." Although MGM had the reputation of a stylistically stodgy plant, that didn't apply when it came to musicals; there, innovation reigned, whether it was Gene Kelly dancing with Jerry the Mouse in *Anchors Aweigh* or Fred Astaire dancing on the ceiling in *Royal Wedding*.

"Freed looked on Mayer as his great benefactor and father figure," said Adolph Green. "He became successful and powerful through L.B., felt he owed everything to L.B. He was always respectful, scared, and proud of their relationship. He was *very* deferential to Mayer. Automatically. He had a cap-in-hand attitude, which was general at the studio. Everybody there had to show an attitude of gratitude, no matter what they may have really felt. "Attitude of gratitude . . . Sounds like a good song, doesn't it?"

(Because of the Freed unit's dependence on talent from the New York theater, there was a large gay component. One day Red Skelton and Esther Williams were walking past a flower bed that was full of pansies nodding in the breeze. Skelton pointed and said, "Look—the Freed unit.")

Working on a level beneath Freed was Jack Cummings, Mayer's nephew. Cummings was a bright, independent man who had adopted Louis as a surrogate father when his own father died young. It didn't stop him from being able to go in and raise a measure of hell with his uncle in a way that nobody else could.

"Jack was highly underrated, probably because he was L.B.'s nephew," said Howard Keel. "Arthur Freed hardly ever talked, but Jack would talk your ear off, and he would admit it when he was wrong. He didn't believe I could do *Kiss Me Kate*—they wanted Olivier or Danny Kaye—and I was the last choice. But after I tested, he said, 'Goddamn, kid, I was wrong. Son of a bitch!' I loved working with Jack; he was the hero behind *Seven Brides for Seven Brothers*. That movie was made in 34 days, and Jack set it up so well I could have shot it. Stanley Donen did a good job, but Jack gave him Michael Kidd, who was not too shabby."

Beneath Cummings was Joe Pasternak, who discovered Deanna Durbin at Universal and made, more or less accidentally, *Destry Rides Again*. Mayer brought him over to MGM in 1941 and for the next twenty-five years, Pasternak churned out consistently successful cornball product, often musicals starring Kathryn Grayson's tremolo or Mario Lanza's alarming bellow. In spite of the fact that he only occasionally worked with A level talent—not Fred Astaire but Van Johnson, not Vincente Minnelli but Richard Thorpe—Pasternak was a candid and happy man whose motto was "Never make an audience think."

Pasternak was almost as hard to take seriously as his movies. When he began using the young Mexican actor Ricardo Montalban, he had trouble pronouncing his name, which usually came out "Richard Mandelbaum." A few times it was "Richard Mountbatten," and at least once it came out "Richard Musclebound."

But all of these men could make their wishes known. When Pasternak wanted Montalban to dance in a movie, Montalban protested that he was nothing more than a social dancer. Pasternak explained that he would be dancing with Cyd Charisse and Ann Miller and they would make him look good. Montalban still resisted. Finally, Pasternak leaned forward and said very quietly, "Listen, Ricardo, if I can't ask you for a favor when I need a favor, when can I ask you for a favor?"

Don Corleone couldn't have phrased it any better.

The musicals were the ultimate extension of Mayer's MGM. "You never stopped studying," remembered Debbie Reynolds. "Ballet, tap, modern dance. Placing the voice properly; how to sing; how to walk and move; how to model, how to hold your hands, how to hold your head, knowing the angle right for the camera; how to do makeup, how to do hair. . . . Anytime you walked on the lot, there was activity, and often music. . . .

"If you didn't like it, you had to be bananas. If you didn't learn from it, you had to be a moron."

When he arrived in Hollywood, Orson Welles played with various projects for his first film. He eventually settled on a project suggested by Herman Mankiewicz and clearly based on the life of William Randolph Hearst, a man with a zest for life and accumulation, but without any underlying spiritual parameters.

By the time *Citizen Kane* was completed, in early 1941, word began leaking out that the movie was about Hearst. He couldn't really sue—there was nothing in the movie that was actionable, and publicity from a lawsuit would just make things worse. Instead the Hearst press decided to ban all mention of the film and began to aggressively report on the movie industry. Not only that, but the Loew's, Fox, and Warner theater chains all refused to book the picture. On January 13, a front-page story in *The Hollywood Reporter* said that the Hearst papers were about to begin attacking the movie industry's hiring of immigrants for jobs that could be performed by Americans.

By itself, this wasn't anything that couldn't be endured, but as a preview of coming attractions from newspapers that had always buried negative stories, it was ugly. Short of the government imposing censorship, there could be nothing worse for the motion picture industry than William Randolph Hearst in a rage.

In February, something was done. Mayer didn't approach RKO president George Schaefer directly; he had Nick Schenck do that. Schenck's offer was succinct: "Louie has asked me to speak to you about this picture. If you will destroy the negative and all prints, he is prepared to pay you the cost of the negative, which he understands is $800,000." The picture had actually cost $686,033, so Mayer was upping the ante so that Schaefer could actually make a small profit. Schaefer didn't even go to his board of directors with the offer, because he thought they might take the money.

By March, the situation was still hanging fire, and Ben Hecht wrote a bridge-burning column in *PM* that laid out the situation: "I can assure you [suppressing the picture] was not done by Mr. Hearst hollering at Mr. Schaefer, under whose aegis the movie was made. Nor was it done by Mr. Hearst threatening Mr. Schaefer with law suits plus his journalistic wrath.

"Mr. Hearst's . . . move was to seek out a softer and sappier target. This he found in the person of Louis B. Mayer. Mr. Mayer is the grand Poo-Bah of Hollywood. He is producing head of Metro Goldwyn Mayer and is not only the highest salaried genius on earth, but the oracle to which Hollywood ever bends its deferential ear. It is an ear, by the way, that bends on a well oiled hinge where Mr. Hearst is concerned."

Hecht mentioned that he had read the script before it went into production and that it was no more about William Randolph Hearst than it was about Prester John—a demonstrable lie, but an effort to give his friend Mankiewicz some cover. There is no reason to doubt Hecht's take on events; his contacts, after all, were impeccable.

None of this was put in writing, of course; we have only George Schaefer's assertions to Bosley Crowther and Pauline Kael that this in fact happened, but there is no reason to doubt it. It *sounds* like Mayer, it *feels* like Mayer.

There were several tribal codes Mayer observed throughout his life:

1. Was it good for MGM, i.e., L. B. Mayer?
2. Not in front of the *goyim*.

These inviolable laws also account for L.B.'s rage when Budd Schulberg's *What Makes Sammy Run?*, the story of an amoral, Jewish rat in heat gnawing on the movie industry, was published that same year. Mayer exploded at Schulberg's father, his old partner on Mission Road. "I blame you for this. God damn it, B.P., why didn't you stop him? How could you allow this? It's your fault. It's an outrage and he ought to be deported." Schulberg pointed out that his son was a native-born American and asked where Mayer wanted him shipped. Catalina?

After *Citizen Kane* was released, Schaefer believed that Mayer began spreading rumors that the RKO head was an anti-Semite, in the hope of driving down the stock and forcing majority owner Floyd Odlum to sell out. At that point, Schaefer said, Mayer planned to buy Odlum's stock at a bargain price and gain control of RKO, just in case he couldn't work out a new contract deal with Nick Schenck. Instead, Odlum fired Schaefer and installed a more commercial management team, which liquidated Welles's Mercury Productions.

The *Citizen Kane* affair didn't affect the friendship between Hearst and Mayer. In 1941, at the low point of Hearst's reputation and influence, Mayer called him "a great man, and a great leader . . . who has always been in the forefront of motion picture and newspaper progress." Later, when Hearst's health began failing, Mayer visited him every week, and he attended Hearst's funeral in San Francisco in August of 1951, at a time when he was having great troubles of his own.

Kane was not the first time Louis played the part of a meddling rabbi for the industry, and it wouldn't be the last. In 1938, when Jackie Coogan was suing his mother for the money he had earned as a child star and the papers were full of the story, he got a phone call at home from Mayer. "Son, we've always been great friends," Mayer began. "I know you're having hard times financially, and you're a married man now. I'd like to help you out. I'll give you $2,500 a week and put you under contract."

Coogan burbled out his gratitude, only to be interrupted. "There's only one condition. You have to drop the case against your mother. No red-blooded American boy sues his mother."

"But Mr. Mayer, I can't stop the suit; my lawyers are working on contingency and I can't stop them now."

"You little son of a bitch! You'll never work in this town again."

From 1939 to 1947, Coogan didn't make a movie. "He worked in nightclubs," said his friend and fellow child star Diana Serra Cary, "and television when it came in. These guys were all intermarried, and they all played cards together, and if one of them wanted you blackballed, you were blackballed."

Most of the time, competition was the order of the day, but when they felt threatened or insulted, the Jews of Hollywood closed ranks. The Bank of America's A. P. Giannini found that out when, during a board meeting, he began railing about Secretary of the Treasury Robert Morgenthau's ongoing investigation of his bank. Giannini vowed that "That god-damned Jew is in for a fight to the finish." Mayer and Joe Schenck both immediately got up and left the room. Several days later they resigned from the Bank of America's board of directors.

The flip side to Mayer's sense of all of Hollywood as his private plantation was his authentic patriarchal largesse. MGM always carried a number of actors who had been stars during the silent days on its payroll, among them King Baggott, Flora Finch, Helen Chadwick, and Frank Mayo. The early Biograph star Florence Lawrence, washed up and broke due to bad career and marital decisions, was put on the MGM payroll at $75 a week, appearing in more than fifty pictures.

It was Mayer's way of providing pensions for people who had been primary forces in the cinema's early days but had seen the business pass them by. Mayer had met Florence Lawrence when she had made that appearance at his theater in Haverhill and signed autographs until the last person had been satisfied. "She kissed all the children, kissed everybody who asked her for an autograph," Mayer told a friend. "I would never allow her to be short of money." Unfortunately, Lawrence gradually despaired of her increasingly shaky health and committed suicide.

"I had been directed by King Baggott years before," remembered Diana Serra Cary, the Baby Peggy of the silent days. "When I was doing extra work, I saw him waiting for the bus. He had been an alcoholic for years, and I thought about going up and speaking to him, but then I thought it might not be a good idea.

"But then I began noticing that Baggott and [Vitagraph star] Florence Turner were always working as extras. Even if there were only five extras in a scene, it seemed that Baggott and Turner and a few others were always the first ones chosen. So I asked about it and was told, 'Oh, they're on Mayer's Panic List. He sees to it that they work.' "

By 1941, MGM was carrying six silent stars under stock contracts, probably about $50 a week for unbilled bits and extra work. If King Baggott wasn't needed as an extra, he worked as a gateman at the studio until his death in 1948. "Baggott loved it," said Mayer's friend Charles Foster. "He liked to talk to the fans that remembered him, and Mayer would stop by all the time to talk to him. Mayer's best friends were all people from the past."

But just as L.B. always had a spot for someone he liked or respected, he never forgot a slight.

Mae Murray had been married to the MGM stalwart Robert Z. Leonard and had starred in *The Merry Widow*, one of the studio's biggest early hits. But she had also been abusive, borderline delusional, and served as the primary inspiration for the character of Norma Desmond in *Sunset Boulevard*. She wrote Mayer a letter begging him to put in a good word for her with the other producers whom he had supposedly influenced not to hire her. "I have a child to support. I need work and I can have work, if you'll allow me. Search your heart for some core of religious feeling." Ida Koverman refused to let Mayer see the letter; although he must have known about the straits she was in, he refused to add her to his list of pensioners.

Mayer had brought Ernst Lubitsch back to MGM for *The Shop Around the Corner* and *Ninotchka*, and George Stevens came in to do *Woman of the Year*, but didn't hang around. "My father never wanted to work at MGM," remembered George Stevens Jr. "He thought it was a producer's studio where the department heads decided what the photography was going to be like. Hepburn called him and asked him to do it, so he did it as a one-shot for Kate."

Another returning prodigal was Al Lewin, who had flounced out of the studio after Thalberg died and gone over to Paramount, but came back to make

The Picture of Dorian Gray. Lewin would stay, off and on, for the rest of his career.

Mayer paid a visit to the *Dorian Gray* set and told star Hurd Hatfield, "I'm glad, Mr. Hatfield, that we're doing a prestige picture again." He might have been less glad had he known that Lewin, a strange, airless director ("I didn't have a great deal of facility, but I loved doing it") would take an amazing 127 days to make the film, over twice the budgeted schedule—more than other troublesome MGM productions like *The Wizard of Oz* and *The Good Earth*, topped only by the ultimate troublesome production: *Ben-Hur.*

Although the picture ended up grossing nearly $3 million, Lewin's extravagance turned a profitable picture into a break-even proposition or, depending on your point of view, a flop *d'estime.* Lewin's pictures weren't actually good, but they had a constipated, oddly compelling air of High Art about them— Michael Powell without the visual flamboyance.

At the same time, Louis signed Charles Laughton to a fat contract that paid him $100,000 a film, an enormous amount for a character star. The key to these hires of men whose sensibility was far removed from Mayer's was that both Lewin and Laughton had been close to Irving Thalberg. For all of the grudges over money and ego that Thalberg represented, anyone who had been close to his late protégé-rival always had Mayer's respect.

The studio put John Gilbert's daughter, Leatrice, under contract as a possibility for the title role in *National Velvet,* which they had purchased for Hunt Stromberg. "My mother [silent star Leatrice Joy] heard about it and said, 'That's the part I want for you,' " remembered Leatrice. "So she did a campaign. Auntie Mame couldn't have done it any better. She got me all dressed up and trotted me down to the studio and we called on Ida Koverman. I'd sit in her lap, then we'd go and see Hunt Stromberg. And then I was invited to meet Mr. Mayer. The office was huge, but I'd met famous people all my life, so I didn't feel any awe."

"What do you want, young lady?" asked Mayer.

"Well," replied the very composed Leatrice, "as I understand it, my father made a lot of money for this studio, and I think it would be nice if you gave me a chance to make some of my own."

There was a moment's stunned silence, then L.B. said, "Well, that's a very good idea." Leatrice was promptly placed under contract. "Mayer could not have been more courteous. My father was never mentioned, but he always liked my mother, I was Leatrice's daughter and he was happy to do her a favor.

Mother was a Christian Scientist and wholesome, a very favorable word in his vocabulary."

But Leatrice ran headlong into some of the less savory aspects of studio life. Benny Thau mentioned that he had some papers and photos of her father that Leatrice should have. He invited her to stop over at his house. They were sitting by the pool having a Coke, when Thau hinted that he might be able to help her get attention at Metro. He then excused himself and came back clad only in a wide-open dressing gown. "I was a virgin in those days," remembered Leatrice Fountain. "I had never seen a naked man before. I was horrified; I just ran. I was scared to death. Those people were dangerous."

The original plan for *National Velvet* had been to shoot on location in England, but the preparations dragged on and the war broke out in 1939, making that impossible. Leatrice Gilbert grew too tall for the part, and was let go, but when the picture was made, by Clarence Brown and Pandro Berman in 1944, she was back at the studio playing a dancing girl in *Kismet* and a small part in *Thirty Seconds Over Tokyo.*

A good part of Louis's job was convincing—or forcing—producers to make the pictures the way he wanted them made, with the casts he wanted. For *Waterloo Bridge*, producer Sidney Franklin wanted to use Laurence Olivier opposite Vivien Leigh. Olivier agreed to do the picture, but Franklin's offer was rescinded by Mayer. A contract player would have to be used, he said; perhaps Robert Taylor. And indeed, Taylor played the part the same way he played every part, adequately and uninspiringly, with the addition of a mustache that seemed to give him more weight.

Mayer understood that, as an actor, Taylor couldn't carry Olivier's eyebrow pencil, but that had nothing to do with it. Taylor was an MGM star and a special protégé and pet of Ida Koverman, who made sure he wasn't taken for granted. If Taylor was going to stay an MGM star, he needed good properties, and *Waterloo Bridge* was assuredly a good property, with a bright young female star. Having to use dull actors like Taylor and Lana Turner was the price producers and directors paid for working at MGM. Besides, as Mayer once told a producer, "Your problem is you only want to work with good actors."

This gradually drove Hunt Stromberg out of the company, even though he had what amounted to an independent unit at the studio, much as David Selznick had some years earlier. Stromberg had been at the studio for eighteen years and was responsible for such films as the *Thin Man* movies, *Red Dust, Treasure Island, Naughty Marietta, Night Must Fall,* and *The Women.* But there were problems behind the scenes; as Joe Cohn would remember, "Hunt Stromberg went on hop."

Frances Goodrich and Albert Hackett remembered that Stromberg began taking morphine because of a slipped disc, but insisted on holding story meetings despite the fact he was hallucinating. The addiction was probably the main reason Mayer allowed Stromberg to leave in February of 1942, with three years still to go on his contract. Stromberg promptly signed a releasing agreement with United Artists and went into independent production. His first picture, *Lady of Burlesque*, with Barbara Stanwyck, made $650,000 profit. *Guest in the House* brought in $50,000 profit. But *Young Widow*, *The Strange Woman*, and *Dishonored Lady*—the latter two starring another MGM refugee, Hedy Lamarr—all tanked. Stromberg's five UA pictures lost a total of $900,000. Without MGM stories and MGM stars, Stromberg's successful touch disappeared. Mayer called Joe Cohn to his office and asked him what he thought of bringing Stromberg back to MGM. Cohn said it would depend on what shape he was in.

Louis could forgive errant talents and welcome them back to the studio, albeit in comparatively menial positions and salaries. But he could go only so far. He would have welcomed prestige filmmakers for long-term relationships—so long as they could have adapted themselves to the MGM manner, the MGM way of doing things. And that they could not do.

Mayer's decisions tended to focus on which stars would be in what picture. Much of the time, he handled things personally. "He was very conscious of the value of his troupe of stars," said Ring Lardner Jr. "Of what would sell best for each of them. Michael Kanin and I worked on a script called *Marriage Is a Private Affair*, and we had written it for a good actress. After we finished the script, Mayer read the synopsis and promptly said, 'That's for Lana Turner.' And we said that would mean we'd have to cheapen it, let somebody else do it. It would have been a super movie, until Mayer made that decision." (The film was eventually made with Turner opposite John Hodiak and James Craig, a supposed replacement for Clark Gable.)

Compared to other studios, writers at MGM worked for the individual producers. "Fox, for instance, was a one-man operation," said Lardner. "Zanuck had a conference on every script with all the people that were concerned. The conference consisted of him talking about his ideas. He had a secretary that took down everything he said, and nothing anybody else said, and then you'd get a copy of Mr. Zanuck's notes. It was a different kind of egomania.

"At Metro, you never thought that Mayer looked at scripts. At Metro you worked with a producer. At Fox, you had a producer, but everybody was waiting to see what Zanuck would say. At Metro, producers had a lot more say."

"Writers were not in on any decisions at Metro except what to order for lunch," said Sidney Sheldon. "Once I was talking to Arthur Freed in his office. His insurance man came in, and the three of us talked for a bit, and then Arthur said to his insurance man, 'I have to look at rushes. Come watch with me.' I was left sitting there, and I was the writer! When I got there, other writers told me, 'Don't expect all your scripts to be shot. One every two or three years is fine with the front office.' "

The downside to being a writer at MGM was explained by Walter Reisch, who knew the upside from having worked on *Ninotchka* and *Gaslight*. "At MGM every picture was either talked to death or to life. They would talk, talk, talk—endless sessions with producers, story editors, directors, writers, actors, other executives, distributors, agents. Everybody had something to say. It never ended. Whenever a picture got made, it was a miracle."

On the other hand, working at MGM under Mayer "was an age like that of Athens in Greece under Pericles." He even installed an in-house drama coach named Lillian Burns whom few people took seriously. When a smart producer like Arthur Freed found a talent he respected, he would often conspire to keep her out of Burns's clutches so the actress wouldn't adopt Burns's repertoire of modified Del Sarte mannerisms—narrowed eyes to indicate displeasure or anger, flared eyes to indicate fear. A show business machine like Mickey Rooney would rhetorically ask, "Did they make me take lessons from her? God, no!"

"She was a failed actress herself, a little woman with quick movements," said Esther Williams. "She married George [Sidney] because she wanted to be part of that dynasty within the studio. It solidified her position." "A dreadful woman," said Cyd Charisse. "A good drama coach? No! she was a dictator. She had this big diamond ring and she'd stand there and say something, and then hold her arm out and admire her ring."

Still, there were talented people who swore by Burns—Debbie Reynolds and Betty Garrett among them. Burns would work with a young talent for weeks on a specific role, even more if she knew they would be working with a weak director. She took particular pride in developing her young charges as people.

"I adored her," said Marge Champion. "Although many of her coaching sessions were about how she coached other people, she was feisty. And she taught me things. Not just for films, but things about living. Steuben glass, for instance. It's all in the attic now, and I don't use it, but she got me into Steuben glass. . . . Lillian was a friend and an older sister."

Burns also served as a sort of ombudswoman for certain delicate problems that could never be taken to Benny Thau, as when Van Johnson noted a certain pungent odor emanating from one of his co-stars. He went to Burns, who went to the actress in question and gave her instructions in feminine hygiene.

"Lillian's great problem," said Terry Kingsley Smith, the son of screenwriter Dorothy Kingsley, "was that if she didn't think you had talent, she couldn't disguise that feeling." L.B. thought the world of Burns, and would tell anybody who would listen that "Lilly can teach a flea how to act!"

Arthur Freed's instinct about Vincente Minnelli had been proven correct. After two years of learning how movies were made and, most importantly, how they were made at MGM, Minnelli found himself directing big-budget films while the studio was still paying him only $1,000 a week, below-market value for A list directors. Nobody questioned Minnelli's talent, although a great many people questioned Minnelli.

"When he was working at Radio City Music Hall, Vincente Minnelli cruised me at Rockefeller Center one day," remembered set decorator Jack Hurd. "We went back to his apartment. He wore makeup, lipstick, and eye shadow—a freak.

"Years later, I show up at MGM and there's Vincente, now a successful director. I went up and introduced myself and he wouldn't acknowledge me. And he was still wearing lipstick and eye shadow! Of course, I'd breached protocol, because at MGM the underlings weren't supposed to speak to producers or directors unless spoken to. At Fox, everybody was just pals, but not MGM.

"A movie studio is like a small town—everybody knows everybody else's business. Vincente wasn't subtle about his gayness, so Judy Garland and everybody else had to know the situation when she married him. Why? Who knows? Add in all the other people who were truly neurotic or crazy, then think about what Mayer had to deal with on a daily basis. His office had to be Crisis Central. If you keep that in mind, he didn't do too badly."

In the summer of 1941, Katharine Hepburn presented Mayer—she always bypassed the studio bureaucracy and dealt directly with him—with seventy-eight pages of a script called *Woman of the Year*, written by Ring Lardner Jr. and Michael Kanin from an idea by Kanin's brother Garson. The script came without the names of its authors. Hepburn told Mayer she wanted $100,000 for the script, $100,000 for herself, $10,000 for her agent, and $1,000 for transportation between Connecticut and California.

Mayer's curiosity was piqued. He consulted Joe Mankiewicz, who liked the script, and figured that it had probably been written by Ben Hecht and Charlie MacArthur, who couldn't put their names on it because they were contractually committed elsewhere.

In many respects, the situation was anomalous. Hepburn recently had a big hit with *The Philadelphia Story*, and MGM very much wanted to stay in business with her. At the same time, Spencer Tracy had been shooting *The Yearling* in Florida for Victor Fleming when, after twenty-one days, the studio pulled the plug. As a result, Tracy was sitting around doing nothing while the studio scrambled to find a suitable project. The *Woman of the Year* script contained a part that was perfect for Tracy.

Mayer eagerly accepted the script, but bridled at the scene in which Katharine Hepburn demonstrates her mastery of languages, including Yiddish. Back came a nonnegotiable dictum: any language was okay—Chinese, Persian—but not, under any circumstances, Yiddish. "There was no explanation of the order, and no way to appeal it," remembered Lardner ruefully. "They wanted to avoid anything that could possibly stir up anti-Semitism."

Over the years, with perfect hindsight, men like Mayer have been castigated for their timidity about appearing too Jewish, their hesitance to use their power in the service of anti-Fascism. But Hollywood was run by Jews within the predominantly Protestant city of Los Angeles. Hollywood was the only place in America where Jews had something approaching absolute power, and Mayer sought to maintain that power by reflecting not merely a Christian point of view, but a Catholic point of view. Mayer was instinctively inclusive; it was nothing less than a mandatory insurance policy, one he believed he could not afford to be without.

The California right wing was deeply suspicious, not merely of leftist Jews, but of *all* Jews. A California state committee on un-American activities noted "quiet Communistic infiltration into the American Jewish Congress," adding ominously that "nine out of twenty-one directors of Warner Bros. are Jews; five out of fifteen directors of Paramount Pictures, Inc. . . . Metro-Goldwyn-Mayer, Inc. and Columbia Pictures have a slight majority of Jews in the directorate."

Likewise, in 1932, Joseph Breen, administrator of the Production Code, had written a letter to a Catholic priest in which he characterized Hollywood as "a rotten bunch of vile people with no respect for anything beyond the making of money. Here we have Paganism rampant and in its most virulent form. Drunkenness and debauchery are commonplace. Sexual perversion is rampant . . . any number of our directors and stars are perverts. Ninety-five percent of these folks are Jews of an Eastern European lineage. They are, probably, the scum of the earth."

The fact of the matter was that anti-Semitism was rife in all facets of American society, from the Senate on down—or, depending on your point of view, from the Senate on up. Years after Breen's letter, senators like Burton Wheeler and Champ Clark were still insisting on an isolationist stance, while rabid anti-Semites such as the isolationist Senator Gerald Nye of North Dakota liked nothing better than focusing on the "Yiddish controllers" of the American movies and theater. "Are you ready to send your boys to bleed and die in Europe, to make the world safe for Barney Balaban and Adolph Zukor and Joseph Schenck?" thundered Nye in August of 1941.

Public anti-Semites like Father Charles Coughlin warned in broadcasts about "world Jewish domination," and a 1938 public opinion poll revealed that 45 percent of Americans believed Jews were less honest than Gentiles in business; 35 percent believed that European Jews were largely responsible for their oppression. Likewise, public opinion polls from 1938 to 1941 said that a third to a half of the public believed that Jews had "too much power in the United States"; after Pearl Harbor, agreement with that proposition rose to 50 percent.

From Mayer's point of view, Nazism was a legalized pogrom, and he had no desire to inadvertently foment one in America. Caution was the watchword, which is why, after the war, he also became anti-Zionist, believing Zionism would lead to nothing but trouble, in spite of the support that the cause received from trusted friends like Mendel Silberberg.

"I don't think the heads of movie companies, and the men they appointed to run the studios, had ever before thought of themselves as American citizens with inherited rights and obligations," wrote Lillian Hellman. "Many of them had been born in foreign lands, and inherited foreign fears. . . . It was possible here to offer the Cossacks a bowl of chicken soup."

Joseph L. Mankiewicz had long been one of Mayer's favorites, a bright young man with a touch of class. But when, in 1942, Mankiewicz began an affair with the twenty-year-old Judy Garland, Mayer blew sky-high. Mankiewicz was on the *Super Chief*, returning to Hollywood from the Menninger Clinic in

Topeka, where his wife was being treated for psychiatric problems—she would later commit suicide—when he encountered Howard Strickling. Mayer was on the train and wanted to see him at once, Strickling said.

When Mankiewicz walked into the compartment, Mayer began screaming. "You have to understand, I have the welfare of all my players at heart and I am talking to you like a father."

"No, you're not," replied Mankiewicz. "You're talking like a jealous old man." As Mayer turned apoplectic, Strickling hurried Mankiewicz out of the compartment.

Mayer's physician, Jessie Marmorston, believed Mankiewicz was wrong about Mayer's feelings for Garland. "He felt Judy Garland was small and ugly and Jewish-[looking]," said Marmorston. "I don't think he wanted her in bed with him. But I think he hated Joe because he used sex to win a girl."

Mayer had not objected to Mankiewicz's affair with Joan Crawford, because he knew that sex would never interfere with Crawford's allegiance to her career. But almost anything could topple Garland's precarious hold on stability. "There were times when I'd think, 'God I wish I had her talent,' " remembered her friend, screenwriter Leonard Gershe. "But there were other times when I'd think, 'God, I'm glad I don't have her temperament.' You could only like Judy on and off, because she tested your friendship so relentlessly. Let's just say I liked her at the beginning."

"Mayer *worshipped* Judy," said Esther Williams. "To be able to present a talent like hers was his reason for living, and in his cold little immigrant's way, he loved her and Mickey."

Back at the studio, Mankiewicz demanded an apology. Mayer's response was to berate him further. "Obviously, Mr. Mayer, this studio isn't big enough for both of us," said Mankiewicz, which caused Eddie Mannix to erupt in laughter. Mankiewicz left MGM to write, produce, and direct at Fox.

Louis had spread elements of power throughout the studio. Even Eddie Mannix could green-light a project, as Sidney Franklin discovered when he went to Mannix with a property about the fortitude of the English during the early days of World War II entitled *Mrs. Miniver.* "It's going to be a very simple story of a little English family, and we more than likely will lose $100,000 on the picture," explained Franklin. "Nevertheless, I think it's mandatory that we make it."

"Okay, Sidney," replied Mannix. "If you feel that strongly about it, go ahead and write your script. I agree with you. Someone should salute England. And if we lose $100,000 that'll be okay, too."

But the picture expanded when Mayer recruited Greer Garson for the title role, in spite of the fact that she was only thirty-three years old and would be playing a woman with an eighteen-year-old daughter. Garson wanted no part of playing a forty-year-old, but Mayer was persuasive. Very persuasive.

"He projected himself into the role of a man who had a strong English orientation," said Jessie Marmorston. "He worked on Greer's mother and offered [them] the arguments that would win: 'I brought you along, you were fat, I had no way of knowing whether you could take off that extra twenty pounds, I put my faith in you when others would not accept you. Now you've got to have the same faith in me.' He talked about honor, worked on her sense of fair play."

Finally, Mayer played his trump card. He picked up the script and began to read. The walls of the Thalberg Building vanished and he stood amidst the rubble of wartime England, proud and defiant against the Luftwaffe. This was the image she could give the world. She was not Greer Garson, an actress worried about her vanity. She was a woman in love with her husband and her family, a woman who loses her daughter to war, but who survives and endures. She was London. No, more than that; she was . . . *England!*

Garson surrendered.

The wartime audience poured an unprecedented amount of money into entertainment, and much of it was spent on watching MGM pictures. *Mrs. Miniver* alone made profits of $4.8 million. As a result, the studio's talent trawl became even more intensive, occasionally resulting in hilarious misalliances, as when the thirty-two-year-old Tennessee Williams was given a six-month trial. He worked for Pandro Berman on the Ring Lardner–Michael Kanin script *Marriage Is a Private Affair*, with its star, Lana Turner, which embarrassed Williams no end. "I think it is one of the funniest but most embarrassing things that ever happened to me, that I should be expected to produce a suitable vehicle for this actress. . . . They want me to give it 'freshness and vitality' but at the same time keep it 'a Lana Turner sort of thing.' I feel like an obstetrician required to successfully deliver a mastodon from a beaver."

Other prospects proved more productive. Mayer had fallen in love with William Saroyan's play *The Time of Your Life* on one of his trips back to New York. Arthur Freed was also an admirer, and Freed and Saroyan both frequented Stanley Rose's bookstore on Hollywood Boulevard. Saroyan was offered a job as an MGM writer. The egomaniacal writer told Mayer that he didn't want to be hired as just another writer, that he had plans and lots of ideas. Saroyan went on to describe his innate qualities at some length, stopping only when Mayer told him that he could hear perfectly well and Saroyan didn't have to shout.

Mayer proposed a "test drive," in which Saroyan could spend a couple of weeks at MGM for $300 a week and expenses. After that, if both parties were willing, they could make a deal. Fair enough.

By the end of January 1942, Saroyan had completed a 158-page screenplay for a film he called *The Human Comedy*. He decided to ask for $250,000 for the screenplay and his services as director. By the first week of February, Mayer told Saroyan that they wanted him to come to work at MGM and they wanted to buy his plays as well. Mayer proposed a price of $50,000 for *The Human Comedy*, and a $1,000-a-week contract as writer and producer or associate producer for the film. Saroyan's counterproposal was $75,000, and $1,500 a week, with Saroyan reporting only to Mayer and all rights to *The Human Comedy* returning to him after five years. He was confident of his ability to finesse Mayer. As he put it, "No Jew can ever cheat an Armenian. The Armenians have been cheating the Jews for centuries."

Mayer didn't blink. "The money won't do you any good," Mayer responded. "It puts you in a high-income bracket. The government will take almost all of it."

Mayer upped the offer to $60,000 for *The Human Comedy*, but the $1,000 a week remained firm. Saroyan signed.

MGM wanted King Vidor to direct the picture. Saroyan wanted Saroyan. There were fierce arguments, until the studio proposed that Saroyan direct a one-reel short to prove that he could make a movie. That seemed reasonable. Saroyan began a brief affair with Norma Shearer while he prepared to direct his first—and only—picture.

The Good Job was shot in five days beginning March 18, 1942. After the picture was cut, gossip began circulating that he had made a stiff. Mary Loos saw the short and remembers it as "very Saroyan—a lot of people meeting in a drugstore and jabbering wittily."

Saroyan was called to Mayer's office and asked Loos to accompany him.

"Young man," began Mayer, "I don't think you're a director. I think you should stick to being a writer. I've looked at your short and I don't understand it."

"Mr. Mayer," replied Saroyan, "it's a string of pearls."

Mayer leaned forward. "The pearls," he said, "are unstrung."

Mayer told him the studio couldn't possibly let him direct a million-dollar picture. Saroyan offered to buy back *The Human Comedy*, but Mayer refused, although he did offer to sell him *The Good Job* for $15,000. Saroyan stormed off the lot to write a nasty play about Mayer and MGM (*Get Away Old Man*), which flopped. The Jew had taken the Armenian.

Someone else would have to direct *The Human Comedy*. By July, Clarence Brown had been assigned to the picture, a fortunate choice, for he was far and away the most lyrical of the MGM directors. Brown began cutting down the script to a shootable length with Howard Estabrook. Brown said that Saroyan's script contained "the nucleus of the story . . . but he never knew when to cut a scene, when the point had been made." (William Ludwig did some writing for last-minute retakes, including the wonderful scene with Darryl Hickman in the library.)

On August 31, Brown began shooting with a cast that included Mickey Rooney and Frank Morgan. In most respects, the film was made under a lucky star: Clarence Brown's wife found Butch Jenkins while walking on the beach; he proved perfect for the part of the youngest brother.

"Mickey Rooney is the closest thing to a genius that I ever worked with," Brown remembered. "There was Chaplin, then there was Rooney. The little bastard could do no wrong in my book. I don't know how he did it, because he never really paid any attention. Between takes, he'd be off somewhere calling his bookmaker, then come back and go into a scene as if he'd been rehearsing it for three days. The scene where he reads the telegram announcing his brother's death—we must have shot that thing four or five times and each time he'd read it as though he'd seen it for the first time. All you had to do with him was rehearse it once."

Darryl Hickman, who pulled off the difficult part of a slightly retarded yet ethereal child amazed at "all those books" in a library, remembered that "I didn't have the slightest idea how to play the part. Then they gave me buck teeth and some glasses and that was it. I got it from the outside in, rather than from the inside out. Clarence Brown didn't say much; the only direction I remember him giving me is, 'Don't blink so much.' That's all. But he was *very* methodical. *Very* painstaking. He took his time until he was good and satisfied."

By November, Saroyan had converted his original script into a novel, which the Book-of-the-Month club took as its February 1943, offering, just before Brown's picture was to be released. The book was a great commercial and critical hit, and Damon Runyon wrote that "This may be one of the greatest novels ever written by an American." From start to finish, the elapsed time was a year.

Saroyan undoubtedly thought Mayer had set him up and never had any intention of letting him direct *The Human Comedy*. Mayer, he would write in his memoirs, "could make or break movie people, in all departments, and he did so whenever desirable or necessary. . . . Anybody who got sarcastic with old L.B., even only in the eyes, giving him only a sarcastic *look*, would soon enough learn that L.B. would take it slow and easy, and then at an unexpected moment take his revenge. Like death itself."

Actually, the idea of letting Saroyan direct was no goofier than letting a songwriter produce musicals—the sort of gamble Mayer was entirely capable of making, so long as Saroyan would have been under the thumb of an experienced producer and cameraman.

The early years of World War II were an unsettling time; Hitler, Mussolini, and Hirohito were winning battle after battle, and the very idea of America seemed in peril. *The Human Comedy* is one of many home front movies that Hollywood was making—*Since You Went Away, Mrs. Miniver, The Clock*—films permeated with yearning and fear, with the awareness of death hovering nearby, and a mystical air that would be as close as American movies have ever gotten to a common thread of potent spirituality, of the bonds between the living and the dead.

The Human Comedy vacillates between the superb and the bathetic. For the former, there is Mickey Rooney's character of Homer Macauley and Frank Morgan's genially soused telegraph operator Willie Grogan; for the latter, there is MGM's vision of the American melting pot, a long tracking shot through a park as every ethnic group known to man ("You can always tell the Armenians by the priests and kids," explains James Craig to Mickey Rooney. "That's what they believe in, God and children") celebrate their national origins in their native costumes, with their native music. (There must have been something in the water on Washington Boulevard in these years. *The Big Store*, the Marx Brothers' 1941 farewell to MGM, features "The Tenement Symphony," a musical statement sung by Tony Martin of the crazed ode to diversity scene in *The Human Comedy*: "The Cohn's pianola/The Kellys and their Victrola/all form a part of my Tenement Symphony . . .")

Still, there is the introduction of Butch Jenkins's Ulysses—evocative, poetic, appealing—the amazing sequence of the city at night, the clown in the window, the sense of desolation in the dark streets, and, last but by no means least, a pre–nose job Robert Mitchum.

Occasionally treacly, sometimes unctuous, *The Human Comedy* remains perhaps the most striking of the home front films that carry emotional devastation in every frame. "Most of my friends detest it," wrote James Agee, before noting that "in its rare successes, it interests me more than any other film I have seen for a good while."

Brown made the picture for $1 million, and it went on to a world gross of $3.8 million, returning $1.5 million to the studio in clear profit. Saroyan was awarded an Academy Award for Best Original Story.

"That's my favorite picture," Brown would say near the end of his life. "Every scene in there came straight from my heart. If a picture is to be any good, it has to be done that way, with total commitment."

It was Mayer's favorite MGM picture as well.

Mayer didn't hold *Get Away Old Man* against Saroyan; when the two men ran into each other at Hollywood Park in 1946, Mayer asked Saroyan to sit in his private box, then said, "I've got a horse in this race and he looks good. *I'm* betting on him. Why don't you bet on him too?" Saroyan refused both suggestions, and put $200 on a different horse. Mayer's horse won, paying six to one.

In the middle of the war, the Office of War Information asked the studios to do something to celebrate the American alliance with Russia. MGM's response was to buy a grim little story called "Scorched Earth," and assign it to Joe Pasternak, who saw it as a great opportunity for a lot of Tchaikovsky on the soundtrack. Pasternak assigned two leftist writers, Paul Jarrico and Richard Collins, to write the screenplay.

"I wouldn't say [Mayer] was enthusiastic about it, but he did do what the government asked him to do," remembered Jarrico. "And when he was told that I was a Communist, he said, 'I know. I wouldn't keep him for a minute if he weren't such a good writer.' "

When the script was finished, Mayer told Jarrico and Collins to take the word "community" out of the script because it was too close to "Communism." He also bridled at the appearance of a collective farm. "Why can't it be just her father's farm?" he asked. There was no private ownership in the Soviet Union, but there were no farming collectives at MGM. The farm issue was fudged.

Mayer assigned Robert Taylor to play the lead, an American orchestra conductor who falls in love with a Russian girl. This was a problem, since politically Taylor was to the right of Mayer and wanted nothing to do with Russia. Mayer managed to talk him into it by declaring *Song of Russia* Taylor's patriotic duty.

Song of Russia made a tidy profit of more than $700,000 on a $1.8 million cost. The trouble the picture had presented seemed to be over; that year, the studio netted $14.5 million—its highest profit since 1937—on an industry record gross of $166 million.

The trouble, however, was not over. In fact, the trouble hadn't even begun.

Chapter
THIRTEEN

WAR RATIONING AFFECTED only the subsidiary talent at MGM—at the commissary, only one pat of butter was allotted for a stack of hotcakes instead of three. But when an assistant director went into the commissary storage area to check up on food for a scene in a picture, he was astonished to see separate stacks of rationed items such as bacon, ham, butter, cheese, sugar, and coffee lined up, each with the name of an MGM executive pasted on the wall above it. The largest stack had "L. B. Mayer" above it; the source of the provisions for the elaborate Sunday brunches at Mayer's beach house suddenly became clear.

As with the food supply, the rules were different at MGM. The studio served as a cornucopia for the favored. If a producer needed a tux, or a morning coat or striped pants for a formal do or wedding, he wouldn't have to actually buy them, he could just go to wardrobe and get outfitted from the stock the studio carried at all times.

The rules were also different in technical matters. The lab was instructed not to print anything like a true black—soft grays were the rule, because heavy blacks or whites were reminiscent of newsreels . . . or RKO. On *Waterloo Bridge*, Mervyn LeRoy was so determined to get true blacks that he used two cameras for the London night scenes and had the film from one camera developed and printed off the MGM lot, so he could get the look he wanted.

MGM developed and printed its own black-and-white footage, which is why its films can be distinguished from those of Paramount or Warners. Technicolor did its own processing, which made MGM's color footage less distinctive than its black-and-white. Natalie Kalmus, the color coordinator on most of the MGM films, tended to work mostly with the art director, in pre-production. "People think that Technicolor was great, loud and garish," said Technicolor's Dr. Richard Goldberg. "But it wasn't quite that way. It wasn't that loud. The original three-strip of *The Wizard of Oz* was slightly flat—low contrast. The colors weren't as saturated as they are today; they were slightly more drab. The [color] density didn't increase at MGM as much as it did at Paramount." Or at Fox, where the remarkable vividness of the Technicolor was largely because the studio focused on primary colors, i.e., red, green, and blue. Besides that, Technicolor did what Technicolor wanted to do. "Technicolor was pretty independent," said Goldberg. "They told the studio—any studio—what was what. Dr. Kalmus ruled with an iron fist. He was a fine gentleman of the old school, and the company had no competition."

One of the studio's premier hits in this period was *Meet Me in St. Louis*, one of those pictures that were miles of bad road but ultimately worth it. "MGM didn't really believe in the picture," remembered the screenwriter Irving Brecher, "but they had a Technicolor commitment they had to use or lose, and there was nothing else appropriate to shoot. Freed did not like the script I was working on with Fred Finklehoffe, then Fred went away, and I was alone, but nobody paid much attention to it. Technicolor became available, and Freed said, 'We have to make this.' He put Vincente Minnelli on it, and I worked with Minnelli.

"Then Mayer asked me to persuade Judy to do the movie. Judy didn't want to do it; Joe Mankiewicz told her, 'Don't do it, the little kid [Margaret O'Brien] will steal the picture.' Freed had tried to persuade her and gave up, and he went to Mayer. Mayer called me and explained the situation. I knew Judy and loved her; she would come over to my house and sing. 'If you can, talk her into it, goddammit,' Mayer said. I said I'd do the best I could.

"So they put her in a room with me and closed the door. 'Judy, I'm not gonna twist your arm and tell you you have to do it. I think the part is burglarproof; I think you'll be a big hit.' Then I read it to her, in a very deceitful way. Every time I got to a line of Margaret O'Brien's, I threw it away. When I got to a line of Judy's, I gave it emphasis. When it was over, she said, 'Well, maybe . . .'

" 'Do the movie, Judy. You won't be sorry.' "

Production on the film was a long slog—it began on November 11, 1943, and finished April 7, 1944—and the script went through the usual multiplicity of hands (original author Sally Benson, Sarah Mason, Victor Heerman, Doris

Gilbert, William Ludwig, as well as credited writers Irving Brecher and Fred Finklehoffe). Margaret O'Brien's mother yanked her off the picture for an unscheduled vacation of twelve days, while Judy Garland's neurotic behavior was slipping into high gear. She complained of headaches, migraines, earaches, a bad stomach, and sinus trouble. She arrived late or not at all. Once she phoned Freed at 4:30 in the morning to say she might not be able to make it to the studio. Another favorite, if slightly bewildering, method of procrastination was to call the studio to warn them that her car "might stall." All told, Garland missed thirteen days of work, with the picture taking seventy days to make rather than the fifty-eight that had been budgeted, at a final cost of $1.7 million.

Minnelli took special care about the set decorations. One daily production report noted that from 3:20 P.M. to 3:26 P.M., the company "[waited] for perfume bottle (special container with satin liner asked for by director)."

"[Minnelli] loved antiques," remembered Margaret O'Brien, "so he was a master at creating that particular era, that Victorian era. He was such a stickler for detail, and he did all of the antiques himself. He went and hunted for them. Every doorknob in the house was an antique doorknob, which I wish I had today. Every ornament on the tree. I'd just stare at that tree in awe. . . . He really created the whole atmosphere and ambience of that film."

O'Brien was undoubtedly Mayer's strangest new star, a young child with a changeling's intensity, who began a rise to prominence in *Journey for Margaret* in 1942 and became a star in *Meet Me in St. Louis*.

"I almost didn't do *St. Louis*," remembered O'Brien. "They didn't want to pay me anything and my mother didn't care. She was a famous flamenco dancer who had worked with the Cansinos; she was a gypsy and lived an Auntie Mame life. She marched into Mayer's office and said, 'I'm taking my daughter home.'

"Now, MGM had a look-alike for every star. . . . If you were a star, they'd hold it over you and threaten to use the look-alike, even though they never would. So my mother disappeared into the Stork Club, and they got the other little girl ready for *St. Louis*. My mother had leverage and she knew it. Mr. Mayer sent out scouts to find us in New York. So they found us and told the other little girl she wasn't going to do the picture. Her father, who was an electrician at the studio, had a nervous breakdown.

"I loved Judy Garland's red dress in the film, so Mr. Mayer had it copied for me. I wore it everywhere, until he got sick of seeing it and said to me, 'Look, Margaret, if you stop wearing the dress, I'll give you a horse.' So one of the horses in his stable became my horse, and I could go out and visit and ride him whenever I wanted. But then the horse started winning races and he took it back." (Mayer also gave a horse to Mickey Rooney, a bay mare named Stereopticon that was about to foal. Rooney tried racing the colt when it hit two, but he only finished in the money once. Mayer never asked for either the mare or her colt back.)

Mayer admired a woman of spirit, and found himself attracted to O'Brien's mother, who, remembers her daughter, "looked like Hedy Lamarr." There was apparently an offer of marriage. Although Mrs. O'Brien liked Mayer, she didn't like him that much, and the proposal was gently refused.

"I didn't find him grandfatherly and he didn't particularly play that part," said O'Brien. "He played the part of a head of a corporation, or perhaps royalty, one who expected you to uphold the position he had found for you. You had to dress a certain way, behave a certain way. If a star was going to the grocery store, you didn't wear jeans. He was terribly concerned with how things *looked*. And it worked; he made stars whose names are still alive today, and some of the movies became classics, and it was because of Mayer's way of doing things.

"Some people have called him a tyrant, but you can't be wishy-washy and create a kingdom. What he was was a businessman who knew how to make motion pictures for his time. All in all, he was fine."

Meet Me in St. Louis emerged as a miraculous triumph that grossed $5 million in America alone, plus ancillaries. (By October 14, 1944, 178,104 copies of the sheet music for Hugh Martin and Ralph Blane's "The Trolley Song" had been sold.) As much as any picture that emerged from Mayer's studio, *St. Louis* is a paean to hearth and home, but the characters have to move through an authentic tunnel of darkness before their devotion to town and family is reaffirmed.

Mayer believed that his greatest discovery in these years was Greer Garson, but posterity would probably vote for Gene Kelly. Mayer had seen the Broadway production of *Pal Joey* that made Kelly a star and gave him the seductive treatment, even telling the dancer that there would be no need for a screen test if he would sign a contract with MGM. The two men shook hands on a deal. A few days later, one of MGM's men in New York contacted the dancer to arrange for a screen test. Kelly was furious and wrote a letter accusing Mayer of lying to him and furthermore, he had no interest in working for MGM. A few months later, David Selznick offered Kelly a contract.

"What about a screen test?" asked the dancer.

"Who said anything about a screen test? Just send your agent over and we'll draw up a contract."

"You sons of bitches are all alike," Kelly said.

An understandably perturbed Selznick asked Kelly what he meant. When Kelly told him, Selznick roared with laughter and said, "Well, *he* might do that, but I won't. I give you my word."

Kelly signed with Selznick, which was a problem, as Selznick didn't make musicals, but Selznick loaned him out to Arthur Freed for *For Me and My Gal*. Mayer had not forgotten Kelly's letter, but allowed Freed to hire the dancer, then bought his contract from Selznick. For the next fifteen years, Kelly defined the MGM musical. For most of that time, Kelly and Mayer existed in a state of steely mutual tolerance. "Gene was a kid from the streets," said Betsy Blair, Kelly's first wife. "He was a natural rebel, and his attitude towards the boss was going to be very irreverent, although he adored David Selznick. But L.B. gave Gene no reason to change his mind."

"During the Communist witch hunts in 1947," Kelly remembered, "Mayer remarked to someone that I couldn't possibly be a Commie because I was a Catholic who loved his mother. The difference between Mayer and [Harry] Cohn was that if Cohn believed me to be a Communist, which I was not, he would have said 'Kelly's a Catholic, *and* he's a Communist. And if he's going to make money for me, I'll put him in my next three pictures.'

"Now Mayer, who was outwardly more respectable than both Cohn and [Billy] Rose put together, I didn't like at all. I could laugh and have fun with Rose and Cohn. But Mayer I avoided."

Professionally, it seemed impossible for Mayer and MGM to make a wrong step during the war years. Louis took a shine to the rushes of a little movie called *Lassie Come Home*, and upgraded the budget from a B film to a cheap A picture. It grossed an amazing $4.5 million worldwide and made a profit of $2 million.

Cinema admissions shot upward, and a very successful film could expect to gross somewhere between $5 and $8 million worldwide, an impossible number for any prewar film other than *Gone With the Wind*. With the market offering such huge returns, Mayer made fewer but more expensive films. The studio cut its release schedule from forty-eight films in 1941–42 to twenty-seven in 1945–46, with average production cost nearly tripling, from $650,000 to $1.68 million. The average MGM picture now cost nearly double the average Hollywood picture, whose cost now stood at $900,000. And the money just rolled in.

The success of the studio was a de facto confirmation of Louis's beliefs and prejudices. He asserted his conventional wisdom everywhere, at the least provocation. The war film *Bataan*—a light rewrite of John Ford's *The Lost Patrol*—was supposed to end on a close-up of the hero firing wildly, hopelessly, at the advancing enemy, the camera creeping forward so that the machine gun filled the screen. Suddenly, the firing was to stop, and the film was to end in silence, as smoke wafted up from the barrel. But Mayer decreed that the dead machine gun must dissolve to a shot of the flag snapping in the breeze, with the resonant voice of Douglas MacArthur on the soundtrack, for a typically rousing propaganda finish.

Then there were personnel problems. Spencer Tracy was always a potential difficulty. Irene Dunne would always remember the production of *A Guy Named Joe* as the "most difficult" picture of her life. From the beginning of *A Guy Named Joe*, Dunne was greeted with incessant, nonstop sexual overtures from her co-star, then in the throes of his supposedly life-altering relationship with Katharine Hepburn, about which more treacle has been spilled than anything since Abelard and Heloise. Tracy wouldn't stop goosing, touching, and rubbing Dunne. When she had to sing "I'll Get By" to him, Tracy leaned over and whispered dirty words into her ear.

The last straw occurred during a take when Tracy was to come up behind her and take her gently by the shoulders. He pressed himself so tightly against her that she could feel his erection pressing into her buttocks.

Dunne was very Catholic, very married, and not the sort of woman who was amused by this kind of behavior. She was not a prude—she had been a leading lady for the Shuberts, and was experienced at fending off passes from producers and leading men. But never had she encountered behavior this unrelenting, this unprofessional. There was no help to be had from director Victor Fleming, who believed that was the way real men behaved—"You're a good-looking woman; you should be flattered," etc. Dunne was not an MGM star, the studio had no vested interest in making her happy, and Tracy was the only big male star they had left on the lot during the war.

Dunne walked up to Mayer's office, assuming that what she was about to do would get her fired. She informed him about what had been going on and said, "Get him to leave me alone. No more innuendoes. No joking. No touching. Nothing. Or I am quitting the film as of today."

During a big scene with Ward Bond, Dunne gave it everything she had. On Monday, Mayer watched the scene and said aloud, "If I'm firing anybody, I'm firing Tracy, not her." He confronted Tracy that same day, and the problems stopped.

Tracy was a model of decorum compared to Lana Turner. Turner was a val-

ued friend to many—"the most natural, the most uncomplicated, the most sincere woman I knew in Hollywood," said Turhan Bey—but she was a dismal,
amateurish actress. If she wasn't marrying them (Mickey Rooney, Artie Shaw,
Lex Barker et al.) she was sleeping with them (Clark Gable, John Garfield).
She was utterly undiscriminating, as was revealed in some tapes Red Skelton
made for a prospective biography:

"Lana Turner and Tony Martin were going together," related Skelton, "and
Lana was trying to make Tony jealous and she was flirting with me all the
time. . . . And finally I went over to Borzage [director Frank, with whom Skelton
was making *Flight Command*] and I said . . . 'God, boy, I've really got it bad.' He
said, 'Go up to her dressing room, throw one into her, and you'll forget it.' So I
did. I came back. I says, 'I don't think it's gonna work. She's really got me.' He
says, 'Well, try it again.' So we went back and she hit the same pose, the same
goddamn dialogue and everything, and that killed that. Through with her."

All this drove Mayer wild; the Loew's executive Charles Moscowitz said
that Mayer once called Turner a "whore" and a "no-good tramp" to her face. A
few months after she married Artie Shaw, Mayer showed up at their front door.
He awkwardly announced that his visit had to do with "our little girl." After
some initial pleasantries, Mayer inquired whether the happy couple was planning on having children.

"Gee, I don't know," replied Shaw. "We're not making plans but we're
doing all the right things. They could come. I'm not taking any precautions.
Why?"

Mayer went on to mention the considerable investment MGM had in
Turner, that she was going to be one of their biggest stars and "It would be disastrous if she had a child. . . . She's a love goddess. And love goddesses don't
have children."

Shaw realized that Mayer wanted the couple to use contraception, but he
also made it clear that he wasn't interested in what Mayer wanted. Very well; a
different line of attack was needed. Mayer had the same conversation with
Turner. A few months later, she became pregnant and had an abortion without
ever telling Shaw. MGM was more important than her marriage, more important than a child.

"Lana was actually a nymphomaniac," remembered her friend Evie Johnson. "She was never satisfied. She was a very nice person, a really good friend,
nothing vicious about her. The first time we met she was eighteen; she was with
Johnny Mascio the agent, and I came out there to visit Ty [Power]. She always
had a way of picking the wrong men; the only one she was ever really in love

with was Ty. And Judy [Garland] was the same way. With her it was Joe Mankiewicz, and later, James Mason."

The male counterpart to Turner was Mickey Rooney, whose rambunctious antics caused Mayer endless trouble. "I've been hearing stories around town," began one typical talking-to. "I hear you've never met a pretty girl that you didn't kiss."

Rooney dodged the implication, and Mayer got serious. "I'm not talking about kissing. I'm talking about fucking. . . . Look, you like being Andy Hardy?"

"Yes, Mr. Mayer."

"Then be—Andy—Hardy."

Rooney demurred, saying what he did on screen was Mayer's business, what he did off screen was his own business, and stormed out of Mayer's office. When Rooney began an affair with Norma Shearer, Mayer went crazy. "You're Andy Hardy!" he bellowed, holding Rooney by the shoulders. "You're the United States! You're a symbol! Behave yourself!"

When Rooney and Ava Gardner got engaged, Mayer again went crazy. "I simply forbid it," he said. "That's all. I forbid it."

"You've got no right to do that," Rooney said. "This is *my* life."

"It's not your life. Not as long as you're working for me. MGM has made your life." Rooney threatened to leave the studio, which he couldn't do. What he could do was become a problem child and hold up the assembly line of Hardy pictures and Mickey and Judy musicals. So Mayer acquiesced to the extent of letting Rooney and Gardner marry, and Rooney acquiesced to the extent of letting Howard Strickling handle the arrangements.

Mayer loved pulling the strings, loved helping people when they were in trouble, and he did it very well. When Carole Lombard found out that Clark Gable was having an affair with Lana Turner, she decided to leave town and go on a bond tour, on which she was killed in a plane crash outside of Las Vegas. The publicist Berdie Abrams had run off to Las Vegas to get married and was at the El Rancho Vegas hotel when she saw Gable and some people from the studio sitting in the lobby. She watched his face crumble when he was told Lombard's body had been found.

After the funeral, Gable returned to the studio to complete *Somewhere I'll Find You* with Turner. Mayer called her in and told her, "You've got to be very patient with him. If his mind should wander, don't be upset, you just be ready at all times. If he wants to come in earlier, you be there before him. If he wants to work through lunch, do it. A lot of the pressure of this picture is going to be riding on your shoulders." Somehow, Gable got through the picture, then enlisted in the air force, where, many believe, he was hoping to get killed.

When the costume designer Irene began missing appointments or appearing for fittings with a handkerchief in front of her face, complaining about incessant bad colds, people began wondering. Mayer would take people aside and quietly explain that Irene was an alcoholic, that she was going through a bad period, but MGM was willing to put up with her because of her ability.

Mainly, though, the studio was fat and happy, and Mayer walked around in seigneurial self-approbation. Even his son-in-law knew how oppressive the atmosphere at Metro could be. In a memo that was dictated but not sent, David Selznick told his father-in-law that "I know how much you hate arrogance in companies and I don't think you have any notion of how much arrogance has grown up at Metro. One of its manifestations is its attitude that it is a privilege to be with Metro, and these people in their right mind would [not] . . . sign with other studios if they had the opportunity to sign with Metro. Please believe me, Dad. This is not the case. Metro simply must understand that there are some people who prefer to be with other studios."

Experienced hands devised ways of working that could ensure their survival within the particular—and peculiar—MGM microcosm. "First," said Donald Ogden Stewart, "you had to try and find out who the star of the picture you were writing was going to be. That's primary. It's very disconcerting to have written something for Joan Crawford and then find out it's actually going to be Lana Turner. Secondly, never tackle a screenplay at the beginning. Let the producer and his writers do a couple of drafts and mess it up. Then, after they've made their mistakes, and they're faced with a shooting date, you can come in and rewrite it and be a big hero. And finally, you had to learn not to let them break your heart."

With such an organization, there was a fair amount of graft in all areas. One New York publicist had a favorite scam that attained the status of legend. He would regularly be assigned to accompany the studio's female stars when they were in New York to make sure they didn't go astray. He would pick them up and take them out to various nightclubs with strict orders to get them back by a certain time. He would arrive at the Stork Club or El Morocco with, say, Lana Turner in tow, then look around for whoever was drinking the best champagne. Walking over to the table full of strangers, he would say, "God, it's so good to see you again, of course you know Lana?"

The stunned host would stutter something about how good it was to see his old friend the movie star, then happily foot the bill for the entire evening's revelry. The next morning, the MGM publicist would write up an expense account and be generously reimbursed for the night on the town he hadn't paid for. He was never caught, and became modestly wealthy from the accumulated expense checks.

Dore Schary was born in Newark in 1905 to Russian immigrants, his father from Riga, his mother from Bialystok. Schary was an industrious Orthodox Jew who had been a *tummler* in the Borscht Belt, working at Grossinger's with Don Hartman and at the Flagler with Moss Hart. Eventually becoming a minor Broadway actor and playwright, Schary arrived in Hollywood as a junior writer in 1932, then fell under the influence of Ginger Rogers's mother, Lela, who produced a play of his at a little theater she ran above Franklin Avenue.

Schary's first tour of duty at MGM was in 1933, writing a script for Marie Dressler and Wallace Beery. Harry Rapf fired him. He was back three years later, and wrote a script called *Boys Town*. Harry Rapf fired him. When *Boys Town* turned out to be a smash hit, Schary was hired back.

A sense of Schary's character can be gauged by his relationship with his wife, Miriam. "He was very devoted to her," said producer and friend Armand Deutsch. "She had been born with a deformed lip, and she looked very peculiar because of it, but he married her and loved her. They had three children. Miriam was . . . strange; she was hampered all her life because of her adjustment to her affliction. She wasn't public at all, wouldn't accompany Schary to things, had nothing to do with studio life. Her domain was her home. Schary was very unusual, different from other executives; he loved his home and children."

He was a man with a benign exterior who cloaked his ambitions with liberal piety. "I thought Dore was my big brother, and he turned out to have clay feet," remembered Irving Brecher. "Do you know what that prick did? I think it was on the Marx Brothers picture *Go West*; I was asked to write it, and they added Dore to the mix. He was my closest friend, so I said fine.

"Schary worked with me for about a week, and I say 'worked' advisedly. He smoked cigarettes and he talked and nothing happened. *Nothing.* I had written an outline on my own and left it on my desk. I went out and the outline wasn't there when I came back. My secretary said that 'Mr. Schary took it.' I go to Jack Cummings's office, and there was Schary, reading my material to Cummings as if he'd written it.

" 'I told him it was yours,' he tried to tell me.

" 'Well, isn't that nice,' I said. I would never, ever have worked with that man again."

Schary was regarded as a young, au courant talent, and as with most of his generation, was part of the left. "If he wasn't a member of the Party himself, he was close to it," said screenwriter Bernard Gordon, later to be blacklisted for his politics. "All of Schary's friends were in the Party. I assumed he was one of those guys."

In 1942, Schary wanted to direct a Paul Gallico story called "Joe Smith, American." When producer John Considine took him to Mayer to get permission to direct, Mayer asked to hear the story. When Schary was finished, Mayer was impressed. "A beautiful story, beautiful story. John, you should buy that story. Now, why do you want to be a director? Why do you want to do a little picture? Why don't you want to do a big picture?"

From there, the conversation evolved into a discussion of the studio's B pictures. Schary thought they could be better, could be used as a laboratory for young directors and writers, apparently not having noticed that that was precisely what they were being used for.

"You can gamble," said the bumptious Schary. "You don't have to worry about finding a big audience because I understand if you just get the cost of your picture back, you're happy. These pictures are made for $250,000, and if you gross $350,000, you've got your money back. Why can't these pictures go out and do $1 million if they're important?"

"You have anything else to say?" asked Mayer. "I'll let you know tomorrow."

The next morning, Schary was told to be in front of the Thalberg Building at 2:00 P.M. Mayer's car was waiting and he invited Schary to accompany him to the racetrack. On the way, he explained that he owned a horse that was running that day. Mayer talked about horses, he talked about his childhood in Canada, he talked about his mother. Mayer's horse lost, but Schary got the impression that it was all right with Mayer; he liked to bet on horses he believed in, and even if they didn't win every time, it was all right as long as they ran a good race. Schary was beginning to understand.

When they got back to Mayer's office, Mayer sat down, shifted his weight to his left hip, and placed his right hand in his pants pocket—a habitual position—and said, "Now, did you mean everything you said yesterday about B pictures?"

"Yes sir, every word."

"All right, you're in charge of all the B pictures in the studio." He went on to explain that Schary could select the stories, pick the cast, the directors, all within the standard budgetary limits, that he would be working with one old studio hand who would ride herd on the money—Harry Rapf. In case of a disagreement between Schary and Rapf, Mayer would arbitrate. "I want to find out whether you know what you're talking about," Mayer said.

It should be noted that Schary's version of these events is the only extant one. Even though he was remarkably consistent about the particulars of his hiring, within the MGM hierarchy the unit was first known as the Rapf unit, then as the Rapf-Schary unit. It would be a violation of Mayer's methods to give authority to a younger, untried man over an older, experienced man. On the other hand, it would have been entirely within Mayer's nature to tell Schary one thing and Rapf another. Schary's version derives from his autobiography, which is outrageously self-serving even by the limited standards of the form, depicting its author as a benevolent Candide always being gifted with one form or another of largesse.

It didn't take long for Schary and Rapf to collide. According to Schary, Harry Rapf bad-mouthed some rushes shot by Jules Dassin and Fred Zinnemann, going so far as to stop the projection. Schary said that creative matters were in his hands, and Rapf said not-so-fast. They waited for Mayer to settle the matter. Mayer settled the matter by screaming at Rapf ("you stupid kike bastard—you ought to kiss this man's shoes . . ."), then fired him, after which Schary rushed to the bathroom to vomit. He had never seen a man gutted by an expert before.

Schary went to Mayer and asked that Rapf be reinstated so long as he didn't interfere with production. According to Maurice Rapf, all of the producers in the Rapf-Schary unit save one signed a petition supporting Rapf and asking that he be reinstated. Whichever version is the truth—and they aren't mutually exclusive—Rapf came back.

Schary's B pictures showed some snap and ambition—*Lassie, Come Home*; *Kid Glove Killer*; *Pilot #5*; *Fingers at the Window*; and *Eyes in the Night* received good reviews, made money (anywhere from $64,000 to $222,000 apiece), and a couple of pictures broke out. *Journey for Margaret* cost only $484,000, and showed a net profit of $561,000, while *Bataan* cost just under $1 million and had a net profit of $1.1 million.

Schary was clearly a rising star, but he would choose to leave the studio after a couple of years, when Mayer killed two pet projects of his, one an allegorical western about Fascism he was writing with Sinclair Lewis, the other an offbeat history of the movies. Schary worked with David Selznick for three years, then took over as production chief at RKO.

Harry Rapf continued the unit for another year and a half, making some good pictures such as *Our Vines Have Tender Grapes* and *The Canterville Ghost*, before the unit was closed down and he was kicked upstairs to the Executive Committee.

Louis was now running the studio as a brilliantly effective CEO. At meetings of the Executive Committee (in 1943, the group included, among others, Eddie Mannix, Al Lichtman, Sam Katz, Ben Goetz, Harry Rapf, Joe Cohn, Dore Schary, Larry Weingarten, James Kevin McGuinness, Pandro Berman, and Joe Pasternak), he occasionally issued fiats, more often guiding and negotiating, especially when it came to contracts with major talent. Occasionally, Mayer would suggest a likely assignment, as when he proposed hiring Sally Benson (*Meet Me in St. Louis*) to write an Andy Hardy picture.

The Executive Committee meetings tended to be structured by star and project, first going through the roster of stars and checking on the material in preparation for each: "WALLACE BEERY: We will require four pictures in the next two years. There should be four projects in work at this time. . . . Mr. Rapf and Mr. Schary are to concentrate on one Beery picture. . . . Ben Goetz is to have Johnny Considine also concentrate on a Beery picture. NOTE: There is to be a report made each week by all of the above producers and executives with regard to the progress being made on BEERY material."

After that, meetings would focus on stories that could be tailored to each personality. Whenever a question came up regarding the suitability of a story, someone was designated to read it to Mayer, although he would give his opinion on material he was familiar with or, in the case of a play or musical, had already seen: "There was mention made that we should consider Noel Coward's *Blithe Spirit*. Mr. Mayer said that if he could get somebody to tell him what the third act would be, he would find a way to buy this property."

Careers were sustained ("We decided to exercise the option on Fred Zinnemann") and ended ("The option on Bobby Readick will not be exercised") and sometimes hung in the balance, as in a December 1942 session, when possible replacements for Myrna Loy in *The Thin Man* series were discussed (the general favorite seemed to be Marsha Hunt).

General business decisions were made, sometimes bad ones, as when the Theater Guild requested an option on an MGM property called *Green Grow the Lilacs*, which they were thinking of turning into a musical with Rodgers and Hart. MGM said they could have the property for what the studio had invested: $35,370.64. With Oscar Hammerstein replacing Lorenz Hart, *Green Grow the Lilacs* became *Oklahoma!*

Mayer was both negotiator and cajoler, looking at film for casting decisions ("It was suggested that Robert Walker who is now appearing in [*Bataan*] should be considered for the leading role in *See Here Private Hargrove*. L. K. Sidney is to show Mr. Mayer the test of Robert Walker"), and coercing touchy stars: "Mr. Mayer is to talk to Miss Crawford regarding *Reunion*. . . . It was decided to assign Jules Dassin as the director for this vehicle if Mr. Mayer could get Miss Crawford's consent to this proposition."

When the necessity arose, Mayer could be stern ("It was suggested by Mr. Mayer that the Vice Presidents re-examine their producers' situations very closely with a view to determination of those who are not clicking."). In the same meeting, he complained about the lack of quick action about which producer would undertake the best-selling Pearl Buck novel *Dragon Seed*. (Pandro Berman took the fall, resulting in one of the worst of all MGM pictures.)

Mayer was concerned with getting the pictures made, but also with making them well. During one meeting, after Harry Rapf said that he didn't want the cost of a particular picture to go over $625,000, Mayer spoke up and "cautioned Mr. Rapf that in the event there is an additional cost to improve the picture, to bring it to his attention."

And at times there was harsh negotiating: "Nelson Eddy asked permission to do a weekly broadcast which would involve his being absent from the studio on Wednesday afternoon of each week. Mr. Mayer was to talk to him and decide whether to ask Nelson Eddy to reduce his contract salary by $1,000 per week for the present term of his contract or giving him the alternative of granting this permission if Eddy gives our company one half of the proceeds of his broadcast monies."

Clearly, Eddy wasn't as well liked as Lionel Barrymore. When the sponsor of Barrymore's radio program wanted to move the broadcast to 4:30 P.M. California time, cutting into the actor's workday, all the studio asked in return was a sixty- or ninety-second commercial for a Metro picture on the show each week. (Occasionally, there are surprises to be found in the minutes of the story meetings; in February 1943, for instance, the Rapf-Schary unit was dutifully considering Isak Dinesen's "The Heroine" "because of Garbo's interest in this material. However, the unit showed no interest in the story.")

Everybody on the Executive Committee was cognizant of the Alpha male.

Occasionally Mayer would snap the leash: "Mr. Mayer thinks that we should bear down on using romantic stories of the type which in the past were laid abroad or in mythical kingdoms in connection with our need for pictures with South American backgrounds."

Nineteen forty-three and 1944 saw the usual tussle about a renewal of Mayer's contract that was complicated by extraneous factors. The wartime income tax was leaving people in Mayer's income category with very little to show for their immense salaries. There was a movement afoot to institute a pension plan for all Loew's employees, which would require some sacrifice on the part of the corporate upper echelon. Mayer and eight other executives finally agreed to hefty salary cuts. In 1941, Mayer had made $704,425.60 and in 1943 $1.138 million. Mayer's salary would decline to $454,266 by 1949, compared to $197,600 for Harry Cohn or $182,000 for Jack Warner (both of whom had ownership participation in their studios, which Mayer did not)—but shortly thereafter he agreed to cap his salary and bonus at $300,000 a year.

However much money he was making, his spiritual prerogatives exceeded his material income. He was now recognized by both friends and enemies as the most powerful man in Hollywood, as well as its primary spokesman.

Mayer's instincts about Greer Garson had been proven correct. *Mrs. Miniver, Random Harvest,* and *The Valley of Decision* all grossed more than $8 million and made profits of over $3 million apiece. *Mrs. Parkington* and *Madame Curie* weren't far behind. L.B. took personal charge of many aspects of her career. He wouldn't let writers speak to her. When a writer was assigned to a new Garson film, he was ordered to watch previous Garson pictures in order to replicate what had been successful. Mayer knew what he wanted and it was already hermetically sealed in the close-ups that permeated her MGM pictures.

Good pictures made money, and even absurdly bad pictures didn't lose as much as they should have. For the 1944–45 season, twenty-six of the studio's twenty-nine releases were profitable, and, of the three failures, only King Vidor's Technicolor production *An American Romance* was a complete debacle (a cost of $2.4 million, a loss of $1.7 million).

On August 27, 1944, Mayer had his first taste of physical disability when he was thrown by a horse and broke his pelvis. The groom hadn't put a check rein on, and as he rode the animal, Mayer cried out to his friends, "He hasn't got the bit in his mouth." The horse heaved up and tossed him in the air. Mayer remained conscious after he hit the ground, saying only "He did it!" After a brief scare over a blood clot in his lung, it became clear that the injury wasn't life-threatening and he would soon be walking and riding again.

But he was laid up in traction for a long time, and the stars at the studio competed to see who could bring him the largest supply of chicken soup as he recuperated. He didn't get back to his desk in Culver City until Christmas, the longest layoff, voluntary or enforced, he'd ever had.

The flush times made even hiring British filmmaker Alexander Korda, Louis's sole corporate error of this period, forgivable. At first, it seemed like a marriage of convenience. Although the two had never cared for each other—"Now they've made the son of a bitch a Lord," exclaimed Mayer when Korda was knighted—Korda, a gifted producer/hustler, had come to the end of his current financial string, and L.B. was going to need an experienced filmmaker to run the MGM British subsidiary. According to Korda's nephew Michael, Nick Schenck agreed to the deal solely because he thought it would fail and he could then use it in his "lifelong struggle to destroy Mayer."

As headquarters for the new postwar MGM British, Loew's purchased the Elstree Studios and one hundred surrounding acres of land. From the beginning, MGM British in Borehamwood had a reputation for glamour and luxury. The studio was outfitted with greenhouses and restaurants good enough to attract the cream of the English stage, not to mention the American stars who would be part of an ongoing corporate lend-lease program.

The plan was for MGM British to eventually equal the Culver City branch. Korda announced future projects calculated to endear him to his boss: *The Hardy Family in England,* and a set-in-England trip for Dr. Kildare. He signed Robert Graves, Graham Greene, James Hilton, and Evelyn Waugh to contracts, and announced a film adaptation of *War and Peace,* among many others.

By the end of 1944, MGM was getting nervous about Korda's spending, and Korda was getting bored with Mayer's supervision. He hated the dinner parties he felt obliged to attend when in Los Angeles; he hated Mayer's peremptory monologues, which tended to revolve around how he had always been right, and Thalberg, Nick Schenck, Sam Goldwyn, and his sons-in-law had always been wrong, not to mention craven and disloyal. At the same time, Korda's own need for Mayer and company had lessened; he had sold his United Artists stock—for which he had paid nothing—for $900,000.

Korda left MGM British at the end of 1945. In a little over two years of profligate operation—he offered the Boulting brothers a $1,000-a-week retainer just so he could have first call on their services after the war!—Korda spent a million pounds of Loew's money and completed exactly one film, a pleasant but minor effort with Robert Donat and Deborah Kerr called *Perfect Strangers*. L.B. would always believe he had been taken. "What's Korda's recipe for an omelet?" he asked rhetorically one day. "First, steal two eggs."

MGM's fascination with England would be largely financial. As of August 1947, 75 percent of the English earnings of foreign films had to stay in England—a devastating blow to Hollywood, withholding as it did three-fourths of the value of its largest export market. MGM had to spend the money in England, so it developed the idea of importing American stars and an American director to mesh with the English crew.

MGM British wouldn't fully kick in until the early 1950s, just about the time Mayer left the studio, when movies like *Ivanhoe, Mogambo,* and *Knights of the Round Table* contributed major profits to the balance sheet. By then, Ben Goetz, the brother of William Goetz, was in charge, and had a suite at Claridge's, a fabulous salary and expense account, but, as cinematographer Freddie Young remembered, "What he didn't know about films would fill a book."

Greer Garson's ascendance made it easy to say goodbye to Norma Shearer, her predecessor as the official MGM Great Lady. Shearer's last two pictures, *Her Cardboard Lover* and *We Were Dancing*, were both resounding commercial and critical failures. "Norma made bad choices in material," said Janet Leigh, a friend of Shearer's in later years. "She was offered *Mrs. Miniver* and she had the ego thing of not wanting to play the mother of a twenty-year-old."

Shearer took her Loew's, Inc. stock and retired. Mayer promptly moved Greer Garson into Shearer's lavishly appointed dressing room and gave her a $30,000 bonus to go along with her new seven-year, no-option contract at $4,000 a week. As long as Mayer was at MGM, nothing was too good for Garson; he even gave her a $5,000 Lincoln Continental convertible and compared her to his favorite horse, Busher, as "a classy filly who runs the track according to orders and comes home with blue ribbons!"

The Queen was dead; long live the Queen.

As for Shearer, "She didn't talk about Thalberg a lot," said Janet Leigh. "She was very happy with Marti [Arrouge, her second husband], who was a wonderful man. She would reminisce once in a while about the studio and Thalberg—how he watched every shot *with* her, every shot *of* her. It must have been a wonderful secure feeling for her. This wasn't in terms of regretting the present, but in the sense that all that was a time that had been and was no more. There was no Norma Desmond thing with her."

While Thalberg was alive, Shearer had respected and admired Mayer but had been wary of him; then had come the period of veiled antagonism because Shearer felt Mayer and the studio had been trying to cheat her out of her rightful percentage of MGM's films. Later on, as she came to contemplate her career and its untimely end, and as Mayer would himself have to cope with changing times and a loss of footing, they would cling together as mutual survivors of years they both realized were the best of their lives.

The chemistry of the studio was further altered in 1943 when Woody Van Dyke passed away at fifty-four. "He was finishing up a picture [*Journey for Margaret*] and recruiting for the Marines at Camp Pendleton," remembered his secretary, June Caldwell. "At Christmas time, he came down with pneumonia and never really recovered. He died on February 5. There was a huge group of men who worked on his pictures, and they were all hysterical when they found out Woody was dead. He was a wonderful man, a gentleman."

By war's end, Mayer and his studio stood securely at the pinnacle of Hollywood. The superb roster of stars, the deluxe budgets that bought the production values of MGM pictures, were the reason for Louis's success. Soon they would be the primary reasons for his failure.

L.B.'s preference was always for strong women, as long as he didn't have to live with them. Jessie Marmorston fit the bill perfectly. She was born in Kiev in 1900 and came to America when she was six. Marmorston's mother died a year later, which made her decide to be a doctor. She got a scholarship to the University of Buffalo and graduated from medical school in 1924, one of two women in her class.

After an initially unsuccessful marriage, in 1933 she married David Perla, a pathologist at Montefiore Hospital in New York and a childhood friend of Irving Thalberg's, with the same damaged heart valve from rheumatic fever. The two couples became friendly. Perla and his wife were the only people with whom Thalberg could discuss his heart problems. When they gave him a first edition of Freud's collected works for his thirty-first birthday, Thalberg wrote them that "Freud has helped me to understand myself and given me courage to confront my particular future, which in the past I had tried to block out." (Presumably a reference to confronting the reality of an early death.)

David Perla died suddenly in June 1940, just as his friend Thalberg had. Shortly thereafter, Marmorston's daughter Norma was diagnosed with asthma. A drier climate was needed, so Marmorston found a clinical appointment at the USC Medical School, and moved to California in the summer of 1943.

Mayer met Marmorston in the midst of a shocking tragedy. Marmorston had begun dating Larry Weingarten, who was a regular at a Sunday poker game with other MGM producers. After a few hours of the boys playing cards, the wives and girlfriends would arrive and everybody would go out to dinner. On October 6, 1942, in the middle of the card game, Bernie Hyman collapsed and died of a massive coronary.

The first of the women to arrive was Marmorston, who sized up the situation immediately. The men were stunned, frozen into place. Marmorston knew Hyman's wife would be arriving soon, and didn't want her to see her husband in his present condition. "We need to take Mr. Hyman upstairs, wash him and change his clothes," she told the butler.

They carried Hyman upstairs, and Marmorston was washing and smoothing his distorted face and combing his hair when she realized that a man with piercing eyes was watching her from the doorway.

"Please go out and close the door, we're busy," she snapped.

"Don't you know who I am? I'm Louis Mayer."

"I don't care who you are, you have no business here. Go downstairs!"

Mayer did as he was told. "Who is that woman?" he asked the stunned men at the base of the stairs.

"That's my doctor," said Larry Weingarten.

"I want her to be my doctor," said Mayer.

Soon after Hyman's funeral, L.B. invited Marmorston to lunch and she took him on as a patient. It was a most unusual relationship. "She saw him almost every day," said Elizabeth Horowitz, Marmorston's daughter. "His car would pick her up from our house at 613 North Cañon Drive. She might stay fifteen minutes, or a half an hour. Sometimes she would give him a B_{12} shot, something for a pickup. I don't think she ever sent him a bill, although I'm not saying he didn't pay for her services. He gave her a car, for instance, and once she was Larry's wife, and in that world, she had a huge practice."

Marmorston was fascinated by Mayer—the sheer emotional size of the man dwarfed anybody she had ever encountered, or ever would again. She intuited that his sex drive was very strong, and remained so even after his cracked pelvis in 1944 and a minor prostate operation.

"His vision was phenomenal; his brain was terrific," Marmorston would recall. "He had powers of logic in making deductions which had no basis in scientific techniques, which came about in the oddest way, but his conclusions were sound."

Marmorston believed that his greatest hunger, his overwhelming desire, was to "belong. He wanted to be a great American." She was amazed by the way he studied people and adjusted his method of handling them according to their personalities and needs. And she quickly realized that his favorite daughter was Edie—she was everything good and tasteful, always said yes to her man. For a man of Mayer's tastes, she was the ideal woman.

L.B. was intensely conscious of his own ugliness and hated it; he believed he looked like a Jewish caricature. What he wanted was to be tall and hand-some; his girlfriends and second wife would not be drop-dead gorgeous, but they would all be tall and sleek—everything he wasn't.

For Mayer, Marmorston was a personality like his mother—a woman who accepted him, loved him, and defended him. He had the MGM wardrobe de-partment design her clothes and told her that he was remembering her in his will. That seemed good enough for Marmorston.

In February 1945, Marmorston married Larry Weingarten and became a member of the extended MGM family. Their house became a happy place full of scientists and people from the movie industry and various waifs whom Mar-morston would take in. A few years later, when Nancy Davis left Benny Thau, devastating the already somewhat depressed executive, he became a perpetual visitor to the house, and the composer Bronislau Kaper spent four weeks there recuperating from gall bladder surgery.

Beyond taking his blood pressure and dispensing appropriate pills, Mar-morston mainly listened to L.B. vent—about Irene and Edie, about their hus-bands, about problems at the studio, about his guilt regarding Margaret. He used Marmorston as a sounding board, a therapist without portfolio.

"It was a very deep friendship," said Elizabeth Horowitz. "He always called her 'Doctor,' and she always called him 'Mr. Mayer.' " L.B. became a regular at Weingarten's parties, and Marmorston's daughter kept her eyes open. "He was a formal little man. I found him intimidating. He had a very powerful person-ality. He was quite serious and talked to me as an adult. Louis was little but not little. He was like David Sarnoff—not tall, but he filled the room.

"My mother liked him and she also respected him. One of the things that drove her and motivated her was his reputation. When he fell in love with Ginny Simms, she tried to influence him not to pursue it, to break it up. She felt it wasn't appropriate. He'd had a wife for forty years, had been identified as an eminent Jew, and he could do better. Not that there was anything wrong with Ginny Simms, but she was much younger and she could be misinter-preted. And because of my mother's personality, she gave Mayer the sense that she had his best interests at heart.

"In those years, the dinner parties were sensational. Cedric Gibbons would come with his wife, Hazel Brooks, and Mayer and all sorts of people. We had a projection room, and people would come to see screenings. I had never believed our life could be like that. I would say to myself, 'Remember these days, it won't be here forever.' But I thought that the world as it was constructed around that industry would always be like that. I always believed MGM would be there."

Mayer continued to be very much involved with his daughters' lives. There were still problems with finagling a proper position for Bill Goetz. To all appearances, Bill and Edie maintained a rock-solid marriage, although he had extramarital relationships with, among others, Joan Bennett. If Edie knew about Bill's dalliances, she never let on.

Darryl Zanuck returned to Fox after his service in the war, and found that Goetz, who had been running things in his absence, had redecorated his office, the swimming pool, barbershop, and steam room. Zanuck's boudoir, a room off his office where he bedded starlets, had been turned into a filing room. More important, Bill Goetz had inveigled some of the creative heavyweights around the lot (Nunnally Johnson, Joe Mankiewicz) to write letters to the board of directors saying that they had never been happier than under his own leadership, implying that they had been miserable peons under Zanuck.

The attempt at undercutting Zanuck failed, and he wouldn't walk onto the lot until Goetz left. Louis sighed, advised his son-in-law to resign, and offered him $10,000 a week to come to MGM. Goetz said no, and L.B. stewed until he went out with the Goetzes to Preston Sturges's restaurant, the Players, where he asked Edie to dance. Once they got on the floor, he put his hands on his hips and said, "So you don't want your husband to work for me?" Edie didn't know what he was talking about, whereupon he informed her of his offer.

On the way home, Edie asked her husband if it was all true. "Yes," he replied. "If I took the job, the first thing I would do is fire your father!" Mayer wrote Goetz a check for $1 million so that he could go into independent production with an outfit called International Pictures, which sent David Selznick into a major snit.

Selznick, under the impression he had some sort of copyright on the word "International," fired off an enraged memo to L.B. in which he called the copycatting "pretty poor thanks for what I had done for Bill. . . . Clearly, he chose to forget what I did for him at the urgings of yourself, of Spyros and Charlie [Skouras] and of Joe Schenck, when he took over Twentieth Century, and I set him up with 3 properties and with cash. . . .

"I have learned that Bill has a short memory, and that among his attributes is not the grace of gratitude. I have learned completely, and often, to my sorrow, how cold-blooded and selfish he can be. I have heard often of the extremes to which he goes to run me down on any and every possible occasion . . . [which] I understand thoroughly . . . is born of envy."

Selznick closed by informing his father-in-law that properties he had dealt to RKO (*Notorious, The Spiral Staircase, The Farmer's Daughter*) could have been handed to Goetz, "if he had only been the possessor of a little more decency and a little more character."

It's probable that Mayer calmed him down by invoking noblesse oblige; at any rate, Selznick never resorted to ads castigating Goetz in the trades as he threatened, and Goetz retained the name International.

Goetz's venture would prove more or less unsuccessful. International's roster of pictures—*Along Came Jones, Belle of the Yukon, Temptation*, and Orson Welles's *The Stranger*, among others—typically included unsuccessful films with major stars and interesting artistic failures. Eventually, International merged with Universal, with Bill as president, meaning that Louis now had a de facto piece of yet another studio.

Bill was now a popular man about town, with many friends who were kept amused by what one friend characterized as a "hard-nosed, sometimes cruel wit. He was a great adapter to life, a quality he had reason to put to daily use." His sister-in-law, Irene, was not amused; as far as she was concerned, he was "a schlep with the filthiest mouth in town."

Part of Bill's adaptive brilliance was in coping with his wife. Armand Deutsch, a good friend of Goetz's, felt that Edie's personality was that of an old-time movie star—Norma Desmond. The Goetz dinner invitations were the number-one invitation in town, and Edie worked at her position with a startling tenacity. Edie's house was furnished as if for a magazine shoot. The appointments were perfection, and the Goetzes employed a Cordon Bleu chef. Her regular guests were the A list: Gable, Power, Niven, Sinatra, Colbert, Stewart—a smattering of top executives, all of whom put up with what Deutsch called "her Machiavellian character" for the sake of Bill's considerable charm and the spectacular Impressionist art collection the couple was amassing.

It seemed as if there was nothing MGM could not do. In 1945 alone, it ambitiously undertook the construction of two of New York's greatest landmarks. For *The Clock*, the studio re-created Grand Central Terminal, while for *Weekend at the Waldorf*, a loose remake of *Grand Hotel*, the studio designed replicas of the hotel's two main lobbies, as well as its Park Avenue façade and entrance hall, guest suites and corridors, and a multitude of offices and rooms. The Waldorf sets occupied 120,000 square feet; the central lobby alone was constructed of walls of Oregon maple burl, trimmed with black marble pilasters and ebony columns with nickel bronze capitals.

Because of this kind of conspicuous construction, the MGM films of this period have an overstuffed, cushy luxuriousness, like an old sofa you sink into to such an extent it's hard to get up. Not stimulating, not innovative, but, if you're in the right mood, astoundingly comfortable.

Like the Pope in Rome, Mayer's opinions were unassailable. When Frank Capra, George Stevens, and William Wyler formed Liberty Productions, Sidney Franklin went to Mayer and told him that MGM should bring the operation to Culver City. No, no, Mayer said; those fellows could break a company. "Let's keep it as it is," he would tell people over and over. "Let's make money." As for smart, innovative directors he would say, "We've got to use these fellows who think, but you can't let them monkey with the system."

One day an eighteen-year-old MGM musician named André Previn was given a ride in Mayer's limo. Mayer asked the group in the car, "Did any of you gentlemen go to the Hollywood Bowl last night?"

Only Previn and Mayer had seen a remarkable performance by Jascha Heifetz.

"What was that weird thing he played?" asked Mayer. "Do you happen to know the name of it?"

Previn assumed Mayer was referring to Sibelius's Violin Concerto, but before he could answer, Mayer continued talking. "No, you can't possibly know, nobody's ever heard of that thing before, he shouldn't play pieces no one's ever heard of, it's ridiculous. Anyway, that's one of the reasons he's not a success."

Previn's breath was sucked out of his body. What could the man mean? Heifetz not a success? Years later, mulling over the moment, he realized what Mayer had meant: Heifetz didn't make movies, specifically MGM movies; therefore Heifetz was not a success.

Still, Mayer had his remarkable eye for talent. He went after the young Montgomery Clift, but the actor didn't want to sign a seven-year contract. Louis finally got him to sign a six-month contract at the end of 1945. Clift found Mayer to have "dashes of Jed Harris lies and Georgie Jessel schmaltz. He told me Leo the Lion is the father of one big happy unsuspended family. And I too will be happy . . . but don't you think you should stay two years and give us four months notice when you want to do a play. . . . They keep throwing Greer Garson in my face—nostrils and all—as a perfect example of what . . . a career can be. Ye Gods!" In later years, Clift could do a good imitation of Mayer in his office at MGM, "like a gangster on a throne," according to Clift.

While new talent struggled for purchase, old talent began to seem slightly shopworn. The studio didn't seem to know what to do with Myrna Loy; it was paying her $3,500 a week, but she wasn't really given anything to do. *Sea of Grass* was planned for her, but when the starting date was postponed, Loy called Benny Thau to find out about the new schedule only to be told that Kate Hepburn had been slotted into the picture. And because of Louis's long-standing dislike of loan-outs, they wouldn't allow anybody else to use her either; when Noel Coward wanted her for Elvira in the movie of *Blithe Spirit*, MGM said no.

Finally, Loy asked for a release from her contract. After much hemming and hawing, Mayer agreed to let her go, provided she would return for any *Thin Man* movies MGM decided to make. She went on to star in a series of hits for other studios—*The Best Years of Our Lives*, and *Cheaper by the Dozen* among them.

L.B. and Sidney Franklin made the decision to reactivate *The Yearling*. This time Franklin handed the picture to Clarence Brown, who would remember that "a film like that, with such enormous logistics, requires ingenuity more than anything else." Brown would retain the second unit footage shot from the abortive effort four years earlier, but he felt the picture had to be entirely recast, especially the part of the young boy, Jody. Brown elected to do most of the work himself. He traveled through the South, visiting schools in seven cities. The teachers thought the quiet, graying man sitting in the back of their classrooms was a building inspector.

"The first time I saw Claude Jarman Jr. he was in the fifth grade at a Nashville school," said Brown. "He was taking down a Valentine display. We talked a bit after class, and I went on to the rest of the cities, but Claude stayed with me. I went back to Nashville to convince Claude and his parents to come back to Hollywood with me."

MGM shipped forty tons of equipment to Florida, and a two-acre zoo was created to house the animals needed for the film. Production began again in the late spring of 1945, and Sidney Franklin found that the painful, abortive 1941 effort had been a preview of coming attractions.

"It was even more of a nightmare than the first attempt," Sidney Franklin would write. Although Brown was, along with Victor Fleming, the premier director on the lot, he was not immune from constant supervision from his producer, who, because of his own directorial past, seemed to regard Brown as his proxy director.

The Florida location was a nightmare of heat and a haze from wildfires that made it extremely difficult to get good Technicolor photography. Since Jarman had never acted before, Brown reverted to his silent film training. "Every word, every action, every gesture was manipulated," said Brown. "The boy was smart enough to do just what I told him. For the hysterics when he has to shoot the deer, I asked him to imagine his mother was dying.

"We actually had an assembly line of pregnant does. When a fawn got too big, we'd simply bring another one in, and since we were in actual production for [a long time] we needed quite a few."

Brown's engineering training was less important than the analytical traits that led him to engineering school in the first place. For the scene that introduces the yearling, the camera tracks with Jody until he comes across the fawn lying in the grass. But the hot lights needed for Technicolor meant that the ground was too warm for the deer to be comfortable, so the fawn would always be standing by the time the camera got to it. After what Brown remembered as six unsuccessful takes, he thought of the solution: a large cake of ice was buried and covered with a thin layer of sand on the desired spot. The fawn immediately lay down right on top of it. "Those are the things that make motion pictures what they are," remembered the director. "You have to be damned ingenious, on your toes all the time."

"Brown's reputation was that he was hard on his crew," remembered Claude Jarman Jr., "but he never asked more of them than he was willing to give himself. Clarence adopted a parental role; I would spend weekends at his home, and practically every evening we would talk about the next day's scenes. It wasn't just a nine-to-five job."

The film was made on an insanely elongated schedule; location work in Ocala and Silver Springs went from April to August of 1945, then Lake Arrowhead in California for three weeks. After that, work proceeded in the studio until January 1946, then returned to Florida for pickup shots and some retakes. Production wrapped in February, and editing and scoring took the rest of the year. The film premiered in December.

MGM carried the cost of the picture as $3.8 million, which undoubtedly included Victor Fleming's first try. The picture was MGM's highest grosser of the year, pulling in $7.6 million worldwide, but only earning profits of $451,000 because of its high costs. Despite the power of Margaret Booth, Brown insisted he edited the film himself, and he probably did; the rhythm is different, more languid, poetic—a child's reverie of his own lost innocence.

Jarman had been paid $600 a week during production on *The Yearling*, and Mayer rewarded him with a $25,000 bonus after the film was released. "Mayer *shepherded* everything," said Jarman. "I had my own tutor, my own makeup man, my own wardrobe man. Everywhere you went, you were surrounded by the same people. You had a family that was looking out for you. He did that, that was the atmosphere he created. For the female stars, it had to be heaven, a warm, fuzzy feeling.

"He genuinely felt he had a moral standard he wanted to achieve in the studio's films. Certain things he would stand for, and certain things he wouldn't. There was no one else remotely like him among the other studio heads."

Mayer could not always articulate what attracted him to one performer while another would leave him cold. He just knew.

"What Mayer had was courage," remembered Janet Leigh. "The buck stopped there. Today, nothing happens without a corporate world conference before a decision can be reached. But when Mayer made a decision, right or wrong, that was it."

Leigh—real name Jeanette Morrison—had been brought to MGM by Norma Shearer, who had seen a photograph of her and was struck by her beauty. The studio was preparing a Hatfield and McCoy picture to be called *The Romance of Rosy Ridge*, for which another young actress was scheduled. "She had done several pictures and she was on the rise," remembered Leigh. "And she was also going with Eddie Mannix, as I understood it. So she was a shoo-in."

But the producer and director and Lillian Burns weren't too sure about the proposed casting, and they had Leigh read a scene for them, which led to a screen test for the part. The test was shown to Mayer on a Saturday night at his house. After he looked at both tests, he simply said, "Well, we go with the new one."

Mayer wanted to meet his new star, so she was brought to his office. "I was all gaga and nervous and scared to death, and I entered this big, long, huge office, with secretaries and this very small man sitting behind this huge desk.

"I sat down and he asked a couple of perfunctory questions—welcome to our family, hope you're happy with us. And then he started to talk about Busher. And I nodded and I kept nodding, even though I didn't know who the hell Busher was.

"So we said goodbye and as I leave the office, I turned to my agent and said, 'Who's Busher?'

" 'His racehorse.' "

In 1947, Irene Mayer Selznick thought it might be interesting to go into the theater. No, no, said L.B., join me at the studio. You want a big job? You can have it. Worried about nepotism? Then start at the bottom. "Why do you think people are in the theater? I'm surprised anyone as intelligent as you can't figure it out. They're there in order to get what you already have, which is position and opportunity in Hollywood. You have friends, you're well-known, you're respected. You've got everything right here. Name one person that didn't wind up broke in the theater." He finally admitted that he needed her; that he was alone and needed Irene's companionship.

But Irene, now separated from Selznick, didn't want to segue from one supreme egotist to another. She needed to be her own woman, so she left for New York. L.B. managed to forgive her; he stepped in and began to broker his daughter's divorce from David Selznick.

Blood is thicker than anything.

The last star to be discovered and built by Mayer was a young tenor from Philadelphia named Alfred Arnold Cocozza, who was rechristened Mario Lanza. Lanza's manager had approached Ida Koverman with some acetates of the singer's audition recordings for RCA. Koverman liked what she heard and played the recordings for Mayer. He was impressed, and then even more impressed when he saw pictures of the singer. Koverman persuaded the management of the Hollywood Bowl to book Lanza during their subscription summer season as a sort of working audition.

Mayer and Koverman both attended the Bowl concert on August 28, 1947. Two days later, Lanza auditioned on the recording stage at MGM. Standing behind a curtain, Lanza sang "Che gelida manina" and Victor Herbert's "Thine Alone." Then Mayer stood up and said, "Gentlemen, you've heard the voice. Now I want you to meet the singer."

Mayer told Lanza the studio would make him a singing Clark Gable, and he was signed for piddling money: $15,000 for his first movie, $25,000 for the second, and $30,000 for the third. With a $10,000 signing bonus, Lanza was handed to Joe Pasternak, but the studio spent an entire year grooming him — production on *That Midnight Kiss* didn't begin until early November 1948. That year involved vocal training, a new diet, a new hairstyle — Pasternak said his hair looked like a horsehair mattress that had burst its seams—and a new wardrobe that emphasized his height rather than his weight.

The tenor quickly proved himself to be among the most obnoxious people ever to walk onto the Culver City lot. He was crude and vulgar—he referred to Ethel Barrymore as "that old bitch"—and he was an egomaniac who squabbled with old MGM hands about how they did their jobs.

But Mayer loved him—"Mr. Mayer would cry every time Mario sang," said Joe Pasternak—and MGM had yet another star on its hands. For his second picture, *The Toast of New Orleans,* MGM gave him a bonus of $25,000 to accompany his contractual salary of the same amount. Mayer had to call Lanza to his office on a regular basis to keep him in some semblance of order, and the singer, who was essentially a big, petulant baby, would get a combination of the soothing Daddy and the angry disciplinarian, emphasis on the former.

L.B. also took the lead in signing some other new blood, including Marge and Gower Champion, whom he went to see several times when they performed at the Mocambo. "We signed with MGM because they gave us a two-picture-a-year deal, and that had to do with Mr. Mayer as well," remembered Marge Champion. "Arthur Freed wanted us very much, and I already knew a lot of people at MGM. It was the ideal studio for us. We were allowed to do everything that we could fit in between the two pictures—Vegas, New York shows, anything at all. Except for television—absolutely no television."

While Cedric Gibbons and Margaret Booth had always been first among equals in terms of the MGM departments, they now had a new addition to their ranks. Johnny Green, the exuberantly egotistical composer of "Body and Soul" and "I Cover the Waterfront," took over the music department. "We want the greatest music department that there has ever been in this entire business," said Mayer with typical expansiveness. "The greatest orchestra and the greatest staff, and we want it managed with the utmost order and system."

"Mr. Mayer, it's going to cost a lot of money to have that kind of a department."

"Well, we've got a lot of money," replied Mayer. Green quickly proved himself as brilliant an administrator as he was a musician, which is not to say he was pleasant. "Johnny Green was a prick," asserted John Waxman, the son of Franz Waxman and the stepson of the Freed unit's Lela Simone. "He was a screamer, always yelling, and he was pedantic. Everyone that knew him hated him."

The first thing Green did was fire twenty-eight of the fifty people in the MGM orchestra, some of whom were just a year or two away from qualifying

for their pensions. A livid Mayer called Green into his office and began by saying Green was cruel, Green was ruthless, and so on.

"The heart of the music operation here is the orchestra," explained Green,
"and every week that that orchestra sits here you are getting poor quality at a dis-
proportionate cost." Green offered to resign with no obligations on the part of
the company.

"You're a pretty feisty guy, aren't you?" said Mayer.

"I'm a killer, Mr. Mayer."

L.B. sat for a minute, then made his decision. "Okay, you run it, and may
God help you."

Green set about replacing the people he had fired, and began rebuilding
Stage 1, the recording stage, at a cost of $250,000. "Johnny was brilliant at using
the system," said John Waxman. "He would call up Richard Rodgers and say,
'I'm doing this concert at the Hollywood Bowl and I want to play something
from *Oklahoma!*' And Rodgers would say, 'But the parts are for a twenty-eight-
person pit orchestra.' And Green would have him send the music anyway, and
Johnny would have his arrangers sketch it out for a hundred pieces, and it didn't
cost Johnny or the Hollywood Bowl anything. All courtesy of L. B. Mayer.

"By doing this, Johnny gave Broadway music a transition to the concert
hall. And with all of his *mishegoss*, he was a great administrator. He hired some
terrific people—Miklós Rózsa, David Raksin, André Previn, Conrad Salinger.
There never would have been a Bernard Herrmann without Johnny Green;
when he was head of music at CBS, he went out of his way to hire Herrmann.

"I remember one day, Johnny called me up and began yelling and screaming about something I'd done, and in mid-sentence he stopped. 'You know,
your dad isn't here, so somebody has to Dutch-Uncle you. Someone has to yell
at you so you'll know what to do.' And he was right."

The studio's greatest strength—its monolithic competence at turning out
smoothly machined parts that could be assembled to make a movie—was
about to become its biggest problem. In the immediate aftermath of World War
II, the studio seemed unsure about tactics—should it make more and cheaper
pictures, or fewer and more expensive ones? In 1945–46, MGM made twenty-
seven pictures at an average cost of $1.68 million; in 1946–47, it made only
twenty, but the average cost had lurched upward to $2.28 million.

Costs were rising, and the net was going down: a profit of $9.7 million in
1945–46 declined to a minor $1.8 million in 1946–47. Something seemed radi-

cally amiss. In 1947–48, sixteen of the studio's twenty-five releases lost money, including such major disasters as *Summer Holiday*, *The Pirate*, and *Desire Me*. Paramount made *The Lost Weekend*, Goldwyn made *The Best Years of Our Lives*, Fox was making *Gentleman's Agreement*, but MGM had no similarly adult offering. The studio wasn't keeping up with the times, and it was showing in its profits. For the fiscal year 1947–48, MGM lost money for the first time in its history—twenty-five pictures made at an average cost of $2.24 million amassed a loss of $6.5 million.

After 1945, the memorable MGM movies tended to be musicals, or exuberant adventures like *The Three Musketeers*—essentially a musical without songs. The studio tried to come up with the bleak thrillers posterity would call film noir, which were increasingly popular, but MGM values were simply not compatible with noir.

The success of Paramount's *Double Indemnity* compelled MGM to step up efforts to produce *The Postman Always Rings Twice*, which it had bought for $25,000 in 1934 but had been forbidden to make by Joe Breen's office. Paramount made inquiries about buying the property, so MGM felt entitled to begin the scripting process around October of 1944. After seven months of back and forth with the Breen office, production got underway in May 1945. Many MGM noirs—*Lady in the Lake*, *The Bribe*—were grim misfires, but the comparatively interesting adaptation of *The Postman Always Rings Twice*, with its unforgettable entrance for Lana Turner in an all-white costume exposing her midriff, was a big hit, with costs of $1.68 million against a world gross of $5 million and a $1.6 million profit. Mayer hated the movie, telling Carey Wilson that he was sorry the studio had made it and that he regarded it as an "evil" film.

There were certain aspects of movies Mayer still regarded as inviolable. He was sitting in the projection room with director-star Robert Montgomery watching rushes for *Lady in the Lake* when a close-up of Audrey Totter came on.

Mayer jabbed Montgomery in the ribs. "Why does her hair look awful?"

"Well, in the previous shot which we haven't done yet she's awakened in the middle of the night," explained Montgomery.

"I don't care if she's coming out of the toilet, her hair can't look like that."

It had been more than ten years since Mayer made precisely the same objection to a close-up of Myrna Loy. Life at MGM.

The conservative business practices of Nick Schenck had helped keep the company profitable during the Depression. But during World War II, record numbers of people flocked to movie theaters, and the companies with the most theaters—Paramount, Fox, and Warners—made the most money. Loew's still had only 135 theaters compared to other companies' five or six hundred (Warners and Fox, respectively) or Paramount's whopping 1,400. MGM made money, a lot of money, but nothing compared to what it could have made.

Production extravagance had become L.B.'s mantra; although MGM's net was declining, its gross was actually the highest in the industry. But the overhead was greatly inflated by legions of executives and producers, and by the way the studio did business. One of Nick Schenck's incontrovertible laws was that percentage deals for talent were impossible, so people like Irving Berlin tended to gravitate to RKO and Paramount. When Berlin sold MGM eight catalogue songs and eight new songs for *Easter Parade*, the studio had to pay him a staggering $600,000 in lieu of any percentage. Mayer didn't blink, just told Arthur Freed to pay the man.

Far more damaging was the top-heavy administrative culture of the studio. In the early days of the company, Mayer and Thalberg had used between three and six producers to make about forty-five movies a year; by 1937, Mayer was using twenty producers to make about the same number of pictures. And by 1941, there were forty producers, even though the studio would shave its output during the war.

The studio culture had never been story-minded but, rather, star-minded. The studio had always defined its task as making two Gables, three Crawfords, two Garbos, and so on for a given year. The stories? They'd think of something. But after the war, the story became as important as the stars, which meant story-oriented executives like Darryl Zanuck were able to adapt, because he didn't have to worry about finding material for a long string of highly paid actors.

The shortsightedness ran all the way up the ladder. The producer Armand Deutsch recalled a meeting he had in New York with Nick Schenck, at which he said that he thought he could be of more use to Loew's, Inc. in New York than Culver City. "Why don't you get me a job at RCA," he volunteered, "and let me do TV. That's the coming thing."

"Oh, Armand," said Schenck. "That'll never be much."

Chapter
FOURTEEN

OF ALL THE HOLLYWOOD STUDIOS, MGM was the most Republican, hence the most anti-Communist. When the Motion Picture Alliance for the Preservation of American Ideals was formed in 1944, the FBI's R. B. Hood estimated that about two hundred of the organization's 225 members worked at MGM. Sam Wood, Norman Taurog, and Clarence Brown were all on the board, Cedric Gibbons was second vice president; James Kevin McGuinness, head of the Executive Committee, was a producer at the studio. Of all the major figures in the Alliance, only Walt Disney was not on the MGM payroll.

After serving as a correspondent with the Marines in World War II, Alvin Josephy had returned to MGM and found that anti-Communism had done the job that the Depression hadn't. "The polarization was much greater after the war. It was a different kind of tumult. Everyone was afraid they might be called a Communist, and they were clamping down on people who were thought to be too far to the left, which hadn't happened at the studio in the 1930s."

"There was never a friendship there that transcended political lines," said Ring Lardner Jr. "I had a speaking acquaintance with John Lee Mahin and Jim McGuinness, and we would have polite exchanges. But I always had the feeling they were saying things when I wasn't there, things about having to put up with radicals and so on."

Richard Goldstone remembered that "the politics were so bad at MGM that the guys who had fought on the side of Spain during the Civil War, the Loyalists, had not worked on [World War II] training films in any capacity.

They were classified as 'premature anti-Fascists.' I always found John Lee Mahin to be an amiable, amicable guy, but [producer] Jim McGuinness and [screenwriter] Harry Ruskin—Oh, boy! And all that animus from the Spanish Civil War carried ten years down the road to HUAC."

McGuinness was a particularly virulent reactionary; he had produced a Red Skelton picture called *Whistling in Brooklyn*, the plot of which revolved around a cab driver who was murdered because he was trying to form a union. McGuinness thought it would be a good idea to rewrite the story so that the murder was the result of the cab driver refusing to join the union. Nat Perrin, the screenwriter, absolutely refused to write that, whereupon everyone ended up in Mayer's office. Mayer listened to both options, and pragmatically said that the original, pro-union story line should remain.

The screenwriter George Oppenheimer believed that after the war, "everybody was out for himself. Pasternak was delighted when Freed had a flop. Freed was delighted when Pasternak had a flop. The heart had gone out of it. [In the cafeteria] the Center Table, with McGuinness, Mahin, and [Howard Emmett] Rogers referred to the writers' table as the Moscow Club."

Also contributing to the problem was bureaucracy. The Executive Committee had put essentially noncreative people like Sam Katz, Al Lichtman, and Joe Cohn in charge of picture-makers, and the committee itself had grown until it included nearly twenty people. "You can't get decisions with that many people, all of whom had opinions," said Sam Marx, recalling a time when Irving Thalberg had made the majority of production decisions by himself.

Perhaps the studio had become too much of a country club; perhaps a harder line was needed. It was decreed that writers would no longer have couches in their office—to cut down on napping—and Eddie Mannix upped the ante by declaring that writers could no longer work at home. The entertainingly insolent Raymond Chandler said that a man as big as Mannix should have the privilege of changing his mind, and worked at home anyway.

For the people on the left, Mayer "was the main enemy," according to Ring Lardner Jr. "He represented the old tradition of dominance by an individual man over the whole company." That he had built the company was irrelevant.

One of Mayer's most valued screenwriters was Dalton Trumbo, who had written three hits in a row (*A Guy Named Joe*, *Thirty Seconds Over Tokyo*, and *Our Vines Have Tender Grapes*). MGM was paying him $3,000 a week or $75,000 a script, as he preferred—top money for a writer, with no layoffs and no morality clause.

When the contract was drawn up, Mayer summoned Trumbo to his office and sat him down in an adjacent armchair. "You sign this contract. You make the first picture, and if it fails, you won't hear a word from anybody. Make another picture, and it's a failure, and nobody will say anything to you. You make another picture, and it fails—not a word! Because the fourth picture will not fail, and that one will make up for the first three."

Fanning the divisive flames was Billy Wilkerson, founder and editor of *The Hollywood Reporter*, and a staunch anti-Communist Catholic—albeit one who would have six wives. "When he was a young man in his twenties" remembered Wilkerson's son Willie, "he had made a trip to Russia and he didn't like what he saw. He put two and two together—if it looked like a duck and quacked like a duck, it was a duck and he didn't want foreign ducks destroying the ducks in his backyard."

Wilkerson's editorials fulminated against Communist infiltration and promoted congressional investigations. Finally, Mayer, with whom Wilkerson had an up-and-down relationship, predicated on what kind of review Wilkerson had given the most recent MGM pictures, called.

"I don't give a shit what my people do in their spare time," said Mayer. "What you're doing is bad for business. Stop it."

"My dad hung up on him," reports Wilkerson. "Mayer was a businessman. Sure, there were moral codes, but he didn't want anything to disrupt the code of commerce."

The call only inflamed Wilkerson more, and he went to Howard Hughes and asked him to get names of likely Communists from Hughes's FBI contacts. Hughes began feeding names to Wilkerson, who began printing them.

Mayer had to do what he was perfectly willing to do—grease palms. The head of the House Un-American Activities Committee in 1945 was a Georgia Democrat named John Wood, who had a lawyer friend named Edgar Dunlap. Mayer paid $25,000 to Dunlap for what the lawyer claimed were services involved in expediting a shipment of Mayer's horses, although why an obscure Georgia lawyer would have been able to cut that particular Gordian knot was unclear. The columnist Drew Pearson clearly implied that some or all of the $25,000 ended up in Wood's pocket, which was, of course, vigorously denied.

Wood never held hearings on the matter of Communist influence in the movie industry. It wasn't until after the elections of 1946, when Mayer's Republicans took control of Congress, that the investigations actually began.

L.B.'s politics had never been in doubt, and they were reinforced when he gave a speech in San Francisco in July of 1947. Communism, he said, "threatens our fundamental concepts of human rights and liberty," and he believed that the movies, along with newspapers and radio, had a duty to portray to the rest of the world the meaning and benefits of American democracy. . . . "A certain nation" did not permit the showing of Andy Hardy movies or, for that matter, any picture in which "freedom loving people are accepted as typical of our democratic way of life. . . .

"Today an undemocratic state is on the march. Its political philosophy is foreign to our traditions." It was not a battle between two countries, he said, or between ourselves, even though "it threatens the way of life upon this planet. It threatens our fundamental concepts of human life and liberty."

Much of this speech is boilerplate Taft Republicanism, but in saying that the Cold War was not between countries, or Americans, Mayer seemed to be seeking a middle ground, an exit strategy to forestall the bloodletting that was already on the horizon. Money had worked, but now things were spinning out of his control.

In September 1947, Mayer hosted an off-the-record dinner in honor of the Ohio isolationist Senator Robert Taft. Attending was the A list of Hollywood conservatives, and even a few Democrats. In the former category were Edward Arnold, Lee Bowman, Clarence Brown, Frank Capra, Norman Chandler (the publisher of the Los Angeles Times), Harry Cohn, Mr. and Mrs. Gary Cooper, Cecil B. DeMille, Walt Disney, Sidney Franklin, Arthur Freed, Cedric Gibbons, Leo McCarey, James Kevin McGuinness, Adolphe Menjou, George Murphy, Walter Pidgeon, Hal Roach, Morrie Ryskind, David O. Selznick, Mendel Silberberg (Mayer's lawyer), Norman Taurog, Benny Thau, and Sam Wood.

In the latter category were William Goetz, Pandro Berman, Eddie Mannix, Edwin Knopf, and at least two - Spencer Tracy and Mervyn LeRoy—who were believed to be in transit from Democrat to Republican. (Tracy would remain a liberal Democrat for the rest of his life.)

At this point, Taft seems to have had a claim on Louis's mind, Louis's heart belonged to the theatricality and charisma of Douglas MacArthur, whom many conservative Republicans wanted to run against Harry Truman in 1948.

The crises in Mayer's life went beyond the political to the personal. After years of separation from Margaret, he decided to move for divorce. Howard Strickling believed that on some level Mayer never forgave himself. There was no way to reconcile all the things Mayer said he believed with the fact that he was leaving his Maggie, the woman who had worshipped him and given him the daughters he adored. He was a hypocrite, and now everybody knew it, most damagingly himself.

"People sucked up to him," said Strickling, "and told him he was doing the right thing, that his wife wanted to make an old man of him by getting him home at night to sit in front of the fire, instead of allowing him his right 'to live,' but he knew deep down it was the wrong thing for him to do. He really hated himself for it."

Strickling believed that Mayer's affection for him was strengthened because he went out of his way to continue as part of Margaret's life. "The poor old lady just wanted to be a simple mother, with her husband and family around her—she cooking for the family and having things just so. If Edie had married a bookkeeper and Irene had married a nice prosperous butcher and all had come home regularly for meals, that would have suited her fine."

Irene remembered that her father was prepared to be generous but didn't trust Margaret to take care of a large lump-sum payment. Mayer suggested a trust fund, the principal to be divided between Irene and Edie on their mother's death. No, said Irene; her mother needed and deserved her independence. L.B. could always get his way with Margaret, but he could never get his way with Irene. Margaret Shenberg Mayer got her settlement with no restrictions.

The settlement was the banner headline of the *Hollywood Citizen-News* for April 28, 1947: "MAYER MUST PAY WIFE $3,250,000." The settlement gave Margaret the Santa Monica house, some other real estate, jewelry, and specified a lump-sum payment of $1.25 million immediately, another $1 million in March 1948, and $500,000 each succeeding March, plus 3 percent interest on the unpaid sums. According to the *L.A. Herald Examiner*, the Mayer settlement was believed to be the highest in the history of American courts.

A short time after the divorce was final, Margaret took a trip to New York and called up her ex-husband's old secretary Florence Browning, who was now working in the Loew's New York office. She asked Browning to accompany her to a play starring the famously over-the-top Yiddish actor Maurice Schwartz. As Schwartz was threatening to bring down the proscenium arch, Margaret turned to her companion. With a little smile and shrug, she whispered, "L.B."

As if all this wasn't bad enough, Mayer's brother Jerry fell ill with cancer and underwent two operations early in 1947 that failed to stem the disease. Louis saw that Jerry had the very best care, and came to visit him often, but there were no overt displays of emotionalism—that was reserved for the studio, for manip-

ulating, for show. Death was serious. In the latter part of September, Jerry fell
into a coma and died at the early age of fifty-six.

"He was caring [about his brother], but under control," said Jerry's son,
Gerald. "He was like that about me, too. He came to see a play I directed, and
attended my graduation from Stanford. I was the only boy named Mayer, the
only one that could pass the name on, and I think that was a factor in his thinking. On the other hand, he didn't leave me any money in his will, but then my
father had been comfortable. That was the way he thought about things." Despite his public religiosity, Mayer was no longer an observant Jew, and the lot
would occasionally be swept by rumors that he was considering converting to
Catholicism, which his brother Jerry always termed "nonsense."

The same day that the *Hollywood Citizen-News* announced Jerry's death,
there was a story announcing that "Studios Will Air Red Hunt, Johnston Says."
Motion Picture Association of America president Eric Johnston announced
that film producers welcomed the House Un-American Activities Committee
inquiry into subversion in the movie business, which was scheduled to begin in
late October.

A couple of representatives of the committee called on Eddie Mannix and
Mayer for individual meetings. The topics were MGM screenwriters Dalton
Trumbo and Lester Cole and the Communist propaganda to be found in *The
Best Years of Our Lives, Margie, Tender Comrade, Mr. Smith Goes to Washing-
ton,* and MGM's *Song of Russia.*

The committee representative, H. A. Smith, never specifically suggested
that MGM discharge putative Communists such as Trumbo, Cole, and Donald Ogden Stewart. "He wanted to find out more as to what I knew who was
Communists because I don't know," said Mayer in a deposition a year later,
lapsing into Casey Stengel's argot. "He argued with me about the Communism, and I said—most of the argument centered around the picture . . . *Song
of Russia,* and I made quite a time about that. He claimed it wasn't free of Communism . . . I asked him to point to the Communism in pictures . . . I wasn't
going to indict no men charging anything. All I am interested in—I got a job to
do. It is for him to show me where the Communism is, not only in ours, but . . .
show me others.

"He couldn't show. I argued, talked. He was mysterious. . . . I didn't pay
any attention. I got nowhere with him. We deadlocked. . . . He was very mysterious. . . . I had nothing to hide and I wasn't going to hide anything. 'Come on,
put it on the table. Let's see what you have got and I will meet it. I will tell you
all I know.' You couldn't get nowhere. He was determined we are full of Com-

munists. Our country is in danger through the pictures, yet he couldn't show in the pictures which one is Communistic. . . . All this menace was hanging over us. I paid no attention to him."

On October 27, 1947, the House Un-American Activities Committee began its investigation of Communist influence in Hollywood. During the initial investigation, ten "unfriendly" witnesses refused to answer the committee's questions, citing their constitutional guarantee of free speech. The ten were promptly cited for contempt of Congress.

Two of the Hollywood Ten, as they came to be known, Dalton Trumbo and Lester Cole, were under exclusive contract to MGM, and the latter had formed a successful alliance with Jack Cummings. A week before the Ten were to appear in Washington, Mayer called Cole to his office. Cole had been working on a script for a movie about Emiliano Zapata—not a project that aroused enthusiasm in the front office, until the Mexican government offered what Cole remembered as $1.5 million in services and equipment in a co-production deal. Suddenly, the story of a Mexican revolutionary was suitable screen material for the most conservative studio in Hollywood. "What the hell," said Eddie Mannix, "Jesus Christ was a revolutionary, too."

"Lester was a very aggressive, noisy, interesting, vital man," remembered the blacklisted writer Bernard Gordon. "He was actually more interesting as a person than as a writer. He wrote one or two good films, but he was a great character, very lively and combative." In other words, a lot like Louis B. Mayer.

"I had notions of what Lester could be," Mayer would remember. "I believed in him terribly. My nephew spoke so highly of him [and] I would have given a great deal for Lester to fix himself so they would stop calling him [a Communist] because I think he is a fine craftsman."

Mayer asked Cole to renounce his brethren, and, according to a deposition Cole gave later, said that the entire matter was the fault of people like James Kevin McGuinness, who had brought the situation to a head by inviting the committee to investigate Hollywood.

Cole said that he thought the Ten had the law on their side, but Mayer exploded.

"I don't give a shit about the law. . . . Break with them. Stick with us. With me. With Jack you'll do what you want. Direct your own pictures? Say so. I believe you'd do great. Dough means nothing. We'll tear up the contract, double your salary. You name it, you can have it. Just make the break."

And then the pitch began rising, the temper spiraling upward. "I know about Communism. I know what happens to men like that. Take that Communist Roosevelt! A hero, the man of the people! And what happened five minutes after they shoveled the dirt on his grave? The people pissed on it! That's what you want, Lester? Be with *us*, be smart. You got kids, think of them."

Cole refused; Mayer fumed.

The first major witness before the congressional committee was Jack Warner, who prominently displayed his yellow streak and babbled. He claimed that he had been under pressure both from Communists and the committee, then said that he had never seen a Communist and wouldn't know one if he did. Robert Stripling, the committee's chief investigator, then pointed out that in private testimony in Washington Warner had named as Communists Alvah Bessie, Gordon Kahn, Howard Koch, Ring Lardner Jr., John Howard Lawson, Albert Maltz, Robert Rossen, Dalton Trumbo, Guy Endore, Emmet Lavery, Irwin Shaw, Clifford Odets, Sheridan Gibney, and Julius and Philip Epstein. Among others. Warner promptly recanted about the Epstein brothers, but only because Julius Epstein was threatening to sue him.

On October 20, 1947, Mayer was called to testify in front of the committee and opened by reading a prepared statement. "I have maintained a relentless vigilance against un-American influences. If, as has been alleged, Communists have attempted to use the screen for subversive purposes, I am proud of our success in circumventing them. . . . It is my earnest hope that this committee will perform a public service by recommending to the Congress legislation establishing national policy regulating employment of Communists in private industry. It is my belief they should be denied the sanctuary of the freedom they seek to destroy."

He went on to enumerate how the studio had produced *Joe Smith, American* as an incentive for defense workers, and had rushed *Mrs. Miniver* into release to counter anti-English feeling. He then fell to a defense of the only problematic picture MGM had: *Song of Russia*, one of several pictures the studios had made (Warners' *Mission to Moscow* was another) during that honeymoon period when the Russians were our allies and Stalin was Uncle Joe.

"It seemed a good medium of entertainment and at the same time offered an opportunity for a pat on the back for our then ally, Russia. . . . We mentioned this to the Government coordinators and they agreed with us that it would be a good idea to make the picture. . . .

"The final script of *Song of Russia* was little more than a pleasant musical romance—the story of a boy and girl that, except for the music of Tchaikovsky, might just as well have taken place in Switzerland or England or any other country on the earth." For corroboration, there was a letter from Lowell Mellett, the chief of the Motion Picture Division of the Office of War Information, who had written that the script "had no political implications, being designed primarily to acquaint the American people with the people of one of our Allied Nations."

Mayer noted that Robert Taylor hadn't liked the project and begged off because he was due to go into the navy. Mayer had called Frank Knox, the secretary of the navy, mentioned all the good that *Mrs. Miniver* was accomplishing, and got Taylor's induction date pushed back.

Under questioning by the committee, Mayer said that he had nothing to fear from Communists because, "they can't get a single thing into our pictures or our studio under our set-up. . . . The only ones that I would have to worry about are the producers, the editors, the executives, because our scripts are read and re-read by so many of the executive force, producers and editors."

When the committee asked if there were any Communists in his employ, Mayer said that "They have mentioned two or three writers to me several times. There is no proof about it, except they mark them as Communists, and when I look at the pictures they have written for us I can't find once where they have written something like that . . ."

"Who are these people they have named?"

"[Dalton] Trumbo and Lester Cole, they said. I think there was one other fellow, a third one . . ."

"Have you observed any efforts on their part to get Communist propaganda into their pictures?"

"I have never heard of any . . ."

"The third individual you mentioned, would that be Donald Ogden Stewart?"

"Yes . . ."

"If you were shown the Communist dues cards of any one of these three individuals, then would you continue to employ them?"

"No, sir."

"By the same token, Mr. Mayer, would you employ a [German-American] Bundist, a known member of the Bund?"

"I have probably had them; I wouldn't employ him knowingly, no sir."

Mayer went on to contradict Jack Warner's earlier testimony, in which Warner had said that great efforts had to be made to avoid Communist writers inserting propaganda. "We haven't had that problem in our studio," said Mayer. "He says he has had it, but I can't say I have had it. . . . I will not preach any ideology except American, and I don't even treat that. I let that take its own course and speak for itself."

Mayer went on to enumerate the anti-Communist pictures MGM had produced: *Ninotchka* and *Comrade X*. As always, Mayer was better on facts than theories; when he was asked what could possibly motivate well-compensated people to embrace Communism, he said, "My own opinion is, Mr. Congressman, which I have expressed many times in discussion, I think they are cracked. It can't be otherwise."

After some more back and forth, Mayer was excused and Ayn Rand was sworn in for a lengthy scoffing session about Mayer's claims for the ideological innocence of *Song of Russia*. Rand eviscerated the film, describing MGM's Moscow as a city of "big, prosperous-looking, clean buildings, with something like swans or sailboats in the background." Robert Taylor mingled with "happy peasants . . . children with operetta costumes . . . manicured starlets driving tractors and the happy woman coming home from work singing." When a Republican congressman named John McDowell asked if nobody smiled in Russia, Rand replied, "Well, if you ask me literally, pretty much no."

Cedric Gibbons had succeeded where Stalin had failed.

From Mayer's point of view, it had been a more or less successful testimony. He had mentioned Trumbo, Cole, and Stewart as people other people thought were Communists while asserting that, as far as he was concerned, they were talented employees, nothing more.

Mayer felt that he was caught in the middle because he was. He was a certified enemy of the left, but many in the right felt he was insufficiently zealous in persecuting the leftists in his employ. It was a feeling amplified when the scurrilous Hearst columnist Westbrook Pegler attacked him for trying to avoid testifying by enlisting one Mickey Rosner, a friend of Frank Orsatti's, as an intermediary to get Mayer excused.

Even Hearst felt Pegler was out of line, and wrote an open letter defending his old friend. He pointed out that Mayer had produced *Ninotchka*, and that "nothing else has appeared on the screen which equaled the effectiveness of that ridicule or offered more devastating exposure of the impractical operation of that particular form of criminal lunacy. . . .

"The committee would do well to run the film *Ninotchka* for its own edification.

"It is the best evidence of Mr. Mayer's contempt for Communism and respect for free American ideals."

"I don't want to blow my own horn," Mayer wrote in protest to the Hearst executive Richard Berlin, "but in running our studios it has always been my policy to examine the complete record of a man, and not to pick out one error or what appears to be an error to condemn him.

"I wonder if Mr. Pegler's actions were analyzed over the course of years if nothing could be found that would be regarded as an error of judgment in all his undertakings.

"I have been a good American ever since the time I came to America; I have been a law abiding and self-respecting citizen. . . . I just want you to figure out for me, if you can, what is the incentive to have self-respect and be a first-class American and then in a matter of what happened in Washington, get a column written such as Pegler wrote. You know how careful I have been that we make no picture that would tend to influence youngsters immorally, or debase the American principles. I think that is my responsibility. Don't you think Pegler should stop and think in a matter of this kind before he writes a column and sends it out special, urging everyone to read it?"

"Mayer was not one of the guys in favor of the blacklist," said screenwriter Bernard Gordon. "He respected Dalton Trumbo, as a writer turning out material who was important to him. And Marguerite Roberts was one of MGM's best writers; she got blacklisted because of her husband, John Sanford."

"They did not care about politics," said the screenwriter Robert Lees, who was named by Sterling Hayden and blacklisted. "Robert Arthur, a producer I worked with a lot at Universal, was a member of the Motion Picture Alliance. One day he and my collaborator Fred Rinaldo got into a political argument. The next day we were talking about our kids and the Dodgers. He was a very good producer and he thought we were good writers and we got along great.

"MGM did their darndest to keep their good writers, whatever their politics. They didn't want to get into that mess, although Jack Warner practically crawled. Basically, the moguls wanted to be Americans first and Jews second."

After the hearings ended, the major motion picture studios were faced with further outside legal and political trouble from the government and other organizations. Anti-Hollywood newspaper editorials began appearing in Kansas and California, and there were protests in North Carolina against Katharine Hepburn, who as a member of the Committee for the First Amendment had publicly supported the Ten.

The most troubling of all of these activities was a threatened boycott by the American Legion, with three million members spread over seventeen thousand posts. Earlier in 1947, protests by the Catholic War Veterans had effectively torpedoed the release of Chaplin's *Monsieur Verdoux*. Loew's theaters helped the boycott by refusing to book *Monsieur Verdoux*, effectively crippling the picture, which grossed only $325,000 in America.

In a deposition, Eddie Mannix was even more open. "A business that is dealing in public favor cannot have a small percentage of the press nor the radio out against them. Whether 50 percent of the press was for them and 50 percent was against them, we suffered. We have always felt that criticism against our industry hurts us where praise does not help us to the same degree. . . .

"We had information, whether true or untrue, that organizations in America were about to put on a campaign against the picture business, particularly against the members who had defied Congress, and if that organized campaign would have taken place, I can assure you that it would have been a very sorry day for our picture business. If the situation, for example [with the Chaplin picture] were reflected throughout the United States of America, they would all have been in the red. There is no question as to that."

If protestors could effectively hobble a movie by Charlie Chaplin, the gold standard for thirty-five years, what could they do to a run-of-the-mill star? (That Chaplin had endured a nasty paternity suit, that *Monsieur Verdoux* was a calculated slap at the triumphalist values of postwar America, and that most critics and audiences slapped back went unnoticed by the moguls.)

And so a meeting was called at the Waldorf-Astoria hotel on November 24 and 25, 1947, for what Mayer would retrospectively characterize as a "two-day wrangle" to address the problems.

Among those present at the Waldorf Conference were Mayer, Joe and Nick Schenck, Nat Spingold, Harry Cohn, Jack Cohn, Sam Goldwyn, Walter Wanger, Eddie Mannix, Albert Warner, Eric Johnston, Samuel Goldwyn, Ned Depinet, Barney Balaban, Y. Frank Freeman, Spyros Skouras, William Goetz, Leo Spitz, J. Robert Rubin, Dore Schary, Henry Ginsberg, Cheever Cowdin, and assorted supporting players and lawyers, including Mendel Silberberg.

Eric Johnston opened the proceedings by saying the movie business belonged to the public, just like baseball, and he pointed to what baseball had done when its reputation had been threatened—elected Judge Landis, banned the so-called Black Sox players, and cleaned house. And now the public, in the form of the American Legion, was rising up; letters were being written; federal censorship was a distinct possibility. It was the movie industry's turn to make a move.

According to one of the participants, there was a long pause, whereupon

Walter Wanger rose and said that he wanted to hear what L. B. Mayer had to say. Mayer got up and started by talking about how he had returned from Washington to Hollywood with some of the Ten and had confronted them, saying, "By God, I should kick the hell out of you sons of bitches, you bastards, taking money from the great American motion picture business that has made it possible for you to live so happily."

He then made a speech that opened the floodgates and the group swung over to Johnston's urgings not to hire anyone who was a known present or former Communist, took the Fifth, or refused to appear before the committee. "The point," said one of the people present, "is that Mayer threw the key block on a signal from Walter Wanger."

Why a conventional liberal like Wanger would have worked in conjunction with a man who had once tried to strangle him is open to question, as is the fact that nobody else remembered Mayer making such a speech.

According to the recollections of both Mayer and Mannix, the substance of Mayer's remarks at the Waldorf was that it was a shame that the industry had been put in the position it was in; that investigating subversion was the business of Congress. "Congress should give us a law," said Mayer. "I shouldn't be the one who tries to judge men. . . . I wasn't afraid of Communists . . . nothing was getting in our pictures, and therefore, I wasn't going to move."

Others began speaking up. "We were told that there had been increasing pressure upon the Board of Directors of the various companies about the problem," remembered Dore Schary. "We were told that various American Legion Posts had begun threats of boycotts of certain films . . . there was a general feeling that the entire industry was under tremendous attack from many quarters in the way of these pressures." Worse, there were more people back in Hollywood who could create further trouble; the HUAC Committee claimed to have the names of seventy-nine Communists working in the studios. Fox had already fired Ring Lardner Jr., and, according to Schary, the Executive Committee of RKO had decided to fire Edward Dmytryk and Adrian Scott.

An awful lot of smoke was being passed off as fire. The groundswell of public anger at Communism in the movies was recalled by Dore Schary as consisting of approximately forty letters; Mayer remembered even fewer coming to his office.

Although Schary had made a principled verbal stand during the Un-American Activities hearings ("Up until the time it is proved that a Communist is a man dedicated to the overthrow of the Government by force or violence, or by any illegal methods . . . I would still maintain his right to think politically as he chooses"), he rolled over at the Waldorf Conference and essentially agreed to the proposition that no Communist or suspected Communist had a right to employment in the movie industry.

The result of the conference was that the studios issued a statement saying they had collectively suspended each of the Hollywood Ten and would not knowingly employ a Communist in the future, thereby initiating the period of the Hollywood blacklist: "We will forthwith discharge or suspend without compensation those in our employ and we will not re-employ any of the Ten until such time as he is acquitted or has purged himself of contempt and declares under oath, that he is not a Communist. . . . We will not knowingly employ a Communist or any member of any party or group which advocates the overthrow of the Government of the United States by force or by any illegal or unconstitutional methods."

There was nothing to be done about the Ten—they had sealed their own fates. The question was what criteria would be applied in the future. Mayer even claimed that he said, "We got to look out for the future that we don't get an innocent person hurt." Unfortunately, as Schary would observe with a straight face, "No machinery had been worked out" for protecting the innocent.

The studio heads have always taken the fall for acquiescing to the blacklist, but it should be remembered that, in those days, New York ran Hollywood. However much power resided in these men who could fire movie stars and green-light pictures, most of them were employees.

"All movie companies are dependent on the House of Morgan," was the way that George Seldes put it, while a prescient, anonymous article in *The Nation* said that "The overlords of the industry are the New York executives who control financing, distribution and the theater chains. The motion-picture business is primarily a real-estate operation, and the real estate is in the hands of men like Loew's Nick Schenck, Paramount's Barney Balaban and Fox's Spyros Skouras."

The key to the result of the Waldorf Conference was its location. "Mayer just wanted to make movies," said playwright and screenwriter Arthur Laurents, "but New York made him back down. The banks made all of them back down. They were afraid of boycotts, they were afraid of the American Legion, and they were afraid of the Catholic church."

A delegation of producers composed of Schary, Walter Wanger, and Eddie Mannix went before the Screen Writers Guild to ask for its acquiescence in blacklisting their own members. They got it.

On December 2, 1947, Dalton Trumbo and Lester Cole were suspended from MGM.

For people like Hugo and Jean Rouverol Butler, the Waldorf Conference was a particularly bitter blow; Schary had been the best man at their wedding, and, said Jean Butler, "had been lovely to Hugo until politics interrupted." Over the years the relationship had cooled as the Butlers grew more radical and Schary less. "By the time of the Waldorf Conference, there was a total estrangement," Jean Butler remembered. When her husband was blacklisted, "there was no possibility of asking for help. Never." It was, as Dalton Trumbo would call it, a time of the toad, predicated on the human fear that the more you have, the more you have to lose.

It was nothing personal, just business. But Trumbo's fellow blacklistee Adrian Scott, who worked for Schary at RKO, didn't want to hear about it. "I'll never forgive him. [Schary] promised to set a precedent, never to fire anyone because he was suspected of being a Communist. Then, as soon as things got hot, he simply let us go."

In a few cases, Mayer did what he could to repair the damage done to innocent people. He told Howard Strickling to give Edward G. Robinson assistance in clearing his name from the blacklist. But in public, Mayer did little, if anything. Mayer remained reluctant to give Robinson a job "for fear of criticism on part of public," according to Bert Allenberg, Robinson's agent, and the actor had some lean years until his career once again picked up.

Lester Cole sued MGM for breach of contract, charging that the studio had fired him without cause. (MGM, as well as the other studios, felt legally justified by invoking the morals clause that was boilerplate in most contracts of the time.)

Mayer took the stand in the case, and when the Loew's attorney asked him about Cole's "immoral" acts, he refused to play the good company man. He had known Lester Cole for more than two years. Cole had written three fine films for MGM. He was on good terms with everyone at the studio. As far as Louis B. Mayer was concerned, Lester Cole's morals were fine.

He was promptly excused, and the attorney read into the record part of a deposition Mayer had given. Referring to the HUAC committee hearings, Mayer said, "I didn't think the industry was wrong and I thought this was just a shoddy way of getting publicity. They asked about Lester Cole and Dalton Trumbo and I said I didn't give a damn whether they were Communists or not. All I'm interested in is getting people to write scripts for me and my responsibility if he is a Communist, a Democrat or Republican is that the ideology is not put on the screen."

As if all this wasn't problem enough, on May 3, 1948, the Supreme Court ruled that the major studios had to sell their theater chains. The Court, in an opinion written by William O. Douglas, decided that the majors had conspired to fix movie admission prices and had used block booking as a means of forcing small exhibitors to take all their output. The decree threatened the studios with dire economic consequences; by 1948, investment in theaters, i.e., real estate, accounted for 93 percent of the investment in the American movie industry (production was only 5 percent). For years, movie companies had actually been real estate companies more than entertainment entrepreneurs.

Loew's wouldn't comply with the order until L.B. was long gone from MGM, but psychologically it was a devastating blow for all the moguls; the decree removed the founding fathers of the industry from exhibition, the business where they had all started their careers, and where they had formed their sense of the public's wants and needs.

In the spring of 1948, after nearly twenty-five years of service with the company that bore his name, Louis B. Mayer still had no standing with the umbrella corporation of Loew's other than as a salaried employee. He was not an officer, just the head of production who, in his words, headed "a group that sits in as a cabinet and I have the veto or approval of what is decided."

Yet, there was still a studio that needed to be run. MGM lent William Powell to Warner Bros. for *Life with Father*, in exchange for Errol Flynn in *That Forsyte Woman*. It seemed a fair exchange, but Warners got the better of it. Lately, it seemed that everybody's films were better—not to mention more profitable—than Metro's, always excepting the musicals.

Clark Gable had come back from the war and made a series of pictures that were, by and large, nothing special, although they made some money. But Gable was older, heavier in body and spirit, and both the public and the studio were aware that something was missing. Audrey Totter dated Gable for a while and, like most people, adored him. "We were at a party with Lana Turner, who had just married Bob Topping. She was covered with jewels and flirting with Clark, showing him her jewelry. It was all gorgeous, and I was fascinated.

" 'Are you admiring Lana's jewelry?' Clark asked me. 'You've got something more important, my dear. Your jewels are inside.' Clark's conversation was limited, mostly about Carole Lombard. But he was a charming, sweet man."

Creatively, MGM seemed at a loss about what to do other than repeat the prewar formula, which was part of the problem. There was consternation at the Loew's offices in New York as well as in MGM's offices in Culver City. Not only that, in 1947, for the first time since the studio's inception, MGM didn't receive any nominations for Best Picture. Schenck began pushing Mayer to do something, anything, and for the first time he had leverage.

The problems of MGM became apparent with the production of *Desire Me*, a melodrama starring Greer Garson, Robert Montgomery, and—on loan from RKO—Robert Mitchum. Production had begun under George Cukor, who disliked both the script and Mitchum, with the actor returning the favor. After a week, the picture was closed down and a procession of new writers began work on the screenplay, originally written by Casey Robinson. Montgomery had to begin work on *Lady in the Lake*, so he left, whereupon Mitchum was moved from the part of Garson's lover to that of her husband.

Mitchum began expressing his displeasure and exhaustion—he was making two other pictures simultaneously—by playing love scenes after eating hamburgers smothered in onions and Roquefort dressing. "Horses don't seem to mind," he observed. During location work at Monterey, Garson almost drowned and hurt her back.

As the budget moved toward $3 million, producer Arthur Hornblow fired Cukor. "After I was taken off *Desire Me*, [only] three colleagues came to visit me," Cukor said. "They were Margaret Booth, the head cutter at Metro, my old assistant, and the cameraman Joe Ruttenberg. They were very sweet and tactful. 'I can just see my own funeral,' I said, 'with only you three coming—and all those hollyhocks.' "

Hornblow had the script rewritten yet again, and then began assigning any director who was free to work on the picture. Jack Conway, Victor Saville, and Mervyn LeRoy all worked on the picture piecemeal until *Desire Me* was finally completed at a staggering cost of $4.1 million.

The studio sat on the picture for more than a year, then it was finally released without any director's credit whatever—a nearly unprecedented indication of a production disaster. (Fox's earlier *Hello Sister* was also released without a directorial credit.) *Desire Me* incurred wretched reviews and a $2.4 million loss.

Mayer's affection for Garson never wavered—not even when she stopped being Benny Thau's mistress and began an affair with, and later married, Richard Ney, the actor who played her son in *Mrs. Miniver*. Although Garson had been a reliable guarantee of high grosses since *Goodbye, Mr. Chips*, the sudden alteration of taste wrought by World War II rendered her starchy image obsolete. Her next picture, *Julia Misbehaves*, reteamed her with Walter Pidgeon, her co-star in *Mrs. Miniver* and *Madame Curie*, and was mildly profitable. But, beginning with *That Forsyte Woman*, Garson never appeared in another MGM film that made money. Expensive Garson pictures like *The Miniver Story* lost $2.3 million; cheap ones like *The Law and the Lady* lost $395,000. There was nothing to be done except eat the losses.

By and large, L.B. was still manufacturing quality goods, but the public's taste was changing.

Producer Edwin Knopf explained why MGM's costs remained so high. The biggest item in any MGM A picture budget was usually the story and script. Since MGM dealt in "known properties," they bought Broadway plays and best-selling books, which were expensive. Say the script and story costs for an A picture were $250,000. If that figure was in the budget, they *had* to spend it. If the picture turned out to be a success and the story and script costs had been, say, only $150,000, it made the producer look good. But if he had spent only $150,000 and the picture failed, he would look very bad indeed, because then Mayer could accuse him of shortchanging the picture, the audience, MGM, and Loew's, Inc.—maybe that extra money could have saved the movie. But if each producer spent up to the full limit of his budget, he could always say that no corners had been cut, he had done everything he possibly could, and wasn't the movie business strange?

This had worked with hundreds of movies, from *Tarzan and His Mate* to *The Wizard of Oz*. But it would rarely work anymore, partially because movie attendance was falling, as were grosses. Mayer and his team could always find new talent—Garson had replaced Shearer, and Deborah Kerr would replace Garson—but they were no longer so adept at sustaining it.

For young directors increasingly used to having some control over their pictures, working at MGM was like disappearing into the smothering embrace of a cloying old auntie. When Elia Kazan checked on to the lot to make *Sea of Grass*, he was stunned to find that the studio had already shot all the second unit footage, designed the sets and costumes. The script was completed and marked "Final." It was clear that upon the completion of shooting, the editing would be done, not by Kazan, but by the studio. All he was expected to do was guide the actors.

Kazan told Walter Plunkett that he was hoping for costumes that would be more indicative of wilderness. "This story is supposed to take place, is it not, in the backcountry?"

"No," Plunkett retorted. "Actually, this picture takes place in Metro-Goldwyn-Mayer land, where you and I are sitting this minute."

Metro was still making movies as if it were 1928, or 1935, or 1943. But those years were gone, directors like Kazan were the future, and they would be increasingly unwilling to bring their projects or themselves to Metro.

Movie attendance began plummeting, going from 80 million per week in 1946 to 67 million in 1948. Nineteen fifty would see attendance at 60 million. The declining market meant that the number of B movies MGM made went from sixteen in 1939–40 to seven in 1942–43 to one in 1947–48. The studio canceled the Hardy films, the Thin Man films, all their formerly profitable B movies. "The peak in film business has been reached," Mayer told Edwin Schallert of the Los Angeles Times. "It is time to prepare for a recession. There will be no sudden collapse, but easy spending will come to a halt."

In a very real sense, this changing of audience tastes would be far more bedeviling—and long-lasting—than the trough wrought by the Depression. The problem then had been obvious—people didn't have enough money for the movies. But in a booming postwar America, people had too much money, as well as other possibilities for diversion. Besides that, the movies didn't have the visceral punch they used to. The movies, L. B. Mayer, and MGM hadn't changed. Audiences had.

Mayer responded with his characteristic vigor and confidence; his ideas had worked before, and would work again. The brightest spots on the lot were the Freed and Pasternak units. But they also made the most expensive films going, so they couldn't have an enormous effect on the bottom line.

As long as attendance and profits held up, there wasn't much Nick Schenck could do. But when theater attendance headed downhill in 1947, so did the studio's fortunes, and Schenck began to be concerned. Sure, The Yearling was a hit, but at what cost?

The MGM version of The Three Musketeers, with Gene Kelly paying a heartfelt homage to Douglas Fairbanks Sr., earned the second highest gross of the decade for the studio, but the film had also cost nearly $4.5 million. The stupefying Green Dolphin Street ran far over budget, with an earthquake sequence that alone cost $1 million. Mayer was shown a rough cut of the unfinished picture and said it looked okay. When Carey Wilson told him the cost was going to hit $4 million, Mayer said he didn't care.

Actually, Green Dolphin Street ended up costing $4.3 million, more than Gone With the Wind, and had a world gross of over $7 million, but only returned a profit of $339,000. The films that were carrying the studio were Esther

Williams musicals like *Fiesta*, *On an Island with You*, and *Texas Carnival*, most of which were grossing in excess of $5 million apiece.

And even Mickey Rooney, heretofore golden at the box office, appeared in two expensive failures in a row: *Summer Holiday* and *Words and Music*. If he was no longer the fresh-faced boy who had captivated the American public, he still had his remarkable talent and he still had considerable commercial appeal—a change-of-pace boxing picture called *Killer McCoy* made a profit of $768,000. But MGM didn't seem interested in lining up more pictures for Rooney and gave him his release.

"We couldn't have Andy Hardy getting married and divorced every year," Mayer said, "so we had to drop the series. Couldn't get someone to take Mickey's place, the public would not have stood for that. People used to call Mickey 'Andy.' He didn't like that, can you imagine?" It was all very sad. Rooney, said Mayer, had never seen $50 a week before he came to MGM, and ended up at $4,000 a week. "Can you imagine the good sense [he] would have needed *not* to have been ruined by that kind of money?"

Yet the stolid leading man Robert Taylor was having a far rockier time adjusting to the postwar box office, with pictures like *High Wall* and *The Bribe* amassing serious losses. But MGM stuck with Taylor because he was the archetypal company man—Mayer was always very impressed that Taylor arrived at the studio every morning wearing a tie and a pin through his collar. Taylor always played the game—showing up for every publicity event the studio asked him to do no matter how menial, speaking against Communism at the HUAC hearings.

On the other hand, Rooney drank too much, married too often, and sustained half the bookies in Southern California. Taylor was obedient and Rooney wasn't. As a result, Robert Taylor lasted at MGM for a full twenty-five years.

Even Arthur Freed was having problems. Between 1946 and 1949, Freed produced eight musicals with budgets that ran between $2 and $3 million. Four of the films were profitable, with a little less than $1 million apiece in profits, but all the profits were wiped out by the huge losses of *Summer Holiday* and *The Pirate*, and the minor losses of *Good News* and *Words and Music*.

Still, the Freed unit was exempt from the strictures that were placed on every other producer. "The Freed unit was a studio within a studio," remembered producer Armand Deutsch. "If I fell a half-day behind schedule, Joe Cohn would be on my back. If Freed fell behind by two weeks—nothing. For one thing, nobody knew how he did what he did."

Part of it was the nebulous nature of the form. Even the stupidest producer or executive could imagine writing or directing. What's so hard about telling people what to say or where to stand? But composing music? Choreographing a dance? Where did *that* come from?

The Freed unit was revitalized by Betty Comden and Adolph Green, who arrived from success on Broadway. MGM had bought their show *On the Town* before it opened on Broadway because Lillie Messinger had called Mayer and told him he had to get this one. "Something happens to your voice, Lillie, when you feel that strongly," Mayer said. The studio paid $250,000 for the show before it opened in December 1944. When Mayer actually saw *On the Town*, he hated it—its modernity, its musical dissonances, the campiness of the book—and vowed that MGM would never film this show.

When Comden and Green arrived on the lot to write *Good News*, they were told that under no circumstances should they mention they had written *On the Town*. As it happened, they didn't meet Mayer for some time, only observed what Comden called "a kindly, white-haired gentleman walking around." When they asked who he was, they were informed it was Louis B. Mayer.

After *Good News*, Comden and Green were assigned a vehicle for Fred Astaire and Judy Garland eventually titled *The Barkleys of Broadway*. Garland dropped out and was replaced by Ginger Rogers. When Mayer saw the film he was transported. *This* was an MGM musical!

"It was about decent, wholesome people having their problems but getting together at the end," remembered Betty Comden. "They worked it out as civilized people should."

"It had everything for him," said Adolph Green. "Clean but active goings-on, balcony scenes with the New York skyline in the background—he specifically referred to those."

Suddenly, Comden and Green were the new pets. They were invited to lunch with Mayer in his private dining room, where he raved about the film, amazed that Comden, "you, this tiny little girl," could have written such a wonderful film. Green remembered his attitude as "hat in hand."

"He had strong feelings about morals and decency," said Comden. "He started reminiscing about the old days and he began talking about King Vidor. 'What a success *The Big Parade* was! We wanted to give him the studio; we allowed him to do whatever he wanted.'

"So, he explained, Vidor did *The Crowd*, a great picture, but not in Mayer's eyes, because of a scene that showed a toilet in a bathroom. 'King, why?' he asked Vidor. 'We all have our natural functions, but we don't put them on the screen.'

"They went back and forth, but Vidor insisted. 'That's life, Louis.' Oh, did that rankle Mayer. And then Mayer said to us, 'And that picture did not make back its negative cost!' To him, there was a direct connection between the toilet and the lack of commercial success."

What so many people didn't realize was that it was never simply a matter of power for L.B. What he was fighting for, what he had always fought for, was his vision of the world.

The success of *The Barkleys of Broadway* removed the onus from *On the Town*. Suddenly the property that Mayer could not countenance went into pre-production—with, it is true, much of Leonard Bernstein's music removed. Mayer thought Gene Kelly's and co-director Stanley Donen's desire to shoot in New York was insane, but allowed two weeks of location work and not an hour more.

The extent of the Freed unit's insulation from the day-to-day *tsimmis* of the studio—and the strength of Mayer's faith in Freed—became evident after the film was made and released. One day, Kelly was passing Mayer in the studio barbershop when Mayer stopped him. "I was wrong about that picture," Mayer said. "You fellows did a good job."

"That was the only discussion I ever had with him about that picture," remembered Kelly.

At the end of 1947, Mayer traveled to New Haven to check out Irene's production of the Broadway-bound *A Streetcar Named Desire*. Irene hadn't wanted him bothering her, so had resisted, but the old man wouldn't be dissuaded. Finally, Irene suggested if he was going to hang around New England, he should visit his grandsons at their respective schools. "Go there and do what?" he wanted to know. Finally, a deal was struck—L.B. would visit his grandsons and Irene would let him see her play in New Haven.

The visits out of the way, he met his exhausted and terrified daughter for dinner, and took charge. He ordered her a shot of whiskey and water on the side, ordered her dinner, and lit her cigarettes for her. Halfway through the meal, he told her she'd eaten enough and she should get to the theater.

After the performance, he hung around on the periphery of Irene's room at the Taft Hotel. Everybody seemed to feel that the play was going to be an artistic success, but nobody was talking a commercial hit. L.B. took his daughter into the bedroom. The people out there, he told her, were goddamn fools.

"They don't know anything. You don't have a hit, you've got a smash. You wait and see. Now get back and don't listen to them."

Afterward, he buttonholed Elia Kazan. It was a great play, he told Kazan, and they were all going to make a fortune, but they had to do one crucial piece of rewriting: after the "awful woman" who'd broken up that "fine young couple's happy home" was taken to an institution, there had to be something to indicate that the young couple would live happily ever after.

Streetcar was one of the indelible dramatic triumphs of the American theater, winning the Pulitzer Prize and establishing Marlon Brando as the godhead of modern acting. And yes, it made a lot of money for everybody. L.B. was beside himself with pride; Irene was the son he had never had. He began giving her very out-of-character lavish presents. She said all she wanted was luggage, which he thought ridiculous: "Luggage you can buy yourself." But he gave her a five-piece set in cherry-red alligator. The year after that it was a gold compact with a scene from *Streetcar* engraved on it from Van Cleef & Arpels and when the road company of *Streetcar* came to Los Angeles, L.B. threw a party complete with an enormous ice sculpture of a streetcar.

A day or two before Christmas of 1948, Irene had a lunch for David Selznick, her father, and Arthur Laurents, who had written a play for her and become part of her social circle.

"One of her boys was headed out the door," remembered Laurents, "and asked Louis for some pocket money. 'Ask your grandmother,' he snapped, 'she got all of it.'

"Anyway, we sat down to lunch and L.B. proposed a toast to some picture David was about to make. And Irene knocked the glass out of her father's hands and said, 'In my house, the first toast is to me.'

"Now, in the real world, people don't act like that, but these people behaved as if they were in one of their own movies. They lived movie lives off screen.

"Irene wasn't afraid of him. She revered him. And she revered David as well. They were all actually very close, but by this time Irene and her sister barely spoke. Edie was just a terrible snob, very interested in being chic and collecting paintings."

There was no artwork in the entrance to the Goetz house, just an eighteenth-century gilt mirror and some Ming and Tang objects. Off to the right was the library, which is where the parties would begin with cocktails and canapés. The room was done in blond maple by Billy Haines, and decorated with Bill

Goetz's collection of first editions, a lot of Vuillards, and a picture of L.B. with Churchill and Hearst. On one side of the living room was a Picasso clown painting, and on the other side, by the double doors that led to the dining room, was a Picasso mother and child. The dining room was in a shade of mustard yellow that was ugly in the daytime but magical at night, when lit by candlelight. Throughout the house there were orchids, for Edie had a greenhouse on the premises.

"Whenever I think of that house, I think of Fred Astaire and Cyd Charisse in *Silk Stockings*," said the writer David Patrick Columbia. "That's what it looked like, a very upscale movie set in an MGM musical. She was a *wonderful* hostess. You would be awed by people in the room, but everybody behaved as if they were Edie's guest, rather than a star. And in her own house, Edie was a nice woman, not favoring Cary Grant or Jimmy Stewart over you. She would show *hauteur* someplace else, but at her house she was very democratic. Her father was so impressed by her femininity, her grooming, her red fingernails, the presence of the best chef.

"Whenever Irene and Edie would talk about each other, they always acted as if they were on the silver screen. The eyebrows would rise and they were Swanson in *Sunset Boulevard*. Irene was mean about Edie, and Edie was mean about Irene. 'I don't know why Irene hates me,' Edie would say, but she said it almost mockingly. There was a very distinct competition as to whom Dad loved the most. I always felt that was the bottom line with both of them."

One of the few things Edie would be sincere about where Irene was concerned was her regret over the Selznick marriage breaking up. "Those girls grew up in a world where the only way you could be legitimate was if you had a man and that man was powerful," said Columbia. "Margaret had lost her man and I think it cost her status in her daughters' eyes. Everybody loved Margaret, she was a very sweet lady, salt of the earth. But they saw that she had been left behind and they were both subconsciously determined that would never happen to them. Margaret was a victim, she got shafted, but L.B. had power, and they were both into that."

Judy Garland's condition had become dangerously unstable. An impossibly needy woman with the strange habit of being sexually attracted to homosexual men, Garland had broadcast for years that Louis B. Mayer was solely responsible for her legion of problems. On *The Pirate*, for instance, out of 135 days of rehearsal, recording, and shooting, Garland was absent for ninety-nine days. To hear Garland tell it, Mayer had gotten her pills to keep her going, pills to keep her from gaining weight, pills to get her to go to sleep. "She felt he was a destructive force," remembered Betty Comden. Others felt that to blame Mayer for what happened to Judy Garland is to imagine that the train wreck could have been averted if only Garland had been working at Warner Bros. or Paramount.

Arthur Freed dismissed such talk out of hand. "All this talk about the oppression. . . . First of all, all the time she was sick or in hospital, Metro paid the bills. Louis Mayer took care of everything." George Sidney agreed, saying, "This widespread notion that the studio somehow destroyed her is nonsense. Her personal life got too much for her."

Garland would also claim that Mayer would entice her to sit in his lap or pat her on the fanny as a means of copping a feel. "Look," said Kathryn Grayson, "Judy drank. And when she drank she would say weird things. I'm sure he never did anything like that. His demeanor was very fatherly at all times. He felt the same way about her as he did me and he never touched me in that way and never thought of me in that way. If you were a lady, you were *always* treated as a lady. And if you were a trollop, you were treated like a trollop, and he didn't like trollops."

Adolph Green believed that "L.B. was the symbol for Judy's problems, but I don't know if the blame can be put at Louis's door. None of it was diabolically planned. There's this misconception that studio heads were this giant group of stern, devilish judges. But they were just trying to get pictures made. 'Try this. It's not working? Then try this.' There was no plan to turn the poor child into a monster. It was accidental bad treatment. Judy Garland was a great performer and a very unhappy girl, with a tough life."

Since the doctors and psychiatrists weren't helping her, maybe a good talk with a sensible person, someone who commanded respect, might have some impact. Mayer thought of the most sensible person on the lot: Kate Hepburn. Hepburn tried, but it didn't help. Nothing did. When Garland's absences put the production of a pleasant little musical called *Summer Stock* in a deep hole, Joe Pasternak told Mayer to cut his losses and cancel the picture. Mayer refused. "Judy Garland has made this studio a fortune in the good days, and the least we can do is to give her one more chance. If you stop production now, it'll finish her." Garland managed to get through the movie, which ran far over schedule, but on the next picture, *Annie Get Your Gun*, the studio finally ran out of patience.

Garland's exhaustion was exacerbated when co-star Howard Keel broke his ankle. Busby Berkeley made Keel do multiple takes of a scene with him gallop-ing on a horse. On the seventh take, the horse stumbled and threw Keel. His spurs caught in the ground and his ankle snapped.

"Buzz was a bad drunk," said Keel. "He didn't drink when I was there, but he was a wild man when he worked. I had done the shot six times, but he didn't care what the actor was doing. All he thought of was the camera."

Berkeley was fired. Instead of shutting the picture down and waiting for Keel's ankle to heal, they attempted to prop him in front of the camera for close-ups and medium shots. But immobility was a problem for new director George Sidney's more flowing visual plan, so they attempted to shoot around him, putting even more pressure on Garland.

"She began to fall apart," said Keel. "She started to lose her hair, and there was a Dr. Feelgood around helping her with shots. And she just fell apart. Fir-ing her was the only tacky thing I ever saw MGM do." Garland's firing precipi-tated a suicide attempt. Mayer visited her during her recuperation, and Garland told him of her mounting financial troubles. Mayer told her that he felt reasonably certain that the company would make her a loan, and pro-ceeded to call Nick Schenck. The conversation didn't last long.

"Mr. Schenck suggests that you go to a charity hospital," Mayer told her. " 'We're not in the money-lending business,' " he said as he put the phone down. He thought for a bit, then said, "You know, if they'll do this to you, they'll do it to me." Mayer proceeded to say he was ashamed of Schenck's behavior, and would personally pay Garland's expenses.

There is a poignance to Mayer's fumbling attempts to understand and help Garland out of the crash dive that was her life. In retrospect, "She loved L. B. Mayer to the end of her life," wrote her daughter Lorna Luft. "In the decade after she left Metro . . . she never blamed L.B. for what had happened to her. She always spoke lovingly of him to us as children and to my father. It was L. B. Mayer who paid for my mother's hospitalizations when she became ill during her years at MGM, even when it was clear she might never be able to make an-other movie for him."

The declining box office meant that someone had to be sacrificed, so Sam Katz, Al Lichtman, and James Kevin McGuinness were all fired, while staffing was cut by 25 percent. The word spread through the studio that Katz would be paid full salary for five years, half salary for two and a half years, would be given stock options, and have his pension advanced. On top of everything else, his chain of theaters would receive MGM films for reduced rentals. Songwriter Harry Ruby banged his fist down on the lunch table so hard that the silverware jumped. "That'll show the son of a bitch!" he said.

The executive producer system was scrapped, and power was centralized in the triumvirate of Mayer, Eddie Mannix, and Benny Thau. Generally, this was felt to be a stop-gap measure; L.B. was regarded as a big-picture man, not a line producer who could tighten the nuts and bolts of twenty to thirty pictures. The MGM way had always been successful, so what was needed was a return to the old MGM way. The cult of personality had worked before, it would work again. Somebody else was needed; somebody like . . . Thalberg.

The drop was not just at Culver City. The number of Hollywood films that grossed $4 million in 1947 was precisely six, compared to twenty-two in 1946. L.B. kept hustling to make good, big pictures. When RKO backed off financing Frank Capra's *State of the Union* because of its $2.7 million budget, Louis picked up the project. "We'll loan Spencer Tracy to Liberty Films if Liberty makes the film at our studio," he explained to Capra. "We'll release it as an MGM picture and that'll still keep Tracy under our banner." The cast was filled out with MGM talent—Hepburn, Van Johnson, Angela Lansbury. But Capra had entered upon what turned out to be a permanent decline, and the finished picture didn't gel for critics, contemporary audiences, or posterity; it grossed $3.5 million, basically breaking even.

At Paramount, Barney Balaban issued a fiat proclaiming that no film could cost more than $2 million. At MGM, $2 million continued to be average.

"Nick would call and say, 'Cut, cut,' " said George Sidney. "And L.B. would say, 'A studio isn't salami, Nick.'

" 'Spend less!'

" 'Spend more!'

"You must realize that L.B. would ask only one question: 'Can you make it better?' It was all he cared about. Once, when I was shooting, he came on the set, got out of his car and saw me riding a new Chapman crane we had rented. 'What's that, boy?' (He always called me 'boy.') I explained what it was, and he asked me, 'Will that help you make a better picture?'

" 'Yes,' I said.

" 'Buy it,' he said.

"This man respected one thing: talent. Harry Cohn used to say, 'If you have talent, I will kiss your ass. If you don't, I will throw you through the window, and I won't open it first.' Mayer's idea was the same."

When Louis had a chance to cut payroll, he wouldn't. Herbert Stothart fell ill early in 1948 with the cancer that would eventually kill him. Contractually, the studio wasn't obligated to pay him his $1,000 a week for periods of illness. But the studio put him on half-salary for an indefinite period.

For the movie business in general, and MGM and Mayer in particular, 1948 would be a tumultuous year of loss and gain, of divestment and investment. In February, L.B. personally bought one of the premier showcase theaters in Manhattan. The Rivoli Theater, built in 1917, had 2,100 seats, fronted on Broadway, and extended back to Seventh Avenue between 49th and 50th Streets. Mayer paid $1.5 million for what was considered one of Manhattan's finest theaters.

At the studio, Nick Schenck wanted a younger man, and Mayer was now forced to agree. A young Irving? L.B. looked around. There was nobody at MGM in that league. He looked elsewhere. David Selznick was a great producer, but he was also nearly bankrupt and Nick Schenck could not have been enthusiastic about hiring a man who seemed to be past his peak.

Everything that you could say professionally about David Selznick you could also say about Walter Wanger. What about Joe Mankiewicz—a fine producer, a brilliant screenwriter and director? He knew MGM, didn't he? As it turned not, Mankiewicz knew MGM all too well, and wouldn't go near the studio or its problems.

And then someone suggested Dore Schary. Sure, he had left MGM after conflicts, but he had energy, creativity, and a warm personality. He had done a good job at Selznick, then had a burst of apparent success at RKO. He also knew the studio and its strengths and weaknesses; he could hit the ground running.

Dore Schary—that was an idea.

On a Sunday in the spring of 1948, Arthur Freed brought a young writer named Richard Brooks to Mayer's house. Mayer was preparing to go to a baseball game, and asked Freed and Brooks to join him. During the game, the conversation turned to Schary, who had recently produced a Brooks novel as *Crossfire* at RKO. The book, about the killing of a homosexual, had been converted into a controversial movie about the killing of a Jew. What, Mayer wanted to know, was Schary's contribution to the picture? Why did he want to make *that* story? Brooks answered all of Mayer's questions and spoke of his high regard for Schary.

Shortly afterward, Lillie Messinger called Schary and asked him to come to Mayer's house for a meeting. Mayer congratulated Schary on the job he had done for Selznick and RKO, then, without any further preliminaries, offered him the job of vice president of production at MGM. Schary was surprised but not stunned; he had recently resigned from RKO after encountering interference from new owner Howard Hughes, and rather thought Mayer was going to offer him an executive producer's job.

Schary told Mayer that he thought MGM was top-heavy with bureaucracy. Mayer countered by telling Schary that he was tired, that he wanted to retire soon. Then he began to reminisce about Thalberg, saying, "believe me, [Irving] was a genius, but he was money-mad. That was his problem. Money—money—that ruined him."

Schary wanted freedom to choose stories and stars, and he wanted final cut of MGM films. Mayer listened, told Schary to stick to his guns and he would tell Nick Schenck what was required. "I'm happy to have you come back home to MGM where you belong," Mayer said by way of farewell. Schary consulted with his former agent, Lew Wasserman, who deeply admired Mayer. But Wasserman was a realist and told Schary the only way it could work would be if he cleaned house: "Get rid of all the executives." Schary disagreed; he believed the system was reasonably sound, just needed energy and new points of view.

At a group lunch, Mayer announced that Schary was returning to MGM. "He worked for us as a writer," said Louis. "And then he went over to other studios, and then one day I called him. 'Dore, we want you,' I said.

" 'Louis, I never left home.' "

Bob Rubin, charged with negotiating Schary's contract, wasn't happy with some of his demands and was frankly suspicious of the new arrival. Even some of Schary's friends had qualms. "Schary had great charm," remembered Richard Goldstone, who had worked with Schary at RKO and would work for him at MGM. "He was a tremendous opportunist for himself, with a streak of ruthlessness. He was a mysophobic—a fear of germs, of contamination. A very large ego. Great artistic pretensions. Great liberal pretensions. A conflicted guy."

Schary insisted on being named head of production, which got Bob Rubin's back up, so the lawyer dropped in a sentence saying that Schary was answerable to "the president, the board of directors, and the head of studio administration," thus handing Mayer an entirely new title and at least apparent control over his new hire.

On July 14, 1948, Schary became vice president in charge of production at MGM "under direction of Louis B. Mayer." His pay was set at $5,000 a week.

When she heard the news, Lillian Burns Sidney marched into Mayer's office. "Now you've done it," she announced. "You've ruined everything."

"Why? What's wrong with Dore Schary?"

"Nothing's wrong with Dore Schary except he only likes 'message pictures.' No musicals, no comedies, no adventures. Just messages. They won't have need for anybody around here. Even you! You'll see."

Mayer was complacent. Why should he worry? Dore was a nice young man. And what could he do, after all? Look at that sign on the roof: Metro-Goldwyn-Mayer. His name. How could they ever take it away from him?

During the contract negotiations, Schary had noted the chemical differences between Mayer and Schenck, noted Mayer's dry, white skin, and Schenck's oily complexion. Schenck walked with short steps, his body angled slightly forward, while Mayer strode aggressively, at a near-trot. Schenck's manners were impeccable, and he stood up to greet nearly everyone, which Mayer seldom did. Schenck was courtly, Mayer was touchy. "If seriously challenged," Schary concluded, "L.B. would maul you to death—Nick would do you in with a cyanide cocktail."

Schary had also been clued in to the relationship—or, rather, the nonrelationship—of the two old men. "Don't trust him," Mayer said. "He'll bring you caviar when you leave New York and flowers in your room when you get back there—but he's only smiles and caviar and roses—the rest of him is all shit. . . . All he knows about movies you could stick in a cat's ass."

From Mayer's point of view, Schary knew the MGM system. Furthermore, his capitulation at the Waldorf Conference intimated that the younger man could be coerced or, if necessary, rolled. Schary was nonthreatening, genial, professorial. But, said Howard Keel, "He was an entirely different kind of producer [from Mayer]. You couldn't help but like Dore, [but] he was indecisive; he'd cast you back and forth. He probably had some idea of taking over. He knew Mayer was not cutting the mustard, and he probably had some things in mind." (It should be noted that Schary cohorts such as Sidney Sheldon and Millard Kaufman seriously doubt that Schary was gunning for his boss.)

In production matters, Schary's liberalism was often expressed with allegorical projects that seemed to derive from medieval morality plays; in other matters, he was a traditionalist, devoted to motherhood and Israel.

Mayer's own feelings about Israel could be characterized as indifference mixed with distrust. Weren't most of the Jews leftists? What had the Jews ever done for L. B. Mayer? When S. N. Behrman, a friend of Israeli leader Chaim Weizmann's, came to talk to him about Israel, Mayer cut him short. "What it comes to is a matter of money, isn't it?" Behrman said that was true. Mayer refused to donate, saying, "When you give them a state, those people will just become Communists."

Mayer undoubtedly felt that Schary's excesses could be regulated; from his days on Mission Road, his achievements had been defined by his excellent taste in production executives, and his ability to control them. Schary was younger, in touch with current trends, he was polite, he was respectful. And he loved his mother! A surrogate son! More importantly, a surrogate David Selznick.

"L. B. MAYER WEDS TODAY; ELOPES WITH LORENA DANKER," read the page one banner headline in the *Los Angeles Examiner* on Saturday, December 4, 1948. They had slipped out of town the night before and taken a train to Yuma, where the service took place in a small room in the Yuma County Jail. Mayer seems to have been in a good mood; just before the ceremony he turned to Sheriff J. A. Beard and told him, "You're just the man I want. You're the best-looking Sheriff I ever saw. Come to Hollywood and I'll give you a job in pictures."

The ceremony was performed by a justice of the peace in two minutes flat. The new Mrs. Mayer wore a fur coat over a tailored suit, while L.B. wore a dark blue double-breasted suit. Mayer planted a quick kiss on his bride; the wedding party, which included Howard Strickling, Whitey Hendry, and Lorena's daughter, Suzanne, headed out in cars.

Reporters who had tailed the couple were thrown off the track by the wedding party switching cars. One photographer's car broke down, and another caught fire. The groom said he was sixty-three; the bride forty-one.

Louella Parsons made the couple sound like Romeo and Juliet, but Hedda Hopper said the flight and pursuit was more like a "B cops-and-robbers production." The *L.A. Mirror* had some fun with the couple, headlining its coverage as "December Wed to—Uh—July," referring to Mayer as "Grandpa," and an "elderly film producer." A day or two later, the pair was discovered honeymooning at Joe Schenck's ten-room Spanish lodge at Arrowhead Springs. When Mayer spotted the photographers, said one, he "was very irate and almost threatening."

Lorena Jones Danker Mayer was a tall, glossy brunette from Georgia, widely liked for her charm and unassuming personality. She began her career in Hollywood as one of Busby Berkeley's showgirls at Warner Bros., appearing in *Gold Diggers of 1933*, *I Loved a Woman*, *Jimmy the Gent*, and *42nd Street*.

She married Danny Danker, vice president of J. Walter Thompson, but Danker dropped dead in a hotel room in 1944 at the age of forty-two, leaving Lorena with a young daughter. (Ten months after the wedding, Mayer adopted Suzanne, Lorena's 12-year-old daughter.)

After Lorena's husband died, she went to work at J. Walter Thompson as well, and earned a reputation as an attractive, well-dressed woman. Charles Feldman said that Lorena was one of Joe Schenck's many girlfriends. Schenck, according to Feldman, made the mistake of giving her a mink coat that wasn't very expensive. Lorena was miffed at the cut-rate gift, and moved on to Mayer.

"Lorena was part of the group that milled around," remembered Mary Loos. "We were all rather surprised when she married Mayer. But she had a daughter and she wanted that girl to have everything she could have."

It was widely believed that Mayer had "begged" her to marry him; Charles Moscowitz, a Loew's executive loyal to Nick Schenck, said that Mayer was so desperate about Danker that he asked Schenck to intercede for him when both Schenck and Danker were visiting Florida one winter.

After the humiliating rejection from Ginny Simms, and Ann Miller, Mayer was gun-shy; he kept calling mutual friends asking them to put in a good word for him with Lorena. Danker told the columnist Dorothy Manners that she found his insecurity charming. Mayer's childlike aspects seemed particularly fascinating for a powerful older man.

Realizing that something besides his personal charm might be called for, Mayer offered to settle $1 million on her daughter by the late Mr. Danker.

"Lorena wasn't that young, she wasn't that pretty, but she was a wonderful lady," remembered Evie Johnson. "She had a great sense of humor. And after he married her, he didn't wander."

"Lorena was superb," said the producer Armand Deutsch. "What compact she made with Louis, I don't know, but she was a great wife to him."

Even Mayer's family liked Lorena; Gerald Mayer called her "very personable. She was a Catholic, a former showgirl, but a very classy lady." Daniel Selznick said that "Lorena was this fabulous, social creature that Maggie had never been, easily one of the two or three most charming women I have ever known. Manipulative, probably. But just so charming, the way she flattered people, the things she noticed, her observations, her memory for names, her ability to schmooze."

A new wife demanded a new home, so L.B. bought—from Mervyn LeRoy—a house at 332 St. Cloud Road in Bel Air. It was large and fashionably modern, nothing like the Spanish haciendas L.B. had lived in since he arrived in California, and it again indulged Mayer's taste for white leather. The entry hall was cream-colored, while the living room had green walls and low-slung white chairs and sofas. A sun parlor was done in red and white, while Mayer's office featured two white leather chairs in front of a white leather table.

"Everything was white," Edie Goetz remembered. "White draperies, white sofa, white rugs. . . . It looked like a hospital room." Ed Willis, a set decorator at MGM, was in charge of decorating the house, and he was in a panic because it all looked terrible, as if it was a "display window in W. & J. Sloane or something." It was what Mayer had demanded, but Edith went to work on her father and suggested some good wallpaper be used for the dining room. In Saint John or Boston, wallpaper was only used when the wall was too dirty to bother with anymore, but Edith got her way and redid the entire house, putting up wallpaper, repainting the walls, coordinating the furniture.

Edie's efforts resulted in a kind of monochromatic blandness. "The house looked like a hotel," said Elizabeth Horowitz, Jessie Marmorston's daughter. "It was comfortable, but it could have belonged to anybody. It was anonymous." The draperies were controlled by electricity, there were lots of terraces, and Suzanne couldn't quite figure out where she fit in amongst such pristine surroundings.

A new wife often implicitly demands a changing of the emotional guard, and Lorena was no exception. "Lorena was Catholic," said Daniel Selznick, "and whenever anything remotely Jewish came up, she would make a reference to 'Your grandfather's former life. He doesn't go to synagogues anymore.' She blanked out all those years. At Santa Monica, and at the house he lived in on Benedict Canyon, there had always been a big photograph of his mother over the bed. But there was no photo of his mother on St. Cloud Road."

Margaret stayed quietly behind, in the house on the beach, sitting in the front bedroom overlooking the Pacific and watching the waves roll in. She had imagined that it was just a question of time until L.B. came back, but his new marriage had changed all that. Her grandson Daniel could tell that she was lonely and heartsick. He couldn't imagine his grandparents apart—they had been married for more than forty years—and neither could Maggie.

"With the most exquisite tact, she would ask me, 'Is she pretty? Is she charming? What is their life like?' And she got lonelier and lonelier. As far as I know, grandfather never contacted her. He would ask me, 'Have you seen your grandmother lately? How is she?' And he would ask my mother about how she was doing, but that was it."

S. N. Behrman ran into Margaret one day in the sales room of the Hattie Carnegie store. When he asked her where she was going, she said, "Nowhere. I like to sit here and watch people come and go."

At least one writer has speculated about suicide attempts, but Daniel Selznick doesn't believe it. "She had no scars on her wrists, or anything like that. I heard at one time that she was *feeling* suicidal, but she wasn't the kind of woman who would have done it. She was vulnerable, certainly, but she was also unusually frightened of anything remotely violent."

And so Margaret Mayer sat by the sea, knowing that her Louis would never come back home.

Chapter
FIFTEEN

IN SOME RESPECTS, Dore Schary was a breath of fresh air. He had a sense of the world beyond the walls of Culver City and, said Sidney Sheldon, "was liberal and compassionate. And he was brilliant on script." You didn't catch him calling all hands to a soundstage for a speech about how they had to be on the lookout for whispers of Communism around the studio, as L.B. did soon after Schary's arrival. "If you laugh now, it could cost you your job," whispered Armand Deutsch to the young contract player Nancy Davis. "Why would I laugh?" she replied, already in the proper mind-set for her future.

Clearly, one of the problems at MGM was overhead, the languorous, top-heavy method of production Mayer had encouraged. "They had a tremendous number of people involved with the studio [who] weren't operating properly," said Schary in analyzing the situation. "Mayer's system of setting individual units within the studio like little independent groups . . . was not working. He had done that to prevent anybody from ever getting control again like Thalberg because he and Thalberg loathed each other. [That] system had fallen apart because the men in charge had not been creative executives."

Schary began by signing up some talent that had more au courant ideas than Robert Taylor. "When I got to MGM, it was a contest, but Dore was winning," remembered James Whitmore, who arrived at the studio after a stint in the Marines during World War II. "I was taken in to meet Mr. Mayer for a welcome-to-the-family talk, but I never quite saw him. He had Venetian blinds behind him, and his desk was raised, and you were in a low chair in front of the dais. It was about three in the afternoon, and the sun was in my eyes. I only saw an outline.

"Dore was the Young Turk coming on. He was a writer and he had some great ideas. He was a *mensch*, a good guy, warm, not pompous at all, and aware of his own shortcomings. Dore was a man willing to accept defeat and failure and did so graciously. Mannix and Thau were company men; they approached actors as children, to be disciplined and cajoled and complimented. Dore was more apt to treat actors as equals."

"In some ways it was a hellhole," said the composer David Raksin, who arrived at Metro around this time. "Their way of doing business, whether conscious or not, was to wear you out with obstinacy and red tape and frustration so that you would not be in danger of doing anything worthwhile. I used to call the place *Strike Up the Bland*.

"It was a producer's studio. The department heads had a great deal of power, but a producer could overrule them. A producer could do anything but make a good picture. It was a place where fire trucks or ambulances were always passing on Washington Boulevard. And when they'd come roaring by, Frank Sinatra would take off his hat in the middle of a take, hold it over his heart, and say 'Another guy made it over the wall.' "

Success had made the studio stiff in the joints and sclerotic. There was considerable young talent in the musical troupe (Debbie Reynolds, Jane Powell), nearly none among writers and directors.

And Exhibit A for the problem was Mayer. When someone proposed doing a biography of the baseball pitcher Monty Stratton, who lost a leg in an accident but made a successful comeback, Mayer didn't want to make the picture. "How do you think people will feel when this man with one leg goes to bat, gets a single, but can't run to first base? How will the pregnant women in the audience feel watching such a disgusting sight?"

Well, among other possibilities, empathy—perhaps even a stirring, inspirational appreciation at watching a fellow human being overcome shattering adversity. The fact that it was *real* adversity, not movie adversity, was the root of Mayer's problem with the picture, and with the entire drift of postwar movies. In any case, he finally went along with the picture, and *The Stratton Story*, helped along by Jimmy Stewart's performance and his pairing with fan favorite June Allyson, proved to be MGM's third most profitable picture in 1949.

The more prescient among the studio's employees recognized that not only MGM but Hollywood in general had fallen behind the times. In one sense, they could hardly help it—tens of millions of people had been slaughtered in

Europe in clear violation of the Production Code, but that couldn't be reflected in the films that were made. More to the point, in 1947, there were only 136,000 television sets in America. In 1948, that figure had jumped to 700,000. On Tuesday nights, Detroit water reservoirs dropped precipitously at 9:00 P.M., as people rushed to the bathroom after Milton Berle's show; nightclubs changed their closing nights from Monday to Tuesday. All this for retread vaudeville and burlesque acts on a flickering black-and-white box. But it was free entertainment, and right there in your living room.

Erich von Stroheim's son Joe came back to MGM to work in the cutting rooms, where he renewed an acquaintanceship with Cotton Warburton, a former USC football star.

"Joe, what are you doing here?" Warburton asked. "Goddamn it, go out there and get in the independent field. Don't come back to a major studio. And if I see you here again, I'll kick your ass."

Schary cut individual budgets an average of 25 percent and tried to institute a more active working schedule for contract players than just a picture or two a year. He also cemented the identification with Thalberg by announcing that he would personally produce a picture or two a year, although unlike Thalberg, he would take credit for those personal productions. A group of stories bought during the war was written off to the tune of $1.1 million, including a few purchased for over $100,000.

After a year of Schary, the studio showed a small profit of $300,000, compared to the previous year's loss of $6.5 million. Schary's personal production of *Battleground*, superbly directed by William Wellman, was a big success, grossing $5 million on a cost of $1.6 million. All this helped everyone overlook the fact that Schary had numerous blind spots, primarily having to do with glossy entertainment—after a preview of *Annie Get Your Gun*, an oblivious Schary told Arthur Freed that the shooting match had to be cut. It was the beginning of a cool contempt on the part of Freed toward Schary.

Richard Goldstone, who had begun in the shorts department in the early 1930s, was now a producer on the lot, and began eating in the executive dining room with Mayer and some of his favorites. "Everybody would talk and everybody would listen to Mayer," remembered Goldstone. "He was interested in what others thought and interested in you hearing what he thought. The talk was mostly about movies, and sometimes he would see into the future very accurately and sometimes he wouldn't. His nemesis was television; he had contempt for it. I remember he once said, 'When television becomes as important as the movies, we will own television.' And it turned out to be the other way around.

"I found him to be a great showman. A great ringmaster. His pretensions were actually aspirations. He was a self-made man, very proud, impeccably dressed and manicured and he enjoyed his prestige and power. The greatest misconception about Mayer is that he was cruel. I saw him do things that were ice-cold, but never cruel."

Mayer has always been assumed to be one with Nick Schenck in believing that TV wasn't a problem, and that MGM could go on doing what it had always done. And in some respects that was indeed the case. When the studio decided to stop making Lassie pictures, screenwriter William Ludwig went to Mayer and said, "Mr. Mayer, the dog gets $250 a week, and the trainer, Rudd Weatherwax, gets $500 a week. That's $750 a week. This dog is worth millions in television, if you ask me."

"You're stupid," Mayer snapped. "We're not interested in television."

But if he shared the myopia of most of his generation of moguls regarding television, he knew that the wind had shifted in other ways. In fact, he knew something was wrong, and that he and his studio would have to adapt. "They keep telling me something new is coming and it's not our MGM kind of movies," he told Richard Brooks. "I don't know, maybe they're right. I don't like the pictures you make—they're not MGM-type pictures—all those dirty fingerprints on the walls. We don't like that. But I don't know what's coming and we're not going to let you go."

Brooks, in later years the underrated filmmaker behind *Elmer Gantry, The Professionals,* and *Looking for Mr. Goodbar,* among others, would talk about this conversation with Mayer with much insight. "You know, these were pretty monstrous bastards who were running the studios at that time. But they gave me a chance—today, you may get one shot, and if you fail, they break your back and forget about you from that time on. Then, you were a part of a system that gave you *another* chance.

"So, MGM gave me opportunity after opportunity and for seven and a half years there I paid my dues and I learned my craft. And I learned it from some great people. The Mayers and the Warners and the Cohns—they did terrible things, but they *loved* movies. I can't say that about many film executives nowadays. They don't even *like* movies."

The instincts that a studio head has to have were not visited upon Dore Schary, as would become obvious as the results of his tenure at RKO played out. Schary had begun at RKO on January 1, 1947, so the results of his efforts there didn't really become visible for about a year. The administration before Schary, 1946 through the first half of 1947, showed a net loss for the studio of $609,000. The results for the following year, mid-1947 to mid-1948—mostly Schary's responsibility—showed a net loss of $5.5 million.

Crossfire, Schary's pet project, was produced for an economical $678,000 and showed a tasty profit of $1.2 million. Other Schary pictures included *They Live by Night*, *Out of the Past*, and *The Set-Up*, tough, bleak noirs that made a little money or lost a little money. But a movie studio is a department store, not a boutique. When it came to the hopefully commercial pictures with which any movie studio has to pay its overhead, Schary had a misguided touch—the John Wayne vehicle *Tycoon* lost over $1 million, *The Miracle of the Bells* lost over $600,000, *I Remember Mama* lost over $1 million, as did *Night Song*. Even an apparently commercial picture like *Mr. Blandings Builds His Dream House* lost $225,000. The next year—when RKO was still burning off some of Schary's productions—was only slightly less disastrous (a net loss of just over $5 million), as such Schary favorites as *The Boy with Green Hair* (loss of $420,000) undercut some mid-range successes.

Contrary to everyone's expectations, Schary got on fairly well with the old guard around Mayer. "The greatest beef they had with him was his predilection for making pictures with a message," said Armand Deutsch. "Mervyn LeRoy would actually say, 'If you want to send a message, go to Western Union.' "

Armand Deutsch was initially Schary's assistant, and was delegated the task of making friends with all of the men that surrounded Mayer—Mannix, Thau, Joe Cohn. "I'm not one of them," Schary told Deutsch. "I'll always be outside of them."

Although Schary now had the primary responsibility of green-lighting films, Mayer still had a good deal of input. As the studio was planning *The Great Caruso*, Mayer called in music director Johnny Green. "I sense that you may seize upon *The Great Caruso* as an opportunity to show off," he began. "You remember that there is no disgrace to melody and making a picture of this kind. I want it to be 'classy,' but I want it to communicate. I want people to be able to identify with it and I am advising you—none of these far out arias—latch on to the familiar ones that everybody loves."

He went on to single out "Celeste Aida" and several others as likely candidates for inclusion. "If I've offended you, I didn't mean to, I just had a hunch that we'd get all kinds of esoteric music in this picture. Don't do it."

He was still capable of terrorizing someone he felt had shortchanged his studio. A writer named John Larkin worked on the treatment and screenplay of a musical called *Two Weeks with Love*. Mayer hated the script and called

Dorothy Kingsley into his office for a meeting about a rewrite. Kingsley found Larkin cowering in a corner as L.B. profanely berated him for his failure. Eventually the writer broke down and began to cry, at which point Kingsley banged her hand on Mayer's desk. "That will be enough, Mr. Mayer! You can't talk to people like that. And furthermore, I will not accept that kind of language."

Mayer was taken aback and, after staring at her for a moment, apologized. Whenever he saw her around the studio, he would tell his coterie, "Uh-oh, boys, watch your language. Dorothy's here."

The old lion was sometimes touchy, and always unpredictable. When Richard Goldstone hired Ramon Novarro to support Joel McCrea in a western called *The Outriders*, Billy Grady told him he was making a big mistake. "There was a terrific feud with Mayer and Novarro," he told Goldstone. Novarro, he explained, was homosexual, and that was not kosher with Mayer.

The first scene to be filmed was a wagon crossing a flooded river. Novarro was in the scene, and just as they were about to get underway a limousine pulled up and Mayer got out. "Ramon!" he bellowed, throwing open his arms. "L.B.!" responded Novarro. As the two men embraced, Goldstone was left to ponder the strange ways of elderly movie moguls.

Lorena's influence impelled Louis to more socializing. "We had dinners at his house a lot," said Evie Johnson. "I always sat next to him because I could talk to him. As a person, I liked him. He could be as nice as can be. Fatherly, with a sense of protection he could give you. He had a lot of different facets to him. I'll never forget something he said about Esther Williams: 'Wet, she's a star. Dry, she ain't.' "

"He gave wonderful parties," remembered the wet star. "Watching Walter Pidgeon light a cigar was a ceremony. L.B.'s house was decorated in Early Pomp. It was a lot of drapes and pillows, very posh. And Lorena was every inch a lady. She always reminded me of Irene Dunne; she had that kind of containment—a wonderful woman. I liked her a lot and L.B. was mad about her. He felt that someone like her gave him class."

If Lorena broadened Mayer's social life, his horizons in other areas remained the same. He sold off the stable he had painstakingly built, partly to finance the divorce settlement from Margaret, partly because, according to Myron Fox, his business manager, there were serious financial benefits that would result, and Lorena had no interest whatever in racing.

The first auction brought in $1.55 million for sixty horses, including L.B.'s beloved Busher, and less successful horses named Main Feature and Make-Up

Man. Harry Warner paid $200,000 for a horse named Stepfather, while Mayer's friend Neil McCarthy bought Busher, so at least he could still visit the horse.

Throughout the auction, Mayer sat quietly, head down, listening to the singsong cadence of the auctioneer. In front of him was a glass of straight bourbon whiskey, which he would occasionally spin around, move forward, then back, but never actually pick up and drink.

The sale set a record for auctions that stood for nearly twenty years. There were more sales over the next three years; by the time he had disposed of the last of his stable in 1950, 248 horses had sold for $4.4 million, while the Perris ranch, valued at only $400,000, was sold off to the Church of Latter Day Saints, who eventually sold it to a potato farmer who kept 162 acres and sold off the remaining 320 acres.

As horses departed, paintings arrived. Collecting art has always been a sideline occupation for movie people, and in the late 1940s Grandma Moses became the latest au courant acquisition. George Sidney suggested Mayer add a couple of Moses canvases to his collection, adding, as an inducement, that she was quite old.

"I don't care how old she is," Mayer snapped, "she's not Renoir." Nevertheless, Mayer took to Grandma Moses in a big way, and ended up buying quite a few of her paintings. Her simple depictions of country life probably reminded him of Saint John, and he liked the fact that her paintings looked the same from every angle. "The simplicity and sweetness appealed to him," said Daniel Selznick. "The distillation of an innocent America, which, in his mind, was the America he was creating movies for. She was an artist who spoke to him. When he looked at a Picasso in my aunt's house, he'd say, 'Tell me what this is, Edie. I don't know what this is.' " From a strictly financial viewpoint, he would have been better off with Renoir, but he didn't care. He liked Grandma Moses and he bought what he liked.

L.B. was still playing the part of Mr. Hollywood, accepting awards for his work on behalf of the United Jewish Appeal, and giving speeches about the responsibilities he felt incumbent on people in charge of the apparatus of modern mythmaking.

When Cardinal Spellman passed through Los Angeles, L.B. hosted a get-together for him at the studio, at which Pat O'Brien, Lionel Barrymore, Ingrid Bergman, Greer Garson, Walter Pidgeon, Tyrone Power, Don Ameche, and Edward Arnold gathered to listen to the Cardinal praise Douglas MacArthur.

A large portrait of Spellman in his red vestments was prominently displayed in L.B.'s library on St. Cloud Road. Mayer, said Edgar Magnin, was attracted to

Spellman's "power, clout, importance." Mayer's grandson Daniel believed that
Catholicism's pomp and respectability was also attractive to him, in the same
way that classical music and ballet were. They were further totems of status for
a man who would always need them.

Within the walls on Washington Boulevard, it seemed that Schary and Mayer
were coexisting, even friendly. Mayer told Schary he respected the way he had
conducted his life, that he didn't run around with women and had a reputation
for being a good family man. "You haven't gotten dirty in Hollywood," Mayer
said.

The minutes of the weekly meetings show Schary taking charge of most
projects, with notations such as "Dore to read." Occasionally, for a difficult picture or a project they were unsure of, they would turn to Mayer, as with the
Robert Taylor vehicle *Conspirator* ("Dore and Thau talk to L.B."), or the musical remake of Lubitsch's *The Shop Around the Corner* ("Meet L.B. for decision."). Other pictures from this period that involved Mayer's input were *Father
of the Bride, East Side, West Side, Kim*, and the remake of *Show Boat*.

For an Esther Williams musical called *The Duchess of Idaho*, it was noted
that "Mr. Mayer and Dore" should listen to the five songs that had been written. With an occasional prospective story, it was noted that "Mrs. [Harriet]
Frank will tell screen play to Mr. Mayer."

People Schary didn't know or didn't want to know, or who maintained a
loftier status than he did, were tossed in L.B.'s lap, as when the studio was interested in Irene Dunne for a picture called *Storm over Vienna*: "Mr. Mayer is
lunching with Irene Dunne today." When the studio was offered a deal to sell a
story, Kenneth MacKenna spoke to Mayer for an okay on the sale and the price.

Musicals were obviously recognized as one of Schary's weak points, for
Mayer was included on projects such as *Lovely to Look At* and *Three Little
Words*. Likewise, when Ethel Barrymore delivered a strong performance in *The
Great Sinner*, Mayer was one of the people pushing to offer her a contract at a
time when the contract ranks were being thinned out and an elderly character
actress was not exactly in a strong bargaining position.

The studio's new emphasis on economy was indicated by the deep concern
over production of Robert Siodmak's pace on *The Great Sinner*. "Fact that
Siodmak is 2 1/8 days behind, plus 1/2 day behind on retakes in first six days was
discussed. Mr. Schary and Mr. Cohn will see dailies this evening and then discuss situation again."

Nobody was immune. A Clark Gable vehicle called *Any Number Can Play* came in with an estimate of thirty-seven shooting days, and a budget of $1.4 million. Joe Cohn was delegated the task of cutting three days off the schedule. The studio backed away from a Preston Sturges script called *Nothing Doing* that was perfect for Gable, probably because it wasn't sure Sturges could be controlled.

At the same time, the studio could be surprisingly indulgent about preparation time for projects regarded as particularly commercial; as of mid-January 1949, writers had been working for forty-six weeks on a sequel to *Mrs. Miniver* with a few months to go before it was expected to be ready, while the script for (the notoriously painstaking) Sidney Franklin production of *Young Bess* was in the works for 119 weeks.

Schary made it a point to be ingratiating and let Mayer know about things that were coming up—an idea of Keenan Wynn's about forming a troupe of players to visit army installations, or informing L.B. that Charles Brackett had left Paramount and signed with Fox without ever seeing what MGM might offer him, as Brackett had promised to do. "My face is covered with egg," wrote Schary, "but a smart fellow I know named L.B. once said, 'This might be a blessing in disguise.'"

Mayer, aware that he might have gotten out of touch, asked Schary to recommend some recent pictures he should see, and Schary suggested *Johnny Belinda*, *The Night Has a Thousand Eyes*, "*Sorry, Wrong Number*," and *An Act of Murder*.

On February 10, 1949, MGM celebrated its twenty-fifth anniversary. There was a week-long conference during which Mayer and Schary outlined their great plans to the sales staff. After a ceremonial lunch, Greer Garson presented Louis with a "silver key of opportunity" just as Will Rogers had given Mayer and Thalberg one on that day twenty-five years earlier.

"When MGM was formed in 1924," Mayer told the audience, "we had six stars and forty acres of land. Today we have thirty-one modern soundstages, sixty stars and five lots covering 176 acres. The motion picture industry will go forward in the years to come just as it has at this studio in the past 25 years. It is to entertainment what the game of baseball is to American sports. And I will remain head of this studio as long as Nick Schenck remains head of the company!"

L.B. went on to pay tribute to all the people who had gone through the last twenty-five years with him—Mannix, Thau, and the rest. "Then he had to introduce Dore Schary," said Adolph Green. "He gave this very involved talk, trying to rationalize why Dore was now there. I don't remember what he said, but whatever it was, none of us were convinced."

Schary announced that the studio would release sixty-seven pictures in 1949–50, compared to twenty-four the previous season. The menu would be broadened, he asserted, but MGM would be sure to keep the favorite recipes too.

The bill of fare for the banquet featured Sarah Mayer's chicken soup and stuffed squab. Dessert was chocolate ice cream in the shape of Leo the Lion, which became the metaphor of the day, and of this period of MGM. "It was a very hot day," remembered Betty Comden, "and all the MGM stars and everybody else were sitting at these long tables. The chocolate lions melted to nothing before we could eat them. When I think about it now, it seems like such an obvious symbol of what ended up happening."

"We had a good relationship," recalled Schary, "but then inevitably and this I must say is absolutely so — it's inevitable when a new guy comes in and the studio suddenly changes complexion that press guys begin to notice it . . . And Mayer began to fret and he disagreed with me about a couple of pictures and . . . he just thought I was making a fool of myself."

"When MGM started," remembered George Sidney, "the picture that really made the studio was *The Big Parade*. And then twenty-five years later, Dore came and made *Battleground*, another war story, and it seemed we had a new company." Mayer would always claim that *Battleground* was the beginning of the end of MGM — because it convinced both Nick Schenck and Dore Schary that Schary was infallible.

In addition to *Battleground*, there was *Adam's Rib*, and a batch of strong musicals led by *On the Town*. MGM boasted eight of the sixteen biggest box-office hits of 1949–50. And while all the other majors had declining profits in 1949, and RKO under Howard Hughes actually suspended operations for a time, MGM's profits rose.

Faced with the perceptible success of his protégé, L.B. began to grow petulant. Schary began playing directly to Nick Schenck, subtly bypassing Mayer and giving Schenck the opening he had wanted for years. Schary was becoming less of a partner, more of a rival, with different tastes in movies, and he was currying favor with Schenck.

Still, the bottom line was improved, so Mayer signed a new five-year deal in May of 1949. He was being paid $3,000 a week plus 6.77 percent of the net up to $500,000 as long as the Loew's retirement plan was in effect.

But a few months after that, in one of his rare interviews with a trade paper (*The Hollywood Reporter*), he blasted elements in the industry that were mak-

ing what he believed were pictures bordering "on the obscene" while pretending to portray "real life stories" or deliver "so-called messages." Moving on from
there, he blasted subversives within the industry, "Communists, leftists, right-
ists. . . . The Communists among others, keep demanding freedom of expression, when what they really want is freedom to bring to the screen filth in
entertainment or leftist messages.

"We in the picture business have a great responsibility to bring to the screen
clean, wholesome entertainment. Our pictures must show religion—love of
our flag and home—respect for father and mother. There are too many who
look at these themes as 'unsophisticated' and lacking the 'realism' of actual life."

He went on to compare the grosses of Andy Hardy to *Ninotchka*, proving
that the unsophisticated made more money than the sophisticated, and said
that crime pictures were "nothing more than a great criminal college for our
youth." Clearly, Mayer had a burr under his saddle, and the burr was making
too many pictures the old man didn't like.

The studio was split along ideological lines; the old guard, within Mayer's
camp or without, sensed a shift in the balance of power and reacted as courtiers
do to the arrival of a new monarch. "Before I left the studio, I knelt on the floor
of your office and received your blessing," Albert Lewin reminded Schary in a
letter. "We both laughed at this . . . but I assure you that, to me, it was not a
facetious gesture. I have often thought of it and have received a kind of moral
support from the recollection at difficult moments. . . . It did not take me long
after your arrival to realize how lucky we were at Metro to have you back. The
results are already so magnificently apparent, and will be increasingly so as
time goes on."

Even Eddie Mannix proved that sycophancy is a movable feast: "Your [sic]
to [sic] nice a guy to be sick and in pain," he wrote Schary from Rome. (Schary's
back had gone out.) "I will visit his Holiness the Pope tomorrow and I ask his
blessing for a complete recovery of your health. . . . What was New York's reaction to [Schary's personal production] *The Next Voice You Hear*? I hope as good
as mine. Cannot get the idea of that picture out of my mind."

Seeing people—*his* people—pay tribute to another, younger man he had
ceded power to, one, moreover, who did not absolutely share his sensibilities,
must have been maddening for Mayer. Frances Marion reported that Mayer
"walked around in his characteristic state of angry superiority. Hatred beat in
him like a strong pulse. It was more than a personal vendetta; he was infuriated
by the lack of faith made evident in the attitude of [Nick Schenck], and the
men who surrounded Schenck."

If the right regarded Schary as the enemy, the left, in the wake of the Waldorf Conference, regarded him as a squishy liberal. His actual constituency was rather small, roughly defined as the New York kids working for Arthur Freed. "We were all on his side," said Betsy Blair. "He was a nice, liberal fellow, intelligent, not a Hollywood executive type."

Creatively, the studio, aside from Arthur Freed, was still off balance. Nineteen forty-nine found MGM trying to respond to the public taste for darker dramas with *Edward, My Son, Border Incident, Caught, Scene of the Crime, Side Street,* and *Tension.* Most of those films were at least okay, and a year later, John Huston's *The Asphalt Jungle* would be a masterpiece. Schary was clearly nudging the studio into the postwar world.

The problem was that audiences weren't very interested. *The Asphalt Jungle,* with a great director at the height of his powers, a modest $1.2 million budget, and spectacular reviews, made a profit of only $40,000. Mayer told John Huston that it was marvelous, simply marvelous, but to others he described it as a picture "full of nasty, ugly people doing nasty, ugly things. I won't walk across the room to see a thing like that."

"There was a terrible exhibitor backlash against noir in 1949 and 1950," says author Eddie Muller. "Exhibitors were rejecting these movies and for commercial reasons. A lot of them were wearing the cloak of 'This is bad for America,' with patriotic editorials, but it was clear that, while these pictures may have played well in urban areas, they were dying in the hinterlands because people didn't want to see that image of metropolitan America. They weren't making enough money with these movies."

Mayer might have been able to tolerate Schary's tastes had there been a market for them, but making pictures for a tiny coterie audience would have struck him as masturbatory. Yet even though the problems at MGM were obvious, it was still a going business. In 1950, the last full year of Mayer's rule, the forty-odd departments that made up the studio turned out sixteen cartoons, twelve short travelogues, nine *Pete Smith Specialties,* 104 newsreels, and forty-one feature motion pictures, among them *Showboat* and *An American in Paris.* MGM may have been having serious financial and creative problems, but it was, industrially and creatively, leagues ahead of any twenty-first-century studio.

But Mayer's fretting grew more volatile. After a meeting in his office, Mayer turned to Schary and reminded him that he had said he would retire in two or three years. But. "I've had second thoughts. What would I do with myself? I'm being honest. What would you do if you were me if you wanted to retire—be honest."

Schary demurred, saying he didn't have Mayer's personal history, his temperament, all the factors that would go into the decision-making process. Mayer persisted.

"Well," said Schary, "I don't know how much you've got, but I assume it's in millions. I think, in your place, I'd travel, write, set up a foundation and administer it to provide ego satisfaction, then I'd set up a fund for destitute people in the industry and do something on behalf of an industry that helped me become successful."

"First," retorted Mayer, "you say that because you're a *kobtzen* [ineffectual pauper]. Second, don't spend my money. And I don't owe this industry or this company a goddamn cent. I got what I got because I deserve it. Nobody gave me anything. Screw the company and screw the stockholders. Listen, why do you think I took a million a year—even if I got only ten cents for every extra dollar—that was so many ten cent pieces and they added up. And furthermore, I've been everywhere, so I don't want to travel."

The bait had been dangled and Schary had gobbled it. He hadn't told Mayer that the studio—and Schary—would be rudderless without Mayer; he hadn't refused to tell Mayer how he should spend his money—always a touchy subject. He hadn't expressed shock and dismay that the old man was actually thinking about leaving.

Mayer was moving past trying to seduce anybody; he couldn't be bothered to hide his true feelings anymore, about Schary or anybody else. He was becoming the most authentic Louis B. Mayer yet.

Mayer tried to talk Schary out of putting his name on individual pictures. "Dore, you know Thalberg never had his name on a picture."

"Well, I don't have my name on all the pictures, I only have them on the pictures I make."

"But he never looked for publicity."

"I don't look for publicity."

"Well, nobody *knew* anything about Thalberg."

"L.B., you know that's not accurate. Everybody knew about Thalberg, and he was given credit for every single picture that came out of Metro, as probably he deserved."

Mayer finally moved to the crux of the matter. "I don't ever have my name on anything. I never look for an interview, I never have a name, I won't talk, I won't talk to a newspaper man: they stink. That's what you should do. You should tell the publicity department that they must tell the press that your name is not to be mentioned."

This wasn't going to happen; even more than Mayer, Schary loved to see his name in the papers and be recognized as a "Leader of the Industry." Schary said that he'd abjure all personal publicity if L.B. would agree to change the name of the company to Metro-Goldwyn-Mayer-Schary.

It was undoubtedly meant as a joke, but like most jokes, there was an element of truth in it as well, a truth Mayer could not abide. Schary was now more important to the company than Mayer was, not just creatively but publicly.

In early 1950, Mayer went to Schary about some oil stock he was letting his friends in on. Schary said that he couldn't afford the minimum shares. Mayer said that was all right, he'd loan him $10,000. Schary gave him a note and bought the stock.

Later, Schary began to feel uncomfortable about the loan and the stock and told his lawyer he wanted to return it to Mayer. Schary and his lawyer went to Mayer's office and the first thing Mayer mentioned was the stock. Schary said he wanted to return it, and Mayer said, "Good, I'm glad to hear that. I only want my friends in on this with me." Schary returned the stock and Mayer tore up the note.

That was Louis B. Mayer: great generosity, great consideration, and great pettiness in equal measure. (Other people would benefit from his largesse without any drawbacks; he gave his caterer $7,500 for a house for her mother, and told her to take the old woman out and spend $1,000 of his money for new dresses.)

Schary was micromanaging the studio in a way that Mayer found obnoxious and egocentric. Everything had to be read, okayed, discussed, and rewritten at his direction. It was a pain, but the initial results seemed to indicate that Schary was in the process of saving the studio.

"It's just a few days over a year since you came back here," wrote Sam Marx in a letter to Schary, "and in that time a lonely frightened studio has changed back to a thriving, exciting place. . . . I often wonder if [Thalberg] would have kept up with these times. I like to think so, I hope so, but I don't know. However, we know about you." Also enthusiastic were Frances Goodrich and Albert Hackett, who wrote Schary, "You can never know what a comfort it is to think of you as the Boss."

When Schary was named Producer of the Year by a New York magazine, a party was held at his house to commemorate the event. One of the guests was a woman who had written an article poking fun at Hollywood parties and their hosts. Armand Deutsch told her, "I wouldn't invite you to one of my parties; you knocked hell out of these people."

Louis overheard the remark and took Deutsch aside. "This is helpful to Metro-Goldwyn-Mayer," he said, his voice trembling with anger. "You keep your mouth shut!"

Communism, which had gradually come to epitomize everything from politics to moviemaking that Mayer saw as threatening, was still much on his mind. "You cannot believe in God and be a Communist because Communism is synonymous with atheism," Mayer said in a speech before the Jewish War Veterans in April 1950. "You cannot call yourself a Communist and call yourself an American because Communism calls for the overthrow of that which is the envy of the world, and that is America."

When Governor Earl Warren vetoed a loyalty oath for state employees, Mayer, Harry Warner, and Harry Cohn asked Warren to attend a dinner at Perino's for a discussion of Communism. Mayer and the rest of the studio heads had supported Warren in his election campaign, and Mayer said that he wouldn't want a Communist to teach his children because the teacher could "poison their minds." Warren got angry and said that if Mayer's children were susceptible to brainwashing by teachers, it was the fault of their parents. "I have four daughters and if a teacher tried to convert them to Communism, I feel certain they would succeed in converting him to democracy."

Only Schary, Bill Goetz, and Darryl Zanuck applauded when Warren stopped speaking. Mayer's response was one of his philosophical shrugs indicating that the fools would have to find out the truth in their own time. But he also indicated that he would never again support Warren.

Charles Foster, the Canadian Air Force pilot Mayer had taken a shine to during the war, was back in town late in 1950 and was invited up to the office in the Thalberg Building. He found a completely different man than the one he had met seven years earlier. "He was very unhappy. He said, 'My days are not long here, because they don't know how to make pictures anymore.' He never called them 'films,' always called them 'pictures.' 'Suddenly, I'm old-fashioned.'

"And in a funny way, I think he did believe he was old-fashioned. I think Schary had convinced him he was old-fashioned, and he felt perhaps Schary was right. MGM hadn't been making money the last year or two he was in charge. I felt he was a very lonely person. He seemed so eager to keep me there.

'It's time I went, Louis.' 'No, no, don't go, stay.' He seemed to want someone to talk to about something, anything at all."

Foster noted that Mayer's best friends seemed to be people scattered around the studio in little jobs, people who had been there since the early days. "Today," he muttered, "everybody I meet wants something from me."

What seemed to be evolving at MGM was a system where Mayer's people approached Mayer, Schary's people approached Schary, and those in the middle worked through committees. When Clarence Brown read William Faulkner's *Intruder in the Dust*, he remembered running, not walking, into Mayer's office.

"I've got to make this picture," said Brown.

"You're nuts," said Mayer, pointing out that the hero was a black man.

"If you owe me anything, you owe me a chance to make this picture."

Had the film been a Schary project, Louis would undoubtedly have fought it tooth and nail, but Brown had earned the right to a personal film and the Faulkner novel was it. "I went through the Atlanta race riots in 1906 [probably 1913]," remembered Brown, his voice shaking with anger. "I saw 15 Negroes murdered by a goddamned mob of white men. That's why I made the film."

Brown compromised to the extent of casting the part of Lucas Beauchamp with Juano Hernandez, a Puerto Rican, because, said screenwriter Ben Maddow, "A black actor would have been going too far for Metro, at the time." He shot the entire film in Oxford, Mississippi—Faulkner's home. "Juano Hernandez was Puerto Rican Negro, and I apologized to him in advance for the way he was going to be treated down there. I am a southerner and I know how they treat Negroes. I told him, 'In Oxford, they're going to treat you in ways you won't like.' He told me not to worry about it, he could control himself."

The film previewed well, but Mayer remained uneasy. He thought Hernandez's character was "too uppity. He ought to take off his hat when he talks to a white man—and he didn't even say thank you to the lawyer." Mayer predicted the film would be a disaster; Schary predicted it would be viewed as one of MGM's proudest accomplishments. They were both right; although Brown made the picture for an economical $988,000, it still lost $614,000. On the other hand, Ralph Ellison said that it was the only black-connected film that whites could see without a black audience present to correct mistaken impressions.

In 1949, Billy Wilder shot *Sunset Boulevard*, the only great movie yet made about the attendant delusions of the movie business. When it was screened before an audience of Hollywood notables at Paramount, Mayer was among the

attendees, and he didn't like what he saw. After the screening, Mayer was standing outside the theater, talking to Eddie Mannix and Joe Cohn, and volubly
proclaiming his distaste. "This Billy Wilder bites the hand that feeds him. He
should be tarred and feathered and run out of town." Some reports indicate that
Mayer even said Wilder should go back to Germany—a remarkably boorish remark in light of the recent horrors.

Wilder overheard Mayer and walked over. "I am Mr. Wilder, and go fuck
yourself." It was not a sentiment that could have been frequently expressed to
Mayer's face for the previous quarter-century. The response was stunned aston-
ishment.

Mayer sensed that his values were being supplanted, and it made him frantic. He would pace up and down in his office, saying, "I don't know what it is,
the picture business. Everyone wants to see *this*," accompanied by a clutch at
his crotch. "Men with dirty faces, women with messed-up hair. Who wants to
look at garbage? We always forget what we're doing! We're making moving pictures! They have to be beautiful! Every frame has to be beautiful!"

At the beginning of 1950, Lillian Ross arrived in Hollywood to spend the next
year and a half hanging around MGM observing John Huston making—and
MGM remaking—*The Red Badge of Courage*. She found a studio that still believed in itself and its ways despite the vagaries of the box office, despite the
Schary insurgence.

"It was Mayer's studio, totally," remembered Ross. "Joe Cohn, and the others surrounding Mayer, all seemed elderly, and they all seemed to pander to
L.B." Ross took one look at Mayer and knew she had found the character every
writer dreams of: "a great old pirate."

"Emotionally, L.B. felt like the bossy uncle at Thanksgiving dinner. He
swore by Andy Hardy, that sentimental immigrant's idea of America. That's
what he always wanted to talk about, but he was also perpetually ruthless and ir-
responsible. But he was gentlemanly, kind, and helpful to *me*."

For a long time, Mayer was effectively shielded from Ross by Howard
Strickling, but when she finally spent time with him he put on a full-tilt performance. The combination of Mayer's white hair, his elegantly tailored blue suit,
his cream-colored office, and the wild emotionalism transfixed Ross.

"He was feeling great and full of himself, getting down on his knees and acting everything out," she remembered. "I was young and naive-looking and I
guess he thought he was impressing me."

While Mayer went through his routine, Arthur Freed sat next to him, looking slightly depressed and parroting banalities designed to reinforce his friend's view of life. "This cultured, marvelous man who produced wonderful movies was a lackey around L.B.," said Ross.

In a way, Ross found Dore Schary more objectionable than Mayer. "He wanted to be thought of as a liberal and good guy, but he did all the genial sweet talk, too. He played the role of an idealist and good guy for all these artistically endowed people—who would make movies that made money. L.B. was a hypocrite who took advantage, but Schary, the good guy, was not a good guy."

John Huston and Mayer had known each other since September 1933, when Huston struck and killed a young woman while driving on Sunset Boulevard. Walter Huston had realized that his son, who had fully earned his reputation as a wild young man, could have his nascent screenwriting career destroyed just as it was beginning. The elder Huston went to Mayer and Marion Davies and asked them to keep the story away from Louella Parsons. Stories swept through the town that MGM and Warner Bros. had kicked in money to keep John out of jail out of their respect for Walter. The grand jury failed to return an indictment; John had supposedly been sober and the light was with him.

When Walter Huston's option was up for renewal, Mayer figured that the actor owed him one, and tried to renew it for another year at the same price, without the agreed upon $500-a-week raise. "Then you don't want to exercise your option?" Walter asked. "We want you to work here," replied Mayer, "but we want to keep you at your current salary." No deal. Huston tore up the contract and went back to New York to do *Dodsworth*, leaving a shocked Mayer to contemplate actors' lack of gratitude.

Mayer and John Huston had a sneaking affection for each other (in his memoirs, Huston called Mayer "a heroic fool"), but they came from two different worlds. Early in Huston's tenure at the studio, Mayer was telling him that he regarded Joe McCarthy as one of the great men of the time. Then he eyed Huston speculatively. "John, you've done documentaries. . . . How about doing one that is a tribute to McCarthy?"

"L.B., you're out of your goddamned mind," snorted Huston.

Huston's first project at MGM had been an adaptation of *Quo Vadis*. Mayer wanted a DeMille-style epic, while Huston and his collaborator, Hugh Gray, were writing about Nero's attempts to destroy the Christians as an analogy to Hitler's attempted destruction of the Jews. One Sunday, Mayer called Huston over to his house for breakfast. He had read the first ninety pages of the script, he told Huston, and it wasn't what he wanted. He told Huston how he had once sang "Eli, Eli" to Jeanette MacDonald in order to show her the emotion she should put into "Ah, Sweet Mystery of Life." "She was so moved, she wept," he said. "She wept! She, who had the reputation of pissing icewater!"

He told Huston that if he could make *Quo Vadis* with that kind of emotion, he, L. B. Mayer, would crawl to Huston on his knees and kiss his hands. To prove it, he crawled over to Huston on his knees and kissed his hands. This is not happening to me, thought Huston.

Schary, on the other hand, had liked Huston's pages, and he suggested letting Nick Schenck adjudicate the dispute. This idea stunned Mayer. Thalberg at his most contentious had never relied on Schenck as an arbiter, because he didn't respect Schenck's opinions about movies.

Schenck said that since *Quo Vadis* had been hanging around the MGM lot as a dead investment for years, any shootable script was an improvement; let Schary have his way. Schenck had taken Schary's side in the argument. Gregory Peck was cast, then came down with an eye infection. The studio decided to put the picture off for a year, and at that point Huston and producer Arthur Hornblow took up *The Asphalt Jungle*.

Huston proposed *The Red Badge of Courage* for the second picture of his two-picture deal. Dore Schary like the idea, but Mayer hated it. Huston was obstinate; so was Schary. Schary was going to go over Mayer's head again. It was at that point that Schary wrote L.B. a placating memo saying "I cannot guarantee that *The Red Badge of Courage* will be a highly successful picture. I can only tell you that . . . I believe it has a chance of becoming a highly important motion picture that will bring honor to the studio, plus every reasonable chance of ultimately making money . . . it is possible that it will be a classic. . . .

"You know that I have not been indifferent to many of your warnings in the past. . . . In this case I really have weighed carefully your own reservations, plus the fact that I know others in the studio dislike this project; but you told me that ultimately the decision to make this picture would have to be mine, and I have been thinking about it in exactly those terms, based on my own confidences and my own evaluation of the risks involved. . . . So, taking a very deep breath and hoping for the best, I would like to go ahead and get the picture started."

Mayer was moved by Schary's memo and called in Huston and producer Gottfried Reinhardt. As far as he was concerned, they could make their movie. To other people, he bitched. "This is thoughts. How are you going to show the boy's thoughts? Nobody will go in. A million and a half. Maybe more. What for? There's no story. . . . I don't say no, but I wouldn't make that picture with Sam Goldwyn's money."

Huston realized that his picture had become the hostage in a shooting war between Mayer and Schary. Whoever won, the picture might lose, so he went to Mayer and volunteered to make another picture besides *The Red Badge of Courage*.

"John Huston, I'm ashamed of you!" thundered the old man. "Do you believe in this picture? Have you any reason for wanting to make it other than the fact that you believe in it?"

"No."

"Then stick by your guns! Never let me hear you talk like this again!"

A few days later, Nick Schenck's decision came down; he agreed with Schary. Again. It was now clear who had the upper hand at Metro-Goldwyn-Mayer. There was one further hurdle: the title, but that seemed to disappear when Hedda Hopper assured her readers that *The Red Badge of Courage* had been written many years earlier and had "absolutely no Commie implications."

The resemblances to a classic tragedy now became obvious: an old Lord who didn't want to go, a young Lord with more than a touch of disingenuousness, plots, counterplots, treachery, and—soon—ingratitude and betrayal in the family. Mayer had always proclaimed his desire for a son, but he wanted a son in the orthodox Jewish tradition—respectful and, above all, subservient. By insisting on forging ahead with pictures Mayer didn't believe in, by insisting on doing it his own way, Schary was, in Mayer's eyes, being disrespectful and willful. The disappointment that L.B. always found in his surrogate sons began to escalate into bubbling rage.

Pre-production on Huston's film didn't get any easier. Producer Gottfried Reinhardt complained that he was in the middle of two Civil Wars—the one on the screen and the one between Mayer and Schary. He would order six hundred uniforms from wardrobe, Schary would okay it, and Mayer would countermand it. Every detail was a crisis.

Reinhardt asked for a meeting. John Huston came along, and Reinhardt was amazed to see Mayer launch into an oration that struck at the very heart of what he hated about the picture, about many pictures.

"Tell me, John, does your wife go to the bathroom?" he began. "Does she pee, John? Does she sit on the toilet and take a crap?" Huston had to admit that she did. "Everybody does!" Mayer said. "You can't live very long if you don't. Does she lock the door, John, when she goes to the bathroom? Tell me, does she lock the door? Why does she lock the door, John? Why does she do that? Why doesn't she open the door and say, 'Come in, everybody. Come in look. I'm taking a pee! That's realism, John! So why doesn't she do that?"

Huston was trying to assemble a sentence, but Mayer continued boring in, cornering the director. "I'll tell you why she doesn't, John. Because it's ugly. It's not pretty, it's not exciting, it's not glamorous to see a woman sitting on a toilet with her dress pulled up and her private parts naked, taking a pee or a crap! It's disgusting. But it's realism, John. It happens many times a day with every woman. She pees and she craps. But she doesn't want other people seeing her do it. So she locks the door, she keeps them out. That's what we do in our pictures. When something is ugly, we lock the door, we keep it out, because we don't want our customers to look at things that are ugly and say, 'Ugh, I don't want to see that!' "

The old man was at his worst now, lunging and lashing out as his footing grew unsure. One Sunday afternoon at Bill Goetz's house, the talk turned to television, and L.B. went into a tirade about the movie industry not making enough family pictures to compete with television, which was making what amounted to cheap family pictures. On top of that, he said, low-end producers of violence were going to poison the well for high-end producers of entertainment. L.B. might never have heard of Gresham's Law, but he understood the way the bad has of driving out the good, and it was hurting the movies with Middle America.

By mid-1950, it was clear that the long knives were out. Such problematic or declining names as Judy Garland, Frank Sinatra, Ann Sothern, Lena Horne, Angela Lansbury, Mary Astor, Edward Arnold, and Edmund Gwenn were leaving the studio.

Around this time, Mayer ran into Esther Williams at Chasen's. "They're kicking me out, Esther. If I start up another studio, would you come with me?"

Williams knew what was going on—everybody at the studio knew—and, while she had a grudging affection for L.B. and couldn't stand Dore Schary, she also knew that no studio other than MGM could make her pictures.

"Thanks, Mr. Mayer," she said, "but where are you going to find a pool like the one on Stage 30? How can I go with you if you don't have a pool?"

"I'll build one," he said.

"No, you won't," she said. "But call me if you do."

The old man looked crestfallen. If Esther Williams wouldn't entertain an offer, what chance did he have with a dry star?

While trying to cope with the rapid alterations of the movie industry, L.B. was still, in many ways, tied to his distant past. His grandson Jeffrey remembered a New York visit with L.B. They lunched at Le Pavillon—Jeffrey noticed his grandfather's habit of refusing any coffee unless it was scalding hot—then got into a waiting limousine and drove south and west, into the heart of the Garment District. The car stopped in front of a dilapidated synagogue that looked as if it could have been relocated to Russia with no alteration whatever.

Mayer and Jeffrey went inside, where the older man put on a yarmulke and a prayer shawl. For over an hour, with tears streaming down his cheeks, Mayer said Kaddish for his mother, for Sarah. It was the anniversary of her death. When he was done, he walked a couple of blocks to compose himself, pressed a $50 bill into his grandson's hand, then got into the limousine and drove off.

Mayer's instincts for what the audience wanted were beginning to fray, but his sense of star talent remained solid. Although at first confused by the young comedy team of Dean Martin and Jerry Lewis ("The guinea's not bad, but what do I do with the monkey?" he said), he eventually came around and offered them the same money that Paramount had. Lewis was inclined to go with MGM, but Mayer wanted approval over all the team's outside work, which Hal Wallis was willing to leave to the discretion of Martin and Lewis. The result was that Paramount signed the hottest comedy team of their generation.

Edie's marriage to Bill Goetz remained strong, as did her opinion of herself. "She took her position as the queen of movie society very seriously," said Dominick Dunne. "She was Hollywood's Mrs. Astor. She kept a rigid caste system at her parties. One of her great friends was Merle Oberon, who had been married to Lucien Ballard—a cameraman. Edie told me that 'It was so difficult when Merle was married to Lucien; it made the men uncomfortable.'"

Edie and Bill's collection of Impressionist art was becoming one of the finest collections in the country. Their house in Holmby Hills had been copied from the nearby Zanuck house—Edie thought Virginia Zanuck's taste was superb. It had the same architect, the same blue shutters, the same placement of the pool. Edie thought all this was the height of fashion, while Irene was horrified, because both she and David Selznick thought the Zanucks were vulgar.

Mary Loos remembered going to a party at Edie's house and termed the paintings "overwhelming. They had a gorgeous projection room, with very comfortable seats. And all of a sudden, a panel with a Monet (I think) lifted up out of sight, and the movie starts: *Wake of the Red Witch* with Vera Hruba

Ralston and John Wayne. From Republic! This was not high style; this was Nouveau Riche, lifting up a great painting to look at a crappy movie, or, for that matter, any movie.

"Unlike Edie, Irene went beyond the fact that she was L. B. Mayer's daughter. She was attractive, she got around, and even when I was a nobody she was nice to me. Edie was an ambitious hostess. She was happily married to one man. That was it."

The breach between the two sisters was far more complicated than appearances suggested. The conventional wisdom had it that Irene was her father's child—cagey, tough, bossy, and humorless. Everybody agreed that she was smart, with her father's sharp eye for quality goods, but without his sentimentality. That was all right as far as L.B. was concerned—he was no laugh riot himself.

Louis, undoubtedly thinking of David Selznick, once told Hedda Hopper that, "If I was married to Irene, I'd hit her. I love her, but I see all her faults." But, said Dominick Dunne, who knew both sisters well, "I just think they were jealous of each other. They were totally different people. Edie was smart, but in a movie sort of way. She did understand the movie business backwards and forwards. I remember that Irving Lazar, whom they all made fun of, slowly became a big social figure. One day I said, 'He's a star,' and Edie said, 'Don't tell me about stars. I know about stars. *Hedy Lamarr was a star!*' "

In some respects, things went on as before. Arthur Freed still came over to L.B.'s house every Sunday for lunch or dinner. Some of the favored employees would also be invited—commanded—and would sit around outside while L.B. played cards inside. When L.B. would take a break from cards, he'd come out to the veranda and dispense wisdom, as when he told Vincente Minnelli that he thought the color in *An American in Paris* should "copy the color in *Coney Island.* In fact, all our color pictures should have that look."

All the evidence indicated that Mayer was on track to become an absent eminence, with a nice office, a secretary, an expense account, and no authority, like Adolph Zukor at Paramount—someone to trot out at anniversaries to talk about the old days and bestow bromides about how the movies' best days still lay ahead. That would have been fine with Schary and it would have been fine with Nick Schenck. But L.B. couldn't leave it at that.

By the end of November 1950, Mayer and Schary rarely communicated directly; if Mayer wanted to give something to Schary, he would send an intermediary like Edwin Knopf, and Schary would reply in a memo. The tone was respectful, even placating, but essentially unyielding, in the vein of "You may very well be right, but this is the way it seems to me . . ."

L.B. began ranting to anyone who would listen, including reporters: "Believe me, I'll be here long after Dore Schary and all the other pricks around him. I've had them sniping at me before. Where in the hell are they now?

"The pictures made by Irving Thalberg and me had heart. They entertained. They made MGM the greatest studio in the history of Hollywood. Let Schary play up to the *schwarzes* and the pinkos. See where it gets him. Do you know what the most successful movies ever made were? Andy Hardy! Clean, wholesome and with heart. Not one goddamn message in them. As for Schary, fuck him!"

MGM was a beseiged Matterhorn, with two climbers. There was only room for one at the peak.

The proverbial handwriting on the wall became clear when Louis was given an honorary Oscar in 1951 for his career achievements in leading MGM for more than a quarter-century. "In 1907, a man entered the infant and precarious motion picture industry," said Charles Brackett in presenting the award. "His vision and passion for quality in films brought him to Hollywood as a producer. In 1925 [actually 1924] he was one of the founders of Metro-Goldwyn-Mayer and for twenty-six years he guided its production policy with foresight, aggressiveness and with a real desire for taste and quality. His instinct and showmanship have found and developed new personalities, bringing the star system into full flower.

"He has always believed in the policy of the greater risk for the greater return. He has encouraged talent in production, writing and direction.

"In addition, he was the founding father of this Academy and has functioned constantly as a powerful force in the entire industry. For this record of achievement, the Academy presents an Honorary Award to Louis B. Mayer."

Mayer's acceptance speech was brief: "My dear friends, this is truly a thrilling experience. I've been formally honored many ways, but this stands out because it comes from the men and women in the industry. I take this honor and with deep humility look forward to years of service to come."

It was the Kiss of Death Award, usually given to someone as they lie dying, or to make amends for an egregious oversight in the past. Louis didn't fit into the latter category, but he was about to symbolize the first very neatly.

L.B. remained very high on Marge and Gower Champion, and, after seeing some rehearsals of their numbers for *Show Boat,* called them into his office. "He spent a few minutes telling Gower how he must keep me simple and pure," remembered Marge Champion. "I was thirty years old but didn't look it. He was raving on and kept saying, 'She's as light as the wind,' and kept blowing his cheeks out to indicate the wind."

Then he came to the point: Marge should play the part of the young dancer in *An American in Paris.* "At this point, I didn't know the man. He was so funny and absolutely charming, and he was trying to talk me into doing something he hadn't even discussed with Gene Kelly."

Terribly flattered, Marge Champion and her husband went home to talk it over. "I said, 'Look, we're not kids. Whatever we have, it's together.' It was Gene Kelly's musical and there was nothing in it for Gower, so I said I didn't want to do the film. So that's what we told our agent."

By November 1950, the Freed unit had spent $1.9 million to make the book and all the other dance numbers for *An American in Paris* when the picture was closed down and Freed requested $500,000 to shoot the concluding ballet. Half a million dollars for one number? In spite of Arthur Freed's track record, Nick Schenck and his staff were very uneasy. Into the breach stepped Mayer.

Vincente Minnelli came to L.B.'s office to show him the sketches for the ballet, derived from artists such as Toulouse-Lautrec and Degas. Mayer nodded approvingly. "My daughters will like that," he said.

"In terms of this ballet," said Alan Jay Lerner, "Mayer played a key role in making the decision to keep the ballet in no matter what the cost. As a matter of fact, that decision was probably one of the last major picturemaking decisions he was to make. . . . I remember very clearly the day that Arthur Freed went up and discussed the whole thing with Mr. Mayer. Freed then came right down and told me that it would be all right. Louis B. Mayer had okayed the money for the ballet."

That he would have to throw his weight behind Freed's ballet couldn't have surprised Mayer; Schenck didn't understand, never had. But Schary obviously didn't understand either, and, when push came to shove, if Schary didn't have the clout to get the ballet past New York, what the hell good was he? (The ballet ended up costing $542,000, for a total budget of $2.7 million. The picture grossed more than $8 million and won the Best Picture Award.)

Mayer's equilibrium could not have been alleviated by a stranger's attempted suicide on March 3, 1951. Paul Salzburg, claiming that he was a human bomb, climbed into Mayer's box at the Santa Anita Handicap and screamed that he was going "to blow up the whole damn joint," although he made an exception for Mayer: "I won't kill you, Mr. Mayer."

Mayer responded coolly and tried to calm the man down. He stroked his arm and quietly asked him what it was he wanted. He kept talking to the deranged man until a bystander laid Salzburg out with a folding chair. Mayer stayed to watch the rest of the races.

Undoubtedly contributing to Mayer's mounting anxiety were events across the Pacific. On April 11, 1951, Harry Truman fired Douglas MacArthur from his position as Commander in Chief of the Far East Command, more or less for insubordination in Korea. Mayer and MacArthur had been friends for some time, and MacArthur had sent some typically stentorian words of praise when Mayer was honored by the Jewish War Veterans in April of 1950.

Mayer was stunned by the firing, writing Herbert Hoover that he was "deeply shocked and grieved," and wiring MacArthur the same day he was fired that "YOU SHOULD NOT WAIT TWO OR THREE WEEKS BUT RETURN AS SOON AS IS HUMANLY POSSIBLE TO OUR COUNTRY SANS UNIFORM TO TELL THE AMERICAN PEOPLE, WHO WORSHIP YOU, THE STORY WHICH WILL TRULY OPEN THEIR EYES."

Schary began negotiating for a new contract that would add stock options to his salary. He got the options (100,000 shares at $16.44 apiece), as did five other executives, and he got heightened authority. Since Mayer had recommended that the executives get the stock options, but had not been allowed to make the announcement to his own people, he took it as a calculated insult. Then there was the matter of the stock options that everybody else had been granted. Everybody but him.

For L.B., who had always been racked by subterranean insecurities, any rejection, no matter how slight, was a devastating insult. It wasn't Schary personally so much as it was what he represented: a future inhospitable to Mayer's vision. The stock option issue had flared up once before, with Thalberg. Now it was here again, setting off all his anxieties. The pressure inside the volcano had been building for three years and now the lava was about to boil over.

It was obvious to everyone that Schary and Schenck were edging the old man toward the door. MGM's profits for 1951–52 would shoot upward to $8.1 million, while the other major studios saw their nets decline for the second straight year. The fact that Mayer would be completely right about the uncommercial nature of *The Red Badge of Courage* was in the future and would have seemed irrelevant. Mayer's twenty-year grudge over the Fox sell-out sparked up again, and he began telling anybody who would listen just what he thought of his boss. And he didn't soft-soap him personally, either.

"Louie, what's wrong?" Schenck asked him on the phone. "Why can't we get together? Let's meet someplace and talk this out."

"No, I've got a temper. If I hit you, I'll kill you, Nick. I'm just waking up and I don't like it."

By the first week in April 1951, the incipient explosion was making the papers. A story ran in the *New York Times* about the conflicts at the studio; it reported that Mayer might be resigning. *Variety* picked it up and noted that Mayer's contract had an out clause: if he resigned before July 31, the resignation would take effect thirty days later. Mayer was not available for comment, and the studio itself said only, "No comment."

When Donald O'Connor checked onto the lot that April to make *Singin' in the Rain*, it was a house divided. "It was difficult to say if it was Mayer's studio or Schary's studio. Dore Schary picked the pictures, but the overall authority rested in Louis B. They were both real nice guys, but in different ways."

Mayer's gnomically mystical casting instinct was still intact. He called Debbie Reynolds in to tell her she'd be Gene Kelly's leading lady in *Singin' in the Rain*. "But I can't dance, Mr. Mayer," she said.

"You'll dance," he said.

Gene Kelly was called into the office to meet Reynolds, and when she reiterated the fact that she couldn't dance, Kelly placatingly turned to Mayer. "L.B., she can't dance."

"She'll dance."

After three months of grueling work, she danced. So let it be written; so let it be done.

By May, Billy Wilkerson was writing editorials in *The Hollywood Reporter* saying "there seems little chance of Mayer and MGM continuing their partnership."

Schary went to ask Mayer if the rumors were true and said he was willing to patch up the quarrel.

"What are you going to do, save my job for me?" snapped Mayer.

Finally, Mayer issued Schenck a blatant challenge in the form of a letter. In it, he said Schary was incompetent, unwilling to listen to anybody else, had a fondness for publicity and an interest in using movies for political propaganda. A choice had to be made, and only Schenck could make it.

Schary or Mayer. Choose.

That, at least, was Schary's recollection of Mayer's letter, which Schenck later showed him. If Mayer did indeed ask his old enemy to make a choice, his judgment had gone seriously awry. Schary had assiduously curried favor with Schenck; Schary had cut costs and made some good pictures that had improved the Loew's bottom line and earned the company Oscar nominations. Finally, Schary was twenty years younger. There was no choice, not really.

It happened suddenly. After a story conference one morning, Schary went in to Mayer's office to talk about some production plans. The phone rang. It was Bob Rubin. "No, I have no intention of talking to Nick Schenck," said Mayer. "Yes of course I have his letter which I suppose you wrote for him. . . . Never, Bob, never. You can tell Mr. Nicholas Schenck that he and Dore Schary can take the studio and choke on it."

He hung up the phone and stared at Schary, waiting for a response.

"What was that all about, L.B.?"

"I know how you and Nick schemed to kick me out, you son of a bitch."

Schary rose and started out of the office.

"Sit down and I'll tell you everything, you little kike," roared Mayer.

Schary went back to his office and rang his lawyer, then Nick Schenck. The next morning, Schary walked into Mayer's office and was again met with a profane barrage. Again Schenck was called. Eddie Mannix, Benny Thau, and L. K. Sidney were rushing around, urging Schary to smooth things over with Mayer, but he wasn't about to walk into the lion's den again.

Twenty-seven years at MGM ended with a May 30 announcement in *Variety*: Louis B. Mayer would tender his resignation within ten days.

The truly odd thing was that, as Schary recognized, the two men had really not had all that many conflicts. Schary had been right about *Battleground*, wrong about *The Red Badge of Courage*. "Most of the time," said Schary, "[Mayer] did not interfere. As a matter of fact, he was quite helpful. On certain properties I wanted to buy—for instance, *Father of the Bride*—the price seemed high, but he said to me, 'Look, even if it's high, buy it, if you have convictions about it.' "

It was probably inevitable; as *Variety* reported, "with Schary 'production chief' and Mayer 'studio head' it was unclear from the start exactly what the demarcation was between them on duties and authority. Originally, the idea was that Mayer would supervise overall production policy, while Schary would handle the day-to-day making of films. It soon became apparent that this wouldn't work, and that Mayer, who had for more than two decades reigned as top man in all Hollywood, resented the powers handed the much-younger Schary."

There can be little doubt that the stock option issue was a red flag purposely waved in front of the maddened old bull. Mayer's contract ran to August 31, 1954, but there was a window for cancellation as of August 31, 1951, so long as notice was given by June 30. The timing couldn't have been an accident.

Robert Rubin, who had never trusted Schary, said that he tried to persuade Mayer not to rise to such obvious baiting, not to play into Schenck's hands. "But he had got past taking my advice," said Rubin.

"By mutual agreement, Louis B. Mayer will no longer be connected with the Metro-Goldwyn-Mayer Studios. Mr. Mayer has given our industry leadership and inspiration, and now in parting, his associates at Loew's wish him success and happiness in his future activities."

Mayer's statement was only marginally less bland than Schenck's: "It has been my honor to have served as head of MGM studio activities since the birth of the company in 1924. I have great pride in its accomplishments and am grateful to the fine men and women of the organization who have established the studio in the high position it has always held. Naturally I regret severing ties and relationships that have been built up over many years, but I leave with my very best wishes to the organization and those connected with it and for its future prosperity and success."

On L.B.'s final day, Howard Strickling had a red carpet laid at the front door of the Thalberg Building. All the executives and secretaries who worked with him gathered on the steps and applauded as he left. "He was so respected," said June Caldwell, Eddie Mannix's secretary.

In their minds, it was the end of an era. In his mind, it was a temporary sidetrack. He would be back.

Mayer's leave-taking of the studio he had built was many things, among them a shot across the bow for the aging men who built the American movie industry. "Mayer, Cohn, these guys were not corporate," said photographer Murray Garrett. "They didn't understand that game, and they didn't want to play that game. Once the corporate structure began moving in, once the guys in the suits began moving in, it was only a matter of time until Mayer and his ilk were moved out."

L.B. was the first mogul to be deposed, and his peers learned the lesson well. Jack Warner fired his son and euchred his older brother out of the company so that what happened to Mayer couldn't happen to him; Harry Cohn held on till he died.

L.B. was defiant. He had no intention of quitting the movie business, he told friends. He fully expected to work harder than he had at any time in the past fifteen years. But some of the wiser heads around Hollywood wondered. "Louis' friends think he'll start an independent studio," wrote Hedda Hopper, "but I doubt it. . . . I know what I'd do if I were in his position. I'd retire gracefully and have fun. It's later than you think. . . . Louis, who has always surrounded himself with a battalion of yes men, is going to find it tough to become a lone wolf."

Nick Schenck almost never discussed firing L.B., although he did tell Bosley Crowther, "It was an irreconcilable situation between Mayer and Schary. One of them had to go. [My] letter to Mayer was a long and absolutely iron-bound summation of his stewardship. [I] made it clear where he stood. He sent through his resignation thereafter." But then Schenck didn't really have to talk about it. Everybody else did it for him.

"When Louis B. Mayer left MGM, that was the end," said Turhan Bey. "Of contract players, of publicity departments who nursed you through the crises of studio life, of the studio life itself. In every meaningful way, it was the end of Hollywood."

PART FOUR

"L. B. Mayer was the guts behind that studio. The guts—and a great, great showman."

—HOWARD KEEL

Mayer signing the contract by which Clark Gable was loaned to David Selznick (center) to star in *Gone With the Wind* in return for Loew's, Inc., taking over distribution of the picture—one of the most mutually advantageous deals in movie history.

Chapter
SIXTEEN

AS MIGHT BE EXPECTED, Mayer loyalists were livid. Howard Strickling believed Schary was personally responsible for Mayer losing his job. Even Mayer's enemies were appalled. Frances Marion hadn't particularly liked Mayer, but she didn't respect Schary as either an administrator or creative executive. "Whatever antagonisms I had harbored against L. B. Mayer," she wrote, "I forgot in those few moments before he left the studio. It was as if you had seen a man being drained of his own blood."

Likewise, Walter Wanger said that "Mayer . . . had a quality that helped make the studio great. He had that paternalism which took people under its wing and made them feel comfortable and good. I think he was the greatest Hollywood executive this business has ever had. . . . I think Dore was an idiot for letting Mayer go. He removed his insurance."

On June 22, *The Hollywood Reporter* printed a long interview in which Mayer talked about his plans and his views on the state of the industry. "There's nothing wrong with the picture business but for the poor pictures, with few exceptions, which have been going to the public. It's incredible to see and hear certain leadership within this business blame everything within this business, television included, for poor business—blame everything but the poor quality of pictures. Naturally the public will not patronize our theaters playing low-quality pictures—they will, however, if the pictures are good. There are specific instances of this right now when a picture like [*The Great*] *Caruso* and a few others are making money.

"I am going to make pictures you can take your mother and your children to see. I am not going to make pictures for the sake of awards or for the critics. I want to make pictures for Americans and for all people to enjoy. When I send my pictures abroad, I want them to show America in the right light—and not that we are a nation chiefly of drunks, gangsters and prostitutes. . . . I am going to make my pictures where I will have the right to make the 'right' pictures— wholesome American entertainment." Putting his money where his mouth was, Mayer promptly sold off 1,500 shares of his Loew's stock, reducing his holdings to only 10,400 shares.

If L.B. expected a mass exodus to follow his own, he was disappointed. "We had contracts," pointed out George Sidney, "and an amazing pension. There were people who wanted to leave, but he was enough of a *mensch* that he begged them to stay. 'You've worked thirty-five years for Loew's; don't walk away from that.' "

MGM was the only studio to have a pension plan, which was instituted in 1944 and kicked in after you'd been there five years. Benefits increased with every succeeding year of employment. Retirement compensation was figured as 15 percent of the employees' average basic earnings for the period of their employment, plus 10 percent of basic earnings that exceeded $3,000, with anything over $200,000 in salary not being figured into the computations. Retirement compensation topped out at $49,700 a year for anybody hired before December 17, 1952. For those hired after that, retirement compensation was essentially cut in half.

People who didn't make as much money as actors got less money—a secretary who retired in the mid-1950s might elect to take a lump sum of around $2,000. It wasn't a rich plan, but it was fully funded by Loew's, and was open to all nonunion personnel.

Sidney worked out his contract until 1954, when he decamped for Columbia. "I didn't really leave the studio," he would say. "They left me."

While Dore Schary had Mayer's moderne office redecorated in red, white, and blue, it became clear that even Arthur Freed would be staying, although it was generally believed that Freed had promised Mayer that if the day ever arrived when MGM didn't want Mayer, it would also mean it couldn't have Freed. "When L.B. left, he left," was the way Freed's friend and biographer Hugh Fordin described his reaction. "Arthur had to get on with it."

Around the lot, nobody mentioned L.B., or if they did it was quietly, behind closed doors. Out of sight, out of mind. In Hollywood at large, the situation was the same. The highly visible Emperor had become the Invisible Man. "It was all ancient history," remembered Leonard Gershe. "Mayer was old news."

Even Hedda Hopper went to ground. In August 1948, just after Schary arrived on the lot, she wrote that "A lot of people ask why I opposed Schary. . . . He expressed pinko sympathies for years in Hollywood and stated on the stand in Washington that he would never fire Eddie Dmytryk and Adrian Scott until it was proven their work was subversive. But when the pressure of the producers was applied to him he proved himself lacking in the courage of his expressed convictions. Americans don't admire a man like that."

Fair enough, proving that the far right and the far left disliked Schary for some of the same reasons. But by October, she was writing that "Schary is winning friends at Metro by his good manners. When he makes an appointment he keeps it. If he finds he'll be late, he phones. And he actually gives out with a yes or a no when a question is put to him."

Over the next five years, Hopper threw an occasional elbow, but mainly played the sycophant's game.

It wasn't until the ominous sound of the guillotine could be heard throughout Hollywood that she again began slamming Schary, criticizing him for refusing to buy *Man of a Thousand Faces*, in spite of the fact that Lon Chaney had been one of the primary reasons for MGM's great initial success. After Schary was safely deposed, she claimed that the two happiest days in her life were when Louis B. Mayer walked into MGM as studio chief, and when Dore Schary was dismissed.

Four months after Mayer left the studio, Dore Schary sat down and drafted a "Dear General" letter to Nick Schenck that constituted a rough sort of manifesto for his regime. Schary spoke of the atmosphere of fear that had permeated the studio after Mayer left—fear that the jobs Mayer had protected would be deleted by executive fiat, fear that the studio was due for a brutal housecleaning, fear that Schary wouldn't be able to do the job.

To assure Schenck that he was indeed capable of doing the job, Schary wrote of stricter budgeting, tighter shooting schedules, a closer relationship of producer to project, earlier discussions of cast and cost, greater selectivity, and better discipline of talent.

But stricter budgeting and tighter schedules wouldn't have helped recent Metro pictures such as *Angels in the Outfield, Callaway Went Thataway, Strictly Dishonorable*, or *The Magnificent Yankee*. Even if those films had been made for $100,000 less apiece, they still would have lost money. As Schary observed, "any TV show for nothing is better than a bad or indifferent movie at $1."

TV made the movie audience more selective; big pictures were grossing more than ever, but programmers were struggling for air, mostly because the 90 million people who had gone to the movies every week in 1946 were down to 54 million in 1951.

Schary proposed cutting overhead, i.e., payroll, and making no more than twenty-four pictures a year, all expressly designed for big grosses. That way the studio wouldn't be forced to make pictures to absorb overhead. It was a perfectly rational approach to the problem, except for the unpleasant fact that Schary's touch for overtly commercial pictures would prove his biggest weakness.

By contract, Mayer had a 10 percent residual interest in every picture MGM made, beginning in 1924. Mayer wanted to sell off his interest in the film library, and beginning November 30, 1951, engaged in a whirlwind series of negotiations.

Among the interested bidders were Lew Wasserman, David Selznick, and Harry Cohn, all of whom were salivating at the prospect of owning a piece of Loew's greatest asset. MGM treasurer Charles Moscowitz said that Mayer's opening offer to his old studio for the rights was $5 million, "But it didn't take Mr. Schenck more than a few minutes to decline." Selznick, Cohn, and MCA all made oral offers of $3 million. Mayer remembered that Loew's countered with $2.5 million, which Mayer refused.

"We got into a lot of talk about the company," remembered Mayer. "You built this thing, now why would you want to put that in hostile hands, etc. When you pay a tax what does it amount to? Well, anyway, we got to where we were going to compromise and I split the difference to $2.75 million and I agreed to take that amount providing it's going to be done within a certain time, because time was running. . . . It is worth many times $3 million, but I wanted to get it out this year, by 1951."

The reason Mayer wanted to make a deal by the end of 1951, and the apparent reason that he made it with Loew's, was that the corporation negotiated a sweetheart deal so that he wouldn't be liable for an onerous tax bite—a deal out of the reach of Selznick or any of the other interested corporations. In a clause that magically appeared in a Senate tax bill, and which appeared nowhere in the House version, L.B.'s payout was taxed at the 26 percent capital gains rate, as opposed to the 91 percent rate for straight income. The deal was linked to Ellsworth Alvord, an MGM tax attorney prominent in Washington political circles.

The First Bank of Boston put up the shockingly low figure of $2.75 million on behalf of MGM. The check was cut on December 14, 1951, and signed by Nick Schenck. Mayer endorsed it in his expansive scrawl and deposited it in his personal account. The accountants had figured that the eight-hundred-odd films made under Mayer's aegis were worth an average of $31,000 apiece, or $3,100 for Mayer per picture.

Had the deal been made in 1941 instead of 1951, the price might have made some sense, but by 1951 television had landed with both feet and film libraries were clearly going to be very valuable. But for the cost of one A picture, and an engineered tax break, Mayer severed his final connection with the company that carried his name. It was undoubtedly the single worst deal since David Selznick sold *Gone With the Wind* to Jock Whitney for $400,000. Only Mayer's bitterness and an overwhelming urge to sever what now seemed an onerous relationship could explain such a bad deal from such a brilliant businessman.

Shortly afterward, it was announced that Mayer had earned $299,999 in his last year of employment ($156,428 in salary, $143,571 in bonuses and profit share) and would be eligible for a yearly MGM pension of $36,142 beginning March 1, 1954.

At MGM, there was a quantum difference. When Michael Powell met Schary he was thunderstruck. This tall, thin bourgeois, with pictures of dogs on the walls of the office that had so recently been the all-white throne room of L. B. Mayer, was now, for little appreciable reason, in charge of the biggest motion picture company in the world.

"Nothing could have shown more clearly how Hollywood had completely failed to understand whence its legendary greatness grew," remembered Powell. "To be in that office with Louis B. Mayer, with Clark Gable, Greta Garbo, and Spencer Tracy on the walls, was to be in a jungle stockade with a watchful rhino. Louis B. ruled by fear, and conquered by trusting to his instinct."

Of course, there were people who preferred Schary, most of them writers. "Mayer represented the boss with a capital B," said David Goodrich, the nephew of screenwriter Frances Goodrich. "He fought the Writers Guild energetically and underhandedly and made a lot of enemies doing it. To people like Frances and Albert [Hackett, her screenwriter husband], Mayer was an overbearing manipulator, a two-faced man who would tell you, on the one hand,

'We're all family here,' and, on the other hand, 'Don't stray too far from what I say or I will crush you.' And he meant it. Schary was a liberal, a writer, and you could say things to him about management that you never could have said to Mayer in a million years."

Schary lured back Joe Mankiewicz to make *Julius Caesar*. Mankiewicz was no Mayer partisan, but he soon learned that he was no Schary partisan either. "Schary carries on the Mayer tradition of the hegemony of the producer," said Mankiewicz, "his pet idea being that the making of a film is a 'group project'— that the whole thing evolves from a team. Look at *The Bad and the Beautiful* as a good example of the consequence of this kind of thinking—a slick, machine-made entertainment that has some good savage moments in it, that looks good, but never gets to the point. . . . Any picture that eight men have to approve is sure to be a piece of crap.

"But you know Dore; he's got that 'one big adult camp' attitude. That's his way of thinking about things; the world will be all right when we can get all the Jews to go to the Catholic churches and the Catholics to go to the synagogues. Dore wants to be the chief rabbi of the MGM synagogue."

Undoubtedly thinking of the Waldorf Conference, Mankiewicz pointed out that Schary "is capable of speaking in a liberal way and rationalizing a very reactionary attitude. He's a rigid moralist with a lack of understanding of sex and women, which shows in MGM pictures. What women stars did he sign? Nancy Davis."

From Schary's point of view, he was in a ludicrously hostile environment. Some measure of the cultural and political problems he faced can be gauged by the MGM star who would claim some fifty years after the events that Schary was a member in good standing of "Carl Foreman's Communist cell," and that he secretly informed to HUAC in Washington, "giving them names they already had in order to clear himself."

Outside the Culver City walls, by 1951 America had 10 million homes with television, a threefold increase from the previous year. It would take only four years for that number to again triple. The impact was so extreme that nearly 6,500 movie theaters closed within three years' time.

In spite of being engaged in a struggle the likes of which it had never before encountered, hampered as it was by the fact that the studios were almost completely undiversified, MGM still held itself aloof. Every other studio made its films available in 16mm for school and nontheatrical use—all except MGM. Every other studio was putting its films on television—all except MGM.

Even Schary partisans would come to realize the strange dichotomy in

Schary's character. "Dore was a relatively mild and decent man," remembered Millard Kaufman. "His problem was his ambivalence. Dore liked to get a lot of people's opinions. When it came to pictures, he was egalitarian, which is a big mistake.

"One day I was in the room with Dore and his assistant Herman Hoffman, when Dore asked Herman something about a script. Herman went through the motions of deep thought, then said, 'Yes and no.' And Dore said, 'If there's one thing I hate more than a yes man, it's a yes-and-no man.'

"I've always remembered that remark. Dore was the first man in power in a studio who could be called a feminist; he was active in the Democratic Party, he had a great deal of intellectual vigor and expressed it in fairly progressive ideas. Yet Dore also attended and approved of the Waldorf Conference that made the blacklist possible. The yes-and-no thing, he could have been talking about himself."

Schary was more immediately approachable than Mayer, less likely to dig in his heels just because they were his to dig in, but he also had less of a grasp of the overall issues. Leslie Caron remembers going to him in tears because of an order that had come down to glamorize her appearance.

"Darling, what can I do for you?" inquired Schary with open arms. Caron presented her case, Schary listening attentively. Finally he said, "My darling, whatever your little heart desires. What film are you on?"

There would be less fear, but also less savvy. "Mayer believed in the star system," said George Sidney. " 'Make it bigger, make it better.' Dore wanted to make movies about little Americans. He got rid of Gable and Tracy and used Jim Whitmore and Nancy Davis; little stories about little people. Size didn't matter to Dore."

Gerald Mayer, L.B.'s nephew, who directed movies for Schary, said that "Schary knew what he was doing, but what he was doing didn't make sense for MGM at that time. L.B. was interested in size, glamour. Schary was interested in issues, which didn't go well with size and glamour. So he started doing smaller pictures. But Dore's interests were not commercially important enough to carry the freight of a large studio, and he didn't have any feel at all for the kind of pictures that could carry the freight."

Schary considered himself a David Selznick protégé, telling people that everything he knew about movies he had learned from Selznick. When the compliment was relayed to Selznick, he snorted and said, "He never finished the course."

On top of Schary's own limitations, there were the limitations of the MGM corporate culture. Robert Wise, who followed Schary from RKO to MGM, said that "Dore had trouble bending MGM to his will." The reason might have been that Schary was attempting to function within the MGM system, a model that was rapidly becoming obsolete. Other studios were decentralizing production in order to cut overhead, and making innovative deals with independent producers. But Schary—undoubtedly at Nick Schenck's urging—was still attempting to operate a centralized production setup, with a reduced but functioning contract system, and star/genre focus.

As far as independents were concerned, the only major deal the studio made in the Schary era was with Sam Goldwyn for *Guys and Dolls*. That picture grossed $13 million, making money for Goldwyn and for MGM, and causing Goldwyn to crow that he was at last part of the organization that carried his name, which was more than L. B. Mayer could say. MGM should have been distributing these kinds of independent pictures years earlier, but *Guys and Dolls* was basically a one-shot.

Old remedies were not going to cure new diseases. Not only wouldn't Nick Schenck deal with independent producers, he adamantly refused to make percentage deals with actors—money from percentage deals was considered capital gains and was taxed at only 25 percent compared to the sky-high rates for straight salaries. For a man like Schenck, actors were waiters, good for delivering the meal. Only a fool would let them in the kitchen.

"By what right do they claim to become owners of the property?" Schenck would say, exploding in anger. "Did they finance the production? Did they take the risk if there is a loss? Did they concern themselves with the huge overhead of the studio? Did they develop the Metro trademark? Who is he? He's nobody. We took him from nobody, we lavished him with lessons and publicity, and now he's the most desired man in the world. Who taught him how to walk? Who straightened his teeth and capped them into that smile. . . . We taught this dumb cluck how to depict great emotions. And now he wants a piece of the action? No! Never!"

The studio let Clark Gable go when he requested more money and a percentage of his film's profits. Other studios were doing it, and had been since Bill Goetz gave James Stewart a piece of *Winchester '73*, but other studios weren't Metro. Gable had never cared for Mayer, but he liked Dore Schary even less. He nursed a grudge for the rest of his life over the studio's failure to give him a tiny piece of *Gone With the Wind*, or even a print of the film—they asked $3,200 for a print, and he refused to pay it. Gable took his pension and went to work for other studios and a lot more money.

"You know," Gable told a friend, "those bastards in the front office didn't give me a farewell party or cake or anything. They didn't even bother to say goodbye." Gable vowed he would never set foot on the MGM lot again. He never did.

MGM seems not to have given a percentage of the profits to any actor since Garbo's holding company got 50 percent of the profits from *Queen Christina* and *The Painted Veil* in the early 1930s. As for directors, they too worked on straight salary. Arthur Freed, by all odds the most successful producer on the lot, also worked for a straight salary until the late 1950s, although over the years, he had received thousands of shares of Loew's stock as bonuses. Besides that, asserted Stanley Donen, Mayer arranged for the studio to buy Freed's song catalogue, giving him a sizable capital gain.

Between Schenck's obstinate adherence to bygone traditions and Schary's own weaknesses, MGM was in the process of making itself obsolete. From 1927 to 1948, MGM won twenty-two Academy Awards; from 1949 to 1968, they would win only seven.

Schary managed to contain costs and show profits, not by increasing the gross, but by cutting overhead. The average cost of an MGM picture in 1947–48 had been $2.2 million. In 1949–50, it was $1.4 million, and in 1950–51 it was $1.3 million. Musicals like *Seven Brides for Seven Brothers* and *Brigadoon* that could have desperately used location footage were shot entirely on the back lot and in airless soundstages. It made financial, if not creative, sense.

Retrenchment was the order of the day. Technicolor gave way to Ansco color; time wastage would be a thing of the past, and temperamental outbursts—are you listening, Mr. Lanza?—would no longer be tolerated.

In July 1952, Nick Schenck journeyed west for a mass meeting of the studio's four thousand employees, where he informed them that while the studio would be making thirty-eight films, there would be reductions in the number of contract employees and executive pay cuts. Anybody earning more than $1,000 a week would have to take a pay cut of from 25 to 50 percent for one year. Schenck himself was taking the pay cut.

Schenck talked to all of the remaining contract actors two at a time, alphabetically. "Keenan Wynn and I went in at the same time," said James Whitmore. "They wanted us to behave, not turn down scripts. And they wanted us to go out on a big public relations tour that they were calling 'Movies Are Better Than Ever.' It was preposterous.

" 'You know, boys,' began Schenck, 'We've got a great MGM family.'

"And I told him I already had a family, a wife and a kid, and I didn't need another one. I have this dislike of organizations that presume to make you a part of them, instead of you making the organization a part of you."

MGM had entered its twilight phase, and people who had been there a long time knew it. "Dore and I became very close, my wife and I and he and his wife," remembered Ricardo Montalban. "We would go to his home once a week and run pictures. And if he wasn't ready to come down and be the host, he would have me come to his room while he got dressed. He was a very likable man, Dore. Down-to-earth, charming, wanted to be considered one of the group. I have nothing but the fondest memories of Dore.

"But I have a dichotomy of feeling about Dore. He was a very intelligent man, a very good writer, he knew motion pictures. But MGM would have lasted longer with Mr. Mayer. He was a showman, and he loved pictures."

Producer Richard Goldstone said, "If L.B. couldn't make it work, there wasn't anybody else who could make it work. Mayer would have been a genius with the wide screen if they'd kept him there. But the company culture catered to spectacle of one sort or another, and other studios were less interested in spectacle and more interested in action and sex. That hurt MGM. And MGM made musicals and then musicals died off."

Esther Williams despised Schary because of what she termed his "supercilious snobbishness. The first thing Dore wanted to know was where you went to college. He didn't like stars, he liked featured players. He liked Jim Whitmore and Nancy Davis. It was so insulting to be told he had no interest in those of us who had worked so hard to be where we were. He was a pseudo-snob. Dore had the kind of snobbery that eliminated people that weren't literary. He was bad casting for a head of a studio; Harry Cohn was a mean man, but he knew the business. Dore Schary should have tried to run a theater for a while."

If Nancy Davis—invariably cited as the dreary essence of Schary's sensibility, even by Republicans—was a pallid presence on screen, she certainly had an impact on Benny Thau. "He was head over heels in love with her, period," remembered Audrey Totter. "Benny was kind of reserved, a little dull. He had dated Frances Gifford for a long time. Anyway, Nancy broke up with him and he had a fit. Finally, her father had to call Benny and say, 'Please leave Nancy alone. She's not interested in you anymore.'

"It's funny, because she tried desperately to be sexy and it wasn't right for her. What was right was to be First Lady. When she met Ronnie, that was it—madly in love. Once we were all sitting in the garden talking. There had been some news stories about flying saucers supposedly landing in New Mexico, and

Ronnie asked me if I thought it was true. Then he said, 'Wouldn't it be wonderful to be President of the United States? Then you could find out about things like that!' "

In the days after he was deposed, Mayer vacillated between talking of nothing else and not talking about the studio at all. When he saw relatives or former employees who were still at MGM, he would never ask what was going on at the old haunt. He would go shopping at the Farmers Market, with his uniformed chauffeur bringing up the rear, and would go into the butcher's locker to personally select prime cuts. He would go for long walks in Bel Air, with the limo trailing behind him. Around town, a crack gained momentum and achieved general circulation: "The old gray Mayer, he ain't what he used to be."

His isolation was only increased by the fact that he had never been particularly friendly with his peer group, and Goldwyn, Warner, and the rest were all still in harness. He opened an office at 9885 Charleville Boulevard in Beverly Hills, from which he called Joe Mankiewicz and offered him a three-picture deal. "He fabricated a whole situation in which we were both the victims of these conspirators at MGM, conveniently forgetting all that had gone before." Mankiewicz let his agent say no.

Mayer owned the screen rights to Sigmund Romberg's *Blossom Time*, but there were still some underlying issues that hadn't been cleared up, and he pursued those, through Paul Koretz, with relentlessness and a total command of detail: "Regarding Chappell release on second thought you may leave mention of document 34 in main agreement with April Productions and add date of quit claim from Chappell to copyright international and from latter to me. Will arrive Friday and desire complete this entire transaction Friday morning."

He maintained his personal generosity, making sure nobody knew about it. When Harry Sherman, producer of the Hopalong Cassidy westerns, financed a couple of big-budget bombs and lost his fortune, he sent a note to L.B. asking for a small loan. Mayer promptly sent the note back with a scribbled P.S. that said $50,000 had been deposited in Sherman's account.

Mayer had endured what he regarded as Bill Goetz's mishandling of one of his horses, but there was much more to come. Your Host ran under the Goetz colors, won the Santa Anita Derby and went into the 1950 Kentucky Derby at 8 to 5. Goetz and his trainer entered the horse in a trial race two weeks before the Derby. The horse won, but Mayer was furious. "You mark what I tell you," he said. "He left his race on that track." Your Host had the post position and was ridden by the great Johnny Longden. It didn't help; he finished ninth in the Derby, as L.B. had predicted.

L.B. might even have been able to countenance Goetz's enthusiasm for Adlai Stevenson in 1952. There were, after all, other Democrats in the Mayer family, Irene among them. L.B. would shrug philosophically and say "She won't listen, she'll have to learn herself." But, as Goetz's friend and partner Armand Deutsch would say, "Bill flaunted his politics. He wasn't just for Stevenson, he played a leading role. 'Fuck 'em,' he said, 'I'll do what I want.' And Mayer just wasn't used to that."

Goetz's main ally in Hollywood's Stevenson contingent was none other than Dore Schary, who asked if he could hold a fund-raising event at Goetz's house. Goetz begged off for all the obvious reasons, so the party was moved to Schary's house, but Schary's invitations read, "William Goetz and I invite you. . . ."

L.B. was apoplectic. There was no way that he could take this as anything other than a calculated slap in the face. As far as Goetz was concerned, his politics were none of his father-in-law's business; as far as Mayer was concerned, he had bought Bill his place at Fox, he had bought Bill his place at International—and Bill repaid him by climbing into bed with Dore Schary.

L.B. stormed, L.B. raved. Edie tried to tell him that Goetz hadn't known that Schary would use the Goetz name, which was highly doubtful; Schary knew how much Mayer hated him and had to know what the response would be at having his name bracketed with Goetz's. The excuse only inflamed Mayer further. "That's a lie! That son of a bitch you're married to is the biggest goddamn liar I've ever known! If Jesus Christ was to come down here and tell me to believe this man I wouldn't be able to!"

Mayer pleaded with his daughter to stop her husband from inflicting this "public outrage." "What do you want me to do, divorce Bill?" she asked. "I've lived with him longer than I've lived with you, and get it through your head, I love him."

Mayer retorted that he would no longer acknowledge Goetz when he saw his daughter. Edie said that was out of the question—Goetz was her husband, entitled to her loyalty. "All right, when you both come in the room, I'll turn my head away," said Mayer.

"That's fine, Dad," Edie said. "Goodbye."

They never spoke to each other again.

Louis B. Mayer—who gave his all in every waking moment, whose emotions were so enormous they needed a movie studio to package them—had to be the best, the most favored, the beloved. For someone to choose a man other than him was a shattering experience. First Nick Schenck had chosen Schary, and now his beloved Edie-La had chosen Bill Goetz, that *momser*. His humiliation was now complete.

"Mr. Mayer expected unchallenged obedience from his daughters," said his nephew Jack Cummings, "unchallenged obedience from everyone in his family. . . . The thing that makes it tragic to me is that she loved her father, and he loved her. He was anguished about it afterwards, but he had taken a stand."

Mayer undoubtedly expected a tearful third-act reconciliation. But he and his daughter were both stubborn, immensely proud people who couldn't admit they were wrong, and Margaret Mayer couldn't broker a reconciliation. The middle ground vanished and it became a point of honor for each of them not to capitulate.

There are no fights as vicious as family fights, when resentments nurtured for decades come tumbling out of the darkest closets. But, for Irene, at least, there was an upside: "When he said, 'My daughter,'" she wrote, "he referred to me."

Communications weren't completely cut off, for Lorena and Edie were friendly, and Mayer's wife kept his daughter appraised of what was going on. Irene's take on this unlikely alliance was a curt, "They take in each other's wash."

Mayer set about rewriting his will and Bill Goetz would wryly note that sponsoring a party for a Democrat in concert with Dore Schary turned out to be "the biggest contribution anyone made to the Stevenson campaign."

On November 19, 1952, the Producers Guild awarded Mayer its Milestone Award in a ceremony at the ballroom of the Biltmore Hotel. Norma Shearer was his guest of honor and saluted him with a speech that called him "the man who more than anyone else helped create the job of the producer as he is known today." She thanked Mayer for giving her "the happiest days of my life, the days which brought me the very most of life." Where that left Marti Arrouge, her second husband, was an open question.

The audience understood to whom Mayer was referring when he said, "I believe in showmanship. . . . I don't make pictures for the Bel Air circuit—private projection rooms. . . . Either you have showmanship or you haven't."

When Mario Lanza's temperamental displays finally led MGM to suspend him, Mayer made himself available to the press, saying, "When you have a rare orchid, you don't stick it in your lawn like a dandelion—you give it special attention and it blooms. In the lawn it would die. If I had stayed at my studio, the studio that I made the greatest in the world, there would have been no trouble with Mario."

Mayer may have been right. "I adored Mario," said the photographer Murray Garrett. "He was crazy, but he was wonderful crazy. A very mixed-up guy, with an overeating problem, a sex problem, a compulsive personality who would literally give you the shirt off his back if he loved you. He was a street guy from Philadelphia, and Schary was helpless to handle him.

"One day, Schary invited Lanza to his house, explaining that he was having a dinner party and wanted Lanza to sing for his friends. Mario nodded, then said, 'My guinea friends are coming out from Philadelphia in two weeks. How about you and your wife come over and write a screenplay for us?' "

"The atmosphere got more tense [at the Freed unit]," said Adolph Green. "Dore wanted meetings to find out what we were up to. He made more demands; he tried to get himself involved more directly. L.B. had his favorites, and he expressed his likings, but he hadn't interfered."

The results were obvious. At the time Mayer left MGM, Freed had three pictures in various stages of production: *An American in Paris, Show Boat,* and *Singin' in the Rain.* All were critical and commercial smashes, and *An American in Paris* won the Best Picture Oscar. But after Mayer left, both the quantity and quality of Freed's work dropped sharply. He averaged one picture a year from 1953 to 1958, and only *The Band Wagon* and *Gigi* were the equivalent of the work done under Mayer's affectionate supervision. L.B. had created Arthur Freed, schooled him in the art of spending in pursuit of perfection, and had always run interference with Nick Schenck to give his lieutenant the tools he needed. Without L.B., Freed was hobbled.

"The ice cold air blew through the third floor," remembered Lela Simone, the Freed unit's music coordinator. "[Freed] detested Schary. He absolutely abhorred him, and vice versa . . . at times there were terrible telephone fights. Very, very difficult."

Performers, even though they're trained to be far more diplomatic than writers and directors, grew to regard Schary with withering scorn. "Dore Schary didn't know what he was doing," said Cyd Charisse. "Please quote me. *He didn't know what he was doing!* He was the biggest mistake they ever made—the beginning of the end. As an example, we were doing a musical called *Meet Me in Las Vegas,* and he was concerned with whether or not he should make this picture, which was already in rehearsal.

"So he called for a reading of the script. A reading of the script! As if that tells you anything about a musical! So we all had to go in there and read the book, except for Dan Dailey, who flatly refused. Then he said he wanted to see a production number. Hermes Pan and I had been knocking ourselves out on a Frankie and Johnny number. Schary wanted to see it from beginning to end. So we did it, and it was a long number that wasn't designed to be done all at once, and I got sick—a dizzy thing in my inner ear. Schary pretended he knew what he was doing, but he didn't have a clue."

In corporate terms, Loew's was adrift. It was the last of the Big Five companies to agree to theater divorcement in 1954, which wouldn't be completed until 1959. (Fox and Warners each signed divorcement decrees in 1951.) The timing couldn't have been worse; the firestorm proliferation of television and the decline of movie attendance devalued Loew's theaters just at the point when they had to find buyers.

Schenck and his peers could have owned television, and on their terms, but they chose to fight it, and thereby lost not merely the battle, but the war. "The studio," said Millard Kaufman, "had a preoccupation with its primary place in the picture business, so it was the last studio in the world to accept TV and turn out TV product. The whole company thought TV was nothing but midgets in a fishbowl, and they were wrong. There was a time when everybody wanted to be with MGM, but with television nobody wanted to be with MGM. So everybody got way the hell ahead of them, and then they got frantic."

"It was a reign of muffled terror," said Leslie Caron. "You did not dare to say, 'Do you know what I saw on TV last night?' One day, [director] Chuck Walters came in with a black eye. Everytime someone asked him about it, he would answer with a joke: 'I said I really liked *I Love Lucy.*' You were not supposed to mention television. It was such a threat."

"Getting MGM into TV was like trying to get an elephant out of the starting gate at Hollywood Park," Sam Marx grumbled.

On the upside, Schary brought John Houseman to the studio, and Houseman produced a series of ambitious, intelligent movies: *Julius Caesar, The Bad and the Beautiful, Executive Suite, Lust for Life.*

Occasionally, Schary's taste for social consciousness produced a solid hit— *Bad Day at Black Rock* (which Nick Schenck violently opposed) or *The Blackboard Jungle*—but whenever he tried to produce an MGM spectacular, the results were dismal in terms of both entertainment and financial results: *Plymouth Adventure, The Prodigal, Raintree County.*

"The fact was that the producer at Metro, in those days, especially if he was successful, made pictures the way he wanted," remembered John Houseman. "He chose the property. He chose the writer. He chose the director. In collaboration with the director, he chose the cast. He chose the editor, the composer . . . he chose everything. I always felt, during those years, that my signature was on those pictures."

This was in the mid-1950s, the time of Kazan, Brando, and Dean, and Houseman was echoing everything Hunt Stromberg would have said twenty years before. Schary's attitude toward directors wasn't much more enlightened than Mayer's. Bringing Wilder, Wyler, Kazan, Huston, or Stevens to Metro would have probably meant throwing the MGM script out, not to mention reducing the authority of the producer. It also would have meant a better movie and, almost certainly, better business at the box office, but that wasn't the MGM way. This failure to move MGM away from a studio-dominated approach to the more personal approach to filmmaking that would dominate in the 1950s and 1960s was Schary's greatest blunder.

After the initial placebo effect of Schary's arrival, when it seemed that he was the reincarnation of Thalberg, things began to slide. Nineteen fifty-four brought $6.3 million in profits, but that was an illusion—a reissue of *Gone With the Wind* turned a major loss into a decent profit. The studio endured disasters like *Jupiter's Darling* (Esther Williams's MGM swan song, which lost $2.2 million). There would be worse to come, as with *The Opposite Sex*, a remake of *The Women*, that brutally revealed how plebeian Schary's taste really was. Recasting a movie that had starred Norma Shearer, Joan Crawford, Rosalind Russell, Paulette Goddard, and Joan Fontaine with June Allyson, Joan Collins, Dolores Gray, Ann Sheridan, and Ann Miller indicated threadbare thinking. And David Miller was no George Cukor. But casting men in the remake and obliterating the original's brilliant gimmick was stupidity that verged on the divine.

In 1949, the first full year of Schary's presence, MGM's share of the market was 22 percent—the same as it had been in 1939. In 1956, Schary's last year, MGM's share of the market had fallen to 17 percent. (The companies that picked up market share were innovators like United Artists and, to a lesser extent, Warner Bros.)

Schary's feel for actresses was abysmal. He failed to sign Marilyn Monroe after *The Asphalt Jungle* and was initially underwhelmed by Grace Kelly—he thought her drab. The studio managed to sign her, but then suspended her three different times because she hated the scripts MGM offered her. Other than John Ford's *Mogambo*, Kelly's signature roles all came on loan-out to Hitchcock—*Rear Window, To Catch a Thief, Dial M for Murder.* At MGM she made low-wattage snoozes: *Green Fire, High Society,* and *The Swan.*

Finally, Schary's considerable passive-aggressive ego flourished when he made himself the public face of the studio by hosting and narrating promotional shorts. It was an act of hubris neither Thalberg nor Mayer would ever have indulged in. Their stars were actors and, beyond that, the studio itself, not the producer, the writer, the director, or the executives.

The primary rules of the game had changed. The studio system that had been devised by Adolph Zukor and L.B. was profoundly paternalistic and profoundly mechanistic. It manufactured movies on an assembly line, as if they were Ford automobiles—a large workforce was necessary. The people running the operation knew best—too much creative debate could slow down the production line.

But once the system began breaking down, the studios no longer needed an assembly line. That meant the talent—on the low end—lost security, but it also meant that—on the high end—the talent gained the upper hand. A movie studio was now less a producer of films than a seducer of talent.

The studio head lost leverage. Under the old system, men like Mayer could use their muscle with their actors, threaten or boycott. But when percentage deals came in, the actors essentially became part owners of each picture they made. The bosses couldn't threaten because they had nothing to threaten with; the employee was now a partner.

Among intimates, Mayer let down his guard and said what he thought. "L.B. was full of hate [about what had happened]," said his nephew Gerald, who saw Mayer often after he was deposed. "He felt he had been screwed. To be the tower of strength for all of Hollywood, and to suddenly have to sit there quietly? To feel that you should be importantly employed, and then to be sitting around Bel Air? That would be very difficult. And it was even more so for Lorena; he was not much of a husband during this period."

At the Mayer house in Bel Air, explosions of temper became common. They could be directed at Lorena, a chauffeur, a maid, or just someone on the telephone. Mayer now existed in a state of constant, barely suppressed rage.

"Lorena had married this very successful man who went to work every morning and came back at night and they went to sneak previews together," said Daniel Selznick. "And all of a sudden the lion was home and he was pacing. She had a wild beast on her hands and she didn't know what to do. His rages and impatience and his frustrations all came out on her. And she had a hell of a temper of her own.

"I couldn't believe the change from when I had visited him at his office in the Thalberg Building. The contrast between the man who knew the first name of everybody on the lot, and the man I saw raging on St. Cloud Road was incredible, but that other life didn't exist for him anymore, and it was heartbreaking; I had never seen him as anything but an incredibly happy, ebullient man.

"And now he was snapping at Lorena, and she was snapping at him, and Suzanne [Lorena's daughter] didn't know where to look and would excuse herself from the table. And Lorena would look at me and say, 'What can I do, Danny?'

"He never turned his rage on me, but I saw him get angry at Jean, his Scottish maid. Now, he had wonderful relationships with his staff; he used to make jokes about Jean's accent. She was an adorable woman, with the face of a British comedienne. And he got angry with her about something and I said, 'Grandpa, you said something mean to Jean.' And he told me to mind my own business.

"It was astounding."

It didn't matter who was listening, Mayer would tell them what he thought, and what he thought tended to revolve around Nick Schenck and Dore Schary, together or singly. "I have more brains in my ass than Nick has in his head," he would snap.

Mary Loos remembered going to a party at Mayer's house. Lorena was downstairs entertaining her friends, while L.B. stayed upstairs. Everybody was having a good time, when a servant came down and asked Lorena to stop the music. "Mr. Mayer is disturbed," said the servant. The band quit, the party drifted away. "Lorena handled the situation with dignity," said Loos. "She had a limited life at this point."

Mayer's attitude toward his stepdaughter was Victorian; Suzanne should be seen and not heard, she should be quiet and respectful to her elders, she should go to bed early. "He was strict with Suzanne," remembered Daniel Selznick, "but he basically let Lorena call the shots. Lorena was a Catholic and Suzanne went to a Catholic school. Lorena brought her up very strictly, to be a virgin until she was married. At one point, Suzanne was going to be a nun; she even did the preliminary novitiate. None of that surprised us, because she'd been so shy; Grandpa expected us to come up with dates for her."

Dan would bring over a friend to St. Cloud Road every Wednesday, in the hopes that the friend would be interested in dating Suzanne. Usually, they weren't. "She was sweet," said Selznick, "but she was so intimidated by her mother. She would always say, 'I can never be my mother.' Suzanne was pretty, but had no sense of movement or how to dress and was painfully self-conscious. And Lorena didn't give her a huge amount of attention." The child rebelled by turning inward and becoming pouty and withdrawn.

Some of L.B.'s friends didn't forsake him. Chrysler chairman K. T. Keller wrote long, chatty letters about how Taft was a better man than Eisenhower, and passed along bon mots from their mutual friend Cardinal Spellman.

In response, Mayer was largely relegated to the sort of gestures of affection that predominate among geriatrics who don't get out much. He enrolled Herbert Hoover in the Fruit-of-the-Month Club, and Hoover dutifully responded with a series of thank-you notes every time a basket appeared on his doorstep at the Waldorf-Astoria. For his part, Hoover made sure to send Louis an inscribed copy of his memoirs, and Mayer told him that he would "keep it beside me, to be read with the care and thought so great a chronicle deserves. Later, it will be a proud addition to my library."

L.B. decided to get back into racing, and bought out Joe Schenck's stock in Del Mar Racetrack, near San Diego, but the magic he had created in the first incarnation of his stables eluded him this time out.

The farm in Perris was long gone, and he didn't want to build another one, so he boarded his small stable in Kentucky. He bred a Preakness winner named Royal Orbit, and a successful horse named Clem. In 1955, Mayer's stable would win $237,000, but that was the only six-figure year he had. He sold Del Mar to oil man Clint Murchison after three years, and it was generally believed that the second incarnation of the Mayer stables lost money.

There were movie opportunities, but none of them seemed quite right. Soon after leaving MGM, Mayer was being romanced by Jerry Wald and Norman Krasna to run their production outfit at RKO, but Mendel Silberberg, Mayer's attorney, didn't trust Wald or Howard Hughes. Hughes thought that perhaps Mayer wanted to go into boutique production à la Goldwyn, and offered him a bargain 20 percent distribution fee. The only problem was that Mayer wanted Hughes to finance the movies, and Hughes wanted Mayer to finance the movies. It was a deal that would do a lot more for Hughes than it would for Mayer. The caravan moved on.

The Hollywood Reporter, which had impeccable connections with Mayer through Billy Wilkerson, went with front-page stories that Mayer was angling for either Columbia or Universal International. Mayer believed that whatever operation he took over would have to offer profit-sharing incentives to sign up top talent, whether in front of the camera or behind. Columbia fell through; Universal fell through.

There had to be something he could turn his hand to, someone that needed him. He thought about buying Republic, but that operation would have had to be completely retooled for major production. Besides, the film library, made up largely of low-end westerns and B movies, was comparatively worthless, so a major revenue source wouldn't be available. Mayer even had some talks with Robert Lippert, a fairly innovative producer of B pictures, about a company in which Mayer would produce four expensive pictures a year while Lippert would make twelve programmers to eat up overhead.

Rumors began to fly about a loose configuration of independent star/producers, a sort of rump United Artists, with Mayer heading up a configuration of Alan Ladd, Gregory Peck, and directors Mark Robson and Robert Wise. Eddie Cantor made inquiries about Mayer producing a picture based on his life.

Nothing happened.

He did pull off a couple of deals outside the movie business, purchasing the northwest corner of Wilshire and Cañon Drive for $475,000. But real estate was comparatively straightforward and far too stolid for a man used to making thirty to forty movies a year. He had to do something to let everybody know L. B. Mayer was still in the game. He hired John Lee Mahin to work as an in-house scriptwriter, producer, and executive for the prospective Mayer company. He bought Lerner and Lowe's *Paint Your Wagon* for $200,000 plus 5 percent of the profits.

But mostly he chafed. There was the occasional speech, as the one he delivered to a group of Catholic newsmen in San Francisco, where he urged that America name an ambassador to the Vatican, eliminate taxes on all privately endowed schools, and allow prayer in schools because "we will have fewer Communists in the country if we achieve this."

Mayer's old secretary Florence Browning and her husband were visiting California from New York and went to MGM for old times' sake. When they saw Ida Koverman, Browning asked about Mayer. "Oh, he's pouting out there in Bel Air," said Koverman. Browning called Mayer's office, and soon he was on the line himself, inviting her to the house and sending his car for her.

When Browning and her husband arrived, he proudly introduced them to Lorena and showed them around the house. Browning thought he seemed bright and confident, but she sensed his loneliness. Her husband, a doctor, found Mayer fascinating—complex, inconsistent, and immature, but still full of his indomitable energy.

On September 30, 1952, *This Is Cinerama* opened at the Broadway Theater in New York to an unprecedented critical and public response. For the first time, the *New York Times* ran a story about a movie on its front page. Cinerama was a spectacular, if cumbersome, screen experience, harnessing three projectors and a very wide, curved screen with a ratio of three to one, marginally improving on Abel Gance's Polyvision of 1927. A few weeks after the opening of *This Is Cinerama*, Mayer became chairman of the board of Cinerama, bringing with him the rights to *Paint Your Wagon*.

Mayer was an attractive bauble for a company that was hoping to seduce the movie industry to a wholesale conversion. Cinerama president Dudley Roberts had been on the verge of refinancing the company to the tune of $20 million, when word hit of Fox's competing—and far less cumbersome—CinemaScope, and the bankers pulled out.

Mayer's salary was set at $1,000 a week and an expense account—short money, but a price he was willing to accept. Louis B. Mayer was back in the movie business.

Charles Foster was now in publicity, and spent some time with a newly energized L.B., who felt that he was allied with the movies of the future, and that creative life was slowly coming back to him.

"You've never worked with me," L.B. told him. "I'd love you to work with me." But Foster didn't think it was a good idea. "Good friends don't always make good workmates," he said. "I found out the truth of that when I worked with Charlie Chaplin for four and a half months on *A King in New York*. Chaplin was a totally different man working than when he wasn't working."

Foster had become friendly with Chaplin and Mayer's sister Ida through their unsuccessful efforts to keep Charles Chaplin Jr. sober. "At this point, Ida was Louis's best friend. He asked Ida about everything and believed everything she told him. He trusted her completely. She was colder than Louis, very businesslike, in spite of the fact she wasn't a businesswoman."

Mayer soon became a presence at the Cinerama offices at 488 Park Avenue and exercised some stock options at the beginning of 1953. Mayer's contract specified that Cinerama had options to buy *Blossom Time* and *Paint Your Wagon*. If the company didn't pick up *Blossom Time* or *Joseph and His Brethren* by February 1, 1953, Mayer was free to sell them elsewhere, while the option on *Paint Your Wagon* was to run until November 1, 1957. Cinerama was obligated to pay Mayer $30,000 for their option on *Paint Your Wagon* even if they didn't choose to make the picture.

Mayer was indeed back in the movie business, but in much the same catch-as-catch-can way he had been thirty-five years earlier. Cinerama was woefully underfinanced and needed a great deal of money to lease and equip theaters and ramp up production. A Cinerama theater could gross up to $250,000 a week, but heavy operating costs for the three projectors and their accoutrements—three projectionists, a sound engineer—took about 50 percent of the gross right off the top. A picture had to play a very long time in a Cinerama theater before it could pay off the conversion costs of the theater, let alone the cost of the movie.

Another complicating factor was the fact that a man named Hazard Reeves was running the division that sold the equipment for the theaters, and Hazard Reeves wanted to sell his machines. So the company had to keep opening theaters in order to keep Hazard Reeves happy, incurring enormous additional overhead with each new operation.

"The problem with Cinerama," remembered Theodore Kupferman, counsel to the company at the time, "was that nobody was actually running things. Lowell Thomas was supposedly president, but whenever we had a board meeting, he'd be writing a script for his daily radio show. When I held a stockholders meeting, I was one of the few people who had any idea what was going on.

"Mayer was brought in to run things, but he didn't want to run things. He didn't want the obligations of it; he wasn't well paid—he was getting $1,000 a week. He was living in California and came in once in a while. They did whatever they could to make him happy. He had a desk big enough to be a billiard table, but since he wasn't there that often, everybody else would use the desk too. Whenever [Cinerama investor] Merian Cooper would come to town, he'd use Mayer's office."

This Is Cinerama was bringing in about $50,000 a week from the four theaters the company had, but that wasn't enough to cover the heavy debt obligations and make another picture. A sequel to *This Is Cinerama* had begun production, but the camera plane was grounded in Crete, and there wasn't enough money to keep it flying.

Cinerama needed money and needed it quickly. Mayer would not make a personal loan, but he got banker Louis Lurie to co-sign a note. Mayer's presence on the Cinerama board helped convince Bankers Trust to loan the company $1.6 million to convert theaters in Detroit, Chicago, Los Angeles, and some other cities.

"He was happy to raise funds," said Theodore Kupferman, "but he wasn't anxious to get involved in any nitty-gritty. When it was time to complete the deal, I suggested that we take the subway, and he was very intrigued. Whenever he came into town with his wife, they were always in limos and stayed on Central Park South, right next to the Essex House. But the subway delighted him."

When the money was on the table and the spotlight hit him, Mayer could still deliver. Lawyer Edward Weisl remembered that Mayer's "enthusiasm was prodigious and he was a great salesman. He would have made a great trial lawyer or actor. Actually, he would have been great in any business. He was successful in real estate, horses, investments, he had a great knack of making friends with important people and surrounding himself with them."

But backstage, waiting for the performance, the situation was different. Gavin Lambert was sent from London to New York to investigate Cinerama for *Sight and Sound* magazine and found "a surprisingly short man. All the stories made you think of an imposing figure, and he wasn't. He was short and stocky and well-spoken, with a decently educated voice. I had expected someone with a much more theatrical manner, and with a heavy accent. But he was well-spoken and extremely friendly.

"He had this nervous tic which caused him to blink a lot. He seemed diminished to me; it was like he'd been defeated. He no longer had an empire, just an office. I suspect that he had been appointed to Cinerama for his name, and that he didn't really have a great deal to do. He didn't seem unenthusiastic, but he wasn't bubbling over. But he'd passed all that, somehow. He was an aging, tired man in a dark suit, who looked like a businessman but was actually an exiled emperor."

Theodore Kupferman's perceptions were only marginally different: "I wouldn't say he was a humorous man, but he wasn't dry either. He wasn't bombastic—you could have a conversation with him. I didn't get a sense that he was genuinely interested in Cinerama as a process. It was a way of coming back into the industry. He still was very energetic; when we went on the subway, he was always walking ahead of me, although I thought he was a little overweight. He knew business, knew all about the financing of things. I'd say he was a very nice man, actually. I think that in the back of his mind he was getting ready to have his fight for MGM, and then he forgot all about us."

By March 1953, Mayer was the largest single stockholder in Cinerama, holding 89,250 shares, 34,000 more than Lowell Thomas and 51,000 more than Merian Cooper. In November 1954, Mayer was instrumental in arranging the deal whereby Cinerama was sold to the Stanley Warner theater company. At this point, Cinerama owed him $80,000 in back salary, $26,000 in expenses, and $30,000 for *Paint Your Wagon*. The company also had the rights to buy back ten thousand shares of his stock at 50 cents a share, which it did, but Mayer wouldn't receive all the money he was due until a week before he died.

That month, two years after he'd assumed the chairmanship of Cinerama, Mayer left the company and took *Paint Your Wagon* and *Blossom Time* with him. Cinerama did not release a second feature until 1955, three full years after its first smash hit.

One of the last times Mayer and Schary were in the same place at the same time was the funeral of Ida Koverman, who died of a heart attack at the age of seventy-eight on November 24, 1954. They all came to Ida's Christian Science funeral: former mayor Fletcher Bowron, agent Abe Lastfogel, journalists Hedda Hopper and Florabel Muir, conservatives Jimmy Stewart and George Murphy, liberal Edward G. Robinson. Earl Warren, J. Edgar Hoover, and Herbert Hoover sent telegrams. Sitting in the front pew reserved for family was L.B. In lieu of flowers, Koverman asked that contributions be sent to the Motion Picture Home. She left an estate of several hundred thousand dollars to a grand-nephew in Maryland.

Chapter
SEVENTEEN

WHAT TO DO WITH *Paint Your Wagon?* Mayer quietly asked Paul Koretz to canvas likely producers to see if anybody wanted to co-produce—i.e., finance—the picture, or even take it over. Since the picture was bound to be expensive, there was a short list of prospective financiers, and Alexander Korda, for one, demurred, saying the picture "is too big an enterprise for us, and also this type of musical is done much better in America than we could do it here." Another avenue blocked, another road closed.

Louis B. Mayer had done one thing for a quarter-century. Could he go back to the days of independent production? Most people in Hollywood believed the answer was no.

"L.B. was not a flexible man, not at all," said Esther Williams. "If your favorite movies were Andy Hardy, how do you perceive the movies that were being made in the 1950s?"

"Mayer was a very sensitive man," said Jane Powell, "and he was very confused when they let him go. He was really a lost soul. He didn't see it coming— how many people do see it coming?—and there weren't that many places to go where he would have been welcome. And where would he have had that kind of power? He was an older man, and I think it deflated him so that it was very hard to think along those lines. He became a beaten man; he became very old.

"Not being wanted is very painful."

Mayer was approached by a young man just out of Yale who was looking for money to start up a magazine devoted to conservative political thought. Cardinal Spellman had suggested Mayer as a likely investor, and William F. Buckley Jr. went to the West Coast to meet some likely investor-contributors.

He spent several hours with Mayer at his office, and found that the forcibly retired producer "spoke most poignantly about his encroaching poverty." Times were bad, he told Buckley; if only he had been here a year ago, "I'd have written you out a check for the whole thing." Since Buckley's goal was the rather sizable amount of $500,000, the remark was taken—and probably meant—as soft-soaping hyperbole.

Buckley's sense of Mayer's conservatism was that he was heavily influenced by the anti-Communist—and largely Catholic—Hollywood faction that included Bing Crosby. Although Mayer promised to make at least a good-faith donation of "a few thousand" to the project that became *National Review*, the check never arrived. Buckley remembered writing a reproachful letter to Mayer before the first issue was published. That didn't shake any cash loose either.

Since L.B. was having trouble making a picture, he began to lend John Lee Mahin to other producers. "He was the best agent I ever had," said Mahin. "He guaranteed me so much, and he'd lend me out at a big profit. He'd take 20 percent, and he'd still make more money than I'd make."

Mayer engaged Philip Yordan to write a screenplay for *Joseph and His Brethren*, the Bible story on which Thomas Mann had based his tetralogy. "I worked on it for ten weeks," remembered Yordan. "I would meet with him once a week, and we would spend several hours together in which I would read him what I had written that week. He could read, but he didn't want to.

"He had very little comment on what I was doing. Each time we talked, he would impress upon me that he was not a writer, that he needed whatever skill I had. He almost had tears in his eyes when he said, 'I wish I could write but I can't. I'm totally dependent on you.' "

Yordan believed that Mayer genuinely wanted to make the picture. He would ask a lot of questions about the Bible. "He asked me to interpret the material; it was old, and he wanted to maintain a sense of the biblical period, but make it contemporary."

Mayer's office was in a bungalow next to a theater on Cañon Drive, just off Wilshire. He would arrive at the office about eleven, work till about 1:30. The sessions were strictly business. It would take about forty minutes to read over the week's pages, and sometimes Mayer would have Yordan read them twice. Then he and Yordan would go to lunch at Romanoff's. "He smelled very fragrant, like he just got out of the shower. He wore fluffy white shirts, with pleats."

At Romanoff's, the two men would discuss politics. "He was a Republican, and talked like a newscaster, a half-hour or so about what was going on in the world." Yordan noticed that Mayer didn't get enthusiastic about anything, although he did talk a lot about real estate. With Yordan, he didn't seem bitter, or preoccupied by what had happened at MGM. "He wasn't a bundle of joy, but he was very polite. He was rather cheerful, a very nice, kindly old man. But he was old for his age. You could see he was sort of burned out."

Yordan found that the difference between Mayer and the other moguls was not intelligence so much as attitude. "Howard Hughes was always nervous, edgy; Goldwyn was always looking to start a conversation with an argument; Cohn was insecure; Jack Warner was scared, but combative—he liked to argue, and always complained about the outside world.

"With Mayer, you were dealing with a man who had absolute power, but didn't have to wield it. It was there. He was enormously wealthy. He was a benevolent despot; you could feel that this was a man on top of the world, who had complete control over himself and everybody else. He was much more secure than the others. The way he acted, he could still have been running Metro. And he let you know it."

Although he was engaged on an open-ended contract, Yordan completed work on the script in ten weeks. Each week, Mayer cut him a check for $2,500, his going rate at the time. "I think I did rather a good job on it," said Yordan.

Mayer had John Lee Mahin take another crack at the script, then sent the result to David Selznick for his opinion, in the hope that Selznick's second wife, Jennifer Jones, would play Potiphar's wife. Selznick was always interested in Mayer's opinions on projects and deals and would often tell his counsel, Frank Davis, "Let's go talk to L.B." The two men would go to Mayer's house, and Davis always found him friendly, cordial, and on top of his game.

Now it was Mayer's turn to ask for advice. Selznick said that he would like to have Jennifer play the part, then spent many pages of one of his famous memos outlining the reasons why she couldn't possibly make the movie from this script. He also dodged what he termed as a "very flattering suggestion" that perhaps Selznick could be associated with the venture.

Selznick obviously believed that Mayer's script was a typical DeMille-style epic. The problem was that "there has appeared only one Cecil B. DeMille. Nothing is more appalling than second-rate DeMille: the result is the vulgarity without the showmanship which makes his work acceptable and even applauded by those of taste, albeit tongue-in-cheek; there is the size and spectacle without discrimination; there is the 'big theater' without the rough but clever balance of characterization and character relationships; there is the indiscriminate use of resources to the ultimate extent, without any realization of why they are being used, but instead only the hope that the sheer weight and volume will produce a result; and there is the final resultant expense without the final resultant gross."

Selznick went on to excoriate the MGM *Quo Vadis* as a precise example of what he was talking about. Since Mayer was going to have to find somebody besides DeMille to direct his picture, Selznick's implication was that Mayer's script had to go in a different direction—an intelligent epic "in quality and integrity of approach . . . add to them idealism worthy of a Thomas Mann, and there will be a motion picture to be remembered for generations."

In October 1953, Selznick upped the ante, obviously concerned about Mayer's emotional state and his temperamental limitations as a producer. The old machinery was clearly breaking down, and he didn't seem to think his ex–father-in-law could retool.

"There are two, and only two, important types of manpower in motion pictures," he wrote to Mayer, "and they are equally rare: the great top executive and the great individual picture maker." Because the studio system was on a morphine drip, there was no way a studio boss schooled in the old system could be expected to outpoint individual picture-makers like Wyler or Huston. Perhaps L.B. should consider some other line of work? "Hoover, Warren, Eisenhower—these man are your intimate friends. . . .

"If I were given the powers of a god or dictator, I would decree that you retire from business endeavor, or at least business endeavors in the motion picture industry . . . to the enjoyment of the rest and fun that you have earned by decades of the most extraordinary devotion to your work. . . . I just cannot stomach the idea of Louis B. Mayer waiting in Harry Cohn's outer office for consultation and for decisions on a commercial enterprise! Surely this would be the motion picture industry turned upside down! . . .

"Temperamentally, your mind is no longer satisfied to deal with the tiny details of picture-making, on an individual picture basis. The enormous contribution you made to the industry was not in these terms, but rather in the building of a great machine, in which you could act in a transcendental capacity, surrounding yourself with the greatest talent available in all branches of the theater arts, and utilizing your unparalleled perspicacity in the selection and management of personalities. . . .

"There has never in all the history of the business been a top executive remotely to compare with you, but you are not equipped by temperament to be limited to a small operation to the details of day-to-day management and control of an individual film."

Mayer could, Selznick thought, wait for MGM to realize the error of its ways and beg him to come back, but that was unrealistic. As for other studio options, there was RKO (*"something* has to be done with RKO . . .") or Warners, if Jack and Harry sold out.

But "the old companies, without exception, are set up for a business that no longer exists. Everything about them is an anachronism: even their physical plants, their studios, are outmoded; their distribution facilities are based upon a quantity and type of product for which there is no longer a market."

Mayer could start up a mini-studio, but Selznick thought that L.B. trying to turn himself into Stanley Kramer—or, for that matter, David Selznick in his heyday—was absurd. Perhaps the best option for *Joseph and His Brethren* was to bring in a director like David Lean, cut a 50-50 deal with Harry Cohn, and then deal with Lean for L.B.'s half.

Selznick urged L.B. to give it up—the movies, his career, his hatred of Nick Schenck and Dore Schary, the latter of whom, at least, was entirely unworthy of it. "Do, please, L.B., think first and foremost of your own happiness and peace of mind, and equanimity. . . . I am not alone in thinking that you are letting your bitterness about your mistreatment at MGM color your thinking to a dangerous extent. Since no one else will tell you, I feel obliged to tell you myself: the extent to which you unburden your heart and soul and mind, in relation to Nick Schenck and Dore Schary, has become a source of town gossip."

It takes a dinosaur to know a dinosaur. Short of slamming the old man over the head with a two-by-four, Selznick could hardly have been more blunt. He summoned every possibility open to Mayer, then dispatched them all as unlikely or unworthy. What he was really saying, of course, is that the times had passed L.B. by, and he was no longer nimble enough to adjust, an assessment that had to have further jostled whatever was left of L.B.'s shaken confidence.

By this time, Mayer was looking to sell his three main story properties, and he put an $800,000 price tag on *Paint Your Wagon, Joseph and His Brethren,* and *Blossom Time,* which he wanted to sell as a group. There were no takers, although he eventually unloaded *Joseph and His Brethren* on Harry Cohn, who had it rewritten by Clifford Odets, among others. The film was never made.

Why couldn't Mayer pull the trigger and make a movie?

Among other things, he hadn't been a line producer for more than a quarter of a century, and he knew it. "In all the years I was [at MGM], Mayer never actually produced a picture," said Sam Katz. "Mayer had isolated himself from production. He had been a producer in his early years, but he had become rusty. He had so isolated himself that he was ill-equipped."

"Why didn't he produce movies?" asked David Brown, Zanuck's story editor at Fox. "Because he wasn't a producer. Zanuck was a producer. His name was on his films. Mayer's name was on the company. Mayer didn't read scripts, he made decisions. He hired talent. Zanuck was hands-on; he selected the writers, he read the scripts, he had editing sessions, he did everything. It takes courage to be a producer; you have to be willing to fail, and you can't legislate success."

Another factor was money. Dore Schary told Bosley Crowther that Mayer had threatened to take many of the top stars at MGM with him as soon as their contracts expired—Esther Williams, Lana Turner, Ava Gardner. But when it came time to actually negotiate and put up the money, he backed off. "He was always great and liberal with the company's money," said Schary, "but tight as hell with his own."

"He wasn't creative in the strict sense," said his nephew Gerald. "He made it possible for others to be creative. Putting together one picture wasn't exciting to him; putting together forty pictures was exciting to him." Now, he was, in David Selznick's phrase, like "Knute Rockne without a football team."

Finally, there was the fear factor. If he made a movie and it failed, it would prove Schenck and Schary to have been right. The fact was that building and running a movie studio had been the perfect job for Louis B. Mayer. The reflected glory of the stars and the pictures had largely compensated for Mayer's own fears and angers. Without all that, his worst nightmares were realized, and his insecurities came roaring out of the closet. Now, he was just an old man that nobody wanted.

"Once he left MGM," said his grandson Dan, "loneliness became a theme in his life again. . . . It immediately manifested itself in his restlessness. He would pace. Watch television. Get up from the television set. Sit back down in front of the television. Since his emotions were on the surface, you'd see it in an instant. Other people would be able to disguise their loneliness cleverly. With him, whatever he was feeling was always evident."

There was one thing that stood out in Philip Yordan's mind about his experience with Mayer. For the entire two and a half months Yordan worked on the script of *Joseph and His Brethren*, there was never a mention of who might star in the picture, or what studio might make it. The entire project had an abstract quality.

Oh, and one other thing: "There were never any interruptions. He never got a phone call all the times I was in his office."

MGM stalwart Clarence Brown completed his career in 1952. "As far as MGM was concerned, Dore Schary was the beginning of the end," Brown said.

Brown was a loyal man, and he remained close to Mayer, accompanying him on a sentimental journey back to Haverhill in 1954 and to Europe in the summer of 1955. Mayer reverted to the passive, dependent aspect of his personality when traveling. Everything from tickets to packing and unpacking was left to somebody else, and he was terrified of being left alone. He couldn't amuse himself, and even left magazine and book purchases to Lorena or Clarence.

In Paris, they stayed at the George V, where they ran into Ricardo Montalban. "Mr. Mayer saw me," remembered Montalban. " 'Ricardo!' he said, putting my arm through his, 'Let's take a walk around the block.' So we talked about things. I told him how much MGM had missed him, and he said, 'I had to leave. I couldn't stand to see my stars doing B pictures or changing their personalities playing something that wasn't suitable for them.' He told me some of his disappointments. He wasn't bitter, just resigned and sad."

The director Vincent Sherman was in Rome that summer, and was passing by the Grand Hotel when he saw Mayer standing by the entrance, waiting for Clarence. Sherman had never met Mayer, but went over and introduced himself, explaining that he had heard laudatory things about Mayer from Joan Crawford. "He was very friendly and appreciative that anybody would come and say hello to him," remembered Sherman. "*He* was appreciative that *I* had recognized him! It was one of the most terrible things I've ever seen in our business."

That year, George Sidney went over to Mayer's house at Christmas. "Come in, boy," Mayer said in welcome. Sidney walked in and noted the large dining room table with only five Christmas cards on it. "Boy, look at that," Mayer said, gesturing at the meager grouping of holiday greetings, a philosophical half-smile on his face.

"I've always wondered if it was a ruse," said Sidney, "wondered if he was playing a scene for me. He was a wonderful actor, you know. But I don't think so. People had just passed him by."

Even Arthur Freed, his creation, his acolyte, didn't call often for lunch, didn't offer to bring L.B. to the occasional screening. The stories Freed could have told Mayer—about screening pictures for Schary at his house, only to have Schary's wife turn down the volume because she didn't like musicals— stayed within the unit.

The initial flurry of speculation about where Mayer would go and what Mayer would do had been replaced by an unhealthy silence. For the first time in nearly fifty years, Louis B. Mayer wasn't the center of attention; for the first time in nearly fifty years, Louis B. Mayer didn't really have anything to do.

Finally, Nick Schenck came to the realization that he had made a mistake. "Schary was a really, really nice man, a lovely man, an intelligent man," said Schenck's daughter Nicola. "But he wasn't a number-one man. He would have been a great vice president, but he didn't have the kind of Hollywood oomph that someone needs to run a studio. When my father liked someone, he liked them unconditionally, 100 percent, and he thought the world of Dore Schary, but . . .

"Let me put it like this. My father and Louis B. were lions—when they spoke, people listened. People didn't pay Dore that kind of attention."

Well, sometimes they did. On February 14, 1954, Schary had appeared on the Ed Sullivan television show to accept congratulations for the studio's thirtieth anniversary, which made prominent mention of all the great films that Schary had had nothing to do with, and no mention of people like Irving Thalberg, David O. Selznick, and Louis B. Mayer.

Selznick and Mayer lashed out. Selznick called Schary's credit hogging a "disgraceful and inexcusable . . . attempt by Dore Schary to present *Gone With the Wind* as an MGM production and, what is worse, to claim, by implication, that it was a picture produced by the present 'team' at the studio. . . . He failed to make the slightest mention of the truly great picture makers whose efforts brought MGM the eminence which it formerly enjoyed. When I made *Gone With the Wind* [Schary] was the entertainment director at Grossinger's."

As for Mayer, he issued an unctuous, nearly hysterical statement invoking God and fate, with overtones of *Et tu, Brute*: "I always pray to God that if there is a wrong I may not commit it. . . . The thing that hurt me most was that Irving Thalberg, the greatest genius the motion picture industry will ever have, was never mentioned. I don't see how Dore Schary dared to stand up there and take bows for pictures he never had any part in. My record speaks for itself. . . . I brought him in and tried to develop him. But he went behind my back and got into cahoots with Nicholas Schenck. . . . After that program, I never prayed so hard except the week when my mother was dying. And my prayers were answered. The American people came to my defense. They have a sense of justice. God bless America."

For Mayer, it had all become one. Schary was a liberal Democrat, so Mayer felt justified in moving further to the right. Mayer even allowed his name to be carried on the roster of the Hollywood Committee for Senator Joseph R. Mc-Carthy, supporting his campaign for reelection. Novelist and screenwriter Rupert Hughes was the chairman, John Wayne, Ward Bond, and Morrie Ryskind were vice chairmen. (The other committee members included C. B. DeMille, Harold Lloyd, Adolphe Menjou, Ray Milland, Dennis Morgan, George Murphy, Leo McCarey, Neil McCarthy, Pat O'Brien, Dick Powell, and Randolph Scott.)

In April 1954, Mayer made a speech praising McCarthy. "The more Mc-Carthy yells, the better I like him," he said. "He's doing a job to get rid of the termites eating away at our democracy. I don't care how many toes he steps on, including mine, as long as he gets the job done.

"I used to consider myself a liberal years ago, but it was the kind of liberalism my father and my friends' fathers taught. That was the liberalism to help others less fortunate than yourself. It's a different kind of liberalism today and a kind I don't like."

In 1954, Edie's daughter Judy was getting married and wrote a letter to her grandfather to tell him. He never replied. Two years later, Judy and her husband were wheeling their new baby past the Plaza, when they were startled to see L.B. walking briskly from the hotel.

"Hello, Grandpa," said Judy. Mayer turned to see who had called him, recognized his granddaughter and got into his waiting limousine. "He walked right by Judy," remembered her husband, Richard Shepherd, "who had nothing to do with the fight, and right by this poor thirty-two-day-old baby who had nothing to do with it either. That's some insight into the nature of the gentleman."

Margaret Mayer spent most of her last years being driven to doctors by her nephew Stanley Hoffman. "She never talked about Louis," said Hoffman. "She faded after the divorce," said her niece Helen Sandler. "She couldn't put a life together and slowly went downhill."

On May 21, 1955, Margaret Shenberg Mayer died of pneumonia at the age of seventy-one. Only Edie was at her bedside. Jack Cummings reported that L.B. was in New York and called him in an agitated state. "Your aunt is dying," he told Cummings, "and I called Irene in Europe and told her. She's not coming to see her mother."

"She was working on *The Chalk Garden* with Enid Bagnold at the time," remembered Cummings. "My uncle was dreadfully disturbed with Irene. She not only did not come to see her mother, she never appeared at the funeral, which she conveniently left out of [her memoirs]."

Shortly before Margaret died, she destroyed all the scrapbooks she had kept chronicling the rise of her beloved L.B. Her will mandated a total of $160,000 in specific bequests to relatives and institutions, and $100,000 trusts for each of her four grandchildren, although Judy Goetz was given the option of taking Margaret's 18-carat emerald-cut diamond ring instead. Houses and personal property were divided between her two daughters, and the remainder of what was estimated as a $3 million estate was placed into trust for the benefit of Irene and Edie.

Mayer was still doodling with the idea of making a movie independently. Agatha Christie's clever play *Witness for the Prosecution* had been a smash hit in both London and New York. In June of 1955, Louis was competing for the screen rights with a bid of $300,000, with Clarence Brown on board as the director. But he was outbid by Gilbert Miller, the producer of the Broadway version of the show, who bid $325,000 and promptly turned around and sold the rights to Edward Small for $435,000.

All around was a sense of diminishment, loss, and increasing eccentricity. Family members noticed that Lorena was growing bitter. This wasn't what she had bargained for. She was supposed to be a carefree trophy wife, basking in the bank account and achievements of her elder statesman husband, but that vision had unaccountably dissolved into marriage to a ranting King Lear.

"We have so few real stars today," Mayer fretted. "The glamour's gone out of the business. Imagine public idols, gods, washing dishes, wearing blue jeans, going to psychiatrists. How can anyone idolize people like that? And look at the profits! They went with the glamour. . . . The stories are ruining the industry. I can't bear to watch them. I often walk out. Pictures are too depressing. I like happy pictures. DeMille still makes spectacles, which I think are wonderful. No art for DeMille—just good pictures, and they make money.

"Today, stars want to produce, directors want to write, everyone wants to be chief cook and bottle washer. So no one does anything very well. In my day, I hired brains to do everything. All I ever did was make a few suggestions—and a few stars."

Even Norma Shearer had begun to fall prey to the irrational. Moss Hart and Kitty Carlisle Hart rented Irving Thalberg's old house from Shearer and her husband, Marti Arrouge. "She would come every week and put artificial flowers in the vases," remembered Carlisle. "Personally. And when she left, I would change them back to real flowers."

Universal announced plans for *Man of a Thousand Faces*, the biographical movie about Lon Chaney, and Norma Shearer chose a young actor named Robert Evans to play Irving Thalberg in the film. For weeks she coached him in Thalberg's mannerisms, made Evans promise not to wear makeup because, "You'll look like a pretty girl."

By this time, remembered Evans, "She looked at Thalberg like a god. Marti was a terrific guy, but she was always in love with Irving—the imagining of what he was. When you die young, you leave an aura behind you. The way we think of Jack Kennedy or James Dean was the way she thought of Irving."

In the middle of 1956, for the first time, Mayer's energy began to flag. He would call Jessie Marmorston in the middle of the night and she'd run over to St. Cloud Road and give him a shot of B_{12}. He was hit with a lung infection diagnosed as pneumonia. On July 4, he received get-well greetings from Herbert Hoover, and responded with a note of palpable gratitude: "I am not surprised to hear from you, just terribly pleased. . . . The fact is that while I am growing stronger every day, I am still unable to be very active. Thanks to the antibiotics, the pneumonia was brought under control right away, but I still have a small spot which takes time to heal completely." He was feeling better in August, but still wasn't up to answering his own correspondence.

In December 1956, during one of his frequent medical tests, a high rate of white blood cells was discovered, indicating, at the least, anemia, and at the worst, leukemia. In line with the medical practice of that era, Mayer was told very little; certainly not of the possibility of leukemia. Marmorston ascribed his general malaise to age, and Mayer settled for that.

Despite his weakened condition, L.B. observed the situation at MGM and saw vulnerability. MGM closed down its cartoon studio and cut the payroll by about 150 people. "After twenty years," remembered Joe Barbera, "there was a phone call, and it was over. We never saw a human being, just a phone call. Were we shocked? A little numb, maybe. It was just so bizarre.

"In essence, we put ourselves out of work. They needed cash and they found that they could reissue Tom and Jerry and make almost dollar for dollar what they'd made originally. I got $12,000 in severance; we weren't in the pension plan; we got taken to the cleaners on that."

No matter—Barbera and Hanna each put up $4,000 and formed a cartoon company that would be the dominant force in television animation for the next twenty-five years.

L.B. began to rethink his options. Forget about production; go in and rescue MGM, bring it back to the pinnacle, where he liked to think it had been when he left. Nick Schenck had now reached the stage where L.B. had been five years earlier—time was working against him, and he was as vulnerable as Mayer had been.

And there was all the East Coast nepotism that was every bit as cozy as Mayer's West Coast nepotism had been. Schenck's nephew was the vice president of the advertising company that billed Loew's for $4 million a year; Schenck's two nieces ran the candy company that had the popcorn and concessions in all Loew's theaters; Schenck had a piece of the company that sold and installed carpeting in Loew's theaters, and so forth.

Nick now refused to talk to Lew Wasserman—whom he regarded as the smartest man he'd ever met—in the afternoon, "because I don't function as well, he's too smart for me after that time."

At the end of 1956, *Time* magazine intimated that Schary was about to be fired. When Schary typed up a statement affirming his intentions to stay on the job, he was told not to issue the statement but to come to New York. There, Dore Schary was removed from his position at MGM. Nick Schenck, who had spent the last several years publicly backing Schary and privately telling him that he was his boy, now told him that he had made up his mind a full year before that Schary had to go. Back in Culver City, the supervisor of the commissary called Schary and asked him to be sure to return all the silverware from his little office dining room.

For the last year under Schary, the studio had shown an operating deficit of $3 million, the heaviest operating loss since the disastrous $6.5 million loss in 1947–48. A little more than a month after he was fired, Schary was informed that under the rules of the Loew's retirement plan, he had not qualified for any benefits.

Loew's gave Schary $150,000 of the $300,000 due him for the last year of his contract, and $850,000 in deferred payments spread over eight years. A million dollars—a veritable golden parachute.

Schary stated in *The Hollywood Reporter* that the reason for his dismissal was "that I made too many speeches and wrote too many articles, and that my participation in the 1956 Presidential campaign on behalf of the Democrats had made for irritation and enmity."

This was absurd; the reason for his dismissal was the hard fact that MGM had had two terrible years in a row. And now the toboggan ride downhill began in earnest. In Culver City, Schary was replaced by Benny Thau. Soon, in New York, Nick Schenck would be replaced as well. Thau was, remembered Millard Kaufman, "a nice, nervous man, a nice kind of dumb guy hopelessly unqualified to be a head of a studio."

Thau was soon succeeded by Sol Siegel, who thought long and hard about taking the job. "The only way I can succeed," he explained to a friend, "is if I fire the people who gave me the vote of confidence to take over the studio." He took the job, didn't fire a soul, and lasted about a year.

Could anyone have stopped the bleeding at MGM? "If they had replaced Mayer with Selznick, Hal Wallis, or Darryl Zanuck," said Walter Seltzer, "they could have pulled it out. But Zanuck wasn't going to leave Fox and Hal Wallis wasn't going to leave Paramount. There was nobody else. Certainly not the guys that ran Universal or RKO or Paramount."

Shortly after Schary was fired, MGM abandoned its traditionally lofty attitude and began making profit participation deals with talent, and began enticing outside stars to the studio on single-picture deals. The studio was also thrown into the television business.

It was all too little too late. "United Artists was doing what the business became," said Frank Davis, David Selznick's lawyer and George Stevens's producer. "Give the independent producers participations. That's how UA attracted talent and that's how the deals got made. By resisting it for so long, MGM lost all their talent and lost out on the future."

Six days before Christmas 1956, Mayer finally said the words: "If the right people in New York get control," he said, he would consider returning as head of MGM. As far as the Los Angeles media was concerned, Napoleon returning to Paris could not have occasioned any more uproar than Mayer returning to Culver City. The L.A. *Herald Express* ran a banner headline on page one: BIG MGM ROW; MAYER MAY RUN STUDIO AGAIN.

That same day, Joseph Tomlinson, a Canadian contractor and hotelier who controlled a quarter-million shares of Loew's stock—about 5 percent of the total—charged that the "company is riddled with nepotism and favoritism." Tomlinson demanded the resignation of five board members, and said that Mayer had offered to take over MGM and make "the lion roar again."

Suddenly, things seemed to be going L.B.'s way. The man whose office phone hadn't rung was suddenly getting wires asking for help. Jack Warner wanted John Lee Mahin to write *The FBI Story*. Unfortunately, Mayer had assigned Mahin to *Blossom Time*. The idea of a movie version of an operetta such as *Blossom Time* in 1957 indicates the extent to which L.B.'s sensibilities stopped evolving about the time of World War II, although there's always a chance it could have been a fluke hit like *The Sound of Music*.

A management consulting team led by C. R. MacBride was hired to make recommendations about the mess at MGM and heard from both sides that Mayer was the key to the troubles as well as the possible solution. MacBride set up an appointment with Mayer and found the old man was still impressive. He held his temper and uttered no diatribes about Schary or Schenck, saying only that they were "misguided men."

What, MacBride wanted to know, would he do with MGM now, in the spring of 1957, to keep it alive? One thing and one thing only, said Mayer. Big pictures. Big pictures exclusively. He would embark on a program of block-busters made by independent units that would be tied up with long-term contracts and given generous profit participation deals. "You have to spend a dollar to make a dollar and ten cents," he told MacBride.

MacBride was impressed; Mayer was honest, sincere, and seemed willing to make the commitment of time and energy that would be necessary. "I will move my bed into the studio in Culver City," Mayer proclaimed. MacBride believed Mayer could still be an effective magnet for attracting top talent. There was only one problem: Mayer would have nothing to do with the company as long as Joe Vogel was there.

That summer, L. B. Mayer's finely tuned organism began to run down. He went through the motions, answered all the birthday wires that came in early in July ("It was a very pleasant day, made more enjoyable by the many wonderful greetings from good friends like yourself . . ."). He had always been extremely vigilant about his health, undergoing nearly obsessive checkups from a variety of doctors, mostly because of his fear of cancer. He grew especially close to Dr. Sidney Farber in Boston. Finally, L.B. was definitively diagnosed with leukemia, prognosis terminal. When Irene came to visit that summer, she was informed of the situation. Irene would remember that while she, Lorena, and Jessie Marmorston all knew the end was near, they all assumed L.B. didn't, which would mean he was a much stupider man than he had been when he was healthy.

In the second week of July, the MGM board of directors convened in Culver City, and Ogden Reid went out to Mayer's house to propose a deal. Would

Mayer accept the presidency of Loew's, Inc.? He said he'd have to think about it. That night he talked to Ed Weisl, a lawyer for Lehman Brothers and Lazard Freres. The next day Mayer told Reid that he couldn't take the job.

C. R. MacBride and Reid were both stunned. They had committed themselves to leading a fight to depose Joe Vogel in favor of Louis B. Mayer, had climbed out on the branch only to have it sawn off behind them. During the next week, various people attempted to convince Mayer to change his mind, but he wouldn't budge.

What had happened between April and July? Although Mayer couldn't have known how little time he had left, he undoubtedly felt his energies waning and may have come to the conclusion that he simply lacked the necessary will. The collapse of the Schary-Schenck regime happened too late for Mayer to attempt a comeback.

On July 23, Joseph Vogel, who had replaced Nick Schenck, let loose the dogs, denouncing Mayer publicly. Mayer, according to Vogel, had "virtually paralyzed the ability of the board of directors to function" as he maneuvered to "seize control" of the company. "The stockholders and the entire motion picture industry are well aware of Mayer's record when he was in supreme command at the studio. During his tenure of twenty-seven years he received over $20,000,000 in compensation. In the last three years of Mayer's sole authority as the studio head in 1947, 1948 and 1949, the pictures released lost about $9 million.

"This is the man who . . . is attempting to recapture his position . . ."

Vogel called for a special stockholders meeting on September 12, precipitating the proxy fight that everybody had feared.

Mayer fired back. Reporters caught up to him on his way to San Francisco, where he tried to have it both ways. "If I had wanted to control the company, I never would have left the job. Vogel is a fool. I don't know what he's talking about. When Vogel took the [chairman's] job, I told him he was a fool to accept it. I don't think he is capable of filling the post, no more capable of it than you would be fighting the heavyweight champion."

When asked if he was trying to depose Vogel, Mayer denied it, saying he was "keeping my hands off." He did admit that he was giving Tomlinson and Meyer advice, but also claimed to be "giving Vogel advice." It didn't make much sense, but the double talk could have derived from Mayer's being flustered and caught off guard.

Even an old partisan like Billy Wilkerson thought the whole thing was unseemly. "Yours is a proud name made famous by the medium of motion pictures," he wrote in an open letter in his newspaper. "You have accumulated a great fortune in the business. By your own acknowledgment you have no desire to return to the full-time duties you formerly administered at the studio or at the company helm. If this is true, what do you want? Is it your desire to contribute to the wrecking of what you helped to build, the greatest single asset in the picture business? . . .

"Why not, Mr. Mayer, use your influence, your judgment that formerly was so sound, in getting the warring factions in this fight together, thereby saving the company millions that will be spent in the fight and many more millions in the loss of time [leading to] zero morale in the company's production activities?"

It was, David Selznick realized, the biggest mistake Mayer had ever made. Time had revealed Schary as a paltry pretender who had no business running a movie studio, and Nicholas Schenck was now on the shelf as well. And here was L.B., aligning himself with second- and third-raters?

But Mayer was imprisoned by his emotions as much as he was by his beliefs. On the one hand, he was slightly bored with pictures; on the other, he hated many of the people who came into the industry after him and regarded them as interlopers. He was filled with resentment about people he didn't like or respect who were making movies, but he couldn't summon the will to compete with them.

Mayer was lonesome and restless. He was disillusioned with politics; his own interest in Republican politics had died with Robert Taft. On a deeper level, David Selznick believed that the old man's insecurity had risen to the surface—he felt he could not associate with the leaders of other industries if he didn't have an equivalent position himself. Any attempt to regain his status, his studio, had been worth whatever risk it entailed.

On July 30, Tomlinson and a few other directors called a rump meeting and elected Mayer to the Loew's board. But under Loew's bylaws, a quorum of seven directors was necessary, and the Tomlinson group had only summoned five. Vogel declared the rump election illegal, and so it proved to be; on August 27, the Delaware court declared that the Mayer and Sam Briskin election was invalid.

Sam Goldwyn watched Mayer's scramblings with fascination, so much so that he bought 10,000 shares of Loew's, Inc. "Here are 10,000 votes against him," he cackled to his son.

By August, Louis was back at Stanford Hospital in San Francisco. Publicly, the doctors professed bafflement over the cause of the anemia and lassitude, and said that there was no sign of leukemia or any other malignancy. Privately, it was clear that the disease was entering its final phase.

They gave him blood transfusions, which helped, and Jessie Marmorston said he "looked very fine." He was feeling good enough to joke with the nurses, said the papers, but it was all window dressing and by this time everybody knew it. Two weeks later he was still in the hospital and doctors were telling straight-faced reporters that there was no sign of malignancy. "If you could see him right now you would think him perfectly well."

Hoover again sent him get-well wishes, and L.B. responded with a note telling Hoover that his letter "was a better tonic than anything the doctors have found to give me." His signature was expanding, growing taller, less constricted, almost sprawling.

After nearly six weeks at Stanford Hospital, Louis was sent home to Bel Air, where a bedroom was turned into a hospital room. He summoned Jessie Marmorston to tend him. Lorena announced that there would be no visitors. L.B. must have been stunned by the loss of his vitality—the increasing diminishment alone would have told him what he was confronting.

Charles Foster was in Los Angeles doing some publicity work when he read in the paper that Mayer had been released from the hospital and dropped him a note telling him he was in town. Two days later, the phone rang. It was Nils, Mayer's factotum, asking if he could come for a quick visit.

Foster arrived at the Bel Air house on a Monday. L.B. was wearing a dressing gown, sitting in a chair, a nurse hovering nearby. "He looked far from well," remembered Foster. "He'd lost weight and had no inspiration about anything at all."

"I haven't much time left," Mayer said. "Is there anything I can do for you before I die?"

Foster was startled. He'd gathered Mayer was ill, but it didn't seem possible that he was dying. "Mr. Mayer, any success I've had in life is because you treated me so well when I was just eighteen years old. You've given me a great deal already."

"You don't want anything? I could leave you money."

"The tears were streaming down my face then as they are now," remembered Foster. "And then he said, 'Everybody wants something from me. You don't want anything. I'll tell you what: I'll tell Jack Cummings that when he does *Paint Your Wagon*, he has to hire you to work on the publicity.' "

They talked for a few more minutes. "It's been a wonderful life," said L.B. "I've offended a few people; I hope I've pleased a lot more." At that, his eyelids began to droop, and his head nodded forward. It seemed he was about to fall asleep.

Foster excused himself and left the house.

Three days later, L.B. was admitted to UCLA Medical Center, suffering from a "reaction of several blood transfusions." Irene flew in from New York for the death watch. The leukemia had caused internal bleeding, and the old man was now also laboring with a kidney infection.

He had terrible abdominal pain from the bleeding; the days blended into each other. September became October, and Mayer hovered between life and death. Going home wasn't an option, but some days he seemed to rally. Basically, the old man was refusing to die.

Sidney Farber came from Boston. Dr. Farber wanted to tell Mayer he was dying, but Irene resisted, feeling that the fact that he hadn't asked the question meant that he didn't want to hear the answer. In fact, both the question and the answer were obvious. Mayer was rarely subtle but always shrewd. What he had acknowledged to an acquaintance like Charles Foster was too deep, too horrible to acknowledge to family and friends.

Kate Hepburn visited. David Selznick visited. Kathryn Grayson visited and remembered that the hospital people "didn't seem to know who he was. We talked about the world, the country, the business. He wanted the studios to control TV; instead, TV ended up controlling the studios. His heart was broken. Schary had done him dirt with the stockholders. He had built the business and he had built MGM and it broke his heart to see what was happening to them both. 'They're wrong,' he said, 'but they won't listen to me. I don't know what to do about it.' He wasn't scared of dying. He wasn't scared of anything except making a bad picture. He believed in God, and thought there was a better place to go. After our visits, I would go out to my car and put my head on the wheel and cry."

Jack Cummings came, and while he was there a needle in Mayer's arm came loose. A look of panic came over Mayer's face, and he sent Cummings out to get a nurse and reattach the needle. A few weeks later, when Cummings was again visiting, the same thing happened, but Mayer now seemed apathetic. After the tube was reattached, he turned his head to his nephew. "It's not going to work," he said. "I can't go on."

Jessie Marmorston moved into the hospital room next to his. There were other primary oncologists, but she was there to make the dying man feel more secure, to take advantage of his confidence in her. "Whatever the treatment was, he wanted her to make sure it was okay," said her daughter Elizabeth.

Jessie's devotion warmed the heart of Irene, who had been somewhat hostile toward Marmorston. Now, at the bedside of a man they both loved, the two women came together in mutual respect. Also keeping faith was Clarence Brown, who was there all day, every day, even though he could only see his dying friend for brief periods. For Brown, as for Mayer, there was no higher virtue than loyalty.

On his last full day of life, Mayer received twenty-two blood transfusions, replacing nearly every drop of blood in his body. He began calling out for Edie, telling Marmorston to bring her to the hospital. "Has she come? Does she know? Is she outside?"

"You'd never forget the scene," Marmorston told Edie later. "He was going to die any minute, and you would never forget that scene."

Irene called Edie to tell her that their father was dying and she should come. "What do you want, Irene," she replied, "a deathbed scene?" Within the family, it was believed that Edie attempted to leave for the hospital but that Bill Goetz forbade it. "Bill may not have believed that Grandpa was dying," said Dan Selznick. "I can hear him with that Ben Gazzara voice and a cigar in his mouth saying, 'Honey, he's not dying. He'll be around for another ten years. *Then* you can go to him.'"

The morphine, the pain, the process of dying caused Mayer to hallucinate; he told Clarence Brown that someone had turned off the drip in his arm. He refused to go to sleep, saying that "some son of a bitch might try to do it again." He told Marmorston that a doctor had hung him upside down so that the blood wouldn't leave his brain. He complained that his beautiful double bed had been stolen, that there was no furniture in his room. Near the end, he drew Howard Strickling close. "Nothing matters!" he whispered. "Don't let them worry you. Nothing matters!"

He slipped into a coma late on October 28. At 12:35 A.M. on Tuesday morning, October 29, 1957, Louis B. Mayer's long journey from Russia to Hollywood finally ended.

Lorena sent out telegrams to those who loved him: "I AM VERY SORRY TO TELL YOU THAT L.B. PASSED AWAY QUIETLY AT ONE THIS MORNING."

That morning, Eddie Mannix got a phone call telling him that L.B. was dead. "The flag is still flying over the Thalberg Building, isn't it?" asked his friend.

"Watch it come down," said Mannix. The flag flew at half-staff for the rest of the week.

The Los Angeles newspapers responded as Mayer would have wished— banner headlines obliterating all other national and local news. "L.B. MAYER DIES" said the *Mirror-News*, as did the *Examiner*. "LOUIS B. MAYER, 72, FILM PIONEER, DIES," said the *Times*.

In *The Hollywood Reporter*, Billy Wilkerson's column began, "Mr. Motion Picture is gone. And with the passing of Louis B. Mayer much more than a man has died. With him also has passed an era, the most fabulous in the history of the entertainment world.

" 'L.B.' was without doubt the most dynamic figure our industry knew. He was a builder, a fighter, a dreamer of practical dreams. He was a giant who left his monument in the towering milestone of progress that marked his tremendous strides. . . . The era he symbolized has been passing long before him. The Hollywood of today is scarcely the Hollywood of his early days on Mission Road. But even then, the uncertainties and challenges were very great. It took a Mayer to meet and conquer them; to provide a leadership that witnessed the growth of the film industry beyond the wildest imagination of its pioneers."

David Selznick went Wilkerson one better: "Louis B. Mayer was the greatest single figure in the history of motion picture production. Even the people of Hollywood know only a small portion of what he did to advance both the industry and the quality of all films. A giant has left the American scene."

Vice President Richard Nixon paid tribute to Mayer as "one of the really great geniuses. . . . Millions of Americans who never had the privilege of meeting him know Louis Mayer through his scores of memorable productions in the entertainment field."

Harry Cohn, who had always been treated by Mayer as a goofy adjutant, said that "In the death of Louis B. Mayer the motion picture industry has lost a great and forceful leader. Mr. Mayer did as much to build the motion picture industry and give it world wide force and influence as any man in its history. . . . He will be missed and mourned for many years to come."

Amidst the reflexive tributes, there was one small dissenting voice. Michael Balcon, a good man with a grudge, was asked by a London newspaper for an appropriate remark. He replied that he had not liked Mayer when he was alive and saw no reason to change his opinion just because the man had died.

On the front page of the same *Hollywood Reporter* that carried the news of Mayer's death, there was a smaller item: "Schary, UA Set 3-Picture Deal."

An autopsy revealed that Mayer had died from "thrombopenia, associated with internal bleeding and leukemia."

Irene and Kate Hepburn took charge of the funeral, while Lorena told Howard Strickling that whatever he thought best was fine with her. Irene wanted the eulogy to be written by her ex-husband. Carey Wilson and John Lee Mahin also worked on it, with MGM publicist Eddie Lawrence spending an entire night running various drafts among the three houses.

Irene and Kate both thought Spencer Tracy should deliver the eulogy, although Tracy seemed unenthusiastic. Some people were worried that he wouldn't show up, but Strickling believed that if Kate said she'd deliver Tracy, she would. And she did.

The services were at noon on Thursday at the Wilshire Boulevard Temple. There were two thousand people inside the temple, three thousand outside—a full house and then some. As the services began, a minute of silence was observed throughout the Hollywood motion picture studios.

L.B. was in an open casket whose bottom half was covered with a blanket of red roses and white carnations; Edie attended without Bill Goetz and was stunned to see how "shriveled and tiny" this man who had once ruled Hollywood looked. Active pallbearers included Clarence Brown, Myron Fox, Mayer's business manager, Nils Lenstrom, his chauffeur, attorneys Neil McCarthy and Mendel Silberberg, Howard Strickling, and former Secretary of Defense Louis Johnson. Honorary pallbearers included Herbert Hoover, Cardinal Spellman, Senator William Knowland and Governor Goodwin Knight, Walter Annenberg, Bernard Baruch, Nate Blumberg, Norman Chandler, Cecil B. DeMille, Frank Freeman, William Randolph Hearst Jr., Mervyn LeRoy, John Lee Mahin, Eddie Mannix, J. Robert Rubin, David Selznick, Joe Schenck, George Sidney, Robert Taylor, Norman Taurog, Benny Thau, Spencer Tracy, Lawrence Weingarten, and Carey Wilson.

Attending was a long list of great figures from Mayer's past and present— Fred Astaire, Norma Shearer, Van Johnson, Cyd Charisse, James Stewart, Eleanor Powell, George Burns, Danny Thomas, Jack Warner, Harry Cohn, Jesse Lasky.

Jeanette MacDonald sang "Ah, Sweet Mystery of Life," and later said that she thought Mayer would have been pleased, as the song "recalled the faraway times he represented."

Spencer Tracy rose to speak the eulogy. "Louis B. Mayer knew people better than all the many things he knew so well. It was because he knew people that he was able to know the other many things.

"Such knowledge of people is a rare privilege. Louis B. Mayer possessed it because from his early childhood he had been intimately involved with human beings in his, and their, struggles. . . . His progress from existence to later fame and fortune came from his knowledge of people and their thinking, for the merchandise he handled was completely intangible. You could not weigh it on a scale, nor measure it with a yardstick, for it was magical merchandise of laughter and tears, of recreation and pleasure, of enlightenment and education. It was nothing more than gossamer; nothing less than a primary human need—entertainment.

"He was a man of contrasts—part sentiment and idealism, part pure practicality.

"At times his temper would rise in indignation when he would discover that someone he loved and trusted had taken such love and trust lightly. It was not so much because of any harm done to him, but more because of the shock to his own faith in that individual. That was the idealist side of him.

"But soon the practical side would come to his rescue. He would say, 'You must never be too surprised when you discover a weakness in someone you respect. This is earth, not heaven,' he'd say, 'and all the religions of earth are only working to make us people of earthly faults more worthy of heaven. People are only human, you know . . .'

"The story he wanted to tell was the story of America—the land for which he had an almost furious love, born of gratitude—and of contrast with the hatred in the dark land of boyhood across the seas. . . .

"Now L.B. is gone from among us, gone from his beloved country—leaving as a bequest to Lorena, his children, his grandchildren and his sisters, the wealth of his self-respect, the swiftness of his gallant spirit, and the native treasure of his humble wisdom, for he was a man of great stature.

"All the rest is history. The shining epoch of the industry passes with him . . ."

At the Home of Peace Cemetery, observed by Lorena, Irene and Edie, his sister Ida and a few relatives, L.B. was interred a few feet away from his loyal acolyte Harry Rapf. His plaque reads:

Louis B. Mayer
Beloved Husband and Father
1885–1957

"How strange, this vacuum he has left," David Selznick wrote to Irene, mourning the man who had been a father to them both. "It is not love that has been lost, nor tenderness, nor even paternal protection. Rather it is as though we had all lived fearfully in the shadow of a magnificent, forbidding Vesuvius, which is now suddenly removed: no more the little arbors huddled up on its slope, no more the threatening lava. . . . You, above all others, know that I never ate of the grapes nor feared the eruptions. Yet I could stand in awe. And I can feel that the world this day is different than all the days of our lives before. . . .

"What power the man had, even over those free of the best and the worst of him alike."

EPILOGUE

The movie mogul as Captain of Industry—L.B. Mayer circa 1948.

"I didn't think I would ever see the day when I
missed Louis B. Mayer. . . . Even if they did four or
five miserable movies they always had to have one or
two films with *class*. There was always a moment
when they said, 'We're going to spend an extra
million on this; we're going to get every movie star we
can, the best director.' In other words, they were
proud of their name. MGM was *proud* of the
musicals that they were able to do with Astaire and
Kelly. That was their *pride*."

— KARL MALDEN

A DAY OR TWO after L.B. died, *The Hollywood Reporter* ran an item reporting
that Edie had been at her father's bedside, causing Irene to erupt in righteous
wrath. "Isn't that terrible?" she yelled at her son Daniel. "Isn't that terrible?"

"Well, that she felt she had to say that, yes, it's pathetic," he replied. "That's
what I cannot tolerate," said Irene. "The dishonesty." Dan pointed out that Bill
Goetz was probably even more upset by the item, but Irene wasn't terribly interested in Goetz's feelings. "Things between mother and Edie deteriorated
badly from that point on," said Dan Selznick.

L.B. might have wanted to take everything with him, but he couldn't have
even if he tried. He left behind a fair amount of real estate holdings — 197 North

Cañon Drive in Beverly Hills (worth $100,000); 9401 Wilshire Boulevard (worth $575,000); 9441 Wilshire Boulevard (worth $1.3 million); 3520 Wilshire Boulevard (worth $82,500); 910 Hartford Way (worth $63,000). In fact, much of Louis's estate was in real estate, including the Mercantile Building in Miami and the Rivoli Theater in New York.

In addition, there were percentages in other properties, some unimproved real estate ($300,000) and pieces of oil fields. He died owning six cars—Dodges and Chryslers—and two theatrical properties: *Blossom Time*, estimated as being worth $250,000, which sounds high, and *Paint Your Wagon*, estimated at $125,000, which sounds low. (Lerner and Lowe were due $30,000 for writing four additional songs.)

L.B. had been conservative financially as well as politically. Life insurance policies brought in nearly $700,000 at his death, and he had an annuity worth $143,716. He had bank accounts scattered around town and across the country—$60,000 at the Bank of America in Culver City, $103,000 at the California Bank in Beverly Hills, $50,000 at the Republic National Bank in Dallas—nearly $3 million in cash overall.

He had some show business holdings—555 shares of common stock in Columbia Pictures, 1,000 shares in American Broadcasting-Paramount Theaters, 41,500 shares of Cinerama, and 3,800 shares of Loew's, Inc. He had many oil, gas, and transportation holdings, including Union Pacific, U.S. Steel, Westinghouse, Standard Oil, General Motors, and other blue chips.

The remnants of the Mayer racing stable consisted of thirty-seven horses and shares and pieces of nearly thirty more. As for accounts receivable, a lot of people had owed L.B. a lot of money for a lot of years. Mitzi Fielding and Sol Baer Fielding were into him for $27,800 in various notes, all without interest; nephew Gerald Mayer had borrowed $10,000 (no interest), as had Vic Orsatti. Adela Rogers St. Johns owed him $5,000 (no interest). There were other outstanding loans from years before, some at interest rates ranging from 3 percent to 5 percent, others gratis—Marie McDonald, an actress who had a brief try at stardom after the war (*Living in a Big Way*), had borrowed $5,000 (no interest) from L.B. in 1946, and hadn't paid back a dime in eleven years. L.B. also held the note for a $26,000 mortgage on 3121 N.E. 7th Avenue in Miami for one Mary Mizell, also without interest.

The estate was originally estimated at $12 million, later downgraded to $9 million, still later downgraded even further. Lorena asked for monthly maintenance of $15,000—rather high in light of her actual overhead (groceries ran about $700 a month)—and was awarded $9,000 a month, because she said that she and her late husband had spent more than $100,000 a year on basic expenses.

The hospital bill for Mayer's illness came to $4,742, and the estate laid out $2,552 for the funeral costs, not including the pricey wall crypt at the Home of Peace Cemetery. Other bills trickled in—the estate owed $12,550 to Mayer's business manager, $60,000 to Victor Canning for a script, $400 for annual dues to the Wilshire Boulevard Temple, and $131.90 for two pairs of gold-framed glasses. In December, the court authorized the auctioning of L.B.'s stable.

Mayer's will had been signed in a firm hand on May 10, 1955, and was admitted into probate on November 11, 1957. The will left Lorena $750,000 in cash, the house at 332 St. Cloud Road in Bel Air, which was appraised at $475,000, and all of his interests in oil, gas, and uranium properties, roughly appraised at $200,000. Lorena's daughter, Suzanne, was left a $500,000 trust fund. Another $500,000 went to Irene, with an additional half-million being set up in trust for Daniel and Jeffrey Selznick.

Louis's sister Ida was given $400 a month for life, Jack Cummings was left $100,000, and Myron Fox and Howard Strickling were left $50,000 apiece. Six servants were given bequests ranging from $2,500 to $5,000, Mayer's secretary received $10,000, and Lorena's sister, brother, and aunt got $10,000 apiece. No mention was made of Jessie Marmorston, who responded by submitting a large bill to the estate—Jack Cummings said it was for $200,000—saying that Mayer had promised her a bequest that would make her financially independent for life. She settled for $27,400.

The snapper was contained in paragraph seven of the will, a curt, disinheriting admonition: "I make no bequest to my daughter, Edith Mayer Goetz, nor to her children, nor to any other member of the Goetz family as I have given them extremely substantial assistance during my lifetime through gifts and financial assistance to my daughter's husband, William Goetz, and through the advancement of his career (as distinguished from that of my former son-in-law, David Selznick, who never requested nor accepted assistance from me) in the motion picture industry."

There it was, the permanent institutionalization of the feud that had long since transcended two daughters jockeying for the position of Daddy's favorite. At long last, Irene was accorded status over Edie, although she never seemed to feel the cost was too high.

The remainder of the estate went to the Louis B. Mayer Foundation, which he set up to underwrite charitable, educational, literary, and scientific ventures, especially medicine. "I refrain from attempting to name these organizations because I do not wish to risk omitting any of them, and because the passage of time may greatly alter the circumstances under which the foundation must make its decisions."

"Lorena was *so* bitter about the will," said Daniel Selznick, "bitter that she didn't get more money than $750,000. 'There are going to be *millions* in this goddamn Louis B. Mayer Foundation?' she asked me. She didn't know what was in the will. Nobody knew, although my mother knew more than anybody else. Later she told me, 'I will be honest with you. Your grandfather wanted to give you a million dollars. That wouldn't have been wonderful, because all the other grandchildren were only getting $250,000 in trust.' She didn't think the money would be worth making enemies of my brother and cousins, and she urged Grandfather to insert the clause that anybody who contested the will would only get $1. And Irene reminded Lorena of that clause, and Lorena was fit to be tied."

As the estate made its way through probate, its value was gradually set at $7.4 million. What was left to the Mayer Foundation after all the individual bequests had been made was $4.5 million. *The Motion Picture Daily* estimated that Louis had been paid $13 million in salary and had a part in another $12 million paid out to the management partners during his tenure at the studio. Add in the millions he received from dispersing his stable and the payout from his percentage of MGM films, and it would seem that he should have died with more money than he did.

But Mayer had the misfortune to live in a time of very high income taxes, so he kept little of the income of his biggest salaried years. For the rest, divorce and his final, failed attempt to reinstate his stable ate up millions.

As Mayer had been an emperor without an empire, as David Selznick lost his studio, William Goetz gained strength. He left Universal International in 1954 and went into independent production. His pictures weren't distinguished, but they were solid commercial entertainments with a patina of social realism (*The Man from Laramie, Sayonara, They Came to Cordura*, among them).

"Goetz wasn't really a producer," said Philip Yordan, who worked for him on a rewrite of *The Man from Laramie*. "He was a delightful man, with a terrific sense of humor, but he was really in the stock market full time. He told me he had over a million in the market. He was a jolly guy, and he never worked a day in his life. His method was to invite a star to have dinner at his home, where they'd be so overwhelmed by his collection of paintings that they'd be honored to do his movie."

After *Sayonara*, Goetz's pictures grew increasingly dismal—*Me and the Colonel, The Mountain Road, Cry for Happy, Assault on a Queen.* Finally, it became a commonplace witticism to say that "Goetz's best pictures are hanging on his walls." He died in August 1969 at the age of sixty-six.

After L.B. died, relations were strained between Lorena and Irene, but that was probably to be expected. "Irene liked Lorena up to a point," said Robert Gottlieb, the editor of Irene's memoir and in her later years her closest friend, "but she didn't find her very interesting. She was grateful to Lorena for taking her father off her back, but she wasn't threatened by her; Irene didn't have the possessiveness of a neurotic woman."

Lorena quickly put the house on St. Cloud Road up for sale. The two-story brick colonial sitting on two acres, the thirty-odd rooms, the dozen bathrooms, the three kitchens, the pool, the tennis courts, the servant's quarters, all went to Jerry Lewis. The price was $350,000, down from the asking price of $450,000 and a great buy.

The estate took years to settle, with Lorena receiving $9,000 a month, a sum later cut to $5,000. In 1961, the federal government received $1.5 million, and the state of California, $2 million. In August 1958, Suzanne Mayer married Veri Dean Keiser Jr., whom she had met while attending Stanford. In December 1961, Lorena was remarried, to Michael Nidorff, a New York business executive.

At one point in the early 1960s, Daniel Selznick was having lunch with Myron Fox, the Mayer Foundation's attorney, and idly asked about his grandfather's papers.

"We burned them," said Fox. "We did it to protect your grandfather's reputation. His grammar wasn't perfect and we wouldn't want anybody to know." The "we" referred to Lorena and Fox, as Dan well knew. "Lorena and Myron were as thick as thieves," he said, "and because of that, decades of motion picture history went into the fire."

In the 1950s, the only female stars developed by MGM were Leslie Caron and Debbie Reynolds. There was no longer any meaningful development of young talent because that cost money that wasn't necessarily apparent on the screen. Cutback followed cutback. In February of 1958, Loew's annual report for 1957 showed a $7.8 million loss from motion pictures, a $4 million profit from theaters, and a $5.5 million profit from MGM Records. The company eked out a $1.3 million profit, attributed solely to its music operation.

One day in 1958, Eddie Mannix went in to argue with Joe Vogel about yet another round of firings. They couldn't fire people who had given their lives to the company, said Mannix. "Okay, Eddie," replied Vogel. "I'll start with you." A stunned, red-eyed Mannix walked across the hall to June Caldwell's desk. "Friday is my last day," he told his secretary. "It's been forty-four years."

He walked out of the Thalberg Building, with Caldwell following. She counseled him to accept an advisory job rather than try to start over and go to Fox, where he had a standing offer. He decided to follow her advice. Eddie moved from the third to the first floor. "He spent five years like that," said Caldwell. "I could see him suffering; they had told him they would include him, but they didn't. He wasn't happy, but he never complained." Eddie Mannix died of heart failure in 1963.

A young man named Roger Mayer (no relation) went to work at MGM. The old regime was still very much a presence—Vincente Minnelli, Chuck Walters, Pandro Berman, Joe Cohn, and Margaret Booth were all holding down the fort. "They talked about L.B. all the time, and it was mostly positive," said Mayer. "They felt that the way Thalberg and Mayer had run the company was good and should be perpetuated." This adherence to the values of a previous generation forced the place into something of a time warp. When someone would suggest changes, the response was likely to be, "Mr. Mayer didn't do it that way."

In the early 1960s, Philip Yordan was ramrodding a series of spectaculars financed by Samuel Bronston when he and his wife were invited to dinner at David Selznick's house. "There was no maid, no cook," said Yordan. "It was a nice dinner, but it was catered. We started late, about nine, and finished at ten-thirty. Then Selznick says, 'Let's go to my office.' I was in there with him until the sun rose, at six in the morning."

Selznick explained that he wanted to produce a picture for Samuel Bronston. "I know I can do something great for him." Yordan asked him what he wanted to make. What book, what play? Selznick picked up the telephone book and said, "I can make a great picture out of this."

The reason he needed Bronston, he explained, was that he couldn't afford a plane ticket to New York. He owned the house and it was a showplace, but it was mortgaged to the hilt. "You must own half a dozen novels or plays," said Yordan. "What about your pictures?"

"No, I've sold everything. I have nothing, nothing at all."

As the night turned into morning, Selznick took Yordan into his bedroom, so he could show Yordan an electric shutter that went up and down a huge glass window. David Selznick liked to watch the sun rise.

Louis B. Mayer's posthumous image was sealed by the publication of Bosley Crowther's 1960 biography. It was a well-researched but sneering hatchet job on a man Crowther regarded as "hideous and vicious . . . pathetic and pitiable." Crowther was an Ivy Leaguer, a good Democrat if not a good democrat, a friend of Dore Schary's and Edie Goetz's, and he made Mayer the villain of his own story. "I wrote about a monster, all right," wrote Crowther, "but if he will make me as much money as Frankenstein's creation, I will be entirely satisfied."

Even those who had competed with Mayer and had no love for him knew the book was slanted and false. Julius Steger, a vice president at Fox, wrote that "it is filled with a lot of names, big and small, worthwhile and many lemons, but mainly many, many untruths."

Jean Howard Feldman, whom Mayer had loved, wrote, "His ravings and tears were kept out of print in those heady days of the 1930s. It's only since his death, when he can no longer defend himself, that he has been attacked by shoddy, inferior writers who seem to delight in taking out their devious little chisels to destroy his memory by degrees. Were he alive today, they would most likely feel honored if he asked them to join him in the commissary for a bowl of chicken matzoh soup."

By the 1960s, MGM was increasingly a studio subsisting on past glories, either in the form of reissues of *Gone With the Wind* or remaking their own or somebody else's classic films, usually badly *(Ben-Hur, Mutiny on the Bounty, The Four Horsemen of the Apocalypse, Cimarron)*. There would be the occasional fluke hit *(Doctor Zhivago, 2001)*, but there was no creative momentum.

By the mid-1960s, said producer Andrew Fenady, "The only people MGM had under contract were Chad Everett and Ralph Taeger. It was on life support." When Fenady made a two-hour TV pilot at MGM in 1967, he hired Robert Taylor—$25,000 for two weeks work. Taylor was a professional, carrying his own makeup case, walking miles from distant locations to his car rather than ask anybody for a ride, asking only that he not have to go to the commissary. "Too many ghosts," he explained.

George Schönnbrunn, who had been interviewed by Mayer in Vienna in 1937, finally got a job at MGM. He was in what was left of the art department and saw the fire sale as it happened. "It was awful. There were constant layoffs.

Sometimes the art department consisted of two people, the head of the depart-ment and his secretary. One year, I didn't have three straight weeks of work.

"They threw everything out, and they wouldn't spend any money. Out went Russian, German, and English magazines dating back to the Crimean War. No new photographs for art department construction were taken; everything MGM had went back to the 1930s. We had to call Universal's research depart-ment all the time."

By 1969, and a net loss of $35,366,000, the studio was taken over by Kirk Kerkorian, who named James Aubrey president of the studio. The answer seemed to be obvious — sell off assets. Lot 2 (the Andy Hardy street, railroad sta-tions, the city street, the Verona square, the wardrobe department) and Lot 3 (the big lake, the waterfront street, the *Meet Me in St. Louis* street, three west-ern streets) were razed and paved over for condos and apartments. Lot 5, where the zoo for the Tarzan films had been, was converted into a small shopping cen-ter; Lots 4 and 6 became industrial parks. Much of the proceeds were diverted into the MGM Grand Hotel in Las Vegas. All that was left was Lot 1 — forty-four acres, twenty-five soundstages, the laboratory — a constricted piece of asphalt.

In 1970, the entire inventory of props and costumes, material lovingly crafted and designed and made by craftsmen over forty years, was sold to the auctioneer David Weisz for $1.4 million. Weisz turned around and held eigh-teen days of auctions and brought in somewhere between $8 and $10 million.

Members of the MGM family went back for the auction, wandering dis-consolately amongst the rows of armoires, gazing at the costumes. It was like the dispersal of the vast warehouse of Charles Foster Kane, "the loot of the world," except what was being sold were pieces of cultural history, the world's patrimony.

Just as MGM had been the paradigm of the Hollywood studio in full flower, now it was another kind of paradigm, the obsolete film city unable to adjust to a world where mass production and long-term contracts were no longer neces-sary, prey to a succession of quit-claim artists who gradually stripped the studio of its assets.

Mary Loos described the event as "one of the sideshows of our time. I went with Gail Patrick several times and I recognized prop men and crew members fondly touching some of the things they had known in more glamorous times. It made me want to weep." Sam Marx also went back. "I wandered around and was so disheartened that I walked out. It was the realization that the great days were really over."

George Schönnbrunn had the job of writing much of the catalogue copy for the props and costumes. There was just one problem. "I had to identify what pictures all the props and costumes had appeared in, and I didn't have the vaguest idea—I just wrote in anything! *Mrs. Miniver, Camille, The Four Horsemen*—I wasn't even in the country when most of those pictures were made. It was idiotic, but that's what happened."

One set of Judy Garland's ruby slippers went for $15,000; a trench coat Gable had worn went for $1,250; Elizabeth Taylor's wedding dress from *Father of the Bride* brought $625. Harlow's nightgown, Brando's coat, Laughton's hat, Shearer's dress. Debbie Reynolds spent upward of $250,000 for costumes for a Hollywood museum.

MGM was now worth more dead than alive, and management acted accordingly. Aubrey ordered Roger Mayer to tell Arthur Freed that management wanted him off the lot. "What do we need that old man in that office for?" Aubrey said.

By 1978, the studio that had been the industry leader in grosses and profits for nearly a quarter-century was seventh in film rentals. Mayer had built MGM to last; it took thirty years of strip-mining to tear it down to bedrock.

In retrospect, it can be seen that Mayer's great gift was to recognize and nurture talent, people like Arthur Freed, Gene Kelly, Judy Garland and the musicians and arrangers who showed them off. "There it is," he would say with his characteristic Napoleonic bravado. "Use it. Make something out of it!"

"I think there's a misapprehension that he was lucky," said his nephew Gerald. "People don't realize the organizational ability he had, to set that place up and run it. It wasn't luck that hired all those good producers; it wasn't luck that led him to find those actors and actresses. Most men won't hire people who can replace them, but he hired Thalberg and Cedric Gibbons and a lot of others.

"Part of the reason he could do that was because his creativity was of a different kind than their creativity. He didn't read; I never heard him relate to things that way. He felt emotions so strongly, and he could visualize how something needed to be presented so that others, who didn't feel things as strongly as he did, could feel those emotions too. He had a kind of genius."

"Mayer was truly a great administrator, in that day when the studio and its organization was the focus of power," said Charles Feldman, who, as an increasingly powerful agent-producer, was the vanguard of the generation that would replace Mayer. "He had or could get the talent, and he was a great manipulator of this pool. He was a tyrant, vindictive, ruthless—but he was good. All the big guys hated him, but they were dependent on him. And he was masterly in the way he would throw them bones.

"But if they had more men in the business with the sort of imagination and daring that Mayer had in the years of his prime, the business would not be wallowing in the slough of despond that it's in today. No matter what you thought about him—whether you liked him or hated him—you had to admit, he had guts!"

In time, the terrible truth of actuarial tables kicked in, and the people who made up the managerial class of Metro-Goldwyn-Mayer began dying off. Benny Thau had a crippling coronary and entered the Motion Picture Home. In his days of power, he had always been preternaturally quiet and soft-spoken, and now that had been mandated by his physical condition. He went to visit Norma Shearer, stricken with Alzheimer's, and asked if she remembered him. She grasped his hand with a strong grip. "Are you Irving?" she asked. Thau died in the Motion Picture Home in July of 1983 at the age of eighty-five; Shearer preceded him in death by a month, at age eighty.

Larry Weingarten died in 1975, Jessie Marmorston in 1980. Joe Cohn remained in his stately house in Beverly Hills, a proud old man even after his mind began to fail. He died in 1996 at the age of one hundred. J. Robert Rubin, the lawyer who had put Marcus Loew, the Goldwyn studio, and L.B. together, died in 1958.

Joe Schenck, everybody's friend, died in 1961 at the age of eighty-two. His brother Nick, L.B.'s great antagonist, died at the age of eighty-eight in 1969, in his beloved Miami Beach.

Louis's sister Ida died at the age of eighty-four in April 1968, and the headlines of her obituaries proclaimed her a "Philanthropist" for her years of labor for the Los Angeles Jewish Home for the Aged. Lorena Mayer Nidorff died in March 1985 at the age of seventy-seven, but only Ida Mayer Cummings chose to spend eternity with L.B., being interred in the niche above her brother.

Dore Schary grew more oracular with age. S. J. Perelman wrote that Schary, "who already in 1936 was the most rabbinical of B picture writers at the writers table we shared at MGM, has . . . become so constipated with his own importance that his smallest pronouncement sounds like Pitt the Elder."

According to Robert Vogel, head of international publicity for MGM, Dore Schary "got to be an absolute monomaniac, living in a condo in Sutton Place." Vogel went to visit him some years after he was deposed and remembered that "I give you my word of honor that the only thing discussed that entire evening was Dore Schary. It was pretty horrible." With time, and Schary's embarrassing independent films (*Lonelyhearts, Act One*), it became clear just how much of a second-rater he had been . . . and how weakened Mayer had been to be picked off by someone like that. Schary died in 1980, just a year after writing his memoirs.

The relationship between Mayer's daughters became increasingly dysfunctional. "Irene thought Edie was Regan *and* Goneril," said Robert Gottlieb. "Irene thought she was a liar. Edie didn't know the truth, didn't care about the truth and had betrayed her parents. She thought that Edie betrayed her father by setting up the Bosley Crowther book. Irene admired her father, she loved her father, and she defended her father. She believed that Edie hadn't cared about her mother, and Irene had adored her mother. *Adored* her."

"Irene was so smart, so interested in everything," said author Steven Bach. "She was very observant and had total recall. She thought of Edie and Bill Goetz with total contempt. Edie gave parties and collected paintings. Irene wouldn't waste her time with that. She had a Cézanne in her apartment, of pears and cheese, and she would serve the same things for dessert. But she never pointed out her Cézanne. Irene was about being smart, being aware, cutting through the bullshit."

"My mother thought Edie was a phony," said Daniel Selznick, "and that her devotion to Bill Goetz was blind—she believed he was nothing more than a good businessman with limited taste. Mother didn't even believe in their art collection. 'Paul Rosenberg picked those pictures,' she'd say. 'You don't think Edie and Bill have the sense to pick that Cézanne or that Van Gogh?' She wouldn't give them credit for anything.

" 'But Aunt Edie's no dumbbell,' I would say.

" 'Clever, use the word clever,' she'd say. 'Intelligent she isn't. Edie's dined out plenty on the fact that I'm a successful Broadway producer; she's gotten plenty of mileage out of that.'

"And Edie was just as focused on Irene. Irene had her father's ear, and he trusted her implicitly on things he wouldn't ever discuss with Edie. Anybody he might be in business with, he would call mother. Edie knew that he didn't turn to her for matters of substance and she was bitterly resentful. Edie was flabbergasted that Irene had this very successful producing career, and she had to take into account that this woman, who she had considered no more than her equal, was clearly her superior, and it bothered the shit out of her."

After Bill Goetz died, Edie continued on in the palatial Holmby Hills house. Edie told intimate friends that the first person she slept with after Billy died was none other than Frank Sinatra. The singer supposedly asked Edie to marry him, which led Edie to the graceless reply, "But, Frank—you're practically a hoodlum!" Sinatra turned on his heel and never spoke to her again. The parties grew less frequent, then stopped, but Edie still took pride in her art collection, her social position in Hollywood, and her house staff, particularly the butler, who had once served the Queen Mother in Buckingham Palace. But on occasions when the butler was elsewhere, and visitors would have a problem with the troublesome front door and ask for help, Edie could only shake her head. "Doors have always been opened for me," she would say.

If she had a single regret, it was that she had never reconciled with her father. "She became obsessed with the fact that she hadn't gone to see him when he was dying," said David Patrick Columbia. "She was the daughter of L. B. Mayer and they had had this terrible falling out and he took it with him to his grave."

Toward the end of her life, Edie was unable to leave her beautiful house because of a degenerative respiratory condition. She died in May 1988 at the age of eighty-two; to the end there was a picture of her father on her Louis XV end table. There was only about $200,000 in liquid assets in the Goetz estate—Edie spent more than $300,000 a year on household expenses—but there were a lot of very fine paintings on the wall.

Irene had published her memoirs in 1983. "When we began, when she started writing and talking about Edie, I told her she was my favorite character," said Robert Gottlieb. "For the rest of our lives, we referred to Edie as 'My favorite character.' At the beginning, Irene didn't think she could go into things with her sister. 'It's too horrible, too disrespectful to the memory of my parents.' By the time we were finished she was castigating herself for going so easy on Edie."

Irene never let go of anything—not her loathing of her sister, not her love for her father. She felt everything as strongly as if it had happened yesterday. Toward the end, she was in great pain. She felt in some strange way that her whole body was misaligned. She began to have trouble with her eyes, and vowed that if she went blind she would kill herself. Nobody doubted her.

"If she said she'd do something, it was done," said Robert Gottlieb. Her great terror was, in her phrase, "losing her marbles." She went out of her way to destroy things, burning her parents' letters and many of her own, leaving only her business correspondence.

Even at the very end of her life, she remained physically strong. Occasionally she would rub Bob Gottlieb's shoulders and her fingers were like steel, matching the strength of will she had inherited from her father.

"Irene never spoke to me about her mother without tears coming to her eyes," said Gottlieb. "Never. The pain of her mother's emotional collapse was one of the worst things that happened to her. She also felt Edie had to be bought a husband, and then her husband had to be bought a career.

"Was it true? I never knew Irene to tell me a lie."

In 1988, Irene made good on a promise her father had made on his deathbed and gave $5 million to the Dana-Farber Cancer Institute in Boston for the establishment of the Louis B. Mayer Research Laboratory. When the eight-story building opened, Irene cut the ribbon and said that Dr. Sidney Farber was "the single most important human being my father had ever known."

The Mayer Foundation donated $250,000 to the Motion Picture Country House for the construction of the Louis B. Mayer Memorial Center, a movie theater, occupational therapy, and a chapel. For the groundbreaking, Mayer loyalists, including Clarence Brown, Arthur Freed, Ramon Novarro, Senator George Murphy, Greer Garson, and Jeffrey and Daniel Selznick attended. When the center was completed, a bust of L.B. was unveiled. The foundation also gave $1 million to the American Film Institute to bankroll its library.

Eventually, Irene asked Robert Gottlieb what he thought should be done about the Mayer Foundation. He told her that the money came from the movies, and should go back into the movies, and so much of it has, endowing a great deal of film restoration, a school for film preservationists at the George Eastman House in Rochester, New York, and other good works. Each year, the Mayer Foundation disburses about $500,000 in grants, split between medical research and film preservation.

Irene Mayer Selznick died in 1990 and was buried in her mother's crypt at Hillside Cemetery.

In one sense, Edie had the last laugh; when the Goetzes' Impressionist art collection was auctioned, it brought $80 million, more than her father's and sister's estates combined. In another sense, Irene got the last laugh. She got a memorial service at the Brooks Atkinson Theater with hundreds of the elite of Broadway and Hollywood mourning one of the most remarkable women they had ever known. But when Edie was interred next to Bill Goetz at Hillside, there was no one in attendance beyond the funeral director and his assistants. Edie had directed there be no service whatever, because, said one family member, "she knew nobody would show up."

Louis B. Mayer was half-educated, but he had a decisiveness, a vehemence that is usually educated out of people somewhere after junior high. While still a small child, he was forced to accept responsibility, to make decisions, to take charge. That, and his wonderful native enthusiasm carried him past men who had superior education but lacked his instincts, and his faith in those instincts.

"L.B. was a terrible reactionary," says Arthur Laurents. "Very corny. He was against anything progressive. His beliefs were deeply held, but he was a hypocrite. The minute they say 'family values,' you just hope they don't open the bedroom door, because then you will see what kind of values they really practice. L.B.'s main, firmly held belief was that what was good for L.B. was good for America.

"On the other hand: the studio he ran *nurtured* people; they had more stars at MGM than they have in all of Hollywood today. And those terrible reactionaries made better pictures than the liberals who run Hollywood now. What are we to make of this?

"The reason is that they knew what they wanted in their movies. They weren't pretentious. L.B. was just out to entertain."

Mayer's legacy survives largely because MGM was one of the few studios with an institutional memory in the form of men and women like Benny Thau, Douglas Shearer, Margaret Booth, Howard Strickling, and Roger Mayer.

Paramount preserved only thirty-seven of its more than one thousand silent features, or about 3 percent. But beginning in the late 1950s and extending over the next ten years, MGM preserved two hundred complete silent features, and nearly all of their sound features, as well as nearly every short and trailer that could be physically preserved, at the cost of about $30 million over the life of the program.

Part of the reason was corporate pride; part was the fact that the company still owned its backlog while Warner Bros. and Paramount had both foolishly sold their old pictures, and part was the fact that it owned MGM Labs, a twenty-four-hour operation, so the copying work could be done in the middle of the night, the lab's downtime. The result is that today we can see a greater proportion of MGM's corporate patrimony than that of any other Hollywood studio.

What else remains? A great deal or very little, depending on your point of view.

The MGM studio is still there, but now it's owned by Sony. The great recording stage is untouched. The dubbing deck is bigger, and the mikes are up-to-date, but, like a European cathedral, the room hasn't been touched for fear of ruining the acoustics.

In the spring of 1986, Kirk Kerkorian sold MGM and United Artists to Ted Turner for $1.5 billion. Turner turned around and sold the studio back to Kerkorian for $780 million, keeping the MGM film library, leaving Turner with four thousand movies. The consensus in the movie business was that Turner had been had. As it turned out, Turner was rewriting Willie Sutton. Film libraries, not banks, turned out to be where the money was. Those four thousand movies provided the foundation for the two television stations and one cable channel that eventually made Turner one of the richest people in America.

Metro-Goldwyn-Mayer itself still exists, after a fashion, but only as a very minor production entity denuded of its film library, or even a home base in the form of a studio.

"I'm biased about L. B. Mayer," said Joseph Newman. "He was always so good to me. He was both a creative man and a businessman. Was he sophisticated? In the sense that we look at sophistication today, no. But I'll tell you what he was: comfortable in his own skin. He believed that what he thought and believed were the things the average man thought and believed. He liked what he was."

His grandson Daniel says that there are two main differences between the Mayer he knew and the Mayer that has been promulgated in popular myth. The first is a vulgarity that had no basis in fact. "I get crazed when I see him portrayed as some sort of a Jewish caricature, chasing women around tables and pinching actresses' asses. . . . He had a circumspect attitude toward women. He put them on pedestals.

"The other thing that people so seldom read was the absolute adoration that the people who worked for him had. People who were there for years. The secretary, the driver, the cook . . . they just adored him. A secretary, I think, had cancer. And he covered the bills and took care of everything. He was a complete father figure to them."

So why has Louis B. Mayer come down to us depicted as a hopeless philistine, vulgar and grasping, with every negative story repeated ad nauseam, while the positive things have gone largely unrecorded?

Mayer believed fervently in success, and he would have achieved it in any business he attempted. He could display a peremptory manner, frustrating a great many people who got their own back after he was dead. And the system he perfected was particularly hard on writers, who never received their proper respect, got kicked around and didn't like it. Writers, it should be remembered, write memoirs. He was a conservative Republican in a business that has traditionally been liberal and Democratic.

And the larger-than-life, overtly escapist, lacquered movies he loved, the kind of movie that serves as insulation for the audience, basically became obsolete. There have been thousands of movies since Mayer's MGM that are equally evasive of reality, but their coarseness and obsessive reliance on violence gives them a contemporaneous feel that takes the edge off their hyperbolically flagrant wish-fulfillment.

The motivating factors in the life of Louis B. Mayer were belonging and acceptance, and fear of losing what he had earned—not so much the money, but the standing and respect. These are factors in everyone's life, of course, but not in the primal way they were for Mayer.

It's no accident that the primary motivation in so many of the great MGM films, from *The Wizard of Oz* to *Meet Me in St. Louis*, from *The Human Comedy* to *The Yearling*, is home—its creation, its preservation, or returning to it.

Home. A place to come to.

Mayer's true home wasn't Saint John or Haverhill or Santa Monica or Bel Air, and it certainly wasn't the small Russian town of Dumier. His true home was the MGM studios in Culver City. After that went away, the money and property held little consolation, so he turned—on Dore Schary, on the people who loved him, on himself.

Mayer lacked an authentic humor, and took himself correspondingly seriously, which meant feelings of inferiority were always threatening to overwhelm him. He had a furious impatience to leave his poor past far behind him, and his primary tool was the hunger for power bred in him by poverty.

The only way Mayer could deal with his aggression and will to power was by cloaking them in a mantle of morality. He would be strong in order to do right, stubborn in order to be just, authoritarian so that he could serve the greater good of depicting democracy in a shining light.

He had extraordinary energy, and an immensely wily intelligence, but he also had a vision, and he consciously used the movies as a matrix for an impressionable public, as examples of how a good life could be lived. True showmanship involves loving and understanding your audience. In today's world, the only knowledge of the audience seems to come from bland demographic research, but Louis B. Mayer felt the audience in his gut and in his passionate heart; the audience was him. He used the movies to test a set of values, and in a modern world in which very few creative people stand responsible for the content of their work, this sounds old-fashioned.

"It's only a movie," they say, which would have led L. B. Mayer to rocket out of his chair, clenching a fist. Only a movie? The movies that had brought him from the Jewish Pale to Bel Air? The movies that gave the world Gable and Garland and Garbo, Gene Kelly and Fred Astaire? *Only a movie?*

Other studios contented themselves with giving an audience two stars; MGM would throw three or four into a single picture, or six or eight. Other studios gave an illusion of opulence, but MGM gave you the real thing. Warners had grit, Fox had girls, and Paramount had Germans—oh, all right, some of them were Austrian—but L. B. Mayer's studio had glamour, gloss, and glitter, not to mention Garbo.

And in the genres in which his studio chose to compete—musicals, high-society melodramas, and polite comedies—no one did it better. Paramount may have had a more tantalizing elegance, and Warners more visceral excitement. But Mayer was not making films for the twenty-first century, he was making films for the early and mid-twentieth century—films to please the audiences of his time, films that did just that.

And all this derived from a man who emerged from Russia and provincial Canada with no natural advantages, few social graces, and a paltry education that gave him what one writer called "a set of values curiously parallel to the dreams of a late Victorian *nouveau riche.*" True enough. But before you condescend, think about where Louis B. Mayer started. Then think about where he finished.

"Mayer was a *man,*" said Ralph Winters. "Dore Schary could write a script, and Dore Schary could make a speech. But Mayer was a *showman.* He had an uncanny knack for picking talent in executives and actors. He knew how to delegate power, which many executives can't. He was more of a businessman than a creator, but don't you think it takes creativity to build a company like MGM? He couldn't write, he couldn't direct, but he had a greatness: *He put the show together.*"

William Saroyan, who loathed him, wrote that Mayer "*made* that studio. It was his. He had made that movie factory, that dream factory, and if you couldn't care for the product, you also couldn't deny that millions of others *did* care for it. And you couldn't deny that the product had earned millions of dollars . . . and made dozens of fantastic reputations."

"There has never been anything like it in the world," says a character at the end of *Meet Me in St. Louis.* "It's where we live," agrees another. "They won't ever tear it down, will they?"

"No," says a little girl. "They will never tear it down. It will be like this forever."

L. B. Mayer undoubtedly believed that to be true, but time proved him wrong. What is left are the films. The best of Louis Mayer—and some of the worst as well—are in those old films. They contain an idealized vision of America, a dream of perfection dreamed by a man, from Dumier, Saint John and Haverhill, Santa Monica and Bel Air, who manufactured them under the usual conditions of waste, chaos, and flagrant displays of human failings. But the cumulative achievement of those films survives, and they constitute a kind of redemption.

Mayer's view of America became America's view of itself—a place and a people more virtuous, more godly, more resilient than anyplace else. His sentimentalization of family had little relationship to any social structure that has ever existed, but such is the force of art that generations of American families attempted to imitate this arbitrary vision, and undoubtedly felt that the failure was in their character, not in Mayer's imagination.

With time, Mayer's larger vision has been supplanted; his hypocrisies have been replaced by crasser hypocrisies. Complacence has replaced belief, braggadocio has replaced humility, cynicism has replaced naïveté, malice has obliterated goodwill. To make certain that nobody ever feels anything, a thick layer of protective irony is invariably applied.

The studio on Mission Road is now a park in a Hispanic neighborhood. Mayer's house at 332 St. Cloud Road in Bel Air has been torn down and replaced by a hideous faux Vegas construct with gold highlights on the balconies. Even the Loew's Building in Times Square was torn down in 1988.

Sooner or later, the grass covers everything.

In Las Vegas, at the MGM Grand Hotel, Mayer's great stars are displayed in murals above the casino. Within the hotel is a glass-enclosed lion habitat, where you can watch the big cats sleep, eat, and play. One of the lions, a quietly lethal-looking specimen, is named Louie B.

Of that, he would surely approve.

Louis B. Mayer's Dream Factory: In front of a spectacular Deco set,
Lionel and John Barrymore play a scene for *Grand Hotel*
observed by Joan Crawford and film crew.

ACKNOWLEDGMENTS

I HAVE NEVER BEGUN a book with more misgivings; I have never been more pleasantly surprised.

To write the life of Louis B. Mayer was the suggestion of Chuck Adams, my editor for nearly fifteen years, whose loyalty and friendship have richly entitled him to be this book's dedicatee.

Bob Bender took Chuck's lateral pass and did some nifty broken-field running to get this book across the goal line. Thank you.

Johanna Li's expertise kept everyone in motion, while the beloved Gypsy da Silva and Fred Chase and Bill Molesky made sure I maintained verb/subject agreement and kept my tenses straight.

Daniel Selznick, grandson of Louis B. Mayer, authorized this book, opened his incredible Rolodex to me, showed me home movies, allowed me access to the Selznick archives at the University of Texas, and sat for long interviews and dozens of phone calls. He showed a remarkable degree of trust.

As he has for all of my books, Jeff Heise once again served as my invaluable research assistant. After nearly thirty years (!) of constant friendship, Jeff and I have developed a sort of intellectual shorthand. Conversation about research parameters is limited. Jeff knows what I want, and I know he'll find it. He's the indispensable man; I couldn't do it without him.

My old friend Jim D'Arc casually mentioned that he had some interesting Mayer material at Brigham Young University. That turned out to be the Bosley Crowther Collection, an impeccably maintained archive of Crowther's research material for his two books on Mayer and MGM, encompassing dozens of interviews with MGM intimates long since gathered to their ancestors. Thanks for the heads-up, Jim.

In Saint John, Harold E. Wright was the man on the ground, thoroughly researching Mayer's time there. In Russia, Viola Gienger went everywhere and did everything. Charles Silver and Ron Magliozzi again welcomed me to the Museum of Modern Art Film Study Center and again supplied me with much valuable material, as did Suzanne Trottier at the Haverhill Public Library, and Joanne Sullivan at the Haverhill Historical Society. Beverly Lindy at the Richard Nixon Library in Yorba Linda pointed me in the right direction. D. J. Turner at the National Film Archive of Canada made it possible to see fragments of L. B. Mayer's very first independent production. And once again I light a candle for Ned Comstock at the University of Southern California, whose generosity and good humor make him remarkable even among his selfless brethren.

I owe a special debt to Jeff Joseph of Sabucat Productions, who supplied me with some rare film of L. B. Mayer giving a speech, permanently dispelling the notion of Mayer as a refugee from the shtetl. In Culver City, Ross Hawkins put me in touch with several MGM veterans and some longtime Culver City residents who gave me solid background on MGM's place in the local firmament. Ross also sent me Sam Marx's invaluable oral history.

To all those who spoke to me about Louis B. Mayer and MGM, my gratitude for your time, and my apologies for the imposition:

Berdie Abrams, Steven Bach, James Bacon, Dick Bann, Joe Barbera, Mary Ellin Barrett, Nicola Schenck Dantine Bautzer, Turhan Bey, Betsy Blair, Michael Blake, Bob Board, Irving Brecher, Herbert Brin, the late Rand Brooks, the late Richard Brooks, David Brown, Hilyard Brown, William F. Buckley Jr., Jean Rouverol Butler, Harry Carey Jr., Marilyn Carey, Leslie Caron, Diana Serra Cary, Marge Champion, Esme Chandlee, Cyd Charisse, David Chierichetti, the late J. J. Cohn, David Patrick Columbia, Betty Comden, Cheryl Crane, the late Hume Cronyn, Frank Davis, Margaret Belgrano deMille, Armand Deutsch, Dominick Dunne, the late Buddy Ebsen, the late Louise Steiner Elian, Robert Evans, George Feltenstein, Andrew J. Fenady, Hugh Fordin, Charles Foster, Leatrice Gilbert Fountain, Devery Freeman, David Friedman, James Garner, Murray Garrett, the late Leonard Gershe, Pat Goldberg, Eve Golden, David Goodrich, Bernard Gordon, the late William Gordon, Robert Gottlieb, Kathryn Grayson, the late Adolph Green, Amy Green, Doris Grumbach, Howard Gutner, Richard Haines, Curtis Harrington, Kitty Carlisle Hart, Ross Hawkins, Darryl Hickman, Stanley Hoffman, the late Elizabeth Horowitz, Margo Howard, Jack Hurd, Edward Jablonski, Claude Jarman Jr., the late Evie Johnson, the late Chuck Jones, Alvin Josephy Jr., Millard Kaufman, the late Howard Keel, Miles Kreuger, Theodore Kupferman, Carla Laemmle, Gavin Lambert, Frances Langford, the late Ring Lardner Jr., Betty Lasky, Arthur Laurents, the late Robert Lees, the late Janet Leigh, the late Mary Anita Loos, Frederica Sagor Maas, the late John Lee Mahin, the late Sam Marx, the late Gerald Mayer, Roger Mayer, Russell Merritt, the late Ann Miller, Ricardo Montalban, Terry Moore, Evelyn Moriarty, Ray Moselle, Eddie Muller, David Nasaw, Joseph Newman, Margaret O'Brien, the late Donald O'Connor, Suzanne Vidor Parry, the late Gregory Peck, Jane Powell, the late Esther Ralston, the late Maurice Rapf, Gene Reynolds, Mickey Rooney, William Rosar, Lillian Ross, Ann Rutherford, the late Joe Ruttenberg, Helen Sandler, the late Nora Sayre, George Schönnbrunn, Budd Schulberg, Walter Seltzer, Sidney Sheldon, Sam Sherman, Vincent Sherman, the late George Sidney, Tina Sinatra, Terry Kingsley Smith, Michael Sragow, George Stevens Jr., Herbert Bayard Swope Jr., Audrey Totter, Edward Baron Turk, Peter Viertel, the late Joe von Stroheim, John Waxman, the late William Wellman, James Whitmore, Willie Wilkerson III, Esther Williams, the late Ralph Winters, Robert Wise, Maria Wrigley, the late Philip Yordan, the late Freddie Young, and Joe Yranski.

There is my small but vital circle at the *Palm Beach Post*, foremost among them Jan Tuckwood, the paper's associate editor, who has always given me the most valuable thing an editor can: absolute trust and freedom, not to mention loyalty. Pat Crowley, Brian Crowley, and Mark Buzek complete a ragged group of musketeers, while Eddie Sears and Tom Giuffrida somehow contrive to keep the beast fed.

Tim Ryback, of the Salzburg Seminar, told me of L. B. Mayer's visit to the same baronial castle that was housing me. At the Screen Actors Guild, Valerie Yaros explained the intricacies of the union movement of the 1930s.

A deep bow to my fellow film historians: Leonard Maltin lent me his interview with Robert Young, and much solid support; Richard Roberts unraveled the mystery of *Dr. Jekyll and Mr. Hyde*; Joseph Carter of Will Rogers Heritage helped far more than he knew. Julie Pearce and her staff at the National Film Theater in London have supported me in both word and deed. David Stenn helped both by giving me some phone numbers and by example. Michael Sragow, with great generosity, took time away from his book about Victor Fleming to share Fleming's MGM contracts with me. Patrick McGilligan plowed through the Dore Schary papers at the State Historical Society of Wisconsin for me, and his advice sharpened sections of the manuscript. Jerry Beck shared the financial information that illuminated the world of the MGM shorts department.

Dennis, Amy, and Adam Doros have been unstinting in their friendship and belief in me for many books and many years.

As I have for longer than either of us cares to think about, I rely on James Curtis for sanity, humor, and the selfless helping hand, not to mention spasms of brutal honesty occasioned by a close reading of the first draft. As all film historians know, Kevin Brownlow is the gold standard. He's also a loyal friend, as was proven when he too threw himself into the thickets of the manuscript.

Ultimately, all indebtedness begins and ends with my wife, Lynn, the perfect writer's wife, the perfect wife. I love you.

—Scott Eyman, January 2000–February 2005
Hollywood–New York–London–Las Vegas–
Vienna–Salzburg–Haverhill– Palm Beach

NOTES

Unless specified in these notes, direct quotations derive from interviews with the author. I consulted the following institutions for research material:

Brigham Young University (BYU)
British Film Institute Special Collections (BFI)
The Museum of Modern Art (MOMA)
The New York Public Library at Lincoln Center (NYPL)
The Herbert Hoover Presidential Library (HHPL)
The Academy of Motion Picture Arts and Sciences (AMPAS)
University of Southern California Library (USC)
University of California at Los Angeles (UCLA)
Ransom Center at the University of Texas at Austin (RCUTA)
State Historical Society of Wisconsin (SHSW)

Also consulted were *Wid's Yearbooks* for 1918–22, as well as *Film Daily Yearbooks* for 1924–30, and the *Historical Atlas of Central Europe* (2002).

Prologue
PAGE
ix The Cukor epigraph derives from *American Film*'s "Dialogue on Film with Cukor" as published in *American Film*, February 1978, which I have combined with material from Gavin Lambert's *On Cukor*, p. 105.
1 In periods of peak production: "Who's Who at MGM 1940," author's collection.
1 Thirty-three actors: Mayer's official biography, 1944, Mayer file, MOMA.
1 "Anywhere from sixteen to eighteen": Wagner, p. 204.
2 It made its own paint: Gottfried, pp. 93–94.
2 Power was supplied: "Who's Who at MGM 1940, 1943," author's collection.

2 Each member of the MGM police: Tornabene, pp. 162–63.

2 "At Warner Brothers, you come in": Harmetz, p. 82.

3 at a sneak preview: Ralph Winters to S.E.

3 "Being . . . at MGM": Dewey, p. 139.

4 "notorious on Broadway": Jack Hurd to S.E.

5 five and a half feet and 175 pounds: L. B. Mayer FBI file, #7-2698, obtained under the Freedom of Information Act.

5 "I have thrown": The details and dialogue of the meeting between Mayer and Evie Johnson were recalled for me by Evie Johnson.

7 "You are talking about the devil incarnate": Hayes to Joseph Yranski, reported to S.E.

7 "Louis B. Mayer was a Jewish Hitler": Dewey, p. 140.

7 "absolutely infallible judgment": Brownlow, *Parade's*, p. 422.

7 "Everything that has been said": Ibid.

7 "Mayer was a great executive": Geist, p. 113.

9 "Placed in his proper perspective": AMPAS, Mayer file, *Variety*, 10-30-57.

9 "desperate men in a bare-knuckle scramble": Kazan, p. 227.

Chapter 1

PAGE

15 The epigraph is from Kobal, p. 649.

17 Jacob was born around 1847: Jacob Mayer death certificate.

17 "Only God knows": *Architectural Digest*, April 1990, "Louis B. Mayer, MGM's Archetypal Studio Head at Home."

17 Jews were forbidden: Lawrence Epstein, *Haunted*, p. 7.

18 In 1882, Alexander III: Joffe, *Pages of the History of the Jews of Belarus*, Minsk, 1996, translated for me by Alexander Michaeltchuk.

18 Eighty percent: Telushkin, p. 8.

18 The usual route: Ibid., p. 9.

19 It's possible that: Viola Gienger, information supplied by the International Association of Jewish Genealogical Societies.

19 Jacob, Sarah, and Lazar: Rabbi Eli Baitch, of the only functioning synagogue in Minsk, founded in 1910, shut down in 1935, reopened in 1980.

20 the first documentary evidence: BYU, Crowther papers, letter, 7-11-58, box 29, f. 9.

20 The Mayer family was living: 1901 Canadian census.

21 "I never picked rags": Charles Foster to S.E.

21 Yet, he once: BYU, Crowther papers, Schary to Crowther, 2-7-58, box 25, f. 3.

21 As late as 1880: Much of the information in this section derives from "The Settlement and Development of the Jewish Community of Saint John," a manuscript in BYU, Crowther papers, box 30.

22 "As the years went by": AMPAS, Mayer file, Wilkerson column, *Hollywood Reporter*, 8-7-57.

23 "He wasn't stealing": *Saint John Evening Times Globe*, 5-1-39, "The Man on the Street."

23 "Mr. Wilson was": Crowther, *Rajah*, p. 20.

23 John Wilson remembered: *Saint John Evening Times Globe*, 5-7-27, "Former School Boy Here Now Is Prince in Movie Kingdom."

23 "Put it to work": MOMA, Mayer file, L. B. Mayer MGM biography, 1944.

24 When he went by the hotel: Higham, *Merchant*, p. 9.

24 "I knew you'd be": *Saint John Evening Times Globe*, 5-1-39, "The Man on the Street."

25 In April 1899: *Saint John Daily Telegraph*, 4-10-1899, p. 3.

25 So Louis was hauled: Server, p. 131.

27 "I have one like that, too": *Saint John Citizen*, 4-15-86, "Louis B. Mayer, from Rags to Riches."

27 On January 3, 1904: BYU, Crowther papers, Mayer naturalization petition, 6-24-12, box 30.

27 "I hadn't the price": *Saint John Evening Times Globe*, 5-2-39, "Movie Magnate's Story of Early Struggles One of Courage and Idealism."

28 "My mother was": Thomson, *Showman*, p. 75.

28 On April 2, 1907: Selznick, p. 7.

Chapter 2

PAGE

30 Then and now: My former colleague Paul Reid gave me chapter and verse on Haverhill, a view confirmed by my own visit there.

31 Stories about the Gem: Altman, p. 4.

31 "What I saw in front of me": Foster, p. 189.

31 Haverhill historians: Haverhill Historical Society, *Haverhill Evening Gazette*, undated, "If Louis B. Had Stayed."

31 The jury-rigged apartment: Haverhill town directories were consulted at the Haverhill Public Library.

31 "Our only assistant": Foster, p. 190.

31 While lugging and painting: BYU, Crowther papers, Charles Shute to Crowther, 10-1-59, box 29, f. 10.

31 "high-class films": Crowther, *Rajah*, p. 29.

32 "you tell me how": USC, Louella Parsons Collection, 2-24-46 broadcast, box 4, f. 31.

32 Mayer was cautious at first: Haverhill Public Library, Mayer file, unsourced clipping, 6-22-40.

32 One employee: Haverhill Public Library, Mayer file, *Haverhill Evening Gazette* clipping, 4-7-39.

32 "Many a . . . girl": Shute interview.

33 He spoke to every Jewish group: Altman, pp. 10–11.

33 "The day my mother": Carey, p. 16.

33 "Manager Mayer": Altman, p. 13.

33 "Mary was a darling": Foster, p. 199.

34 "The Colonial is the zenith": Altman, p. 22.

35 On June 24, 1912: BYU, Crowther papers, certificate of naturalization #266993, box 30.

35 "Mr. Louis B. Mayer": Gabler, p. 87.

35 "He would spend a dollar": BYU, Crowther papers, Daniel Shea to Crowther, 8-29-59, box 29, f. 8.

35 You could shoot exteriors: Crowther, *Rajah*, p. 51.

36 Irene and Edie were regular attendees: BYU, Crowther papers, Charles Shute to Crowther, 10-1-59, box 29, f. 10.

36 That winter, David Perkins: Perkins to Crowther.

37 Years later: Gene Reynolds to S.E.

37 He also incorporated: BYU, Crowther papers, incorporation papers, box 31, f. 8.

37 "He wasn't like": Gabler, p. 90.

38 "I shall be crossing": Higham, *Merchant*, p. 22.

38 "Do not grieve, Louis": LeRoy, p. 135.

39 "Only God was more important": Kobal, p. 307.

39 "No kind of emotion": Selznick, p. 8.

39 "I do things": Ibid.

40 "We all gave it": Shute to Crowther.

40 Mayer paid $4,000: Berg, *Goldwyn*, p. 43.

40 "I would rather attend": BYU, Crowther papers, Weisl interview, box 31, f. 6.

40 The Lasky pictures: Altman, p. 29.

40 Rudy would come down: Shute to Crowther.

40 By 1913, the Mayer boys: Saint John city directory listing for Jacob Mayer, 1913.

41 When he went to New York: Shute to Crowther.

41 The Aitken brothers: Nelson and Jones, p. 154.

41 Associate producer Roy Aitken: BYU, Crowther papers, Aitken letter, 9-1-58, box 29, f. 8.

41 "I pawned everything": Gish, p. 157.

41 The figure he remembered paying: Haverhill Public Library, Mayer file, clipping dated 9-10-27.

41 Mayer formed a company: Crowther, *Rajah*, p. 49.

42 In his first year: Ibid., p. 50.

Chapter 3

PAGE

43 Lichtman's plan was to: Hampton, pp. 131–32.

43 Among its films: Ramsaye, p. 713.

43 In January 1915: Ibid., p. 714.

43 Richard Rowland, a lurid fashion plate: Jobes, p. 180.

43 Capitalization was $300,000: Maturi and Maturi, p. 43.

44 "Mayer looked up to him": BYU, Crowther papers, Browning to Crowther, 1-30-58, box 30.

44 "If we had a popular star": AMPAS, Mayer file, *American Weekly*, 6-8-58, "What Makes a Star."

44 "scenarios for Francis X. Bushman": Maturi and Maturi, p. 45.

45 "The Mall and Alhambra theaters": Ibid., p. 71.

45 Edie Mayer remembered: Higham, *Merchant*, p. 28.

46 L.B. pledged money: Altman, p. 47.

46 Cochrane said to give Mayer: BYU, Crowther papers, Cochrane interview, box 24, f. 4.

46 As with all the other homes: Columbia, "Sisters of Celluloid," *Quest* (1994).

46 "It is a sin": Selznick, p. 12.

47 When he went: Columbia, "Sisters of Celluloid," *Quest* (1994).

47 Mayer "handled Irene and Edie": Ibid.

47 "He worshipped the ground": Ibid.

47 While Maggie played the piano: Selznick, p. 18.

48 he talked a lot about: Ibid., p. 21.

48 "He was the very first movie star": *New Yorker*, 8-8-88, p. 24.

48 "I'm not sure": Selznick, p. 18.

48 "Mayer's idea was": BYU, Crowther papers, Rubin interview, 7-27-53, box 25, f. 2.

49 "Watch what I say": Thomson, *Showman*, p. 25.

49 "the pawnbrokers": BYU, Crowther papers, Schaefer to Crowther, 9-22-58, box 30.

50 At some point: BYU, Crowther papers, Stewart letter, box 25, f. 2.

50 "They were saying": Crowther, *Rajah*, pp. 55–56.

50 Anita Stewart Productions, Inc.: BYU, Crowther papers, Stewart Corporation papers, box 25, f. 2.

51 A 1917 release: BYU, Crowther papers, Vitagraph financial statement, box 25, f. 2.

51 To point up: Bodeen, *From Hollywood*, p. 123.

51 by mid-1918: Jobes, p. 180.

52 "Everybody told Mayer": BYU, Crowther papers, Rubin interview, 3-14-55, box 25, f. 2.

52 "Mr. Louis Mayer": Altman, p. 77.

52 Her deal with Mayer: Federal Trade Commission testimony by J. D. Williams of the First National Circuit, 5-9-23.

52 "I was completely happy": BYU, Crowther papers, Stewart letter.

53 "It is with a tinge": BYU, Crowther papers, *Exhibitor's Herald*, 11-8-19, box 30.

53 In association with Nate Gordon: *Wid's Daily Yearbook*, 1919–20, no page numbers.

53 There were caricatures: Ibid.

55 By 1915: *L.A. Times*, 8-27-91, "L.A. Redux: The City Then and Now."

56 "it made a profit": Foster, p. 195.

56 "THANKS FOR EXPRESSION": Crowther, *Rajah*, p. 69.

56 A young girl named Margaret Booth: AMPAS, Booth oral history.

57 "I'll bet you'd be surprised": Sam Marx, *Mayer and Thalberg*, p. 23.

57 "You can't run a house": Selznick, pp. 66–67.

57 Browning remembered: BYU, Crowther papers, Browning interview, 1-30-58, box 30.

58 "Mayer was very shy and speechless": BYU, Crowther papers, Myers to Crowther, box 23, f. 4.

58 "The business managers": Schulberg to Kevin Brownlow.

59 By this time: Gabler, p. 284.

59 "Sunday was a sturgeon": Schulberg, p. 115.

59 "My difficulties with Mayer": BYU, Crowther papers, Neilan letter, undated but 1953, box 25, f. 2

60 Alfred E. Green ended up: Spears, p. 291.

60 A little over a year: Williams testimony.

60 "You can't use my name": BYU, Crowther papers, Rubin to Crowther, 3-4-58, box 30.

60 Louis admired Hedda Hopper's flair: Day, p. 91.

61 "high hokum of Mother Love": Brownlow letter, 4-30-03.

62 "Those [other] girls *have*": Selznick, p. 52.

62 "He was a very cagey fellow": Ibid., p. 89.

62 He would talk with such enthusiasm: BYU, Crowther papers, Marion to Crowther, 10-31-53, box 25, f. 1.

62 "I worship good women": Marion, p. 99.

62 "I like your scenario": Ibid.

63 "I kept backing away": Miriam Cooper, *Dark Lady*, pp. 160–61.

63 "Can't you tell the headmistress": Gabler, p. 272.

63 "as many loyal friends": Fairbanks, *Salad Days*, p. 36.

63 "Their intellectual and cultural standards": Easton, p. 31.

63 "If you have the right values": Gabler, p. 292.

64 "If this keeps up": Yallop, p. 242.

64 "When I was 18": Farber and Green, p. 46.

64 "He was a forceful": Gabler, p. 81.

64 But Mayer's desire for quality: Crowther, *Rajah*, p. 88.

64 *Thy Name Is Woman:* Soares, p. 369.

65 "He would suddenly pitch forward": Schulberg to Brownlow, courtesy of Kevin Brownlow.

65 "He was a very emotional man": Schulberg, p. 122.

66 "Be smart, but never show it": Gabler, p. 107.

66 He would wear his coat: Roddy McDowall to S.E.

66 "He was trying to imitate": McGilligan, *Film Crazy*, p. 154.

66 "John Stahl made": BYU, Crowther papers. Carey Wilson to Crowther, 4-24-58, box 30.

66 "a hard task-master": Brownlow, *Parade's*, p. 302.

67 "a striking Italianate face": Coffee, p. 64.

67 "He had a boyish quality": Sidney Franklin autobiography, p. 179, courtesy of Kevin Brownlow.

67 "When you were shown into his office": Coffee, p. 64.

67 "Irving was an invalid": Sam Marx oral history, Culver City Historical Society, courtesy of Ross Hawkins.

68 Laemmle was impressed: *N.Y. Times*, 5-13-28, "Mr. Thalberg Returns from Europe."

68 "he was a keen observer": BYU, Crowther papers, Cochrane to Crowther, box 24, f. 4.

68 "Irving," he implored: Koszarski, *Evening's Entertainment*, p. 89.

69 "It is hard to . . . explain": Puttnam, p. 4.

69 "Wait a while": Crowther, *Lion's*, p. 77.

69 When Thalberg sent Hedda Hopper: AMPAS, Mayer file, Hopper column, 5-18-44.

69 "See that line": Ibid.

70 "brothers under the skin": BYU, Crowther papers, Frances Marion to Crowther, 10-31-53, box 25, f. 1.

70 "Mayer backed out": AMPAS, Booth oral history.

70 "determined to get Irving": BYU, Crowther papers, Browning to Crowther, 1-30-58, box 30.

72 "Loew wanted to know": Lewis and Lewis, p. 150.

72 "We thought that the Goldwyn product": BYU, Crowther papers, Schenck to Crowther, 1-4-54, box 25, f. 4.

72 Creatively, Goldwyn: BYU, Crowther papers, Meredyth to Crowther, 3-3-54, box 25, f. 1. Mathis's overall stewardship of the Goldwyn product is also attested to by Victor Seastrom's letter to Crowther, 2-2-54, box 31, f. 1.

72 Nick Schenck asked Rubin: BYU, Crowther papers, Rubin to Crowther, 3-14-55, box 25, f. 2.

73 Marcus Loew was born: Crowther, *Lion's*, p. 19.

73 "I was poor": Gabler, p. 19.

73 Loew was not particularly religious: BYU, Crowther papers, David Loew to Crowther, box 24, f. 7.

73 He didn't gamble: BYU, Crowther papers, Schenck to Crowther, 1-4-54, box 25, f. 4.

73 He was a diminutive man: BYU, Crowther papers, box 21, f. 10.

74 But the two men: *Fortune*, December 1932, "Metro-Goldwyn-Mayer," p. 118.

74 "That was on Tuesday": *N.Y. Times*, 5-2-26, "Marcus Loew's Start."

74 In January 1908: *Fortune*, August 1939, "Trust Everyone but Cut the Cards," p. 29.

74 According to their naturalization registrations: Higham, *Merchant*, p. 63.
74 both in Rybinsk: Joe Schenck, N.Y. *Times*, *Variety* and Associated Press obituaries, MOMA.
74 Contrary to the stories: Nicola Schenck to S.E.
75 One of their employees: Affron, p. 204.
75 Nick built an elaborate: Nicola Schenck to S.E.
75 In one chapter: Pizzitola, p. 105.
75 Nick and Joe Schenck signed a note: BYU, Crowther papers, box 24, f. 7.
75 Within a year: Gomery, *Shared Pleasures*, p. 30.
75 "You must want a big success": Hay, p. 14.
76 "We sell tickets": Puttnam, p. 100.
76 He converted an old warehouse: MOMA, Joseph Schenck file, *Classic Images* #138, December 1986, "The Joseph Schenck Studio," by Gene Fernett.
76 The terms of the deal: Crowther, *Lion's*, p. 51.
76 The Loew's State Theater: Altman, p. 90.
76 Loew's plans dwarfed Mayer: *Wid's Yearbook 1920–21*, p. 435.
77 Mayer was in the middle: Schulberg, p. 147.
77 "When you stop to think about it": Marx, *Mayer and Thalberg*, p. 46.
77 "Well, come on, Louis": Cotta Vaz and Barron, p. 46.
77 "Thalberg can do the job": Sam Marx, *Mayer and Thalberg*, p. 48.
77 "we had a producing company": BYU, Crowther papers, Arthur Loew deposition, 9-22-38, box 22, f. 4.
78 "To set your percentage": Sam Marx, *Mayer and Thalberg*, p. 48.
78 His company had capital stock: N.Y. *Times*, 4-18-24, "$65,000,000 Movie Merger Completed."
78 a roster of story properties: BYU, Crowther papers, box 23, f. 1.
79 The three men would divide: Crowther, *Lion's*, p. 81.
79 "I think we'll": Coffee, p. 95.

Chapter 4
PAGE
81 "Organization is responsible": *Film Daily*, 6-7-25, p. 7.
83 "the keystone of the arch": Griffith, p. 79.
83 "While Mayer was ambitious": BYU, Carey Wilson to Crowther, 4-24-58, box 30.
84 Mayer moved most of his: Crowther, *Lion's*, p. 82.
84 "Without warning": Schulberg, p. 154.
84 "Then," he said: Farber and Green, p. 27.
84 it was "not a difficult transition": AMPAS, Cohn oral history.
85 "I have been warned": AMPAS, Mayer file, *Variety*, 11-1-57.
85 "OK gang": Schulberg, p. 149.
85 "I knew the speeches": BYU, Neilan letter to Crowther, undated but 1953, box 25, f. 2.

85 The speech, Neilan explained: BYU, Neilan to Crowther, 5-14-57, box 21, f. 12.

85 "I fully realize": Schulberg, p. 150.

85 "he got a big office": BYU, Selznick to Crowther, 4-20-53, box 25, f. 4.

86 He kept a very sharp eye: Gerald Mayer to S.E.

86 He told them what to think: Selznick, p. 65.

86 "He was a very": Ibid., p. 68.

86 "Met von Stroheim": Irene Mayer Selznick's diaries are in her archive at the Special Collections of Boston University.

88 He went ahead and wrote a script: BYU, Seastrom letter to Crowther, 2-2-54, box 31, f. 1.

89 "It's Metro-Goldwyn-Mayer": Haver, p. 25.

89 "They were amazingly farsighted": AMPAS, Cohn oral history.

89 "If the first set": Foster, p. 346.

89 a knack for picking talent: Marion, p. 133.

89 Frances Marion: BYU, Marion letter to Crowther, 10-31-53, box 25, f. 1.

90 Along the way: Maas, p. 69.

90 Mayer revered Thalberg's gentleness: BYU, Wilson to Crowther, 4-24-58, box 30.

90 When a prominent: Mayer to Renée Adorée, 5-25-27, private collection.

90 When Norma Shearer bridled: *Fortune*, December 1932, "Metro-Goldwyn-Mayer," p. 120.

91 A panicked Boardman: Jordan Young, *Entertain*, p. 128.

91 "worm-eaten desk": Finch and Rosenkrantz, p. 226.

91 There was a metal staircase: Maurice Rapf to S.E.

91 Nearby was a fig tree: Dance and Robertson, pp. 75–76.

91 Thalberg had a Pacific Electric: Schatz, p. 118.

91 "We previewed in Highland Park": AMPAS, Booth oral history.

92 "Thalberg was an intuitive person": BYU, Crowther papers, Gibbons to Crowther, undated, box 24, f. 4.

92 "I'm 25": Bob Thomas, *Thalberg*, p. 119.

92 Sam Marx said: Flamini, *Thalberg*, p. 232.

92 "I don't like the seduction scene": Forslund, p. 226.

92 "He was an extremely complex personality": Coffee, pp. 98–99.

93 "He was thoughtful": Dietz, p. 157.

94 "It's a modern version": MOMA, Hilliker Collection, 4-24-25.

94 "We weren't a penny ante": Shorris and Bundy, p. 43.

94 The preferred production method: MOMA, Hilliker Collection, letter dated 6-5-25.

94 The first year of operations: The campaign book is in the Lincoln Center Library for the Performing Arts.

95 "There are no waits": NYPL, Lincoln Center, Mayer file, "Quality Production Under Mayer Regime," 7-19-24.

95 "His arm was under her robe": Dowd and Shepard, *King Vidor*, p. 55.

96 "My sympathies are all": Carey, p. 66.

96 "We felt he was": BYU, Schenck to Crowther, 1-4-54, box 25, f. 4.

96 "It's a travelogue": Powell, *A Life*, p. 150.

96 "When we came to Culver City": Bruskin, p. 12.

96 "My argument was": BYU, Crowther papers, Neilan to Crowther, undated but 1953, box 25, f. 2.

97 "Ten hours in a concrete box": The first part of the quotation is from *New Yorker*, 8-8-88, p. 22; the second part is from Selznick, p. 56.

98 *Variety* reported: *Variety*, 7-23-24.

98 but Joe Cohn still had to: AMPAS, Cohn oral history.

98 After fourteen weeks: Koszarski, *The Man*, pp. 169–70.

99 "We knew you had": Curtiss, p. 219.

99 "$25,000 and boat fare": BYU, Crowther papers, Brabin to Crowther, box 24, f. 4.

99 Dozens of actors: UCLA, *Ben-Hur* files, f. 1.

100 On May 2, 1924: UCLA, *Ben-Hur* files, Schenck to Loew, 5-2-24, f. 8.

100 "terrible. They'd got huge sets": Brownlow, *Parade's*, p. 394.

100 "It is almost beyond": Flamini, *Thalberg*, p. 61.

101 On Sunday, June 8, 1924: Soares, p. 78.

101 "Niblo had been a pet of Erlanger's": BYU, Crowther papers, Wilson to Crowther, 4-24-58, box 30.

101 "Personally, I will be": UCLA, *Ben-Hur* files, Niblo to Mayer, 5-20-24, f. 8.

101 Ramon Novarro was getting: UCLA, *Ben-Hur* production files, "*Ben-Hur* sailing dates," undated, f. 1.

102 "If our company": Crowther, *Rajah*, p. 108.

102 "conditions here generally": These and the next several quotations are from a précis of cables in the UCLA *Ben-Hur* files.

103 "Imagine a company": UCLA, *Ben-Hur* files, Niblo to Mayer, 9-2-24, f. 12.

104 When Mayer arrived: Brownlow, *Parade's*, p. 397.

104 On October 20, Carey Wilson: UCLA, *Ben-Hur* files, Wilson to Thalberg, 10-20-24, f. 13.

104 Thalberg responded: UCLA, *Ben-Hur* files, Thalberg to Wilson, 10-21-24, f. 13.

105 "Look at that girl!": Paris, p. 81.

105 One of the production managers: UCLA, *Ben-Hur* files, Aronson to Mayer, 11-28-24, f. 14.

105 "Frankly, I want to say": UCLA, *Ben-Hur* files, Aronson to Mayer, 12-11-24, f. 15.

105 On January 2: UCLA, *Ben-Hur* files, Niblo and Aronson to Mayer, 1-1-25.

106 on Saturday, January 3: Irene Selznick diaries, 1-3-25, Boston University Special Collections.

106 This extortionate demand: Soares, p. 90.

106 Besides having to make: Ibid., p. 92.

106 To take one day: UCLA, *Ben-Hur* files, Daily Production Report, 3-2-25, f. 1.

107 "After having a long talk": UCLA, *Ben-Hur* files, Niblo to Mayer, 7-2-25, f. 22.

108 "The Bethlehem star": UCLA, *Ben-Hur* files, Niblo to Mayer, 8-25-25, f. 23.

108 The studio filled the vast: UCLA, *Ben-Hur* files, interoffice communication, 10-2-25, f. 25.

108 Joe Cohn would admit: AMPAS, Cohn oral history.

108 Fred Niblo would utter: *N.Y. Times*, 1-3-26, "Niblo Talks About Work in Filming *Ben-Hur.*"

109 On December 31, 1925: UCLA, *Ben-Hur* files, Schenck to Thalberg, 12-31-25, f. 27.

109 The Culver City end of the production: Soares, p. 331.

109 "It seemed impressive": *New Yorker*, 8-8-88, p. 23.

109 Clearly, this story: I owe a great debt to T. Gene Hatcher, who took time from completing his definitive book about the three screen versions of *Ben-Hur* to share some of his documents with me and shepherd me through them.

Chapter 5

PAGE

111 Exhibitor J. J. McCarthy: *Variety*, 2-1-28, "6 Road-Show Film's History," p. 9.

111 He showed the picture: Bob Thomas, *Thalberg*, p. 72.

112 *The Big Parade* was one of two: *Variety*, 1-20-88, Merritt, "Roadshows Put on the Ritz," p. 93.

112 In October 1925: Crowther, *Lion's*, p. 119.

113 "[We were] the crème de la crème": William Haines to Fred Lawrence Guiles, private collection.

114 The dominating principal: Schatz, pp. 45–46.

114 Hearst's deal was a gold mine: Nasaw, p. 346.

114 "They were mentioned": Haines to Guiles, author's collection.

115 Hearst's twenty-two daily newspapers: Carey, p. 116.

115 In moments of special emphasis: Selznick, p. 84.

115 "When Hearst got his first newspapers": Pizzitola, p. 226.

115 "I would suggest": Ibid., p. 227.

115 A week later: Ibid., p. 228.

116 When the Loew and Mayer families: Nasaw, p. 394.

116 "The news reels should be": Ibid.

116 "This is to notify you": Jobes, p. 257.

117 "Why don't you get together": Schwartz, p. 8.

117 In any case: *Variety*, 11-13-2002.

117 "I found that the best way": AMPAS, Mayer file, *American Weekly*, 6-8-58, "What Makes a Star."

117 "You should explain": BYU, DeMille papers, DeMille to Mayer, 11-25-29, box 294, f. 3.

118 "We are splitting their ranks": BYU, DeMille papers, undated Mayer memo, box 294, f. 31.

118 The industry's prevailing: McDougal, *Privileged Son*, p. 107.

118 Besides Thalberg: Behlmer, *Memo*, p. 9.

118 Hyman was good-natured: Crowther, *Lion's*, p. 119.

118 Stromberg's references: Stewart, p. 198.

119 Another of Thalberg's bright young men: Felleman, p. 1.

119 "Harry Rapf came from Warner Brothers": AMPAS, Cohn oral history.

121 In 1928 a developer: *Leonard Maltin's Movie Crazy*, Autumn 2002.

121 "My father was mad": Paris, p. 80.

121 MGM was going to tear up: Forslund, p. 193.

122 MGM kept a slush fund: BYU, Crowther papers, Loew's minutes, 5-19-37, box 22, f. 3.

122 Around the studio: Forslund, p. 222.

122 "I can still feel agony": BYU, Crowther papers, Seastrom to Crowther, 2-2-54, box 31, f. 1.

123 "Is that man crazy": Jensen, p. 23.

123 "Do you think the American farmer": Ibid., p. 28.

123 There were twenty-seven writers: Haver, pp. 26–27.

123 They instituted Sunday morning: Harmetz, p. 12.

123 "Everything is done in conference": MOMA, Hilliker files, Hilliker letter, 6-5-25.

124 "Metro—you might as well be": McGilligan, *Backstory*, p. 75.

124 One of L.B.'s few dictums: Saville, p. 103.

124 "No, Louis, they're signed": McGilligan, *Backstory*, p. 250.

124 Lillian Gish was welcomed: Oderman, p. 140.

124 Gish was going to be paid: Affron, p. 205.

124 "You? You? You?": Oderman, p. 151.

125 Gish told her biographer: Paine, pp. 224–25.

125 when the picture was completed: BYU, Crowther papers, Marion to Crowther, 10-31-53, box 25, f. 1.

126 "Mayer didn't get the returns": Oderman, p. 168.

126 "I was used to working": Lillie, pp. 178–79.

126 Jacob Mayer would occasionally arrive: BYU, Crowther papers, Ross Willis to Crowther, 7-28-59, box 29, f. 10.

126 "never really liked his father": BYU, Crowther papers, Margaret Wills to Crowther, 9-8-59, box 29.

126 Two thousand mourners: Altman, p. 161.

127 "continually solicitous": Dietz, p. 109.

128 "You look at that": Gabler, p. 113.

129 "He thinks we're a bunch of bad boys": Sam Marx, *Gaudy*, p. 73.

129 Mayer and Nick Schenck clashed: Carey, p. 123.

130 "I came out": June Caldwell to S.E.

130 Beneath the surface geniality: *Vanity Fair*, David Stenn, "It Happened One Night . . . at MGM," April 2003.

131 If Mannix felt: Day, p. 265.

131 Benny Thau was a booker: Sam Marx, *Mayer and Thalberg*, p. 113.

131 Greer Garson was Thau's mistress: Kotsilibas-Davis and Loy, p. 208.

131 likewise, Joan Crawford: Schulberg, p. 381.

132 "They wanted to see": Ingram, "Art Advantage of the European Scene," undated, unsourced clipping in author's collection.

132 The distractions didn't work: Soares, p. 141.

133 He and his lover: Alan Brock to Joe Yranski, courtesy of Yranski.

133 "I was blind": Haines to Fred Lawrence Guiles, private collection.

133 "If Gilbert would have hit": AMPAS, Joe Cohn oral history.

134 On the other hand, Boardman: Boardman to Fred Lawrence Guiles, private collection.

134 In 1926, L.B. decided: *Architectural Digest*, April 1990, "Louis B. Mayer: MGM's Archetypal Studio Head at Home."

135 Thalberg's house: MOMA, *Screenland*, undated, "The Home of the Irving Thalbergs."

135 Irene Mayer remembered: Paris, p. 135.

135 "How dare you socialize": Columbia, "Sisters of Celluloid," *Quest*, 1994.

135 L.B. was doing a fair amount: Higham, *Merchant*, p. 104.

136 About $18 million was collected: MOMA, Mayer file, *N.Y. Herald Tribune*, N.Y. *World* clippings, both 6-28-27.

136 It was revealed: Watkins, p. 19.

136 The indictments were thrown out: McDougal, pp. 131–33.

137 Koverman was one of the invisible: USC, Koverman clipping file, Koverman obituary, 11-25-54.

138 Years later, at Corbaley's funeral: Sam Marx, *Gaudy*, p. 27.

138 But Mayer hated the picture: Dowd and Shepard, p. 289.

138 Mayer hated *The Crowd*: Adolph Green to S.E.

139 Seastrom remembered: BYU, Crowther papers, Seastrom to Crowther, 2-2-54, box 31, f. 1.

139 "Mr. Mayer heard": Oderman, p. 177.

139 They had a serious argument: Affron, p. 222.

139 "They all point to": Ibid., p. 223.

139 "I hardly think": Ibid., p. 234.

140 L.B. usually played the sycophant: HHPL, Commerce papers, Mayer to Hoover, 9-2-24, box 388.

140 "GET BUSY WITH [HOOVER]": HHPL, Commerce papers, Ida Koverman correspondence, Mayer to Koverman, 12-2-27, box 360.

140 "Strictly confidential to yourself": HHPL, Commerce papers, Hoover to Mayer, 1-2-26, box 388.

140 "Pending the construction": HHPL, Commerce papers, Hoover to Mayer, 9-21-26, box 388.

140 "when you are finally elected": HHPL, Campaign and Transition papers, Mayer to Hoover, 8-10-28, box 47.

140 "While I never had": HHPL, Campaign and Transition papers, Mayer to Hoover, 11-6-28, box 118.

141 Mayer began acting as: HHPL, Ida Koverman 1929–33 file, Koverman wire, 6-8-31, box 675.

141 All of these appointments: HHPL, L. B. Mayer 1929–32 file, Mayer to Richey, 3-19-29 and 4-24-29; Richey to Mayer, 8-6-32, 8-10-32, box 728.

141 "Mr. Mayer decided": BYU, Crowther papers, Hoover to Crowther, 7-8-58, box 29.

141 The Republican financier: BYU, Crowther papers, Lurie to Crowther, 7-30-59, box 29, f. 7.

141 "He most certainly": HHPL, Louis B. Mayer 1929 file, Presidential Personal File, Fort to Richey, 6-4-29, box 172.

141 "I understand that you": HHPL, Presidential Personal File, box 172.

142 "This is another small boy": HHPL, Ida Koverman general correspondence— Campaign and Transition, Koverman to Richey, 1-28-29, box 41.

142 A squeaking mouse: Beauchamp, p. 234.

142 As he wrote Thalberg: Crafton, p. 326.

143 The tip-off: Crowther, *Rajah*, p. 143.

144 Loew's had expanded: Ibid., p. 144.

144 Nick Schenck had offered: Sam Marx, *Mayer and Thalberg*, p. 98.

144 According to William Fox's account: Sinclair, p. 90.

145 At this point: Leatrice Gilbert Fountain to S.E.

145 According to both Mayer: Crowther, *Rajah*, p. 149.

145 "He wanted as much": Sam Marx, *Mayer and Thalberg*, p. 126.

145 Mayer would later tell: Sinclair, p. 91.

145 "All the important leaders": BYU, Crowther papers, Hoover to Crowther, 7-8-58, box 29.

146 Mayer would always deny: Crowther, *Rajah*, p. 148.

Chapter 6

PAGE

148 "Gilbert always drove": BYU, Crowther papers, Strickling to Crowther, box 25, f. 6.

148 As Joe Cohn pointed out: AMPAS, Joe Cohn oral history.

149 When a young MGM director: Gabler, p. 214.

150 The next day: Blake, *Lon Chaney*, p. 271.

150 A few weeks later: Eyman, *Speed*, p. 357.

151 Whatever grudges L.B. held: Carey, p. 111.

151 Whoever came to the Santa Monica house: Berkman, p. 88.

151 On April 18: Jacob Mayer death certificate.

151 Jacob left an estate: AMPAS, Mayer file, *L.A. Herald* obituary, 5-20-30.

151 Yetta Mayer was operating: Higham, *Merchant*, p. 160.

152 "MGM happens to be": *Fortune*, December 1932, "Metro-Goldwyn-Mayer," pp. 118–20.

153 "an injured lion": Beauchamp, p. 301.

154 "I'm going to build up": Bob Thomas, *Thalberg*, p. 255.

154 Wanger was worried: Bernstein, p. 83.

154 Mayer didn't like: Ibid., p. 86.

154 "There were a lot of alterations": Pizzitola, p. 298.

154 Wanger's diary: Wanger's diary is at SHSW.

155 "L. B. Mayer had a theory": Marx with Anobile, *The Marx Bros. Scrapbook*, p. 210.

155 A movie called *China Seas*: Schatz, p. 107.

156 The MGM record: Bach, p. 99.

156 "Sometimes writers worked": Meryman, p. 159.

156 When the rainbow script: Coffee, p. 126.

157 "Well, that's a very nice": Ibid., p. 187.

157 "find scenes that worked": Stempel, p. 75.

157 "If he shoots a scene": Marx with Anobile, p. 206.

158 "I was really just": *N. Y. Times*, 3-24-35, "W. S. Van Dyke Discusses Donkeys and Directors."

158 "I resent simpering idiots": Cannom, pp. 296–98.

158 "The trouble with most movie people": Behlmer, *Van Dyke*, p. 90.

159 "I consider the director": Sam Marx, *Mayer and Thalberg*, p. 96.

161 When he finally did sign: I am greatly indebted to Fleming's biographer Michael Sragow for sharing some of Fleming's contracts with me, to wit: 10-9-31, 7-29-32, 8-17-32, 6-10-33, and 2-15-34.

161 Edie and Bill wanted: Crowther, *Rajah*, p. 157.

162 And so, on March 30, 1930: *Architectural Digest*, April 1992, "William Goetz: Prolific Producer's Holmby Hills Collection."

162 As far as Irene was concerned: Robert Gottlieb to S.E.

162 That ferocious meeting: Selznick, p. 145.

163 "Dear little mother": Thomson, *Showman*, p. 141.

163 Without a releasing agreement: Haver, p. 68.

163 "They were men": Berg, *Goldwyn*, p. 163.

164 "because our people": Sam Marx, *Mayer and Thalberg*, p. 170.

164 "He's not a well man": Swanson, pp. 69–70.

165 The comedian was to get: Eleanor Keaton and Vance, p. 164.

165 "They'll ruin you": Blesh, p. 298.

166 "Jackie, the whole studio": Zollo, p. 246.

166 Mayer and Thalberg tried: Meade, pp. 200–201.

166 "Maybe half a dozen": Ibid., p. 213.

166 Keaton countered: Dardis, p. 209.

166 He blamed Mayer: Ibid., p. 188.

167 With all the delusional grandiosity: Meade, p. 216.

167 Sam Marx remembered: Turk, p. 131.

168 MacDonald basked: Ibid., p. 155.

168 He was elected: AMPAS, Mayer file, *L.A. Daily News* clipping, 7-10-35.

168 He was presented: AMPAS, Mayer file, *L.A. Examiner* clipping, 1-12-34.

168 "I have observed": AMPAS, Mayer file, *L.A. Herald* clipping, 6-3-32.

168 He campaigned for him: AMPAS, Mayer file, unsourced, undated clipping.

169 Hearst was appalled: Crowther, *Rajah*, p. 196.

169 "Show business owns": NYPL, Mayer file, *Variety*, 6-21-32.

169 L.B. and the former President: HHPL, Ida Koverman correspondence, 1933–54, box 116.

170 One friend of Mayer crony Frank Orsatti: Higham, *Merchant*, p. 158.

170 Tabs were kept: Ibid.

170 While the market value: Schatz, p. 159.

170 "Irving, that is silly": BYU, Crowther papers, Mayer deposition, box 24, f. 3.

172 It was finally agreed: Crowther, *Lion's*, pp. 193–95.

172 "Mayer never denied": Lambert, *Shearer*, p. 185.

172 A few years later: BYU, Crowther papers, Rubin interview, box 25, f. 2.

172 An electrocardiogram: BYU, Crowther papers, Philip Newmark, M.D., letter, 1-17-33, box 22, f. 1.

174 Thalberg closed: I'm deeply indebted to James Curtis for sharing this remarkable document with me. Norma Shearer gave Bosley Crowther a slightly different draft, in his papers at BYU.

175 "More than any single person": Lambert, *Shearer*, p. 152.

175 On February 8: BYU, Crowther papers, Thalberg letter, 2-8-33.

175 "Dear Irving": Crowther, *Rajah*, p. 167.

177 "I was deeply and sincerely": Ibid., p. 169.

178 Ramon Novarro: Beauchamp, p. 424.

178 For the executive staff: BYU, Crowther papers, Loew's minutes, 7-18-32, box 22, f. 3.

179 On Wednesday, March 8, 1933: The date is attested to by Walter Wanger's diary for 1933, at SHSW.

179 Barrymore announced: Kotsilibas-Davis, *The Barrymores*, p. 146.

179 After the meeting: Sam Marx, *Gaudy*, p. 88.

180 "Oh, that L. B. Mayer": Schwartz, p. 10.

180 As the screenwriter: Mosley, pp. 124–25.

180 Schenck brought to the table: Farber and Green, p. 53.

180 Mayer would eventually: Custen, p. 176.

181 Selznick's share was divided: Thomson, *Showman*, pp. 159–60.

181 "Goetz wouldn't recognize": Custen, p. 176.

181 "How could you humiliate": Gussow, p. 62.

181 "Bill is a born thumbtack": Mosley, p. 151.

181 "He was a very good assistant": Gussow, p. 63.

181 "It got so I couldn't hire": BYU, Crowther papers, Katz interview, undated, box 30.

183 He assured Schenck: BYU, Crowther papers, Thalberg to Schenck, box 22, f. 2., 10-13-33 and 12-5-33.

183 When Edward VIII: Lardner, p. 83.

183 "We argued and won him over": Haver, p. 156.

183 When Selznick showed him: AMPAS, Mayer file, *Kansas City Star*, 10-15-33, "In Night Flight a Studio Drama Found a Happy Ending."

184 The approach was made: Thomson, *Showman*, p. 189.

184 L.B. had to try: Ibid., p. 186.

185 One was Fanny Holtzmann: Berkman, p. 85.

186 "You don't spit": Ibid., p. 99.

186 "Mayer didn't even": Bruskin, p. 159.

186 Nicholas Schenck stepped in: Maltin and Bann, p. 65.

186 Roach always dealt directly: Richard Bann to S.E.

187 Mayer grabbed Wilcox's hand: Crowther, *Rajah*, p. 139.

187 The famous chicken soup: Finch and Rosenkrantz, p. 57.

187 "Mr. Mayer wanted everything right": AMPAS, Margaret Booth oral history.

188 As for L.B.: Day, p. 83.

188 All the employees: Ibid., p. 74.

188 The directors' table: Rapf, p. 51.

188 When gossip columnist Louella Parsons: Finch and Rosenkrantz, pp. 132–33.

188 Once, he was in New York: BYU, Crowther papers, Phillips to Crowther, 1-17-58, box 30.

189 "I remember distinctly": Gabler, p. 190.

189 It's entirely possible: Doherty, p. 261. Also, Mae West told the author in 1972 that she regularly dropped particularly base lines in her scripts in order to have something to give up in order to keep material she really wanted.

190 "Mr. Breen goes to the bathroom": Leff and Simmons, p. 63.

190 "Well, it usually has": Mamoulian to Kevin Brownlow, courtesy of Brownlow.

191 On the set: Paris, p. 305.

191 "Oh, a critic!": William Haines to Fred Lawrence Guiles, private collection.

191 Mayer took personal charge: Lee, p. 203.

191 In the January 1933: Ibid., p. 240.

192 Mayer made the trek: BYU, Crowther papers, Strickling to Crowther, box 32, f. 5.

192 Dressler died on July 28, 1934: Lee, pp. 260–61.

192 Dietz was invited: Dietz, pp. 186–87.

Chapter 7

PAGE

193 "Mayer had a reputation": Sam Marx, *Mayer and Thalberg*, p. 121.

193 Margaret was beginning: AMPAS, Mayer file, *L.A. Examiner* and *Hollywood Citizen-News* clippings, 9-9-33.

193 Mayer told Eddie Mannix: Sam Marx, *Mayer and Thalberg*, p. 225.

194 He tried to seduce: Anita Page to S.E.; and Villeco, pp. 137–38.

194 More compliant: Schulberg, pp. 484–85.

195 "He couldn't get laid": Sam Marx, *Mayer and Thalberg*, p. 225.

195 "Mayer was a Puritan": Ibid., p. 226.

195 "Mayer thought *that*": Carey, p. 181.

195 If Orsatti noticed: Grady, p. 247. Although Grady does not mention Orsatti by name, it's clear who he's talking about.

195 "an intense personal interest": McCarthy, p. 321.

196 "We just did a lot of walking": BYU, Crowther papers, Strickling to Crowther, 12-3-58, box 27, f. 9.

196 "As God hears me": Sam Marx, *Mayer and Thalberg*, p. 228.

197 "You sing your psalms": Ralston to S.E.

198 Reinhardt took Mayer: Reinhardt, p. 307.

198 "I didn't say": BYU, Crowther papers, Feldman to Crowther, 11-21-58, box 27, f. 9.

199 "Why should I loan": Crowther, *Rajah*, p. 229.

199 "L.B. was the czar": Feldman to Crowther.

200 The details were fuzzy: Mitchell, p. 80.

200 A well-funded apparatus: Ibid., p. 200.

201 Thalberg stared at the man: Viertel, p. 206.

201 As he explained: Maurice Rapf to S.E.

201 Thalberg ordered Carey Wilson: BYU, Crowther papers, Wilson to Crowther, 4-28-58, box 30.

202 "We don't go in for that": McDougal, *Privileged Son*, p. 141.

202 Mayer mobilized the advertising: Josephy, pp. 96–97.

202 Standing in line: Mitchell, p. 304.

203 "He knows how to salvage junk": Ibid., p. 310.

203 "Before Louis Mayer": Ibid., p. 435.

203 L.B. basked: Ibid., p. 535.

204 "they had to balance": Gabler, p. 342.

204 "Thalberg, not Mayer": BYU, Crowther papers, Montgomery interview, box 32, f. 5.

205 "Why have anything to do": Robert Lees to S.E.

205 "Those writers are living": Mitchell, p. 81.

205 "I'll show that Jew bastard": Rapf, p. 96.

206 "If anybody tries to threaten you": Schwartz, p. 76.

206 "I have no intention": Perelman, p. 9.

206 In 1937: AMPAS, Mayer file, *L.A. Examiner* clipping, 4-9-39. Income tax statistics derive from IRS Statistics of Income, Individual Income Tax Returns.

207 "Mayer was a brilliant": Sam Marx, *Gaudy*, p. 92.

207 Rosalind Russell remembered: BYU, Crowther papers, Russell interview, box 25, f. 2.

207 Color, he explained: AMPAS, Mayer file, unsourced clipping, 8-17-32.

207 "You can't shout": AMPAS, Mayer file, *L.A. Times*, 2-17-38.

208 "Whenever Mayer sneezed": Capra, p. 164.

208 "Most of the": Jessel, p. 194.

208 There were three suites: Kotsilibas-Davis and Loy, p. 120.

209 "Each of them wanted": Schary, p. 77.

210 One of the department no-nos: Knox, p. 151.

210 Gibbons set up: Hambley and Downing, p. 54.

210 As Preston Ames: Ibid., p. 59.

211 "I haven't held": *Film Comment*, May-June 1978, George Jenkins interview, p. 46.

211 "Whether it fitted": Hambley and Downing, p. 59.

211 "The behavior of a molecule": *Pacific Coast Musician*, 10-2-37, p. 20, William Rosar Collection.

212 "He was God": *Film Music Notebook*, vol. 4, 1978, Bronislau Kaper interview, p. 21.

212 if somebody's option: *Film Music Notebook*, vol. 3, 1977, John Green interview, p. 22.

213 "Because she's *better*": Armand Deutsch to S.E.

213 The director would rehearse: Worsley, p. 31.

214 Until the advent of Edith Head: Chierichetti, *Hollywood Costume*, pp. 14–15.

214 "Adrian always played down": Gutner, p. 120.

214 Adrian was a fiend for work: Ibid., p. 9.

215 Strickling was a kind: Berdie Abrams to S.E.

215 If Clark Gable: Tornabene, pp. 126–27.

215 While Hendry worked: Goodman, p. 325.

216 "I always thought": Wallace, p. 20.

217 When a story needed: Berdie Abrams to S.E.

217 "MGM created a certain": Madsen, *Stanwyck*, p. 117.

217 The shoeshine stand: Worsley, p. 11.

218 The projection room: Ibid., p. 12.

218 "I used to wander": Farber and Green, pp. 247–48.

219 "He kept his word": Ibid., p. 250.

219 "We do make a good picture": Al Hirschfeld to Kevin Brownlow, courtesy of Brownlow.

220 "The secret of Clark's surviving": Tornabene, p. 211.

220 Gable's attitude: Ibid., p. 296.

222 Douglas Fairbanks Jr.: Fairbanks, *Salad Days*, pp. 192–93.

222 Edward Bernays: BYU, Crowther papers, Bernays letter, box 21, f. 12.

222 "Don't worry about that": Coffee, p. 100.

222 Hawks proceeded to tell: John Lee Mahin to S.E.

223 Once, Beery invited: Darryl Hickman to S.E.

223 "She was really lovely": Robert Young to Leonard Maltin, transcript courtesy of Maltin.

225 "Too many stars stay": Tapert, p. 86.

225 Thalberg went directly: Lambert, *Shearer*, p. 222.

225 "When a producer tells me": Sam Marx, *Mayer and Thalberg*, p. 246.

226 *Romeo and Juliet* was in production: Ibid., p. 255.

226 Mayer thought Thalberg's plans: Lawrence, p. 221.

226 Sam Marx remembered: Sam Marx, *Gaudy*, p. 87.

226 "You're what I always": Coffee, pp. 101–2.

227 "So you had": Ibid., p. 174.

227 Marion Davies claimed: Guiles, *Marion Davies*, p. 279.

228 "Louis had been after me": Steen, pp. 173–74.

228 When an agent: L. B. Mayer FBI file, #62-44507, obtained under the Freedom of Information Act.

228 He asked that: Arce, p. 234.

229 In January 1936: AMPAS, Mayer file, *L.A. Herald*, 1-28-36.

229 On June 2, 1936: McBrien, p. 194.

230 but the composer went to Mayer: Ibid., p. 207.

230 "Would you mind": Bob Thomas; *Thalberg*, p. 277.

230 "never backed up": BYU, Crowther papers, Strickling to Crowther, box 25, f. 6.

230 In the first week: *Saint John Evening Times Globe*, 9-2-36, "The Man on the Street."

230 "MGM has been trying": AMPAS, Mayer file, *Motion Picture Herald*, 9-5-36.

231 He saw *Tudor Rose:* BFI Special Collections, Balcon Collection, Thalberg to Balcon, 7-1-36.

231 Around this time: BYU, Crowther papers, box 22, f. 2.

231 As the fall of 1936 approached: MOMA, Thalberg file, "What Does a Producer Do," undated clipping.

231 But Franklin knew: Franklin autobiography, p. 239, courtesy of Kevin Brownlow.

232 The funeral was: Madsen, *Wyler*, p. 153.

232 "They won't miss him": *Fortune*, August 1939, "Trust Everyone but Cut the Cards," p. 104.

232 That, at least: Sam Marx to S.E.

232 But Norma Shearer told friends: Lambert, *Shearer*, p. 233.

Chapter 8

PAGE

237 "If anything can be done": Crowther, *Lion's*, p. 239.

237 and $4.49 million: Flamini, *Thalberg*, p. 7.

237 "Every son of a bitch": Altman, p. 209.

237 "I will debate you": BYU, Crowther papers, Edward Weisl interview, box 31, f. 6.

238 "Nobody can be": Sam Marx, *Mayer and Thalberg*, p. 240.

238 "I wish I could say the same": Winters, p. 25.

238 "If you come across": Altman, p. 210.

238 "Thalberg envisioned": Turk, p. 196.

238 "Mr. Mayer was infuriated": Rosenberg and Silverstein, p. 113.

239 In the early part of 1936: Nielsen and Mailes, p. 21.

240 "Just handle it, Louis": Altman, p. 200.

240 At one negotiating session: Murphy, "Say, Didn't You Used to Be George Murphy," excerpted in Sylvester, p. 275.

240 "There is no room": Altman, p. 202.

241 Mayer was petulant: *Nation*, 4-2-38, Morton Thompson, "Hollywood Is a Union Town."

241 The 1940 trial: MOMA, Joe Schenck file, Associated Press obituary, 10-23-61.

241 "We had about 20 percent": Altman, p. 185.

241 They were given producer contracts: David Brown to S.E.

242 As a result: Turk, p. 220.

242 "I understand Mr. L.B.": Ibid., p. 235.

243 "I could feel the temperature falling": Ibid., p. 220.

243 She was promptly summoned: Brenner, pp. 189–92.

244 Al Lichtman, the head of sales: BYU, Crowther papers, Lichtman interview, box 24, f. 7.

244 "I owe you a duty": Crowther, *Rajah*, p. 222.

245 It was a very rich contract: Author's collection.

245 the largest profit percentages: BYU, Crowther papers, box 22, f. 4.

246 "Mayer was less involved": Lewis, p. 105.

246 "It's a good thing": Ibid., p. 102.

246 "[Mayer] was not only": Ibid., pp. 102–5.

247 "He had no morality": Ibid., pp. 106, 219.

247 "a fascinating figure": Ibid., p. 113.

247 After Edward VIII abdicated: Shorris and Bundy, pp. 118–19.

247 In November of 1937: The scripts for the *Good News* shows are in the MGM collection at USC.

249 "I don't discover stars": USC, Parsons Collection, 2-24-46 broadcast, box 4, f. 31.

249 He began to be honored: AMPAS, Mayer file, *L.A. Examiner*, 2-24-38, "Louis B. Mayer to Be Honored at Banquet." The other honors accorded Mayer also derive from clippings in that same file.

250 Nick Schenck came out to Hollywood: BYU, Crowther papers, Loeb interview, 4-22-58, box 30.

250 In fact, Thalberg had left: Lambert, *Shearer*, p. 242.

250 "I must go back to work": Ibid., p. 244.

250 In the twenty years after: Crowther, *Lion's*, p. 240.

251 "Norma is brilliant": Tapert, p. 86.

251 In 1936: Gomery, *Hollywood Studio*, p. 59.

251 "He was the only American": Saville, p. 99.

251 Denham was the most lavish: Troyan, p. 62.

252 Garson proved: Ibid., pp. 63–64.

252 "MGM spent more money": Saville, p. 126.

252 It was on this trip: Maria Koretz Wrigley to S.E.

253 The two had developed: BFI, Balcon papers; see, for instance, Balcon to Thau, 4-21-36.

253 "I was given": Balcon, p. 103.

253 According to Benny Thau: Leff, pp. 23–24.

254 Balcon got the distinct impression: Balcon, p. 112.

254 Donald Ogden Stewart: Stewart, p. 231.

255 At the end of December 1937: Franklin autobiography, p. 256, courtesy of Kevin Brownlow.

256 "His [Duvivier's] name is not": Lambert, *Shearer*, p. 260.

257 "I always got my Oscars": BYU, Crowther papers, Gibbons interview, box 24, f. 4.

257 "You're doing": Morley, pp. 150–52.

258 Fadiman made an appointment: Shorris and Bundy, p. 114.

259 On January 10, 1938: Thomson, *Showman*, p. 265.

259 The deal that was finally struck: Haver, pp. 251–52.

259 "During the same conversation": Thomson, *Showman*, p. 281.

260 "They'd stone Christ": Flamini, *Scarlett*, p. 239.

260 At the end of 1940: Haver, p. 330.

261 David Selznick's home movies: I'm indebted to Daniel Selznick for showing me these fascinating films.

261 "He had a wonderful": Thomson, *Showman*, pp. 436–37.

261 "My mother said": Carey, p. 4.

261 By 1939, the bonuses: AMPAS, Mayer file, 1940 *Film Daily* clipping.

262 There were 16,250 movie theaters: *Fortune*, August 1939, "Trust Everyone but Cut the Cards," p. 30.

263 "Grow a mustache": Ross Hawkins to S.E.

263 "His face turned almost purple": Esther Williams, *The Million Dollar Mermaid*, p. 90.

263 "Louis B. Mayer had an enormous ego": Ibid., p. 94.

264 As S. J. Perelman once snarled: Perelman, p. 26.

264 "He hated Irving Thalberg!": McLelland, pp. 40–41.

264 "I started out to be": Mary Loos to S.E.

264 Adrian told Stromberg: Gutner, pp. 178–79.

264 In May 1939: *Saint John Evening Times Globe*, 5-18-39, "Louis B. Mayer Offers Advice to N.B. Youths."

265 The community also wanted: BYU, Crowther papers, Wolfie Cohen interview, 1-3-58, box 30.

265 "I can't prove this": Carey, p. 152.

265 "Along comes a Clark Gable": Tornabene, p. 129.

266 "The idea of a star": AMPAS, Mayer file, *American Weekly*, 6-8-58, "What Makes a Star."

267 "We need your *manpower*": Guiles, *Paradise*, p. 101.

267 "So you think": Geist, p. 75.

267 "He hated writers": BYU, Crowther papers, Mankiewicz interview, box 32, f. 5.

Chapter 9

PAGE

268 First, he spent $600,000: AMPAS, Mayer file, *L.A. Examiner*, 2-12-38; *L.A. Times*, 12-24-40.

269 Soon, a code developed: Crowther, *Lion's*, p. 286.

269 Katz had grown to respect Mayer: BYU, Crowther papers, Katz interview, box 30.

269 according to Jack Baker: Finch and Rosenkrantz: p. 290.

269 "As he had his own": Gabler, pp. 264–65.

270 But after going to a lot of trouble: AMPAS, Mayer file, *L.A. Times*, 1-18-41.

270 Mayer had his own small bungalow: Crowther, *Rajah*, p. 251.

271 "If Colonel Bradley": Ibid., p. 252.

271 L.B.'s brother Jerry: AMPAS, Robert Vogel oral history.

273 The unit was eventually housed: Adams, p. 51.

274 Beginning in 1943: Barrier, p. 410.

274 "The industry as a whole": Skretvedt, pp. 331–32.

275 The upshot of all this: Richard Bann to S.E.

275 By the early part of 1937: AMPAS, MPAA Collection, *Three Comrades* file, Gyssling to Breen, 4-8-37.

275 "As this book deals": Ibid., 12-29-37.

276 At this point: Lawrence Epstein, *Haunted*, p. 99.

276 "a serious indictment": Miller, *Censored*, p. 111.

277 "the shot showing the drums": AMPAS, MPAA Collection, *Three Comrades* file, Breen to Gyssling, 5-16-38.

277 Mayer once told screenwriter George Oppenheimer: BYU, Crowther papers, Oppenheimer interview. box 29, f. 12.

277 "Warner Bros. had guts": Kelly, p. 146.

277 By 1940, only MGM: Hake, p. 131.

277 "Louis Mayer was only thinking": AMPAS, Robert Vogel oral history.

280 Sidney wanted the lines: Kanfer, p. 260.

280 "Motion pictures are nothing more": Goodman, p. 317.

280 "What do you mean": Ibid., p. 313.

281 "Original thinking": Saville, p. 105.

281 "In their thirty years together": Selznick, p. 262.

Chapter 10

PAGE

283 Often, he played a nine-ball: Saville, p. 110.

283 After dinner: AMPAS, Mayer file, *Reader's Digest*, June 1947, "The Unchallenged King of Hollywood."

283 On Sunday mornings: MOMA, Mayer file, *New Yorker*, 3-28-36 and 4-4-36; also confirmed by Dan Selznick.

284 "damn near as big": Wellman, p. 226.

285 Among the roles: BYU, Crowther papers, Schary interview, 2-7-58, box 25, f. 3.

285 "He was stubborn": BYU, Crowther papers, Willis to Crowther, 7-28-59, box 29, f. 1.

287 "proceed to show them": *Saint John Evening Times Globe*, 12-30-30, "Louis B. Mayer Tells Story of Business Life."

287 "He spoke Yiddish": Paris, p. 81.

288 The girl would stand": Grady, pp. 245–46.

288 When Irene Hervey: Higham, *Merchant*, p. 307.

288 "Mayer respected brains": AMPAS, Joe Cohn oral history.

288 "Mayer prided himself": AMPAS, Robert Vogel oral history.

289 One of Mayer's ambitions: BYU, Crowther papers, Freed interview, box 24, f. 5.

289 Many MGM contractees: Ricardo Montalban to S.E.

290 Once he woke up: Margaret O'Brien to S.E.

291 Likewise, when a messenger boy: Shorris and Bundy, p. 318.

291 "L. B. Mayer was a great romantic": Miller, p. 130.

291 Once an actor asked Benny Thau: Robert Young to Leonard Maltin, courtesy of Maltin.

292 Robert Young remembered: Ibid.

293 Mayer's power: McGilligan and Buhle, *Tender*, p. 205.

294 "I just want to be": BYU, Crowther papers, Mayer deposition, 7-15-38, box 22, f. 6.

294 When the lights came up: Server, p. 120.

294 Elizabeth Taylor's mother, Sara: Heymann, p. 51.

294 He was the sort: Finch and Rosenkrantz, p. 87.

295 "Not for an instant": Edward G. Robinson, p. 191.

295 "If you delivered for them": McGilligan and Buhle, *Tender*, p. 576.

295 "I asked him what he thought": Muller, pp. 31, 48, 197.

295 Once, he was trying: BYU, Crowther papers, Behrman interview, 1-16-58, box 32, f. 5.

296 He liked to listen: BYU, Crowther papers, Marmorston interview, 4-27-58, box 30.

296 "My grandfather": Shorris and Bundy, p. 297.

297 Ida Mayer Cummings: I'm indebted to Elaina Archer for some of Ida Mayer Cummings's business correspondence.

297 Jack Cummings remembered Mayer: Shorris and Bundy, p. 50.

298 When Mayer was presented: Jackie Cooper, p. 181.

298 "I would sit next to him": Gabler, p. 216.

298 At one gathering: Ibid., p. 252.

299 Mayer was voluble: Esther Williams to S.E.

299 When his grandchildren: Dan Selznick to S.E.

299 His table manners were lusty: BYU, Crowther papers, Schary interview, 2-7-58, box 25, f. 3.

299 "If 75 percent": AMPAS, Mayer file, *Reader's Digest*, June 1947, "The Unchallenged King of Hollywood."

300 When Lillie Messinger: Fordin, p. 93.

300 He preferred two-handed games: Sam Marx, *Mayer and Thalberg*, pp. 164–65.

300 At Hillcrest: Gabler, p. 275.

301 "Don't put one thought": AMPAS, Mayer file, *Saturday Evening Post*, 11-16-63, "The Best Angel God Ever Saw."

301 "Mr. Mayer looked at us": Primack, p. 118.

301 When Walter Pidgeon: Foster, p. 203.

302 "Even the extras": Harmetz, pp. 42–43.

302 After a few days of shooting: Saville, p. 113.

303 "Don't sit over there": Aumont, p. 75.

304 *Variety* editorialized: Parish and Bowers, p. 42.

304 Ayres had been a pacifist: Bakewell, p. 122.

304 Mayer hurriedly recalled: Slide, pp. 20–21.

304 Ayres was granted 4-E status: Bakewell, p. 138.

305 When the government thought: The interviews with his peers are contained in L. B. Mayer FBI file, #7-2698, obtained under the Freedom of Information Act.

306 A friend of Mayer's: Charles Foster to S.E.

Chapter 11

PAGE

307 On June 26, 1942: The chronology and details of the aborted extortion demands derive from Mayer's FBI file and the coverage of the *L.A. Times* in Mayer's file at AMPAS.

312 To accommodate: Worsley, p. 17.

312 During one War Bond rally: Ibid., p. 18.

312 He once looked straight: Kirkwood, p. 116.

313 "Everybody says I'm a fool": BYU, Crowther papers, Wilson interview, 4-24-58, box 30.

313 Margaret blamed L.B.: Gabler, p. 392.

313 "I am leaving Margaret": Saville, p. 175.

314 One headline read: AMPAS, Mayer file, unsourced clipping, 6-13-44.

314 "I was just very aware": Gabler, p. 392.

314 There was a kind of reciprocal bond: I'm indebted to David Thomson for this insight.

314 Edwin Knopf, then the head: Elizabeth Horowitz to S.E.

315 Arthur Hornblow's chauffeur: Barzman, p. 118.

316 "Mayer often saw to it": BYU, Crowther papers, Reinhardt interview, box 32, f. 5.

316 "When a man": AMPAS, Mayer file, *New Theater*, 9–35, "Mayer of MGM."

316 Marilyn Maxwell was also thought: Evie Johnson to S.E.

317 Screenwriter Dorothy Kingsley: Terry Kingsley Smith to S.E.

317 In 1944, Ann Miller: Ann Miller, *High Life*, pp. 116–21.

319 When Vic Orsatti: Ibid., p. 148.

319 When Arthur Hornblow Jr.: Day, p. 117.

319 "He's stupid": Freedland, p. 215.

Chapter 12

PAGE

320 On the cast's first day: Harmetz, p. 11.

320 L.B. issued a memo: Foster, p. 209.

320 Roger Edens arranged: Mann, *Behind the Screen*, p. 274.

321 "I live and breathe": *Hollywood Reporter*, 70th anniversary, November 2000, p. 89.

321 When Horne was loaned out: Lena Horne, *Lena*, p. 164.

321 "He was the most honest man": Berg, *Kate*, p. 162.

322 After the first preview: Carey, p. 249.

322 "Look out for yourself": LeRoy, p. 135.

322 "If Mayer thought": Day, p. 101.

323 "If a man wants": Isherwood, *Diaries*, p. 67.

324 "You can visit the Hardys": USC, MGM Collection, *Chicago American*, 3-29-38, box 228.

324 Even Damon Runyon: USC, MGM Collection, file on *Judge Hardy's Children*, *L.A. Examiner*, 4-25-38.

325 "The best pictures": AMPAS, Mayer file, *American Weekly*, 6-8-58, "What Makes a Star."

325 "A boy may hate": Crowther, *Rajah*, p. 239.

325 The screenwriter William Ludwig: Server, p. 118.

326 Mayer called Seitz in: BYU, Crowther papers, Carey Wilson interview, 4-28-58, box 30.

327 This tic of Wilson's: Maas, p. 73.

327 Mayer agreed: Server, p. 118.

327 "We discovered": Ibid., p. 115.

328 "Mervyn LeRoy has got": Kobal, p. 641.

328 "Don't get overly dramatic": Hugh Fordin to S.E.

328 "The thing that astounded me": Davis, p. 8.

328 After Oz: Fordin, p. 8.

329 "Freed's talent": AMPAS, Lela Simone oral history.

329 Freed's office featured: Knox, p. 11.

330 "I have gone shopping": USC, Freed Collection, *Meet Me in St. Louis*, box 55, Benson to Freed, undated.

330 When Freed went to the Plaza Hotel: Fordin, p. 31.

330 When Judy Garland would see him: Betsy Blair to S.E.

330 a sense of zest and history: Sanders, pp. 313–14.

331 "a very *sexy* horn line": Friedhofer, p. 68.

331 Working on a level beneath: Bruskin, p. 58.

332 Mayer brought him over: *Films in Review*, February 1985, "Joe Pasternak."

332 "You never stopped studying": Reynolds, pp. 63–64.

334 Mayer exploded: Schwartz, p. 166.

334 "a great man": AMPAS, Mayer file, *L.A. Examiner*, 6-3-41.

334 when Hearst's health: Nasaw, p. 598.

335 Giannini vowed: Bonadio, pp. 260–61.

335 "She kissed all the children": Charles Foster to S.E.

335 Lawrence gradually: Foster, p. 162.

336 By 1941: Dumaux, p. 170.

336 She wrote Mayer: Sam Marx, *Mayer and Thalberg*, p. 147.

337 Mayer paid a visit: *Scarlet Street*, Spring 2001, "Picture Perfect: Hurd Hatfield."

338 Taylor was an MGM star: Ida Koverman speaks of her affection for Taylor in an April 14, 1948, letter to Larry Richey, HHPL, Ida Koverman correspondence, 1933–1954, box 116.

339 Frances Goodrich: Goodrich, p. 125.

340 "At MGM every picture": McGilligan, *Backstory 2*, p. 235.

342 He consulted Joe Mankiewicz: Leaming, p. 387.

342 A California state committee: Gerald Horne, *Class Struggle*, p. 69.

342 Likewise, in 1932: Staggs, p. 53.

343 "Are you ready": Affron, p. 291.

343 a 1938 public opinion poll: Lawrence Epstein, p. 107.

343 Likewise, public opinion polls: Hogan, pp. 258, 535.

343 "I don't think": Gabler, p. 374.

344 When Mankiewicz walked into: Geist, p. 113.

344 "He felt Judy Garland": BYU, Crowther papers, Marmorston interview, 4-29-58, box 30.

344 Mayer's response: Geist, p. 114.

344 Even Eddie Mannix: Sidney Franklin autobiography, p. 298.

345 "He projected himself into": BYU, Crowther papers, Marmorston interview, 4-29-58, box 30.

345 He worked for Pandro Berman: Tennessee Williams, *Selected Letters*, pp. 450–51.

346 Mayer proposed: Leggett, p. 89.

346 By the first week of February: Ibid., p. 94.

346 "No Jew can ever cheat an Armenian": Crowther, *Rajah*, p. 243.

346 "The money won't": AMPAS, Mayer file, *Saturday Evening Post*, 11-16-63, "The Best Angel God Ever Saw."

347 William Ludwig did some: USC, MGM script collection, *Human Comedy* file.

349 "I've got a horse in this race": AMPAS, Mayer file, *Saturday Evening Post*, 11-16-63, "The Best Angel God Ever Saw."

349 "I wouldn't say": McGilligan and Buhle, *Tender*, p. 339.

Chapter 13

PAGE

351 But when an assistant director: Worsley, p. 40.

351 The lab was instructed: Vidor, *Filmmaking*, p. 167.

353 One daily production report: Kaufman, p. 40.

353 "He was such a stickler": Thompson, p. 117.

354 Mayer also gave a horse: Rooney, *Life*, pp. 143–44.

354 Kelly was furious: Hirschorn, pp. 83–84.

355 "During the Communist": Ibid., pp. 112–13.

356 But Mayer decreed: Garnett, p. 257.

356 Irene Dunne: *Film Comment*, January-February 1980, "Irene Dunne," p. 30.

356 The last straw occurred: Dunne spoke of this episode to both Joe Yranski and David Chierichetti, who independently confirmed it for me.

357 "Lana Turner and Tony Martin": from transcripts in the author's collection.

357 He awkwardly announced: *L.A. Times Magazine*, 8-6-2000, "Artie Shaw Talking."

358 "I've been hearing stories": Lambert, *Shearer*, p. 274.

358 When Rooney and Ava Gardner got engaged: Rooney, *Life*, p. 164.

358 When Carole Lombard found out: Berdie Abrams to S.E.

358 "You've got to be very patient": Turner, *Lana*, p. 80.

359 In a memo: RCUTA, DOS to LBM, 7-15-41.

359 Experienced hands: *American Film*, July-August 1982, "Don Stewart in Exile," p. 36.

359 One New York publicist: Margaret O'Brien to S.E.

361 In 1942, Schary wanted to direct: McGilligan, *Film Crazy*, pp. 197–99.

362 According to Schary: Schary, p. 125.

363 At meetings of the Executive Committee: SHSW, Schary papers, box 107, f. 11–12. See meetings dated 1-6-43, 1-20-43, 12-15-42, 12-22-42, 5-6-42, and 1-6-43.

365 When a writer was assigned: Peary, p. 390.

365 Mayer remained conscious: BYU, Crowther papers, Marmorston interview, 4-29-58.

366 He didn't get back: AMPAS, Mayer file, *L.A. Times*, 12-26-44.

366 Although the two had never cared: Korda, p. 156.

366 As headquarters: Kulik, p. 283.

366 He hated the dinner parties: Korda, p. 174.

367 L.B. would always believe: Higham, *Merchant*, p. 332.

367 As of August 1947: Puttnam, pp. 162–63.

367 As long as Mayer: Troyan, p. 152.

368 While Thalberg was alive: Gavin Lambert to S.E.

368 After an initially unsuccessful marriage: Background for this section derives from an interview with Elizabeth Horowitz, Jesse Marmorston's daughter.

368 When they gave him a first edition: Flamini, *Thalberg*, p. 155.

369 "His vision was phenomenal": BYU, Crowther papers, Marmorston interview, 4-29-58.

370 He had the MGM wardrobe department: Dan Selznick to S.E.

371 If Edie knew about Bill's dalliances: Columbia, "Sisters of Celluloid," *Quest*, 1994.

371 More important, Bill Goetz: Behlmer, *Hathaway*, p. 201.

371 where he asked Edie to dance: Farber and Green, p. 52.

371 Selznick, under the impression: RCUTA, DOS to LBM, 7-31-46.

372 Bill was now: Deutsch, p. 110.

372 "a schlep with the filthiest mouth": Berg, *Kate*, p. 162.

373 "We've got to use": BYU, Crowther, Gottfried Reinhardt interview, box 32, f. 5.

373 One day an eighteen-year-old: Previn, pp. 19–20.

373 Clift found Mayer: Bosworth, p. 104.

374 The studio didn't seem: Kotsilibas-Davis and Loy, p. 192.

374 "It was even more": Franklin autobiography, p. 374. Other citations in this section are from the same source, pp. 375, 376, 378.

377 In 1947, Irene Mayer Selznick: Thomson, *Showman*, p. 503.

377 The last star: Bessette, pp. 57–58; other citations for this section involve pp. 60, 61, 73.

378 The first thing Green did: *Film Music Notebook*, Vol. 3, 1977, "John Green Interview," p. 24.

380 Mayer hated the movie: BYU, Crowther papers, Carey Wilson interview.

380 Mayer jabbed Montgomery: Audrey Totter to S.E.

381 Loew's still had only 135 theaters: Gomery, *Shared*, pp. 61–62.

381 When Berlin sold MGM: Fordin, pp. 219–20.

381 And by 1941: Schatz, p. 360.

Chapter 14

PAGE

382 When the Motion Picture Alliance: Roberts and Olson, p. 331.

383 McGuinness thought: Server, pp. 149–51.

383 The screenwriter George Oppenheimer: BYU, Crowther papers, Oppenheimer interview, box 25, f. 1.

383 The entertainingly insolent Raymond Chandler: Chandler, p. 131.

383 MGM was paying him: Cook, p. 159.

384 Mayer paid $25,000: AMPAS, Mayer file, Pearson clipping, 6-12-50.

384 Communism, he said: AMPAS, Mayer file, *L.A. Examiner*, 7-8-47; "MGM News," 7-11-47.

385 Attending was the A list: Hoover, Post-Pres. Individuals, box 113, Julius Klein file, Klein to Hoover, 9-17-47.

386 "People sucked up": BYU, Crowther papers, Strickling interview, box 32, f. 5.

386 Mayer suggested a trust fund: Selznick, p. 264.

386 A short time after: BYU, Crowther papers, Browning interview, 1-30-58, box 30.

387 "He wanted to find out more": SHSW, Schary papers, Mayer deposition, 3-10-48.

388 Cole had been working: Cook, p. 197.

388 "I had notions": SHSW, Schary papers, Mayer deposition, 3-10-48.

388 Cole said that he thought: Cole, p. 272.

389 "I have maintained": Mayer's testimony was retrieved from the Florida Atlantic University's Government Archives, with the help of my colleague Eliot Kleinberg.

391 Even Hearst felt: AMPAS, Mayer file, *Variety*, 10-30-47.

391 "I don't want to blow my own horn": HHPL, Westbrook Pegler papers, box 27, Mayer to Richard Berlin, 11-17-47.

393 Loew's theaters helped: Balio, *United Artists: The Company Built by the Stars*, p. 214.

393 Among those present at the Waldorf Conference: The roster of attendees is drawn from depositions given by Dore Schary, L. B. Mayer, and Eddie Mannix in SHSW, Schary papers.

393 Eric Johnston opened: The substance of Johnston's remarks was recalled by Mayer in a deposition of March 10, 1948, in SHSW, Schary papers.

394 According to one of the participants: BYU, Crowther papers, Schlaifer interview, box 30.

394 According to the recollections: Mannix deposition in SHSW, Schary papers, p. 96.

394 "Congress should give us": SHSW, Schary papers, Mayer deposition, 3-10-48.

394 "We were told": SHSW, Schary papers, Schary deposition, 3-17-48.

395 Mayer even claimed: SHSW, Schary papers, Mayer deposition, 3-10-48.

395 Unfortunately, as Schary would observe: SHSW, Schary papers, Schary deposition, 3-17-48.

395 "The overlords of the industry": *Nation*, 6-28-52, "Hollywood Meets Frankenstein," reprinted in Bromley, p. 172.

396 "I'll never forgive him": *Take One*, vol. 7, no. 8, July 1979, Gerald Peary and Patrick McGilligan, "Dore Schary."

396 He told Howard Strickling: SHSW, Schary papers, William Hebert to Dore Schary, 1-16-51.

396 Mayer remained reluctant: SHSW, Schary papers, Allenberg to Schary, 1-11-51.

396 Mayer took the stand: Cole, pp. 299–300.

397 "a group that sits": SHSW, Schary papers, Mayer deposition, 3-10-48.

398 "After I was taken off": Lambert, *On Cukor*, p. 254.

398 Jack Conway, Victor Saville: I'm indebted to Michael Sragow for sharing some of the fruits of his research from his forthcoming book on Victor Fleming.

399 Producer Edwin Knopf: Powell, *A Life*, pp. 529–30.

399 When Elia Kazan: Kazan, p. 307.

400 "The peak in film business": AMPAS, Mayer file, *L.A. Times*, 3-22-47.

400 When Carey Wilson told him: BYU, Crowther papers, Wilson interview, 4-22-58, box 30.

401 "We couldn't have Andy Hardy": AMPAS, Mayer file, *American Weekly*, 6-8-58.

402 "Something happens to your voice": Fordin, p. 257.

403 "I was wrong about that picture": *American Film*, March 1985, "Who Could Ask for Anything More," p. 73.

403 At the end of 1947: Selznick, p. 307.

404 Afterward, he buttonholed: Kazan, p. 345.

405 On *The Pirate*, for instance: Fordin, p. 212.

405 To hear Garland tell it: Evie Johnson to S.E.

406 Arthur Freed dismissed such talk: Kobal, p. 647.

406 Mayer thought of the most sensible person: Hepburn, p. 215.

406 "Judy Garland has made this studio": Hirschorn, p. 163.

407 "She loved L. B. Mayer": Luft, pp. 41–42.

407 Songwriter Harry Ruby: David Raksin to S.E.

408 But Capra had entered: McBride, *Capra*, pp. 536–40.

409 But the studio put him: Deal memo dated 4-25-44, addendum 1-27-48, courtesy of William Rosar.

409 L.B. personally bought: AMPAS, Mayer file, *Motion Picture Daily*, 2-24-48.

409 On a Sunday: Fordin, p. 254.

410 Schary told Mayer: Schary, pp. 173–74.

410 Bob Rubin: BYU, Crowther papers, Rubin interview, 3-14-55, box 25, f. 2.

411 When she heard the news: Reynolds, p. 262.

411 During the contract negotiations: Schary, p. 178.

411 "Don't trust him": Schary, pp. 179, 231.

412 When S. N. Behrman: BYU, Crowther papers, Behrman interview, box 32, f. 5.

412 Louella Parsons made: The wedding details are drawn primarily from clippings in AMPAS, Mayer file, among them *L.A. Mirror*, 12-4-48; *L.A. Daily News*, 12-7-48; *Hollywood Citizen-News*, 12-7-48.

413 Charles Feldman said: BYU, Crowther papers, Feldman interview, 11-21-58, box 27, f. 9.

413 Charles Moscowitz: BYU, Crowther papers, Moscowitz interview, 6-4-54.

413 Realizing that something besides: Margaret O'Brien to S.E.

415 S. N. Berhman ran into: BYU, Crowther papers, Behrman interview, box 32, f. 5.

Chapter 15

PAGE

416 "If you laugh now": Deutsch, p. 199.

416 "They had a tremendous number": SHSW, Schary papers, Schary seminar, 7-19-77, p. 31.

418 On Tuesday nights: Epstein, *Haunted*, p. 130.

418 after a preview: Fordin, p. 283.

419 "They keep telling me": Richard Brooks to S.E.

420 The next year: RKO grosses are from the C. J. Tevlin ledger, as enumerated by Richard Jewell in *Historical Journal of Film, Radio and Television*, vol. 14, no. 1, 1994.

420 As the studio was planning: *Film Music Notebook*, vol. 3, 1977, "John Green Interview," p. 25.

420 Mayer hated the script: Terry Kingsley Smith to S.E.

422 Throughout the auction: AMPAS, Mayer file, *L.A. Examiner*, 2-28-47; other citations for this section include the *L.A. Times* for 6-18-50, also at AMPAS, and MOMA, Mayer file, *Thoroughbred of California*, December 1976, "Louis B. Mayer, California Breeder of the Century."

422 A large portrait: Gabler, p. 285.

423 "You haven't gotten dirty": BYU, Crowther papers, Schary interview, 2-7-58, box 25, f. 3.

423 The minutes of the weekly meetings: All these are in SHSW, Schary papers, 8-27-48, 9-13-48, 10-12-48, 11-9-48, 11-23-48.

424 "My face is covered": SHSW, Schary papers, Schary to Mayer, 11-6-50.

425 "We had a good": SHSW, Schary papers, Schary seminar, 7-16-77.

425 Mayer signed a new: AMPAS, Mayer file, *Motion Picture Herald*, 7-30-49.

425 But a few months after that: AMPAS, Mayer file, *Hollywood Reporter*, 7-7-49.

426 "Before I left": SHSW, Schary papers, Lewin to Schary, 4-4-50.

426 Even Eddie Mannix: SHSW, Schary papers, Mannix to Schary, 5-19-50.

426 Frances Marion reported: Marion, p. 323.

427 "full of nasty": Grobel, p. 336.

427 After a meeting: Schary, pp. 233–34.

428 Schary demurred: SHSW, Schary papers, Schary seminar, 7-16-77.

429 Schary said he wanted to return it: BYU, Crowther papers, Schary interview, 2-7-58, box 25, f. 3.

429 Other people would benefit: Higham, *Merchant*, p. 349.

429 "It's just a few days": Schatz, p. 454.

429 Also enthusiastic: Goodrich, p. 183.

430 "You cannot believe in God": AMPAS, Mayer file, *L.A. Herald Express*, 4-13-50.

430 Only Schary, Bill Goetz: Schary, p. 220; support of Earl Warren is in Schary's proposal for the book in his files at SHSW.

431 When Clarence Brown: McGilligan, *Film Crazy*, p. 60.

431 Brown compromised: McGilligan, *Backstory* 2, p. 172.

431 Ralph Ellison said: Buhle and Wagner, p. 394.

432 After the screening: Crowe, p. 255.

432 "I don't know what it is": BYU, Crowther papers, Schary interview, 2-7-58, box 25, f. 3.

433 John Huston and Mayer: Grobel, pp. 159–60.

433 Then he eyed Huston: Huston, p. 135.

433 One Sunday, Mayer: Ibid., pp. 175–76.

434 Schenck said that since: Crowther, *Lion's*, p. 259.

434 "I cannot guarantee": SHSW, Schary papers, Schary to Mayer, 6-9-50.

434 "This is thoughts": Altman, p. 243.

435 Huston realized: Huston, pp. 177–78.

435 There was one further hurdle: Eels, p. 289.

435 Reinhardt asked for a meeting: BYU, Crowther papers, Reinhardt interview, box 32, f. 5.

436 One Sunday afternoon: Curtis, *Tony Curtis*, p. 103.

437 His grandson Jeffrey: Carey, p. 4.

437 Although at first confused: Levy, *King of Comedy*, p. 94.

437 Edie thought all this was: Dan Selznick to S.E.

438 "If I was married to Irene": Edward Epstein, *Portrait*, p. 81.

438 By the end of November 1950: SHSW, Schary papers, Schary to Mayer, 11-27-50.

439 L.B. began ranting: Bacon, p. 121.

439 "In 1907, a man": AMPAS, Mayer file, *L.A. Mirror*, 4-2-51.

440 "In terms of this ballet": Knox, p. 147.

441 Mayer responded coolly: AMPAS, Mayer file, *L.A. Times* and *L.A. Herald Examiner*, 3-3-51, 3-4-51.

441 Mayer was stunned: HHPL, Mayer correspondence, 1949–57, box 145, Mayer to Hoover, Mayer to MacArthur, both 4-11-51.

442 "Louie, what's wrong?": Crowther, *Lion's*, p. 298.

442 *Variety* picked it up: AMPAS, Mayer file, *Variety*, 4-9-51.

443 After a story conference: Schary, pp. 235–36.

443 "Most of the time": SHSW, Schary papers, Columbia University, Schary oral history, November 1958.

443 as *Variety* reported: NYPL, Mayer file, *Variety*, 5-30-51.

444 Robert Rubin: BYU, Crowther papers, Rubin interview, box 25, f. 2.

444 "By mutual agreement": AMPAS, Mayer file, *Variety*, 6-27-51.

445 "Louis' friends think": SHSW, Schary papers, Hopper columns, 4-12-51 and July 1951.

445 "It was an irreconcilable": BYU, Crowther papers, Schenck interview, box 25, f. 2.

Chapter 16

449 "Whatever antagonisms": Beauchamp, p. 363.

449 "Mayer . . . had a quality": BYU, Crowther papers, Wanger interview, box 32, f. 4.

449 "There's nothing wrong": AMPAS, Mayer file, *Hollywood Reporter*, 6-22-51.

450 Mayer promptly sold off: AMPAS, Mayer file, *Variety*, 6-27-51.

450 MGM was the only studio: BYU, Crowther papers, retirement plan, box 24, f. 5.

450 a secretary who retired: June Caldwell and Roger Mayer to S.E.

451 Even Hedda Hopper: All these column items are from a précis made up by a somewhat paranoid Dore Schary of Hopper's mentions of his name in SHSW, Schary papers.

451 Four months after Mayer left: SHSW, Schary papers, undated Schary letter to Schenck.

452 the 90 million people: U.S. Census, Historical Statistics of the United States, 1960.

452 MGM treasurer Charles Moscowitz: AMPAS, Mayer file, *Variety*, 5-27-53.

452 "We got into a lot of talk": BYU, Crowther papers, Mayer deposition, box 23, f. 4.

453 Shortly afterward: AMPAS, Mayer file, *Motion Picture Herald*, 1-12-52.

453 "Nothing could have shown": Powell, *Million Dollar Movie*, p. 200.

454 "Schary carries on": BYU, Crowther papers, Mankiewicz interview, box 32, f. 5.

456 "By what right": Altman, pp. 237–38.

456 He nursed a grudge: Tornabene, p. 345.

459 "The old gray Mayer": Goodman, pp. 451–52.

459 "He fabricated a whole situation": Geist, p. 222.

459 "Regarding Chappell release": Koretz collection, undated but 1952.

459 When Harry Sherman: Tuska, *Filming of the West*, p. 487.

459 "You mark what I tell you": Crowther, *Rajah*, p. 301.

460 "She won't listen": Carey, p. 278.

460 "That's a lie!" Crowther, *Rajah*, p. 304.

461 "Mr. Mayer expected": Farber and Green, p. 61.

461 "They take in each other's wash": Dan Selznick to S.E.

461 "I believe in showmanship": AMPAS, Mayer file, *L.A. Examiner*, 11-20-52; *Hollywood Citizen-News*, 11-21-52.

461 "When you have a rare orchid": Bessette, p. 91.

462 "The ice cold air": AMPAS, Lela Simone oral history.

464 "The fact was that the producer": *Film Comment*, March-April 1975, "John Houseman: The Producer's Signature," p. 21.

464 In 1949, the first full year: Finler, *Hollywood Story*, p. 35.

466 "I have more brains": BYU, Crowther papers, Schoenfeld interview, box 23, f. 14.

467 Some of L.B.'s friends: HHPL, K. T. Keller correspondence, box 107.

467 He enrolled Herbert Hoover: HHPL, Mayer correspondence, 1949–57, box 145, 4-8-52, 5-8-52.

467 He bred a Preakness winner: MOMA, Mayer file, *Thoroughbred of California*, December 1976, "Louis B. Mayer, California Breeder of the Century."

467 Soon after leaving MGM: This section derives from NYPL, *Variety*, 5-7-52, as well as AMPAS, Mayer file, *Variety*, 5-7-52.

468 Mayer even had some talks: AMPAS, Mayer file, *Variety*, 6-6-52.

468 He did pull off a couple of deals: AMPAS, Mayer file, *L.A. Times*, 12-1-51.

468 There was the occasional speech: AMPAS, Mayer file, *L.A. Herald Express*, 2-4-52.

468 Mayer's old secretary: BYU, Crowther papers, Browning to Crowther, 1-30-58, box 30.

469 Mayer's contract specified: BYU, Crowther papers, Margolin to Crowther, date obscured, box 30.

470 Mayer's presence on the Cinerama board: Balio, *American Film Industry*, p. 428.

471 Lawyer Edward Weisl remembered: BYU, Crowther papers, box 31, f. 4.

471 By March 1953: AMPAS, Mayer file, *Variety*, 3-18-53.

472 They all came: USC, *L.A. Examiner* files, Ida Koverman file.

Chapter 17

PAGE

473 Since the picture was bound to be: Koretz files, Korda to Koretz, 1-3-55.

474 He spent several hours: William F. Buckley Jr. letter to S.E.

474 "He was the best agent": McGilligan, *Backstory*, p. 259.

475 "there has appeared": Behlmer, *Memo*, p. 417.

476 "There are two, and only two": RCUTA, DOS to LBM, 10-1-53.

477 By this time: AMPAS, Mayer file, *Variety*, 10-14-53.

477 "In all the years": BYU, Crowther papers, undated Katz interview, box 30.

478 "He was always great and liberal": BYU, Crowther papers, Schary interview, box 25, f. 3.

478 "Once he left MGM": Gabler, p. 413.

479 Mayer reverted to the passive: Clarence Brown to S.E.

479 The stories Freed could have told Mayer: Hugh Fordin to S.E.

481 Mayer even allowed his name: BYU, DeMille papers, box 1168, f. 4.

481 "The more McCarthy yells": AMPAS, Mayer file, *Variety*, 4-7-54, 4-13-54.

481 "He walked right by Judy": Farber and Green, p. 62.

481 On May 21, 1955: AMPAS, Mayer file, *L.A. Herald Examiner*, 5-22-55.

481 "Your aunt is dying": Farber and Green, p. 65.

482 In June of 1955: Sikov, p. 399.

482 "We have so few real stars today": AMPAS, Mayer file, *American Weekly*, 6-8-58, "What Makes a Star."

483 In the middle of 1956: AMPAS, Mayer file, *L.A. Herald Examiner*, 6-22-56.

483 "I am not surprised": HHPL, L. B. Mayer correspondence, 1949–57, Mayer to Hoover, 7-31-56, box 145.

484 And there was all the East Coast nepotism: Altman, p. 260.

484 Nick now refused: SHSW, Schary papers, Schary seminar, 7-17-77, p. 38.

484 For the last year: Fordin, p. 396.

484 A little more than a month: SHSW, Schary papers, Ellerbrock to Schary, 1-1-57, box 108, f. 3.

484 Loew's gave Schary: Schary, p. 315.

484 Schary stated in *The Hollywood Reporter*: Bromley, p. 179.

485 "If the right people": AMPAS, Mayer file, *L.A. Herald Express*, 12-19-56.

485 Jack Warner wanted: USC, Warner collection, Warner to Mayer, 1-29-57, box 68, f. 1.

486 A management consulting team: Crowther, *Rajah*, p. 318.

486 "I will move my bed": Ibid.

486 "It was a very pleasant day": Koretz Collection, Mayer to Koretz, 7-15-57.

486 In the second week: Crowther, *Rajah*, p. 319.

487 On July 23: AMPAS, Mayer file, *L.A. Mirror-News*, 7-23-57.

487 Even an old partisan: AMPAS, Mayer file, *Hollywood Reporter*, 7-29-57.

488 On a deeper level: BYU, Crowther papers, Selznick interview, 1-10-58, box 25, f. 3.

488 Sam Goldwyn watched: Berg, *Goldwyn*, p. 484.

489 Publicly, the doctors professed: AMPAS, Mayer file, *L.A. Times*, 8-29-57.

489 Two weeks later: AMPAS, Mayer file, *L.A. Mirror*, 8-29-57.

489 Hoover again sent him: HHPL, Mayer correspondence, 1949–57, Mayer to Hoover, 8-3-57, box 145.

490 A look of panic: Crowther, *Rajah*, p. 326.

491 "Whatever the treatment was": Elizabeth Horowitz to S.E.

491 Also keeping faith: BYU, Crowther papers, Selznick interview, 1-10-58, box 25, f. 3.

491 On his last full day of life: Gabler, p. 424.

491 Irene called Edie: Columbia, "Sisters of Celluloid," *Quest*, 1994.

491 Near the end: BYU, Crowther papers, Strickling interview, box 23, f. 14.

491 Lorena sent out telegrams: HHPL, Mayer correspondence, 1949–57, Mayer to Hoover, 10-29-57, box 145.

492 "Watch it come down": June Caldwell to S.E.

492 The Los Angeles newspapers: AMPAS, Mayer file.

493 Irene and Kate Hepburn: BYU, Crowther papers, Strickling interview, 4-27-58, box 30.

493 Edie attended without Bill Goetz: Farber and Green, p. 63.

493 Spencer Tracy rose: BYU, Crowther papers, box 30.

Epilogue

PAGE

500 In fact, much of Louis's estate: AMPAS, Mayer file, *Variety*, 3-31-61.

500 The estate was originally estimated: AMPAS, Mayer file, *L.A. Times*, 1-11-58.

501 Mayer had promised her: BYU, Crowther papers, Marmorston interview, box 30.

501 The remainder of the estate: AMPAS, Mayer file, *L.A. Herald Examiner*, 12-3-57.

502 its value was gradually set: AMPAS, Mayer file, *Hollywood Citizen-News*, 8-22-59, 6-21-62.

502 *The Motion Picture Daily*: AMPAS, Mayer file, *Motion Picture Daily*, 10-30-57, p. 3.

503 After *Sayonara*, Goetz's pictures: The best analysis of William Goetz's career is contained in Allen Eyles, "Universal and International," in *Focus on Film #30*, June 1978.

503 The price was $350,000: Shawn Levy, *King of Comedy*, p. 231.

503 In 1961, the federal government: AMPAS, Mayer file, *Variety*, 3-31-61.

503 In August 1958: AMPAS, Mayer file, *L.A. Herald Examiner*, 6-25-58.

503 In December 1961: AMPAS, Mayer file, *L.A. Times*, 12-17-61.

505 "hideous and vicious . . . pathetic and pitiable": BYU, Crowther papers, Crowther to Wills, 8-12-59, box 29.

505 "I wrote about a monster": BYU, Crowther papers, Crowther letter, 4-25-60, box 29.

505 "it is filled with a lot of names": Koretz Collection, Steger to Koretz, 7-25-60.

505 "His ravings and tears": AMPAS, Mayer file, *Hollywood Reporter*, 1-22-82.

506 "one of the sideshows of our time": *Film Comment*, Fall 1970, p. 74.

507 By 1978: Balio, *American*, pp. 552–53.

507 "Mayer was truly a great administrator": BYU, Crowther papers, Charles Feldman interview, box 27, f. 9.

508 "Are you Irving?": Lambert, *Shearer*, p. 352.

508 "who already in 1936": Perelman, p. 206.

508 "I give you my word of honor": AMPAS, Robert Vogel oral history.

510 There was only about $200,000: Columbia, "Sisters of Celluloid," *Quest*, 1994; *Architectural Digest*, April 1992, "Prolific Producer's Holmby Hills Collection."

511 "the single most important human being": MOMA, Mayer file, *Boston Globe*, 6-14-88.

511 The Mayer Foundation donated: AMPAS, Mayer file, *Variety*, 1-29-81.

511 But when Edie was interred: Columbia, "Sisters of Celluloid," *Quest*, 1994.

512 In the spring of 1986: Gomery, *Shared Pleasures*, p. 270.

515 "a set of values curiously parallel": AMPAS, Mayer file, *L.A. Times*, 4-6-60, "The Book Report."

515 William Saroyan, who loathed him: AMPAS, Mayer file, *Saturday Evening Post*, 11-16-63, "The Best Angel God Ever Saw."

BIBLIOGRAPHY

Aberdeen, J. A. *Hollywood Renegades*. Los Angeles: Cobblestone, 2000.

Adams, T. R. *Tom and Jerry: Fifty Years of Cat and Mouse*. New York: Crescent, 1991.

Adamson, Joe. *Tex Avery: King of Cartoons*. New York: Da Capo, 1990.

Affron, Charles. *Lillian Gish: Her Legend, Her Life*. New York: Scribner's, 2001.

Aitken, Roy, and Al P. Nelson. *The Birth of a Nation Story*. Middleburg, Va.: Denlinger, 1965.

Allvine, Glendon. *The Greatest Fox of Them All*. New York: Lyle Stuart, 1969.

Allyson, June, with Frances Spatz Leighton. *June Allyson*. New York: Putnam, 1982.

Altman, Diana. *Hollywood East: Louis B. Mayer and the Origins of the Studio System*. New York: Birch Lane, 1992.

Arce, Hector. *Groucho*. New York: Putnam, 1979.

Astor, Mary. *A Life on Film*. New York: Delacorte, 1971.

Aumont, Jean-Pierre. *Sun and Shadow*. New York: Norton, 1977.

Bach, Steven. *Dazzler: The Life and Times of Moss Hart*. New York: Knopf, 2001.

Bacher, Lutz. *Max Ophuls in the Hollywood Studios*. New Brunswick: Rutgers University Press, 1996.

Bacon, James. *Hollywood Is a Four Letter Town*. Chicago: Regnery, 1976.

Bakewell, William. *Hollywood Be Thy Name*. Metuchen, N.J.: Scarecrow Press, 1991.

Balcon, Michael. *A Lifetime of Films*. London: Hutchinson, 1969.

Balio, Tino. *United Artists: The Company Built by the Stars*. Madison: University of Wisconsin Press, 1976.

Balio, Tino (ed.). *The American Film Industry*. Madison: University of Wisconsin Press, 1985.

Barbera, Joe. *My Life in 'Toons*. Atlanta: Turner, 1994.

Barrier, Michael. *Hollywood Cartoons*. New York: Oxford, 1999.

Barrios, Richard. *Screened Out*. New York: Routledge, 2003.

Barrymore, Lionel (with Cameron Shipp). *We Barrymores*. New York: Appleton-Century-Crofts, 1951.

Barsacq, Leon (ed. by Elliot Stein). *Caligari's Cabinet and Other Grand Illusions*. Boston: New York Graphic Society, 1976.

Barzman, Norma. *The Red and the Blacklist*. New York: Thunder's Mouth, 2003.

Basquette, Lina. *Lina: DeMille's Godless Girl*. Fairfax: Denlinger's, 1990.

Basten, Fred. *Glorious Technicolor*. South Brunswick: A. S. Barnes, 1980.

Baxter, John. *Buñuel*. London: Fourth Estate, 1994.

Beauchamp, Cari. *Without Lying Down*. New York: Scribner's, 1997.

Behlmer, Rudy. *W. S. Van Dyke's Journal: White Shadows in the South Seas and Other Van Dyke on Van Dyke*. Lanham: Scarecrow Press, 1996.

Behlmer, Rudy (ed.). *Henry Hathaway: An Oral History*. Lanham: Scarecrow Press, 2001.

——. *Memo from David O. Selznick*. New York: Viking, 1972.

Behrman, S. N. *People in a Diary*. Boston: Little, Brown, 1972.

Bellamy, Madge. *A Darling of the Twenties*. Vestal: Vestal Press, 1989.

Belton, John. *Widescreen Cinema*. Cambridge: Harvard University Press, 1992.

Bendersky, Joseph W. *The Jewish Threat: Anti-Semitic Politics of the U.S. Army*. New York: Basic, 2000.

Berg, A. Scott. *Goldwyn*. New York: Knopf, 1989.

——. *Kate Remembered*. New York: Putnam, 2003.

Berkman, Edward. *The Lady and the Law*. Boston: Little, Brown, 1976.

Bernds, Edward. *Mr. Bernds Goes to Hollywood*. Lanham: Scarecrow Press, 1999.

Bernstein, Matthew. *Walter Wanger: Hollywood Independent*. Berkeley: University of California Press, 1994.

Bessette, Roland L. *Mario Lanza: Tenor in Exile*. Portland: Amadeus, 1999.

Blake, Michael. *Lon Chaney: The Man Behind the Thousand Faces*. Vestal: Vestal Press, 1993.

——. *A Thousand Faces*. Vestal: Vestal Press, 1995.

Blesh, Rudi. *Keaton*. New York: Macmillan, 1966.

Bodeen, DeWitt. *From Hollywood*. South Brunswick: A. S. Barnes, 1976.

——. *More from Hollywood*. South Brunswick: A. S. Barnes, 1977.

Bonadio, Felice. *A. P. Giannini: Banker of America*. Berkeley: University of California Press, 1994.

Bosworth, Patricia. *Montgomery Clift*. New York: Harcourt, Brace & Jovanovich, 1978.

Boutelle, Sara Holmes. *Julia Morgan—Architect*. New York: Abbeville, 1995.

Bowers, Ronald. *The Selznick Players*. South Brunswick: A. S. Barnes, 1976.

Brady, Frank. *Citizen Welles*. New York: Scribner's, 1989.

Brenner, Marie. *Great Dames: What I Learned from Older Women*. New York: Crown, 2000.

Bromley, Carl (ed.). *Cinema Nation: The Best Writing on Film from The Nation*. New York: Thunder's Mouth/Nation Books, 2000.

Brown, Kelly R. *Florence Lawrence, the Biograph Girl*. Jefferson: McFarland, 1999.

Brownlow, Kevin. *Napoleon*. New York: Knopf, 1983.

———. *The Parade's Gone By*. New York: Knopf, 1968.

Bruskin, David. *Behind the Three Stooges: The White Brothers*. Los Angeles: Directors Guild of America, 1993.

Budd, Mike (ed.). *The Cabinet of Dr. Caligari*. New Brunswick: Rutgers University Press, 1990.

Buhle, Paul, and Dave Wagner. *Radical Hollywood*. New York: New Press, 2002.

Calder-Marshall, Arthur. *The Innocent Eye*. New York: Harcourt, Brace & World, 1966.

Cannom, Robert. *Van Dyke and the Mythical City Hollywood*. Culver City: Murray & Gee, 1948.

Capra, Frank. *The Name Above the Title*. New York: Macmillan, 1971.

Carey, Gary. *All the Stars in Heaven*. New York: Dutton, 1981.

Carringer, Robert. *The Making of Citizen Kane* (revised edition). Berkeley: University of California Press, 1996.

Chandler, Raymond (ed. by Dorothy Gardiner and Katherine Sorley Walker). *Raymond Chandler Speaking*. Berkeley: University of California Press, 1997.

Chaplin, Saul. *The Golden Age of Movie Musicals and Me*. Norman: University of Oklahoma Press, 1994.

Chierichetti, David. *Hollywood Costume Design*. New York: Harmony, 1976.

———. *Mitchell Leisen: Hollywood Director*. Los Angeles: Photoventures, 1995.

Clarke, Mae (ed. by James Curtis). *Featured Player*. Santa Barbara: Santa Teresa Press, 1996.

Coffee, Lenore. *Storyline: Recollections of a Hollywood Screenwriter*. London: Cassell, 1973.

Coghlan Jr., Frank. *They Still Call Me Junior*. Jefferson: McFarland, 1993.

Cole, Lester. *Hollywood Red*. Palo Alto: Ramparts, 1981.

Columbia, "Sisters of Celluloid," *Quest* (1994).

Cook, Bruce. *Dalton Trumbo*. New York: Scribner's, 1977.

Cooper, Jackie (with Dick Kleiner). *Please Don't Shoot My Dog*. New York: Morrow, 1981.

Cooper, Miriam (with Bonnie Herndon). *Dark Lady of the Silents*. Indianapolis: Bobbs-Merrill, 1973.

Cooper, Stephen. *Full of Life*. New York: North Point, 2000.

Cotta Vaz, Mark, and Craig Barron. *The Invisible Art*. San Francisco: Chronicle, 2002.

Cotten, Patricia Medina. *Laid Back in Hollywood*. Los Angeles: Belle, 1998.

Crafton, Donald. *The Talkies*. New York: Scribner's, 1997.

Crawford, Joan (with Jane Kesner Ardmore). *Portrait of Joan*. Garden City: Doubleday, 1962.

Crowe, Cameron. *Conversations with Wilder*. New York: Knopf, 1999.

Crowther, Bosley. *Hollywood Rajah: The Life and Times of Louis B. Mayer*. New York: Holt, 1960.

————. *The Lion's Share.* New York: Dutton, 1957.

Curtis, James. *James Whale: A New World of Gods and Monsters.* London: Faber & Faber, 1998.

Curtis, Tony, with Barry Paris. *Tony Curtis.* New York: Morrow, 1993.

Curtiss, Thomas Quinn. *Von Stroheim.* New York: Farrar, Straus & Giroux, 1971.

Custen, George F. *Twentieth Century's Fox.* New York: Basic, 1997.

Dance, Robert, and Bruce Robertson. *Ruth Harriet Louise and Hollywood Glamour Photography.* Berkeley: University of California Press, 2002.

Dardis, Tom. *Keaton: The Man Who Wouldn't Lie Down.* New York: Scribner's, 1979.

Davies, Marion (ed. by Pamela Pfau and Kenneth Marx). *The Times We Had: Life with William Randolph Hearst.* Indianapolis: Bobbs-Merrill, 1975.

Davis, Ronald L. *The Glamour Factory.* Dallas: Southern Methodist University Press, 1993.

Day, Beth. *This Was Hollywood.* London: Sidgwick & Jackson, 1960.

DeMille, Cecil B. *Autobiography.* Englewood Cliffs: Prentice Hall, 1959.

De Toth, André (ed. by Anthony Slide). *De Toth on De Toth.* London: Faber & Faber, 1996.

Deutsch, Armand. *Me and Bogie.* New York: Putnam, 1991.

Dewey, Donald. *James Stewart: A Biography.* Atlanta: Turner, 1996.

Dick, Bernard. *The Merchant Prince of Poverty Row.* Lexington: University Press of Kentucky, 1993.

Dietz, Howard. *Dancing in the Dark.* New York: Quadrangle/Times Books, 1974.

Dmytryk, Edward. *Odd Man Out: A Memoir of the Hollywood Ten.* Carbondale: Southern Illinois University Press, 1996.

Doherty, Thomas. *Pre-Code Hollywood.* New York: Columbia University Press, 1999.

Douglas, Kirk. *The Ragman's Son.* New York: Simon & Schuster, 1988.

Dowd, Nancy (with David Shepard). *King Vidor: A Director's Guild of America Oral History.* Metuchen: Scarecrow Press, 1988.

Drew, William M. *Speaking of Silents.* Vestal: Vestal Press, 1989.

Dumaux, Sally A. *King Baggot.* Jefferson: McFarland, 2002.

Dunning, John. *On the Air.* New York: Oxford, 1998.

Eames, John Douglas. *The MGM Story.* New York: Crown, 1982.

Easton, Carol. *No Intermissions: The Life of Agnes de Mille.* Boston: Little, Brown, 1996.

Edelman, Rob, and Audrey Kupferberg. *Angela Lansbury: A Life on Stage and Screen.* Secaucus: Citadel, 1999.

Eels, George. *Hedda and Louella.* New York: Putnam, 1972.

Epstein, Edward Z. *Portrait of Jennifer.* New York: Simon & Schuster, 1995.

Epstein, Lawrence J. *The Haunted Smile: The Story of Jewish Comedians in America.* New York: Public Affairs, 2001.

Essoe, Gabe. *The Films of Clark Gable.* New York: Citadel, 1970.

Everson, William K. *Classics of the Horror Film.* Secaucus: Citadel, 1974.

Eyman, Scott. *Mary Pickford.* New York: Donald I. Fine, 1990.

——. *The Speed of Sound*. New York: Simon & Schuster, 1997.

Fairbanks Jr., Douglas. *A Hell of a War*. New York: St. Martin's, 1993.

——. *The Salad Days*. New York: Doubleday, 1988.

Farber, Stephen, and Marc Green. *Hollywood Dynasties*. New York: Ballantine, 1985.

Fawkes, Richard. *Opera on Film*. London: Duckworth, 2000.

Felleman, Susan. *Botticelli in Hollywood*. New York: Twayne, 1997.

Fenin, George, and William K. Everson. *The Western*. New York: Grossman, 1973.

Fields, Ronald. *W. C. Fields by Himself*. Englewood Cliffs: Prentice Hall, 1973.

Finch, Christopher, and Linda Rosenkrantz. *Gone Hollywood: The Movie Colony in the Golden Age*. Garden City: Doubleday, 1979.

Finler, Joel. *The Hollywood Story*. New York: Crown, 1988.

——. *The Movie Directors Story*. New York: Crescent, 1985.

Fitzgerald, F. Scott (ed. by Matthew J. Bruccoli). *A Life in Letters*. New York: Scribner's, 1994.

Flamini, Roland. *Scarlett, Rhett and a Cast of Thousands*. New York: Collier, 1978.

——. *Thalberg: The Last Tycoon and the World of MGM*. New York: Crown, 1994.

Fleischer, Richard. *Just Tell Me When to Cry*. New York: Carroll & Graf, 1993.

Fordin, Hugh. *The World of Entertainment: The Freed Unit at MGM*. Garden City: Doubleday, 1975.

Forslund, Bengt. *Victor Sjostrom: His Life and Work*. New York: New York Zoetrope, 1988.

Foster, Charles. *Stardust and Shadows*. Toronto: Dundurn, 2000.

Franklin, Sidney A. (with Kevin Brownlow). "We Laughed and We Cried" (unpublished autobiography).

Freedland, Michael. *The Warner Bros*. New York: St. Martin's, 1983.

Friedhofer, Hugo (ed. by Linda Danly). *The Best Years of His Life*. Lanham: Scarecrow Press, 1999.

Friedrich, Otto. *City of Nets*. New York: Harper & Row, 1986.

Fuller, Samuel. *A Third Face*. New York: Knopf, 2002.

Gabler, Neil. *An Empire of Their Own*. New York: Crown, 1988.

Gardner, Gerald. *The Censorship Papers*. New York: Dodd, Mead, 1987.

Garnett, Tay. *Light Your Torches and Pull Up Your Tights*. New Rochelle: Arlington House, 1973.

Garrett, Betty (with Ron Rapoport). *Betty Garrett and Other Songs*. Lanham: Madison, 1998.

Geduld, Harry M., and Ronald Gottesman. *Sergei Eisenstein and Upton Sinclair: The Making and Unmaking of Que Viva Mexico!* Bloomington: Indiana University Press, 1970.

Gehman, Geoff. *Down but Not Quite Out in Hollow-Weird: A Documentary in Letters of Eric Knight*. Lanham: Scarecrow Press, 1998.

Geist, Kenneth. *Pictures Will Talk: The Life and Films of Joseph L. Mankiewicz*. New York: Scribner's, 1978.

Giddins, Gary. *Bing Crosby: A Pocketful of Dreams*. Boston: Little, Brown, 2001.

Gilbert, Julie. *Opposite Attraction: The Many Lives of Erich Maria Remarque and Paulette Goddard*. New York: Pantheon, 1995.

Gish, Lillian (with Ann Pinchot). *The Movies, Mr. Griffith, and Me*. Englewood Cliffs: Prentice Hall, 1969.

Goldenson, Leonard. *Beating the Odds*. New York: Scribner's, 1991.

Gomery, Douglas. *The Hollywood Studio System*. New York: St. Martin's, 1986.

——. *Shared Pleasures*. Madison: University of Wisconsin Press, 1992.

Goodman, Ezra. *The Fifty Year Decline and Fall of Hollywood*. New York: Simon & Schuster, 1961.

Goodrich, David L. *The Real Nick and Nora*. Carbondale: Southern Illinois University Press, 2001.

Gottfried, Martin. *Balancing Act: The Authorized Biography of Angela Lansbury*. New York: Kensington, 2000.

Grady, Billy. *The Irish Peacock*. New Rochelle: Arlington House, 1972.

Griffith, Richard. *The Movie Stars*. Garden City: Doubleday, 1970.

Grobel, Lawrence. *The Hustons*. New York: Scribner's, 1989.

Guiles, Fred Lawrence. *Hanging On in Paradise*. New York: McGraw-Hill, 1975.

——. *Marion Davies*. New York: McGraw-Hill, 1972.

Gussow, Mel. *Darryl F. Zanuck: Don't Say Yes Until I Finish Talking*. Garden City: Doubleday, 1971.

Gutner, Howard. *Gowns by Adrian*. New York: Abrams, 2001.

Hake, Sabine. *Popular Cinema of the Third Reich*. Austin: University of Texas Press, 2001.

Hambly, John, and Patrick Downing. *The Art of Hollywood*. London: Thames, 1979.

Hampton, Benjamin. *History of the American Film Industry*. New York: Dover, 1970 (reprint of 1931 edition).

Harmetz, Aljean. *The Making of The Wizard of Oz*. New York: Delta, 1989.

Harvey, Stephen. *Directed by Vincente Minnelli*. New York: Harper & Row, 1989.

Haskin, Byron (ed. by Joe Adamson). *Byron Haskin*. Metuchen: Scarecrow Press, 1984.

Haver, Ronald. *David O. Selznick's Hollywood*. New York: Knopf, 1980.

Hay, Peter. *MGM: When the Lion Roars*. Atlanta: Turner, 1991.

Heisner, Beverly. *Hollywood Art*. Jefferson: McFarland, 1990.

Henabery, Joseph. *Before, In and After Hollywood*. Lanham: Scarecrow Press, 1997.

Hepburn, Katharine. *Me: Stories of My Life*. New York: Knopf, 1991.

Herman, Jan. *A Talent for Trouble*. New York: Putnam's, 1995.

Heymann, C. David. *Liz: An Intimate Biography of Elizabeth Taylor*. New York: Birch Lane, 1995.

Higham, Charles. *Cecil B. DeMille*. New York, Scribner's, 1973.

——. *Charles Laughton: An Intimate Biography*. Garden City: Doubleday, 1976.

——. *Merchant of Dreams: Louis B. Mayer, MGM, and the Secret Hollywood*. New York: Donald I. Fine, 1993.

———. *Orson Welles: The Rise and Fall of an American Dreamer*. New York: St. Martin's, 1985.

Hirschfeld, Al. *Hirschfeld's Hollywood*. New York: Abrams, 2001.

Hirschhorn, Clive. *Gene Kelly*. New York: St. Martin's, 1984.

Hogan, David J. (ed.). *The Holocaust Chronicle*. Lincolnwood: Publications International, 2000.

Hopkinson, Peter. *Split Focus*. London: Hart-Davis, 1969.

Horne, Gerald. *Class Struggle in Hollywood*. Austin: University of Texas Press, 2001.

Horne, Lena (with Richard Schickel). *Lena*. Garden City: Doubleday, 1965.

Huston, John. *An Open Book*. New York: Knopf, 1980.

Hutchisson, James (ed.). *A DuBose Heyward Reader*. Athens: University of Georgia Press, 2003.

Isherwood, Christopher. *Diaries*, vol. 1. New York: HarperCollins, 1996.

Jacobs, George, and William Stadiem. *Mr. S: My Life with Frank Sinatra*. New York: HarperCollins, 2003.

Jensen, Jytte (ed.). *Benjamin Christensen: An International Dane*. New York: Museum of Modern Art, 1999.

Jessel, George. *So Help Me*. Cleveland: World, 1944.

Jobes, Gertrude. *Motion Picture Empire*. Hamden, Conn.: Archon Books, 1966.

Johnson, Nunnally. *The Letters of Nunnally Johnson*. New York: Knopf, 1981.

Josephy Jr., Alvin M. *A Walk Towards Oregon*. New York: Knopf, 2000.

Kalmus, Herbert. *Mr. Technicolor*. Absecon: MagicImage, 1993.

Kanfer, Stefan. *Groucho: The Life and Times of Julius Henry Marx*. New York: Knopf, 2000.

Kashner, Sam, and Nancy Schoenberger. *A Talent for Genius*. New York: Villard, 1994.

Kaufman, Gerald. *Meet Me in St. Louis*. London: British Film Institute, 1994.

Kazan, Elia. *A Life*. New York: Knopf, 1988.

Keaton, Buster (with Charles Samuels). *My Wonderful World of Slapstick*. New York: Da Capo (reprint), 1982.

Keaton, Eleanor, and Jeffrey Vance. *Buster Keaton Remembered*. New York: Abrams, 2001.

Kelly, Andrew. *Filming All Quiet on the Western Front*. London: Tauris, 1998.

Kirkwood, Pat. *The Time of My Life*. London: Robert Hale, 1999.

Knox, Donald. *The Magic Factory*. New York: Praeger, 1973.

Kobal, John. *People Will Talk*. New York: Knopf, 1985.

Kobler, John. *Damned in Paradise: The Life of John Barrymore*. New York: Atheneum, 1977.

Korda, Michael. *Charmed Lives*. New York: Random House, 1979.

Koszarski, Richard. *An Evening's Entertainment*. New York: Scribner's, 1990.

———. *The Man You Loved to Hate*. New York: Oxford University Press, 1983.

———. *Von: The Life and Films of Erich von Stroheim*. New York: Limelight, 2001.

Kotsilibas-Davis, James. *The Barrymores: The Royal Family in Hollywood*. New York: Crown, 1981.

Kotsilibas-Davis, James, and Myrna Loy. *Myrna Loy: Being and Becoming*. New York: Knopf, 1987.

Kulik, Karol. *Alexander Korda: The Man Who Could Work Miracles*. New Rochelle: Arlington House, 1975.

Lally, Kevin. *Wilder Times*. New York: Holt, 1996.

Lambert, Gavin. *Nazimova*. New York: Knopf, 1997.

——. *Norma Shearer*. New York: Knopf, 1990.

——. *On Cukor*. New York: Capricorn, 1973.

Lamour, Dorothy (with Dick McInnes). *My Side of the Road*. Englewood Cliffs: Prentice Hall, 1980.

Lardner Jr., Ring. *I'd Hate Myself in the Morning*. New York: Thunder's Mouth Press/Nation Books, 2000.

LaSalle, Mick. *Complicated Women*. New York: St. Martin's, 2000.

Lasky, Betty. *RKO: The Biggest Little Major of Them All*. Englewood Cliffs: Prentice Hall, 1984.

Lasky, Jesse L. *Whatever Happened to Hollywood?* New York: Funk & Wagnalls, 1975.

Laurents, Arthur. *Original Story By*. New York: Knopf, 2000.

Lawford, Lady May (with Buddy Galon). *Mother Bitch*. Brookline Village: Brandon, 1986.

Lawrence, Jerome. *Actor: The Life and Times of Paul Muni*. New York: Samuel French, 1975.

Leaming, Barbara. *Katharine Hepburn*. New York: Crown, 1995.

Lee, Betty. *Marie Dressler: The Unlikeliest Star*. Lexington: University of Kentucky Press, 1997.

Leese, Elizabeth. *Costume Design in the Movies*. New York: Dover, 1991.

Leff, Leonard. *Hitchcock and Selznick*. New York: Weidenfeld & Nicolson, 1987.

Leff, Leonard, and Jerold Simmons. *The Dame in the Kimono*. New York: Grove Weidenfeld, 1990.

Leggett, John. *A Daring Young Man*. New York: Knopf, 2002.

Lennig, Arthur. *Stroheim*. Lexington: University Press of Kentucky, 2000.

Lerner, Alan Jay. *The Street Where I Live*. New York: Norton, 1978.

LeRoy, Mervyn (with Dick Kleiner). *Mervyn LeRoy: Take One*. New York: Hawthorn, 1974.

Levy, Emanuel. *George Cukor: Master of Elegance*. New York: Morrow, 1994.

Levy, Shawn. *King of Comedy: The Life and Art of Jerry Lewis*. New York: St. Martin's, 1996.

Lewis, David (ed. by James Curtis). *The Creative Producer*. Metuchen: Scarecrow Press, 1993.

Lillie, Beatrice (with James Brough). *Every Other Inch a Lady*. Garden City: Doubleday, 1972.

Longstreet, Stephen. *All Star Cast*. New York: Crowell, 1977.

Loos, Anita. *Kiss Hollywood Good-Bye*. New York: Viking, 1974.

——. *The Talmadge Girls*. New York: Viking, 1978.

Louvish, Simon. *Man on the Flying Trapeze*. New York: Norton, 1997.

Luft, Lorna. *Me and My Shadows*. New York: Pocket, 1998.

Maas, Frederica Sagor. *The Shocking Miss Pilgrim*. Lexington: University Press of Kentucky, 1999.

MacAdams, William. *Ben Hecht: The Man Behind the Legend*. New York: Scribner's, 1990.

Madsen, Axel. *Stanwyck*. New York: HarperCollins, 1994.

——. *William Wyler*. New York: Crowell, 1973.

Maltin, Leonard. *The Art of the Cinematographer*. New York: Dover, 1978.

——. *The Great Movie Shorts*. New York: Bonanza, 1972.

——. *Hollywood: The Dream Factory*. New York: Popular Library, 1976.

——. *Of Mice and Magic*. New York: McGraw-Hill, 1980.

Maltin, Leonard, and Richard W. Bann. *The Little Rascals: The Life and Times of Our Gang* (second edition). New York: Crown, 1992.

Mankiewicz, Joseph L. (with Gary Carey). *More About All About Eve*. New York: Random House, 1972.

Mann, William J. *Behind the Screen*. New York: Viking, 2001.

——. *Wisecracker*. New York: Viking, 1998.

Manso, Peter. *Brando*. New York: Hyperion, 1994.

Marion, Frances. *Off with Their Heads*. New York: Macmillan, 1972.

Marx, Arthur. *Goldwyn*. New York: Norton, 1976.

Marx, Groucho. *The Groucho Phile*. Indianapolis: Bobbs-Merrill, 1976.

Marx, Groucho (with Richard Anobile). *The Marx Bros. Scrapbook*. New York: Darien House, 1973.

Marx, Sam. *A Gaudy Spree*. New York: Franklin Watts, 1987.

——. *Mayer and Thalberg: The Make-Believe Saints*. New York: Random House, 1975.

Mast, Gerald. *The Comic Mind* (second edition). Chicago: University of Chicago Press, 1979.

Maturi, Richard, and Mary Buckingham Maturi. *Beverly Bayne, Queen of the Movies*. Jefferson: McFarland, 2001.

McBride, Joseph. *Frank Capra: The Catastrophe of Success*. New York: Simon & Schuster, 1992.

——. *Hawks on Hawks*. Berkeley: University of California Press, 1982.

McBrien, William. *Cole Porter*. New York: Knopf, 1998.

McCarthy, Todd. *Howard Hawks: The Grey Fox of Hollywood*. New York: Grove, 1997.

McClelland, Doug. *Forties Film Talk*. Jefferson: McFarland, 1992.

McDougal, Dennis. *The Last Mogul*. New York: Crown, 1998.

——. *Privileged Son: Otis Chandler and the Rise and Fall of the L.A. Times Dynasty*. Cambridge: Perseus, 2001.

McGilligan, Patrick. *Film Crazy: Interviews with Hollywood Legends*. New York: St. Martin's, 2000.

——. *Fritz Lang: The Nature of the Beast*. New York: St. Martin's, 1997.

——. *George Cukor: A Double Life*. New York: St. Martin's, 1991.

McGilligan, Patrick (ed). *Backstory*. Berkeley: University of California Press, 1986.

——. *Backstory 2*. Berkeley: University of California Press, 1991.

McGilligan, Patrick, and Paul Buhle. *Tender Comrades*. New York: St. Martin's, 1997.

Meade, Marion. *Buster Keaton: Cut to the Chase*. New York: HarperCollins, 1995.

Medavoy, Mike, with Josh Young. *You're Only as Good as Your Next One*. New York: Atria, 2002.

Meryman, Richard. *Mank: The Wit, World and Life of Herman Mankiewicz*. New York: Morrow, 1978.

Miller, Ann (with Norma Lee Browning). *Miller's High Life*. Garden City: Doubleday, 1972.

Miller, Frank. *Censored Hollywood*. Atlanta: Turner, 1994.

——. *MGM Posters*. Atlanta: Turner, 1994.

Minnelli, Vincente (with Hector Arce). *I Remember It Well*. Garden City: Doubleday, 1974.

Mitchell, Greg. *The Campaign of the Century*. New York: Random House, 1992.

Mordden, Ethan. *The Hollywood Musical*. New York: St. Martin's, 1981.

Morley, Sheridan. *Tales from the Hollywood Raj*. New York: Viking, 1984.

Mosley, Leonard. *Zanuck: The Rise and Fall of Hollywood's Last Tycoon*. Boston: Little, Brown, 1984.

Muller, Eddie. *Dark City Dames*. New York: HarperCollins, 2001.

Napley, Sir David. *Rasputin in Hollywood*. London: Weidenfeld & Nicolson, 1990.

Nasaw, David. *The Chief*. Boston: Houghton Mifflin, 2000.

Nelson, Al P., and Mel Jones. *A Silent Siren Song*. New York: Cooper Square, 2000.

Newquist, Roy. *Conversations with Joan Crawford*. Secaucus: Citadel, 1980.

Nielsen, Mike, and Gene Mailes. *Hollywood's Other Blacklist*. London: BFI Publishing, 1995.

Noble, Peter. *Hollywood Scapegoat*. London: Fortune, 1950.

Nolan, Frederick. *Lorenz Hart*. New York: Oxford University Press, 1994.

Oderman, Stuart. *Lillian Gish: A Life on Stage and Screen*. Jefferson: McFarland, 2000.

O'Leary, Liam. *Rex Ingram: Master of the Silent Cinema*. Dublin: Academy Press, 1980.

Paine, Albert Bigelow. *Life and Lillian Gish*. New York: Macmillan, 1932.

Paris, Barry. *Garbo*. New York: Knopf, 1994.

Parish, James Robert, and Ronald Bowers. *The MGM Stock Company*. New Rochelle: Arlington House, 1973.

Peary, Danny. *Close-Ups*. New York: Workman, 1978.

Peary, Gerald, and Danny Peary. *The American Animated Cartoon*. New York: Dutton, 1980.

Perelman, S. J. *Don't Tread on Me: Selected Letters*. New York: Knopf, 1987.

Peters, Margot. *The House of Barrymore*. New York: Knopf, 1990.

Phillips, Gene D. *Creatures of Darkness: Raymond Chandler, Detective Fiction and Film Noir*. Lexington: University of Kentucky Press, 2000.

Pizzitola, Louis. *Hearst Over Hollywood*. New York: Columbia University Press, 2002.

Powell, Michael. *A Life in the Movies*. New York: Knopf, 1987.

———. *Million Dollar Movie*. New York: Random House, 1995.

Preminger, Otto. *Preminger: An Autobiography*. Garden City: Doubleday, 1977.

Previn, André. *No Minor Chords*. New York: Doubleday, 1991.

Price, Victoria. *Vincent Price: A Daughter's Biography*. New York: St. Martin's, 1999.

Prideaux, James. *Knowing Hepburn and Other Curious Experiences*. Boston: Faber & Faber, 1996.

Primack, Bert (ed.). *The Ben Hecht Show*. Jefferson: McFarland, 1993.

Puttnam, David. *Movies and Money*. New York: Knopf, 1998.

Ralston, Esther. *Some Day We'll Laugh*. Metuchen, N.J.: Scarecrow Press, 1985.

Ramsaye, Terry. *A Million and One Nights*. New York: Simon & Schuster, 1926.

Rapf, Maurice. *Back Lot: Growing Up with the Movies*. Lanham: Scarecrow Press, 1999.

Reinhardt, Gottfried. *The Genius*. New York: Knopf, 1979.

Reynolds, Debbie (with David Patrick Columbia). *Debbie: My Life*. New York: Morrow, 1988.

Rivkin, Allen, and Laura Kerr (ed.). *Hello, Hollywood*. Garden City: Doubleday, 1962.

Roberts, Jerry (ed.). *Mitchum: In His Own Words*. New York: Limelight, 2000.

Roberts, Randy, and James S. Olson. *John Wayne: American*. New York: Free Press, 1995.

Robinson, David. *Chaplin: His Life and Art*. New York: McGraw-Hill, 1985.

Robinson, Edward G. (with Leonard Spigelgass). *All My Yesterdays*. New York: Hawthorn, 1973.

Rooney, Mickey. *I.E.: An Autobiography*. New York: Putnam, 1965.

———. *Life Is Too Short*. New York: Villard, 1991.

Rosenberg, Bernard, and Harry Silverstein. *The Real Tinsel*. New York: Macmillan, 1970.

Rotha, Paul. *Robert J. Flaherty: A Biography*. Philadelphia: University of Pennsylvania Press, 1983.

Sanders, James. *Celluloid Skyline*. New York: Knopf, 2001.

Saroyan, Aram. *William Saroyan*. San Diego: Harcourt Brace Jovanovich, 1983.

Saville, Victor (with Roy Moseley). *Evergreen: Victor Saville in His Own Words*. Carbondale: Southern Illinois University Press, 2000.

Schary, Dore. *Heyday*. Boston: Little, Brown, 1979.

Schatz, Thomas. *The Genius of the System*. New York: Pantheon, 1988.

Schickel, Richard. *D. W. Griffith: An American Life*. New York: Simon & Schuster, 1984.

Schulberg, Budd. *Moving Pictures: Memories of a Hollywood Prince*. New York: Stein & Day, 1981.

Schwartz, Nancy Lynn. *The Hollywood Writer's War.* New York: Knopf, 1982.

Scott, Evelyn F. *Hollywood: When Silents Were Golden.* New York: McGraw-Hill, 1972.

Selznick, Irene Mayer. *A Private View.* New York: Knopf, 1983.

Sennett, Robert S. *Setting the Scene: The Great Hollywood Art Directors.* New York: Abrams, 1994.

Server, Lee. *Screenwriter.* Pittstown: Main Street Press, 1987.

Seton, Marie. *Sergei M. Eisenstein.* New York: Wyn, 1951.

Sherman, Eric. *Directing the Film.* Boston: Little, Brown, 1976.

Sherman, Vincent. *Studio Affairs.* Lexington: University Press of Kentucky, 1996.

Shipman, David. *Judy Garland.* New York: Hyperion, 1992.

Shipman, Nell. *The Silent Screen and My Talking Heart.* Boise: Boise State University Press, 1987.

Shorris, Sylvia, and Marion Abbott Bundy. *Talking Pictures.* New York: New Press, 1994.

Sikov, Ed. *On Sunset Boulevard.* New York: Hyperion, 1998.

Silver, Alain, and James Ursini. *What Ever Happened to Robert Aldrich?: His Life and His Films.* New York: Limelight, 1995.

Sinclair, Upton. *Upton Sinclair Presents William Fox.* Los Angeles: Sinclair, 1933.

Skal, David, and Elias Savada. *Dark Carnival: The Secret World of Tod Browning.* New York: Anchor, 1995.

Skretvedt, Randy. *Laurel and Hardy: The Magic Behind the Movies.* Beverly Hills: Past Times, 1994.

Slide, Anthony. *Actors on Red Alert.* Lanham: Scarecrow Press, 1999.

Smith, Amanda (ed.). *Hostage to Fortune: The Letters of Joseph P. Kennedy.* New York: Viking, 2001.

Soares, André. *Beyond Paradise: The Life of Ramon Novarro.* New York: St. Martin's, 2002.

Spears, Jack. *Hollywood: The Golden Era.* Secaucus: A. S. Barnes, 1971.

Sperling, Cass Warner, and Cork Millner. *Hollywood Be Thy Name.* Rocklin: Prima, 1994.

Staggs, Sam. *All About All About Eve.* New York: St. Martin's, 2000.

Steen, Mike. *Hollywood Speaks.* New York: Putnam, 1974.

Stempel, Tom. *Framework.* New York: Continuum, 1988.

Stenn, David. *Bombshell: The Life and Death of Jean Harlow.* New York: Doubleday, 1993.

Sterling, Bryan B., and Frances N. Sterling. *Will Rogers in Hollywood.* New York: Crown, 1984.

Stewart, Donald Ogden. *By a Stroke of Luck!* New York: Paddington, 1975.

Swanson, H. N. *Sprinkled with Ruby Dust.* New York: Warner, 1989.

Swindell, Larry. *Charles Boyer: The Reluctant Lover.* Garden City: Doubleday, 1983.

——. *Screwball: The Life of Carole Lombard.* New York: Morrow, 1975.

——. *Spencer Tracy.* New York: New American Library, 1969.

Sylvester, Christopher. *The Grove Book of Hollywood.* New York: Grove, 1998.

Talmey, Allene. *Doug and Mary and Others*. New York: Macy-Masius, 1927.

Tapert, Annette. *The Power of Glamour*. New York: Crown, 1998.

Taylor, John Russell. *Strangers in Paradise*. New York: Holt, Rinehart & Winston, 1983.

Telushkin, Rabbi Joseph. *The Golden Land: The Story of Jewish Immigration to America*. New York: Harmony, 2002.

Thomas, Bob. *Astaire: The Man, the Dancer*. New York: St. Martin's, 1984.

———. *Clown Prince of Hollywood*. New York: McGraw-Hill, 1990.

———. *Joan Crawford*. New York: Simon & Schuster, 1978.

———. *Selznick*. Garden City: Doubleday, 1970.

———. *Thalberg: Life and Legend*. Garden City: Doubleday, 1969.

———. *Walt Disney*. New York: Hyperion, 1994.

Thomas, Tony. *Music for the Movies*. South Brunswick: A. S. Barnes, 1973.

Thompson, Frank. *Great Christmas Movies*. Dallas: Taylor, 1998.

Thomson, David. *Rosebud: The Story of Orson Welles*. New York: Knopf, 1996.

———. *Showman: The Life of David O. Selznick*. New York: Knopf, 1992.

Tormé, Mel. *It Wasn't All Velvet*. New York: Viking, 1988.

Tornabene, Lyn. *Long Live the King*. New York: Putnam, 1976.

Troyan, Michael. *A Rose for Mrs. Miniver: The Life of Greer Garson*. Lexington: University Press of Kentucky, 1999.

Trumbo, Dalton (ed. by Helen Manfull). *Additional Dialogue*. New York: Evans, 1970.

Turk, Edward Baron. *Hollywood Diva*. Berkeley: University of California Press, 1998.

Turner, George E. *The Cinema of Adventure, Romance and Terror*. Hollywood: ASC Press, 1989.

Turner, Lana. *Lana: The Lady, the Legend, the Truth*. New York: Dutton, 1982.

Tuska, Jon. *Close-Up: The Contract Director*. Metuchen: Scarecrow Press, 1976.

———. *The Filming of the West*. Garden City: Doubleday, 1976.

———. *The Vanishing Legion: A History of Mascot Pictures*. Jefferson: McFarland, 1982.

Yallop, David. *The Day the Laughter Stopped*. New York: St. Martin's, 1976.

Vidor, King. *On Filmmaking*. New York: David McKay, 1972.

———. *A Tree Is a Tree*. New York: Harcourt, Brace, 1953.

Vieira, Mark. *Sin in Soft Focus*. New York: Abrams, 1999.

Viertel, Salka. *The Kindness of Strangers*. New York: Holt, Rinehart & Winston, 1969.

Villeco, Tony. *Silent Stars Speak*. Jefferson: McFarland, 2001.

von Sternberg, Josef. *Fun in a Chinese Laundry*. New York: Macmillan, 1965.

Wagner, Walter. *You Must Remember This*. New York: Putnam, 1975.

Walker, Alexander. *Dietrich*. New York: Harper & Row, 1984.

———. *Garbo*. New York: Macmillan, 1980.

Wallace, David. *Hollywoodland*. New York: St. Martin's, 2002.

Wapshott, Nicholas. *Carol Reed*. New York: Knopf, 1994.

Warren, Patricia. *British Film Studios*. London: Batsford, 2001.

Watkins, T. H. *The Hungry Years: A Narrative History of the Great Depression in America*. New York: Holt, 1999.

Watts, Stephen (ed.). *Behind the Screen: How Films Are Made.* New York: Dodge, 1938.

Webb, Michael (ed.). *Hollywood: Legend and Reality.* Boston: Little, Brown, 1986.

Welles, Orson, and Peter Bogdanovich. *This is Orson Welles.* New York: HarperCollins, 1992.

Wellman, William. *A Short Time for Insanity.* New York: Hawthorn, 1974.

Williams, Esther (with Digby Diehl). *The Million Dollar Mermaid.* New York: Simon & Schuster, 1999.

Williams, Tennessee. *The Selected Letters of Tennessee Williams.* New York: New Directions, 2000.

Winters, Ralph. *Some Cutting Remarks.* Lanham: Scarecrow Press, 2001.

Worsley, Wallace (ed. by Charles Ziarko). *From Oz to E.T.: Wally Worsley's Half-Century in Hollywood.* Lanham: Scarecrow Press, 1997.

Young, Freddie (with Peter Busby). *Seventy Light Years.* London: Faber & Faber, 1999.

Young, Jeff. *Kazan—The Master Director Discusses His Films.* New York: Newmarket, 1999.

Young, Jordan. *Let Me Entertain You.* Beverly Hills: Moonstone, 1988.

Zimmer, Jill Schary. *With a Cast of Thousands.* New York: Stein & Day, 1963.

Zinnemann, Fred. *A Life in the Movies.* New York: Scribner's, 1992.

Zollo, Paul. *Hollywood Remembered.* New York: Cooper Square, 2002.

INDEX

Page numbers in *italics* refer to illustrations.

Abrams, Berdie, 216, 358
Academy Awards, 138
  LBM and, 117, 439
  statuette of, 209, 210
Academy of Motion Picture Arts and Sciences,
    439
  salary cuts recommended by, 179, 180
  unions and, 117–18, 180
actors:
  appearing at LBM's Haverhill theaters,
    33–34
  in 1918 Hollywood, 54
  percentage deals for, 456–57, 465, 485
  unions and, 117, 240–41
actors, MGM, 1, 3
  black, 218, 320, 321, 431, 436
  classes offered to, 4, 291, 311, 332–33, 340–41
  exodus of, 436
  in MGM merger, 83–84
  obligations of, 4, 292
  option renewal and, 291
  sexuality and, 4–6, 131, 132–34, 193, 292–93,
    303, 331, 421
  see also stars, star system, MGM; *specific
    actors*
Adams, Maude, 33
Adam's Rib, 292, 425
Adorée, Renée, 61, 78, 79, 111, 132
Adrian, 153, 162, 213–15, 243, 264, 303
Adventures of Robin Hood, The, 257
Agee, James, 349
Aitken, Harry and Roy, 41–42
Alco Films, 43, 44
alcoholism, 6, 165–67, 185, 186, 190, 215, 336, 359
Alexander (Alex) theater, 91
All Quiet on the Western Front, 304

Allyson, June, 5, 290, 417
Alvord, Ellsworth, 453
American Feature Film Company, 39–42
American Film Institute, Louis B. Mayer
    Foundation and, 511
American in Paris, An, 10, 427, 438, 440, 462
American Legion, threatened movie boycotts
    of, 392–93, 394
American Red Cross, 1940 MGM rally for,
    279
American Romance, An, 365
Ames, Preston, 210
Anchors Aweigh, 303, 331
Andy Hardy series, 1, 3, 8, 9, 219, 323–27, 358,
    400, 401, 432, 439, 473
  cast of, 324, 325, 326
  costs of, 324–25, 326
  scripts for, 323–24, 325, 326, 327
  symbolism of, 324, 358
Anita Stewart Productions, Inc., 50–53
Annie Get Your Gun, 406, 418
Annie Laurie, 99, 139
anti-Semitism:
  in American society, 342–43
  of Italy's Fascist government, 274
  in Los Angeles, 63, 204, 342, 343
  movie moguls and, 49, 63, 96, 152, 163, 335,
    342–43
  Nazism and, 198, 204, 278
  in Russia, 17–18, 203
Any Number Can Play, 423–24
Arab, The, 84, 95, 96
Arbuckle, Fatty, 63, 76, 86
Arlen, Harold, 328
Aronson, Al, 103, 105, 106
Arrouge, Marti, 367, 461, 483

Arsene Lupin, 156
Asphalt Jungle, The, 427, 464
Assignment in Brittany, 304
Astaire, Adele, 39, 331
Astaire, Fred, 331, 332, 402, 405, 499, 515
Atonement of Gösta Berling, The, 104–5, 125
Aubrey, James, 506, 507
Aumont, Jean-Pierre, 303–4
Authors League, 205
Avery, Tex, 273
Ayres, Lew, 4, 7, 304

Babes in Arms, 246, 328
Babes on Broadway, 330–31
Bach, Steven, 509
Bad and the Beautiful, The, 454, 463
Baggott, King, 335, 336
Bainter, Fay, 8
Baker, Jack, 269
Balaban, Barney, 395, 408
Balaban & Katz, 237, 239, 304
Balcon, Michael, 231, 253–54, 492
Band Wagon, The, 10, 462
Bank of America, investigation of, 335
Barbera, Joe, 273, 274, 303, 403
Barker, Reginald, 61, 90
Barkleys of Broadway, The, 10, 402, 403
Barrett, Mary Ellin, 127, 241
Barretts of Wimpole Street, The, 157, 225, 227
Barrymore, Ethel, 12, 378, 423
Barrymore, John, 12, 53, 108, 188, 232, 517
Barrymore, Lionel, 9, 12, 108, 179, 188, 232,
    248–49, 291, 304, 324, 364, 517
Bartholomew, Freddie, 224
Barton Fink, 12
Bataan, 356, 362
Bates, Jeanette, 311
Battleground, 418, 425, 443
Bayne, Beverly, 44, 45
Beard, J. A., 412
Beebe, Lucius, 135
Beery, Wallace, 12, 61, 180, 220, 222–23, 262, 360,
    363
Behrman, S. N., 156, 157, 182, 295–96, 300, 412,
    415
Belasco, David, 26, 66, 113, 157
Bell, Monta, 98, 120
Bellamy, Ralph, 7
Benchley, Robert, 156, 272–73
Ben-Hur (1925), 99–110, 112, 337
    cast of, 99, 100, 101, 102–3, 104, 107, 118, 132,
    309
    chariot race of, 107–9
    costs of, 99, 101, 102, 103, 106, 107, 109
    directors of, 99, 100, 101, 102, 103, 104, 105,
    106–7, 108–9
    Goldwyn and, 71, 72, 77, 78, 84, 99–101, 106
    LBM and, 100, 101, 102–3, 104, 105–6, 107, 108,
    130

locations and sets for, 99, 100, 102, 103, 105,
    106, 107–8, 109, 110
    Thalberg and, 100–101, 104, 108, 109
Ben-Hur (1959), 110, 505
Bennett, Constance, 149
Bennett, Joan, 198, 320, 371
Benson, Sally, 330, 352, 363
Berkeley, Busby, 407, 412
Berle, Milton, 34, 418
Berlin, Irving, 127, 381
Berlin, Richard, 392
Berman, Pandro, 228, 239, 316, 338, 345, 363,
    364, 504
Bern, Paul, 156, 222
    death of, 170, 222, 308
Bernays, Edward, 222
Bernstein, David, 143
Bernstein, Leonard, 403
Best Years of Our Lives, The, 374, 380, 387
Beverly Hills, Calif., 199
Bey, Turhan, 287, 291–92, 357, 445
Big Parade, The, 111–12, 118, 124, 132, 138, 402–3,
    425
Big Store, The, 279, 280, 348
Bioff, Willie, 239–41
Biograph, 49
Birth of a Nation, The, 44, 52, 61
    distribution of, 41–42
Blackboard Jungle, 463
Blair, Betsy, 322, 330, 331, 335, 427
Blithe Spirit, 363, 374
Blossom Time, 459, 469, 477, 486, 500
Boardman, Eleanor, 90–91, 133, 134
Boheme, La, 113, 124, 139
Bolger, Ray, 328
Bond, Ward, 356
Booth, Elmer, 56
Booth, Margaret, 56, 64, 66, 70, 92, 142, 187, 213,
    231, 375, 378, 398, 504, 512
Born to Dance, 229–30
Borzage, Frank, 98, 278
Boston, Mass., 19, 27, 46
Boston American, 47
Boston Opera, 35
Bow, Clara, 70
Bowes, Edward, 99, 100
Boyer, Charles, 198–99
Boys Town, 256, 360
Boy with Green Hair, The, 420
Brabin, Charles, 84, 99–100, 101, 103, 106
Brackett, Charles, 193, 302, 424, 439
Brando, Marlon, 404
Brecher, Irving, 119, 257, 258, 301, 311, 352, 353,
    360–61
Breen, Joe, 189, 190, 276, 277, 342–44, 380
Brewster, Eugene, 116
Brewster's Millions, 40
Brice, Fannie, 248
Briegleb, William, 312

Brigadoon, 457
Brin, Herbert, 297
Brisbane, Arthur, 47, 108, 115
Briskin, Sam, 488
Broadway Melody of 1940, 246
Broadway Rhythm, 317
Broadway Theater (Lawrence, Mass.), 36
Broadway to Hollywood, 156
Bronson, Betty, 107
Bronston, Samuel, 504
Brooks, Rand, 260, 291
Brooks, Richard, 409, 419
Brown, Clarence, 7, 113–14, 115, 157, 189, 197,
    265, 280–81, 338, 347, 374–76, 431, 479, 491
Brown, David, 128, 478
Brown, Harry Joe, 181
Brown, Nacio Herb, 327
Browne, George, 239–41
Browning, Florence, 57–58, 70, 143, 387, 468–69
Browning, Tod, 151–52
Brownlow, Kevin, 61, 100, 133, 134
Brulatour, Jules, 240
Buchman, Frank, 278
Buckley, William F., Jr., 473–74
Burns, George, 34, 312
Burns, Lillian, *see* Sidney, Lillian Burns
Bushman, Francis X., 44–45, 48, 104, 106, 107,
    308–9
Butler, Hugo, 327, 396
Butler, Jean Rouverol, 323–24, 327, 396

Cabanne, Christy, 101, 103, 106–7
Cabinet of Dr. Caligari, The, 71
Cabin in the Sky, 320, 321, 330
Caldwell, June, 220, 315, 316, 368, 444, 504
Calling Dr. Gillespie, 304
Cameraman, The, 165
cameramen, 117
Cameron, Don, 268
Cameron, Robert, 51
Camille, 228, 229, 237
Canada, Canadians:
    Jewish migration to, 18
    LBM's generosity to, 301–2, 310–11
    Mayer family in, *see* Saint John, New
        Brunswick
    at MGM, 301–2, 311
Capitol Theater (New York City), 78, 324
Capra, Frank, 208, 373, 408
Carey, Harry, 232
Caron, Leslie, 329, 455, 463, 503
Carré, Ben, 210
Carroll, Harrison, 216
cartoons, MGM, 273–74, 483
Cary, Diana Serra, 335, 336
Catholicism, Catholics, 413, 414, 466
    LBM and, 342, 423
Catholic War Veterans, 393
Catledge, Turner, 202

Cerf, Bennett, 206
Chalk Garden, The, 481–82
Champ, The, 174
Champion, Gower, 378, 440
Champion, Marge, 340–41, 378, 440
Chandlee, Esme, 216, 217
Chandler, Harry, 118, 136, 200
Chaney, Lon, 68, 78, 89, 113, 122, 123, 451, 483
Chaplin, Charlie, 10, 45, 48, 86, 134, 165, 200,
    221, 232, 275–76, 347, 393, 469
    LBM and, 60, 108, 164
Chaplin, Charles, Jr., 469
Chaplin, Mildred Harris, 60, 61
Charisse, Cyd, 329, 332, 340, 405, 462–63
Chester, C. M., 248
Chevalier, Maurice, 167, 174
chicken soup, at MGM commissary, 90, 187–88
China Seas, 155–56, 159, 182, 226, 229
Christensen, Benjamin, 123
CinemaScope, 469
Cinematograph Act (1928), 251
Cinerama, 469–72
    financing of, 470–71
    sale of, 471–72
Citizen Kane, 333–34
Clift, Montgomery, 373–74
Clock, The, 348, 372
Cochrane, Robert, 46, 68
Coffee, Lenore, 67, 92–93, 157, 226–27, 230
Cohan, George M., 330, 331
Cohen, Emanuel, 244
Cohn, Harry, 10, 57, 179, 180, 193, 198, 202, 208,
    240, 241, 298, 301, 315, 355, 365, 408, 430,
    445, 452, 458, 475, 477
Cohn, Joe, 84, 89, 94, 98, 99, 108, 119, 133–34,
    148, 157, 245, 288, 339, 363, 401, 420, 424,
    432, 504, 508
Colbert, Claudette, 198, 312
Cold War, 385
Cole, Lester:
    blacklist and, 395, 396
    HUAC and, 387, 388–89, 390, 391
Collins, Richard, 349
Colman, Ronald, 159, 174, 258
Colonial Theater (Haverhill, Mass.), 16, 34–35,
    36, 39, 40
Columbia, 10, 178, 179, 239, 240, 262, 450,
    468
Columbia, David Patrick, 405, 510
Comden, Betty, 402, 406, 425
    MGM musicals and, 331, 402
Committee for the First Amendment, 392
Communist Party, Communism, 180, 197, 361
    and HUAC investigations, 387–92
    Jews and, 201, 342
    LBM and, 200, 349, 355, 384–85, 390–92,
        394–97, 416, 426, 430, 433, 468, 481
    movie industry and, 254, 295, 355, 387–97,
        416, 426

Comrade X, 391
Confessions of a Nazi Spy, 278
Conquest, 198, 210–11
Considine, John, 361
Conway, Jack, 398
Coogan, Jackie, 72, 83, 84, 334–35
Coolidge, Calvin, 85, 87, 137
Cooper, Gary, 232, 258, 312
Cooper, Jackie, 165–66, 178, 183, 223, 224
Cooper, Merian, 179, 180, 470, 471
Corbaley, Kate, 64, 138, 153, 186, 226, 299–300
Cosmopolitan, 114
Cosmopolitan Pictures, 71, 143
    MGM and, 78, 84, 114–17, 227
    Warners and, 227
Coughlin, Charles, 343
Cowan, Ada, 24, 230
Coward, Noel, 363, 374
Craig, James, 339
Crawford, Joan, 8, 131, 135, 149, 158, 191, 197, 208,
    214, 220, 241, 262, 264, 289, 344, 479, 517
Crosby, Bing, 262, 474
Crossfire, 409, 420
Crowd, The, 120, 138, 226
Crowd Roars, The, 159, 160
Crowther, Bosley, 334, 445, 478
    LBM biography of, 505, 509
Cukor, George, ix, 157, 160, 183, 221, 225, 264,
    292, 398, 464
    Gone With the Wind and, 259, 260
    homosexuality of, 133, 303
Culver City, Calif., 2, 71
Culver City Historical Society, 155
Cummings, Ida Mayer (sister), 19, 38, 62, 151,
    296, 469, 494, 501
    Jewish Home for the Aged and, 297, 508
Cummings, Jack, 47, 239, 289, 360, 388, 461,
    481–82, 489, 490, 501
    Freed unit and, 331–32
    LBM and, 86, 239, 331–32
Cummings, Nathan, 27

Daily Variety, 240, 241
Dana-Farber Cancer Institute, Louis B. Mayer
    Research Laboratory of, 511
Dangerous Age, The, 66
Daniels, William, 120
Danker, Danny, 413
Dassin, Jules, 271, 293–94, 362
David Copperfield, 183, 212, 230
Davies, Marion, 71, 84, 86, 95, 114–15, 153, 227
Davis, Frank, 475, 485
Davis, Jerry, 290
Davis, Nancy, 370, 416, 454, 458–59
Dawn, Norman, 70
Day, Richard, 305
Day at the Races, A, 237
Deep Cliff Farm, 270
de Mille, Agnes, 63

DeMille, Cecil B., 40, 53, 93, 106, 117–18, 136,
    141, 164, 182, 185, 214, 249, 262, 475–76, 482
de Mille, William, 62, 63
Democrats, Democratic Party, 460
    and 1934 California gubernatorial race,
    200–203
Depression, Great, 3, 146, 152, 227, 231, 324, 380,
    400
Desire Me, 380, 398
Destry Rides Again, 332
Deutsch, Armand, 8, 372, 381, 401, 413, 416, 420,
    430
Devil Is a Sissy, The, 223
Dietrich, Marlene, 312
Dietz, Howard, 71, 94, 127, 192, 325
Dillon, Josephine, 148
Dinner at Eight, 157, 191, 192, 210, 259
directors, Louis B. Mayer Productions and, 56,
    59–60, 61, 62–63, 66–67, 78, 83
directors, MGM, 1, 66, 99, 113, 114, 121, 152, 154,
    157–61, 224–25, 267
    casting of, 224–25
    era of, 97
    in MGM merger, 83–84
    in MGM's system, 157, 159, 280–81, 399,
    464
    system challenged by, 95–99, 159
    Thalberg and, 92, 95–99, 157, 159
Disney, Walt, 142, 232, 382
Dmytryk, Edward, 394, 451
Dodsworth, 117, 433
Donat, Robert, 367
Donen, Stanley, 332, 403, 457
Dorn, Philip, 304
Double Indemnity, 380
Doubling for Romeo, 209
Douglas, William O., 397
Dracula, 151
Dragon Seed, 291–92, 364
Dramatists Guild, 188–89
Dressler, Marie, 9, 157, 191–92, 194, 223, 266,
    360
Dr. Jekyll and Mr. Hyde (Louis Meyer; 1920),
    53–54
Dr. Jekyll and Mr. Hyde (Paramount; 1920),
    53
Dr. Jekyll and Mr. Hyde (1941), 160
Dr. Kildare series, 291, 326
Dubrey, Claire, 191, 192
Duchess of Idaho, 423
Dull, O. O. "Bunny," 315
Dumier, Ukraine, 18, 19, 34
Dumont, Margaret, 280
Dunlap, Edgar, 384
Dunne, Dominick, 437, 438
Dunne, Irene, 356, 423
Durante, Jimmy, 166
Durbin, Deanna, 311, 332
Duvivier, Julian, 252, 256

Eagle, The, 113
East Coast-West Coast divide:
    deposition of moguls in, 444–45
    Hollywood blacklist and, 395
    Nicholas Schenck vs. LBM in, 129, 131, 172,
        243–45
    Thalberg and, 175, 183
Easter Parade, 10, 381
Eastman Kodak, 240
Ebsen, Buddy, 299
Eddy, Nelson, 167–68, 230, 242, 255, 364
Edens, Roger, 320, 331
Edington, Harry, 101, 102, 104, 106
Ed Sullivan Show, 480
Educational Comedies, 186
Edward VIII, King of England, 247
Edwards, Frances, 312
"Eli, Eli," 434
Elliott, George C., 33, 34, 35, 40
Ellis, Havelock, 66
Ellison, Ralph, 431
Eminent Authors, 71
EPIC program, 200, 201, 202
Epoch Corporation, 41–42
Erté, 123
Estabrook, Howard, 347
Evans, Robert, 483
Everett, Chad, 505
Everyman, 198
Exhibitor's Herald, 53
Exit Smiling, 126

Fadiman, William, 247, 254, 258
Fairbanks, Douglas, Jr., 63, 131, 159, 222
Fairbanks, Douglas, Sr., 57, 106, 108, 135, 138,
    200, 232, 400
Family Affair, A, 219, 324
Famous Players Film Corporation, 43, 44
Famous Players-Lasky, 44, 49, 54, 164
Farber, Sidney, 486, 490, 511
Farnum, William, 33
Faulkner, William, 431
Federal Bureau of Investigation (FBI), 382
    Grace-Lipton extortion case and, 308
    LBM and, 228
    moguls interviewed on LBM by, 305
Feist, Felix, Jr., 201
Feldman, Charles, 194, 196, 198–99, 413, 507–8
Feldman, Jean Howard, 195–96, 197, 198, 505
Fenady, Andrew, 505
film editing, film editors, 56, 213
    and mass production of movies, 66–67
    unions and, 117
Film-Kurier, 275
film noir, 380, 427
film preservation, Mayer Foundation and, 511
Finklehoffe, Fred, 352, 353
Firefly, The, 248
First National, 43, 49, 64, 113, 138

Fitts, Buron, 216
Fitzgerald, F. Scott, 152, 155, 268, 275
Fleming, Victor, 142, 160–61, 225, 226, 328, 342,
    356, 374, 375, 398
Flesh and the Devil, 113, 114, 134
Flint, Motley, 136
Florida, and movie industry relocation, 200
Flynn, Errol, 258, 259, 397
Flynn, John "Bodger," 32
Fordin, Hugh, 328, 450
For Me and My Gal, 10, 355
Fortune, 1932 article about MGM in, 152–53, 214
Foster, Charles, 310–11, 336, 430–31, 469, 489–90
Fountain, Leatrice Gilbert, 133, 148, 242, 337–38
Four Horsemen of the Apocalypse, The, 71, 72, 96
Fox, 143, 170, 179, 217, 239
    Joseph Schenck and, 127, 173, 180, 371
    Movietone Corporation of, 144
    theaters of, 146, 262
Fox, Myron, 421, 501, 503
Fox, William, 49, 53, 143–46
Foy, Brian, 245
Frank, Harriet, 423
Frankenstein, 151
Franklin, Sidney, 67, 120, 226, 231, 232, 239, 252,
    255–56, 315, 338, 344, 373, 374–75, 424
Freaks, 151–52
Freed, Arthur, 10, 168, 239, 327–31, 340, 341, 345,
    352, 353, 381, 383, 406, 409, 432–33, 440
    creative instincts of, 329, 330
    firing of, 507
    LBM and, 327–29, 330, 331, 438, 450, 457,
        479, 507
    management style of, 328–29
    Schary and, 418, 462
Freed unit, 10, 168, 327–33, 378, 401, 403, 479
    atmosphere of, 329–30
    movies produced by, 10, 328, 332, 352–54, 355,
        381, 401–3, 405–7, 418, 427, 440, 442, 457,
        462–63
    mystique of, 401–2
    producers of, 331–33
    revitalization of, 402–3
Freeman, Devery, 254, 290–91
Freeman, Frank, 305
Freud, Sigmund, 368
Friedman, David, 262
From Here to Eternity, 272
Fury, 219

Gable, Clark, 8, 11, 12, 148, 155, 157, 180, 220–21,
    224, 228, 232, 243, 249, 255, 266, 289, 301,
    312, 339, 357, 423–24, 448, 455, 456–57, 515
    background of, 148, 221
    development of, 149, 221, 265
    Gone With the Wind and, 258–59, 456
    and Lombard's death, 358–59
    MGM contract of, 148–50
    personality and charisma of, 220, 397

Gabler, Neal, 204
Gabriel Over the White House, 154, 155
gangster movies, 300
Garbo, Greta, 8, 12, 114, 120, 135, 149, 157, 167,
    190–91, 198–99, 208, 229, 241, 251, 266, 302,
    323, 364, 515
    abortive marriage of Gilbert and, 133–34
    character of, 220
    LBM and, 105
Garden of Allah, The, 132
Gardner, Ava, 294, 358, 478
Garland, Judy, 8, 224, 255, 272, 299, 321, 325, 328,
    330–31, 352–54, 402, 436, 515
    LBM and, 343, 405–6, 407, 507
    Minnelli's marriage with, 341
    temperament of, 344, 353, 405–7
Garrett, Betty, 340
Garrett, Murray, 444, 462
Garson, Greer, 8, 131, 251–52, 288, 345, 365, 367,
    374, 398–99, 424
Gaslight, 3, 340
Gaumont-British, 231, 251, 253
Gaynor, Janet, 174, 191, 215
Gem theater (Haverhill, Mass.), 30–31, 44
Gentleman's Agreement, 380
German-American Bund, 204, 390
Gershe, Leonard, 344, 451
Giannini, A. P., 335
Gibbons, Cedric, 71, 92, 134, 153, 187, 188,
    209–11, 232, 249, 257, 269, 280, 371, 378, 391,
    507
    MGM style and, 209, 210, 211
Gibney, Sheridan, 66
Gifford, Frances, 255, 458
Gigi, 10, 462
Gilbert, John, 12, 84, 89, 95, 111, 118, 124, 132, 149,
    189, 190, 337
    LBM and, 133–34, 148, 164, 185–86, 195,
    316
    MGM contract with, 147, 186–87
    talkies and, 147–48, 149
Gillespie, Arnold, 210
Girl Philippa, The, 51
Gish, Dorothy, 75, 88
Gish, Lillian, 41, 75, 88, 107, 124–26, 139–40
Gish, Mary, 75
Glyn, Elinor, 78, 95
Godsol, Frank, 71, 72, 99
Goetz, Ben, 363, 367
Goetz, Edith Mayer, 28, 33, 36, 37, 53, 59, 64,
    88, 230, 370, 414
    death and burial of, 510, 511
    education of, 62, 63, 161
    as hostess, 372, 404, 405, 437–38, 509, 510
    Irene's relationship with, 47, 88, 404, 405,
    438, 499, 509, 510
    and LBM's death and funeral, 493, 494,
    499
    LBM's final illness and, 491, 510

    LBM's relationship with, 46–47, 55, 56, 57,
    62, 64, 65–66, 86, 88, 135, 161, 180–81, 297,
    386, 405, 460–61, 481, 501
    LBM's will and, 501
    Margaret and, 481, 509
    personality of, 46, 47, 161, 372, 404, 405, 437
Goetz, Judy, 481, 482
Goetz, William, 367, 430, 491, 499, 502–3, 505
    affairs of, 371
    art collection and home of Edith and, 372,
    404, 405, 437–38, 502–3, 509, 510, 511
    as independent producer, 371–72, 456,
    502–3
    LBM and, 180, 181, 371–72, 459–61, 501
    marriage of Edith and, 161–62, 194, 371, 437,
    460–61, 511
    Selznick and, 371–72
Going Hollywood, 227
Goldberg, Richard, 352
Goldstone, Nat, 329
Goldstone, Richard, 272, 277, 382–83, 410,
    418–19, 421, 458
Goldwyn, Blanche, 40
Goldwyn, Sam, 11, 49, 108, 179, 459
    Goldwyn Company and, 71, 164
    LBM and, 40, 164, 456, 459, 488
Goldwyn Company, 164
    deterioration of, 71–72
    Loew and, 72, 78, 100
    in MGM merger, 72–73, 76–79, 83–84, 144,
    209
    movies of, 71, 72, 77, 78, 98, 99–101
    studio facilities of, 71, 72
    talent at, 72, 83–84, 122, 209
Gone With the Wind, 102, 221, 355, 400, 453, 480,
    505
    directors of, 161, 259, 260
    Gable and, 258, 448
    MGM deal on, 259, 260
    profitability of, 260–61, 464
    script patching on, 260
    Selznick and, 258–60, 480
    as Selznick vs. MGM picture, 259
Goodbye, Mr. Chips, 228, 252, 254, 256, 398
Good Earth, The, 182, 226, 228, 229, 231, 237, 243,
    337
Good Job, The, 346, 347
Good News, 328, 401, 402
Good News of 1938, 247–49
Goodrich, David, 453–54
Goodrich, Frances, 180, 205–6, 339, 429, 453
Gordon, Bernard, 2, 388, 392
Gordon, Nathan, 45–46, 49, 51, 53, 321
Gordon, Sally, 46
Gordon, William, 45, 46
Gordon-Mayer Film Corp., 49
Gordon-Mayer Theatrical Company, 45–46
Gottlieb, Robert, 503, 509, 510–11
Goulding, Edmund, 120, 229, 231, 238

Go West, 89, 360
Grace, Meyer Philip, 307–8
Grady, Bill, 288, 421
Grand Hotel, 209, 257, 372, 517
Grant, Cary, 312
Grauman, Sid, 138
Gray, Hugh, 433
Grayson, Kathryn, 211–12, 263, 316, 332, 406, 490
Great Caruso, The, 420, 449
Great Dictator, The, 275–76
Great Secret, The, 45
Great Sinner, The, 423
Great Waltz, The, 243
Great Ziegfeld, The, 117, 330
Greed, 72, 77, 78, 84, 95, 97
Green, Adolph, 406, 424
    MGM musicals and, 331, 402, 462
Green, Alfred E., 60
Green, Johnny, 378–79, 420
Green Dolphin Street, 400
Green Grow the Lilacs, 363–64
Green Hat, The, 182
Griffith, D. W., 41, 49, 97, 125, 158
Griffith, Richard, 83
Grumbach, Doris, 73
Guilaroff, Sydney, 251
Guiles, Fred Lawrence, 133
Guy Named Joe, A, 3, 5, 356
Guys and Dolls, 456
Gyssling, George, 275, 276

Hackett, Albert, 180, 339, 429, 453
Haines, William, 84, 113, 114–15
    homosexuality of, 4, 5, 7, 132–33
Hamilton, Lloyd, 186
Hanna, William, 273, 274, 484
Hanna-Barbera Company, 484
Hanson, Lars, 125
Harburg, E. Y. "Yip," 328
Harlow, Jean, 8, 155, 157, 178, 221–22, 241, 323
Harman, Hugh, 273
Hart, Kitty Carlisle, 197, 482–83
Hart, Moss, 482–83
Hatfield, Hurd, 337
Hatrick, Eddie, 116, 143
Haverhill, Mass., 479
    LBM's theaters in, *see* Colonial theater; New Orpheum theater; Orpheum theater
    as mill town, 30, 32
Haverhill Evening Gazette, 32
Haverhill Record, 33
Hawks, Howard, 222
Hayden, Sterling, 392
Haydon, J. Charles, 54
Hayes, Helen, 7
Hays, Will, 64, 275
Hayton, Lennie, 320
Hayward, Susan, 160

Head, Edith, 214
Hearst, William Randolph, 7, 47, 71, 75, 154, 191, 206, 227
    and California gubernatorial race (1934), 200, 201–2
    Citizen Kane and, 333, 334
    and Fox Movietone Corp., 144
    LBM and, 115–16, 153, 154, 169, 227, 333, 334, 391
    MGM and, 78, 84, 114–17, 154, 217
    radio station of, 140
Hecht, Ben, 301, 333–34, 342
Heifetz, Jascha, 373
Hellman, Lillian, 205, 343
Hell's Angels, 221
Hendrickson, Floyd, 322
Hendry, Whitey, 2, 215–16, 412
Hepburn, Katharine, 264, 298, 319, 321–22, 336, 341–42, 356, 374, 406, 408, 490, 493
Hernandez, Juano, 431
Herrmann, Bernard, 379
Hervey, Irene, 288
He Who Gets Slapped, 88–89, 95
Hickman, Darryl, 223, 347
High Noon, 272
Hill, George, 111, 142, 226
Hillcrest Country Club, 56, 164, 204, 268, 283, 300
Hilliker, Katherine, 123–24
Hirschfeld, Al, 219
His Hour, 95
Hitchcock, Alfred, 253, 292, 465
Hitler, Adolf, 276, 277, 348, 433
Hoffman, Herman, 455
Hoffman, Stanley, 281–82, 481
Holden, Fay, 324, 326
Hollywood, Calif.:
    LBM's move to, 53, 55, 56–57
    in 1918, 54
    movie industry and growth of, 199–200
    outdoor shooting in, 57
Hollywood Bowl, 296–97, 373, 377
Hollywood Citizen-News, 386, 387
Hollywood Park, 268, 270, 349
Hollywood Reporter, 184, 203, 304, 333, 384, 425–26, 442, 449, 467–68, 484, 492, 499
Hollywood School for Girls, 63
Hollywood Ten, 388, 392, 394, 395, 396
Holtzmann, Fanny, 150–51, 185–86
Home of Peace Cemetery, 494, 501
homosexuality, 4–6, 123, 132–33, 303, 331, 421
Hood, R. B., 382
Hoover, Herbert, 85, 137, 140–42
    election of, 140–41, 144
    LBM and, 137, 140–41, 144, 145–46, 163, 168–69, 441, 467, 489
Hoover, J. Edgar, 228
Hope, Bob, 262, 292, 316
Hopkins, Bob, 155

Hopper, Hedda, 52, 60–61, 63, 69, 78, 188, 214, 255, 412, 435, 438, 445, 451
Hornblow, Arthur, Jr., 315, 319, 398, 434
Horne, Lena, 320, 321, 436
Horowitz, Elizabeth, 369, 370–71, 414, 491
horror movies, 151–52
Houseman, John, 463, 464
House Un-American Activities Committee (HUAC), 383, 387–91
    LBM's bribe of, 384
    Schary and, 394–95
Howard, Jean, see Feldman, Jean Howard
Howe, James Wong, 280
Hudson, Rock, 6
Hughes, Howard, 384, 467, 475
Human Comedy, The, 3, 4, 8, 114, 346–49
    cast of, 347, 348
    director of, 346–47, 348, 349
Human Comedy, The (Saroyan), 347
Hunchback of Notre Dame, The, 68, 69, 78
Hurd, Jack, 341
Huston, John, 427, 433–36
Huston, Walter, 154, 178, 311, 433
Hyman, Bernard, 118, 173, 189, 237, 245, 246, 302, 369

"I'll Get By," 321, 356
Important News, 273
independent producers, 163, 456
    see also Goetz, William; Selznick, David O.; Selznick, Irene Mayer
Ingram, Rex, 72, 83, 84, 95, 96, 98, 100, 101, 120, 131–32
Internal Revenue Service, Thalberg and, 145
International Alliance of Theatrical Stage Employees (IATSE), 239–41
International Pictures, 371–72
"In the Still of the Night" (Porter), 230
Intruder in the Dust, 431
Irene (costume designer), 359
Isherwood, Christopher, 279, 323
Ising, Rudolf, 273
isolationists, 343, 385
Israel, LBM and, 411–12
Italy, 274–75
It Can't Happen Here (Lewis), 275
It Happened One Night, 221

Jackson, Horace, 107
Jarman, Claude, Jr., 374, 375, 376
Jarrico, Paul, 349
Jazz Singer, The, 185
Jean (maid), 466
Jenkins, Butch, 224, 347, 348
Jerry the Mouse, 303, 331
Jessel, George, 208
Jesse L. Lasky Feature Play Company, 40, 44
Jewish Home for the Aged (Los Angeles), Cummings and LBM fundraising for, 297

Jewish War Veterans, 430, 441
Jews, Judaism:
    Ashkenazi vs. Russian, 26, 68–69
    Communists and, 201, 342
    immigrant, 17, 18, 26, 49, 129, 203–4, 343
    in Israel, 411–12
    LBM's family and, 21, 45, 59
    in Los Angeles, 59, 90, 163, 185, 204, 268, 342–43
    Mayer family and, 19, 21–22
    Nazism and, 198, 204, 250, 276, 433
    Russian persecution of, 17–18, 203
    in Saint John, 20, 21–22, 38, 265
    Sephardic, 26, 33
Joe Smith, American, 277, 361, 389
Johnson, Evie, 5–6, 12, 224, 287, 357–58, 413, 421
Johnson, Van, 4–6, 332, 341, 408
Johnston, Eric, 387, 393, 394
Jones, Jennifer, 475
Jones family movies, 323
Joseph and His Brethren, 469–76
Josephy, Alvin, 202, 206–7, 219, 382
Journey for Margaret, 294, 353, 362, 368
Joy, Leatrice, 242, 337–38
Judge Hardy's Children, 324
Julia Misbehaves, 399
Julian Petroleum Company, 135–36
Julius Caesar, 454, 463
junk dealers, 20–28, 39, 59
Jupiter's Darling, 464

Kael, Pauline, 334
Kalmus, Natalie, 352
Kanin, Garson, 341
Kanin, Michael, 339, 341, 345
Kaper, Bronislau, 198, 212, 370
Katz, Sam, 181, 245, 246, 255, 276, 363, 407–8, 477–78
    LBM and, 237–38, 269
Kaufman, Millard, 130–31, 411, 455, 485
Kaye, Danny, 292, 332
Kazan, Elia, 9, 399–400, 404
Keaton, Buster, 7, 72, 76, 83, 84, 89, 95, 142, 165–67, 292
    LBM and, 165, 166, 195, 279–80
    rehired by MGM, 279–80
Keel, Howard, 332, 406–7, 411, 447
Keller, K. T., 467
Kelly, Gene, 299, 303, 322, 330, 354–55, 400, 403, 440, 442, 499, 507, 515
Kelly, Grace, 464–65
Kent, Sidney, 179
Kerkorian, Kirk, 506, 512
Kerr, Deborah, 367, 399
Keyes, Asa, 136
Kidd, Michael, 332
Kiki, 113
King Kong, 208
Kingsley, Dorothy, 317, 341, 420

Kiss Me Kate, 332
Klaw and Erlanger, 99, 109
Knopf, Edwin, 206, 239, 314–15, 399, 439
Korda, Michael, 366
Koretz, Paul, 252–53, 459, 473
Korngold, Erich Wolfgang, 212
Koverman, Ida, 5, 64, 136–37, 140, 142, 167, 188,
        213, 255, 263, 287, 298, 302, 316, 323, 336,
        337, 338, 377, 468, 472
Kramer, Stanley, 477
Krasna, Norman, 219, 467
Kupferman, Theodore, 470, 471

Lady in the Lake, 380, 398
Laemmle, Carl, Jr., 189
Laemmle, Carl, Sr., Thalberg and, 68, 69, 172
Laemmle, Rosabelle, 68, 70
L.A. Herald Examiner, 386, 492
L.A. Herald Express, 485
Lamarr, Hedy, 8, 252, 263, 316, 339, 438
Lambert, Gavin, 172, 303, 471
L.A. Mirror, 412, 492
Lang, Fieldsie, 220
Lang, Fritz, 219
Lang, Richard, 220
Langford, Frances, 220
Langley, Noel, 302
Lansbury, Angela, 408, 436
Lanza, Mario, 167, 255, 332, 377–78, 461–62
Lardner, Ring, Jr., 254, 339, 341, 345, 382, 383,
        394
Larkin, John, 420–21
Lasky, Jesse, 40, 53
Lassie, Come Home, 3, 327, 355
Lassie movies, 114
    for television, 419
Last Tycoon, The (Fitzgerald), 152, 155, 268
Laughlin, Mike, 212
Laughton, Charles, 157, 228, 337
Laurel and Hardy movies, 186, 221, 274
Laurents, Arthur, 395, 404, 512
Lawrence, Florence, 34, 335
Lazar, Irving, 438
Lean, David, 477
Lee, Harriet, 311
Lees, Robert, 156, 205, 206, 219, 239, 272–73, 327,
        392
Leigh, Janet, 3–4, 367, 376–77
Leigh, Vivien, 253, 338
Leisen, Mitchell, 211, 214
Leonard, Robert Z., 84, 98, 225, 238, 248, 336
Lerner, Alan Jay, 440, 468, 500
Lerner, Michael, 12
LeRoy, Mervyn, 257, 258, 301, 302, 328, 351, 398,
        413, 420
Lewin, Albert, 119, 182, 231, 232, 238–39, 336–37,
        426
Lewis, David, 12, 246
Lewis, Jerry, 437, 503

Lewis, Sheldon, 53, 54
Lewis, Sinclair, 362
Lewton, Val, 190
Liberty Productions, 373, 408
Lichtman, Al, 43, 244, 245, 246, 259, 363, 407
Lillie, Beatrice, 126
Lippert, Robert, 468
Lipton, Channing Drexel, 307–8
Lipton, Lew, 307, 308, 309
Lipton, Mrs. Lew, 308, 309
Little Nellie Kelly, 330
Little Robinson Crusoe, 84
Loeb, Edwin, 57, 69, 250
Loew, Arthur, 77–78
Loew, Caroline Rosenheim, 73, 126, 143
Loew, David, 73
Loew, Marcus, 186
    business acumen and work ethic of, 73, 74, 75
    as exhibitor, 74, 75–76
    illness and death of, 126, 131
    LBM and, 116, 119, 127
    MGM and, 72–73, 76–78, 83, 94, 102, 127
    and MGM-United Artists merger attempt,
        108
    personality of, 73, 75
Loew's, Inc., 3, 7, 10, 503–4
    Depression and, 146, 152, 380
    favoritism and nepotism at, 484, 485
    Fox purchase and, 143–46, 442
    Gaumont-British and, 251
    Gone With the Wind and, 259
    LBM and, 78–79, 112, 244–45, 261–62,
        319, 365, 397, 425, 441, 444, 450, 452–53,
        487
    MGM and, 3, 72, 73, 76–79, 94, 102, 107, 109,
        111, 112, 117, 127–29, 130, 152, 170–72, 173–75,
        176, 180, 182, 184, 186, 225, 231, 237–38,
        239–40, 242, 243–45, 250, 251, 255, 258,
        261–62, 275, 299, 304, 380, 381, 395, 407,
        408, 409, 424, 440, 442–43, 444, 445, 450,
        451–52, 456, 457–58, 503
    proxy fight at, 487–88
    Schenck brothers and, *see* Schenck, Joseph;
        Schenck, Nicholas
    theaters of, 74, 75, 76, 129, 143–44, 152, 262,
        381, 393, 397, 463
Loew's State Building, 76
Loew's State theater, 76, 325
Lombard, Carole, 220, 232, 259
    Gable and, 358–59, 397
Loos, Anita, 93, 131, 135, 156, 264
Loos, Mary, 93, 131, 135, 264, 313, 346, 413,
        437–38, 466, 506
Los Angeles:
    Jewish community of, *see* Jews, in Los
        Angeles
    movie industry unions and, 118
Los Angeles Country Club, 268
Los Angeles Examiner, 412

Los Angeles Times, 118, 136, 188, 200, 201–2, 297, 307, 400, 492
Los Angeles Zoo, 55
Louis B. Mayer Foundation, 27, 501–2, 503, 511
Louis B. Mayer Productions, Inc., 37, 50–78, 226
   financial problems and shortfalls at, 58, 65
   MGM merger and, 77–79, 83, 84
   Mission Road studio of, 55–56, 57, 58–60, 62, 76, 77, 84
   movies made by, 52, 53, 59, 60, 61, 76–77
   profitability of, 64–65
   talent at, 50–53, 56, 59, 60, 61, 64, 66–67, 70, 77, 78, 83, 308
   Thalberg at, 68–70, 77–78
Louise, Ruth Harriet, 90, 140
Love, 113, 120
Love Finds Andy Hardy, 324–25
Lovely to Look At, 423
Lowe, Frederick, 468, 500
Loy, Myrna, 199, 220, 265, 280, 320, 374
Lubitsch, Ernst, 94, 107, 118, 148, 153, 167, 229, 259, 289, 302, 336, 423
Ludwig, William, 294, 325, 327, 347, 352, 419
Luft, Lorna, 407
Lurie, Louis, 141, 470
Lux Radio Theatre, 249

Maas, Fredericka Sagor, 10, 138
MacArthur, Charles, 118, 342
MacArthur, Douglas, 290, 356, 385, 422, 441
MacBride, C. R., 486, 487
McCarthy, J. J., 111
McCarthy, Joseph R., 433, 481
McCarthy, Neil, 271, 422
McCoy, Tim, 114, 291
MacDonald, Jeanette, 167–68, 241–43, 253, 279, 298, 434
McDowell, Claire, 102–3
McDowell, John, 391
McGuinness, James Kevin, 155, 188, 205, 206, 363, 382, 383, 407
Mack, Joseph, 30, 31
Madame Curie, 256, 365
Maddow, Ben, 431
Magnin, Edgar, 163, 297, 422–23
Mahin, John Lee, 188, 222, 237, 254, 255, 260, 382, 383, 468, 474, 475, 486, 493
Malden, Karl, 499
Mamoulian, Rouben, 190–91
Man, Woman and Sin, 120
Man from Laramie, The, 502
Manhattan Melodrama, 224
Mankiewicz, Herman, 333, 334
Mankiewicz, Joseph L., 7, 202, 218, 219, 238, 267, 276, 277, 316, 342, 343–44, 352, 358, 409, 454, 459
Mann, Thomas, 474, 476
Manners, Dorothy, 413

Mannix, Bernice, 130
Mannix, Eddie, 130–31, 135, 145, 154, 173, 189, 193, 205, 207, 220, 232, 239, 255, 256, 259, 260, 276, 279, 300, 330, 344, 363, 376, 387, 388, 393, 394, 395, 408, 420, 424, 426, 432, 443, 444, 491–92, 504
Mannix, Toni, 232
Man of a Thousand Faces, 451, 483
March, Fredric, 232
Mare Nostrum, 96
Margie, 387
Marie Antoinette, 255–57
   art direction on, 220, 255, 257
   costumes for, 214, 264
   scripting of, 182, 255
   stars of, 225, 227, 256, 257
Marion, Frances, 62, 64, 89–90, 142, 153, 253, 426, 449
Marmorston, Jessie, 64, 344, 345, 368–70, 414, 483, 486, 489, 490–91, 501
Marriage Is a Private Affair, 339, 345
Marsh, Oliver, 243
Martin, Dean, 437
Martin, "Docky," 217
Martin, Mary, 247
Martin, Tony, 3, 348, 357
Martin and Lewis, 437
Marx, Groucho, 157, 280
Marx, Harpo, 280
Marx, Sam, 7, 68, 92, 149, 152, 155, 180, 186, 193, 196, 202, 207, 218, 226, 238, 267, 383, 429, 463, 506
Marx Brothers, 167, 228, 232, 279, 280, 292, 348, 360
Mascot, 133
Massey, Ilona, 255, 316
Master of Women, 70
Master Photoplays, 41–42
Mata Hari, 174
Mathis, June, 71, 72, 99, 100, 101, 102, 103
Mayer, Gerald, 25, 54, 134, 198, 204, 296, 317, 318, 387, 413, 455, 465, 478, 507
Mayer, Jacob, 17, 18, 19–21, 40, 134, 185, 324
   businesses of, 19, 20–26, 27
   death of, 151
   LBM's relationship with, 23, 25, 26, 62, 126, 150–51
Mayer, Jerry, 19, 20, 25, 31, 36, 51, 320
   bird collection of, 271
   illness and death of, 386–87
   as studio manager, 56, 151, 204, 273
Mayer, Lorena Jones Danker, 412–14, 468, 486, 489, 493
   appearance of, 412, 421
   career of, 412–13
   Edith Goetz and, 461
   elopement of LBM and, 412
   home of LBM and, 413–14, 501, 503
   as hostess, 421

Irene Selznick and, 503
LBM's relationship with, 412, 413, 421,
    465–66, 479, 482
LBM's will and, 500–501, 502
Mayer, Louis B., *iv*, 16, 236, 448, 497
    Academy and, 117–18, 138
    aggression and ruthlessness of, ix, 7, 8, 9,
        10–11, 12, 22, 26, 60, 63, 64, 87, 90, 98, 119,
        129, 134, 188–89, 199, 253–54, 279–80, 305,
        432, 514
    America and, 6, 34–35, 48, 49, 183, 203–4, 287,
        297, 310, 324, 325, 370, 385, 392, 422, 432,
        450, 512, 516
    anger and combativeness of, 48, 54, 98, 199,
        285, 296, 301–2, 362, 388, 420–21, 428–29,
        435, 442, 465–66, 482, 514
    appearance of, 5, 20, 21, 22, 27, 28, 34, 40, 44,
        50, 57, 63, 70, 187, 284, 295, 310, 312, 314,
        318, 329, 370, 376, 402, 432, 471
    art collection of, 422
    audience taste and needs understood by, 9, 11,
        33, 40, 89, 142, 149, 183, 190–91, 266, 274,
        288, 298, 299, 324, 437, 449, 453, 513, 514
    belief system and picture values of, 6, 8–12,
        38, 48, 53, 56, 62, 64, 70, 85, 89, 95, 98,
        124–25, 149, 163–64, 185, 203–4, 219, 220,
        224, 230, 264, 280, 294, 300, 316, 321, 323,
        324, 325, 355–56, 376, 402–3, 417, 426, 432,
        435–36, 439, 440, 449–50, 482, 486, 512,
        513–15, 516
    birthplace and birthdate of, 18–19, 34, 35, 188
    brainstorms of, 247, 292
    as caricatured in popular art, 12, 513
    childhood and adolescence of, 17, 18–27, 294,
        511–12
    Citizen Kane affair and, 333–34
    civil rights and, 320–21
    class and breeding as important to, 21, 57,
        68–69, 168, 206, 252, 290, 421
    as dancer, 312–13, 318
    deposition of, 443–44, 449–51, 459, 473, 477
    earthy directness of, 295, 435–36
    education of, 10, 24, 26, 230, 287, 322, 511, 512,
        515
    emotionalism of, 8, 57, 58, 65, 90, 123, 124,
        142, 162, 163–64, 187, 188, 196, 197, 198, 205,
        230, 231, 263, 282, 284, 289, 291, 303, 310,
        312, 317, 318, 323, 386, 432, 434, 488, 505,
        507
    energy and exuberance of, 62, 297, 298–99,
        300, 312–13, 318, 469, 471, 512
    as exhibitor, 11, 16, 39–50, 53, 54, 95
    family background of, 10, 17–19
    as father, 46–47, 53, 55, 56–57, 62, 63–64,
        65–66, 86–88, 135, 161–63, 180–81, 261, 297,
        386, 403–4, 405, 413, 460–61, 466
    film library of, 452–53, 512–13
    final illness and death of, 9, 85, 483, 489–91,
        493–94

finances, 78–79, 112, 178, 180, 244–45, 261–62,
    319, 365, 425, 453, 502
food and, 90, 187–88, 299
frugality of, 40–41, 69
generosity of, 27, 36, 37, 46, 50, 180–81, 250,
    261, 271, 281–82, 305, 306, 310–11, 335–36,
    354–55, 406, 407, 429, 459, 513
and Grace-Lipton extortion trial, 307–9
as grandfather, 261, 269–70, 283–84, 296, 299,
    403, 481
grudges and hatreds of, 10, 37, 60, 131–32,
    133–34, 148, 164, 185–86, 198–99, 226–27,
    247, 261, 279–80, 302, 308–9, 316, 335, 336,
    465, 481, 488, 501
health of, 65, 104, 164, 369, 483, 486, 487
homelife of, 27–28, 29, 31, 33, 35, 36, 46,
    47–48, 55, 56, 57, 61–62, 63–64, 65–66,
    86–88, 134–35, 161–63, 185, 281–82, 283–84,
    289, 296, 297, 385–86, 482
honors and awards bestowed on, 27, 168,
    249–50, 264–65, 439, 441, 461
insecurities of, 58, 64, 65, 66, 90, 129, 163, 187,
    294, 413, 441, 478, 479, 488, 514
integrity of, 192, 269, 295, 321, 322
Jewish identity and spirituality of, 21, 45, 59,
    90, 185, 250, 278, 297, 313, 335, 342, 343,
    411–12, 414, 437, 513
legacy of, 9, 13, 512–13, 515–16
loneliness of, 478, 479, 488
management skill and style of, ix, 4, 7–12, 36,
    47, 56, 57, 59–60, 70, 77, 81, 83, 84, 89, 90,
    111, 151, 154–55, 166, 183, 187, 190–91, 194,
    199, 207, 216, 228, 245–46, 247, 249, 253–54,
    256, 269, 281, 284, 286, 287–89, 297–98, 301,
    311–12, 315, 319, 323, 370, 507
MGM decentralization and, 173, 174, 181,
    182
and MGM illegitimate activities, 170, 218
MGM merger and, 77–79, 83, 84, 102
and MGM power struggle, 430–31, 432, 434,
    435, 436, 438–39, 441, 442–44, 445
middle name of, 35
morality and, 63–64, 95, 98, 124–25, 135, 185,
    195, 221, 247, 264, 280, 316, 376, 402, 514
narcissism of, 10, 47, 50, 57, 247, 285
negotiating tactics of, 132, 226–27, 288, 291,
    303–4, 311–12, 322–23
nepotism and, 185, 312
office of, 4, 5, 82, 85, 91, 239, 282, 284, 337,
    374, 376, 416–17, 450, 453
papers of, 503
parents of, *see* Mayer, Jacob; Mayer, Sarah
parties of, 135, 289, 292, 298–99, 312–13, 351,
    366
paternalism of, 5, 6, 11, 22, 64, 69, 90, 120, 135,
    181, 191, 220, 248, 249, 263, 285, 289–90, 291,
    293, 302, 310, 312, 319, 323, 335–36, 378, 421,
    449, 465, 513
peer-held reputation of, 305–6, 507

Mayer, Louis B. (*cont.*)
    politics and political connections of, 136–37,
        140–41, 145, 154, 155, 159, 163, 168–69,
        200–204, 216, 218, 229, 250, 295, 305–6, 321,
        349, 355, 383, 384–85, 390–92, 394–97, 416,
        426, 430, 433, 452–53, 460, 474, 475, 481,
        488, 500, 512, 513
    post MGM, 467–68, 474–80, 482, 484, 485,
        486–87
    as powerful and feared, 10, 12, 26, 90–91, 253,
        282, 283, 284, 290, 292, 293–94, 295, 296,
        301, 316, 323, 354, 365, 370, 374, 420–21, 453,
        475, 495, 507, 514
    racing stable of, 268–71, 291, 301, 353–54,
        365–66, 377, 421–22, 459–60, 467, 500, 502
    respectability craved by, 9, 21, 57, 63, 142, 168,
        292, 423
    routines of, 283–84
    Saint John and, 23, 24, 27, 35, 230–31, 264–65
    as scrap and junk dealer, 20–28, 29, 39, 59, 70
    as self-made man, 294–95, 322, 419, 514
    showmanship and self-promotion of, 8, 11,
        18–19, 32, 33, 46, 52, 94–95, 179, 269, 285,
        315, 419, 447, 458, 461, 514, 515
    stunted emotional development of, 26, 39,
        142, 281, 317
    talent recognized and nurtured by, 7, 104–5,
        149, 154, 228, 233, 238, 243, 251–52, 263,
        265–66, 288, 311, 354, 365, 377–78, 440, 442,
        455, 507, 512
    as theater owner and manager, 30–37, 39–40,
        53, 54, 70
    threatened resignation of, 244
    tributes to, 492
    voice of, 287, 471
    wealth of, 41, 42, 135, 244, 271, 500–501, 502
    wives of, *see* Mayer, Lorena Jones Danker;
        Mayer, Margaret Shenberg
    women and, 8, 25, 64, 185, 193–98, 213, 221,
        283, 294, 308, 309, 316–19, 329, 353, 368–71,
        413, 513
    work ethic of, 22–23, 24, 25, 35, 39, 45, 46, 52,
        55, 56, 89, 244, 284, 321
    World War II and, 3, 168, 277, 278–79, 304,
        305, 312, 345–81, 417–18
    Zionism and, 343, 411–12
Mayer, Margaret Shenberg, 28, 33, 46, 47, 151,
    185, 187, 404, 461
    appearance of, 28, 261, 313
    children of LBM and, *see* Goetz, Edith
        Mayer; Selznick, Irene Mayer
    death of, 481–82
    health of, 193, 194, 197, 281, 481, 511
    as hostess, 134, 313
    intelligence of, 28, 39
    LBM's marriage and relationship with, 28, 39,
        47–48, 55, 56, 59, 87, 90, 142, 161, 162, 185,
        193–94, 197–98, 229, 281, 287, 297, 313–14,
        370, 386, 405, 414, 482

LBM's separation and divorce from, 313–14,
    317, 385–86, 414–15, 421, 481
    Louis B. Mayer Productions and, 55–56, 62
    as mother, 46, 161, 162, 197, 386, 482
    personality of, 28, 47, 194, 197, 198, 314, 386,
        415
    theater business and, 31, 32, 36
Mayer, Roger, 504, 507, 512
Mayer, Rudolph, 19, 25, 31, 40, 51, 150–51, 204
    death of, 151
    theater business and, 38
Mayer, Sarah, 27
    appearance of, 21, 25
    death and burial of, 38, 46, 265, 437
    Jacob and, 19
    LBM's relationship with, 19, 21, 22, 23, 38, 39,
        46, 47, 65, 265, 284, 300, 324, 370, 414, 437
Mayer, Suzanne Danker, 412, 413, 414, 466–47,
    501
Mayer, Yetta, 19
Mayer's ganze mishpocheh, MGM as, 185
Mayer Stock Farm, 270–71, 422
Maytime, 205, 229, 231, 238, 246
MCA, 452
Meet Me in Las Vegas, 463
Meet Me in St. Louis, 1, 3, 10, 300, 352–54, 515
    casting of, 352, 353
    script of, 330, 352–53
    sets of, 353, 506
Mellett, Lowell, 390
Mendoza, Tony, 208
Menzies, William Cameron, 211, 259
Merriam, Frank, in California gubernatorial
    race, 200–204
Merritt, Russell, 41
Merry-Go-Round, 97
Merry Widow, The, 95, 98–99, 112–13, 148, 226,
    229, 336
    preview of, 98–99
Messinger, Lillie, 300, 402, 409
Metro-Goldwyn-Mayer (MGM):
    art department of, 209, 210, 211, 372–73, 506
    ascendance of, 152
    board of, 173, 174
    and California gubernatorial race (1934),
        200–203
    caste system at, 287, 341, 351
    Christmas parties at, 188, 218, 316
    commissary of, 90, 151, 152, 187–88, 218, 271,
        312, 320, 351
    costume department at, 123, 153, 213–15, 264,
        351, 359
    debauchery and gambling at, 169, 188, 218
    decentralization of, 173, 174, 181–83
    dedication ceremony for, 84–85
    department heads of, 209–15
    Depression and, 146, 152
    editorial department of, 64, 213, 375, 378,
        504

elitism of, 2–3, 138, 285, 359, 373, 454
Executive Committee of, 245, 257, 293–94, 363–65, 383
executive life at, 315, 316
first picture of, 88–89
first year campaign book of, 94–95
first year productions of, 112–13
formation of, 3, 72–73, 76–79, 83–85
in *Fortune* article (1932), 152–53
and Fox purchase of Loew's, 143, 144, 145, 146, 442
graft at, 359–60
Hays office and, 95, 154, 189–90, 275, 276, 380
Hearst and, 78, 84, 114–17
as Hollywood gold standard, 2, 3, 7, 11, 12, 13, 93–94, 113, 120, 121, 199, 207–8, 220, 279, 281, 286, 292, 294, 303, 368, 515
institutional memory of, 512–13
integrated facilities at, 320
layoffs and economizing at, 407–18, 423–24, 451, 452, 457–58, 503–4, 505–6
layout and physical plant of, 1–2, 3–4, 84, 91, 94, 123, 152, 208, 217–18, 424, 506
Loew's, Inc., and, see Loew's, Inc., MGM and
logo and motto of, 1, 3, 10, 13, 71, 425
media and, 114–17, 125–26, 188, 201, 215–16, 247–49, 429–30
music department at, 198, 211, 212–13, 378–79
Nazi Germany and, 275–77
and participation deals, 456–57, 485
pension plan at, 450, 456, 484
police department of, 2, 215–16
political schisms at, 254–55, 382–84
power struggle and coup at, 426, 427, 429, 431, 432, 434, 435, 436, 438–39, 441, 442–44, 445, 449
present-day, 13, 512–13
profits and losses at, 3, 112, 152, 170, 173, 178, 179, 180, 237, 262, 355, 379–80, 381, 397, 407, 427, 441, 464, 484, 504, 506
publicity and, 4, 114–15, 116, 123, 192, 215–17
on radio, 247–49
Red Scare and, 254, 295, 355, 382–85, 387–97, 411, 416, 427, 451, 454, 455
relatives as LBM's employees of, 185
salary cuts at, 178–79
Schary at, 361–63, 409–12, 416–49, 450–52, 453–59, 462–65, 472, 478, 479, 480–81, 484–85, 508
scripting process at, 156–57
selling off assets of, 506–7
shorts department of, see shorts, shorts department, MGM
silent film stars at, 335–36
sound department of, 142, 143, 211–13, 226
storytellers at, 138, 226, 299–300, 423
television and, 418, 419, 436, 463, 485, 512–13
Thalberg Building at, 239

after Thalberg's death, 12, 232–33, 237–39, 241, 244–46, 249, 256, 320
triumverate at, 408
twenty-fifth anniversary conference of, 424–25
twilight of, 458, 479, 483–86, 503–4, 505–7
unions and, 131, 204–6, 240–41, 254, 255, 395, 453
United Artists merger attempt with, 108
as victim of changing times and tastes, 8–9, 12, 380, 381, 398–401, 417–19, 506
VIP tours at, 285–86
"Metro-Goldwyn Picture, Produced by Louis B. Mayer, A" credit, 89, 90
Metro Pictures Corporation, 44–45, 51, 76, 83
founding and organizing of, 43–44
Loew and, 72, 76
Louis B. Mayer Productions and, 64–65
MGM merger and, 72, 76–79, 83, 84, 144
Meyer, Louis, 53–54
MGM British, 366
British film laws and, 251, 367
heads of, 253–54, 366–67
studios of, 251, 252, 366
MGM Grand Hotel, 506, 516
MGM Labs, 512
MGM Records, 504
Miles Brothers, 31
Miller, Ann, 197, 271, 291, 319, 332
LBM's courting of, 317–19, 413
Min and Bill, 191, 223
Minnelli, Vincente, 159, 330, 332, 341, 352, 353, 438, 440, 504
Mitchum, Robert, 348, 398
Mockery, 123
Mogambo, 367, 465
Monroe, Marilyn, 464
Monsieur Verdoux, 10, 393
Montalban, Ricardo, 4, 221, 458, 479
Montgomery, Robert, 149, 194, 204, 220, 240–41, 279, 305, 380, 398
Moore, Matt, 61
Moral Rearmament, 278
Morgan, Frank, 160, 347, 348
Morgenthau, Robert, 335
Morley, Robert, 256, 257
Mortal Storm, The, 278
Moscowitz, Charles, 357, 413, 452
Moselle, Ray, 216
Moses, Grandma, 422
Motion Picture Alliance for the Preservation of American Ideals, 382, 392
Motion Picture Association of America (MPAA), 387
Motion Picture Country House, Louis B. Mayer Memorial Center at, 511
Motion Picture Daily, The, 502
Motion Picture Director, 109
Motion Picture Home, 472, 508

movie exhibitors, 31, 39–50, 72, 74, 75–76, 397
  Birth of a Nation and, 41–42
  Citizen Kane affair and, 333
  MGM favored by, 262
movie industry:
  anti-Communism and, 382–85, 387–92, 401, 430
  anti-labor stance of, 117–18, 239–41
  audience taste and, 417–19
  Citizen Kane affair and, 333–34
  Depression and, 3, 146, 152, 380, 400
  English foreign film earnings law and, 367
  and 1934 California gubernatorial race, 200–203
  Fascist threat and, 275–77, 279
  LBM as spokesman for, 249, 333–35, 365, 422
  LBM's adoration of, 322
  organized crime and, 239–41
  as real-estate operation, 76, 152, 395, 397
  Red Scare and, 203, 254, 295, 355, 382–97, 411, 416, 427, 451, 454, 455
  sex and drug scandals in (1921–22), 63–64
  Waldorf conference and, 393–95, 411, 427, 454, 455
  World War II and, 3, 256, 345–81, 417–18
movie moguls, Jewish, 459
  America and, ix, 6, 12, 49, 392
  anti-Semitism and, 49, 63, 96, 152, 163, 335, 342–43
  audiences understood by, ix, 49, 76, 397
  commonalities of, 9, 49, 75–76, 335, 419
  demonization of, 406
  deposition of, 444–45
  differences in attitude between, 475
  LBM as seen by, 305–6
  non-Jewish wives of, 8, 412–14
  politics of, 203, 305–6
  WASP movie moguls vs., 49
  as womanizers, 193, 321
  see also specific moguls
movies:
  acquired in MGM merger, 84
  declining grosses and attendance at, 399, 400, 408
  Jewish immigrants and, 33, 49
  mass production of, 66, 67, 93, 95, 112, 114, 126, 174, 279, 465
  orphan, 97, 139
  television and, 381, 418, 419, 452, 453, 463, 512–13
  see also specific movies
movies, MGM:
  anti-Communist, 391
  anti-Nazi, 275–77, 278
  B movies, 114, 246, 324, 325, 326, 330, 361–63, 400
  censorship and, *see* Production Code
  costs of, 106, 211, 355, 379, 399, 452, 457
  film noir, 380, 427
  horror, 151–52, 300
  look of, 120–21, 153, 186–87, 209, 210, 211, 246, 272, 280, 294, 351–52, 373, 438
  message pictures, 420
  musicals, *see* musicals, MGM
  previews of, 91–92, 98–99, 139, 149, 187, 298, 322, 325
  production and picture values of, 3, 8–9, 38, 49, 70, 85, 89, 93–94, 95, 99, 111, 120, 132, 149, 153, 157, 163–64, 174, 175, 182, 183, 185, 189–90, 208, 218–19, 220, 224, 230, 273, 274, 280, 300, 303, 321, 323, 324, 365, 376, 380, 399, 400, 402–3, 408, 417, 419, 420, 426, 435–36, 439, 440, 449, 455, 486, 512, 513–14, 516
  remakes of, 505
  scoring of, 212–13
  sequels of, 208
  shorts, *see* shorts, shorts department, MGM
  silent, look of, 120–21
  sound and, 12, 139, 142, 143, 147–50, 153, 167–68, 211–13
  standout scenes (from 1930s), 157
  targeted audience for, 89, 93–94, 118, 121, 273, 274, 299, 427, 514, 515
  World War II and, 3, 256, 344–45, 346–50
movie theaters:
  divorcement of, 397, 463
  in Haverhill, Mass., 30–37, 39
  in Saint John, 26–27
  Southern, black-themed movies in, 321
  studio-connected, 74, 75, 76, 129, 143–44, 152, 262, 381, 393, 397, 463
Moving Picture World, 44–45, 54
Mr. Deeds Goes to Town, 117
Mrs. Miniver, 3, 256, 344–45, 348, 365, 367, 389, 390, 398, 399, 424
Mr. Smith Goes to Washington, 387
Muller, Eddie, 427
Murray, Mae, 84, 87, 95, 98, 336
musicals, MGM, 9, 245, 397, 499
  Eddy-MacDonald operettas, 167–68
  Freed unit and, *see* Freed unit
  Kelly and, 355
  as LBM's greatest legacy, 10
  production time for, 246
  profitability of, 397, 427, 440
  quality of, 10, 331, 420
  Schary and, 418, 423, 440, 462–63
Mussolini, Benito, 201, 348
  movie-making ambitions of, 274–75
Mussolini, Vittorio, 274
Mutiny on the Bounty, 157, 226, 228, 249
Myers, Anna, 90
Myers, Carmel, 58, 90
Myers, Israel, 90
Mysterious Lady, The, 99, 120

Nagel, Conrad, 84, 117
Nasaw, David, 227
Nation, 395
National Association for the Advancement of Colored People (NAACP), 320–21
National Review, 474
National Velvet, 3, 114, 271, 337
Naughty Marietta, 167, 338
Navigator, The, 84, 95
Nazi Germany, MGM and, 275, 276, 277
Nazis, Nazism, 198
   American, 204, 278
   Hays Office and, 275–77
   LBM and, 277, 343
NBC radio network, 247
Neilan, Marshall, 56, 59–60, 72, 84, 85, 96–97, 98
Newcombe, Warren, 210
New Deal, 206
Newman, Joseph, 119–20, 229, 231, 233, 238, 241–42, 513
New Masses, 276–77
New Orpheum theater (Haverhill, Mass.), 32, 35, 36–37
newsreels, 116, 144, 201
New Theater, 316
New York Times, 202, 442, 469
Next Voice You Hear, The, 426
Ney, Richard, 398
Niblo, Fred, 61, 66, 77, 78, 79, 83, 95, 99, 120, 226
   Ben-Hur and, 101, 102, 103, 104, 105, 106, 107, 108–9
Night at the Opera, A, 157, 228, 279
Night Flight, 183–84
Nimitz, Chester, 290
Ninotchka, 259, 281, 302, 336, 340, 391, 426
Nixon, Richard, 492
Nolan, Mary, 130
Northwest Passage, 246, 256
Nosler, Lloyd, 106, 109
Nothing Doing, 424
Novarro, Ramon, 4, 61, 77, 133, 167, 178, 421
   in *Ben-Hur,* 101, 107, 118, 132
Nye, Gerald, 343

Oberon, Merle, 437
O'Brian, John Lord, 146
O'Brien, Dave, 272
O'Brien, Margaret, 290, 352, 353–54
O'Connor, Donald, 442
Oderman, Stuart, 126
Odets, Clifford, 243, 477
Odlum, Floyd, 334
Oklahoma!, 364, 379
Olcott, Sidney, 34, 310, 311
Old Music, 251, 252
One Clear Call, 61
On the Town (movie), 10, 402, 403, 425

On the Town (show), 402
operettas, Eddy-MacDonald, 167–68
Oppenheimer, George, 155, 277, 300, 383
Opposite Sex, The, 464
organized crime, 239–41
Orpheum theater (Haverhill, Mass.), 31–32
Orsatti, Frank, 170, 185, 194, 195, 198, 238, 300, 305, 317, 318, 391
Orsatti, Vic, 305, 317, 318, 319
O'Sullivan, Maureen, 189, 190
Our Dancing Daughters, 120, 209
Our Gang shorts, 186, 274
Outriders, The, 421
"Over the Rainbow," 328

Page, Anita, 194, 196
Paine, Arthur Bigelow, 125
Paint Your Wagon, 472, 489, 500
   LBM and, 468, 469–70, 473, 477
Palisades Amusement Park, 75, 130
Palmer, Ernest, 52
Palmer, Kyle, 463
Pan, Hermes, 463
Paradise Park, 74, 75
Paramount Pictures, 3, 44, 53, 66, 93, 94, 113, 138, 152, 162, 167, 170, 173, 174, 220, 239, 244, 262, 305, 336, 342, 351, 352, 380, 381, 395, 397, 408, 431, 437, 485, 512, 515
   Depression and, 152
   drug scandal at (1921–22), 63–64
   movie theaters of, 152, 262, 381
   World War II and, 381
Parry, Suzanne Vidor, 112
Parsons, Louella, 188, 217, 250, 412
Passion Play, The, 32, 33
Pasternak, Joe, 225, 239, 332, 363, 377–78, 383, 406
Patrick, Gail, 506
Pearson, Drew, 384
Pearson, Virginia, 54
Peck, Gregory, 434
Pegler, Westbrook, 241, 391–92
Pembroke (Loew estate), 126
Perelman, S. J., 206, 263, 508
Perfect Strangers, 367
Perils of Pauline, The, 75
Perkins, David, 36–37
Perrin, Nat, 383
Pete Smith Specialties, 272, 427
Philadelphia Story, The, 264, 281, 285, 292, 342
Photoplay, 96, 125, 126
Pickford, Jack, 33, 34
Pickford, Mary, 33–34, 44, 48, 51, 59, 108, 135, 138, 297, 310
Picture of Dorian Gray, The, 337
Pidgeon, Walter, 301–2, 311, 312, 399
Pirate, The, 10, 380, 401, 405–7
Pirosh, Robert, 206
Plunkett, Walter, 399–400

Porter, Cole, 229–30
Possessed, 189
Postman Always Rings Twice, The, 380
Powell, Dick, 290
Powell, Eleanor, 168, 229
Powell, Jane, 417, 473
Powell, Michael, 96, 453
Powell, William, 157, 174, 208, 220, 265, 266,
    320, 397
Power, Tyrone, 357–58
Previn, André, 373, 379
Pride and Prejudice, 228, 229
Pringle, Aileen, 95, 125–26
Prisoner of Zenda (1922), 120
Prisoner of Zenda (1937), 159
producers, MGM, 118, 256, 381
    in Freed unit, 331–33
    hegemony of, 89, 156, 263–64, 267, 417, 454,
        464
    LBM's choice of stars forced on, 338–39
    Thalberg's producers at, *see* Hyman, Bernard;
        Lewin, Albert; Rapf, Harry; Stromberg,
        Hunt; Thalberg, Irving
Producers Guild, Milestone Award of, 461
Production Code, 130
    anti-Nazi movies and, 275, 276, 277
    anti-Semitism and, 342–43
    MGM and, 95, 125, 154, 189–90, 275, 276, 277,
        380
    Paramount and, 64
Prohibition, 170

Quality Street, 120
Queen Christina, 155, 157, 190–91, 457
Quimby, Fred, 273
Quirk, James, 126
Quo Vadis, 433–34, 476

Raboch, Al, 101, 103, 106, 107
radio, MGM on, 247–49
Rainer, Luise, 214, 243, 253
Raksin, David, 213, 379, 417
Ralston, Esther, 196–97
Rambova, Natacha, 213–14
Rand, Ayn, 391
Random Harvest, 256, 365
Rapf, Harry, 84, 88, 91, 96, 118, 119, 131, 135, 156,
    173, 206–7, 245, 360, 362, 363, 364, 494
Rapf, Matt, 207
Rapf, Maurice, 91, 107, 108, 119, 131, 134, 146,
    166, 169, 183, 187, 197, 204–5, 207, 210, 362
Rapf-Schary unit, 361–63, 364
RCA, 381
readers, 156
Reagan, Ronald, 458–59
Rear Window, 292
Red Badge of Courage, The, 432, 434–36, 441–42,
    443
Red Dust, 157, 161, 254, 338

Red Scare, 203, 254, 295, 355, 382–97, 411, 416,
    427, 451, 454, 455
Reeves, Hazard, 470
Reid, Ogden, 486–87
Reinhardt, Gottfried, 316, 434, 435
Reinhardt, Max, 198
Reisch, Walter, 252, 340
Remarque, Erich Maria, 275, 304
Report on Blacklisting (Cogley), 240
Republic, 468
Republicans, Republican Party:
    and 1934 California gubernatorial race,
        200–203
    Koverman and, 136–37
    LBM and, 136–37, 140, 141, 145, 168–69,
        200–203, 384–84, 475
Reynolds, Ben, 103
Reynolds, Debbie, 332–33, 340, 417, 442
Reynolds, Gene, 160, 187–88, 291
Rinaldo, Fred, 219, 239, 272, 392
Rin Tin Tin, 114
Riptide, 182, 189
Ritchie, Robert, 251, 252, 253
Rivkin, Allen, 175
Rivoli Theater (New York City), 409
RKO, 3, 179, 220, 228, 239, 309, 351, 372, 381,
    467, 477
    and *Citizen Kane* affair, 333, 334
    finances of, 170, 262, 420, 425
    Red Scare and, 394, 396
    Schary and, 396, 409, 410, 419–20
Roach, Hal, 186, 274–75
Roach and Mussolini (RAM) Productions,
    274–75
Road pictures, 262
Robbins Corporation, 245
Roberts, Beatrice, 316
Roberts, Dudley, 469
Roberts, Marguerite, 295, 392
Roberts, Richard, 53
Robertson, John S., 99
Robinson, Bill, 39
Robinson, Edward G., 278, 295, 396
Rodgers, Richard, 379
Rogers, Ginger, 402
Rogers, Will, 191, 209, 424
Rogue Song, The, 212
Romance of Rosy Ridge, The, 376
Romanelli, Carlo, 55
Romeo and Juliet, 45, 219, 225, 226, 230, 264
Romm, May, 313
Rooney, Mickey, 12, 127, 223–24, 249, 255, 288,
    304, 325, 330–31, 340, 347, 348, 357
    Andy Hardy movies and, 325, 326, 401
    LBM and, 323, 354, 358
Roosevelt, Franklin D., 154, 169, 206, 219, 229,
    231, 388
Rosalie, 230
Rose, Billy, 355

Rose Marie, 167
Ross, Lillian, 432–33
Rosson, Hal, 221, 246
Rouverol, Aurania, 323–24
Rowland, Richard, 43, 49, 51
Royal Theater (Brooklyn, N.Y.), 74
Royal Wedding, 331
Rózsa, Miklós, 379
Rubin, J. Robert, 44, 51–52, 172, 508
   and Fox's Loew's purchase, 143, 144, 145
   Metro Pictures and, 43–44, 48–49
   MGM and, 72, 77, 78, 79, 102, 112, 129, 172,
      176, 178, 180, 184, 244, 324, 410, 443, 444
Ruby, Harry, 408
Runyon, Damon, 324, 347
Ruskin, Harry, 383
Russell, Rosalind, 207
Russia, 17–18, 74, 127, 129
Rutherford, Ann, 1–2, 3, 221, 243, 311, 322–23, 326
Ruttenberg, Joe, 398
Ryerson, Florence, 169

Saint John, New Brunswick, 18, 20–27, 31, 40
   Jewish community of, 20, 21–22, 38, 265
   LBM and, 23, 24, 27, 35, 230–31, 264–65
   Pidgeon and, 301–2
Sale, Chic, 273, 324
Salinger, Conrad, 331
Salt, Waldo, 327
Salzburg, Paul, 440–41
Samuel Goldwyn, Inc., 164, 179, 258, 292,
   380
Sandler, Helen, 28, 194, 282, 481
Sanford, John, 392
San Francisco, 167, 226
San Luis Obispo, Calif., Morro Strand at, 121
Santa Anita racetrack, 268, 269, 270, 441
Santa Monica, 134–35
Santé, Luc, 222
Saroyan, William, 345–48, 449, 515
Sartov, Hendrik, 125
Satan Sanderson, 44
Saunders, John Monk, 308, 309
Saville, Victor, 251, 252, 254, 281, 301, 302, 398
Sayonara, 502, 503
Scarlet Letter, The, 124–26, 139
Schaefer, George, 333, 334
Schallert, Edwin, 400
Schary, Dore, 209, 360–63, 429, 430, 453,
   462–65, 492, 505
   character and temperament of, 410, 411, 417,
      433, 454–55, 458, 465
   dismissal of, 451, 484–85
   LBM and, 412, 423, 424, 425, 426, 427–29, 434,
      435, 438–39, 441, 442, 443, 445, 449, 453,
      460–61, 466, 472, 477, 486, 508, 509
   liberalism of, 360, 394–95, 410, 411, 416, 427,
      433, 451, 454, 455, 481, 484
   marriage and family of, 360, 423, 479

at MGM, 361–63, 409–12, 416–49, 450–52,
   453–59, 462–65, 472, 478, 479, 480–81,
   484–85, 508
   picture values of, 420, 455, 463
   Red Scare and, 394–95, 396, 411, 427, 451, 454,
      455
   at RKO, 396, 409, 410, 419–20
   Selznick and, 409–10, 455
   Thalberg and, 408, 418, 428
Schenck, Joseph, 74–75, 135, 138, 198, 200, 335,
   508
   background of, 74, 127
   Bioff and, 241
   LBM and, 100, 180, 313, 412, 467
   Loew's and, 75, 100
   MGM and, 165
   personality of, 127, 128
   as producer, 76, 113, 130
   Selznick and, 184
   20th Century-Fox and, 127, 173, 180, 371
   womanizing of, 321, 413
Schenck, Louis, 74
Schenck, Nicholas, 86, 96, 148, 333, 508
   actors' percentage deals and, 456, 457
   background of, 74, 127
   and Fox purchase of Loew's, 143, 144, 145, 146,
      442
   LBM and, power plays of, 10, 127, 128, 129,
      144–46, 184, 186, 230, 231, 235, 237–38,
      243–45, 252, 299, 334, 366, 395, 411, 413, 426,
      434, 438, 441, 442–43, 444, 445, 452, 453,
      466, 477, 486
   Loew's and, 72, 75, 76, 127–29, 143, 144, 145,
      146, 170–72, 244, 251, 262, 275, 395, 484, 485
   MGM and, 72, 73, 107, 109, 128–29, 130,
      170–72, 173–75, 176, 180, 182, 184, 186, 225,
      231, 237–38, 239, 242, 243–45, 250, 255, 258,
      275, 299, 304, 380, 381, 395, 407, 408, 409,
      424, 440, 442–43, 444, 445, 451–52, 456,
      457–58
   Schary and, 425, 426, 434, 443, 451–52, 456,
      461, 480, 484
   television and, 381, 419, 463
   Thalberg and, 170–72, 173–75, 182, 225, 230,
      237, 244, 434
   20th Century Pictures and, 180
   on continuing validity of silent movies, 142
Schenck, Nicola, 128, 129, 480
Schenck, Pansy, 258
Schertzinger, Victor, 83
Schönnbrunn, George, 505–7
Schulberg, Ad, 59, 65, 251
   LBM's affair with, 194, 309
Schulberg, B. P., 58–59, 70, 84, 113, 194, 334
Schulberg, Budd, 47, 55, 58–59, 65, 84, 91, 216,
   240, 314, 334
Schultz, Bobby, 286
Schwartz, Maurice, 386
Scott, Adrian, 394, 396, 451

Scott, Randolph, 196–97
scrap business, 20–28, 29, 39, 59
Screen Actors Guild, 240–41
Screen Playwrights, 205, 206, 254, 255
Screen Writers Guild, 254, 395
Sea of Grass, 374, 399–400
Seastrom, Victor, 84, 88–89, 92, 97–98, 121–22, 123, 125, 139
Seaton, George, 155, 206, 327
Seawright, Roy, 274–75
Seely, Walter, 43
Seitz, George B., 253, 325, 326
Seldes, George, 395
Select Pictures, 49
Seltzer, Walter, 285–86, 289, 485
Selznick, Daniel, 10, 25, 261, 269–70, 287, 296, 298, 299, 314, 403, 404, 413, 414, 415, 422, 423, 466–67, 478, 499, 501, 502, 503, 509, 513
Selznick, David O., 49, 114, 409, 412, 437, 452, 485, 488, 490, 502
  financial problems of, 504–5
  Goetz and, 371–72
  as independent producer, 163, 184, 258–61, 354–55, 371–72, 448, 455, 475, 477, 480
  Irene and, 162–63, 180–81, 194, 313–14, 404, 438
  Kelly and, 354–55
  LBM and, 162–63, 180–81, 183–84, 261, 303, 314, 371–72, 475–77, 493, 495, 501
  MGM and, 173, 174, 183–84, 224, 259, 338
  personality of, 183, 296
  Schary and, 409–10, 455
  Thalberg and, 173, 174, 183, 184
Selznick, Irene Mayer, 26, 28–29, 33, 36, 39, 48, 59, 64, 85, 97, 100, 104–5, 109, 121, 133, 156, 166, 230, 259, 260, 281, 287, 370, 372, 437, 502
  death of, 511
  education of, 62, 63, 161
  intelligence of, 87, 509
  and LBM's death and funeral, 493, 494
  LBM's final illness and, 486, 491
  LBM's relationship with, 46–47, 48, 55, 56–57, 62, 64, 65–66, 86, 87, 135, 161, 162–63, 180–81, 184, 261, 297, 386, 403, 404, 405, 438, 460, 461, 482, 490, 495, 501, 509
  Margaret and, 481–82, 509, 510–11
  marriage of, *see* Selznick, David O.
  memoirs of, 503, 510
  personality of, 47, 161, 162, 163, 181, 261, 438, 510
  as producer, 403–4, 481–82, 509, 511
  teenage diaries of, 86–88
Selznick, Jeffrey, 163, 261, 270, 296, 299, 403, 404, 437, 501
Selznick, Lewis J., 49, 162
Selznick, Myron, 49, 259
Seven Brides for Seven Brothers, 332, 457

Shakespeare, William, 225
Shaw, Artie, 357
Shea, Daniel, 35
Shearer, Douglas, 89, 143, 211–12, 213, 226, 512
Shearer, Norma, 61, 78, 79, 86, 89, 90, 122, 143, 149, 172, 191, 208, 222, 226, 227, 228, 251, 255, 256, 257, 346, 367–68, 376, 399, 461, 482–83, 508
  retirement of, 225, 367
  Thalberg and, 70, 175, 225, 232, 237, 250–51, 367, 483
  Thalberg contract and, 250–51, 368
Sheldon, Sidney, 340, 411, 416
Shenberg, Hyman, 27, 28, 185, 197
Shenberg, Rachel, 28
Shenberg family, MGM positions of, 312
Shepherd, Richard, 481
Sherman, Harry, 459, 479
Shop Around the Corner, The, 259, 281, 336, 423
shorts, shorts department, MGM, 186, 205–6, 271–75, 427
  animated, 273–74, 483
  anti-Nazi propaganda in, 277
  LBM and, 272, 277
  Miniature series, 277
  star system in, 272–73
Show Boat, 427, 440, 462
Show People, 120–21
Shubert, Lee, 72
Shubert organization, 71, 72, 75
Shute, Charles, 31, 32, 39, 40
Sidney, George, 128, 158, 160, 235, 268, 271, 300, 311, 331, 340, 406, 407, 408, 425, 450, 479
Sidney, Lillian Burns, 311, 340–41, 411
Sidney, L. K., 268, 280, 443
Sidney, Sylvia, 194
Siegel, Sol, 485
Sight and Sound, 471
Silberberg, Mendel, 200, 204, 343, 467
Silk Stockings, 405
Simms, Ginny, 317, 370, 413
Simone, Lela, 329, 378, 462
Sinatra, Frank, 417, 436, 509–10
Sinclair, Upton, 145
  in California gubernatorial race (1934), 200–203, 204
Singin' in the Rain, 442, 462
Siodmak, Robert, 423
Skelton, Red, 292, 331, 357, 383
Skouras, Charles, 371
Skouras, Spyros, 371, 395
Slickum, 217–18
Smith, Genevieve, 242
Smith, H. A., 387–88
Smith, Pete, 85, 272
Smith, Terry Kingsley, 341
Socialism, and California gubernatorial race, 200–203
Somewhere I'll Find You, 358–59

Song of Russia, 349–50, 387, 389–91
Son of Kong, 208
Sony, MGM owned by, 512
Sowing the Wind, 61
Spanish Civil War, 382–83
Spanish flu epidemic, 53
Speak Easily, 166
Spellman, Francis Cardinal, 289, 422–23, 467, 473–74
Spite Marriage, 142
Spitz, Leo, 239
Squaw Man, The, 40
Stack, Robert, 278
Stahl, John M., 56, 61, 66–67, 78, 83
Stalin, Joseph, 389
Stanwyck, Barbara, 295, 339
stars, movie:
  fans and, 50
  at Louis B. Mayer Productions, 50–53, 59, 60, 61, 70
stars, star system, MGM, 1, 12, 114, 153, 199, 217, 220–24, 228, 241, 243, 262, 338–39, 357, 358
  and advent of sound, 147–50
  in armed forces, 304, 359, 390
  contract negotiations with, 149–50, 288, 303–4, 311–12, 321, 354–55
  dependency of, 217, 322
  discovery and development of, 104–5, 149, 154, 221, 265–66, 288–89, 292–93, 311–12, 354, 358–59, 365, 373–74, 377–78, 406, 503, 507, 512
  dressing rooms of, 208, 220, 367
  exodus of, 436
  freezing out and blackballing of, 90–91, 243, 290, 304, 308–9, 316, 335
  juveniles, 224, 352, 353–54
  LBM on writing for, 30
  LBM's seduction of, 8, 11, 44, 51, 53, 90, 165–66, 295, 373–74, 442
  in MGM merger, 83–84
  percentage deals and, 456, 457
  problem, 12, 132–34, 165–67, 170, 185–86, 195, 215–16, 217, 341, 356–59, 377–78, 461–62
  publicity department and, 2, 215–17
  salary cuts for, 178–80
  as studio centerpiece, 4, 8, 93, 114, 149, 155, 157, 164, 174, 220, 263, 381, 455, 465, 515
  treatment of, 220, 224, 263, 289–90, 322
  as types, 220
State of the Union, 408
Steger, Julius, 505
Steiner, Max, 184, 212
Stempel, Tom, 157
Sternberg, Josef von, 93, 99, 153
Stevens, George, 336, 373, 485
Stevens, George, Jr., 336
Stevenson, Adlai, 460
Stewart, Anita, 50–53, 59–60, 61

Stewart, David Ogden, 118, 254, 255, 359
  Red Scare and, 387, 390, 391, 395
Stewart, James, 247, 272, 273, 278, 304, 417, 456
Stiller, Mauritz, 104, 105
Stone, Lewis, 324, 326
Stormy Weather, 321
story editors, 138, 156
Stothart, Herbert, 211, 212–13, 226, 243, 408–9
Stratton Story, The, 417
Streetcar Named Desire, A (show), 403–4
Strickling, Howard, 2, 132, 148, 172, 191, 195, 196, 197, 215–17, 223, 230, 232, 242, 265, 285, 298, 313–14, 344, 358, 385–86, 396, 412, 432, 449, 491, 501, 512
Strike Up the Band, 281, 328
Stripling, Robert, 389
Stroheim, Erich von, 72, 77, 84, 86, 95, 97–99, 99, 148, 232, 279, 316, 418
Stroheim, Joe von, 418
Stromberg, Hunt, 91, 118–19, 173, 237, 238, 245, 246, 255, 257, 262, 264, 337, 338–39, 464
Student Prince in Old Heidelberg, The, 118
studios, studio system, 465, 477
  Academy and, 117, 179, 180
  creators of, *see* movie moguls, Jewish
  decentralized production in, 456
  film libraries of, 452–53, 512–13
  IATSE paid off by, 239–41
  salary cuts at, 178–80
  star- vs. story-centered, 381
  television and, 381, 418, 419, 452, 454, 463
  and theater chain divorcement, 397, 463
Sturges, Preston, 424
Sullavan, Margaret, 278
Summer Holiday, 380, 401
Summer Stock, 406
Sunset Boulevard, 11, 121, 336, 405, 431–32
Supreme Court, U.S., 397
Swope, Herbert, Jr., 127, 128

Taeger, Ralph, 505
Taft, Robert, 385, 488
Tale of Two Cities, A, 212, 219, 259
Talmadge, Constance, 76, 86, 165
Talmadge, Norma, 51, 76, 86, 105, 113, 128, 135
Tarzan and His Mate, 189–90
Tarzan movies, 159, 208
Taylor, Elizabeth, 224, 271, 294
Taylor, Robert, 160, 247, 248, 255, 272, 289, 314, 315, 338, 349, 390, 391, 401, 416, 423, 505
Taylor, Sam, 126
Taylor, Sara, 294
Technicolor, 351–52
television:
  film libraries and, 453, 513
  studios and, 381, 418, 419, 452, 454, 463
Tender Comrade, 387
"Tenement Symphony, The," 348
Tennessee Johnson, 320–21

Tess of the D'Urbervilles, 84, 95, 96–97
Thalberg, Irving G., ix, iii, 12, 13, 67–70, 87, 88,
    89, 90, 100–101, 133, 150, 151, 154, 165, 189,
    198–99, 219, 222, 224, 328, 337, 368, 383,
    408, 418, 424, 439, 480, 507
  acquisitiveness of, 135, 145, 170, 171–72, 198,
    204, 208, 410
  birth and childhood of, 67–68
  business model and management style of, 92,
    99, 139, 147, 157, 173–75, 428
  death and funeral of, 12, 67, 172, 231–32, 281
  estate of, 237, 250–51
  and Fox purchase of Loew's, 144, 145
  health of, 67–68, 92, 164, 170, 172–73, 176, 177,
    181, 229, 231
  independent unit of, 182–83, 226, 228–29, 230,
    238
  LBM and, 12, 69–70, 77, 90, 111, 118, 119, 120,
    123, 132, 144–45, 164, 170–72, 173, 175–78,
    181, 183, 187, 208–9, 225–26, 228–29, 230,
    231–32, 233, 237–39, 241, 246, 249, 250–51,
    264, 416
  legend of, 11–12, 92, 93, 120, 122, 152–53, 170,
    172, 410
  at Louis B. Mayer Productions, 68–70, 77–78
  marriage of, *see* Shearer, Norma
  MGM merger and, 78–79, 83, 84
  and 1934 California gubernatorial race,
    200–201, 203
  office of, 91, 153, 229, 231
  personality of, 67, 90, 92–93, 118, 119, 120, 123,
    125, 145, 147, 183, 204
  production schedules of, 226
  salary and profit sharing of, 69, 79, 112, 170,
    171–72, 178, 180, 182, 250–51, 441
  Saturday morning meetings of, 91
  unionization and, 204–5, 206, 241
  at Universal, 68–69, 97, 118
  women and, 93
  work ethic of, 67, 231
That Forsyte Woman, 397, 399
That Midnight Kiss, 377
Thau, Benny, 131, 179, 205, 207, 239, 245, 251,
    253, 255, 257, 276, 291, 294, 300, 338, 341,
    370, 374, 398, 408, 420, 424, 443, 458, 485,
    508, 512
theater, 26, 36–37
Thin Man, The movies, 157, 208, 338, 374, 400
This Is Cinerama, 469, 470
Thomas, Lowell, 470, 471
Thomson, Kenneth, 240–41
Thorpe, Richard, 159, 160, 225, 332
Three Comrades, 275–77
Three Little Words, 423
Three Musketeers, The, 380, 400
Thy Name is Woman, 64–65, 77
Tibbett, Lawrence, 167
Time, 484
Time of Your Life, The (Saroyan), 345

Toast of New Orleans, The, 378
Toby the Hunchback, 50
Tom and Jerry cartoons, 273, 274, 483
Tomlinson, Joseph, 485, 487
Tomorrow Never Comes, 219
Tone, Franchot, 182, 240–41
Tortilla Flat, 161
Totter, Audrey, 295, 303, 380, 397, 458–59
Tourneur, Jacques, 272
Tourneur, Maurice, 113
Tower of Lies, The, 122
Tracy, Spencer, 8, 215, 220, 249, 266, 342, 356,
    385, 408, 455
  LBM's eulogy given by, 85, 493–94
Trader Horn, 1, 110
Tree of the Garden, The, 88
Trevor, Claire, 196
Triangle Film Company, 71
Truman, Harry, 241, 385, 441
Trumbo, Dalton, 383–84
  Red Scare and, 387, 388, 390, 391, 395,
    396
Tucker, George Loane, 52, 56, 61
Tugboat Annie, 191, 223, 257
Turner, Florence, 336
Turner, Lana, 257, 338, 339, 345, 357–59, 397,
    478
Turner, Ted, 512–13
20th Century-Fox, 3, 251, 321, 331, 341, 344, 380,
    395, 469, 504, 515
  creative method at, 280–81
  Red Scare and, 394
  script conferences at, 339, 340
  technicolor at, 352
  theaters of, 262, 381, 463
  World War II and, 381
20th Century Pictures, 180–81
Two Weeks with Love, 420–21

Unholy Three, The, 150
unions:
  Academy and, 117–18, 180
  corruption of, 204, 239–41
  MGM and, 131, 204–6, 240–41, 254, 255, 395,
    453
  writers and, 204–6, 254, 255, 395, 453
United Artists, 108, 113, 127, 147, 178–79, 275,
    339, 366, 464, 485, 512
Universal City, 56–57
Universal International, 372, 468, 502
Universal Pictures, 3, 6, 46, 68–69, 97, 118, 287,
    309, 332, 483, 485, 506
Upstage, 120

Vajda, Ernest, 179, 255
Valentino, Rudolph, 72, 99, 113, 149, 213–14
Van Dyke, W. S. "Woody," II, 157–60, 225, 226,
    232, 256–57, 259, 326, 368
Variety, 9, 45, 169, 304, 442, 443–44

Vidor, King, 64, 72, 84, 91, 95, 98, 111, 112, 114, 120–21, 124, 132, 133, 157, 226, 227, 346, 365, 402–3
Viertel, Peter, 220
Viertel, Salka, 220, 279, 323
Virginia Pearson Photoplays, 54
Virtuous Wives, 52, 53, 61
Vitagraph Company, 49, 50–53, 74
Viva Villa!, 222
Vogel, Joseph, 486, 487, 488, 504
Vogel, Robert, 91, 154, 271, 277, 288–89, 508
Voice of Bugle Ann, The, 211

Wagner Act (1935), 205, 240
Wald, Jerry, 189, 467
Waldorf Conference (1947), 393–95, 411, 427, 454, 455
Wallis, Hal, 2, 245, 286, 437, 485
Wallis, Minna, 148
Walsh, George, 99, 100, 101
Walsh, Miriam Cooper, 63
Walsh, Raoul, 62–63
Walters, Chuck, 463, 504
Walthall, Henry B., 125
Wanger, Walter, 153–55, 173, 195, 198, 199, 305, 320, 394, 395, 409, 449
War Bonds, MGM rally for, 312
Warburton, Cotton, 418
War Department, U.S., 277, 349
War Information Office, U.S., 349, 390
Warner, Harry, 107, 179, 180, 257, 270, 305, 315, 422, 430, 444–45, 477
Warner, Jack, 11, 107, 180, 203, 245, 257, 286, 298, 311, 315, 319, 365, 444–45, 475, 477, 486
    HUAC testimony of, 389, 390, 392
Warner Brothers, 2, 107, 114, 119, 138, 148, 173, 174, 180, 189, 202, 227, 239, 247, 286, 331, 342, 351, 397, 412, 464, 477, 515
    anti-Nazi movies and stance of, 277, 278
    film library of, 512
    movie theaters owned by, 262, 381, 463
    production bureaucracy at, 245
    sound and, 143, 212
Warren, Earl, 430
Warren, Harry, 2–3
Wasserman, Lew, 410, 452, 484
Waterloo Bridge, 256, 281, 338, 351
Waxman, Franz, 267, 329, 378
Waxman, John, 267, 328–29, 378, 379
Wealth Recovery Tax, 206
Weber, Lois, 56, 111
Weekend at the Waldorf, 372–73
Weingarten, Lawrence, 239, 245, 363, 369, 370, 508
Weisl, Edward, 471, 487
Weissmuller, Johnny, 190
Weizman, Chaim, 412
Welch, Jack (father), 37

Welch, Jack (son), 37
Wellman, William, 159, 259, 284, 418
What Makes Sammy Run? (Schulberg), 334
What! No Beer?, 166–67
Wheelwright, Ralph, 215–16
Whistling in Brooklyn, 383
Whitbeck, Frank, 217
White, Jack, 96, 186
White, Walter, 320–21
Whitmore, James, 416–17, 455, 457–58
Whitney, Jock, 261, 453
Wilder, Billy, 118, 209, 302, 431–32
Wilkerson, Billy, 184, 203, 384, 442, 467–68, 487–88, 492
Williams, Esther, 11, 255, 263, 283, 287, 300, 311, 312, 331, 344, 400–401, 421, 423, 436, 458, 464, 473, 478
Williams, Tennessee, 345
William Selig Studio, 54–55
Willis, Edwin, 170, 255, 414
Willis, Ross, 285, 286–87
Wilshire Boulevard Temple, 185, 297, 493
Wilson, Carey, 66, 83, 85, 101, 102, 104, 105, 156, 201, 203, 232, 239, 255, 277, 313, 325, 326, 327, 493
Wilson, John, 23, 27, 230
Winchell, Walter, 228
Winchester '73, 456
Wind, The, 139–40
Wings, 138
Winters, Ralph, 147, 160, 209, 213, 238, 245, 298, 515
Wise, Robert, 456
Witchcraft Though the Ages (Häxan), 123
Witness for the Prosecution, 482
Wizard of Oz, The, 10, 212, 214, 264, 281, 285, 337, 352
    directing of, 161, 260, 328
Woman of the Year, 322, 336, 341–42
Women, The, 260, 264, 281, 338, 464
Wood, John, 384
Wood, Sam, 12, 157, 232, 237, 260
Woods, Al, 71
Woolf, Edgar Allan, 169
Words and Music, 401
World of Our Fathers (Howe), ix
World War I, movie scripts about, 51–52
World War II, MGM and, 3, 168, 277, 278–79, 304, 305, 312, 345–81, 417–18
Worsley, Wallace, Jr., 68, 218
Wrangell, Basil, 104, 231
Wrench, Herbert, 291
writers, MGM, 152, 154, 155–57
    blackballed and blacklisted, 295, 308, 309, 361, 388, 392, 394, 395–97
    in junior-writer program, 327
    LBM and, 124, 155, 205, 226–27, 263–64, 267, 301, 307, 308, 309

writers, MGM (*cont.*)
  Schary and, 453–54
  schism among, 254–55, 382–83
  status of, 254, 263–64, 267, 339–40, 513
  Thalberg and, 67, 92, 93, 124, 138, 155–56, 174, 204–5
  unionization of, 204–6, 254, 255, 395, 453
Writers Guild, 204–6, 453
Wyler, William, 373
Wynn, Keenan, 5–6, 424, 457

Yank at Oxford, A, 253, 254
Yankwich, Leon, 308–9
Yearling, The, 114, 256, 342, 374–76
Yiddish, 21, 26, 38, 185, 186, 287, 342
Yordan, Philip, 319, 474–75, 478, 502–3, 504–5
York Theatre (New Brunswick), 26–27

Young, Robert, 217, 223, 225, 247, 249, 278, 291, 292–93
Young Bess, 424
You're Only Young Once, 324
Yranski, Joe, 121

Zanuck, Darryl, 11, 173, 180, 181, 193, 203, 280–81, 339, 340, 381, 430, 437, 478, 485
Zanuck, Virginia, 437
Zapata, Emiliano, 388
Ziegfeld, Florenz, 330
Zimbalist, Sam, 161, 239
Zinneman, Fred, 159, 271, 272, 362
Zionism, 343, 411–12
zoo, at MGM, 1
Zukor, Adolph, 43, 44, 49, 64, 74, 93, 343, 438, 465